EUCOTAX Series on European Taxation

VAT Exemptions

EUCOTAX Series on European Taxation

VOLUME 37

Series Editors:

Prof. Dr Peter H.J. Essers
Prof. Dr Eric C.C.M. Kemmeren

Fiscal Institute Tilburg/Center for Company Law, Tilburg University

Prof. Dr Dr h.c. Michael Lang

WU (Vienna University of Economics and Business)

The titles in this series are listed at the back of this volume.

EUCOTAX Series on European Taxation

VAT Exemptions

Consequences and Design Alternatives

Edited By

Rita de la Feria

Eucotax

Wolters Kluwer
Law & Business

Published by:
Kluwer Law International
PO Box 316
2400 AH Alphen aan den Rijn
The Netherlands
Website: www.kluwerlaw.com

Sold and distributed in North, Central and South America by:
Aspen Publishers, Inc.
7201 McKinney Circle
Frederick, MD 21704
United States of America
Email: customer.service@aspenpublishers.com

Sold and distributed in all other countries by:
Turpin Distribution Services Ltd
Stratton Business Park
Pegasus Drive, Biggleswade
Bedfordshire SG18 8TQ
United Kingdom
Email: kluwerlaw@turpin-distribution.com

Printed on acid-free paper.

ISBN 978-90-411-3276-5

Printed and Bound by CPI Group (UK) Ltd, Croydon, CR0 4YY.

To Conor,
ATMS
To Pílar and Tomás,
Born on 20 June 2011

List of Editor and Contributors

Sijbren Cnossen is Professor at the Economics Faculty of the University of Pretoria and Emeritus Professor of Economics at Maastricht University and of Tax Law at Erasmus University Rotterdam. He has served with the Fiscal Affairs Department of the IMF and the Dutch Tax Service and has been a consultant to the OECD, European Commission, IMF, World Bank, Harvard Institute for International Development and the US Agency for International Development.

Rita de la Feria is Professor at the Durham Law School, University of Durham, UK; Programme Director at the Oxford University Centre for Business Taxation, UK; and Visiting Professor at the Law Faculty, University of Lisbon, Portugal. She served as adviser to the Portuguese Government on VAT Policy between 2011 and 2012.

Timothy Edgar is Professor at Osgoode Hall Law School, York University and the Faculty of Law, the University of Sydney. He has served as a consultant to the Department of Finance, the Canada Revenue Agency, the Australian Treasury Department, New Zealand Inland Revenue (Policy Advice Division), the OECD and the IMF. He is also a co-editor of the *Canadian Tax Journal*.

Joachim Englisch is Professor at Muenster University, where he holds the Chair for Tax Law and Public Law.

Pierre-Pascal Gendron is Professor of Economics at The Business School, Humber College Institute of Technology and Advanced Learning, Toronto, Canada. He is a member of the Expert Roster for the Fiscal Affairs Department of the International Monetary Fund.

Harry Grubert is a senior research economist in the Office of Tax Analysis in the US Treasury Department. He received a PhD from the Massachusetts Institute of Technology.

Walter Hellerstein is Distinguished Research Professor and Shackelford Professor of Taxation at the University of Georgia School of Law, Athens, Georgia, USA.

Richard Krever is Director of the Taxation Law and Policy Research Institute and Head of the Department of Business Law and Taxation at Monash University, Melbourne, Australia.

Richard Lyal is a legal adviser to the European Commission.

Yoram Margalioth is Professor at the Tel Aviv University Faculty of Law.

Rebecca Millar is Professor of law at the Faculty of Law at the University of Sydney.

Alan Schenk is Distinguished Professor at Wayne State University in Michigan, and he teaches at the Law School. He is currently on the editorial board of the *International VAT Monitor*. For over 15 years, has served as Technical Advisor for the International Monetary Fund legal department, drafting and reviewing VATs for countries in Africa, the Caribbean and Eastern Europe.

Howell H. Zee is Professor of Economics, Xiamen University; Senior Fellow, Monash University; and Consultant, IMF.

Summary of Contents

Table of Contents

Preface

Exemptions are arguably the most controversial feature of VAT regimes. They constitute exceptions to the principle of VAT as a tax on consumption – a tax levied on all commodities supplied for consideration by a taxable person, with systematic offsetting of tax charged on commodities purchased as inputs, against tax due on outputs. Contradicting this rule, exempt supplies do not carry any output tax, nor do they entitle the recipient to input tax deductions in respect of the tax incurred on acquisitions relating to those supplies.

In traditional VAT systems, like those in place in European countries, exemptions constitute a sizable portion of the potential tax base. Whilst this was already the case when the first VAT systems were introduced in Europe in the 1950s and 1960s, it is much more so today as a result of the exponential growth of traditionally exempted sectors of the economy, such as the financial services and healthcare sectors. Moreover, parallel to the growing economic relevance of these exempted industry sectors, the difficulties – and potential economic distortions – that are caused by VAT exemptions also appear to be on the increase, if the number of cases arriving to the Court of Justice of the European Union is anything to go by. Modern VAT (GST) systems, such as those applied in New Zealand, Australia, Canada and Israel, started appearing in the 1980s and are today prevalent everywhere else in the world apart from Europe. In these systems the number of exemptions is typically significantly smaller, and alternative legal designs for taxing specific sectors of the economy under a VAT have been attempted. However, not all modern VATs have opted for the same design alternatives, with different countries opting for different solutions as regards traditionally exempted sectors. Furthermore, sufficient time has elapsed since their introduction to allow for an unbiased assessment of those solutions.

Against this background, questioning the existence of VAT exemptions appears to be both timely and fundamental. Are VAT exemptions desirable and/or unavoidable, or are alternative legal designs possible and/or necessary? And if alternative designs are available and required, which of these represents the best solution to doing away with exemptions? Thirty years since the first appearance of modern VATs on the world stage, is it time to consider a shift in regime design and progress towards a *post*-modern VAT?[1]

It was with a view to providing answers to these questions that an interdisciplinary conference, bringing together economists and lawyers working and researching on VAT, was organized at Oxford University in April 2010, under the theme *VAT Exemptions: Consequences and Design Alternatives*. The aim of the event was to provide a systematic and comprehensive legal and economic analysis of exemptions, as well as to assess potential design alternatives - both those that have already been attempted in some countries around the world, and others that have not yet been attempted anywhere. A special issue of the *International VAT Monitor*, published in late 2011, was the first of two publications to have resulted from this conference.[2] The papers included in that special issue offer an in-depth analysis of the state of current law in Europe and further afield as regards VAT exemptions, and highlight the difficulties caused by the existence of exemptions, in particular those relating to the calculation of the right to deduct. This volume constitutes the second publication emerging from the conference; its focus being more explicitly on tax policy. The chapters included here provide a comprehensive discussion of the future of VAT exemptions, and an investigation of potential VAT design alternatives. Our sincere ambition is that the high-calibre contributions included within these two complementary publications will make a valuable contribution to the discussion around the need for, and the alternatives to, VAT exemptions.

Finally, in a project as testing as this one was there are always many people and institutions to thank. The Oxford University Centre for Business Taxation provided generous financial support and assisted with organizing the conference under unprecedented logistical challenges, by virtue of the travel chaos that ensued from the Icelandic volcanic ash-cloud that swept across Europe at the precise time of the conference, leaving many speakers stranded. Special thanks are due in this regard to Jane O'Hare and Clare Ruthven-Stuart for all their help. Michael Devereux and Judith Freedman - respectively Director and Legal Research Director of the Centre for Business Taxation - were constant presences throughout this whole process, and I am, as ever, grateful for their wisdom, and their continuous and relentless support. Two referees, an academic economist and an academic lawyer, who have preferred to remain anonymous, thoroughly reviewed all the chapters included in this volume with no reward beyond further contributing to this debate, and for no other reason than their strong commitment and dedication to high academic standards. Lindsay Loomer, copy editor for this project and personal friend, worked tirelessly on all the chapters, liaising directly with both the authors and the publisher. Lijntje Zandee, my publishing editor at Kluwer Law International for nearly ten years, was as always supportive and helpful throughout. My final words however are of personal gratitude towards the authors of the contributions to this volume. They have contended with a long and arduous

1. The use of the expression post-modern is not meant in the cultural sense of 'postmodernism', but rather to express the shift from a modern VAT to a new, improved VAT.
2. R. de la Feria & H. van Kesteren (eds.), *Special Issue: VAT Exemptions – Consequences and Design Alternatives*, 22 International VAT Monitor 5 (2011).

editorial process, and I am extremely grateful for their outstanding patience and unwavering commitment to this project.

Rita de la Feria
Durham, January 2013

List of Tables and Figures

Tables

Figures

Part I

Exemptions: General Considerations

CHAPTER 1

Ending VAT Exemptions: Towards a *Post*-Modern VAT

Rita de la Feria and Richard Krever*

§1.01 INTRODUCTION

Struggling to rebuild its economy three years after the end of the Second World War, the French government decided to try a unique gamble, rebating the turnover tax borne by a selected range of enterprises exporting their goods. The hope was that the increase in exports from a more competitive and efficient export sector would more than offset the initial revenue cost of the refunds. The gamble paid off and the experiment was extended a few years later to more turnover tax transactions.[1] By the 1960s, plans were put in place to transform the entire turnover tax system to one that would rebate the turnover tax all the way along the production chain to the final consumer, shifting the turnover tax from an inefficient compounding tax on production or sales to an efficient and fair tax on final consumption. Europe was on the path to a value added tax.[2]

* We are grateful to our discussant Stephen Smith, and to participants at the conference for comments received therein. All remaining errors are our own. This paper forms part of the work undertaken under ESRC Grant RES-060-25-0033.

1. At the time, the introduction of the value added tax was characterized as 'an invention of the first order', and France as an 'innovator in taxation': see C.S. Shoup, *Taxation in France*, 8(4) Natl. Tax J. 325–344 (1955).
2. An earlier VAT had been enacted in 1953 at state level in Michigan in the United States, but without the VAT's invoice-credit format that now prevails around the world. For an analysis of this earlier VAT see C.W. Lock, D. Rau & H. Hamilton, *The Michigan Value-Added Tax*, 8(4) Natl. Tax J. 357–371 (1955); and J.A. Papke, *Michigan's Value-Added Tax After Seven Years*, 13(4) Natl. Tax J. 350–364 (1960). A VAT had also been enacted in 1950 in Japan but was repealed a few years later, prior to commencement; see M. Bronfenbrenner, *The Japanese Value-Added Sales Tax*, 3(4) Natl. Tax J. 298–314 (1950); and A. Schenk, *Japanese Consumption Tax: The Japanese Brand*, 42 Tax Notes 1625 (1989).

From Europe to the rest of the world, the new value added tax (VAT) quickly spread, becoming what has been described as an unparalleled tax phenomenon,[3] and the most important event in the evolution of tax structure in the last half of the twentieth century.[4] Yet, despite its overwhelming popularity and its undeniable appeal in its pure form, in practice VATs applied around the world are – to different degrees – imperfect with exemptions, an anathema to the logic of the VAT,[5] being a common and significant design imperfection in many of those tax systems.[6] Not only do they constitute exceptions to the core principle of VAT as a tax on consumption, but they are also equally perceived as being particularly damaging to the efficiency and neutrality of the tax.[7] In European countries, where VAT was first introduced, exemptions constitute a very sizable – and growing – portion of the potential tax base. In most other countries around the world, where a VAT was enacted later, the number of exemptions is typically significantly smaller and alternative legal designs for taxing specific sectors of the economy that are exempt under the European VAT have been adopted. However, whether considering a traditional VAT – like that applied in European countries – or a modern VAT – such as that applied in New Zealand, Australia or Canada – questions remain over the suitability of exemptions.[8] Are VAT exemptions, in the words of one contributor to this volume, a necessary evil, an unnecessary evil, or no evil at all?[9] Thirty years since the first appearance of modern VATs on the world stage the debate on (or battle against) exemptions continues, and if anything has actually intensified.[10] Is it time to consider a shift in tax design and progress towards a *post*-modern VAT?[11]

The various chapters in this volume attempt to answer these questions through in-depth analysis of existing exemptions and consideration of alternative legal designs – both of those designs that have already been attempted in different countries around the world, and of others that are as yet untested. It would be impossible to do justice in this introductory chapter to the wealth of knowledge and insight displayed in all these contributions. Our aim, therefore, is merely to bring together in a systematic

3. A.A. Tait, *Value Added Tax – International Practice and Problems* 3 (International Monetary Fund 1988).
4. S. Cnossen, *Global Trends and Issues in Value Added Taxation*, 5(3) Intl. Tax & Pub. Fin. 399–428 (1998).
5. I. Crawford, M. Keen & S. Smith, *Value-Added Tax and Excises*, in *Dimensions of Tax Design – the Mirrlees Review* 275–422 (S. Adam, T. Besley, R. Blundell, S. Bond, R. Chote, M. Gammie, P. Johnson, G. Myles & J. Poterba eds., Oxford University Press 2010).
6. V. Lenoir, *April 1954–April 2004 – VAT Exemptions: The Original Misunderstanding*, 10 European Taxn. 456–459 at 459 (2004). The multiple rates found in some jurisdictions, particularly in European countries, constitute another serious deviation from the theoretically ideal VAT.
7. See OECD, *Consumption Tax Trends 2010*, at 15 (OECD Publishing 2011).
8. The expression 'modern VAT' to classify this new, improved VAT model, as opposed to the 'traditional VAT' used in Europe, appears to have been coined by L. Ebrill, M. Keen, J-P. Bodin & V. Summers, *The Modern VAT* (International Monetary Fund 2001).
9. See J. Englisch, *The EU Perspective on VAT Exemptions*, Ch. 2 in this volume.
10. As predicted by L. Ebrill (n. 8 above), at 198.
11. As referred to in the Preface to this volume, the use of the expression 'post-modern' is not meant in the cultural sense of 'postmodernism', but rather to express the shift from a modern VAT to a new, improved, VAT.

fashion all the various topics discussed therein, as well as to offer our own thoughts on the future of VAT exemptions.

In section §1.02, we start with general considerations on VAT exemptions, discussing their origins, namely through consideration of their historical roots in the European model and the attempt to limit their scope in modern VATs; and then consider the concept of exempt supplies, particularly when compared to that other similar concept of out-of-scope supplies. In section §1.03, we delve deeper into the concept of out-of-scope activities and analyse the two main types of activities which fall within this concept: those that are deemed to be out-of-scope for reason of the type of supply in question (out-of-scope supplies), and those that are regarded as out-of-scope because of the nature of the supplier (out-of-scope suppliers). In section §1.04, typical exemptions are analysed in detail. We consider first the so-called merit or concessional exemptions, such as those typically applied to healthcare, cultural activities and education services; and we then move on to technical exemptions, applied to what is known as difficult-to-tax supplies, namely gambling, immovable property and financial and insurance services. We conclude in section §1.05 with considerations on the current state-of-play as regards VAT exemptions and potential alternative designs, and on a possible move to a *post*-modern VAT.

§1.02 GENERAL CONSIDERATIONS ON VAT EXEMPTIONS

[A] On the Origin of Exemptions

The theoretical roots for the VAT were sown shortly after the First World War when an American scholar and a German industrialist separately, but almost at the same time, wrote papers setting out proposals for the tax. The timing of the first proposals remains unclear, with one later scholar attributing the first articulation to T.S. Adams, a leading public finance scholar in the US.[12] However, it is more likely that industrialist Carl Friedrich von Siemens' pamphlet slightly preceded Adams' work by a year.[13] Ironically, neither advocate for the VAT viewed their proposals as reforms for turnover taxes; rather, both saw it as a possible substitute for corporate income tax, which they thought to be inferior to a tax that ultimately fell only on final consumption. It is almost certain that neither was aware of the other's contributions to the subject.

As is so often the case, the ultimate adoption of the VAT had little to do with the grand theoretical concerns of academics or industrialists, but rather was a response to, on the ground, pragmatic considerations. At the time VAT was adopted in France, there were two models for final consumption taxes that eliminated cascading taxes on

12. See R.W. Lindholm, *The Origin of the Value-Added Tax*, 6(1) J. Corp. L. 12 (1980). Lindholm suggests Adams had supported the concept from 1911, although his earliest papers on the topic appear to date from 1921: see T.S. Adams, *Fundamental Problems of Federal Income Taxation*, XXV Q. J. Econ. 553 (1921).
13. Cf. von Siemens, *Veredelte Umsatzsteuer* (Siemensstadt 1919), who cites his brother, Wilhelm von Siemens, as originator of the proposal: see R.A. Musgrave, *Schumpeter's Crisis of the Tax State: An Essay in Fiscal Sociology*, 2 Evolutionary Econ. 89–113, at fn.9 (1992).

business, which distorted business decision-making and encouraged possibly inefficient practices such as vertical integration. The first was the retail sales tax (RST), adopted in most sub-national jurisdictions in North America, which avoids tax on business through a suspension system: the tax is, in theory, suspended on any supplies made to registered enterprises making acquisitions for business purposes. The VAT in contrast, imposes tax on every supply, be it to a registered business or final consumer, but then rebates, through a refundable input tax credit, any tax borne on business acquisitions. Each business will collect tax on the full value of its supplies but only remit a net amount after recovering all tax on inputs used for business purposes. It will pay tax on the entire price to the supplier but then recover it from the customer and only remit the portion of the VAT collected equal to the value added at that stage. Thus, while VAT is paid by the purchaser on the full value of supply, the seller only passes on to the government a slice of the tax received equal to the tax on the excess of the sale price over the value that has previously been taxed. Only if no part of the value has been subject to tax previously (all the inputs were entirely tax free) would the tax remitted be the same as the tax collected. The title 'value added tax' refers therefore to the mechanics of the remittance system, not the intended tax base, which is the full value of the supply.[14] For that reason, a number of modern VAT systems have adopted the name 'Goods and Services Tax' (GST) to reflect the tax base as opposed to the remittance method.

Although an ideal RST and an ideal VAT should be economically equivalent,[15] in practice their differences, in particular as regards the remittance method, may affect their economic impact[16] and administrative efficiency. Since the time of adoption of the RST and VAT, there has been, therefore, an ongoing debate on the relative merits of the two bases.[17] Proponents of VAT argue - amongst other aspects - that it is more

---

14. Ebrill et al. illustrate the difference with a restaurant meal in a tax regime in which raw food products are entirely free of tax from the farmer through wholesaler through retailer, see n. 8 above. The value added by the restaurant may represent only a small amount of the final selling price but if the sale of raw food is tax free while restaurant meals are taxable supplies, the entire value of the meal will be taxed at the restaurant level.
15. See W. Hellerstein, *Comparing the Treatment of Charities under Value Added Taxes and Retail Sales Taxes*, Ch. 5 in this volume. See also S. Cnossen, *VAT and RST: A Comparison*, 35 Canadian Tax J. 3 (1987); M. Gillis, P. Mieszkowski & G. Zodrow, *Indirect Consumption Taxes: Common Issues and Differences Among Alternative Approaches*, 51(4) Tax L. Rev. 725–774 (1996); C.H.E McLure & W. Hellerstein, *Congressional Intervention in State Taxation: A Normative Analysis of Three Proposals*, 31 State Tax Notes 721–735 (2004); and M. Keen & S. Smith, *VAT Fraud and Evasion: What Do We Know and What Can Be Done?*, LIX(4) Natl. Tax J.L861–887(2006).
16. See S. Fedeli, *The effects of the interaction between direct and indirect taxation: the cases of VAT and RST*, 53(3-4) Pub. Fin. 385–418 (2003). On the economic impact of who remits tax, see also J. Slemrod, *Does It Matter Who Writes the Check to the Government? The Economics of Tax Remittance,* LXI(2) Natl. Tax J.L 251–275 (2008).
17. The key issues in the debate are surveyed in R. Bird & P-P. Gendron, *The VAT in Developing and Transitional Countries* Ch. 3 (Cambridge U. Press 2007), 'Is VAT Always the Answer?'. The relative merits of the two versions of a 'final consumption' VAT were considered in S. Cnossen, *The Technical Superiority of VAT or RST*, in *Australian Tax Reform in Retrospect and Prospect* 325–359 (J.G. Head ed., Australian Tax Research Foundation 1989), and later debated at some length in N. Leccisotti & M. Maré, *On the Presumed Technical Superiority of VAT*, 9(3)

resistant to losses through fraud because of the incremental collection on the way,[18] while proponents of the RST argue a VAT system which offers refundable tax credits all the way up an economic chain may actually be more susceptible to fraud. They also argue the churning - collection of VAT and subsequent upfront refund in cases where the buyer would use acquisitions to make supplies over a long period - is inefficient and costly to businesses that have to fund finance for the period between remittance and refund. In response to this particular concern, the VAT in many jurisdictions has moved to adopt the RST model and suspend any tax - via a zero-rating mechanism - on supplies in a range of circumstances such as sales of going concerns[19] or intra-group supplies.[20]

This debate did not feature in the initial decision to adopt the VAT in Europe. The first moves towards a VAT in France consisted of a slight tinkering of an existing tax to provide refundable input tax credits in limited circumstances.[21] The very gradual expansion of the program in France pointed the way to a method by which existing European turnover taxes could be transformed into final consumption taxes, without replacement with a radically new tax such as a RST. The Neumark Committee, appointed by the European Commission to assess tax impediments to and options for a common market, suggested in 1962 that Europe's existing turnover tax systems could follow the French example and be easily shifted to a final consumption tax through the use of input tax credits,[22] a proposal which has been characterized as

---

Australian Tax Forum 259–269 (1992) and S. Cnossen, *Misunderstanding VAT: A Comment on 'On the Presumed Technical Superiority of VAT'*, 9(3) Australian Tax Forum 271–276 (1992).

18. For a recent view on why VAT is a preferred form of taxation, see S. Cnossen, *A VAT Primer for Lawyers, Economists and Accountants*, 55(4) Tax Notes Intl. 319–332 (2009).
19. In the EU, Articles 19 and 29 of the Council Directive 2006/112/EC of 28 November 2006 on the common system of value added tax, OJ L347 of 11 December 2006, 1-118, hereafter 'EU VAT Directive' allows Member States to consider that no supply of goods or services has taken place on sales of ongoing concerns. On the EU Court of Justice interpretation of these rules, see recent commentary by G. Richards, *Finanzamt Ludenscheid v. Christel Schriever: shedding more light on transfers as a going concern*, 2 British Tax Rev. 151–153 (2012).
20. In the EU, Article 11 of the EU VAT Directive gives Member States the option to introduce a VAT grouping scheme, although it does not provide any guidelines on its design. Consequently just over half of the EU Member States have introduced a VAT grouping scheme, but with legal designs that vary greatly. On this topic see European Commission, *Communication from the Commission to the Council and the European Parliament on the VAT Group option provided in Article 11 of Council Directive 2006/112/EC on the common system of value added tax*, COM(2009) 325 final, 2 July 2009; A. van Doesum & G.J. van Norden, *T(w)o become one: the communication from the Commission on VAT grouping*, 6 British Tax Rev. 657–667 (2009); and J. Swinkels, *The phenomenon of VAT groups under EU law and their VAT-saving aspects*, 21(1) Intl. VAT Monitor 36–42 (2010). Australia, New Zealand, Canada and Singapore are just some of the other countries which also allow VAT/GST groups; for a general overview of the applicable rules in these countries, see P. Stacey, *A rational basis for setting GST and VAT grouping thresholds*, 17(3) Intl. VAT Monitor 186–190 (2006); R. Millar, *Time is of the Essence: Supplies, Grouping Schemes and Cancelled Transactions*, 7(2) J. Australian Taxn. 132–195 (2004); and R. Thomas, *Leaving a GST group – Is a Clean Exit Possible?*, 9(6) Australian GST J. 73–76 (2009).
21. The work of M. Lauré was particularly influential in the French process of adopting a VAT: see M. Lauré, *La Tax à la Valeur Ajoutée* (2d ed., Librarie du Receuil Sirey 1953) and M. Lauré, *Au Secours de la TVA* (Presses Universitaires de France 1957).
22. Also known as the Fiscal and Financial Committee, the Neumark Committee was set up by the European Commission to assess the manner by which the disparities of public finance within

'audacious'.[23] In light of the recommendations of the Neumark Report, the European Commission submitted legislative proposals which envisaged the adoption by Member States of a common system of VAT that followed the fundamental principles of the French VAT system.

The final proposal by the European Commission deviated from the majority recommendation of the Neumark Committee that the VAT operate up to but not including the final retail stage, instead calling for the adoption of a full VAT through all stages of production and sales. The mandatory rollout throughout the Community commenced with promulgation in 1967 of the Commission's First and Second VAT Directives[24] and by 1973 all original members of the EEC had transformed their turnover taxes into VATs. Ten years later, motivated by the introduction of VAT as a Community own resource, and in an attempt to address the existing divergence of VAT national systems, a blueprint for common rules, the Sixth VAT Directive, was approved amidst high expectations,[25] and effectively regarded at the time as a new 'European VAT Code'.[26] As this new VAT legislation became part of the *acquis communautaire*, the introduction of a VAT system, subject to the rules set out therein, became a pre-condition for accession of any countries subsequently joining the European Economic Community, its successor the European Community and today's European Union.

This redesign of the turnover tax into a VAT enjoyed significant advantages over the adoption of a new tax base, particularly in terms of the administration, compliance and acceptance by the business community. The VAT could be presented to this group as a continuation of the existing turnover tax with a benefit in the form of full recovery by businesses of all taxes incurred on acquisitions. To this day, in Europe the VAT is often referred to both unofficially and officially as a 'turnover tax'.[27]

Winning over the business community, however, was not the only political challenge faced by proponents of the VAT. An equal, and perhaps greater, challenge was achieving acceptance by those who would ultimately be most affected by the move to a comprehensive tax on final consumption, the consumers. To gain the acceptance needed for the change, the first VAT contained a wide range of implicit subsidies by

---

Member States could prejudice the establishment of a common market; included within this mandate was the potential harmonization of turnover taxes: see *The EEC Reports on Tax Harmonisation – The Report of the Fiscal and Financial Committee and the Report of the Sub-Groups A, B and C* (Amsterdam: IBFD Publications, 1963).

23. See B. Terra and P. Wattel, *European Tax Law* 200–201 (4th ed., Kluwer Law International 2005).
24. OJ 71 of 14 April 1967, 1301–1312.
25. Sixth Council Directive 77/388/EEC of 12 May 1977 on the harmonization of the laws of the Member States relating to turnover taxes, OJ L145 of 13 June 1977, 1. For a detailed analysis of the process which preceded the approval of these Directives and ultimately led to the introduction of VATs in European countries, see R. de la Feria, *The EU VAT System and the Internal Market* 47–56 (IBFD 2009). See also J. Englisch (n. 9 above).
26. P. Miconi, *Razões Justificativas da Introdução de um Sistema de Imposto sobre o Valor Acrescentado*, 244/246 *Ciência e Técnica Fiscal* at 429 April/June (1979); and A.E. Genot, *Fiscal Harmonisation and European Integration: A 1978 Appraisal*, 3 European L. Rev. 355–369, at 360 (1978).
27. See Article 113 of the Treaty on the Functioning of the European Union.

way of reduced rates for some types of supplies and 'exemptions' for selected other types of supplies, which often replicated those that had been in place under the previous turnover taxes.[28] Alongside these concessional quasi-subsidy exemptions were a number of exemptions adopted for 'technical' reasons, namely the perceived difficulties of fitting these supplies into the ordinary VAT regime. The most significant examples of such supplies are financial and insurance services, some types of transactions on immovable property and gambling services. The implication is that these activities would ideally have been subject to VAT, but pragmatic considerations determined that they be exempt. Preparatory work to the Sixth VAT Directive confirms this reasoning.[29] Crucially, all the exemptions included in European VAT legislation, both concessional and technical, have been from the outset mandatory in nature. While the EU legislator allowed Member States to depart from the rules set out therein in many other areas of the tax, such as the application (or not) of reduced rates, insofar as exemptions are concerned Member States are in principle obliged to apply them, and cannot to this day deviate from what is set out at European level. The fact that there are a few exceptions - where Member States have retained some level of discretion as regards the application of exemptions - does not take away from this general rule.[30]

The theoretical economic neutrality advantages of the VAT, its potential for enhanced compliance as a consequence of multi-stage collection and invoicing, and its proven ability to raise significant revenues, led advisors from Europe and international organizations such as the International Monetary Fund (IMF) to recommend adoption of a VAT in their development models,[31] and over the next decades approximately 150 nations adopted taxes they called VATs.[32] In practice, few of these were VATs in the European sense of applying in a relatively comprehensive fashion to goods and services

28. See S. Cnossen, *What Rate Structure for a Value-Added Tax?*, 35(2) Natl. Tax J. 205–214, at 209 (1982); and V. Lenoir (n. 6 above), at 456–457.
29. European Commission, *Proposal for a Sixth VAT Directive on the harmonisation of legislation of Member States concerning turnover taxes – Common system of value added tax: uniform basis of assessment*, COM(73) 95, 20 June 1975, Bulletin of the European Economic Communities, Supplement 11. See also the Hutchings Report, which was a broad consultation on VAT and financial services undertaken by the tax authorities in the then six Member States in close liaison with the industry, European Commission, *Les Operations Financières et Bancaire et la Taxe sur la Valeur Ajoutée*, Working Document XIV/241/71, June 1971.
30. Article 137 of the EU VAT Directive allows Member States to grant taxable persons the option to tax in respect of financial services and immovable property; and under Article 133 of the Directive Member States may make the granting of some concessional exemptions conditional on specific requirements. On this point see J. Englisch (n. 9 above).
31. For an assessment of the comparative advantages of VAT, as well as other historical and practical reasons for its spread, see L. Ebrill et al. (n. 8 above), at 4–13; M. Keen & B. Lockwood, *The Value-Added Tax: its Causes and Consequences*, 92(2) J. Dev. Econ. 138–151 (2010); and R.M. Bird & P-P. Gendron (n. 17 above), at 16 et seq. For a critical view of the IMF approach to tax reform, including its role on the spread of VAT, see M. Stewart & S. Jogarajan, *The International Monetary Fund and Tax Reform*, 2 British Tax Rev. 146–175 (2004).
32. A complete list as of 2007 can be found in A. Schenk & O. Oldman, *Value Added Tax – A Comparative Approach* app. A. (Cambridge University Press 2007).

while providing a robust input tax credit system to avoid cascading taxes on business-to-business transactions. Some only applied to goods and others provided at best limited input tax credits.[33]

Attempts to enact VAT systems outside of Europe revealed some of the shortcomings of the European model. While European tax administrations had long turnover tax experience that could be applied to develop administration systems capable of handling the complexities of multiple VAT rates and concessional exemptions, the complexity of the European model was beyond the capabilities of administrations in developing countries. More significantly, the resulting narrow base required exceptionally high - and, outside of Europe, politically unsustainable - standard rates to raise sufficient revenue, and there was considerable concern with respect to the economic costs of biases and embedded tax in a multi-rate, multiple exemption VAT system.

An alternative model appeared in 1984 with the enactment in New Zealand of what has become known as the modern VAT - in contrast to the traditional European VAT. Like its European counterpart, the New Zealand GST uses invoices to track acquisitions and determine entitlement to refundable input tax credits (invoice-credit method). Unlike the European VAT, however, the New Zealand VAT has a single, and consequently much lower, standard rate with no reduced rate(s), no merit concessional exemptions and limited exemptions for technical reasons.[34] From the mid-1980s onwards, most non-European VAT laws have followed the modern VAT model and while most have adopted one of the foundation principles of the New Zealand law, a single rate, few have adhered as closely as New Zealand to the second principle of no concessional exemptions or exclusions. In addition to rejecting the use of exemptions to subsidize particular activities or types of consumption, the modern VAT showed it was possible to apply the VAT to many types of supplies that had been classified as too difficult to tax under the traditional VAT, and therefore, appropriate for exemption. It illustrated how gambling services, certain types of immovable property transactions, some types of insurance services, and entities such as government departments, public bodies and charities, could all be included in the VAT system.

Not all modern VATs have opted for the same design alternatives as New Zealand, with different countries opting for different solutions as regards traditionally exempted sectors. Moreover, even the modern VAT had its limits at the time it first appeared, the most significant of which was the maintenance of the traditional VAT's exemption for financial services. A quarter century after its introduction, the model for the modern VAT, the New Zealand's GST law, finally addressed in part this remaining

33. China being one of the most well-known examples of both these phenomena: see W. Cui & A. Wu, *China*, in *The Future of Indirect Taxation – Recent Trends in VAT and GST Systems Around the World*, EUCOTAX Series on European Taxation 159–190 (T. Ecker, M. Lang & I. Lejeune eds., Wolters Kluwer 2012); and X. Yang, *Merger of Business Tax into VAT in China*, 2 Intl. VAT Monitor 120–123 (2009).

34. On the introduction of the GST in New Zealand, see in particular R. Douglas, *The New Zealand GST Policy Choice and its Political Implications*, in *GST in Retrospect and Prospect* 3–11 (R. Krever & D. White eds., Thomson Brookers 2007); R. Green, *Consulting the Public in Developing a GST*, in *GST in Retrospect and Prospect.* 13–25 (R. Krever & D. White eds.); and J. Todd, *Implementing GST – Information, Education, Co-ordination*, in *GST in Retrospect and Prospect.* 27–43 (R. Krever & D. White eds.).

exemption, perhaps in the process paving the way to the consideration of a post-modern VAT.

[B] What Are Exemptions?

The term 'exempt supplies' is used in most VAT systems to describe supplies that do not bear output tax – the supplier need not collect or remit any tax in respect of the supply – and do not entitle the recipient to any input tax credits in respect of tax borne on acquisitions related to the making of the supply.[35] The irony of the term is not lost on VAT experts, even if other economic players, particularly final consumers, are misled by the terminology. From the perspective of registered businesses an 'exempt' supply in the VAT system is actually a taxable supply, while a 'taxable' supply is actually an exempt supply. As there is no recovery of input tax embedded in the price of exempt supplies, the cost of the tax included in the price must be borne by the business that acquires the exempt supply and can only be recovered if the tax is passed on to customers. A taxable supply, on the other hand, is tax-free to a registered business customer as the tax can be recovered through the input tax credit system. Ultimately, both taxable and exempt supplies are taxed supplies from the perspective of the final consumers – albeit at different levels – with an explicit tax levied on the first type of supply, and a (smaller) embedded tax included in the cost of the second.[36]

Unlike the case with an explicit tax levied on taxable supplies, measurement of the tax embedded in the cost of an exempt supply may be problematic, as it is dependent on various factors. The level of VAT embedded in the price of an exempt supply will depend on the value of services provided by the supplier making the exempt supply and the character of supplies up the supply chain. Where there is little labour input in the supply and relatively little mark up by the supplier for his or her work in making the supply available, the embedded VAT may not be far below the VAT that would have been charged had the supply been taxable.[37] If most of the value of the supply is attributable to the labour input of the person making the supply and that person draws upon few inputs to provide the labour, the rate of embedded tax relative to the value of the supply may be small.

The Organisation for Economic Co-operation and Development (OECD) has identified a range of standard exemptions which vary greatly across member nations,

35. Some label these supplies as 'exempt without credit' - both outside Europe, e.g., Brazil, and within Europe, e.g., Portugal - while Australia uses the term 'input taxed supplies', both alternatives being more accurate in terms of the effect of the rules applicable to supplies of this type.
36. As Keen puts it, when referring to the financial services exemption, 'business users pay too much tax (in the sense that the normal crediting mechanism of the VAT would wipe out such input VAT ...), while final consumers pay too little (because the value added by the financial institutions is not taxed)'; see M. Keen, *The Taxation and Regulation of Financial Institutions*, IIPF Musgrave Lecture (2010).
37. Of course the level of the mark up may itself be influenced by the amount of embedded VAT. Depending on the price elasticity of the products offered or/and the competitiveness of the market, the supplier might not be able to set prices that reflect the full extent of the embedded VAT, having instead to decrease its profit margin.

with significant differences between European nations and other members. Generally, jurisdictions outside the EU have a very limited number of exempt supplies. In contrast, exemptions proliferate in Europe. Standard exemptions in European countries include postal services, transport of sick/injured persons, hospital and medical care, human blood, tissues and organs, dental care; education, sporting activities, cultural services (excluding radio and television broadcasting), charitable work, non-commercial activities by non-profit organizations, certain fund-raising events, the supply of land and buildings (including letting of immovable property), betting, lotteries and gambling, insurance and reinsurance, and a range of financial services including loan intermediary services and capital raising operations. Beyond these core items are exemptions covering a wide diversity of sectors such as legal aid, passenger transport, public cemeteries, waste and recyclable material, water supply, precious metals and certain agricultural inputs.[38]

Two other types of supply may replicate the effect of an exempt supply in the VAT: out-of-scope supplies made by VAT registered suppliers and supplies made by out-of-scope suppliers. The first of these is a supply that falls outside the scope of the VAT legislation, either for technical reasons related to its design or as a result of narrow judicial interpretations of provisions in the VAT law. Whether an out-of-scope supply will bear embedded input tax in the same manner as an explicitly exempt supply will depend on the technical design of the input tax credit measures in the VAT law. In cases where the entitlement to input tax credits for acquisitions is not directly tied to the use of those acquisitions in making taxable supplies, the supplier will be able to recover the input VAT and the supply will be tax-free. If, however, the law only allows input tax credits where the acquisition is directly connected with a taxable supply, the out-of-scope supply will bear embedded VAT in the same manner as explicitly exempt supplies.

The second type of supply that can replicate the effect of an exempt supply is a supply made by an out-of-scope supplier. Suppliers may fall outside the scope of a VAT law for three reasons. First, they are taxable enterprises with turnovers less than the threshold for compulsory registration under the VAT law. Second, they may be excluded from the definition of taxable enterprises as a result of a narrow definition in the VAT law or narrow judicial interpretation of the concept of taxable enterprise. Third, they may be explicitly excluded from the operation of the VAT system by the relevant legislation.

§1.03 ACTIVITIES OUTSIDE THE SCOPE OF VAT

[A] Out-of-Scope Supplies

The use of restrictive terminology in VAT legislation or the effect of restrictive judicial interpretation of terms used in the law can leave supplies made by registered persons

38. See OECD (n. 7 above), at 76–81. See also R. Bird & P-P. Gendron, who offer a sample of exemptions applicable in some countries outside the OECD; see n. 17 above, at 121–123.

(or persons who are required to be registered) as out-of-scope supplies, often also referred to as non-taxable supplies. The result is an under-taxation of supplies to final consumers and over-taxation of business customers.

Occurrences of out-of-scope supplies by registered businesses are found in both the EU traditional VAT and the modern VAT. Many instances in the former are attributable to the 'direct and immediate link' doctrine developed in the European Court of Justice in the 1980s. The doctrine established as a condition of a taxable supply that there be a direct (and formal) link between a supply and payment (consideration) received in respect of that supply.[39] Thus, for example, a voluntary payment to a person making supplies at large would not be treated as consideration for a taxable supply in the traditional VAT.[40]

Another source of out-of-scope supplies found in both the traditional and modern VAT is a narrow understanding of 'supply' to exclude, for example, supplies of inaction, supplies made at large and involuntary supplies. An example of the first is the fulfilment of a non-competition covenant or agreement to cease activities upon receipt of consideration for non-performance.[41] An example of the second is the assumption by an entity of social or economic responsibilities or undertakings in return for payment.[42] An example of the third is an expropriation of property where the supply is the result of compulsory acquisition by the acquirer, not voluntary disposal by the vendor.[43]

A third cause of out-of-scope supplies is the characterization of some dealings in financial securities such as shares and bonds by an otherwise fully taxable enterprise as investment activities undertaken by the firm rather than part of its business activities. If the impugned transactions constitute a significant enough portion of the enterprise's activities, the entire enterprise may be tainted as an out-of-scope person, not engaged in requisite economic activities.[44]

---

39. The doctrine was first introduced in Cases 154/80, *Staatssecretaris van Financien v. Cooperatieve Verenigning Cooperatieve Aardappelenbewaarplaats GA (Dutch Potato)* [1981] ECR 445; and 102/86, *Apple and Pear Development Council (APDC) v. Commissioners of Customs and Excise* [1988] ECR 1443.
40. See Case C-16/93, *R. J. Tolsma v. Inspecteur der Omzetbelasting Leeuwarden* [1994] ECR I-743, a case involving a street musician receiving 'donations' from passers-by. The approach used by the Court to exclude the transaction in that case from VAT is analysed in A. Schenk & O. Oldman (n. 32 above), at 120. The nexus required by courts to establish the link between consideration and a supply has been more relaxed in some cases. See for example Case C-498/99, *Town & County Factors Ltd v. Commissioners of Customs & Excise* [2002] ECR I-7173.
41. See, for example, Case C-215/94, *Mohr v. Finanzamt Bad Segerberg* [1996] ECR I-959, where a farmer was paid to withdraw from milk production.
42. See, for example, *Chatham Islands Enterprise Trust v. CIR* (1999) 19 NZTC 15,075 (Ct of A) (NZ) where a trust received funds from the government after agreeing to assume responsibility for what were previously government responsibilities; and *CIR v NZ Refining Co Ltd* [1997] 18 NZTC 13,187 (Ct of A) (NZ) where a company received a payment from the government in return for an agreement to stay in business following deregulation.
43. *Hornsby Shire Council and Federal Commissioner of Taxation* (2008) AATA 1060 (AAT) (Australia) where a local government expropriated property owned by a registered enterprise.
44. See, for example, Cases C-333/91, *Sofitam SA (formerly Satam SA) v. Ministre chargé du Budget*, [1993] ECR I-3513; C-4/94, *BLP Group plc v. Commissioners of Customs & Excise* [1995] ECR I-983; C-80/95, *Harnas & Helm CV v. Staatssecretaris van Financiën* [1997] ECR I-745; C-98/98, *Commissioners of Customs and Excise v. Midland Bank plc* [2000] ECR I-4177; C-16/00, *Cibo Participations SA v. Directeur régional des impôts du Nord-Pas-de-Calais* [2001]

[B] Out-of-Scope Suppliers

As noted earlier, there are three groups of suppliers that may fall outside the scope of VAT law. The first are businesses that would otherwise be subject to VAT but with turnovers below the compulsory VAT threshold; the second are entities that fall outside the scope of the tax as a result of judicial interpretations of legislative charging provisions; the third are entities explicitly prevented from registering by legislative exclusions. The first category of out-of-scope supplier is common to the traditional VAT and the modern VAT. The second and third types of out-of-scope supplier are found most often - albeit not exclusively - in the traditional European VAT systems.

[1] Unregistered Businesses

Most VAT laws, both traditional and modern, contain registration 'thresholds' that exempt small businesses from compulsory registration and inclusion in the VAT system, although the thresholds vary widely across countries.[45] These registration thresholds were not always well perceived. When VAT initially appeared on the world stage, the general view was that the ideal VAT threshold should be zero, and therefore the usual expert advice was to set the threshold as low as possible.[46] This view was in line with optimal taxation theory which stated at the time that differentiation of tax liability based on firm size violates production efficiency.[47] A number of disadvantages to establishing a registration threshold were cited to buttress the case for no or very low thresholds.

The first disadvantage - or advantage, if the rationale is to enhance the competitive position of small firms - of thresholds is that they may distort competition between those above and below the trigger point, particularly in the case of firms selling directly

ECR I-6663; C-465/03, *Kretztechnik AG v. Finanzamt Linz* [2005] ECR I-4357; C-437/06, *Securenta Göttinger Immobilienanlagen und Vermögensmanagement AG v. Finanzamt Göttingen* [2008] ECR I-597; and C-29/08, *Skatteverket v. AB SKF* [2009] ECR I-10413. For comprehensive discussion on this jurisprudence see A. van Doesum & G.J. van Norden, *The Right to Deduct under EU VAT*, 5 Intl. VAT Monitor 323–329 (2011); and P. Melz, *Activities Outside the Scope of VAT and Exempt Activities*, 5 Intl. VAT Monitor 330–331 (2011). See also R. de la Feria, *When Do Dealings in Shares Fall Within the Scope of VAT?*, 1 EC Tax Rev. 24–40 (2008); J. Englisch, *The Future of Indirect Taxation – Recent Trends in VAT and GST Systems Around the World*, EUCOTAX Series on European Taxation 159–190 (T. Ecker, M. Lang & I. Lejeune eds., Wolters Kluwer 2012), at 549–585; D.R. Jensen & H. Stensgaard, *The distinction between direct and general costs with regard to the deduction of input VAT – the case of acquisition, holding and sale of shares*, 4(1) World Tax J. 3-32 (2012); A. van Doesum, H. van Kesteren & G.-J. van Norden, *Share disposals and the right of deduction of input VAT*, 19(2) EC Tax Rev. 62–73 (2010); G. Richards, Skatteverket v AB SKF: *exploring the impact on input tax recovery on the boundary between exempt transactions and non-business activities*, 3 British Tax Rev. 273–275 (2009); and C. Amand, *VAT: deductibility of the costs of issuing new shares – the direct and immediate link test*, 5(3) EC Tax J. 203–230 (2001).

45. Several developed countries with good tax administrations, such as Spain, have thresholds of zero, so that every business regardless of how small, must register for VAT, see OECD (n. 7 above), at Table 3.9.
46. See R. Bird & P-P. Gendron (n. 17 above), at 115.
47. See P. Diamond & J.A. Mirrlees, *Optimal Taxation and Public Production I: Production Efficiency*, 61(1) Am. Econ. Rev. 8–27 (1971).

to final consumers. In the case of business customers, the apparent lower VAT included in the cost of supplies from unregistered suppliers is negated by the fact that these suppliers cannot issue tax invoices and no input tax credits are available to recover the embedded VAT included in the supplies. In contrast, the fully taxable supply made by the registered supplier is free of tax after input tax credits are claimed. The registered business customer will thus almost always prefer to limit acquisitions to those supplied by registered persons. To ensure smaller businesses are not at a competitive disadvantage relative to larger firms with turnovers greater than the registration threshold, most VAT systems provide for voluntary registration by smaller firms that may wish to supply registered businesses. On the other hand, small businesses supplying to final consumers may find it advantageous to remain as unregistered suppliers. Their customers will bear the entire cost of embedded VAT included in the price of goods and services acquired by the suppliers, but incur no tax liability in respect of the value added by the suppliers. As final consumers are indifferent between tax that is embedded in the price and tax that appears on a tax invoice as a separate line before the total amount payable, unregistered suppliers will be able to attract non-business customers so long as the embedded tax is less than the explicit tax charged by registered businesses.

The ability of unregistered businesses to make de facto exempt supplies provides small businesses with a slight competitive advantage in some cases, or with a better ability to compete in the face of the economies of scale and volume purchase pricing available to larger registered competitors. It might be argued that this competitive advantage given to unregistered firms is desirable as it tends to be the smaller and hence presumably poorer traders that are relatively advantaged and the implicit subsidy of reduced taxation meets vertical equity concerns.[48] On the other hand, an indirect subsidy delivered by way of reduced consumption tax liability is a very crude redistribution instrument that is impossible to target effectively. To the extent the implicit subsidy keeps less efficient smaller firms afloat,[49] the economic consequences may be counter productive and it might actually further growth by firms approaching the threshold, creating a bunching of firms just below the threshold and an absence of firms for some distance above it.[50] A recent study seems to confirm this possibility, not solely by finding a clustering of companies just below the threshold, but also suggesting that masquerading behaviour - either in the form of avoidance or evasion - in order to fall outside the scope of VAT may be commonplace.[51]

The second disadvantage of establishing a registration threshold is the loss of potential revenue. This aspect must, however, be seen in the context of administrative and compliance costs. The initial view dismissing the benefits of registration thresholds above zero implicitly assumed that there were little or no additional administrative and

48. M. Keen & J. Mintz, *The Optimal Threshold for Value-Added Tax*, 88 J. Pub. Econ. 559–576, at 564 (2004).
49. Smaller firms tend to be less efficient than their larger competitors; see A. Schenk & O. Oldman (n. 32 above), at 77–79.
50. M. Keen & J. Mintz (n. 48 above), at 568.
51. See K. Onji, *The Response of Firms to Eligibility Thresholds: Evidence from the Japanese Value-Added Tax*, 93(5-6) J. Pub. Econ. 766–775 (2009).

compliance costs from the low threshold. The evidence now suggests that firm-size differentiation can indeed be part of an optimal tax system when there are fixed-per-firm cost elements in the administrative costs of running a tax system.[52] In fact, bringing every small business into the VAT system increases administrative costs exponentially, and the additional VAT collected may be largely absorbed as costs in collecting the tax. Therefore, even if some revenue is forgone by dropping small taxpayers, in most countries any revenue loss could be likely recouped by removing the high administration costs of assessing numerous low-return taxpayers who universally account for relatively little VAT revenue.[53]

Additional rationales for low thresholds concern the interest of tax authorities in gathering information and assessing participants in the shadow economy. Since good tax administration rests on information, it has been argued that including the largest possible share of the economic activity in the tax base has the advantage of capturing as much information as possible; it may also be that dipping as deeply as possible into the pool of potential taxpayers will lead to catching some 'hidden whales'.[54] Neither of these reasons is particularly convincing, however. There has been no evidence of concealed VAT profit windfalls waiting to be uncovered through broader assessment of small businesses.

Optimal tax administration analysis now suggests the VAT registration threshold should be determined by balancing collection costs against the marginal value of additional tax revenues.[55] Interestingly, the older and more current views are not reflected in distinctions between traditional VAT and modern VAT jurisdictions' practices. Some traditional VAT systems such as those in place in the Czech Republic, France, Ireland, Slovak Republic and the United Kingdom apply a high threshold compared to those applied in modern VAT systems such as Australia, Canada or New Zealand.[56] To the extent to which these thresholds reflect conclusions on the relative cost of administration relative to revenue collection, there may be room for improvement of administration processes in some jurisdictions.

[2] Deemed 'Non-business' Enterprises

The definition of taxable person for VAT purposes varies from jurisdiction to jurisdiction, but a common feature to all definitions is the requirement that the person be carrying on economic activities – a stipulation intended to exclude private household activities. A significant point of departure between the traditional and modern VAT systems, however, is the approach taken by courts when interpreting phrases such as 'business', 'enterprise' or 'economic activities' used within those definitions. In

52. See D. Dharmapala, J. Slemrod & J.D. Wilson, *Tax Policy and the 'Missing Middle': Optimal Tax Remittance with Firm-Level Administrative Costs,* J. Pub. Econ. 95, 1036–1047 (2011).
53. M. Keen & J. Mintz (n. 48 above). In this regard, it is also worth noting that in most countries reportedly 'a surprisingly small number of VAT registrations, sometimes less than a few dozen, account for 80% to 90% of VAT collections', see R. Bird & P-P. Gendron (n. 17 above), at 115.
54. See R. Bird & P-P. Gendron (n. 17 above), at 120.
55. See M. Keen & J. Mintz (n. 48 above).
56. See OECD (n. 7 above), at tbl. 3.9.

modern VAT jurisdictions, these terms tend to be given wide interpretations - prima facie, an entity with a significant number of employees, making substantial acquisitions, owning or renting commercial property, and so forth is carrying on economic activities and would be treated as a taxable person under the modern VAT.[57] They would thus be able to register and claim input tax credits, even if they make no taxable supplies - the test for eligibility for input tax credits in the modern VAT is whether the acquisitions are related to carrying on the person's enterprise and do not give rise to personal consumption, rather than whether they are directly used to make taxable supplies.

In contrast, courts in traditional VAT jurisdictions - in particular the EU Court of Justice - have read down the notion of an 'economy activity'[58] through a phenomenon of what has been designated elsewhere as creeping case law,[59] so it rarely extends beyond activities involving supplies for consideration in the course of an ongoing business. Three key groups left out of the scope of economic activity by the narrow concept, and thus of the ability to make taxable supplies or creditable acquisitions, are mutual business organizations, holding companies and investment companies. All these enterprises play intermediary roles in the economy, reflecting no final consumption, but nevertheless incur unrecoverable input tax on acquisitions as a result of their exclusion from the VAT system by the judicial interpretations.

The exclusion from the business concept of mutual organizations applies where an organization carrying on substantial activities absorbs all its income into making supplies to its members.[60] If the body's members are not final consumers, the designation of the organization as a non-business entity results in over-taxation with members unable to claim input tax credits on their membership fees that are in turn used in part or in whole to acquire taxable services through the mutual organization.

57. On the definition of 'enterprise' under Australian GST law, see R. Millar & D. McCarthy, *Australia*, in *The Future of Indirect Taxation – Recent Trends in VAT and GST Systems Around the World*, EUCOTAX Series on European Taxation 159–190 (T. Ecker, M. Lang & I. Lejeune eds., Wolters Kluwer 2012), 21–96, at 32–33; on the definition of 'commercial activity' under Canadian GST law, see M. Abbas & A.J. Cockfield, *Canada*, in *The Future of Indirect Taxation – Recent Trends in VAT and GST Systems Around the World*, EUCOTAX Series on European Taxation 159–190 (T. Ecker, M. Lang & I. Lejeune eds., Wolters Kluwer 2012), 109–141, at 114–116; and on the concept of 'taxable activity' under New Zealand GST law, as interpreted by the courts in that country, see P. Blanchard, *Some Basic Concepts of New Zealand GST*, in (R. Krever & D. White eds.) (n. 34 above), 91–101.

58. In the language used in Article 9 of the EU VAT Directive.

59. The term is used to describe the phenomenon whereby the introduction of a general principle in a given judgment has demanded extra qualifications, and explanations by the Court in subsequent decisions, resulting in the accumulation of a complex body of case law, riddled with factual minutiae: see R. de la Feria (n. 44 above), at 24–25.

60. For example, the UK House of Lords has held that the activities of the Institute of Chartered Accountants (UK) in ensuring accountants adhere to certain standards are undertaken without a view to profit and thus do not constitute a business, a threshold test for a taxable person in the UK: see *Institute of Chartered Accountants in England and Wales v. Commissioners of Customs and Excise* [1999] STC 398.

The designation by European courts of holding companies as non-taxable persons that are unable to claim input tax credits[61] results in unrecoverable tax becoming embedded in business to business transactions that involve no final consumption, generating the biases that the VAT was intended to eliminate.[62] Despite calls for reform,[63] and indeed the European Commission's recognition of the problem, there seem to be no immediate plans to address the problem in the traditional VAT.[64]

The third group sometimes left out of the scope of economic activity amounting to a business are investment and financial companies, often situated within a corporate group. By using the services of a financial member to source debt and capital and invest excess capital, a corporate group may realize significant economies of scale benefits, reducing costs and increasing returns. As noted previously in the context of out-of-scope supplies, an enterprise that carries on some financial transactions might find the transactions are characterized as passive investment activities rather than business activities and if the scale of these transactions relative to the entire operations of the enterprise is significant, the entire enterprise may be characterized as an out-of-scope enterprise not engaged in business-like economic activities. Lending operations by a factoring company[65] or making annual financing loans to subsidiaries[66] will be considered business activities, as would a fund manager's ongoing investing for the purpose of generating gains,[67] but the managed sale of an investment portfolio will not

---

61. This interpretation of the EU VAT Directive was initially introduced by the EU Court of Justice in the *Polysar* case in the early 1990s: see Case C-60/90 [1991] ECR I-3111, a judgment that at the time 'seemed innocuous enough in itself'. See P. Farmer, *Taxable persons and the 'Private Life' of Companies*, 2 EC Tax J. 41–48, at 42 (1997). The doctrine has been reinstated and developed in later decisions, which indicate that a holding company may qualify as an eligible enterprise where different exceptions apply. For an analysis of this case law from both a European perspective and that of national courts, see R. de la Feria (n. 44 above); and J. Englisch, *Input VAT Deduction by Holding Companies – German Practice and Community Law*, 2 Intl. VAT 172–179 (2007).
62. For a principle-based analysis of the EU Court of Justice jurisprudence on holding companies see R. de la Feria, *A Natureza das Actividades e Direito à Dedução das Holdings em Sede de IVA*, 4(3) Revista de Finanças Públicas e Direito Fiscal (2011).
63. See recently M. Aujean, *Harmonization of VAT in the EU: Back to the Future*, 3 EC Tax Rev. 134–143 (2012).
64. In 2010, the European Commission seemed to be considering a review of the VAT treatment of holding companies: see *Green Paper on the Future of VAT – Towards a simpler, more robust and efficient VAT system*, Communication from the Commission to the European Parliament, the Council and the European Economic and Social Committee, COM(2010) 695 final, 1 December 2010; for a comment see A. van Doesum & G.J. van Norden, *EU2011, EUtopia and EU2020: the European Commission's Green Paper on the Future of VAT*, 3 British Tax Rev. 253–272, at 263–267 (2011). However, by the following year the issue seemed to have been dropped from the Commission's immediate plans; see *Communication on the Future of VAT – Towards a simpler, more robust and efficient VAT system tailored to the single market*, Communication from the Commission to the European Parliament, the Council and the Economic and Social Committee, COM(2011) 851 final, 6 December 2011.
65. Cases C-305/01, *Finanzamt Gross-Gerauv v. MKG-Kraftfahrzeuge Factoring GmBH* [2003] ECR I-6729; and C-93/10, *Finanzamt Essen-NordOst v. GFKL Financial Services AG* [2011] ECR I-000.
66. Case C-77/01, *Empresa de Desenvolvimento Mineiro SGPS SA (EDM) v. Fazenda Publica* [2004] ECR I-4295.
67. Case C-8/03, *Banque Bruxelles Lambert v. Etat Belge* [2004] ECR I-10157.

cross this threshold.[68] The borderline is murky at best and the narrowing of the economic activity concept can result in a compounding VAT liability on enterprises seeking a more efficient allocation of resources and skills within a company group.

[3] Government Departments, Other Public Sector Bodies, and Charities

While the treatment of supplies by governments and government bodies attracts much comment and generates many tax disputes and consequent case law, in many cases the question is of little importance in practical terms. The clearest case where the tax status of a government body is irrelevant is where the government that levies the VAT provides monopoly services such as issuing passports or issuing spectrum licences.[69] All customers for the former will be individuals and the acquisition will be private consumption. It makes no difference to the customers if the government charges a lower price and imposes VAT or charges a higher price and has no VAT. A supply such as a telecommunications spectrum licence, on the other hand, will only be acquired by a registered enterprise in the course of a business. When calculating how much to bid for the supply, this customer should be indifferent between a higher price that includes a recoverable VAT component or a lower price that is exempt from VAT, provided it knows beforehand whether the supply will be taxable or not.

Difficulties may arise if the character of a monopoly supply is not made clear prior to the supply being made. If, for example, the government has assumed a supply did not include VAT and the customer assumed it did, the customer may overpay for an acquisition from the government. Alternatively, it may be the customer that assumes the supply is exempt and bids a lower price, later seeking a windfall by claiming the lower amount was VAT-inclusive. Leaving the cases of poor prior communication aside, however, the character of monopoly supplies is relatively unimportant so long as both the government and customers agree beforehand on that character and the government or customer, as need be, adjust their prices or bids respectively.

In terms of the government that levies the VAT, the treatment of government bodies under the VAT will only affect the budget allocation between departments. For example, if the police and army can register and claim input tax credits, their acquisition costs will fall and a smaller funding allocation from the central budget will be needed. If they cannot register, their acquisition costs will rise and the government will fund them with higher direct budget allocations rather than lower allocations combined with input tax refunds.

The treatment of lower tier governments and government bodies is much more problematic in the VAT. Two distinct sets of issues arise – should taxes paid to lower tier governments be treated as consideration for taxable supplies and should lower tier

68. Case C-155/94, *Wellcome Trust Ltd v. Commissioners of Customs and Excise* [1996] ECR 1-3013.
69. Examples of litigation seeking to determine whether VAT is included in the price of these supplies include Cases C-284/04, *T-Mobile Austria GmbH and Others v. Republic of Austria* [2007] ECR I-5189; and C-369/04, *Hutchison 3G UK Ltd and Others v. Commissioners of Customs & Excise* [2007] ECR I-5247.

governments be allowed to register for VAT purposes or should they be kept out of the VAT system and thus treated in effect as persons making out-of-scope supplies?

Agreeing to pay a particular level of taxes (by way of the democratic process) results in forgoing consumption that could otherwise be acquired with the funds used to pay taxes. It can be argued consequently that taxes paid to a democratically elected government are simply another form of consideration for taxable supplies, the supplies being the public goods and services provided by the government and desired by the taxpayers who agree to pay higher taxes and reduce other consumption. On this basis, modern VAT systems may treat taxes paid to lower tier governments as consideration for taxable supplies.[70] The practice is relatively rare, however.

The second issue, whether lower tier governments should be allowed to register for VAT purposes and claim input tax on all acquisitions, not just those used to make taxable supplies that compete with supplies offered by private sector businesses, is a matter of great concern in all jurisdictions and one that leads to considerable political tension and litigation. If lower tier governments are not able to register and claim input tax credits on all their acquisitions, there will be a transfer of tax revenues from the lower tier governments to the higher level government that levies the VAT. The lower tier governments will be forced to raise local taxes to pay non-recoverable VAT on all their acquisitions.

This problem does not arise in modern VAT systems that allow all enterprises to register without regard to whether they are public or private, or for profit or not for profit. In these jurisdictions, lower tier governments simply register within the ordinary VAT system.[71] In other jurisdictions, particularly those modelled after the traditional European VAT with its narrower definition of enterprise that excludes governments, lower tier governments commonly bear a non-recoverable VAT burden on acquisition, resulting in a transfer of funds to the central government. There have been ongoing discussions about the need for a European-wide solution but to date there have been no effective steps taken to resolve the problem.[72] In the meantime, alternative solutions

70. New Zealand, for example, treats most taxes paid to lower tier governments as consideration for taxable supplies. The Australian legislation provides for similar treatment but delegates to the Treasurer the power to specify that some taxes should in effect be treated as consideration for exempt supplies. In practice, therefore, and for political reasons Australian Treasurers have excluded almost all lower tier government taxes from the VAT system.

71. To overcome constitutional issues, lower tier governments in Canada are registered under a separate system that parallels the national GST system.

72. In 2000, the Commission published a VAT strategy aimed at improving the operation of the Internal Market. Under the heading 'other potential future priorities', the Commission set out the areas which it considered warranted a thorough review. The first item on this list was the treatment of subsidies, public authorities and services in the public interest: see *A Strategy to Improve the Operation of the VAT System within the Context of the Internal Market*, Communication from the Commission to the Council and the European Parliament, COM(2000) 348 final, 7 June 2000. The Commission's intention to reform the VAT treatment of public bodies was reiterated in 2003 in their review and update of the VAT strategy. It stated then that preparatory work for reform of this area was already under way, and despite its complexity, a final proposal would be presented in the fourth quarter of 2004: see *Review and Update of VAT Strategy Priorities*, Communication from the Commission to the Council and the European Parliament, COM(2003) 614 final, 20 October 2003. Yet, six years on, the Commission has not only failed to do so, but equally there are no obvious signs of an intention to initiate the

have been developed at the national level to address the problem of tax transfer from lower tier governments to the government levying the VAT. The most common solution is to establish a parallel regime that allows lower tier governments to file returns in the parallel regimes and claim refunds of all or part of their input tax. While these refund schemes have the advantage of eliminating the bias towards self-supply and away from outsourcing, they, too, give rise to difficulties.[73]

The VAT treatment of government departments and other public sector bodies and charities marks another point of departure between the modern and traditional VAT, with these entities treated as out-of-scope suppliers in the European VAT.

Public bodies are a concept set out (and defined) in EU law,[74] and the special VAT status of these entities is largely an issue only in the traditional VAT. In broad terms, a public body is an entity established by, and largely funded by, a government but which operates outside any government department. An example is a national sports institute or arts organization.

The special rules for public bodies in the traditional VAT are in essence an anachronism derived from the roots of the European VAT in turnover taxes.[75] Today's European VAT law makes a distinction between 'commercial' supplies made by a public body that competes in the market with private profit-making entities and other supplies that are not seen to be offered in competition to supplies from private sector enterprises.[76] EU legislation treats public bodies as out-of-scope suppliers to the extent their supplies are non-commercial supplies, presumably on the assumption that there is some merit to their outputs that deserves a subsidy. The economic distortions and compliance consequences of dissecting and characterizing an organization's outputs may be significant,[77] with a bias towards self-supply and opportunities for aggressive planning and avoidance.[78] At the same time, the treatment of these bodies as out of

consultation process, which would usually precede such a move. See M. Aujean, *Application of VAT to Public Bodies: The EU VAT System, Current Issues and Proposals*, in *VAT in Africa* 71–79, at 79 (R. Krever ed., Pretoria University Press 2008).

73. See R. de la Feria, *The EU VAT Treatment of Public Sector Bodies: Slowly Moving in the Wrong Direction*, 37(3) Intertax 148–165, at 161–162 (2009).
74. For example, Article 1(9) of the Procurement Directive defines public body or, in the terms of the definition, a 'body governed by public law' as any body '(a) established for the specific purpose of meeting needs in the general interest, not having an industrial or commercial character; (b) having legal personality; and (c) financed, for the most part, by the State, regional or local authorities, or other bodies governed by public law; or subject to management supervision by those bodies; or having an administrative, managerial or supervisory board, more than half of whose members are appointed by the State, regional or local authorities, or by other bodies governed by public law'.
75. As Advocate-General Jacobs of the Court of Justice so clearly stated in the *Waterschap Zeeuws Vlaanderen* case: 'It is inherent in the existence of exceptions to the VAT system that they will interfere to some extent with the application of the principles of neutrality and of equality treatment. Whatever the merits of the decision to treat public sector bodies as final consumers, it forms an integral part of the Directive. In that and in comparable situations, the treatment of taxable persons and persons excluded from the VAT system will inevitably be different': see Case C-378/02, *Waterschap Zeeuws Vlaanderen v. Staatssecretaris van Financien* [2005] ECR I-4685, at para. 38.
76. See Article 13 of the EU VAT Directive.
77. See R. de la Feria (n. 73 above).
78. Cases C-223/03, *University of Huddersfield* [2006] ECR I-1751 and C-63/04, *Centralan* [2005] ECR I-11087.

scope suppliers to the extent they make non-commercial supplies at best amounts to an inefficient and ill-targeted subsidy.

Unlike public bodies, the concept of charitable organizations is common to both traditional and modern VAT jurisdictions. Their VAT treatment is not consistent, however. In the European traditional VAT systems, charities are treated as out-of-scope suppliers, unable to register and claim input tax credits. The result is input taxation of their charitable supplies, an uneven and perhaps illogical government levy on their activities. In some modern VAT jurisdictions, the activities of charities are viewed as economic activities in the broader sense, even if they are not for profit, and the bodies will be considered taxable persons, able to recover input tax on acquisitions and thus eliminate any embedded tax on their supplies of charitable goods or services. This is not the case in all modern VAT jurisdictions, however. In fact, while there appears to be a consensus that the VAT system should not be modified to deal with the perceived problem of charities,[79] in practice the exclusion of charities from the scope of VAT is not limited to traditional VAT jurisdictions,[80] with some countries, such as Canada, adopting a 'middle-ground' approach.[81]

§1.04 PARTICULAR CATEGORIES OF EXEMPTIONS

[A] Merit / Concessional Exemptions

The original designation of many types of exempt supplies as exempt was based not so much on clearly articulated policy objectives but rather on pragmatic political goals, as designers of the VAT sought to replicate the impact of the predecessor turnover taxes and deflect concerns about the tax on beneficiaries of previous concessions. Over time, two *ex post facto* rationales have been offered for the concessions. The first is based on vertical equity concerns, with the exemption of essential products said to diminish the natural regressivity of a VAT. The second is based on the alleged benefits of subsidizing particular types of consumption that yield positive externalities, with exemptions seen as a way of increasing consumption of so-called merit goods.

Once it is accepted that exemptions for merit goods amount to tax expenditures, the concessions should be subject to the same cost-benefit analysis as direct expenditure programs: what are the objectives of the exemptions and are there alternative spending or subsidy programs that might achieve the intended social and distributional goals more efficiently and fairly.

The equity / countering regressivity rationalization for exemptions derives from the fact that the proportion of income that is saved reduces as income reduces, with the

79. See W. Hellerstein (n. 15 above); and W. Hellerstein & H. Duncan, *VAT Exemptions: Principles and Practice*, 128 Tax Notes 989–999 (2010).
80. In fact, the OECD lists New Zealand and Turkey as the sole exceptions, see n. 7 above.
81. For an analysis and defence of this middle-ground approach see P.P. Gendron, *VAT Treatment of Public Sector Bodies: The Canadian Model*, Ch. 3 in this volume; for a critique to this approach in defence of the full-taxation model, see R. Millar, *Smoke and Mirrors: Applying the Full Taxation Model to Government under the Australian and New Zealand GST Laws*, Ch. 4 in this volume.

lowest income earners using all their income for consumption and diverting none to savings. As a consumption tax falls only on income used for consumption and exempts income that is applied to savings, consumption taxes fall more heavily on lower income persons than on higher income persons in terms of the proportion of income derived by those persons. The vertical equity principle guiding the design of the income tax suggests that tax should rise as a proportion of income if income is a valid measurement of ability to contribute to public goods and services. A consumption tax that yields the opposite outcome is troublesome for those adhering to this notion of vertical equity and the use of taxation as a tool for redistribution. Exemptions for commodities that form a higher percentage of the spending budget of lower income persons are seen as a way of reducing the tax burden on these persons and thus increasing their consumption capability.

Exemptions as a social welfare measure fare quite badly compared to the alternative of full taxation and targeted income support, and constitute a blunt instrument for redistribution.[82] They come at a significant revenue cost to the government, a cost that far exceeds the benefit derived by lower income persons. Even though consumption of any particular commodity will represent a lower percentage of the total income of a wealthy person compared to the consumption of a poorer person, in absolute terms the high income person is likely to spend more on the commodity.[83] If the item were fully taxed and low income persons compensated for the tax by direct payments, the government could return the tax to lower income persons and have additional revenue left over to apply to other redistributive programs.[84] In this sense, lower income persons may be much worse off with a tax system that contains exemptions designed to assist them than they would be in a tax system with no exemptions and redistribution of the excess revenue raised under a more neutral tax base.[85]

The 'positive externalities' rationale for exemptions derives from a belief that the market price for some types of supplies does not fully reflect the overall benefits from consumption of those supplies and government intervention to subsidize consumption of those goods is desirable. The assumption is that exempt supplies would be less costly to final consumers than fully taxable supplies, as they would bear VAT on inputs up to

82. J. Creedy, *Indirect Tax Reform and the Role of Exemptions*, 22(4) Fiscal Stud. 457 (2001).
83. Cnossen has argued that VAT is regressive with respect to income but not necessarily with respect to consumption: see S. Cnossen, *The Value-added Tax: Key to a Better Tax Mix*, 6(3) Australian Tax Forum 265–281 (1989). Davis and Kay provide amusing examples with reference to the United Kingdom to illustrate the shortcomings of using the VAT structure as mean to diminish its regressivity: see E.H. Davis & J.A. Kay, *Extending the VAT base: problems and possibilities*, 6(1) Fiscal Studies 1-16 at 11–12 (1985).
84. Godbout and St. Gerny show that with tax credits targeted at lowest income individuals in place, the effective tax rate of consumption taxes increases with income, see C. Godbout & S. St. Gerny, *Are Consumption Taxes Regressive in Quebec?*, 59(3) Canadian Tax J. 463–493 (2011).
85. Ballard and Shoven conclude using US data that using exemptions to partially offset the effects of replacing income tax with a VAT would do little to mitigate the adverse distributional impact of such a change: see C.L. Ballard & J.B. Shoven, *The Value-Added-Tax: The efficiency cost of achieving progressivity by using exemptions*, in *Modern Developments in Public Finance: Essays in Honor of Arnold Harberger* 109–129 (M.J. Boskin ed., B. Backwell 1987).

the final supplier stage but not on the value added by the final supplier. While there are a number of exempt supplies in this class in the traditional VAT, they are rare in modern VAT systems.

The 'merit' benefits of many exempt goods and services in the traditional VAT are questionable and to the extent subsidies by way of exemption may stimulate greater consumption of target goods and services, the costs of subsidizing in this manner are likely to be significant. From a legal perspective these exemptions give rise to definitional and interpretative problems, create difficulties in calculating the portion of deductible VAT, and constitute an incentive to engage in aggressive tax planning. For these reasons merit exemptions tend to result in substantial - and increasing - litigation, which in turn results in substantial compliance and administrative costs. In Europe, the steady increase in references from national courts to the EU Court of Justice, focusing on the interpretation of these exemptions,[86] or the application of tax planning schemes by universities and hospitals,[87] is not only significant, but also symptomatic of two factors. The first is the outdated nature of these exemptions, unfit to deal with a new economic environment, where competition between public and private bodies is a common occurrence; the second is the pressure to increase efficiency in the provision of public services, which has resulted in an increase in subcontracting and outsourcing.

The quantitative costs[88] and qualitative effects in terms of distortions of consumption and investment decisions may be significant. The exemptions erode the tax base, create tax cascading and create bias towards self-supply and away from outsourcing. Importantly, they also tend to be inefficient mechanisms for subsidizing chosen types of supplies, as much of the effective subsidy is likely to be capitalized into a higher price for the exempt supplies either through inefficient production (the producers of the exempt supplies do not have to compete on a level playing field with producers of other supplies), or profit taking as the suppliers sell the subsidized supplies into a market that does not subsidize substitute types of consumption.[89]

The results of the cost-benefit analysis as applied to merit / concessional exemptions is therefore particularly negative: not only is it unclear whether they

86. For recent examples see cases C-86/09, *Future Health Technologies Limited v. The Commissioners for Her Majesty's Revenue and Customs* [2010] ECR I-5215; C-156/09, *Finanzamt Leverkusen v. Verigen Transplantation Service International AG* [2010] ECR I-11733; and C-237/09, *Belgian State v. Nathalie De Fruytier* [2010] ECR I-4985.
87. See for example cases C-419/02, *BUPA Hospitals Ltd, Goldsborough Developments Ltd v. Commissioners of Customs and Excise* [2006] ECR I-1685; C-223/03, *University of Huddersfield Higher Education Corporation v. Commissioners of Customs & Excise* [2006] ECR I-1751; and C-63/04, *Centralan Property Ltd v. Commissioners of Customs & Excise* [2005] ECR I-11087.
88. See R. Bird & P.-P. Gendron (n. 17 above).
89. Whether exemptions actually affect prices downwards is unclear. This is essentially for two reasons. Exemptions actually increase input tax costs, which will be at least partially passed on from the suppliers to the customers. Additionally, studies on the impact on prices of reduced VAT rates seem to indicate that concessions of this type do not necessarily affect prices, and that prices are more likely regulated by the competitiveness of the market in question, as well as the price elasticity of the given product: see R. de la Feria & M. Walpole, *VAT Rates Structures – A Case of Political Obstacles to Optimal Tax Policy* 3–5 (Paper presented at the Australasian Tax Teachers Association Annual Conference 2010).

accomplish any of the social and distributional objectives that they set out to achieve, but they also carry significant costs beyond the mere loss of potential revenue.[90]

[B] Technical Exemptions

Three categories of exempt supplies found particularly in traditional VAT systems are often explained as necessary or appropriate for technical reasons rather than as part of a policy to deliver subsidies through the tax system. The implication is that these activities should ideally be subject to VAT, but pragmatic considerations regarding the perceived difficulty of subjecting these transactions to the VAT led to their exemption from the tax. These three types of supplies are supplies of immovable property, financial services and pooling services, including insurance and gambling. Where these activities were not exempt as a matter of principle in order to attain specific benefits, but because of uncertainty as to how the VAT might apply to them, a cost-benefit analysis – similarly to that conducted for merit / concessional exemptions – may not have been appropriate when the VAT was first adopted in Europe. This is no longer the case. Other key questions include what are the legal and economic collateral costs of excluding these transactions from full taxation and how might the traditional VAT transition to include these transactions within the scope of VAT.

[1] Immovable Property

It is commonly asserted that no OECD members fully include all types of immovable property within their VAT base[91] and that the treatment of at least some immovable property transactions as exempt is nearly universal.[92] The common misconception arises because some types of immovable property are taxed in modern VAT systems in the same manner as second-hand goods, using a pre-payment system to accommodate sales by unregistered owners of residential premises.

VAT systems commonly distinguish between two types of immovable property – residential premises and other types of property which would include all commercial property. Immovable property other than residential premises is usually taxable under VAT, while residential premises are normally subject to special rules. The application of the ordinary VAT rules to property other than residential premises ensures that input tax credits are available on properties purchased by businesses, and that no non-recoverable VAT is embedded in the cost of these properties. An exception to this rule is found in the European traditional VAT system where, as a consequence of historical factors deriving from the treatment of immovable property under predecessor turnover

90. Gendron reaches similar conclusions, see P.-P. Gendron (n. 81 above). See also S. Cnossen, *Value-Added Tax and Excises: Commentary*, in *Dimensions of Tax Design – the Mirrlees Review* 275–422 (S. Adam, T. Besley, R. Blundell, S. Bond, R. Chote, M. Gammie, P. Johnson, G. Myles & J. Poterba eds.) (n.5 above).
91. OECD (n. 7, above) at tbl. 3.1.
92. R.F. Conrad, *Comments on VAT and Housing*, 63 Tax L. Rev. 471 (2010).

tax regimes,[93] a supply of both residential property and other (commercial) property may be treated as an exempt supply under default rules. To overcome the problem of embedded non-recoverable VAT for business customers, European VAT laws that use this default rule commonly provide for optional characterization of the supply as an ordinary taxable supply, thus providing qualifying purchasers with entitlement to input tax credits.[94] These rules are, however, themselves problematic. The optional nature of some of these rules results in a complex and non-transparent system that is subject to considerable variation across Europe.[95] In addition, various European countries apply additional or alternative taxes on transfers of immovable property, so that extra rules are needed to prevent overlapping taxation between these taxes and the VAT.[96] It is unsurprising that European rules on the VAT treatment of immovable property have given rise to significant litigation.[97]

Under modern VAT systems, the initial sale of residential premises is treated as an ordinary taxable supply, while subsequent sales are deemed to be exempt supplies. The rule that the original sale is a taxable supply and subsequent sales are exempt supplies is intended to replicate for residential premises the ordinary VAT treatment of second hand goods such as consumer durables. In the case of other second hand goods, the initial sales of the new goods are usually taxable supplies made by a registered retailer and later sales are out-of-scope sales, the equivalent of exempt supplies, because the private owners of the goods are not registered or are not making the supplies in the course of an enterprise.

The treatment of second-hand goods supplied by private sellers as out-of-scope (or effectively exempt) supplies reflects the nature of consumer durables as assets with an effective life stretching over a number of years. In a sense, the person buying consumer durable goods is acquiring assets that amount to savings. The consumption takes place as the assets are used (and depreciate) over their lives. In a truly comprehensive VAT world, all consumers of durables would be registered and entitled to input tax credits on their acquisitions and then be subject to tax as the assets are used and generate consumption benefits to the owner. It would, however, not be feasible to levy tax on this basis for every consumer durable purchased. Fortunately, the initial value of an asset when acquired is equal to the present value of the future consumption over the life of the asset and thus VAT calculated on the purchase price will equal the present value of the tax that would have been levied on consumption over the life of the asset.

Since the purchase price of a consumer durable equals the present value of consumption over the entire life of the asset, the initial purchaser will have paid VAT

93. S. Cnossen, *VAT Treatment of Immovable Property*, in V. Thuronyi, *Tax Law Design and Drafting* Ch. 7 (IMF 1996).
94. Article 137(1)(b), (c) and (d) of the EU VAT Directive.
95. For an overview of the VAT treatment of the various types of immovable property transactions, see S. Cnossen, *A Proposal to Improve the VAT Treatment of Housing in the European Union*, Ch. 7 in this volume, at Table 7.1.
96. *Ibid.*, at Table 7.2.
97. See e.g. Cases C-269/03, *Vermietungsgesellschaft and Objekt Kircheberg* [2004] RCR I-8067; C-184/04, *Undenkaupungin kaupunkin* [2006] ECR I-3039; and C-246/04, *Turn-und Sportunion Waldburg* [2006] ECR I-589.

on the entire future consumption from the asset. If the asset is sold over the course of its effective life, the second hand price will represent the depreciated value of the tax-inclusive price. The initial buyer will thus be able to recover from the next owner an amount equal to the VAT component of the remaining value of the asset and the next owner will bear a cost that includes this embedded VAT amount. The government is indifferent as it has already received the full VAT when the asset was initially sold but the burden of the VAT is automatically allocated correctly between all the persons who use it as a consequence of the fact that the value of second hand goods is based on the VAT-inclusive price of new goods.

The VAT treatment of residential premises rests on the same principles as assets that may be sold as second-hand assets. The initial price of the property is based on the present value of future consumption so levying VAT on the first sale of residential premises and treating remaining sales as out-of-scope supplies (or economically equivalent exempt supplies) should yield the appropriate VAT outcome. In practice, therefore, taxing new residential property is a proxy for the VAT that would be payable on the flow of housing services.[98] However, unlike ordinary consumer durables, residential premises have a high value and the sale price of residential property will often place sellers above the registration threshold. As a consequence, in the absence of specific legislative measures, later sales of residential property would not be out-of-scope supplies. To obtain this outcome, VAT systems specify that sales of residential property other than the initial sale are exempt supplies (with European VAT regimes sometimes extending exempt treatment to the initial sale).

While the system of taxing consumer durables at the time of purchase and treating subsequent private sales as out-of-scope supplies should yield the appropriate tax treatment of these assets, it may not fully tax the value of consumption from residential premises. Unlike consumer durables that have a limited life, the underlying real property in residential premises does not waste and most often rises in value over the longer term, even if the physical structure on it declines in value. In theory, the initial sale price of residential premises should include the present value of anticipated profits that will be realized when the property is sold as second hand residential premises, in which case the initial sale price should include the present value of consumption by subsequent owners. It may be difficult, however, for the market to measure all anticipated future rises in the value of a residential property as it moves through a potentially unlimited number of subsequent owners. Also, the present value of very distant consumption may be so low that it does not materially affect the present price of an asset. For example, the value of a 90-year lease of residential premises may be almost the same as the value of freehold title in the same property. If the initial sale price of residential premises does not fully capture the value of all future consumption from the property, later owners of property will not bear VAT on the full value of their consumption. The general implication, therefore, is that future increases - or decreases - in the value of residential property will be excluded from the VAT base.

98. S. Cnossen (n. 93 above).

Imposing VAT on the initial sale of residential premises may thus prove to be a flawed surrogate means of taxing the full value of consumption by subsequent owners. The theoretically correct tax could be imposed by treating all sales of residential premises as taxable sales, registering every homeowner, allowing input tax credits on purchase and collecting monthly VAT on the imputed rental consumption by owner-occupiers.[99] This alternative is neither administratively nor politically feasible, however, leaving the VAT on initial sale the only second-best alternative open to governments wishing to tax this consumption.[100] One alternative approach that has been suggested is a margin scheme that would subject the increased value of consumption by purchasers of appreciated residential premises to VAT, replacing the transfer taxes and stamp duties currently applicable in many countries to the sale of residential property – which are highly distortionary.[101]

The logic behind taxation of the initial sale of residential premises and out-of-scope or exempt treatment for subsequent sales extends to rent. If the rental supply of residential premises is treated as an exempt supply, the buyer of property will not be able to recover the tax incurred to acquire the premises and the unrecovered VAT will be embedded in all future rental payments. As with supplies of residential premises by way of sale, this surrogate means of taxing consumption value may miss the full value where property appreciates. But once again, the theoretically correct alternative, in this case allowing all landlords to register and claim input tax credits on the purchase of rental property and then impose VAT on rental payments, is neither administratively nor politically feasible.[102]

[2] Financial Services

All VAT tax systems have special rules for a category of supply known as financial services, with almost all treating them as exempt supplies. There are, however, significant differences in the definition of financial supply and the rationale for special treatment across VAT systems. Subject to many variations on the borderline of each type, the broad category embraces three distinct types of supply. The first comprises

99. By using owner-occupied property directly, the owner realizes a benefit equal to the benefit that would have been received had it been rented to another person. The consumption value or imputed rental value of owner-occupied premises is included in the income tax base of some income taxes. However, no country applies VAT to the imputed rental value of owner-occupied premises.
100. For an discussion of these alternatives see also S. Poddar, *Taxing of Housing Under a VAT*, 63 Tax L. Rev. 444–470 (2010); G.J. Harley, *Dilemma for GST Tax Policy Designers – Land Transactions*, in (R. Krever & D. White eds.) (n. 34 above), 213–241; M. Smith, *GST and Immovable Property Transactions in New Zealand – Some Interpretative Issues*, in (R. Krever and D. White eds.) (n. 34 above); M. Evans, *The Value-Added Tax Treatment of Immovable Property – An Antipodean Context*, in (R. Krever and D. White eds.) (n. 34 above); and R.F. Conrad and A. Grozou, *Immovable Property and VAT*, in *VAT in Africa*, 81–112 (R. Krever ed., Pretoria University Press 2008).
101. S. Cnossen (n. 93 above).
102. For a detailed proposal on the appropriate VAT treatment of the various types of immovable property transactions, see R. Millar, *VAT and Immovable Property: Full Taxation Models and the Treatment of Capital Gains on Owner-Occupied Residences*, Ch. 8 in this volume.

intangible ownership rights in legal persons or relations. Examples include shares,[103] interests in unit trusts or mutual funds, and interests in pension or superannuation funds. The second comprises financial intermediary services for loans, the function of banks and similar organizations that link lenders (depositors) and borrowers. The third consists of pooling intermediary services such as lotteries or insurance where a service provider collects funds from a range of persons and allocates the pool to a select group of winners (in the case of lotteries) or losers (in the case of insurance).

[a] Investments in Ownership Rights

The first type of financial supply - investments in ownership rights - gives rise to difficulties in the VAT system because a large number of persons acquiring these assets are individuals who are not registered for VAT purposes. In theory, a consumption tax should never be levied on investments; the tax is supposed to fall on consumption and not touch savings. This outcome follows automatically if the consumption tax is imposed as an annual expenditure tax that measures consumption as income and withdrawals from savings minus amounts invested (everything that is not invested is assumed to be used for consumption).[104] This is difficult to achieve, however, in a transaction based consumption tax that relies on registration, tax invoices, and refundable input tax credits as a means of removing tax on non-consumption acquisitions. It would be administratively impossible to apply the normal VAT rules to supplies of intangible ownership assets and then register all investors acquiring these supplies and process input tax refunds for the VAT imposed on the supplies.

The over-taxation of investments caused by the current characterization of these investments as exempt financial supplies undermines one of the economically desirable attributes of a consumption tax, namely its complete non-application to savings and investments. A possible solution to the problem in the context of the VAT mechanism is to treat these supplies as zero-rated. Such treatment would present its own challenges, however. Identifying appropriate types of financial assets to be subject to a zero-rating rule could be difficult and identifying qualifying ancillary expenses such as legal, accounting, or investment advice would also be problematic as these services are also used for both personal consumption and the acquisition or maintenance of investments.[105]

[b] Loan Intermediary Services

The second type of financial supply, the loan intermediary service offered by financial institutions to lenders and borrowers, fits awkwardly in the ordinary VAT system for several reasons. To begin with, it is difficult to measure the value of this service as no

103. Although not all dealings in shares are regarded as exempt under European VATs, see R. de la Feria (n. 44 above).
104. This form of consumption tax was advocated in Institute for Fiscal Studies (J. Meade, committee chair), *The Structure and Reform of Direct Taxation* (Meade Report) (1978).
105. This solution and potential difficulties are explored in detail in H. Grubert & R. Krever, *VAT and Financial Services: Competing Perspectives on What Should Be Taxed*, Ch. 9 in this volume.

explicit fee is charged for it. Rather, lenders and borrowers pay for it in the spread between interest paid to lenders and by borrowers. While it is possible to measure the value on an institutional basis and have the institution remit VAT implicitly charged to customers, it is difficult to attribute specific charges to individual depositors and borrowers, a step that would be necessary for the intermediary to issue tax invoices so investors and business customers could recover the VAT.

These difficulties explain in part why the traditional VAT treated loan intermediation supplies as exempt supplies and why most modern VATs followed suit. The result was over-taxation of business borrowers and lenders and private depositors (all of whom in theory should have borne no VAT burden on their investments or borrowings) and under-taxation of private borrowers. Some jurisdictions that have followed the modern VAT model have since shifted to alternative rules to try and mitigate these outcomes. For example, the tax borne by registered business customers can be removed by zero-rating loan intermediation services provided to these customers or treating all services that are not strictly intermediary services paid by way of interest rate spreads as ordinary taxable supplies.[106]

It is likely that other countries using the modern VAT model will shift to these post-modern VAT rules over time. Europe has considered these and other reform options,[107] with some European countries already giving financial institutions an option to be taxed under VAT.[108] Reform has stalled in recent times, however, more for fiscal reasons than for theoretical or practical considerations. Treating loan intermediation services to business customers and private investors may be wrong as a matter of policy and may lead to significant economic distortions, particularly where the tax compounds along the supply chain, but the over-taxation does generate a lot of revenue.[109] The revenue loss that would result from the return of input VAT to business

106. For a description of the New Zealand experience, the first jurisdiction to zero-rate intermediary financial supplies to business customers, see M. Pallot, *Financial Services under New Zealand's GST*, 5 Intl. VAT Monitor 310–315 (2011). Singapore has an alternative regime intended to accomplish the same result; Australia provides financial institutions with generous input tax credits on a range of inputs used by financial intermediaries, see M. Walpole, *The Miraculous Reduced Input Tax Credit for Financial Supplies in Australia*, 5 Intl. VAT Monitor 316–323 (2011); and South Africa treats all financial services as taxable supplies if the fees for the services can be identified. For a comparative analysis of these alternatives see also A. Schenk & H.H. Zee, *Financial Services and the Value-Added Tax*, in *Taxing the Financial Sector – Concepts, Issues, and Practices* 60–74 (H.H. Zee ed., International Monetary Fund 2004); T. Edgar, *Exempt Treatment of Financial Services Under Value-Added Tax: An Assessment of Alternatives*, 49(5) Canadian Tax J. 1133–1219 (2001); and H.H. Zee, *VAT Treatment of Financial Services: A Primer on Conceptual Issues and Country Practices*, 34(10) Intertax 458–474 (2006).
107. For a review of attempted reforms over time, see R. de la Feria, *The EU VAT Treatment of Insurance and Financial Services (Again) Under Review*, 2 EC Tax Rev. 74–89 (2007). One of the reforms which was under strong consideration was the transplantation of the Australian system: see R. de la Feria & M. Walpole, *Options for Taxing Financial Supplies in Value Added Tax: EU VAT and Australian GST Models Compared*, 58(4) Intl. & Comp. L. Q. 897–932 (2009).
108. For an analysis of the option to be taxed applied in some EU Member States, see R. de la Feria & B. Lockwood, *Opting for Opting In? An Evaluation of the Commission's Proposals for Reforming VAT for Financial Services*, 31(2) Fiscal Stud. (2010).
109. The revenue collected through over-taxation resulting from exemptions has been calculated in the United Kingdom to be 15% of the total VAT yield: see R. de la Feria, *Partial-Exemption Policy in the United Kingdom*, 21(2) Intl. VAT Monitor 119–123, at 22 (2010).

consumers of financial intermediary services and private depositors might not be as significant as feared, as full taxation of financial services provided to final consumers might go some way to compensate for removal of the over-taxation of business depositors and borrowers and private depositors.[110] There could nevertheless be a net revenue loss and governments seeking to reform the current treatment would thus need to find the political courage to recover the lost revenue elsewhere either through base-broadening or higher rates and furthermore to explain that the broadening or rate increases are needed to relieve banks and business of tax, a difficult sell at the best of times.[111]

Many VAT systems, particularly those following the traditional VAT model, compound the problem of over-taxation of businesses and investor users of loan intermediary services and under-taxation of customer users by extending exempt supply treatment to a range of ancillary services offered by financial institutions and similar organizations even though the value of these ancillary services can be easily ascertained and the ordinary VAT tax rules applied to these supplies.[112] Refining the definition of financial services in these jurisdictions so these ancillary supplies are no longer treated as exempt supplies would be a relatively simple way to begin reform of this area.[113] Europe is taking a step in this direction, with negotiations ongoing with a view to approving legislation which would redefine financial supplies for the purposes of exemptions.[114]

---

110. See calculations for loss of revenue under the current European Commission's proposals for reform of VAT on financial and insurance services in R. de la Feria & B. Lockwood (n. 108 above). In a recent paper, Buettner and Erbe provide an analysis of revenue and welfare effects associated with the application of a VAT exemption to financial services using a general equilibrium model. Using German data, they conclude that the revenue effects of removing the exemption would be positive, but quite small: see T. Buettner & K. Erber, *Revenue and Welfare Effects of Financial Sector VAT Exemption*, CESifo Working Paper (June 2012). It is worth noting however that Germany is one of the few European countries that already allow financial institutions an option to tax their financial supplies, a factor that could help explain these limited revenue effects.
111. Concern about the undertaxation of the financial sector is now at the centre of the discussions on the introduction of a new tax on the financial sector, see in particular European Commission, *Proposal for a Council Directive on a common system of financial transaction tax and amending Directive 2008/7/EC*, COM(2011) 594 final, of 28 September 2011, and accompanying documentation; J. Vella, C. Fuest & T. Schmidt-Eisenlohr, *The EU Commission's Proposal for a Financial Transaction Tax*, 6 British Tax Rev. 607–621 (2011); and M. Keen, *Rethinking the Taxation of the Financial Sector*, 57(1) CESifo Econ. Stud. 1–24 (2011).
112. While the bundling of ancillary services under the financial services umbrella has been significantly limited in Europe by the ruling of the Court of Justice in *Accenture*, Case C-472/03, *Staatssecretaris van Financien v. Arthur Andersen & Co. Accountants c.s.* [2005] ECR I-1719, the EU VAT Directive itself - and the interpretation given to it by the EU Court of Justice - deems many transactions that are not strictly intermediary services to be exempt financial services: see R. de la Feria (n. 107 above).
113. Edgar better summarizes the tax policymakers technique at play: 'modify the application of exemption through partial reform alternatives intended to suppress one of the perceived distortions', in T. Edgar, *The Search for Alternatives to Exempt Treatment of Financial Services Under a Value-Added Tax*, in (R. Krever and D. White eds.) (n. 34 above), 131–161, at 147.
114. The legislative proposals currently on the table envisage the re-definition of financial services, introduction of a cost-sharing group allowing economic operators to pool investments and re-distribute the costs of these investments to the members of the group, exempt from VAT, and introduction of an option to tax: see Commission of the European Communities, *Proposal for a Council Regulation laying down implementing measures for Directive 2006/112/EC on the*

Much more is known today about how to tax financial supplies under VAT than was the case just 20 years ago. The experience of some modern VAT jurisdictions with methods to prevent overtaxation of financial intermediary services to registered businesses may lead to general agreement that businesses should not bear tax on these services under a post-modern VAT. Developing a consensus on the optimal method of taxing loan intermediary services provided to unregistered consumers may prove more elusive.

[c] Intermediary Pooling Services

Intermediary pooling services are found in arrangements such as gambling lotteries or insurance where a service provider collects funds from a range of persons and allocates the pool to selected participants in the arrangements. In the case of insurance, a financial intermediary pools contributions from policy holders and distributes amounts from the pool to those who suffer losses. In the case of gambling, the financial intermediary pools contributions from gamblers and distributes amounts from the pool to winners.

The traditional VAT exempted insurance services for technical reasons – at the time the VAT was adopted, policy makers had to consider ways of measuring and taxing the value of intermediary services while reconciling options with the separate insurance taxes in place in many jurisdictions. As is the case with loan intermediation services discussed earlier, customers of insurance services are businesses that would be over-taxed if these services were treated as exempt services or consumers who would be undertaxed. This exemption gives rise to significant difficulties, and over the years it has been the source of much litigation in Europe.[115] In fact, it was a decision from the EU Court of Justice on the interpretation of the insurance exemption in a case concerning outsourcing, which led to the ongoing review of the exemptions applicable to financial and insurance services.[116] As a result, current negotiations include proposals to include some insurance services in the tax base.[117]

---

common system of value added tax, as regards the treatment of insurance and financial services, COM(2007) 746 final, 28 November 2007; and Commission of the European Communities, *Proposal for a Council Directive amending Directive 2006/112/EC on the common system of value added tax, as regards the treatment of insurance and financial services*, COM(2007) 747 final, 28 November 2007. However, negotiations at the Council of Ministers have concentrated primarily on discussions over clarification and re-definition of exemptions.

115. See amongst others Cases C-349/96, *Card Protection Plan Ltd (CPP) v. Commissioners of Customs and Excise* [1999] ECR I-973; C-240/99, *Forsakringsaktiebolaget Skandia (publ)* [2001] ECR I-1951; C-8/01, *Assurandor-Societetet, acting on behalf of Taksatorringenv Skatteministeriet* [2003] ECR I-13711; C-308/01, *GIL Insurance Ltd, UK Consumer Electronics Ltd, Consumer Electronics Insurance Co. Ltd, Direct Vision Rentals Ltd, Homecare Insurance Ltd, Pinnacle Insurance plc v. Commissioners of Customs and Excise* [2004] ECR I-4777; C-425/06, *Ministero dell'Economia e delle Finanze v. Part Service Srl* [2008] ECR I-897; and C-242/08, *Swiss Re Germany Holding GmbH v. Finanzamt München für Korperschaften* [2009] ECR I-10099.
116. Case C-472/03, *Staatssecretaris van Financien v. Arthur Andersen & Co. Accountants c.s.* [2005] ECR I-1719. For a detailed analysis of the background to the ongoing review see R. de la Feria (n. 107 above).
117. See n. 114 above.

The technical problems that led to the classification of insurance services as exempt within the traditional European VAT appear to have been solved by VAT designers in many modern VAT systems and to avoid the overtaxation and undertaxation problems that flow from exempt treatment, modern VAT systems commonly treat non-life insurance services as ordinary taxable supplies. The inclusion of insurance intermediary services within the scope of the VAT has not, however, been extended to intermediary services for life insurance which are so far universally exempt, perhaps in part due to the savings component in some types of life policies.

The traditional VAT also exempted gambling services in part because of uncertainty by the designers over how the intermediary services should be measured and taxed.[118] However, as with loan intermediation services, it is possible to measure and collect tax on the value of the service to all customers, if that value is calculated at the level of the pooling service provider. Since all participants in a gambling pooling arrangement are assumed to be final consumers, there is no need to allocate the value to individual participants and issue tax invoices. Accordingly, many modern VAT systems have relatively simple rules to impose tax on gambling services (including the provision of casino gambling and lotteries), with the value of the service being the difference between bets collected by the intermediary service provider and winnings paid out.[119] Although the EU VAT Directive provides EU Member States with an option to tax gambling services, exemption remains the more common approach in the traditional VAT. Judicial interpretations have limited the possibility of extending the exemption to ancillary activities,[120] but conversely also limited the ability of EU Member States to selectively remove the exemption from particular types of gambling, on the basis of the respect for the principle of fiscal neutrality.[121]

§1.05 CONCLUSION: TOWARDS A *POST*-MODERN VAT

Exempt supplies and out-of-scope supplies with economic outcomes similar to those of exempt supplies are found in abundance in the traditional VAT and to a lesser extent in the modern VAT. These lead to overtaxation of business and undertaxation of final consumers. The efficacy of explicit exemptions that supposedly further equity or merit good objectives is questionable and the logic for retaining all exemptions supposedly needed for technical reasons is no longer convincing.

---

118. Article 135(1)(i) of the EU VAT Directive.
119. See A. Schenk, *Gambling and lotteries*, in (R. Krever ed.) (n. 72 above), 47–70. There is an argument that this approach undertaxes the consumption of gamblers and that the gross amount should be taxed, rather than merely the margin. This issue is explored further in Y. Margalioth, *VAT on Gambling*, Ch. 6 in this volume.
120. See Case C-89/05, *United Utilities plc v. Commissioners of Customs & Excise* [2006] ECR I-6813.
121. See Cases C-283/95, *Fischer, Karlheinz v. Finanzamt Donaueschingen* [1998] ECR I-3369; C-453/02, *Finanzamt Gladbeck v. Edith Linneweber* [2005] ECR I-1131; C-58/09, *Leo-Libera* [2010] ECR I-5189; C-260/10, *Commissioners of Her Majesty's Revenue and Customs v. The Rank Group plc* [2011] ECR I-000; C-464/10, *Belgian State v. Pierre Henfling and Others* [2011] ECR I-000. For a recent analysis of these cases see R. de la Feria, *Rank Group. VAT exemption on gambling. Principle of fiscal neutrality. Court of Justice*, 1 Highlights & Insights European Taxn. (2012).

It has been said that 'the taxation systems of the major developed countries will grow to resemble each other more and more', with the spread of VAT being offered as an example of this phenomenon.[122] A close examination of VAT systems, however, reveals significant divergences in practice. Historical factors that led to multiple rates and multiple exemptions in the traditional European VAT were not present in most jurisdictions outside the EU and adopters of a modern VAT model were able to avoid these features of the traditional VAT, for the most part adopting single rates and substantially limiting the number of exemptions. Even these more limited exemptions have imposed economic and administrative costs, however, prompting some modern VAT jurisdictions to explore post-modern alternatives, particularly in the sphere of financial supplies, but also in respect of supplies by SMEs and registration thresholds.

At present the attention is on another possible tax policy transfer, this time in the opposite direction: from modern VATs to the traditional VATs, a transplantation of the modern VAT model for taxing traditionally exempt transactions to the traditional VAT systems. However, there are intrinsic complications to tax policy transfer and regional specificities are a normal occurrence. This is precisely one of the reasons public policy transfer in general, and tax policy transfer in particular, is perilous at the best of times.[123] Lack of information on the real effects of the tax policy in the country of origin will aggravate the dangers. In this context, a debate regarding the adoption by traditional European-style VATs of the modern VATs' approach of taxing specific supplies must be well-informed. Accepting the inherent risks of tax policy transfer in this case might be unavoidable if reform is ultimately the wisest way forward. If such a transfer is going to succeed, however, it is necessary to realize not solely what are the advantages of the modern VAT model but equally what are its limitations. Understanding their weaknesses might lead to a post-modern VAT: one which takes into account the weaknesses of modern VATs and aims to overcome them.

Indeed, there is already a realization that modern VATs are not a complete panacea. Undoubtedly they are an improvement on the traditional VAT exemption model. They have solved some of the difficulties encountered under the traditional VAT but it is less clear whether they have solved all, or to what extent they have given rise to new problems. Various chapters in this volume draw attention to some of these problems such as the difficulties caused by the rebate system applicable to public sector bodies and charities in Canada or the definitional and planning problems caused by the input tax credits model applied to Australian financial services. Additionally recent research has shed new light over the VAT treatment of some transactions which until now had been relatively untapped; this is the case for example with the treatment of supplies by SMEs and the optimal level of registration threshold.

Table 1.1 summarizes the treatment of specific transactions under traditional, modern, and post-modern VAT. The transactions highlighted in grey represent those where significant departures between modern and post-modern VAT are proposed.

122. See R.K. Osgood, *The Convergence of the Taxation Systems of the Developed Nations*, 25(2) Cornell Intl. L. J. 339–347, at 339 and 343 et seq. (1992).

123. See D.P. Dolowitz & D. Marsh, *Learning from Abroad: The Role of Policy Transfer in Contemporary Policy-Making*, 13(1) Governance: Intl. J. Policy & Admin. 5–24 (2000).

One recurrent issue throughout this volume and during the conference discussions at Oxford which preceded it - particularly insofar as technical exemptions are concerned - is the definition of consumption. In all chapters regarding technical exemptions the key when considering alternative designs has been the concept of consumption. It has therefore become clear that one of the main challenges of the post-modern VAT will be a rather unexpected one: not about feasible legal designs or about economic consequences, but one with an intrinsically philosophical nature, one about philosophy of tax. That is, how to conceptually define what constitutes consumption for the purposes of a consumption tax.

Table 1.1 Treatment of Specific Supplies under Traditional, Modern and Post-modern VAT

	Traditional VAT		*Modern VAT*	*Post-modern VAT*
	Treatment	*Rationale*	*Treatment*	*Treatment*
No direct consideration	Out-of-scope supplies	Out-dated legal wording and judicial interpretation	Full taxation	Full taxation
SMEs	Out-of-scope suppliers (varying thresholds)	Vertical equity versus widening of tax base	Out-of-scope suppliers (varying thresholds)	Out-of-scope suppliers (high threshold)
Non-business enterprises	Out-of-scope suppliers	Out-dated legal wording and judicial interpretation	Full taxation	Full taxation
Public sector bodies	Out-of-scope suppliers	Out-dated legal wording and judicial interpretation	Full taxation	Full taxation
Merit goods and services	Exempt	Vertical equity Positive externalities	Full taxation (or exempt or zero-rated)	Full taxation
Immovable property	Exempt (option to tax commercial property)	Difficult-to-tax	Full taxation of commercial property Exemption of residential property (except first sale)	Full taxation of commercial property First sale of residential property taxable
Financial intermediary services	Exempt(option to tax)	Difficult-to-tax	Exemption model Zero-rating of B2B model	Full taxation
Non-life insurance services	Exempt	Difficult-to-tax	Full taxation	Full taxation
Gambling	Exempt	Difficult-to-tax	Full taxation	Full taxation (margin model)

CHAPTER 2

The EU Perspective on VAT Exemptions

Joachim Englisch*

§2.01 INTRODUCTION

As early as 1967, the Member States of the European Community – six at that time – agreed to harmonize their national systems of turnover taxes, based on what is now Article 113 TFEU[1] (ex Article 93 EC). As a model, they chose the French system of value added tax (VAT)[2] that had also been deliberated in other Member States like Germany, establishing a general, multi-stage but non-cumulative turnover tax in the First and Second VAT Directives.[3] These first two VAT Directives laid down only the general structures of the system so as to ensure neutrality of competition regarding both intra-Community and intra-State trade. Member States were still almost entirely free to provide for exemptions in their national VAT systems.[4] But in its 1973 proposal for a

* I am deeply grateful for the comments made by my discussant Richard Lyal. I would also like to express my gratitude for the suggestions and comments made by two anonymous referees. Any eventual errors are all mine.

1. Treaty on the Functioning of the European Union, OJ C 83/94, entry into force on 1 December 2009.
2. Cf. C. Celorico Palma, *O IVA e o mercado interno – reflexões sobre o regime transitório,* Cadernos de Ciência e Técnica Fiscal 178 1998, 53 et seq.
3. First Council Directive 67/227/EEC of 11 April 1967 on the harmonization of legislation of Member States concerning turnover taxes, OJ L71/1301 of 1967, and Second Council Directive 67/228/EEC of 11 April 1967 on the harmonization of legislation of Member States concerning turnover taxes – Structure and procedures for application of the common system of value added tax, OJ L71/1303 of 1967, respectively.
4. Cf. Art. 10 of the Second VAT Directive. However, the Commission had stressed in the explanatory memorandum of the preceding proposal of the Second VAT Directive that 'it is highly desirable to limit the number of exemptions as far as possible', cf. '*Proposition d'une Deuxième Directive du conseil en matière d'harmonisation des législations des états membres relatives aux taxes sur le chiffre d'affaires concernant la structure et les modalités d'application du système commun de taxe sur la valeur ajoutée*' of 13 April 1965, IV/COM(65) 144 (final), 15.

Sixth VAT Directive, the EC Commission envisaged a far greater degree of harmonization including, inter alia, rules on a limited number[5] of uniform and compulsory tax exemptions.[6] This list of exemptions had been drawn up having regard to the exemptions already existing in the Member States;[7] the Commission obviously was not willing to engage into disputes as to whether all of these exemptions were really well-founded.[8] Likewise, the Commission maintained the principle that input VAT on goods and services used for the purpose of exempt transactions should not be deductible, without any further explanation.[9] When the Sixth VAT Directive was finally adopted in 1977 after only minor amendments, these concepts became binding for the Member States.

Since then, over 30 years have passed. The Sixth VAT Directive has been replaced by the EU VAT Directive, and the harmonized system of VAT is now being implemented in 27 Member States. Over the course of time, the rules related to exemptions have proven to be a major source for legal dispute.[10] They have been associated with distortions of competition, and most VAT planning activities revolve around the system of exemptions. As in other VAT jurisdictions, this begs the question whether exemptions are really a necessary evil, or whether they are rather unnecessarily evil (so that the system should be amended), or whether they are no evil at all?

However, there are some peculiarities inherent to the harmonized system of VAT that make it worthwhile to dedicate a chapter specifically to the EU perspective on exemptions. First, the EU constitutes a supranational institution founded on the rule of law (cf. Article 2 EU) that recognizes fundamental rights, freedoms, equality and other

5. Cf. Case C-149/97 *The Institute of the Motor Industry v. Commissioners of Customs and Excise* [1998] ECR I-7053, para. 18; Case C-307/01 *Peter d'Ambrumenil and Dispute Resolution Services Ltd v. Commissioners of Customs & Excise* [2003] ECR I-13989, para. 54; Case C-445/05, *Werner Haderer v. Finanzamt Wilmersdorf* [2007] ECR I-4841, para. 16: the provisions of the Sixth VAT Directive (now EU VAT Directive) on tax exemptions are exhaustive.
6. The harmonization of VAT exemptions was chiefly motivated by the desire to make VAT a suitable source of Community revenue by ensuring a uniform basis of assessment and thus a uniform collection in all Member States, cf. C. Amand, *Are VAT Exemptions Compatible with Primary EU Law?*, 21 Intl. VAT Monitor 41 et seq. (2010), with further references to preparatory documents for the VAT directives; R. de la Feria, *The EU VAT System and the Internal Market*, 54 et seq. (IBFD 2009); see also recital 11 of the Preamble to the Sixth Directive.
7. Cf. Explanatory Memorandum to the *Proposal for a Sixth Council Directive on the harmonization of Member States concerning turnover taxes*, submitted to the Council by the Commission on 29 June 1973, COM(73) 950, 15. For further references, see Amand (n. 6 above) 411, 413, who points to the traditional exemptions of the German turnover tax preceding the European harmonization of VAT in particular.
8. See also S. Cnossen, *How Much Tax Coordination in the European Union?*, 20 Intl. Tax and Pub. Fin. 625, 627 (2003): 'The rationale for most exemptions must be found in the history of their adoption, not in their underlying economic or administrative logic.' See furthermore in R. Krever (ed.), *VAT in Africa*, 9, 16 (Pretoria University Law Press 2008), who points out that an expansive list of exemptions was adopted so as to win the support of the business sector in the (formerly six) Member States, by making the shift from traditional turnover taxes to a VAT appear a rather minor one.
9. Cf. Explanatory Memorandum (n. 7 above), 18.
10. Cf. Amand (n. 6 above), 409: 'The VAT exemptions are probably the most complex aspect of the European VAT system.'

constitutional principles. As a consequence, the entire body of harmonized VAT law, including the provisions relating to exemptions, is subject to quasi-constitutional review. Second, the relevant Directives have always clearly stated that harmonized VAT is an indirect tax on consumption expenditure[11] designed to burden the final consumer even though collected by economic operators as taxable persons.[12] As a consequence, the assessment of exemptions from a legal perspective must bear in mind this presumption when analysing possible repercussions for business and for final consumers. Finally, the fact that VAT is harmonized at EU level but mostly implemented through national VAT Acts constitutes a particular challenge with regard to its uniform and principle-based interpretation.[13]

This chapter will focus on exemptions available for intra-State transactions only. These exemptions are characterized, in principle, by the non-deductibility of input VAT for any supplies that become cost elements of the exempt transactions. This kind of exemption needs to be distinguished from exemptions that do not preclude the right to deduct input VAT. As a general rule, these latter exemptions are available exclusively for cross-border transactions so as to ensure taxation in conformity with the destination principle;[14] they are equivalent to zero-rating exports.

The chapter is organized as follows: It sets out with a short overview of both the harmonized and the non-harmonized aspects of the EU system of exemptions, and a brief analysis of the way they are interpreted by the Court of Justice of the European Union (CJEU) Having thus sketched the legal framework, the chapter then discusses the constitutional standards as well as some economic and tax policy benchmarks by which the different types of exemptions provided for in the EU VAT system should be assessed. Based on these findings, the subsequent section carries out a critical analysis of seven possible rationales for those exemptions. Finally, the exclusion of input VAT deduction will be scrutinized.

As a caveat, it should be mentioned that this chapter is not primarily intended to provide a tax policy analysis of VAT exemptions in general. Instead, it is mainly dedicated to the legal issues associated with exempt supplies, with special emphasis on the constitutional and institutional framework of the present EU VAT system. Nevertheless, due consideration will also be given to economic insights, particularly when

11. As regards the present version of the common system of VAT, cf. Art. 1 (2) of the EU VAT Directive see also, in greater detail, J. Englisch, *Value Added Tax and Direct Taxation: Similarities and Differences*, in *Value Added Tax and Direct Taxation*, 1, 25 et seq. (M. Lang, P. Melz & E. Kristofferson eds., IBFD 2009); O. Henkow, *Financial Activities in European VAT: Theoretical and Legal Research*, 67 (Kluwer Law International, Eucotax Series on European Taxation 2008); B. Terra & J. Kajus, *A Guide to the European VAT Directives 2010: Introduction to European VAT*, 249 et seq. (IBFD 2010).
12. Case C-10/92, *Maurizio Balocchi v. Ministero delle Finanze dello Stato* [1993] ECR I-5105, para. 25; Case C-271/06, *Netto Supermarkt GmbH & Co. OHG v. Finanzamt Malchin* [2008] ECR I-771, para. 21; A. González, *Fraude y delito fiscal en el IVA*, 19 et seq. (Marcial Pons 2008); W. Reiß, *Steuerrecht*, § 14 para. 1 (20th ed., K. Tipke & J. Lang ed., Schmidt (Otto) 2010); H. Stadie, *Umsatzsteuerrecht*, paras. 1.15 and 1.18 (Otto Schmidt 2005).
13. See also Amand (n. 6 above), 409, 410: The occasional 'lack of obedience [with respect to CJEU judgments] leads to serious distortions of competition and legal uncertainty ...'.
14. Cf. B. Genser & Winker, *Measuring the Fiscal Revenue Loss of VAT Exemption in Commercial Banking*, 54 Finanzarchiv 563 (1997).

analysing the EU system of exemptions in the light of the primary Union law requirements of neutrality, proportionality, and consistency. As the reader will notice, there is a considerable degree of congruence between the constitutional and the economic standards of assessment, even insofar as the latter are now influenced by optimal taxation theory. The main differences seem to be that a constitutional review can only ask for a reasonable rather than an optimal degree of compliance with the aforementioned and other benchmarks;[15] moreover, it will accept a welfare decrease resulting from particular features of the tax system more readily, insofar as the former constitutes a corollary of the protection of individual human rights.[16]

§2.02 OVERVIEW OF THE SYSTEM OF EXEMPTIONS IN EU VAT

Different from what might be expected, not all aspects of VAT are harmonized in the common system of EU VAT. As regards exemptions in particular, some key aspects still remain at the discretion of Member States. Furthermore, the responsibility for interpreting the VAT exemptions is shared by national courts and the Court of Justice of the European Union (CJEU), although the latter may usually claim ultimate authority in this regard.

[A] Harmonized Aspects of Exempt Transactions

[1] The Exemption List of Articles 132 to 136 of the EU VAT Directive

Articles 132 to 136 of the EU VAT Directive provide an enumerative list with more than 30 compulsory exemptions. Most of these exemptions concern the supply of services. They have been subdivided into two categories by the Community legislator: Exemptions for certain activities in the public interest, and exemptions for other activities. The first category encompasses, inter alia: certain postal services, the supply of medical care, the supply of services and of goods closely linked to welfare and social security work by public entities or charitable organizations, and certain educational and cultural services. Among the transactions that fall into the second category are: insurance transactions, certain financial services, the leasing or letting of immovable property, and supplies of land or buildings that meet certain conditions. As a general rule, the exemptions listed in the aforementioned provisions of the EU VAT Directive are *objective* exemptions that refer to certain features of the exempt supply,[17] rather

15. For further explanation, see below at §2.03[B][2][d].
16. As regards the preference for utilitarianism under optimal taxation theory, see L. Kaplow, *A Fundamental Objection to Tax Equity Norms: A Call for Utilitarianism*, 48 Natl. Tax J. 497 et seq. (1995); J. Tiley, *Revenue Law*, 14 (6th ed., Hart Publishing 2008). See also R. Bird & P.-P. Gendron, *The VAT in Developing and Transitional Countries*, 70 et seq. (Cambridge University Press 2007), who distinguish between tax-specific equity (the traditional legal approach) and overall equity, or welfare effect, of the tax and budgetary system (the approach of most modern economists).
17. Cf. Case C-305/01, *Finanzamt Groß-Gerau v. MKG-Kraftfahrzeuge-Factoring GmbH* [2003] ECR I-6729, para. 64.

than *subjective* exemptions reserved exclusively to suppliers with certain personal characteristics.[18] However, with respect to some objective exemptions, only taxable persons who also meet certain subjective criteria (being a non-profit organization, for example) will be eligible for the exemption at issue.[19]

[2] Exclusion from the Input VAT Deduction Scheme

Pursuant to Article 168 of the EU VAT Directive, all of the exemptions contemplated in Articles 132 to 136 of the EU VAT Directive imply a denial of input tax deduction for any VAT charged in the price for supplies used for the purpose of carrying out the exempt transaction. The exclusion from the substantial scope of the input VAT deduction will only exceptionally be reversed for certain cross-border transactions where the state of destination is a third country. If input supplies are only partially used for exempt transactions, there will be granted a pro rata deduction of input VAT, as specified in Articles 173 et seq. of the EU VAT Directive.

[3] The Mandatory Character of the Directive's Provisions

Member States may not deviate from the above system of compulsory exemptions without a right to deduct input VAT unless expressly authorized to do so. Such authorization can be granted either by the Directive itself, or by a decision of the Council that is in itself empowered to grant a waiver with respect to mandatory provisions under certain conditions, especially based on Article 395 of the EU VAT Directive.[20] By contrast, Article 131 of the EU VAT Directive, which stipulates that Member States are to lay down the conditions for exemptions in order to ensure the correct and straightforward application of the exemptions, and to prevent any possible evasion, avoidance, or abuse, does not authorize Member States to modify the subject-matter of the exemptions envisaged by the Directive.[21]

If a Member State does not (properly) transpose an exemption that is provided for by the Directive into its national VAT laws, then the taxable person might be entitled to rely directly on the Directive to claim the exemption if this turns out to be favourable for him. According to settled case law, such direct effect only presupposes that the provisions of a directive appear, as far as their subject-matter is concerned, to be

18. J. Frink, *Der Ausschluss des Vorsteuerabzugs bei der Ausführung steuerfreier Umsätze im Umsatzsteuerrecht*, 85 (Roderer Verlag 2002); E.A. Poblet, *Manual del IVA*, 392 (3d ed., Teixeira Da Silva 2006). The French VAT terminology is more precise in this regard, because it distinguishes between an objective 'exoneration' and a subjective 'exemption', cf. P. Mollard, La TVA suisse et la problématique des exonérations, *Archiv für schweizerisches Abgaberecht*, 443, 448 (ASA 1994).
19. See also Case 107/84, *Commission of the European Communities v. Federal Republic of Germany* [1985] ECR 2655, para. 13.
20. Cf. Art. 395 (1) of the EU VAT Directive: 'The Council, acting unanimously on a proposal from the Commission, may authorise any Member State to introduce special measures for derogation from the provisions of this Directive, in order to simplify the procedure for collecting VAT or to prevent certain forms of tax evasion or avoidance.'
21. Cf. Case C-97/06, *Navicon SA. v. Administración del Estado* [2007] ECR I-8755, para. 27.

unconditional and sufficiently precise.[22] In a similar vein, if a Member State does provide for an exemption that is neither contemplated in nor authorized by the Directive, then the taxable person may rely directly on the Directive to claim an input tax credit if this turns out to be more favourable for him than the exemption.[23] In any event, the EU Commission can initiate infringement proceedings against a Member State that deviates from the Directive without proper authorization.

[B] Non-Harmonized Aspects of Exempt Transactions

[1] Option for Taxation

Pursuant to Article 137 of the EU VAT Directive, Member States may grant taxable persons a right of option for taxation in respect of a limited number of exempt transactions: certain financial transactions, the supply of buildings or land, and the leasing and letting of immovable property. The predominant purpose of this authorization is to provide Member States with a mechanism to counter VAT cascading in Business-to-Business (B2B) transactions that might occur due to the denial of a right to deduct input VAT on supplies used for exempt transactions. Even when they decide to provide that right of option, Member States are, in principle, free to restrict the scope or set forth certain prerequisites as they deem fit. At present, only very few Member States have altogether excluded that feature from their national VAT system. On the other hand, hardly any Member States grant an option to taxation for the entire range of supplies that could qualify by virtue of Article 137 of the EU VAT Directive, and most States have established additional requirements.[24]

[2] Special Scheme for Small Enterprises

The EU VAT Directive authorizes Member States to exempt taxable persons whose annual turnover is below a certain threshold. The threshold is determined on an individual basis for each Member State, as laid down in Articles 284 to 288 of the EU VAT Directive. This special scheme for small enterprises constitutes a personal or subjective exemption;[25] in particular, any enterprise covered by its substantive scope that does not opt out is not entitled to deduct any input VAT. With the notable exception of Spain, all Member States currently provide for a registration threshold; however, the threshold differs considerably depending on the respective country.[26]

---

22. See, for instance, Case C-193/91, *Finanzamt München III v. Gerhard Mohsche* [1993] ECR I-2615, para. 17.
23. See also Case C-228/05, *Stradasfalti Srl v. Agenzia delle Entrate – Ufficio di Trento* [2006] ECR I-8391, para. 66.
24. See, in greater detail, W. van der Corput & F. Annacondia, *EU VAT Compass*, 481 et seq. (IBFD 2009/2010).
25. Likewise I. Crawford, M. Keen & S. Smith, *Dimensions of Tax Design: The Mirrlees Review*, 275, 309 (Mirrlees et al. eds., Oxford University Press & Institute for Fiscal Studies 2010); H. Stadie, *Das Recht des Vorsteuerabzugs*, 152 (Otto Schmidt 1989).
26. For further details, consult van der Corput & Annacondia (n. 24 above), 413 et seq.

[3] Deductible Portion of Input VAT Regarding Mixed-Use Purchases

In the case of goods or services used by a taxable person both for exempt and for taxed transactions, only such proportion of the input VAT as is attributable to the taxed transactions shall be deductible.[27] By default, the deductible portion is calculated pro rata by putting the entire taxable turnover in proportion to the taxed turnover, as specified in Articles 174 et seq. of the EU VAT Directive. However, Member States may have resort to alternative, more precise measures to calculate the deductible portion. These measures are stipulated in Article 173 (2) of the EU VAT Directive.

[4] Aspects of Minor Importance

Finally, there are some aspects of minor importance that are not fully harmonized within the EU: Member States are authorized to make certain exemptions subject to certain conditions or to restrict their scope by virtue of Articles 133, 135 (2) 2 of the EU VAT Directive. Some Member States may also abstain from implementing certain exemptions which are, in principle, compulsory (cf. Articles 370, 375 et seq. of the EU VAT Directive). And conversely, some may exempt certain transactions which constitute, in principle, taxed transactions (cf. Articles 371, 375 et seq. of the EU VAT Directive). Finally, some Member States have negotiated, as part of their transition to the common system of VAT, the authorization to zero-rate certain transactions which constitute, in principle, taxed or exempt transactions (cf. Articles 375 et seq. of the EU VAT Directive).

[C] Interpretation of Exemptions Within the EU VAT System

[1] General Observations

The interpretation of the provisions relating to VAT exemptions is initially a task to be mastered by the Member State's national tax administrations and courts, but it is the Court of Justice of the European Union (CJEU) that has ultimate jurisdiction in this regard insofar as the disputed provision constitutes a fully harmonized element of the common system of VAT. The CJEU comprises some of Europe's brightest judges. But it is not a court that is specialized in tax law, nor have any of its chambers been designated to deal specifically with disputes concerning taxes, or VAT in particular. For that reason, the Court faces peculiar challenges in developing a coherent body of case law – especially as the sheer number of judgments on VAT issues now well exceeds 500 and has thus expanded considerably since the first cases were decided in the 1970s. Regarding the interpretation of VAT exemptions in particular, the problem is aggravated by the lack of a clear and consistently implemented rationale for many of the exemptions.[28]

---

27. Cf. Art. 173 (1) of the EU VAT Directive.
28. For extensive analysis, see below at §2.04.

According to settled case law of the CJEU, the exemptions provided for in the Directive have, as a general rule, their own independent meaning in Community law and must therefore be given a Community definition.[29] This will only exceptionally be different when the exemption, as contemplated in the EU VAT Directive, makes express reference to the law of the Member States for the purposes of determining its meaning and scope.[30] Furthermore, the CJEU has consistently held that exemptions from VAT should be interpreted 'strictly' because they constitute exceptions. This restrictive stance was never explained further by the Court. It could be regarded as an implicit acknowledgement of the aforementioned difficulties of rational interpretation, or as carried by the desire to pursue as far as possible the fundamental concept of VAT as a *general* tax on consumption expenditure, as laid down in what is now Article 1 (2) of the EU VAT Directive.

However, the Court's approach has repeatedly been criticized as too simplistic by prominent scholars. A distinguished Advocate General observed that the provisions on exemptions 'should not be whittled away by interpretation ... As a corollary, limitations on exemptions should not be interpreted narrowly, but nor should they be construed so as to go beyond their terms. Both the exemptions and any limitations on them must be interpreted in such a way that the exemption applies to that to which it was intended to apply and no more.'[31] This criticism had its impact on the Court's jurisprudence,[32] and in recent times, the CJEU has made express reference also to the need for systematic interpretation and purposive construction.[33] It should be noted, however, that the CJEU still relies heavily on a literal interpretation of exemptions. The Court is very reluctant to interpret them beyond their wording, i.e. to apply them by

29. Cf. Case C-2/95, *Sparekassernes Datacenter (SDC) v. Skatteministeriet* [1997] ECR I-3017, para. 21; Case C-326/99, *Stichting 'Goed Wonen' v. Staatssecretaris van Financiën* [2001] ECR I-6831, paras. 47 et seq.; Case C-572/07, *RLRE Tellmer Property sro v. Finanční ředitelství v Ústí nad Labem* [2009] ECR I-7501, para. 15; Case C-473/08, *Ingenieurbüro Eulitz GbR Thomas und Marion Eulitz v. Finanzamt Dresden I* [2010] ECR I-907, para. 25; Case C-237/09, *Belgian State v. Nathalie De Fruytier* [2010] ECR I-4985, para. 21; and the case law cited there. For critical comments regarding the exemption for the letting of real estate, see Opinion Statement of the CFE on the distinction between taxable and VAT exempt letting of immovable property, submitted in November 2009. However, the statement ignores the international distortions of competition that might arise in case of a national interpretation due to a possible denial of a credit also in B2B transactions.
30. Case C-433/08, *Yaesu Europe BV v. Bundeszentralamt für Steuern* [2009] ECR I-11487, para. 18.
31. AG Jacobs, Opinion of 13 December 2001, Case C-267/00, *Commissioners of Customs & Excise v. Zoological Society of London* [2002] ECR I-3353, paras. 18 et seq. Likewise Terra & Kajus (n. 11 above), 697; H. Stadie, *Umsatzsteuergesetz: Kommentar*, 479 et seq. (Otto Schmidt 2009).
32. For further details, see F. Schulyok, *The ECJ's Interpretation of VAT Exemptions*, 4 International VAT Monitor 266, 267 et seq. (2010). It should be noted, though, that the Court has de facto never relied on the 'strict interpretation' formula alone when it handed down its judgments on VAT exemptions, and also in its early judgments.
33. See, for example, Case C-434/05, *Stichting Regionaal Opleidingen Centrum Noord-Kennemerland/West-Friesland (Horizon College) v. Staatssecretaris van Financiën* [2007] ECR I-4793, para. 16; Case C-284/03, *État belge v. Temco Europe SA* [2004] ECR I-11237, para. 17; Case C-156/09, *Finanzamt Leverkusen v. Verigen Transplantation Service International AG*, [2010] ECR I-11733, paras. 23 et seq. For further references, see Terra & Kajus (n. 11 above), 234 et seq., and the case law cited there.

analogy, even when their purpose and objective would suggest such an approach.[34] Along the same lines, the CJEU has also refused to construe an exemption narrower than its seemingly clear and unambiguous wording would suggest.[35]

In order to identify the principles or public policy goals underlying an exemption, the CJEU has frequently referred to the Directive's preamble,[36] but it has also drawn inspiration from the normative context and overall system of the Directive.[37] The CJEU has also resorted to somewhat more formal contextual arguments relying on the positioning of the exemption at issue within the Directive's sections or sub-sections.[38] Furthermore, the Court has occasionally referred to the legal history of the provision at issue insofar as the relevant considerations are published and thus accessible to the taxpayer.[39] Therefore, the explanatory memoranda accompanying the respective legislative proposal made by the Commission are also relevant.[40] Another valuable source of interpretation is provided by comparing the various language versions of the Directive.[41] By contrast, the interpretation of exemptions needs not necessarily be reconciled with similar definitions or concepts in other sources of secondary EU law that deal with the subject-matter of the exemption. However, it must be carefully examined on a case-by-case basis if contextual, historical, or teleological arguments support the consideration of other legal provisions beyond the ones contained in the VAT Directives.[42]

34. A negative example in this regard is the case *Seeling*, cf. Case C-269/00, *Wolfgang Seeling v. Finanzamt Starnberg* [2003] ECR I-4101; for critical comments, see Reiß 2010 (n. 12 above), § 14 para. 89.
35. Cf. Case C-29/08, *Skatteverket v. AB SKF* [2009] ECR I-10413, paras. 46 et seq.
36. See, for example, Case C-327/94, *Jürgen Dudda v. Finanzamt Bergisch Gladbac* [1996] ECR I-4595, para. 22; Case C-357/07, *The Queen, on the application of TNT Post UK Ltd. v. The Commissioners for Her Majesty's Revenue and Customs* [2009] ECR I-3025, para. 48.
37. See, for example, Case 122/87, *Commission of the European Communities v. Italian Republic* [1988] ECR I-2685, para. 10; *Goed Wonen* (n. 29 above), para. 53; Case C-280/04, *Jyske Finans A/S v. Skatteministeriet* [2005] ECR I-10683, paras. 34 et seq.
38. See, for example, *Institute of the Motor Industry* (n. 5 above), paras. 18 and 21.
39. Cf. Case C-372/88, *Milk Marketing Board of England and Wales v. Cricket St. Thomas Estate* [1990] ECR I-1345, para. 19; *SDC* (n. 29 above), para. 22; Case C-384/98, *'D' v. 'W'* [2000] ECR I-6795, para. 16; see also Terra & Kajus (n. 11 above), 237 et seq., and the case law cited there.
40. Cf. Case C-98/07, *Nordania Finans A/S and BG Factoring A/S v. Skatteministeriet* [2008] ECR I-1281, para. 22; Case C-174/08, *NCC Construction Danmark A/S v. Skatteministeriet* [2009] ECR I-10567, para. 30. By contrast, declarations recorded in Council minutes in the course of preparatory work leading to the adoption of a directive cannot be used for the purpose of interpreting that directive where no reference is made to the content of the declaration in the wording of the provision in question, cf. Case C-375/98, *Ministério Público and Fazenda Pública v. Epson Europe BV* [2000] ECR I-4243, para. 26.
41. Cf. Case C-296/95, *The Queen v. Commissioners of Customs and Excise, ex parte EMU Tabac SARL, The Man in Black Ltd, John Cunningham* [1998] ECR I-1605, para. 36; *Institute of the Motor Industry* (n. 5 above), para. 16; *MKG-Kraftfahrzeuge-Factoring* (n. 17 above), paras. 67 et seq.; Case C-498/03 *Kingscrest Associates Ltd. and Montecello Ltd v. Commissioners of Customs & Excise* [2005] ECR I-4427, para. 26. See also Terra & Kajus (n. 11 above), 226 et seq., and the case law cited there.
42. Cf. Case C-349/96, *Card Protection Plan Ltd (CPP) v. Commissioners of Customs & Excise* [1999] ECR I-973, paras. 17 et seq.; Case C-363/05, *JP Morgan Fleming Claverhouse Investment Trust plc and The Association of Investment Trust Companies v. The Commissioners of HM Revenue and Customs* [2007] ECR I-5517; *TNT Post UK* (n. 36 above).

Finally, the CJEU has repeatedly held that whenever the wording of secondary Community law is ambiguous, preference should be given to the interpretation which renders the provision consistent with the EU treaties, and with the fundamental rights protected by the EU legal order 'or with the other general principles of Community law'. In the area of VAT, this convincing approach has materialized in an accentuated role of the principle of fiscal neutrality in the interpretation of exemptions.[43] In particular, the scope of an exemption must be construed, at least within the limits set by its wording,[44] so as to ensure that similar goods and supplies of services, which are thus in competition with each other, are treated equally.[45] Thus, unless specified otherwise, the status of the entity providing the supply (public body, charity, profit-oriented entity, etc.), should not be relevant.[46]

By virtue of the provisions on Community loyalty,[47] national tax administrations and courts must interpret the exemptions enshrined in their respective national VAT statutes in a manner consistent with the corresponding provision of the of the EU VAT Directive, taking into account the rules of interpretation discussed above. Arguably, this obligation can now also be derived from the more specific provision of Article 291 (1) TFEU. The authorities and courts of the Member States must also make sure that they do not rely on an interpretation which would be in conflict with the various fundamental rights protected by the Community legal order or with the other general principles of Community law.[48] Insofar as the Directive grants - exceptionally - discretion to the Member States regarding the scope or conditions of an exemption, it must not be construed so as to impair fiscal neutrality.[49]

---

43. See, for example, Case C-246/04, *Turn- und Sportunion Waldburg v. Finanzlandesdirektion für Oberösterreich* [2006] ECR I-589, para. 34; Joined Cases C-453/02 and C-462/02, *Finanzamt Gladbeck v. Edith Linneweber* (C-453/02) and *Finanzamt Herne-West v. Savvas Akritidis* (C-462/02) [2005] ECR I-1131, paras. 24 et seq. See also Y. Martínez Muñoz, '*El principio de neutralidad en el IVA en la doctrina del TJCE*', Civitas. Revista española de Derecho Financiero 145 (2010): 145, 184.
44. This limit is emphasized by Schulyok (n. 32 above), 266, 269 et seq.; however, an application by analogy should also be allowed for to ensure conformity with primary union law requirements, so long as it can be defended as *interpretatio praetor legem* rather than *interpretatio contra legem*.
45. See, for example, Case C-216/97, *Jennifer Gregg and Mervyn Gregg v. Commissioners of Customs & Excise* [1999] ECR I-4947, para. 20; Case C-169/04, *Abbey National plc and Inscape Investment Fund v. Commissioners of Customs & Excise* [2006] ECR I-4027, para. 68; Case C-540/09, *Skandinaviska Enskilda Banken AB Momsgrupp v. Skatteverket*, [2011] ECR I-01509 paras. 20 and 36. See also Martínez Muñoz (n. 43 above), 145, 184. The Court's case law is not entirely consistent in this regard, though, as can be seen in *Verigen Transplantation Service International* (n. 33 above), paras. 30 et seq.
46. See, in this regard, also A.A. Tait, *Value-Added Tax: International Practice and Problems*, 69 (International Monetary Fund 1988).
47. Cf. Case 14/83, *Sabine von Colson and Elisabeth Kamann v. Land Nordrhein-Westfalen* [1984] ECR 1891, para. 26.
48. Cf. Case C-101/01, *Criminal proceedings against Bodil Lindqvist* [2003], ECR I-12971, para. 87; Case C-305/05, *Ordre des barreaux francophones et germanophone and Others v. Conseil des ministres* [2007] ECR I-5305, para. 28.
49. Cf. *JP Morgan Fleming Claverhouse* (n. 42 above), paras. 22 and 43; Case C-58/09, *Leo-Libera GmbH v. Finanzamt Buchholz in der Nordheide* [2010] ECR I-5189, paras. 34 et seq.

[2] *Specific Topics of General Interest*

[a] *Complex Transactions*

When a taxable transaction comprises a bundle of elements and acts, only some of which would qualify for an exemption if each element was viewed in isolation, the question arises as to whether the remaining elements nevertheless fall under the scope of the exemption, too, because they form part of a single transaction for VAT purposes. A similar problem surfaces in the context of the place of supply rules that differentiate between supplies of goods and supplies of services, and furthermore require more specific classifications, based on the objective characteristics of the transaction within each category of supply.

By and large, the Court has developed identical criteria in the context of either of the aforementioned scenarios in order to decide whether a composite or complex transaction really constitutes one single supply, and if so, which element(s) should be regarded as being characteristic. According to settled case law, every transaction must normally be regarded as distinct and independent. However, a transaction which comprises a single supply from an economic point of view should not be split artificially.[50] This can be confirmed where two or more elements or acts supplied by the taxable person to the customer are so closely linked that they form, objectively, a single, indivisible economic supply.[51] Such is also the case where one or more elements are to be regarded as constituting the principal service, whilst one or more elements are to be regarded, by contrast, as ancillary services which share the tax treatment of the principal service. In particular, a service must be regarded as ancillary to a principal service if it does not constitute for customers an aim in itself, but a means of better enjoying the principal service supplied.[52]

However, it must not go unnoticed that there is also a fundamental difference between the delimitation of the scope of an exemption, on the one hand, and of a place of supply rule, on the other hand. In the latter case, the question at issue will tend to focus on which proxy for the destination principle should apply in B2B transactions. In Business-to-Customer (B2C) trade, the analysis will usually determine whether the destination principle applies at all.[53] As a general rule, considerations of a tax-technical nature dominate this assessment. By contrast, the application of an exemption usually implies the conferral of a tax privilege upon the final consumer or, exceptionally, upon the taxable person, which must be justified by overriding reasons of public interest.[54]

---

50. Cf. Case C-276/09, *Everything Everywhere Ltd. v. Commissioners for Her Majesty's Revenue & Customs*, [2010] ECR I-12359, paras. 21 et seq., and the (settled) case law cited there.
51. Cf. Case C-41/04, *Levob Verzekeringen BV and OV Bank NV v. Staatssecretaris van Financiën* [2005] ECR I-9433, paras. 20 and 22; Case C-111/05, *Aktiebolaget NN v. Skatteverket* [2007] ECR I-2697, paras. 22 et seq.; Case C-425/06, *Ministero dell'Economia e delle Finanze v. Part Service Srl* [2008] ECR I-897, para. 53; Case C-88/09, *Graphic Procédé v. Ministère du Budget, des Comptes publics et de la Fonction publique* [2010] ECR I-1049, para. 19.
52. Aktiebolaget NN (n. 51 above), para. 28; *Part Service* (n. 51 above), paras. 51 et seq.; *Tellmer Property* (n. 29 above), para. 18; *Graphic Procédé* (n. 51 above), para. 24.
53. For further details, see Terra & Kajus (n. 11 above), 485 et seq.
54. See, in this regard, below at §1.03[B].

Therefore, two additional aspects come into play, both of which have occasionally already been relied on by the Court. First, it is appropriate to take into account the objective pursued by the exemption - provided that it is discernible - in order to determine whether those elements of the composite transaction at issue that would not by themselves qualify for the exemption are indeed closely linked or of a merely ancillary nature to the qualifying elements.[55] Second, the extension of the exemption must not lead to serious distortions of competition that would infringe the fundamental principle of fiscal neutrality.[56] In general, this calls for a restrictive approach towards assessing complex transactions in the context of VAT exemptions.

[b] Outsourcing

The denial of input VAT deduction that corresponds with a VAT exemption[57] provides an incentive for vertical integration of business, contrary to the principle of fiscal neutrality. The outsourcing of constituent elements of an exempt transaction to a legally independent service provider will imply an additional and irrecoverable VAT burden for the supplier of the exempt goods or services,[58] if his subcontractor does not benefit from the exemption himself. To alleviate these negative effects, the CJEU has developed a set of criteria whose fulfilment will permit to include the activities realized by the subcontractor in the scope of the exemption. According to settled case law, they must, viewed broadly, form a distinct whole, fulfilling in effect the specific, essential functions of a transaction described in the exemption at issue.[59] By contrast, mere material or technical supplies which do not share the characteristic features that distinguish the exempt transaction from other supplies, such as the making available of a system of information technology, are not covered by the respective exemption.[60]

55. Cf. Joined Cases C-394/04 and C-395/04, *Diagnostiko & Therapeftiko Kentro Athinon-Ygeia AE v. Ypourgos Oikonomikon* [2005] ECR I-10373, paras. 22 and 25; *Bundesfinanzhof*, 10 December 2009, Case V R 18/08, BFHE 227, 528.
56. Cf. *Diagnostiko & Therapeftiko Kentro Athinon-Ygeia* (n. 55 above), paras. 32 et seq.; see also *Tellmer Property* (n. 29 above), para. 22. However, see also *Everything Everywhere* (n. 50 above), para. 31, regarding the reverse situation of an ancillary element of a supply that would be exempt if assessed in isolation. Here, the Court did not esteem the neutrality principle very highly, probably well aware of the serious and indeed disproportionate complications that the exemption of a minor part of an integrated supply and the ensuing need to determine and apply a pro rata for the calculation of the deductible input VAT would imply.
57. For further details, see below at §2.05.
58. See also - with respect to public sector entities that carry out non-taxable or exempt transactions - Copenhagen Economics & KPMG, *VAT in the Public Sector and Exemptions in the Public Interest, Final Report for TAXUD/2009/DE/316* (Copenhagen: Colophon 2011), 10 et seq., 13.
59. Cf. *SDC* (n. 29 above), para. 66, Case C-235/00, *Commissioners of Customs & Excise v. CSC Financial Services Ltd.* [2001] ECR I-10237, para. 25; *Abbey National* (n. 45 above), para. 70.
60. Cf. *SDC* (n. 29 above), para. 66; *Abbey National* (n. 45 above), para. 71.

The jurisprudence of the Court thus requires that the outsourced supply forms a well-matched and clearly definable composition of goods and/or services ('distinct whole') which, having regard to its inherent and objective characteristics,[61] features core elements of the exempt transaction that characterize and distinguish the latter ('specific functions') and contributes significantly to the performance of the exempt transaction as contemplated in relevant provision ('essential functions'). For the sake of fiscal neutrality, the latter criterion in particular should not be applied overly strictly. However, it is not sufficient, all by itself, that the supply by the subcontractor constitutes an indispensable element of the exempt transaction.[62]

§2.03 BENCHMARKS FOR THE ANALYSIS OF EXEMPTIONS

Pursuant to the preamble and to Article 1 of the EU VAT Directive, the common system of EU VAT intends to establish a VAT that is harmonized as between Member States, neutral with respect to competition between economic operators, and designed as a general tax on expenditure for consumption exactly proportional to the price of the goods and services. As in other jurisdictions with a comprehensive VAT or GST, exemptions constitute an 'alien matter' within the tax system.[63] They raise concerns regarding both optimal tax policy and constitutional requirements of the tax system. The following section will elaborate on the respective benchmarks insofar as they are relevant, before applying them to the specific rules to be examined. Tax policy aspects will only be discussed rather briefly, as the chapter intends to contribute to the debate mainly from a legal perspective.

[A] Tax Policy Considerations

[1] Neutrality

According to the modern theory of public finance, a key requirement for a good tax system is that it should ideally not interfere with the efficient allocation of resources.[64] As a general rule, a tax system should therefore be neutral with respect to the decisions of market agents (the supply and the demand side) in the absence of market failure.[65] There is a common belief among economists that, considering information

61. Special reference to the objective characteristics is also made by S. Heidemann, *Die Umsatzsteuerbefreiungen von Finanzdienstleistungen*, 216 (Duncker & Humblot GmbH 2008).
62. Cf. *CSC Financial Services* (n. 59 above), para. 32.
63. Likewise F.J. Sánchez Gallardo (ed.), *Guía del Impuesto sobre el Valor Añadido*, 289 (8th ed., CISS Wolters Kluwer 2006); H.G. Ruppe, *'Unechte' Umsatzsteuerbefreiungen*, in *Steuerrechtsordnung in der Diskussion, Festschrift für Klaus Tipke*, 457 (461) (J. Lang ed., Otto Schmidt 1995).
64. Pars pro toto J.E. Stiglitz, *Economics of the Public Sector*, 458 et seq. (3d ed., W. W. Norton & Company 2000).
65. Pars pro toto Tiley (n. 16 above), 11.

asymmetries and the reality of political decision-making, 'best practice ... strongly indicates that the consumption base of the VAT should be defined as broadly as possible and that all goods and services should be taxed at a uniform rate' in order to promote fiscal neutrality.[66] One of the main arguments brought forward in favour of a comprehensive VAT in this context is that it leaves relative factor prices unchanged.[67] By contrast, exemptions are hardly ever fully neutral with respect to competing goods or services. Moreover, the neutrality requirement extends also to the organization of business activities. Finally, any national tax system – or in the case of the EU VAT, the European tax system – should also not cause distortions in international commerce.[68] With respect to both aspects, the 'input taxation' effect inherent to the 'standard' EU VAT exemption causes problems.[69]

Insofar as an incentive or disincentive for certain behaviour not following market rationale is desired by the legislator contrary to the neutrality principle, or a correction of market outcome is intended, it should be achieved in the most efficient way possible (and therefore possibly not as a tax measure). However, unlike direct personal taxes, VAT as an indirect tax is often ill-suited to pursue extra-fiscal policy goals through tax concessions. VAT laws only address the taxable person in his function as a tax collector, rather than the final consumer who is supposed to be the final taxpayer and who is therefore normally intended to ultimately benefit from most objective exemptions.[70] Exemptions therefore often cannot be tailored to their objective without producing free-rider effects due to the impossibility of making their grant dependent upon the fulfilment of certain personal criteria by the recipient of the supply at issue.

It is also worth mentioning that VAT exemptions may diminish or aggravate the distortions caused by the respective system of direct personal taxes.[71]

66. Cf. S. Cnossen, 'Commentary', in Mirrlees et al. (n. 25 above), 370; S. Cnossen, *Global Trends and Issues in Value Added Taxation*, 5 Intl. Tax Pub. Fin. 399 (1998). See also Crawford et al. (n. 25 above), 275, 286 et seq.: uniform taxation of all commodities tends to be the best guarantee for neutrality of taxation; likewise R.F.W. van Brederode, *Systems of General Sales Taxation*, 46 (Kluwer Law International 2009).
67. Cf. K.B. Bhatia, *Value-Added Tax and the Theory of Tax Incidence*, 19 J. Pub. Econ. 203, 209 et seq. (1982).
68. Cf. van Brederode (n. 66 above), 47; J.E. Meade, *The Structure and Reform of Direct Taxation*, 20 (George Allen & Unwin 1978).
69. To be discussed below at §2.05[a][1].
70. Cf. P. Tonner, *Umsatzsteuerbefreiung heilberuflicher Leistungen*, 30 (Mensch & Buch 2005); for an in-depth analysis, see below at §2.03[B][2][b].
71. See the different examples given by P. Gottfried & W. Wiegard, *Exemption versus Zero Rating: A Hidden Problem of VAT*, 46 Journal of Public Economics 307, 325 et seq. (1991), on the one hand; and by A. ab Iorwerth & J. Whalley, *Efficiency Considerations and the Exemption of Food from Sales and Value Added Taxes*, 35 Can. J. Econ. 166, 173 et seq. (2002).

[2] *Simplicity and Administrative Efficiency*

A tax system should not cause disproportionate or even excessive costs for those affected, taking into account both compliance costs of the taxpayer and administrative costs of the tax authorities.[72] This requires a tax system to first implement its fundamental principles as consistently as possible so as to maintain structural simplicity and enhance legal certainty. This aspect also calls for a comprehensive design of VAT.[73] Since exemptions are by definition exceptions,[74] they add complexity to the tax system. In particular, they tend to give rise to difficult interpretive questions regarding the delimitation of their scope.[75] The resulting increase in compliance costs and risks for business will also tend to reduce the benefits of the exemption for the taxpayer.[76] Moreover, in the EU context, these drawbacks are particularly severe, because exemptions are supposed to be interpreted uniformly in all Member States,[77] and this has proven to be an almost insurmountable task for national tax administrations and courts.[78] Second, a balanced trade-off may be required between the individual assessment of all the circumstances that should matter for the scope of an exemption pursuant to its underlying objective, and the lower administrative costs corresponding to a higher degree of standardization.[79]

[3] *Transparency*

Considerations of public choice and political accountability call for transparency of the tax system.[80] In the context of VAT exemptions, this implies that it should be clear who the intended beneficiary is, and that these intentions should not be incongruous with economic reality. Moreover, the extent of the tax concession ensuing from an 'exemption' should not be left in the shadows of tax technicalities and market mechanisms which ordinary citizens (and voters) find hard to grasp. It can already be stated here

---

72. Cf. W. Gale & J. Holtzblatt, *The Role of Administrative Issues Tax Reform: Simplicity, Compliance and Administration*, in *US Tax Reform in the 21st Century*, 179 and 185 (G.R. Zodrow & P. Mieszkowski eds., Cambridge University Press 2002).
73. Cf. Cnossen 2010 (n. 66 above), 370.
74. Cf. P. Hoffsümmer, *Steuerbefreiungen für Inlandsumsätze*, 3 (Peter Lang 2009); Martínez Muñoz (n. 43 above), 145, 183.
75. Cf. A. Camenzind, N. Honauer & K.A. Vallender, *Handbuch zum Mehrwertsteuergesetz*, 235, para. 652 (2d ed., Haupt Verlag 2003); Heidemann (n. 61 above), 38 et seq.; D.G. Raboy, *The Value Added Tax: Orthodoxy and New Thinking*, 87, 92 et seq. (M.L. Weidenbaum, D.G. Raboy & E.S. Christian Jr., eds., Springer 1989). For some very nice examples, see Tait (n. 46 above), 70 et seq.
76. Cf. van Brederode (n. 66 above), 132; Camenzind et al. (n. 75 above), 236, para. 654; Krever (n. 8 above), 9, 17.
77. See above at §1.02[C][1].
78. The latter, supranational problem could be alleviated by implementing measures at the EU level – in particular, Council Regulations based on Art. 397 of the EU VAT Directive – but the Commission and the Council have so far been reluctant to enact such measures.
79. For instance, an exemption for books that is intended to promote the consumption of a seemingly meritorious good might refrain from making further distinctions, thus also covering 'profane' books such as train timetables. For further examples, see Tait (n. 46 above), 74.
80. Pars pro toto J.E. Stiglitz & B. Schönfelder, *Finanzwissenschaft*, 416. et seq. (Oldenbourg 2000).

that with respect to exemptions without credit, the Australian term 'input taxation' would therefore be clearly preferable.

[4] Flexibility

The fact that within the EU, the exemptions listed in the EU VAT Directive are supposed to be uniformly granted has additional drawbacks. Such a harmonized system of mandatory exemptions may force certain social and economic policy priorities upon individual Member States even though the respective national government may not, by itself, want to pursue such policies. Member States may thus be forced to forgo revenue and raise it otherwise by increasing the regular VAT rate or other taxes.[81] This is a particularly harsh consequence for new Member States who must, as a general rule, accept the catalogue of 'standard' exemptions without ever having influenced it. By contrast, a restrictive approach to exemptions in the European VAT Directives would not hinder Member States from pursuing their eventual non-tax policies, either by resorting to direct subsidies, or through concessions in other, non-harmonized taxes. These considerations call for a strict limitation of exemptions.

[B] Constitutional Requirements

It is suggested that within the EU, exemptions and the distortions caused by exemptions do have an additional (quasi-) constitutional dimension.

[1] General Observations

Pursuant to Article 2 EU, the European Union is founded on, inter alia, freedom, equality, and the rule of law, and it is based on a society in which justice prevails. Article 6 (1) EU specifies further that 'the Union recognises the rights, freedoms and principles set out in the Charter of Fundamental Rights of the European Union, which shall have the same legal value as the Treaties'. Moreover, Article 6 (3) EU adds that 'fundamental rights, as guaranteed by the European Convention for the Protection of Human Rights and Fundamental Freedoms and as they result from the constitutional traditions common to the Member States, shall constitute general principles of the Union's law'. All Community institutions are bound to respect these superior principles of EU law, in particular when enacting rules of secondary EU law. The enactment of VAT legislation constitutes no exception in this regard, as the CJEU has demonstrated

81. Admittedly, these taxes could be fine-tuned so as to correlate closely to a certain exemption, e.g., by imposing an insurance tax at the standard VAT rate so as to compensate for the exemption of insurance services. However, it is suggested here that such specific excise duties may not wholly undermine the exemption stipulated by the Directive, hence distortions or shortcomings will (have to) remain, even apart from the denial of a right to deduct input tax which will be discussed later on.

on various occasions.[82] For that reason, exemptions need to be justified insofar as they constitute a prima facie infringement of the equality principle, a freedom right, or any other general principle referred to in Articles 2 and 6 EU.

According to Article 3 (3) 1 EU, the EU shall establish an internal market. Pursuant to Article 26 (2) TFEU, the internal market shall comprise an area without internal frontiers in which the free movement of, inter alia, goods and services is ensured. Precisely in order to ensure the establishment and the functioning of the internal market, the competence to adopt provisions for the harmonization of legislation concerning turnover taxes has been conferred upon the Union in Article 113 EU. Consequently, exemptions also need to be justified insofar as they constitute a prima facie infringement of the guarantees of free movement of goods (Articles 34 et seq. TFEU and Article 110 TFEU) or of the freedom to provide services (Article 56 TFEU). It should be noted though that such an infringement will only exceptionally occur; usually with regard to those aspects of the exemption regime that have not as yet been fully harmonized.[83] For example, Article 135 (1)(g) exempts the management of special investment funds 'as defined by Member States'. If a Member State proceeds to define as beneficiaries only investment funds established under national law, as Germany did until a few years ago, this constitutes an obstacle to the freedom to provide services within the meaning of Article 56 TFEU.

As a general rule, the provisions on prohibited State aid stipulated in Article 107 TFEU are not applicable to VAT exemptions; this has also been acknowledged by the Commission.[84] Under Article 107 (1) TFEU, 'any aid granted by a Member State or through State resources in any form whatsoever which distorts or threatens to distort competition by favouring certain undertakings or the production of certain goods shall, in so far as it affects trade between Member States, be incompatible with the common market'. The CJEU has convincingly pointed out that those parts of the VAT system which are set up by Community legislation and must be uniformly implemented by all Member States do not meet the condition of intervention by the State and therefore do not constitute State aid within the meaning of Article 107 (1) TFEU.[85]

82. It should be noted, though, that so far the CJEU has never declared void any provision of the VAT Directives on grounds of a presumed incompatibility with superior principles of EU law.
83. Cf. Hoffsümmer (n. 74 above), 29 et seq.
84. Cf EU Commission, Report on the implementation of the Commission notice on the application of the state aid rules to measures relating to direct business taxation, 9 February 2004, C (2004) 434, para. 72.
85. Cf. Case C-460/07, *Sandra Puffer v. Unabhängiger Finanzsenat, Außenstelle Linz* [2009] ECR I-3251, paras. 67 to 71; Case T-351/02, *Deutsche Bahn AG v. Commission of the European Communities* [2006] ECR II-1047, para. 100 u. 103. See also Opinion of AG Jacobs, Case C-482/99, *France v. Commission* [2002] ECR I-4397, para. 54, who convincingly pointed out that 'the second alternative in Article 87(1) [now Art. 107 (1)] of the Treaty (aid granted through State resources) ... serves only to preclude circumvention of the State aid rules through decentralised or privatised distribution of aid. That means however that where aid is granted under the second alternative through State resources the measure must be the result of action of the Member State concerned.'

[2] *Relevant Constitutional Principles*

For the reasons given above, the main standard of quasi-constitutional review of any VAT exemption in the context of the common system of EU VAT are the fundamental rights and general principles which are binding upon the Union legislator. In the context of VAT, and with regard to exemptions in particular, the following rights and principles are specifically relevant.

[a] Fiscal Neutrality for Business as a Corollary of the Equality Principle

It is settled case law that the equality principle has to be considered a fundamental right[86] and thus constitutes one of the fundamental and general principles of Union law.[87] Its character as a superior principle of EU law was recently enhanced when Article 20 of the Charter of Fundamental Rights became legally binding for almost all Member States, pursuant to Article 6 (1) EU Treaty as amended by the so-called Lisbon Treaty. Sometimes also denominated as general principle of non-discrimination, equal treatment requires, according to the CJEU, that similar situations not be treated differently and different situations not be treated alike unless such treatment is objectively justified.[88] In recent years, the CJEU has even repeatedly held that in the field of VAT, the principle of fiscal neutrality is 'the' reflection of the fundamental principle of equal treatment.[89]

86. Case C-292/97, *Kjell Karlsson* [2000] ECR I-2737, paras. 37 et seq.; Case C-442/00, *Ángel Rodríguez Caballero v. Fondo de Garantía Salarial (Fogasa)* [2002] ECR I-11915, paras. 31 et seq.; Case C-177/05, *María Cristina Guerrero Pecino v. Fondo de Garantía Salarial (Fogasa)* [2005], ECR I-10887, para. 26; Case C-81/05, *Anacleto Cordero Alonso v. Fondo de Garantía Salarial (Fogasa)* [2006] ECR I-7569, para. 37. See also T. Tridimas, *The General Principles of EU Law*, 60 (2d ed. Oxford University Press 2006).
87. Joined Cases C-27/00 and C-122/00, *The Queen v. Secretary of State for the Environment, Transport and the Regions, ex parte Omega Air Ltd.* (C-27/00) and *Omega Air Ltd. , Aero Engines Ireland Ltd. and Omega Aviation Services Ltd. v. Irish Aviation Authority* (C-122/00) [2002] ECR I-2569, para. 79; Case C-334/03, *Commission of the European Communities v. Portugal* [2005] ECR I-8911, paras. 23 et seq.; Case C-27/95, *Woodspring District Council v. Bakers of Nailsea Ltd.* [1997] ECR I-1847, para. 17; Case C-127/07, *Société Arcelor Atlantique et Lorraine and Others v. Premier ministre, Ministre de l'Écologie et du Développement durable and Ministre de l'Économie, des Finances et de l'Industrie* [2008] ECR I-9895, para. 23.
88. See, to that effect, joined Cases C-248/95 and C-249/95, *SAM Schiffahrt GmbH and Heinz Stapf v. Bundesrepublik Deutschland* [1997] ECR I-4475, para. 50; *Karlsson* (n. 86 above), para. 39.
89. Cf. *Kingscrest Associates* (n. 41 above), paras. 54 et seq.; joined Cases C-443/04 and C-444/04, *H. A. Solleveld* (C-443/04) *and J. E. van den Hout-van Eijnsbergen* (C-444/04) *v. Staatssecretaris van Financiën* [2006] ECR I-3617, para. 35; Case C-106/05, L.u.P. *GmbH v. Finanzamt Bochum-Mitte* [2006] ECR I-5123, para. 48; Case C-240/05, *Administration de l'enregistrement et des domaines v. Eurodental Sàrl* [2006] ECR I-11479, para. 55; Case C-309/06, *Marks & Spencer plc v. Commissioners of Customs & Excise* [2008] ECR I-2283, paras. 47 and 49; Case C-484/06, *Fiscale eenheid Koninklijke Ahold NV v. Staatssecretaris van Financiën* [2008] ECR I-5097, para. 36; *Puffer* (n. 85 above), para. 53. Hence, fiscal neutrality should properly be regarded as a VAT-specific sub-principle of the more fundamental principle of equal treatment, instead of the reverse. For an in-depth discussion, see J. Englisch, Gemeinschaftsgrundrechte im harmonisierten Steuerrecht, in *Zukunftsfragen des deutschen Steuerrechts*, 39 et seq. (W. Schön & E.M. Beck eds., Springer 2009); for a different opinion, see de la Feria (n. 6 above), 262 et seq.

Fiscal neutrality as interpreted by the Court of Justice[90] precludes, as already mentioned, treating similar goods or similar economic transactions which are in competition with each other differently for VAT purposes.[91] Occasionally, the CJEU has also stressed the requirement of organizational neutrality of VAT.[92] Moreover, the principle of fiscal neutrality is also conceived by the CJEU to require, as a general rule, a full relief of the taxable person with respect to the VAT burden payable or paid in the course of taxable economic activities.[93] This latter aspect is closely related to the conception of VAT as a tax on consumer expenditure, rather than business expenses.[94] The constitutional status that must be attributed to the neutrality principle as a presumed reflection of the equality principle implies that any infringement must serve legitimate conflicting interests or policies and do so in a proportionate manner.[95]

It should be noted that the CJEU has recently decided that different from the equality principle, the principle of fiscal neutrality would be merely a 'fundamental principle underlying the common system of VAT established by the relevant Community legislation' and therefore the 'subject of detailed rules' that may deviate from it without need for justification.[96] Against the background of the above conclusions, it is respectfully submitted that the CJEU's reasoning is inconsistent, or is at least misleading, and should not establish a model for future case law. If fiscal neutrality is presumed to be a or even 'the' reflection of equality in the area of VAT, then any VAT regime that does not comply with the requirements of fiscal neutrality must, by definition, ultimately also constitute an infringement of the equality principle, to be justified according to the standards developed for such infringements.

[b] Fair Taxation of Final Consumers as a Corollary of the Equality Principle

It is the common constitutional tradition of (almost) all Member States of the EU to inseparably link tax equality with the notions of tax equity and tax fairness.[97] The

90. For a thorough analysis of the Court's case law on fiscal neutrality, see also Martínez Muñoz (n. 43 above), 145, 149 et seq.
91. Cf. Case C-283/95, *Karlheinz Fischer v. Finanzamt Donaueschingen* [1998] ECR I-3369, paras. 21 and 27; Case C-481/98, *Commission v. France*, [2001] ECR I-3369, para. 22; Case C-109/02, *Commission v. Germany* [2003] ECR I-12691, para 20; Case C-382/02, *Cimber Air A/S v. Skatteministeriet* [2004] ECR I-8379, para. 24; *Eurodental* (n. 89 above), para. 46; *Navicon* (n. 21 above), para. 21; Case C-162/07, *Ampliscientifica Srl and Amplifin SpA v. Ministero dell'Economia e delle Finanze and Agenzia delle Entrate* [2008] ECR I-4019, paras. 25 et seq.
92. Cf. Case C-453/05, *Volker Ludwig v. Finanzamt Luckenwalde* [2007] ECR I-5083, para. 35.
93. Cf. Case C-400/98, *Finanzamt Goslar v. Brigitte Breitsohl* [2000] ECR I-4321, para. 37; *Puffer* (n. 85 above), para. 47.
94. See, for instance, *Fiscale eenheid Koninklijke Ahold* (n. 89 above), para. 36. See also *Frink* (n. 18 above), 63 et seq.; *Heidemann* (n. 61 above), 30; W. Reiß, *Der Verbraucher als Steuerträger der Umsatzsteuer im Europäischen Binnenmarkt*, in (J. Lang ed., n. 63 above), 433, 440.
95. As regards the specific requirements of the proportionality principle, see below at (c).
96. Cf. *NCC Construction* (n. 40 above), paras. 41–43.
97. Cf. the country reports in G.T.K. Meussen (ed.), *The Principle of Equality in European Taxation* (Kluwer 1999); K. Tipke, *Europäisches Steuerverfassungsrecht – Eine rechtsvergleichende Übersicht*, in *Staaten und Steuern, Festschrift für Klaus Vogel*, 561, 567 et seq. (P. Kirchhof, et al., eds., C.F. Müller 2000).

legislator is thus constitutionally required, in the field of taxation, to plausibly pursue a reasonable concept of tax fairness in a consistent manner, in principle without privileging or discriminating against any individual taxpayer. This should therefore also be the standard of review to be derived from the right to equal treatment enshrined in Article 20 of the Charter of Fundamental rights, even though the CJEU has not as yet pronounced itself accordingly.[98]

Obviously, the requirement of tax fairness has to be observed with respect to the final taxpayer, rather than with respect to the tax collector.[99] Considering the conceptual basis of the EU system of VAT, this calls for equal tax burdens on comparable consumption expenditure. As a general rule that can be inferred from Articles 2 and 9 of the EU VAT Directive: only a business carrying out taxable supplies for consideration is liable to VAT. By virtue of Article 1 (2) of the EU VAT Directive, though, the EU system of harmonized VAT has to be conceived, for the purposes of legal analysis, as a 'general tax on consumption'. Hence, the EU VAT has been designed as an indirect tax (as opposed to a direct, personal expenditure tax) on consumption expenditure. The incidence of the tax is therefore presumed and intended to rest with final consumers.[100]

Admittedly, this statutory incidence need not coincide with the effective division of the tax burden between suppliers and consumers that depends, predominantly, on demand and supply elasticities.[101] It does also not take into account second order effects of a possible decrease in trade volume, resulting welfare losses, eventual production inefficiencies, etc. Notwithstanding these acknowledgements, the principle of equal treatment will have to be applied, in the field of VAT, based on the *intended* (first order) effects of taxation. From the perspective of constitutional law, the legislator enjoys a margin of appreciation regarding the actual effects of statutory provisions - including tax laws - as long as its assumptions are not manifestly erroneous or the envisaged effects have been demonstrated not to occur on a regular basis.[102] Furthermore, the legislator cannot be held accountable for merely indirect

---

98. In addition, the Union legislator is also bound by the non-discrimination standard enshrined in Art. 14 of the European Convention on Human Rights (ECHR), which in combination with the right to a peaceful enjoyment of possessions laid down in Art. 1 of Protocol No. 1 also offers protection against discriminatory taxation, cf. the landmark judgment of the European Court of Human Rights (ECR) 23 October 1990, App. No. 11581/85, *Darby v. Sweden*, §§ 30 et seq.; see also ECR 19 July 2005, App. No. 6638/03, *P.M. v. United Kingdom*, § 28; ECR 29 April 2008, App. No. 13378/05, *Burden v. United Kingdom*, §§ 59 et seq. However, the Court has so far only objected to arbitrary imposition of tax burdens and has not as yet specified on any further requirements regarding the justification of a deviation from a consistent implementation of the respective tax fairness standard.
99. Cf. K. Tipke, *Steuer und Wirtschaft* (1992): 102, 105; for a more detailed discussion, see also J. Englisch, *VAT and General Principles of EU Law*, in *Traditional and Alternative Routes to European Tax Integration*, 231, 257 (D. Weber ed., IBFD 2010).
100. See also Krever (n. 8 above), 9, 10, regarding the typical contemporanean VAT in general.
101. Cf. Bird & Gendron (n. 16 above), 71; van Brederode (n. 66 above), 29 et seq.; as regards demand elasticities in particular, see also Raboy & Massa in Weidenbaum et al. (n. 75 above), 39, 56 et seq.
102. Cf. *SAM Schiffahrt und Stapf* (n. 88 above), para. 25; *Omega Air* (n. 87 above), para. 65; see also German Constitutional Court 9 July 1969, Case 2 BvL 20/65, BVerfGE 26, 302 (312); German Constitutional Court 7 July 1969, Case 2 BvL 3/66, BVerfGE 27, 111 (127).

repercussions of its tax legislation on the economy and social welfare if the incidence of such second order effects cannot be clearly assessed on a general basis. However, the legislator must at least ensure that its own conception (and perception) of the tax at issue is in compliance with the aforementioned standards of tax equality.

This calls for equal and fair taxation of the final consumers who are intended to be the final taxpayers, under the presumption – or, if preferred: legal fiction – that the VAT burden is shifted forward onto them.[103] In economic terms, this requirement tends to be equivalent to demanding that, in principle, relative prices remain unchanged after VAT is imposed. It is important to note that from a constitutional perspective, what ultimately matters with respect to the equality principle is not that consumer preferences remain undistorted,[104] but rather that the distribution of the tax burden is evenly oriented according to an equitable indicator of taxpaying capacity (i.e. consumption expenditure).[105]

Remarkably, some scholars argue that equality in VAT should be restricted to the principle of paying the same tax for *similar* goods.[106] This stance indeed comes close to reducing the impact of the equality principle regarding both the interpretation and (quasi-)constitutional review of VAT to the principle of fiscal neutrality. Under such a premise, no justification is needed under the equality principle insofar as the exemption is neutral in itself (i.e. if it covers an all-encompassing group of competing goods or services).[107] An exemption for certain goods and services could not be constitutionally objected to regardless of whether a convincing rationale could be brought forward in its defence, and independent of an eventual lack of proportional and coherent implementation, as long as all similar (directly competing) goods and services benefit from the exemption.

It is suggested here that such a narrow approach falls short of the concept of VAT as a *general* tax on consumption expenditure. Under such a premise, set forth by the Union legislator, an equal amount of expenditure must also be taxed equally, regardless of whether the expense is incurred for similar or for different goods or services.[108] One could also argue that, in a European Union committed to the achievement of justice in the exercise of its competences, only such a broad perspective complies with the fundamental principle of tax fairness as the most significant reflection of the

103. As regards the plausibility of this presumption, cf. C. Carbonnier, *Who Pays Sales Taxes? Evidence from French VAT Reforms, 1987–1999*, 91 Journal of Public Economics 1219 et seq. (2007); E. Christian in Weidenbaum et al. (n. 75 above), 17, 26 et seq.); Raboy & Massa in Weidenbaum et al. (n. 75 above), 39 et seq.; Raboy in Weidenbaum et al. (n. 75 above), 69, 73 et seq.
104. This might be a concern under a freedom right analysis, cf. R. Wernsmann, *Verhaltenslenkung in einem rationalen Steuersystem*, 345 et seq. (Mohr Siebeck 2005)
105. Some prefer to denominate this 'the legal neutrality' of VAT, cf. van Brederode (n. 66 above), 46; however, in the context of the harmonized EU VAT system this term is slightly confusing, because the CJEU uses a legal concept of neutrality that refers exclusively to effects of VAT on taxable business.
106. Cf. S. Hemels, in Lang et al. (n. 11 above), 35, 40 and 47; in a similar vein H. Stadie, *Umsatzsteuer im Europäischen Binnenmarkt*, 275 (R. Seer ed., Otto Schmidt 2009).
107. Obviously, distortions might then still arise due to the ensuing denial of input VAT taxation, which is an aspect to be assessed separately, though.
108. Likewise Frink (n. 18 above), 65 et seq.

equality principle in the field of taxation. Quite a few scholars will even equate fairness regarding the taxation of consumption expenditure as a particular expression of the ability-to-pay principle even if it does not take the form of a personal expenditure tax.[109] However, this assessment and the opalescent notion of ability to pay in the various tax jurisdictions need not be discussed in the present context in order to assert that exemptions must be justified per se because they constitute an infringement of the principle of equal taxation of consumption expenditure.

[c] The Proportionality Principle

The scope and extent of an exemption must furthermore respect the general principles of proportionality[110] and consistency.

Even if there exists - as can usually be expected - a legitimate objective underlying the exemption at issue which serves important policies relating to the public interest, a restriction on the general principles and freedoms guaranteed by the EU Treaties (and of the equality principle, in particular) may be justified only if the relevant measure is appropriate to ensure the attainment of the objective in question and only if it does not go beyond what is necessary to attain that objective.[111] The necessity requirement is a modified standard of Pareto efficiency firmly established in the case law of the Court as the second leg of the proportionality principle. In addition, the legitimate interest must also be an overriding one, which implies a weighing and balancing of the breach of the principle of equal taxation and the policies underlying the exemption.[112] It should be noted that the application of the principle of proportionality is disputed in the context of the equality principle. The Court's case law is

109. Cf. Poblet (n. 18 above), 112; González (n. 12 above), 19 et seq; A. Amatucci, *L'Ordinamento Giuridico Della Finanza Pubblica* (Jovene 2007), 82; G. Break, *The Value-added Tax*, in *The Promise of Tax Reform*, 128, 139 (J. Pechman ed., Prentice-Hall 1985); J. Casalta Nabais, *O Dever Fundamental de Pagar Impuestos*, 480 et seq. (Almedina 2004); Coimbra Silva, *Tributação sobre o Consumo*, 321 (331) (Silva, Bernades & Fonseca eds., São Paulo 2008); A. Comelli, *IVA comunitaria e IVA nazionale*, 998 et seq. (CEDAM 2000); P. Herrera Molina, *Capacidad Económica y sistema fiscal*, 456 (Tirant Lo Blanch 1998); R. Lobo Torres, *Tratado de Direito Constitucional Financeiro e Tributário, Volume II: Valores e Princípios Constitucionais Tribuários*, 310 (Renovar 2005); Mollard (n. 18 above), 443 (463); H.G. Ruppe, *Umsatzsteuergesetz*, 3rd ed. (facultas.wuv Universitäts, 2005), Einf para. 32; C. Sullivan, *The Tax on Value Added*, 4 and 20 (Columbia University Press 1965); See also Englisch, in Lang et al. (n. 11 above), 1, 22 et seq. with further references.
110. Cf. landmark ruling Case 11/70, *Internationale Handelsgesellschaft* [1970], ECR 1125, para. 15; N. Emiliou, *The Principle of Proportionality in European Law* (Kluwer 1996), 134 et seq.; F. Jacobs, *Recent Developments in the Principle of Proportionality in European Community Law*, in *The Principle of Proportionality in the Laws of Europe*, 1 (E. Ellis ed., Hart Publishing 1999).
111. See, for example, Case C-479/04, *Laserdisken ApS v. Kulturministeriet*, [2006] ECR I-8089, para. 53; for further references, consult X. Groussot, *General Principles of Community Law*, 153 (Europa Law Publishing, 2006); Jacobs, in (Ellis ed., n. 110 above), 2.
112. Cf. Case 181/84, *Man* [1985] ECR 2889, para. 20; Case 265/87, *Schräder* [1989] ECR 2237, para. 4; Case C-331/88, *Fedesa* [1990] ECR I-4023, paras. 6 and 13; Case C-26/90, *Wünsche* [1991] ECR 4961, paras. 12 et seq.; Case T-76/890, *ITP / Kommission* [1991] ECR II-575, paras. 78 et seq.; G. de Búrca, *Yearbook of European Law*, 105, 113 (Oxford University Press 1993).

inconsistent in this regard.[113] However, if one assumes that tax fairness as an expression of equality of taxation constitutes a (quasi-)constitutional value and individual right, then the legislator should not be permitted to compromise it any further than is necessary and appropriate.[114]

Furthermore, the CJEU has repeatedly held, in the context of an infringement of the fundamental freedoms enshrined in the TFEU, that legislation is appropriate to ensuring attainment of the objective pursued only if it genuinely reflects a concern to attain it in a consistent and systematic manner.[115] The same should apply, by analogy, in case of a breach of a general principle of EU law. It is suggested here that legal inconsistency implies arbitrary measuring by a double standard contrary to the principle that all parties should stand equal before the law.

[d] Judicial Restraint

With respect to all the above principles, judicial review must not be overly strict, because the CJEU must not - and indeed shows no inclination to - usurp the power of political decision-making reserved to the legislating institutions of the EU (i.e. to the Commission, the Council, and Parliament). Judicial restraint is required so as to avoid undermining the principle of institutional balance which requires that each of the EU institutions must exercise its powers with due regard for the powers of the other institutions.[116] Therefore, as already mentioned, a margin of appreciation must be conceded to the Union legislator; only obvious violations of the aforementioned principles can - and must - lead to the invalidity of the respective exemption or related provision. Moreover, generalizing assumptions must be accepted unless they are unrealistic or if the subject-matter is too diverse for too broadly standardized rules.

It should be noted that judicial restraint should not be mistaken for giving the legislator *carte blanche* in the area of European tax law, particularly with respect to VAT exemptions.[117] And while it seems appropriate to acknowledge a prerogative of the legislator with respect to a prognostic assessment of the impact of an exemption upon its introduction, the proportionality principle implies that the legislator must also monitor its effects and any subsequent developments carefully. If an exemption that

113. See, for instance, Case 267/88 a.o., *Wuidart a.o.* [1990] ECR I-435, paras. 27 et seq.; Case C-126/04, *Heinecken* [2005] ECR I-331, paras. 21 et seq., on the one hand (mere review of the legitimacy of a possible justification for unequal treatment); Case C-273/97, *Sirdar* [1999] ECR I-7403, para. 26; *Karlsson* (n. 86 above), paras. 44 et seq.; *Arcelor* (n. 87 above), paras. 47 and 59, on the other hand (strict scrutiny, also regarding necessity and proportionality *strictu sensu*). See also T. Kingreen, *European Fundamental Rights and Freedoms*, § 18 paras. 8 et seq. (D. Ehlers ed., de Gruyter Recht 2007); S. Manolkidis, *The Principle of Equal Treatment in EC Law*, para. 5.37 (A. Dashwood & S. O'Leary eds., Sweet & Maxwell 1997).
114. See also Hoffsümmer (n. 74 above), 127.
115. See, for example, Case C-169/07, *Hartlauer* [2009] ECR I-1721, para. 55; Case C-153/08, *Commission / Spain* [2009] ECR I-9735, para. 38; Case C-169/08, *Regione Sardegna*, [2009] ECR I-10821, para. 42; Case C-137/09, *Josemans*, [2010] ECR I-13019, para. 70; Case C-161/09, *Kakavetsos-Fragkopoulos*, [2011] ECR I-915, para. 42.
116. Cf. Case C-70/88, *Parliament v. Council* [1990] ECR I-2041, para. 22; Case C-133/06, *Parliament v. Council* [2008] ECR I-3189, para. 57.
117. Likewise Hoffsümmer (n. 74 above), 10 et seq.

could originally be justified turns out to be ineffective or if it has outlived its purpose, the legislator is under a duty to amend or repeal it. It is indeed somewhat astonishing that in over 30 years of judicial review of the Sixth VAT Directive and its successor Directive, the Court has never declared void any provision contained in the Directive on grounds of a presumed violation of general principles of EU law.[118]

§2.04 CRITICAL ANALYSIS OF THE RATIONALE FOR THE EXEMPTIONS OF THE EU SYSTEM

There are various rationales given for the exemptions that are currently enshrined in the EU VAT Directive. Some are broadly indicated by the title that chapter 2 of Title IX of the Directive carries: 'activities in the public interest'. More detailed reasons for exempting certain supplies are laid down in the explanatory memorandum to the Commission's proposal for the Sixth Directive. However, those explanations cover only a fraction of all exemptions contemplated in Articles 132 et seq. of the EU VAT Directive. Therefore, most justifications must be inferred from the substantive scope and the prerequisites of the exemption at issue; this is also the approach chosen by the CJEU when the Court elaborates on the objective for an exemption. In the following, we will analyse seven possible rationales for the 'standard' VAT exemptions of the harmonized EU system, preceded by some general remarks on the perspective to be adopted when assessing VAT exemptions.

[A] General Observations

As an indirect tax on consumption, VAT has a twofold impact: with respect to economic operators who are taxable persons and therefore liable to pay VAT and with respect to final consumers from whom the tax is supposed to be collected as the intended final taxpayers. This peculiarity, which distinguishes VAT from a direct tax on income or a personal expenditure tax, implies that there exist two potential beneficiaries of a tax exemption: either the taxable person (i.e. the business), or the final taxpayer (i.e. the final consumer).[119] Insofar as exemptions are intended to have a subsidizing effect, their justification therefore depends on a correct identification of the intended beneficiary.[120]

118. It is pointed out by de la Feria (n. 6 above), 279 et seq., that 'a more radical attempt by the Court to resolve the problems of the EU VAT system could ultimately lead to a legal vacuum'. While this assessment certainly highlights the need for judicial restrain (cf. Hoffsümmer (n. 74 above), 47), it cannot relieve the Court of its duty to assert the supremacy of general principles and fundamental rights in harmonized areas of tax law, as it already does in other, non-tax areas of legislation where the Court can also only annul but not reform legislation. It is suggested here that by doing so, the CJEU would probably sharpen the legislator's awareness of these supreme guidelines for VAT law design and thus contribute significantly to a better system of VAT.
119. See also Mollard (n. 18 above), 443, 453.
120. Likewise Weidenbaum & Christian, in Weidenbaum et al. (n. 75 above), 1, 10. For a different opinion, cf. Hoffsümmer (n. 74 above), 73: In the context of a VAT type consumption tax, exemptions can only be justified if they provide relief for (final) consumers. However, this

Personal (subjective) exemptions will tend to subsidize the taxable person, as long as most competitors are not eligible for the exemption. The equilibrium price in the market should then not be significantly affected by the exemption,[121] hence the privileged operators can charge gross prices as if they were liable for VAT and can thus make greater profits or compensate for extra-fiscal competitive disadvantages. A good example is the exemption for transactions carried out by blind persons[122] that some Member States have maintained by virtue of the authorization granted in Article 371 of the EU VAT Directive.[123]

Objective exemptions will usually have the primary effect and aim to lower the tax burden of the final consumers who are recipients of the exempt supply, at least if they cover all directly competing goods or services.[124] As explained above, the European-style VAT is based on the theory that under conditions of competition, the tax for which the economic operator is liable will be wholly shifted forward onto his customer and, ultimately, onto the final consumer. It should already be noted[125] that exemptions generally do not provide complete relief from VAT (due to a corresponding denial to credit input VAT corresponding to the exempt supply), but relieve from tax only the value added by the exempt trader.[126]

At least in B2C transactions, an exemption should thus lead to a decrease of marginal costs equivalent to the VAT on the value added by the taxable person.[127] This implies a reduction of the tax wedge between demand and supply prices corresponding to the reduced VAT burden (i.e. the arithmetic product of the VAT rate and the value added by the exempt trader), even though the ensuing new equilibrium price need not fully reflect this due to second order effects. Therefore, according to the inherent logic of VAT, it is the final consumer who under a legal analysis must normally be held to directly benefit from objective exemptions.[128] Insofar as the exempt traders also benefit due to the second order effects – e.g. an increased turnover volume – these indirect and rather remote effects could hardly justify an exemption as a proportionate measure, because direct subsidies would obviously be much more efficient instruments for that purpose.

---

stance seems too rigid; since tax exemptions do not fit into the system of a general tax on consumption (expenditure) and therefore need to be justified, anyways, it is not conceivable why possible justifications should a priori be limited to effects concerning the final taxpayer rather than the taxable person. But as Hoffsümmer (n. 74 above), 74, correctly points out, also under the latter premise exemptions aimed at the taxable person usually cannot be justified as proportional, as shall be demonstrated below.

121. See also the caveat provided for in Annex X Part B (5) to the EU VAT Directive regarding the exemption for transactions carried out by blind persons or by workshops for the blind.
122. See also Frink (n. 18 above), 114 et seq.; P. Kirchhof, *Umsatzsteuer Gesetzbuch*, § 11 para. 104 (Verlagsgruppe Hüthig-Jehle-Rehm 2008); Stadie 2009 (n. 31 above), 607.
123. Cf. Ruppe 2005 (n. 109 above), § 6 para. 291.
124. See also Frink (n. 18 above), 141.
125. See below at §2.05.
126. Cf. van Brederode (n. 66 above), 127; Genser & Winker (n. 14 above), 563 et seq.; Raboy in Weidenbaum et al. (n. 75 above), 87, 97; Tait (n. 46 above), 50.
127. See also Sánchez Gallardo (n. 63 above), 289; L. Pérez Herrero, *La Sexta Directiva Comunitaria del IVA*, 202 (Cedecs Editorial 1997); K. Löhr, *Das umsatzsteuerrechtliche Optionsrecht für Vermietungsumsätze*, 105 et seq. (Duncker & Humblot, 2003).
128. Cf. Kirchhof (n. 122 above), § 11 para. 5.

Exceptionally, objective exemptions may be assumed to subsidize primarily the taxable person, if the taxable person operates in a market that is typically characterized by little price flexibility due to political or other constraints. In certain sectors of the economy such as education or cultural activities (such as opera, theatre and other artistic performances), the majority of economic operators are state-controlled and will sustain costs that exceed the turnover they generate. Therefore, they depend on subsidies to carry out their activities. Since the prices they charge are already below uncontrolled market prices, a decrease in the VAT burden will not result in a price reduction, only in a reduced need for direct subsidies.[129]

In the following paragraphs, the most relevant of possible justifications for the exemptions contemplated in the EU VAT Directive will be discussed.

[B] Expenditure Not Indicating any Taxpaying Capacity

Some of the compulsory exemptions contemplated in Article 132 of the EU VAT Directive and granted 'for certain activities in the public interest' can by defended, in principle, by considerations of tax equity or tax fairness because the expenditure incurred for the exempt supplies should arguably not be deemed to indicate taxpaying capacity. One may reasonably assume that the obligation to pay taxes without receiving any directly related or equivalent consideration in return can (only) be regarded as equitable because according to contemporary concepts of tax fairness, every person who is integrated into society or who has, to a certain degree, become connected with society should be under a solidary obligation to contribute to that society's common good. However, such a solidary responsibility presupposes that the taxpayer has certain funds – as indicated by income, wealth or expenditure: i.e. funds that he or she earns, owns or spends – at his or her *free disposal.*[130] Insofar as he or she depends on these funds to pay for essential personal needs or for those of dependent family members, this person should not be assumed to be under a social responsibility to nevertheless contribute to covering the costs of public welfare and public goods; hence the corresponding income, wealth or expenditure does not indicate chargeable financial resources.

Even though transfer payments (social assistance) to the poor, and higher income tax allowances for households that pay income tax, are often considered a viable alternative to direct tax relief,[131] they are not fully equivalent from a constitutional perspective. They are an inferior choice when expenditure for essential goods or services can (exceptionally) be relieved from VAT sufficiently targeted even though

129. Cf. explanatory memorandum to the German VAT Act implementing the former Sixth VAT Directive, Bundestags-Drucksache V/1581, 5.

130. Cf. M. Lehner, *Einkommensteuerrecht und Sozialhilferecht*, 41 et seq. (Mohr Siebeck 1993); J. Lang, *Steuerrecht*, § 4 para. 113 (20th ed., Tipke & Lang eds., Otto Schmidt 2010); L. Schemmel, *Entlastung lebensnotwendiger Ausgaben von der Mehrwertsteuer*, 48 (Karl-Bräuer-Institut des Bundes der Steuerzahler 2009).

131. Not the least by the European Commission, cf. European Commission, cf. *Report from the Commission to the Concil*, COM(82) 885 final, 17 January 1983, reproduced in Intertax 1983, 137 (139).

VAT is levied as an indirect, impersonal tax. On the one hand, respect for human dignity requires that taxation must not push individuals who could otherwise sustain themselves (in particular, low-income workers) into relative poverty and social assistance programs, even though this could be avoided by a tax concession without significant 'spill-over' to non-essential expenditure. On the other hand, the increase of lump-sum income tax allowances for VAT on expenditure for essential needs will not guarantee vertical tax equity, at least with respect to those items where individual spending differs (e.g., medicine). Even if allowances were personalized, their compensatory effect would differ under a progressive income tax diametrically opposed to requirements of vertical tax equity.

Exemptions that are potentially justified partially or primarily on grounds of these kinds of tax equity considerations are, inter alia, the supply of hospital care and closely related activities,[132] the provision of (other) medical care,[133] the supply of services by dental technicians,[134] and the supply of transport services for sick or injured persons.[135] Expenditure for medicine and pharmaceuticals could also be considered to qualify for a tax concession based on the above consideration, at least if only available by prescription. However, the EU VAT Directive does not allow for an exemption of such supplies.[136] Moreover, the exemptions stipulated for the supply of services and for goods closely linked to welfare and social security work,[137] or to the protection of children and young persons,[138] probably fall into this category as well. According to the CJEU and also the German Constitutional Court, this is also true for the supply of basic postal services.[139] Some scholars would also consider the exemption for the leasing and letting of residential housing to be justified on grounds that it spares expenditure for essential personal needs from taxation.[140]

In the context of VAT as an indirect tax, it is unavoidable that wealthy or high-income consumers can avail themselves of the relevant tax exemptions, too, just like poorer members of society.[141] However, this does not per se put into question the legitimacy of these kinds of exemptions. Contrary to commonly held beliefs[142] shared

132. Cf. Art. 132 (1) (b) of the EU VAT Directive.
133. Cf. Art. 132 (1) (c) of the EU VAT Directive.
134. Cf. Art. 132 (1) (e) of the EU VAT Directive.
135. Cf. Art. 132 (1) (p) of the EU VAT Directive.
136. Instead, Member States may apply a reduced rate by virtue of Art. 98 of the EU VAT Directive. Only very few Member States such as Ireland and Malta have been granted a derogation from the general rule and may exempt medicine (with credit, i.e. by way of zero-rating).
137. Cf. Art. 132 (1) (g) of the EU VAT Directive.
138. Cf. Art. 132 (1) (h) of the EU VAT Directive.
139. Cf. *TNT Post UK* (n. 36 above), para. 33: 'essential needs'; German Constitutional Court, 9 February 2010, case 1 BvL 1/09, Neue Juristische Wochenschrift 2010, 505.
140. Cf. Kirchhof (n. 122 above), 141 et seq.; Reiß in Seer (n. 106 above), 9, 46. By contrast, the CJEU refers only to reasons of social policy, cf. *Goed Wonen* (n. 29 above), para. 52; likewise Stadie 2009 (n. 31 above), 530.
141. This effect has been pointed out by, e.g., Frink (n. 18 above), 147; Reiß (n. 12 above), § 14 para. 88.
142. See, inter alia, Gottfried & Wiegard (n. 71 above), 307, 308; Krever (n. 8 above), 9, 18 et seq.; Raboy in Weidenbaum et al. (n. 75 above), 87, 91 et seq.

by the EU Commission,[143] exemptions granted wholly or primarily on grounds of tax equity considerations of the kind discussed so far do not focus on a redistribution of wealth, nor do they derive their justification from the objective to mitigate the seemingly[144] regressive effects of VAT. Instead, they merely acknowledge that certain expenditures do not indicate an individual's taxpaying capacity,[145] regardless of the personal circumstances of the consumer.

Moreover, many times, and with respect to health care services in particular, the corresponding expenditure is not roughly the same for every (final) taxpayer, but rather varies considerably. As already mentioned, the exemption of related supplies could in principle also be justified by considerations of vertical tax equity. Even though the expenditures of two individuals in a certain period of time may be the same – whether relatively high or relatively low – it does not indicate the same capacity and solidary obligation to contribute to public sector activities if one of them has had to spend considerably more on essential goods or services than the other. The allegation that an exemption for essential expenditure must be regarded as highly inefficient because the majority of consumption of 'necessities' is attributable to families with incomes in excess of poverty level (i.e. to middle-class and upper-class households)[146] misses the point with respect to the categories of exemptions discussed in this section.

It has to be acknowledged, though, that under VAT as an *indirect* and transaction-based tax on consumption, expenditure related to the subsistence minimum cannot be spared from taxation by applying the targeted approach of *personal*

143. Cf. Communication from the Commission to the Council and the European Parliament on VAT rates other than standard VAT rates, 5 July 2007, COM(2007) 380 final, 5: '... improving equity... In this respect, the study finds that for the improvement of income distribution in a Member State, reduced VAT rates are effective only when the share of consumption expenditure of goods/services subject to a reduced rate (out of the total consumption expenditure) differs sufficiently between low and high-income groups and is stable over time.'

144. From a life-cycle perspective, taking into account also inheritance taxation, it is probably more correct to consider VAT a proportional rather than a regressive tax, see also van Brederode (n. 66 above), 44; Crawford et al. (n. 25 above), 275, 285. And even when income is chosen as the standard against which distributive effects are to be assessed, a VAT need not necessarily be regressive, or if so, only slightly, cf. the surveys provided by Bird & Gendron (n. 16 above), 72 et seq.

145. This does not preclude the possibility that certain exemptions could be justified by either aspect. For example, a tax concession for the supply of food might be justified on grounds of a very generous generalization that expenditure for food is typically incurred to pay for the minimum subsistence. However, under a stricter approach, this might not seem an acceptable assumption because frequently the type, quality and/or quantity of food consumed exceeds what would be considered minimum standards in the respective society (to be assessed, e.g., in the light of legislation on social assistance). A tax concession might then nevertheless be introduced to add a certain element of progressivity into the VAT system (as discussed in the next section), because empirical data shows that low-income households use a comparatively higher portion of their income to buy food. In such a situation, a conscious choice on part of the legislator is required as to which justification should carry a VAT concession for the good or service at issue, because the decision predetermines the question whether the supply at issue should be zero-rated or could rather also be maintained or be replaced by a mere rate reduction; for further discussion, see below at §2.05[B][2]. In the EU VAT system, the supply of food is not exempt. But most foodstuff qualifies for a reduced rate; moreover, some Member States have retained a right to exempt it with credit (zero-rating).

146. Cf. Raboy in Weidenbaum et al. (n. 75 above), 87, 92.

taxes on income that usually provides for a lump-sum allowance and special deductions for specific needs. Instead, the legislator has to resort to generalizing assumptions as to whether certain goods or services can be classified, by referring to their objective features and characteristics, as covering the essentials of life. Moreover, in order to avoid spill-over effects that would run counter to the principle of tax equity, an exemption can be justified on these grounds only if expenditure incurred for such goods or services is typically limited to the costs of subsistence. Hence, both qualitative and quantitative criteria related to the subsistence minimum have to be met in order to reasonably defend an exemption for the supply of certain goods or services as a measure that promotes tax equity. Moreover, the exemption should not cause excessive compliance or administrative costs. Otherwise, it is preferable to accept certain shortcomings with respect to this objective, which are inherent to the technical design of VAT, and to refer the taxpayer to a (partial) compensation by way of higher income tax allowances or to social assistance.

The attempt to justify the exemption concerning the leasing or letting of residential housing on the same basis of tax equity considerations as discussed above is highly questionable, because the exemption covers supplies ranging from public housing to the letting of luxury apartments. This exemption can hardly be defended on grounds of vertical tax equity and is not sufficiently targeted in order to relieve only expenditure incurred for essential human needs.[147] As regards the exemptions related to the health care sector, they require a particularly close analysis. The corresponding goods and services do cover essential needs, and expenses will usually be incurred only to the extent deemed necessary to restore health or alleviate suffering. However, in almost all EU Member States, the prices for medical care are highly regulated and thus generally inflexible in order to contain costs. A full taxation of related transactions would often not impose an additional burden on insurance systems and – ultimately – patients as final consumers,[148] but it would negatively affect the profits and income of hospitals and doctors, or lead to an increase of government subsidies. For these reasons, it is hard to justify that the EU VAT Directive stipulates a mandatory exemption for supplies of hospital and other medical care regardless of the regulatory context in several Member States.

Even if an exemption justified on grounds of tax equity considerations can be regarded as proportional, especially considering the margin of discretion to be conceded to the legislator, it can still be open to challenge due to a lack of consistency as to scope and prerequisites. In Germany, for instance, the exemption for the provision of medical care had until recently been transposed into national law in broad wording that was also understood to cover cosmetic surgery, regardless of its motivation.[149] Obviously, the inclusion of such services does not constitute a coherent alignment of the exemption to concerns of tax equity.[150]

147. Likewise Hoffsümmer (n. 74 above), 145 et seq.
148. See, in this regard, R. Peffekoven, *Zur Reform der Mehrwertsteuer* (Initiative Neue Soziale Marktwirtschaft- INSM GmbH 2010), 32.
149. For further details see Reiß (n. 12 above). § 14 para. 90.
150. Cf. *d'Ambrumenil* (n. 5 above), paras. 57 et seq., and case law cited therein. See also the detailed restatement of relevant CJEU jurisprudence by Terra & Kajus (n. 11 above), 712 et seq.

Another example is the exemption for 'public' postal services laid down in Article 132 (1)(a) of the EU VAT Directive. which has been interpreted by the CJEU to be reserved to suppliers of universal postal services in the entire territory of a particular Member State (irrespective of the agent's status as a public or private law entity).[151] As a consequence, not all basic postal services are exempt, but only those offered by suppliers with universal coverage. While both concepts were still congruent when the Sixth Directive was adopted, because all Member States had state monopolies in the postal sector at that time, the subsequent liberalization of these services has led to an asymmetric impact of the exemption. It would nowadays have to be regarded as inconsistent if its legitimacy were based – as is sometimes suggested – on the intention to decrease the tax burden on expenditure for essential needs. And if one were to consider that the exemption might then instead be justified as a subsidy to the economic agent itself, in order to compensate for the higher costs associated with the obligation to provide universal postal service,[152] this would hardly seem appropriate. The same effect could be reached much more efficiently and transparently by direct subsidies.

However, the efforts undertaken by the Commission to reform the VAT treatment of postal services by abolishing the exemption[153] have so far been frustrated by the Council. Meanwhile, the CJEU has refused to enter a thorough proportionality analysis and has merely declared that suppliers of universal postal services operate in a different legal context than other suppliers of postal services, hence the fiscal neutrality of VAT should not be assumed as being affected.[154] It is respectfully submitted that this kind of reasoning is highly unsatisfactory. It ignores economic reality; economic surveys show that the tax exemption is distorting competition significantly in European postal markets,[155] even when taking into account the moderating effect of the denial of input VAT deduction.[156] From a normative perspective, the position of the CJEU fails to adequately reflect that fiscal neutrality as a VAT-specific expression of the equality principle focuses on equal conditions of competition for suppliers of goods and services that are considered similar – i.e. substitutable – by their consumers, and that the legal context of their supply matters in the comparability analysis only insofar as it has an impact on this particular similarity concept.

151. Cf. *TNT Post UK* (n. 36 above), para. 36.
152. See, in this regard, H. Dietl, C. Jaag, M. Lang & U. Trinkner, *Competition and Welfare Effects of VAT Exemptions*, 11 B.E. J. Econ. Anal. Pol. 1, 22 (2011). Since the exemption contemplated in Art. 132 (1) (a) of the EU VAT Directive. is granted for the provision of all universal postal services by the privileged supplier, it effectively enables qualifying companies to cross-subsidize costly services in rural areas by extra-profits made by the provision of services in urban areas.
153. Cf. *Proposal of the Commission for the amendment of the VAT treatment of services provided in the postal sector*, COM (2003) 234, 5 May 2003, and the amended Proposal COM (2004) 468, 8 July 2004.
154. Cf. *TNT Post UK* (n. 36 above), para. 37.
155. Cf. Dietl et al. (n. 152 above), 1, 16 et seq. with further references.
156. For further details on this aspect, see below at §2.05[A][3].

[C] Social Policy and Redistributive Effects

Some compulsory or transitional exemptions that are contemplated in the EU VAT Directive have been justified on grounds of social policy or tax impact distribution. Even though this kind of justification is also somewhat related to aspects of tax equity and tax fairness, the corresponding exemptions should be distinguished from the tax relief measures discussed above that address a presumed lack of relevant taxpaying capacity. In the latter case, relief should not be at the discretion of the EU legislator, insofar as it is technically feasible to integrate it without significant spill-over or overcompensation effects into the design of VAT as an indirect and thus 'impersonal' tax. Moreover, the final consumer should then be fully shielded from any tax burden. By contrast, the exemptions analysed in the following sections can either be characterized as subsidies ('tax expenditure') that are motivated by aspects of social policy, or that serve to enhance the redistributive effects of VAT – both objectives will indeed often go hand in hand. Their introduction into the harmonized system and their extent can be regarded as a deliberate choice on part of the legislator that must, however, respect the requirements of proportionality and consistency.

Social policy concerns have been brought forward as ancillary motives for the exemption related to the granting of consumer credit,[157] and they have furthermore been identified as the main reason underlying the exemption of the management of special investment funds.[158] This is particularly striking since both of these exemptions are listed in Article 135 (1) of the EU VAT Directive. under the heading 'exemptions for other activities', rather than being included in the list of Article 132 (1) of the EU VAT Directive. concerning 'exemptions for activities in the public interest'. Moreover, if one were to disagree with the attribution of any of the exemptions discussed above to the category of tax relief measures that reflect a lack of taxpaying capacity, one would at least have to consider whether they can be justified on grounds of social policy reasons. In particular, this seems to be the position of the Commission and the CJEU with respect to the exemption provided for the letting and leasing of residential housing.[159]

Different from exemptions justified on grounds of a lack of taxpaying capacity, exemptions that are motivated by the 'mere' objectives of social policy or redistributive effects can be regarded as consistent and legitimate only if either one of the following two scenarios applies.

First, if it has been demonstrated or may at least reasonably be assumed that the exempt supplies benefit predominantly final consumers with relatively low income and relatively little wealth. This is arguably the case, for example, regarding social welfare services that specifically target youth or elderly persons with few resources.[160] By

157. Cf. Case C-455/05, *Velvet & Steel Immobilien und Handels GmbH v. Finanzamt Hamburg-Eimsbüttel* [2007] ECR I-3225, para. 24; *Skandinaviska Enskilda Banken* (n. 45 above), para. 21.
158. Cf. *Abbey National* (n. 45 above), para. 62; see also Heidemann (n. 61 above), 123.
159. Cf. *Goed Wonen* (n. 29 above), para. 52; see furthermore explanatory Memorandum to the *Proposal for a sixth Council Directive on the harmonization of Member States concerning turnover taxes*, submitted to the Council by the Commission on 29 June 1973, COM(73) 950, 15.
160. See, for example, Art. 132 (1) (g) and (h) of the EU VAT Directive.

contrast, even acknowledging a margin of appreciation to be conceded to the legislator, a sufficiently focused impact can hardly be presumed regarding the granting of consumer credit.[161] For the reasons already discussed above, it is also highly questionable whether the exemption concerning the leasing or letting of immovable property could be defended as proportional and consistent on grounds of social policy considerations. Similar objections could be raised with regard to the exemption available for the management of investment funds.[162]

Second, if the exemption is intended to enhance the redistributive effects of VAT by introducing an element of (indirect) tax progression,[163] it must be shown that low-income households typically spend a significantly higher portion of their income on the exempt items or services than households in the higher income deciles.[164]

In economic literature, it is sometimes suggested that VAT concessions on grounds of social policy or income redistribution are unnecessary, at least in developed countries such as the EU Member States, because income tax and income-support measures would achieve the same objective equally well or even better with less distortions and at lower compliance and administrative costs.[165] If such a conclusion were indeed obvious, the respective VAT exemptions would have to be considered disproportionate under a constitutional scrutiny based on primary Union law. However, some caution seems appropriate in this regard. In order to be equally targeted as a VAT exemption on social policy grounds, both additional social assistance programs and income tax allowances also require additional administrative resources and cause additional compliance costs, and they may also give rise to definitional problems and invite misclassification. By contrast, mere lump-sum payments or (in the tax context) lump-sum deductions are less precise; they risk under- or overcompensation, and in the case of social assistance, also the (ab)use for other than the intended consumption by the recipients.[166] As regards exemptions granted due to concerns of tax impact

---

161. As regards, for example, the situation in Germany, see J. Schupp et al., *Repräsentative Analyse der Lebenslagen einkommensstarker Haushalte*, 81, 86 and 90 (Bundesministerium für Gesundheit und Soziale Sicherung 2003).
162. However, a tax concession for financial services of this kind could be defended as a measure to avoid distortions between a self-supply of portfolio management services and the investment through collective investment vehicles. Moreover, as shall be discussed below at (g), the cost of such management services does not constitute consumption expenditure and should therefore be relieved from VAT.
163. See, in this regard, also van Brederode (n. 66 above), 34.
164. Under this premise the objective of reducing regressive effects of VAT or – more precisely – introducing an element of tax progression into VAT is not called into question by the fact that the expenditure of households in higher income deciles on the exempt items or services is higher in absolute amounts than the corresponding expenditure of low-income households; for a seemingly different opinion, see Cnossen 1998 (n. 66 above), 399, 409 et seq.
165. Cf. Cnossen 2003 (n. 8 above), 625, 628. See also R. Bird, 'Commentary', in Mirrlees et al. (n. 25 above), 363, 366; Crawford et al. (n. 25 above), 275, 277, 284. See furthermore Bird & Gendron (n. 16 above), 76 and 126 et seq., who point out the differences between developed and developing countries in this regard; likewise the special study by Boccanfuso et al., Can the removal of VAT Exemptions support the Poor? The Case of Niger, CERDI, Etudes et Documents, E 2011.6, 5 et seq.
166. See, in this regard, R. Hickel, *Brauchen wir eine Reform des Mehrwertsteuersystems?*, 90 Wirtschaftsdienst 585, 589 (2010).

distribution, they can be more easily replaced by direct transfers or income tax measures,[167] but not without certain drawbacks.[168]

Notwithstanding the above, it will in any event be necessary to scrutinize both kinds of exemptions with respect to their proportionality *strictu sensu*. Each VAT exemption should be assessed on whether it strikes a reasonable balance between its objective and its negative implications for social welfare. This assessment must also take into account the combined superior and inferior aspects of alternative measures. Under such an approach, empirical evidence suggests that a VAT exemption of 'basic' goods and services intended to smoothen the distributive impact of VAT is indeed disproportionate because it is much less efficient than income tax or income enhancing measures,[169] and only – if at all – slightly superior with a view towards administrative and public acceptance issues.

Finally, it should be noted that even if a VAT concession of this kind can be regarded as legitimate and proportionate, this does not automatically imply that the exemption *without credit* is the best, or is at least an acceptable, instrument to implement such a VAT relief.[170]

An exemption may exceptionally also be granted on grounds of social policy in order to benefit the taxable person rather than the final consumers. The only straightforward example in the common system of VAT are transactions carried out by blind persons or by workshops for the blind[171] which may be maintained by certain Member States by virtue of Article 371 of the EU VAT Directive. It seems questionable whether such exemptions constitute an appropriate and coherent measure to ensure the attainment of their social objective.[172] The amount of aid conveyed through the exemption will increase with the volume of turnover of the taxable person, unrelated – or even in inverse relation – to his or her need for social assistance.

[D] Reasons of Cultural or Educational Policy/Meritorious Services

Another set of mandatory exemptions contemplated in the common system of VAT pursues objectives of cultural and educational policy, including the promotion of sport

167. As regards the positive New Zealand experience in this context, see I. Dickson & D. White, 'Commentary', in Mirrlees et al. (n. 25 above), 387 399 et seq.; see also the comments made on 404.
168. For an in-depth discussion of possible difficulties (in the similar context of reduced VAT rates), see R. Ismer, A. Kaul, W. Reiß & S. Rath, *Analyse und Bewertung der Strukturen von Regel- und ermäßigten Sätzen bei der Umsatzbesteuerung unter sozial-, wirtschafts-, steuer- und haushalts-politischen Gesichtspunkten*, 201 et seq. (German Ministry of Finance 2010). This issue will not be explored further here, because food as the most obvious contender for an exemption on grounds of redistributive policy is actually not exempt under the standard EU VAT rules; it merely qualifies for a reduced rate (that could, of course, also be questioned for the reasons given above).
169. Cf. Crawford et al. (n. 25 above), 275, 300 et seq., and the references cited there. See also Krever (n. 8 above), 9, 19; Tait (n. 46 above), 70.
170. For further discussion of this aspect, see below at §2.05.
171. See explanatory memorandum to the corresponding provision in the German VAT Act, Bundestags-Drucksache V/1581, 5.
172. Likewise Stadie 2009 (n. 31 above), 608; very critical Mollard (n. 18 above), 443, 448, n. 15.

or physical education. This can be assumed, in particular, with respect to the following exempt supplies: the provision of children's or young people's education, school or university education, vocational training or retraining, the supply of certain cultural services, the supply of certain services closely linked to sport or physical education, and the non-commercial activities carried out by public radio and television bodies. These exemptions concern activities which are arguably of societal value,[173] so that the related supplies provide 'meritorious' goods and services to the final consumer. The legislator can thus, in principle, promote their consumption through a tax concession. The policy considerations underlying such exemptions therefore constitute legitimate reasons to deviate from the principles of fiscal neutrality and tax fairness.[174]

However, insofar as an exemption that pursues legitimate objectives is designed to benefit the final consumer, it should be considered proportional only if the legislator may reasonably assume that a significant number of potential consumers would abstain from having recourse to these services, or consume them to a significantly lower degree, if they were (fully) burdened with VAT. Economic surveys suggest that such an assessment can generally be accepted as reasonable for supplies related to physical education in sport clubs, etc.,[175] and probably for higher education services,[176] taking into account the margin of appreciation to be granted to the Union legislator.

By contrast, economic research indicates that the price responsiveness of the demand for cultural services tends to be relatively low.[177] Present consumers of such services would not markedly change their consumption patterns if VAT were charged at the regular rate, nor would the exemption contribute significantly to attracting consumers who are habitually alien to such activities. Exemptions that promote such activities with the stated aim of incentivizing consumer behaviour could furthermore be objected to because of their paternalistic approach.[178] For instance, under the current rules of EU law, the purchase of an opera ticket is exempt from VAT, whereas the purchase of a theme park ticket is not. Furthermore, such distortive effects infringe the neutrality principle without good reason.[179] Finally, very difficult borderline issues

173. As regards education in particular, see also L. Ebrill, M. Keen & J.-P. Bodin, *The Modern VAT*, 93 et seq. (International Monetary Fund 2001). For a different opinion regarding cultural services and services linked to sport or physical education see Cnossen 2010 (n. 66 above), 370, 382.
174. Cf. Hoffsümmer (n. 74 above), 123.
175. Cf. P. Wicker, *Perspektiven und Grenzen der Beitragsfinanzierung von Sportvereinen*, 197 et seq. (summary at 314 et seq.) (German Sport University Cologne 2009).
176. A comprehensive meta-study carried out in the US came to the conclusion that there is a certain degree of price responsiveness among college and university students, in particular among less selective public institutions, cf. L. Leslie & P. Brinkman, *Student Price Response in Higher Education: The Student Demand Studies*, 58 J. Hr. Educ. 181, 198 et seq. (1987), and the studies cited therein. These results are probably also true for EU Member States.
177. Cf. B. Seaman, *Handbook of the Economics of Art and Culture*, Chapter 14, 424 et seq. (V. Ginsburgh & D.Throsby eds., North-Holland 2006), and the references cited therein.
178. See also Hoffsümmer (n. 74 above), 121: 'arbitrary'; in a similar vein, Mollard (n. 18 above) 443, 463.
179. Likewise Cnossen 1988 (n. 66 above), 399, 404.

may arise when taxpayers and authorities have to classify certain services as either exempt cultural services or as taxed service of a different quality.[180]

Against this background, the exemptions for cultural services should be regarded as disproportionate insofar as they are intended to benefit final consumers. However, some of those exemptions may also have been conceived to benefit the taxable person. Under such a premise, assuming that the exemption functions as a subsidy for the economic operator, the legislator enjoys a greater margin of appreciation as to which sectors and organizations should be eligible for the exemption. The corresponding exemptions therefore can withstand constitutional scrutiny, aside from their implications for the input VAT credit. Nevertheless, good tax policy, taking into account efficiency considerations and the transparency principle, would replace such exemptions with direct subsidies.

[E] Avoidance of Double Tax Burdens

Some exemptions have originally been granted by the Member States prior to VAT harmonization to mitigate an accumulation of turnover taxation and the levy of special excise or stamp duties.[181] It is quite probable that they were incorporated into the Sixth VAT Directive against this historical background, as well as for additional considerations. This can be assumed, in particular, for the supply of insurance services, for transactions relating to bets and lotteries, for certain financial services like the supply of shares and other securities, and to some extent for the supply of real estate.[182] All of these transactions are at least partially exempt under Article 135 (1) of the EU VAT Directive. With respect to financial services in particular, such an objective would also provide a consistent explanation for the exclusion of the management or safekeeping of shares from the scope of the exemption.

It should be noted that over the course of the last decades, and in the light of the modernization of many Member States' tax systems, this originally legitimate justification[183] has become a rather weak one. It does not provide, by itself, a sound reason why the conceptually superior system of VAT as a general tax on consumer expenditure should partially yield to historically overcome excise taxes which can be levied or abolished by Member States at their discretion.[184] It is thus the Member States that should be held responsible for a double tax burden rather than the European system of harmonized VAT. Admittedly, some Member States with a strong emphasis on fiscal

180. Cf. Tait (n. 46 above), 83.
181. Cf. D. Dziadkowski, *Sinn und Widersinn von Steuerbefreiungen im Mehrwertsteuersystem : kritische Anmerkungen zu unechten Steuerbefreiungen*, 55 Umsatzsteuer-Rundschau 87, 89 (2006); Reiß (n. 12 above), § 14 para. 92.
182. Cf. Peffekoven (n. 148 above), 32; Stadie 2009 (n. 31 above), 515 and 522. As regards insurance services in particular, see also J. Swinkels, *EU VAT Exemption for Insurance Transactions*, 18 Intl. VAT Monit. 262 (2007); as regards real estate, see Bird & Gendron (n. 16 above), 84. However, the supply of real estate might also have been designated as exempt supply due to the difficulties of determining the consumption element inherent to the acquisition and use of this durable good, cf. Ebrill et al. (n. 173 above), 98.
183. Cf. Dziadkowski (n. 181 above), 87, 89.
184. Cf. Mollard (n. 18 above), 443, 463 et seq.

federalism may find it hard to integrate certain excise taxes and stamp duties into VAT and abolish them as independent taxes because revenue allocation between the federal level and the sub-national level may differ for each kind of tax. However, this problem could be solved by granting a generous transition period towards more uniform commodities and service taxation.

To summarize, the Union legislator should not consider it necessary to exempt a transaction merely because it might be subject to national excise or stamp duties. Moreover, if the exemption is not matched by a corresponding excise or stamp duty within a certain Member State, its effect will go beyond what is necessary to attain its objective, hence the mandatory and uniform nature of the exemptions at issue seems ill-founded. It is therefore suggested that for proportionate justification, one should rather search for reasons that might justify levying a separate and often lower tax – instead of VAT – in the first place. These might be technical reasons, as could be brought forward in the case of bets and lotteries, or with a view towards certain financial services, or for reasons of tax equity in the case of certain insurance services.

[F] Hard-to-Tax Supplies/Avoidance of Undue Compliance Burdens

Some exemptions are based on considerations of administrative efficiency with respect to the assessment and collection of the tax, as well as on the desire to avoid undue compliance burdens.

The personal exemption for small enterprises – the so-called registration threshold provided for in all but one national VAT system of EU Member States – can be justified by the objective to avoid excessive compliance burdens for these economic operators.[185] If no such personal exemption were available, the ensuing compliance burden might indeed be considered a disproportionate infringement of the fundamental right to conduct a business (compare Article 16, Charter of Fundamental Rights). Moreover, the registration threshold also reduces administrative costs because the tax administration has to monitor a smaller number of taxable persons whose accounts tend to be better kept.[186] Arguably, the legislator has a wide margin of discretion in this regard. The weighing and balancing of the conflicting aspects of a distortion of competition and/or unequal tax burdens of final consumers against relief for business and administrative efficiency[187] will also depend on the broader regulatory context and level of development of each Member State.[188] It can therefore be defended that the Directive sets only maximum thresholds.

185. Cf. Bird & Gendron (n. 16 above), 120; Crawford et al. (n. 25 above), 275, 309; Ebrill et al. (n. 173 above), 90; Ruppe 2005 (n. 109 above), § 6 para. 12. See also Stiglitz (n. 64 above), 465 et seq. Empirical support for the above thesis is provided by Dickson & White et al. (n. 167 above), 387, 394 et seq., who refer to two major New Zealand surveys showing that GST/VAT compliance costs are very regressive; this is affirmed by Krever (n. 8 above), 9, 19.
186. Cf. Cnossen 1988 (n. 66 above), 399, 402.
187. See, in this regard, also Dickson & White (n. 167 above), et al., 387, 402; Massa in Weidenbaum et al. (n. 75 above), 237, 247 et seq.
188. See also van Brederode (n. 66 above), 123 et seq., regarding the factors to be taken into account when fixing the relevant threshold.

In a similar vein, the exemption for leasing and letting of immovable property is officially based on the avoidance of disproportionate compliance and administrative costs,[189] in addition to the considerations of vertical tax equity or social policy discussed (and dismissed) above. According to the CJEU, leasing or letting of real estate is normally a relatively passive activity that does not generate significant added value.[190] Taxing it would not yield much extra revenue (as compared to the present exemption without credit) but would impose significant compliance burdens on a great number of landlords who are not otherwise liable for VAT.[191]

Based on such reasoning, an exemption for the leasing and letting of *residential* housing can be regarded as justified. The assumption that the letting of such property provides for only a relatively small contribution to value added, whereas the number of private landlords and thus potential taxpayers is large, seems defendable taking into account a margin of appreciation to be conceded to the Union legislator.[192] It can also be defended to provide for an objective exemption in addition to the subjective registration threshold (small business exemption).[193] Such reasoning would neglect the presumed peculiarity of letting and leasing of residential housing, namely the relatively small amount of value added which can reasonably raise concerns of disproportionate administrative costs beyond the standard threshold. By contrast, it is questionable whether this is equally true for commercial rents. It is therefore consistent, but insufficient, to exclude the supply of hotel accommodation and parking sites, and the letting of permanently installed equipment and machinery from the scope of the exemption.[194] In general, it does cause unnecessary and thus disproportionate complications that the exemption (without credit) is not limited to residential housing.[195]

Closely related to exemptions intended to avoid excessive compliance and administrative costs are those for 'hard-to-tax' services. Traditionally, it has been assumed that it is impossible or at least overly complex to assess the taxable base for certain categories of services within the framework of a transaction-based multi-stage

189. Cf. Explanatory Memorandum (n. 7), 15: '... it should be noted that in the Member States the letting of immovable property is generally exempted on technical, economic and social grounds.'
190. Cf. *Goed Wonen* (n. 29 above), para. 52, with further references to legislative history; confirmed in *Temco Europe* (n. 33 above), para. 20.
191. For critical comments, see Kirchhof (n. 122 above), § 11 para. 36, who objects that landlords have to file tax reports and keep tax records anyways because they are usually liable to income tax; hence, a VAT liability would not imply any significant additional compliance or administrative costs. However, in the author's view the Community legislator should have a margin of appreciation regarding the relative severity of the added VAT compliance and administrative burden; it should furthermore be acknowledged that VAT liability is also associated with additional compliance *risks* for both the taxable person and the tax administration. This is also not fully reflected in the critical statement made by Hoffsümmer (n. 74 above), 147 et seq.
192. For instance, the gross added value by letting of dwellings excluding imputed rent of owner occupiers accounted for only approx. 3% of overall value added in the UK in 2010 (estimate, based on a homeownership rate of approximately 70% and the data provided by the UK Office for National Statistics, *The Blue Book 2010*, 104). By contrast, there are an estimated 1 million private landlords in the UK (according to a 2007 Mintel study), most of whom will not already be registered for VAT on grounds of other economic activities.
193. For a different opinion, see Hoffsümmer (n. 74 above), 147.
194. Cf. Art. 135 (2) (a) to (c) of the EU VAT Directive.
195. For a detailed discussion, see Cnossen 1988 (n. 66 above), 399, 405 et seq.

tax such as VAT. The exemption for betting, lotteries and other forms of gambling laid down in Article 135 (1) (i) of the EU VAT Directive has been based 'on practical considerations' of this kind.[196] In the view of the Commission, such activities are 'ill-suited to taxation on a value-added basis and are better dealt with by means of special taxes'.[197] It has furthermore been pointed out that the exemption for the letting of residential housing can also be defended as a reflection of the difficulties inherent to the taxation of the imputed rental value of owner-occupied property. If the latter cannot be properly assessed, the former should also not be taxed to maintain fiscal neutrality.[198]

In a similar vein, it has frequently been stated that the financial services listed in Article 135 (1) (b) to (g) of the EU VAT Directive have originally been exempted because the taxable base was presumed to be difficult to calculate.[199] In particular, the cost of the service is often included in a margin and thus cannot be determined easily.[200] This argument has been advanced in literature, for example, with respect to transactions concerning the supply or exchange of currency, bank notes and coins used as legal tender.[201] Similar reasons have been put forward to justify the exemption available for depositing and account-keeping services,[202] for the granting of credit,[203] and for insurance services.[204] The Commission pointed out in 2006 that 'the decision of

196. Cf. *Leo-Libera* (n. 49 above), para. 24.
197. Cf. Explanatory Memorandum (n. 7 above), 16; likewise B. Terra & P. Wattel, *European Tax Law*, 308 (5th ed., Alphen aan den Rijn 2008). See also A. Schenk *VAT in Africa*, 47, 53 et seq. (R. Krever ed., Pretoria University Law Press 2008), who proposes to tax casinos and other operators of games of chance based on gross margins rather than on a transaction basis, albeit as an integral part of the VAT.
198. Cf. Bird & Gendron (n. 16 above), 82 et seq.; Cnossen 1988 (n. 66 above), 399, 405; Krever (n. 8 above), 9, 24 et seq. See also van Brederode (n. 66 above), 191.
199. Cf. *Velvet & Steel* (n. 157 above), para. 24; Crawford et al. (n. 25 above), 275, 306; Ebrill et al. (n. 173 above), 90 et seq.; Henkow (n. 11 above), 88 et seq. with further references. This view is questioned by Amand (n. 6 above), 409, 414, who refers to some statements made by Maurice Lauré about the motivation of the French legislator for the exemption of financial services implemented in France in 1954.
200. For further details, see Ebrill et al. (n. 173 above), 94 et seq.; H. Grubert & R. Krever, 'VAT and Financial Services: Competing Perspectives on What Should Be Taxed', Ch 9, this volume; Heidemann (n. 61 above), 111 et seq., and 116 et seq.
201. Cf. Reiß (n. 12 above), § 14 para. 91. For a different opinion, see H. Friedrich-Vache, *Verbrauchsteuerkonforme Umsatzbesteuerung von Finanzdienstleistungen* (Otto Schmidt 2005), 248: the availment of the exchange service does not constitute consumption on part of the recipient of the service and should therefore not be subject to tax in the first place. However, in the author's view this could only be assumed if the exchange service were intrinsically linked to a savings/investment activity rather than a corollary to consumption, which is arguably not the case, though, cf. Heidemann (n. 61 above), 72.
202. Cf. Hoffsümmer (n. 74 above), 151.
203. Cf. Henkow (n. 11 above), 6 et seq. with further references. It should be noted, though, that the main argument in this regard is an economic one which is based on the view that a bank, by offering the possibility of interest-bearing deposits, on the one hand, and by lending money to other economic agents, on the other hand, essentially provides intermediation services for its depositors and borrowers, hence the taxable base should be the value added by this intermediation activity, i.e. the difference between the respective interest rates for depositors and borrowers (after subtraction of an implicit fee for depositing services), which is hard to determine under a transaction based tax such as VAT, cf. Grubert & Krever (n. 200 above).
204. Cf. Swinkels (n. 182 above), 262.

the Council [in 1977 upon the adoption of the Sixth VAT Directive] was to exempt financial services and insurances, mainly for pragmatic reasons since the technical difficulties could not be readily overcome. These consisted mainly in the impossibility of establishing taxable amounts and the amounts of deductible VAT without generating unacceptable administrative charges and without creating legal and accounting complexity for both economic operators and Member States' fiscal authorities.'[205]

Even though the Commission also referred to 'the perceived political sensitivities associated with imposing VAT on consumers' as an additional motive for the exemption of financial services, the latter was probably only an ancillary concern.[206] It also goes a step too far to demand that all financial services 'charged for in form of a fee ... can and should be fully taxed',[207] even though the calculation of the taxable base indeed does not raise any conceptual difficulties in such cases. Their exemption can nevertheless be defended on grounds of the neutrality principle, insofar as the service at issue could also be charged implicitly in a margin, which will usually be the case.

However, it is appropriate to emphasize that exemptions for technical reasons imply a particular duty of the legislator to monitor technical developments, especially in the affected sector of the economy. An exemption is not necessary any more - and thus becomes a disproportionate interference with the principle of tax equality - once technical or economic changes or new developments in economic theory would make it feasible to tax the transactions at issue.[208] Furthermore, and from the provision's inception, the disadvantages associated with the exemption (less legal certainty due to the need to determine its scope; eventual infringements of the neutrality principle and of the principle of equality of taxation) must not outweigh the technical difficulties of taxing the transactions at issue. As regards financial services in particular, it seems that their exemption is still tenable despite the taxation techniques that have meanwhile been proposed and discussed as possible alternatives.[209]

[G] Non-consumptive Nature of Related Expenditure

It has already been demonstrated in the context of the above discussion of tax equity objectives that exceptionally, an exemption will promote rather than contradict essential principles underlying VAT as a tax that intends to allocate the fiscal burden in proportion to individual taxpaying capacity as indicated by consumption expenditure.

---

205. European Commission, *Consultation paper on modernizing the Value Added Tax obligations for financial services and insurance*, 2006, 2. For critical comments, see Friedrich-Vache (n. 201 above), 213 et seq.
206. As Henkow (n. 11 above), 90, remarks, the exemptions would otherwise have been included in Art. 132 of the EU VAT Directive (ex-Art. 13A Sixth Directive) titled 'Exemptions... in the public interest'. For a different opinion, see Friedrich-Vache (n. 201 above), 212 et seq.
207. Cf. Crawford et al. (n. 25 above), 275, 306.
208. Likewise Mollard (n. 18 above), 443, 462.
209. For a more extensive discussion, see van Brederode (n. 66 above), 146 et seq.; Cnossen 1988 (n. 66 above), 399, 407 et seq.; Crawford et al. (n. 25 above), 275, 306 et seq. Since opinions of economic scholars on the issue are divided and there is no clear 'best practice' as yet established, the continuation of the present system cannot be regarded as obviously disproportionate. Likewise Bird & Gendron (n. 16 above), 97.

This will arguably also be the case when the expenses incurred for the exempt supply cannot be considered expenditure made for the purpose of *consumption* even though they are not incurred in the course of taxable business. In a recent judgment, the CJEU acknowledged that there exists a sphere of activities which constitute neither an economic activity relating to transactions that are taxable under the common system of VAT, nor an activity related to private consumption of goods or services.[210]

This could in particular be assumed for private financial investments that do not yield any direct utility for the investor (such as the acquisition of bonds, shares, and other securities), but rather constitute a mere transformation of money into another form of monetary asset representing the potential for future consumption.[211] The same applies for (cash value) life insurance premiums or pension insurance premiums, insofar as the respective premium consists of a savings element.[212] Since the European-style VAT has explicitly been conceived as a general tax on *consumption* (expenditure), one might therefore assume that any such transaction should not be burdened with VAT.[213] In the same vein, directly related services such as financial investment advisory services should also be spared from taxation,[214] because they constitute expenses caused by private saving activities rather than consumption expenditure. This would be consistent with the usual deductibility of any such costs under a Haig-Simons income tax or a personal expenditure tax.[215] Since a VAT refund might be considered to be technically unfeasible, because it would seemingly require private individuals to register for VAT, the second-best solution might then be an exemption of the corresponding supplies. By contrast, the granting of a consumer credit that is now exempt pursuant to Article 135 (1) (b) of the EU VAT Directive should rather constitute a taxed transaction - were it technically feasible - because it is directly related to private consumption.[216]

---

210. Cf. Case C-515/07, *Vereniging Noordelijke Land- en Tuinbouw Organisatie* (VNLTO) [2009] ECR I-839.
211. Cf. Frink (n. 18 above), 145; Heidemann (n. 61 above), 57 et seq.; H.-H. Heidner, *Umsatzsteuergesetz*, § 4 Nr. 8 para. 2 (9th ed., Bunjes & Geist eds., C.H. Beck 2009); Hoffsümmer (n. 74 above), 151; J. Kraeusel, *Umsatzsteuergesetz*, loose-leaf commentary, § 4 Nr. 8 para. 27 (Reiß, Kraeusel & Langer (Stollfuß 2010); Ruppe 1995 (n. 63 above), 457, 464; Ruppe 2005 (n. 109 above), § 6 para. 98. For a different opinion, see Stadie in Seer (n. 106 above), 143, 149 et seq.
212. See also Hoffsümmer (n. 74 above), 137; Kirchhof (n. 122 above), § 11 para. 24. However, Kirchhof ignores that part of the insurance premium constitutes a premium for the coverage of biometric risks and thus, arguably, consumption expenditure. The exemption also of this element of the premium can thus only be justified on grounds of administrative efficiency, because tax authorities can hardly be expected to verify the pertinent information that would have to be furnished by the insurance companies, cf. Hoffsümmer (n. 74 above), 137 et seq.
213. This is suggested by Camenzind et al. (n. 75 above), 235 et seq., para. 653; Ruppe 2005 (n. 109 above), § 6 para. 12.
214. For a different opinion regarding related services, cf. Frink (n. 18 above), 145; Heidemann (n. 61 above), 91 et seq., and 101 et seq.
215. See, in this regard, also the references to economic debate on financial intermediation and VAT provided by Grubert & Krever (n. 200 above); Henkow (n. 11 above), 80 et seq.
216. Likewise Heidemann (n. 61 above), 93; Kirchhof (n. 122 above), § 11 para. 46; for a different opinion see Friedrich-Vache (n. 201 above), 220 et seq.; Reiß (n. 12 above), § 14 para. 91; W. Reiß, *Cahiers de droit fiscal international, Vol. 88b: Consumption Taxation and Financial Services* (IFA ed., Sdu Uitgevers 2003), 351 (372).

In a similar vein, many scholars contend that the expenditure for the acquisition of raw land, the supply of which might be exempt pursuant to Article 135 (1) (k) of the EU VAT Directive,[217] does not relate to consumption but rather to an investment and savings activity.[218] It could also be argued that expenditure for (higher) education and vocational training is an investment rather than a consumption activity. It has long been accepted in economic and legal literature that education is a consumption good as well as an investment good,[219] and it would not be obviously unreasonable to argue that in today's modern labour markets, the investment aspect is clearly the dominating one.[220]

Admittedly, the present system of the harmonized European VAT does not distinguish between expenditure for private use and enjoyment of goods and services, on the one hand, and the use of goods or services for personal savings, or other non-taxable activities which arguably do not constitute private consumption, on the other hand. As a general rule, there is no tax relief available for the latter kind of activities. From the final taxpayer's perspective, the scope of the tax is thus not strictly limited to expenditure for private consumption. Hence, it would seemingly be inconsistent to single out financial services related to the acquisition of shares, educational services, etc., on grounds of a presumed non-consumptive nature of related expenditure. But one could also come to a different assessment, concluding that it is indeed the standard denial of VAT relief for supplies used for other activities than individual private consumption which is prima facie inconsistent and in need of justification, whereas the exemption for goods and services which are typically acquired only in order to carry out such activities would, in principle, correspond to the specific principles of tax fairness underlying the VAT system and to its inherent economic rationale. Such has been the conclusion of some prominent scholars, and this position is also shared by the author of this chapter.

Obviously, an assessment of the consistency of the exemptions for financial services, as required by the equality principle, depends on whether the above explanation for them should be accepted, or whether the justifications that have

217. Article 135 (1) (k) of the EU VAT Directive exempts the supply of land which has not been built on other than the supply of building land.
218. Cf. Hoffsümmer (n. 74 above), 131; Ruppe 2005 (n. 109 above), § 6 para. 192; Tait (n. 46 above), 80 et seq. (albeit with some qualifications). For a different opinion, see Söhn, *Steuer und Wirtschaft*, 1, 7 et seq. (1976). See also Henkow (n. 11 above), 69, 78 et seq.
219. See, for instance, C. Gross, *Tax Treatment of Education Expenses: Perspectives from Normative Theory*, 55 University of Chicago Law Review 916 (930 et seq.) (1988) ; J.K. McNulty, *Tax Policy and Tuition Credit Legislation: Federal Income Tax Allowances for Personal Costs of Higher Education*, 61 California Law Review 1, 18 et seq. (1973) ; J. Schaafsma, *The Consumption and Investment Aspects of the Demand for Higher Education*, 11 The Journal of Human Resources 233 (240 et seq.) (1976) ; T.W. Schultz, *Resources for Higher Education: An Economist's View*, 76 The Journal of Political Economy 327, 330 (1968) ; L.E. Vila, *The Non-monetary Benefits of Education*, 35 European Journal of Education 21 (22 et seq.) (2000)
220. Cf. L.C. Argrett, *Tax Treatment of Higher Education Expenditures: An Unfair Investment Disincentive*, 41 Syracuse Law Review 621 (1990) (638 et seq.: consumption element is 'insignificant'); R. Ismer, *Bildungsaufwand im Steuerrecht*, 15 et seq (Otto Schmidt 2006) . This has also been the position adopted by the German Federal Tax Court in the context of personal income taxation, cf. Federal Tax Court 28 August 2008, Case VI R 35/05, BStBl II 2009, 108, 110; Federal Tax Court 27. Mai 2003, Case VI R 33/01, BStBl II 2004, 884, 885.

originally been brought forward for those exemptions can still be regarded as relevant and convincing. For instance, based on the above premise, it would seem inconsistent to exclude the management or safekeeping of shares from the scope of the exemption under Article 135 (1) (f) of the EU VAT Directive.

Along the same lines, some other exemptions that certain Member States are authorized to maintain by virtue of Article 371 of the EU VAT Directive and Annex X Part B could be regarded as compliant with the concept of VAT as a general and equitable tax on consumption. In particular, public expenditure for the supply, modification, repair, maintenance, chartering and hiring of fighting ships or aircraft used by State institutions need arguably not be burdened with VAT. These inputs for the provision of public goods and services do not imply identifiable supply transactions to individual consumers or other individual customers.[221] Moreover, insofar as they are funded through taxation they cannot be linked to individual (consumption) expenditure.[222] And even if one were to characterize the use of such input supplies as 'collective' consumption that is realized by a public entity,[223] such consumption would not indicate individual taxpaying capacity. However, the latter aspect is precisely what the equality principle is concerned with, because a fair and equitable tax is one that distributes the overall tax burden fairly among individuals. It is neither inherent to such a concept nor does it make much sense to have the state contribute its 'fair share' to its own funding needs.[224]

However, if one were to follow this reasoning, then obviously the fragmentary and non-compulsory nature of the corresponding exemptions must be objected to as inconsistent implementation of the underlying rationale. For instance, supplies related to military equipment in general would then have to be exempt. Adopting an even broader perspective, it also becomes obvious that itemized exemptions cannot be relied on as a comprehensive remedy for unjustified VAT burdens of public sector entities, even if they were granted with credit, i.e. in the form of zero-rating. Most supplies made to such entities will also be demanded by private customers, and to make the exemption dependent on customer status would inject considerable complexity into the system. Therefore, the superior approach would be the extension of the

221. As regards this requirement under the EU VAT Directive as interpreted by the CJEU, see Case C-384/95, *Landboden Agrardienste* [1997] ECR I-7387, para. 23. From a conceptual viewpoint, this requirement is debatable, cf. M. Aujean, P. Jenkins & S. Poddar, *A New Approach to Public Sector Bodies*, Intl. VAT Monit. 144, 146 et seq. (1999).
222. See also M. Aujean, P. Jenkins & S. Poddar (n. 221 above), 144, 147: 'the link is too remote'. However, fees charged for public services should in any event be taxable and, as a general rule, taxed; likewise (but with preference for full taxation of the public sector) Bird & Gendron (n. 16 above), 93.
223. This 'traditional thinking' is mentioned – and rejected – by M. Aujean, P. Jenkins & S. Poddar (n. 221 above), 146.
224. Cf. Kirchhof (n. 122 above), § 4 para. 4; D. Pohmer, *The Value-Added Tax. Lessons from Europe*, 91, 94 (Aaron ed., Brookings Institution 1981) . Cnossen 1988 (n. 66 above), 399, 403, argues that 'application of the VAT... has the advantage of confronting policymakers more directly with the full cost of public intervention.' However, this reasoning comes close to a *petitio principii*; VAT should be a cost factor only if the recipients of public goods and services – or private sector entities subsidizing the recipients – do have to make payments that can be sufficiently linked to these public sector supplies.

taxable sphere of public sector entities to all activities for which they receive a consideration from the private sector, and the implementation of refund schemes – such as currently operated in some EU Member States and in Canada[225] – for the remainder of (in particular: redistribution) activities.[226]

[H] International Tax Competition

For a Member State of the EU, there is little need to implement exemptions in order to match similar exemptions in other Member States that could undermine the competitiveness of taxable persons established in the former. As a general rule, exemptions are uniform within the entire EU, so that the phenomenon of international tax competition is essentially reserved to the application of a reduced tax rate, with respect to which Member States enjoy a wide margin of discretion. However, it cannot be excluded that certain service providers compete, to a significant degree, with suppliers from third countries who benefit from traditional tax exemptions. In particular, certain financial services may fall into this category.[227]

Of course, under a model VAT where the taxation of all international trade is firmly and wholly based on the destination principle, there should be hardly any room for international tax competition and thus hardly any need to match exemptions in foreign jurisdictions in order to prevent competitive disadvantages for domestic business. Foreign suppliers who offer their goods and services to customers in the domestic market would then have to calculate with the same VAT burden as their domestic competitors. Under this premise, the level of taxation in other jurisdictions could, at most, influence a citizen's choice of habitual abode or domicile. But considering the relative (lack of) importance of this aspect in comparison with other factors that determine a person's place of residence, this would be a rather hypothetical and negligible effect.

It would only exceptionally be otherwise with respect to products and services which are typically consumed immediately when they are supplied, which moreover provide the same degree of utility to an average consumer regardless of where they are consumed, and which are so expensive that an average consumer would be willing to travel to another jurisdiction in order to acquire the supply there. For example, a family pondering a theme park vacation in Europe might be attracted to a certain jurisdiction through lower prices due to a VAT exemption. Moreover, with a view to the indirect effect that a VAT exemption usually has on the volume of turnover, economic agents, too, could make the choice where to offer their supplies dependent upon the existence of an exemption in such a scenario. This could be the case, for instance, for the organizers of huge sporting events such as world soccer championships. It is noticeable

225. Cf. Copenhagen Economics & KPMG (n. 58 above), 80 et seq.
226. See also M. Aujean, P. Jenkins & S. Poddar (n. 221 above), 145 et seq. As regards some of the possible shortcomings and trade-offs that have to be addressed when implementing a refund scheme, see Bird & Gendron (n. 16 above), 92 et seq.
227. This is also suggested by Kirchhof (n. 122 above), § 11 paras. 47 and 51, with respect to the granting of credit and regarding account-keeping services.

in this regard that some Member States are indeed authorized to still exempt admission to sporting events by virtue of Article 371 of the EU VAT Directive.

However, the reality of European VAT is a different one. For B2C transactions, with respect to which asymmetrical exemptions could convey a competitive advantage, the default rule in the harmonized system of VAT used to determine the place of supply for services and thus the relevant tax jurisdiction is still the *supplier's* place of management or fixed establishment, cf. Article 45 of the EU VAT Directive. Thus, the origin principle still prevails for B2C services, and services in turn make up for the great majority of exempt transactions. Therefore, the maintenance of certain exemptions (not necessarily the ensuing denial of input VAT deduction)[228] can possibly also be justified by the intention to fend off distortions of competition to the detriment of service suppliers established within the EU. For example, should the Union legislator decide to abolish the exemptions currently provided for the management of investment funds or the granting of credit, third-country financial services providers who are domiciled in a jurisdiction where these services are still exempt or not subject to VAT would enjoy a competitive edge over companies that offer similar services from within the EU.[229]

At first sight, one could object that it is unnecessary and thus disproportionate to keep exemptions merely based on the above considerations, because a superior alternative would be to change the place of supply rules. Pursuant to the 'switch-over' clause of Article 59a of the EU VAT Directive, Member States may already consider the place of supply of a service, if situated outside the Community, as being situated within their territory if the effective use and enjoyment of the service takes place within their territory, in order to prevent distortion of competition. If that rule were enhanced to become a compulsory one, the destination principle would prevail over the origin principle whenever a service is taxed under the EU harmonized system but is usually exempt under the VAT/GST rules of third countries. However, a closer look reveals that such an approach cannot be considered a feasible alternative unless proper tax assessment and tax collection in the Member State of destination could be ensured, even though the taxable person cannot be audited by that Member State, and the recipient of the supply has neither an incentive nor an obligation to report to the tax authorities. Considering the present degree of international cooperation in VAT matters, the Community legislator may in general reasonably assume that the maintenance of an exemption is the better solution.

It should be noted that under the premise that serious international tax competition is really the motive underlying an exemption, the latter does not constitute a tax privilege for the taxable person. To the opposite, such an exemption is necessary in order to avoid that the taxable person, who cannot shift the asymmetrical VAT burden contrary to its concept as a tax to be borne by the final consumer, suffers from distortions of competition that would infringe the neutrality principle. The exemption also does not have to be justified as a breach of the principle of equality of consumer taxation, because the latter is not primarily caused by the exemption as such, but rather

228. See the discussion below at §2.05[B][4].
229. Cf. H. Heidner, *UStG*, § 4 Nr. 8 para. 45b (11th ed., in Bunjes ed., C. H. Beck 2012).

by the fact that consumers could avoid a VAT burden by substituting the taxed domestic services with exempt or untaxed services provided by third-country suppliers. Notwithstanding these considerations, the pressures of international tax competition provide a legitimate and proportional justification for a VAT concession only as long as no agreement can be reached with relevant third countries to tax the relevant services in an internationally coordinated reform.

§2.05 NON-DEDUCTABILITY OF INPUT VAT

The input tax credit granted under a VAT system ensures that, ideally, only consumption expenditure is taxed[230] in proportion to the price of goods and services, as contemplated in Article 1 (2) of the EU VAT Directive. This is a fundamental principle of the common system of VAT established by the relevant EU legislation,[231] and the main distinction from preceding turnover taxes. As a general rule, under the EU system of VAT the credit can be claimed only insofar as input goods and services are used for the purposes of taxed transactions, pursuant to Article 168 of the EU VAT Directive. The denial of an input tax credit as a consequence of carrying out exempt transactions has been referred to as the 'original sin'[232] of the common system of VAT.[233]

[A] General Observations

[1] Technical versus Substantive Coherence

Admittedly, the nexus between the exemption of a transaction, on the one hand, and the ensuing non-deductability of any input VAT for supplies that have been used to carry out the exempt transaction,[234] on the other hand, is *technically* coherent if the 'principle of deduction' contemplated in the common system of VAT since its inception is understood to require a correlation between input tax and output tax.[235] This is indeed suggested by what is now Article 1 (2) of the EU VAT Directive and Article 168

230. Cf. Gottfried & Wiegard (n. 71 above), 307, 308.
231. Cf. Case C-107/10, *Iztok 3*, [2011] ECR I-000, paras. 31 et seq., and the case law cited therein.
232. Cf. Opinion of AG Ruiz-Jarabo Colomer 22 February 2005 in *Kingscrest Associates* (n. 41 above), heading before para. 14. See also the references cited by Mollard (n. 18 above), 443, 445. Ebrill et al. (n. 173 above), 83, refer to this feature as an 'aberration in terms of the basic logic of VAT'.
233. It was already contemplated in Art. 11 (2) of the Second VAT Directive.
234. Cf. Art. 168 of the EU VAT Directive *a contrario*. An input supply is generally deemed to have been used for a specific output transaction if the former constitutes a 'direct' cost component of the latter, cf. Art. 1 (2) of the EU VAT Directive; see also Case C-4/94, *BLP Group* [1995] ECR I-983, paras. 18 et seq.; Case C-98/98, *Midland* [2000] ECR I-4177, paras. 20 and 30; Case C-408/98, *Abbey National plc v. Commissioners of Customs & Excise* [2001] ECR I-1361, paras. 25 et seq.; *AB SKF* (n. 35 above), para 57. For further details, see G. W. Kofler, *Vorsteuerabzug*, 105 (107 et seq.) (Achatz & Tumpel eds., Linde-Verlag 2005).
235. This is emphasized by Stadie in Seer (n. 106 above), 143, 151. Likewise de la Feria (n. 6 above), 142 et seq., who concludes that the ensuing restrictions to the right to deduct in case of exempt supplies are therefore coherent with the principles of EU VAT.

of the EU VAT Directive. But such technical consistency of the mechanism of input VAT deduction, if assessed in isolation, does not imply that the inherent limitation of a credit or refund for input VAT also forms a consistent and integral part of the overall system of VAT.[236] To the contrary, any element of harmonized EU VAT must comply with – and therefore has to be scrutinized in the light of – the essential requirements of fiscal neutrality (in the sense of equal taxation of competing supplies and suppliers, and of relieving business entirely from any substantive VAT burden), and it has to respect the principle of equality of taxation of consumer expenditure. Any shortcomings in this regard need special justification.[237]

[2] Ill-Conceived Origins and Lack of Judicial Awareness

Historically, none of these fundamental principles and considerations seems to have been much of a concern when the rules on exemptions and the ensuing restrictions with respect to input VAT credit and refund were drawn up.[238] Indeed, the denial of input VAT credit or refund is probably a relic of the past perception of VAT as a special form of transactional turnover tax on business output.[239] For some governments, it seemed 'out of the question to grant [exempt] business sectors that do not contribute to the collection of tax revenue a refund for taxes paid by other businesses'.[240] However, in the harmonized system of European VAT such a conception of value added tax is no longer in conformity with its fundamental orientation as a tax on

236. Likewise Ruppe 1995 (n. 63 above), 457, 469 et seq.; K. Tipke, *Die Steuerrechtsordnung*, 999 (vol. II, 2. ed., Otto Schmidt 2003).

237. The CJEU routinely limits the scope of the principle of VAT neutrality to economic activities 'subject in principle to VAT', cf. Case C-188/09, *Profaktor*, [2010] ECR I-07639, para. 20; Case C-438/09, *Dankowski*, [2010] ECR I-000, para. 24; Case C-277/09, *RBS Deutschland Holdings*, [2010] ECR I-14009, para. 38; settled case law. However, this is a mere restatement of the status quo under the present directives, rather than a normative statement based on the Court's own – and correct – characterization of the principle of fiscal neutrality as a VAT-specific manifestation of the equality principle, whose scope cannot be limited by referring to the shortcomings of the secondary Union law that it is supposed to control. For an extensive critique, see above at §2.03[B][2][b].

238. Only the European Parliament pointed out that the number of exemptions contemplated in the Commission's proposal for the Sixth VAT Directive '... must remain limited...[because] the tax applied at an earlier stage [than retail stage] is retained in the price of the entrepreneur's end product as supplied to the customer, which means that the turnover tax paid by the ultimate consumer is not exactly proportional to the price of the product or service ...'; cf. European Parliament, Documents of session 1973–1974, Document 360/73 of 14 February 1974, as cited by Amand (n. 6 above), 409, 410, 411.

239. Cf. Ruppe 1995 (n. 63 above), 457, 469 et seq.

240. Cf. explanatory memorandum to the 1963 draft of a German VAT Act, Bundestags-Drucksache IV/1590, 26; similar concerns have been raised in the explanatory memorandum to the Austrian VAT Act 1972, as cited by Ruppe 2005 (n. 109 above), § 6 para. 15. This line of reasoning can be regarded as paradigmatic for the predominant approach to exemptions at the time when the first VAT Directives were enacted. The same idea is obviously also underlying Art. 99 (2) of the EU VAT Directive that deals with reduced VAT rates and stipulates that 'each reduced rate shall be so fixed that the amount of VAT resulting from its application is such that the VAT deductible ... can normally be deducted in full', hence refunds for VAT levied at former stages from other businesses should be avoided.

consumption,[241] as it has been expressly formulated in Article 1 (2) of the EU VAT Directive, and as is apparent from various provisions of this Directive.[242]

For the purposes of constitutional scrutiny, it must therefore be assumed that according to the now-prevailing theory of VAT, the non-deductible VAT is *supposed* to be implicitly shifted on the recipient of the supply in the price of the goods or services. This would seem to be within a margin of appreciation and generalization to be conceded to the legislator, notwithstanding the fact that empirically, the incidence of VAT depends not only on the design of VAT legislation, but also on a variety of marketplace factors that are beyond control of the legislator. Otherwise, the fundamental principle that harmonized European VAT is a tax on consumption to be borne by the final consumer rather than by the taxable person would be blatantly infringed without any apparent justification.[243] It should be noted, that the CJEU is seemingly not yet fully aware of the implications of the consumption tax principle for the non-deductability of input VAT.[244]

[3] Infringement of the Neutrality Principle and Other Shortcomings

Even under the premise that non-deductible input VAT is ultimately born by the recipient of the exempt supply, its effects are incompatible with virtually all of the tax policy and constitutional benchmarks discussed above.

With respect to exempt B2C transactions at the retail stage, the non-deductibility of input VAT implies that only the tax burden of the final layer of value added is removed.[245] This mechanism thus converts a tax 'exemption' into a mere reduction of the tax burden, the exact scale of which is not discernible for the consumer.[246] Hence, the wording and the effect of the relevant rules is not in conformity with the principle of transparency of tax burdens. Moreover, the non-deductibility of individually divergent (although possibly sector-specific) input VAT injects an element of arbitrariness

241. In German literature, this has been pointed out by Friedrich-Vache (n. 201 above), 41; Kirchhof (n. 122 above), § 11 para. 55; Stadie in Seer (n. 106 above), 143, 152; K.M. Teichmann, *Der Verlust des Vorsteuerabzugs im steuerfreien Bereich der Mehrwertsteuer* (Rechtswissenschaftliche Fakultät, 1975), 140. See also Krever (n. 8 above), 9, 13: A consumption-type VAT is not a tax on value added; its denomination as such refers merely to the mechanism by which the tax operates.
242. In particular, the entitlement of taxable persons (acting as such) to an input VAT deduction or credit, and the provisions on taxable self-supplies for private purposes.
243. This has already been firmly established in the PhD thesis written by K.nud M. Teichmann in 1975, cf. K.M. Teichmann, *Der Verlust des Vorsteuerabzugs im steuerfreien Bereich der Mehrwertsteuer*, 101 et seq. (1975). Likewise W. Reiß, *UStG*, loose-leaf commentary, Einführung UStG, para. 46 (Reiß, Kraeusel & Langer eds., Stollfuß 2007).
244. Cf. Case 8/81, *Becker* [1982] ECR 53, para. 44; *Puffer* (n. 85 above) (Action brought 2007), para. 59; see also Opinion of AG *Saggio* in Case C-98/98, *Midland Bank* [2000] ECR I-4179, para. 18.
245. See above at n. 126.
246. Cf. van Brederode (n. 66 above), 130; Camenzind et al. (n. 75 above), 236, para. 655: 'taxe occulte'; Heidemann (n. 61 above), 38; Mollard (n. 18 above), 443 , 454 et seq.; H. Söhn, no 218 above, 26 Stadie 1989 (n. 25 above), 151; H. Stadie in Rau/Dürrwächter, *UStG*, loose-leaf commentary (Köln: Otto Schmidt), Einf. paras. 283 and 438 et seq.; Tait (n. 46 above), 52 et seq.; Terra & Kajus (n. 11 above), 281; V. Thuronyi, *Comparative Tax Law*, 321 (Kluwer Law International 2003).

into the determination of the final tax burden, contrary to the principle of equal taxation.[247] Depending on an unknown and often also unpredictable amount of input VAT incurred (and on the ratio between capital, intermediate goods and external services used as input, on the one hand, and in-house labour not carrying a VAT burden, on the other hand), the tax relief ensuing from the provisions on exempt supplies will range from anywhere between coming close to zero-rating and applying the regular tax rate. Such a disparate impact constitutes, by itself, a prima facie infringement of the principle of equality of taxation at least insofar as it affects the same type of exempt transactions. For example, it requires some explanation why the provision of high-tech medicine services should bear a relatively higher implicit VAT burden than equally expensive medical care that is provided by a general practitioner who hardly incurs any input VAT.

With respect to exempt B2B transactions, the non-deductibility of input VAT can compromise the destination principle[248] and provoke cascading effects,[249] which have been referred to as 'perverse tax repercussions' by an Advocate General.[250] The tax is thus converted into a partial tax on investment,[251] contrary to its conception. This undermines its neutrality and impairs production efficiency.[252] In particular, the denial of input tax deduction creates an incentive for vertical integration - a self-supply bias - and thus distorts market decisions about optimal business organization.[253] The outsourcing of constituent elements of an exempt transaction to a legally independent service provider will imply an additional and irrecoverable VAT burden for the supplier

247. Likewise Ruppe 2005 (n. 109 above), § 6 paras. 16 et seq.; Tonner (n. 70 above), 31 et seq.
248. For further details, consult Ebrill et al. (n. 173 above), 88. See also Cnossen 2003 (n. 8 above), 625, 627; Crawford et al. (n. 25 above), 275, 305.
249. For further details, consult Copenhagen Economics & KPMG (n. 58 above), 48; Ebrill et al. (n. 173 above), 85; Frink (n. 18 above), 85 et seq.; Gottfried & Wiegard (n. 71 above), 307, 308; Sánchez Gallardo (n. 63 above), 289 et seq.; Raboy in Weidenbaum et al. (n. 75 above), 87, 97; Ruppe 2005 (n. 109 above), § 6 para. 16; B. Forgách, *UStG*, loose-leaf commentary (Reiß, Kraeusel & Langer eds., Stollfuß 2010), § 15, para. 23; Tait (n. 46 above), 50; Terra & Kajus (n. 11 above), 280; see also Poblet (n. 18 above), 391: 'efecto de piramidación del gravamen'.
250. Cf. Opinion of AG Ruiz-Jarabo Colomer 22 February 2005 in *Kingscrest Associates* (n. 41 above), para. 15.
251. Cf. Crawford et al. (n. 25 above), 275, 292, 305; Gottfried & Wiegard (n. 71 above), 307, 319 and 323. For a different - but unfounded - opinion, see Stadie 2005 (n. 12 above), para. 10.68.
252. As regards the requirement to leave capital goods and intermediate goods untaxed so as to not distort production decisions and thus achieve production efficiency under the assumptions of the Diamond-Mirrlees production efficiency theorem see P. A. Diamond & J. A. Mirrlees, *Optimal Taxation and Public Production I: Production Efficiency*, 61 Am. Econ. Rev. 8 et seq.(1971). As regards the strength of this argument also when the underlying assumptions of Diamond and Mirrlees are not fully met, see the considerations following this footnote; see furthermore Crawford et al. (n. 25 above), 275, 283.
253. Cf. Bird & Gendron (n. 16 above), 89; van Brederode (n. 66 above), 130; Cnossen 1988 (n. 66 above), 399, 404; Cnossen 2003 (n. 8 above), 625, 627; Crawford et al. (n. 25 above), 275, 305; Dietl et al. (n. 152 above), 1, 8 et seq., and 22 et seq.; Ebrill et al. (n. 173 above), 86 et seq.; K. M. Teichmann (n. 241 above), 119 et seq.; Terra & Kajus (n. 11 above), 281. See also Pérez Herrero (n. 127 above), 201 et seq.

of the exempt goods or services,[254] and is thus avoided unless efficiency gains exceed the additional VAT burden. Moreover, this tends to favour large firms over their smaller competitors due to economies of scale. The same logic applies to labour-saving investment decisions, because the capital asset to be acquired for this purpose is burdened with irrecoverable input VAT, whereas in-house labour is not.[255]

These detrimental effects could be avoided to a large degree in a B2B context if taxable persons had an option to treat their supplies to other businesses as taxed transactions. However, the Directive contemplates an option for taxation only with respect to very few exemptions, and moreover leaves its implementation at the discretion of the Member States.

With respect to all kinds of exempt transactions, the non-deductibility of input VAT is also objectionable due to an increase of compliance and administrative costs. This is especially the case when taxable persons carry out both taxed and exempt supplies in the course of their business.[256] For them it is necessary to establish and apply often complex criteria for a sufficient economic link between a particular input transaction and a taxed output transaction with a right to deduct.[257] In the case of mixed use of input supplies, a realistic but also feasible formula to determine the pro rata deduction must be decided upon and consistently applied. If based on a simple formula like turnover ratios, this apportionment will be 'inherently arbitrary' and provide tax planning opportunities.[258] Otherwise, it will be complex and will frequently give rise to disputes between the taxpayer and tax authorities. It should also be noted that with respect to capital goods, the initial deduction must arguably be adjusted when, due to subsequent changes in their use, the appropriate deduction is significantly higher or lower than that to which the taxable person was originally entitled.[259] The adjustment mechanism, too, results in an increase of complexity (i.e. in higher compliance and administrative costs). Moreover, different rules as regards the calculation of the deductible pro rata in each of the 27 EU Member States[260] lead to international distortions of competition.[261] But even wholly exempt traders may have resort to complex tax planning strategies, such as the interposition of foreign fixed establishments that are situated in a jurisdiction where no exemption applies, or artificial and abusive schemes.

Finally, some of the exemptions provided for in the EU VAT system are asymmetric, because they apply only for some of the firms or economic agents within

254. Cf. Ebrill et al. (n. 173 above), 86 et seq.; Swinkels (n. 182 above), 262. See also – with respect to public sector entities that carry out non-taxable or exempt transactions – Copenhagen Economics & KPMG (n. 58 above), 10 et seq., 13, 51.
255. Cf. Copenhagen Economics & KPMG (n. 58 above), 13.
256. Cf. Cnossen 2010 (n. 66 above), 370, 382; Crawford et al. (n. 25 above), 275, 305.
257. Cf. Bird & Gendron (n. 16 above), 89 and 99.
258. Cf. Cnossen 1988 (n. 66 above), 399, 406 et seq., incl. footnote 19; Genser & Winker (n. 14 above), 563, 567; see also van Brederode (n. 66 above), 136. As regards groups of companies in particular, they may be incentivized to manipulate their transfer prices, as acknowledged by the special provision of Art. 80 of the EU VAT Directive.
259. This is provided for by Arts 184 et seq. of the EU VAT Directive.
260. There is a lack of (full) harmonization in this regard, cf. Art. 173 of the EU VAT Directive.
261. Cf. Amand (n. 6 above), 409, 415.

the relevant market sector. A prominent example is the supply of postal services discussed above, which are exempt only under the condition that the operator provides universal postal service within the respective Member State.[262] In these instances, the denial of input VAT deduction will reduce the price advantage that the exempt firms enjoy over their non-exempt competitors in B2C transactions and with respect to business customers who cannot deduct VAT themselves (since they, too, are exempt traders). However, at the same time the cost disadvantage of not being able to deduct input VAT will translate into a competitive disadvantage with respect to taxed business customers who can deduct invoiced VAT but not the 'taxe occulte' resulting from a shift of irrecoverable input VAT incurred by their supplier. The net effect on the competitive position of the exempt firms in the market will depend mainly on two factors: the fraction of non-labour inputs for the supplies at issue (input VAT on labour can be avoided by insourcing it, although often at the cost of some efficiency loss), and the fraction of non-taxable or exempt customers.[263] Since the former factor in particular can only be estimated, and since it may also change over the course of time (e.g., due to technical innovations, or between different Member States), the denial of input VAT deduction obscures the extent – if any – of the privilege conveyed by the exemption.

It is submitted that in the Union legal order, these severe deficiencies of the link between taxation of output transactions and deduction of input VAT are not a mere 'inconvenience'.[264] They must not be accepted as 'a consequence of a deliberate choice on the part of the Community legislature',[265] as if the latter could liberate itself from any constitutional requirements in the area of taxation. Rather, if measured by the standards established – but unfortunately not consistently enforced – by the CJEU itself and discussed above at §2.03[B], the denial of input VAT deduction infringes primary Union law and the VAT-specific principles to be derived from it. If one takes the constitutional dimension of the principle of fiscal neutrality seriously, such an infringement has to be justified or the rule responsible for it must be declared in breach of superior Union law and thus void. It would then be up to the Union legislator to amend the of the EU VAT Directive.

[B] Possible Justifications in the Context of Different Categories of Exemptions

[1] Admissible and Inadmissible Justifications

As regards possible justifications for the denial of an input VAT credit, it should first be pointed out that mere revenue effects[266] can never serve as a valid justification within

262. See, in this regard, Art. 132 (1) (a) of the EU VAT Directive, as interpreted by *TNT Post UK* (n. 36 above), para. 36.
263. See, in this regard, Dietl et al. (n. 152 above), 1 and 3 et seq.
264. Cf. Explanatory Memorandum (n. 7 above), 15.
265. Cf. *Seeling* (n. 34 above), para. 54; Case C-72/05, *Wollny* [2006] ECR I-8297, paras. 46–48; in a similar vein, Case C-378/02, *Waterschap Zeeuws Vlaanderen* [2005] ECR I-4685, para. 43.
266. Obviously, total tax revenue under an exemption exceeds that under zero-rating, cf. Gottfried & Wiegard (n. 71 above), 307, 310 and 326.

the framework of a constitutional analysis.[267] If government needs additional revenue, it must not overburden individual taxpayers contrary to requirements of tax fairness and to equal taxation according to individual taxpaying capacity. Instead, it must distribute the higher tax burden equally.[268] Insofar as the VAT exemption pursues extra-fiscal objectives unrelated to tax equity considerations of the aforementioned kind, its extent may be subject to budgetary constraint, but not in a way that renders the exemption internally incoherent.

The same applies for a possible variation of such considerations, according to which the treasury should always be entitled to keep at least the revenue that has been collected at earlier stages of production.[269] Such an argument was possibly a legitimate one prior to the harmonization of turnover taxes, as long as the latter were conceived as a tax on the value added, because under such a premise it could seem consistent that only the value added by the taxable person who qualifies for an exemption should be truly exempt from VAT. However, the common system of EU VAT has been firmly based on the concept of an indirect tax on (expenditure for) consumption from its very inception, which necessarily implies a shift of perspective to the tax burden of the final consumer.

Against that background, the original concern of the Commission that the granting of an input VAT credit or refund would inevitably imply an increase of the regular tax rate[270] might adequately reflect the political constraints that the Commission faced in drafting its proposal on a harmonized system of VAT, but it cannot be regarded as relevant in the context of a constitutional review of the rules on exemptions. Indeed, when exemptions are too costly for Member States, they should be abolished already for this reason, insofar as they are not (exceptionally) mandated by considerations of tax equity, administrative efficiency, or the design of VAT as a tax on final consumption.

The denial of an input VAT credit can therefore be regarded as justified, if at all, primarily on grounds of the tax policy or extra-fiscal policy objectives underlying the exemption itself. Since the output and input consequences of an exemption are not intrinsically linked in the sense that granting an input VAT credit would be *technically* unfeasible if the corresponding output transactions are exempt, the legitimacy of privileging certain supplies is not in itself sufficient justification. Instead, it will be necessary to show that the 'input taxation' of a particular category of exempt supplies, and its negative consequences, are a proportionate corollary of the purpose based on which the exemption itself can be regarded as justified. A comprehensive analysis of the compatibility of the non-deductibility of input VAT with superior principles of EU

267. As regards an economist's viewpoint, see Ebrill et al. (n. 173 above), 94. The need to raise the standard VAT rate to compensate for the revenue cost of zero-rating was also a major concern of the EC Commission, cf. Report from the Commission to the Council, COM(82) 885 final, 17 January 1983, reproduced in *Intertax* (1983): 137, 138.
268. This is also the position adopted by the German Constitutional Court, cf. Constitutional Court 9 December 2008, joined cases 2 BvL 1/07 a.o., BVerfGE 122, 210 (at 236 et seq), and the case law cited there.
269. See the references in n. 240 above.
270. Cf. explanatory memorandum of the preceding proposal of the Second VAT Directive (n. 4 above), 16.

law - and the principles of tax equality, consistency and fiscal neutrality in particular - therefore has to distinguish between the different types of objectives of the provisions on exempt supplies.

[2] No Justification in the Context of Equity-Based Exemptions

Insofar as an exemption can be regarded as legitimate and indeed required because the expenditure incurred for the exempt item or service by a final consumer *typically* does not indicate any taxpaying capacity, regardless of the amount spent, any form of 'input taxation' through a denial of a right to deduct input VAT is obviously inconsistent. Tax equity requires that such goods and services - the cost of which can clearly be identified as expenditure related to the minimum subsistence, even when considering the restrictions to such an approach in the context of VAT as an indirect tax - must not be made more costly by imposing a VAT burden. Relief for such expenditure that is typically incurred for indispensable items and services in order to satisfy essential human needs must be granted in full, excluding both explicit *and implicit* VAT burdens. Hence, effective zero-rating of the corresponding supplies would be appropriate.[271]

In economic literature, it is often pointed out that zero-rating or the application of a reduced rate implies an increase in the number of assessable taxable persons and may thus result in additional compliance and administrative costs.[272] This seems to have been an argument against zero-rating for the Commission, too.[273] However, it can be expected that any additional costs will to some degree already be offset by the elimination of the costs and possible distortions associated with the calculation and verification of the pro rata VAT deduction in case of mixed-used input supplies[274] by taxable persons who carry out both taxed and exempt supplies (partially exempt traders).[275] Moreover, any remaining negative welfare effects are very likely to be (over-)compensated by a reduction in tax planning schemes,[276] and due to efficiency gains by removing the barriers for outsourcing and the other distortive effects of input taxation discussed above. It is also noteworthy that economic analysis suggests that the additional compliance costs for formerly exempt businesses that are associated with a transition to zero-rating are relatively low.[277] To some extent (although considering the nature of the goods and services at issue, probably only to a small extent), the shift

271. Likewise Ruppe 1995 (n. 63 above), 457, 461 et seq. See also Kirchhof (n. 122 above), § 11 para. 37 (with respect to the leasing and letting of residential apartments and housing).
272. Cf. Ebrill et al. (n. 173 above), 91; Gottfried & Wiegard (n. 71 above), 307, 327; Raboy in Weidenbaum et al. (n. 75 above), 87, 98. See also Cnossen 1988 (n. 66 above), 399, 400; Tait (n. 46 above), 50.
273. Cf. EC Commission, cf. Report from the Commission to the Council (n. 267 above) 137, 138.
274. Cf. Ebrill et al. (n. 173 above), 88 et seq.
275. This is also admitted by Gottfried & Wiegard (n. 71 above), 307, 327.
276. Cf. Mollard (n. 18 above), 443, 473.
277. See Copenhagen Economics & KPMG (n. 58 above), 19 et seq., 149 et seq., regarding the similar issue of establishing refund schemes for public sector entities. These findings can probably be explained to a large degree by the fact that often, bookkeeping and recording requirements for VAT may already be demanded for income tax purposes.

towards a system that permits input VAT deduction may also reduce VAT cascading within the system and thus enhance investment. Finally, only a relatively small number of taxpayers would have to be additionally registered for zero-rating if one accepts that the letting of residential housing is not included within the category of exemptions discussed here.

Some also argue that zero-rating would be welfare decreasing if implemented in a revenue neutral fashion (by increasing the standard VAT rate), because this can generally be observed when the gap between the lowest and the highest rate widens.[278] Due to the higher VAT relief effect of zero-rating, it is also conceivable that the legal uncertainty with respect to the exact borderlines between privileged products and services, on the one hand, and regularly taxed goods and services, on the other hand, gives rise to even fiercer disputes between taxable persons and tax authorities.[279] However, in the author's view, neither these concerns nor a remaining net increase of administrative costs – if any – can tilt the balance of the proportionality analysis. One should be aware that by legal standards, the constitutional dimension of the argument for zero-rating essential supplies (insofar as the corresponding expenditure can be targeted sufficiently precise within the system of an impersonal indirect tax such as VAT) outweighs efficiency concerns as well as a possible welfare decrease that might occur under the condition of revenue neutrality of a reform, unless the net negative effects could reasonably be assessed as grave. The margin of discretion and appreciation of the Union legislator is thus significantly reduced in this regard.

By contrast, if mere reasons of *social policy* are underlying an exemption, it may reasonably be assumed that a mere reduction in the tax burden is sufficient to realize the social objectives pursued by the (European) legislator. Since this is the actual effect of an exemption without credit, it cannot be concluded a priori that the latter is inconsistent with respect to the pursuance of its underlying objective. Notwithstanding this acknowledgement, it would still be more appropriate to tax such supplies at a lower than regular rate instead.[280] Such an approach could be fine-tuned so as to yield the same tax revenue, and it would not distort the functioning of the system and would render a clearer picture of the extent of aid.[281] The insistence on the antiquated tradition of denial of input VAT deduction therefore is disproportionate.

278. Cf. Bird & Gendron (n. 16 above), 123; Gottfried & Wiegard (n. 71 above), 307, 325; see also Krever (n. 8 above), 9, 19, concerning VAT concessions in general: '... increasing gap... exacerbates the economic distortions ...'
279. For some examples, see Tait (n. 46 above), 53 et seq.
280. Likewise Bird & Gendron (n. 16 above), 110; Dziadkowski (n. 181 above), 87, 91; see also M. Aujean, P. Jenkins & S. Poddar (n. 221 above), 148.
281. This has rightfully been pointed out by Gottfried & Wiegard (n. 71 above), 307, 309; Heidemann (n. 61 above), 144 et seq., and 146 et seq.; Ruppe 1995 (n. 63 above), 457, 462; H. Söhn (n. 218 above), 27; See also Mollard (n. 18 above), 443, 473, who regards this solution as second-best, if a complete abolition of tax concessions should not be politically feasible. The transparency and political accountability aspect is also highlighted by Ebrill et al. (n. 173 above), 91.

[3] Other Instances of Insufficient Justification

If theatres, museums, or other institutions that predominantly pursue activities in the public interest on a non-profit basis are intended to be subsidized by granting an exemption for their supplies, the same criticism applies. Admittedly, equality of taxation with respect to final consumers might not be impaired if the privileged traders are in the minority so that the exemption will not have a noticeable influence on consumer prices, and the privileged operators will thus be able to fix prices as if VAT were charged. Moreover, in the (exceptional) case of a personal exemption intended to subsidize the taxable person, a limitation of the fiscal aid to the value added by the taxable person might prima facie seem plausible.[282] Thus, the denial of deduction is not necessarily counterproductive. However, for the reasons set out above, it is unnecessarily distortive and furthermore produces arbitrary results.[283] It complicates the system without any real need; a rate reduction would therefore be preferable should zero-rating be regarded as a step too far or too costly.

If the avoidance of double burdens resulting from the simultaneous application of VAT and excise or stamp duties were to be accepted as a valid justification for certain exemptions, the denial of input VAT deduction is obviously inconsistent, because it will lead to the persistence of a double burden.[284]

As explained above, several exemptions and especially those regarding financial services can be justified – and should be maintained – in order to avoid a tax burden on expenditure that does not reflect consumer spending, but rather constitutes savings or investment, or is directly linked to such activity. Such services must then also not be implicitly 'input taxed' by way of denying an input tax credit.[285] It has to be acknowledged, though, that scholars of economy and law have not as yet reached consensus as to the exact dividing line between consumption and savings, and regarding the adequate treatment of related services, in the field of financial transactions. The same applies to a lesser agree for the supply of land. Regarding educational services, the extent of the consumption element inherent to their use is debatable. Therefore, any political decision on these aspects that is based on a reasonable and consistent theory of the concept of consumption vs. savings and investment will have to be accepted as compatible with the requirements of superior principles of law and their VAT specifications. Insofar as the legislator assumes consumption expenditure, an exemption without credit might then be justified insofar as it can be maintained on grounds of administrative efficiency or for technical reasons.

282. Cf. Ruppe 1995 (n. 63 above), 457, 467 et seq.
283. See also Ruppe 1995 (n. 63 above), 457, 463.
284. See also Frink (n. 18 above), 119 et seq.; Ruppe 1995 (n. 63 above), 457, 467; Ruppe 2005 (n. 109 above), § 6 para. 257; K. M. Teichmann (n. 241 above), 123 et seq.
285. Likewise Ruppe 2005 (n. 109 above), § 6 para. 99.

[4] *Partial Justification Where Taxing Output Would Be Hard or Inefficient*

As analysed above, some exemptions can be justified because taxation of output supplies is technically unfeasible or would result in considerable complexity of the tax system, thus arguably causing high compliance burdens and excessive costs. Here, an 'input taxation' might be defended despite the distortions that it causes, because it ensures that there will be at least some form of tax burden placed on the consumer of such services, in accordance with the concept of VAT as a tax on expenditure for consumption.[286] Admittedly, the denial of input VAT may in itself also result in higher compliance and administrative costs, insofar as it becomes necessary to determine an adequate pro rata for the input VAT deduction for suppliers of both exempt and taxed services. This can affect private landlords and real estate companies in particular, when they let partially to business tenants and partially to private tenants, provided the respective Member State grants an option to taxation for B2B supplies.[287] But it is far from obvious that this occasional complication compromises the objective of technically feasible and efficient taxation underlying the exemption to the same degree as taxing the output supplies would.[288] At present, it is therefore not inconsistent to exempt such services without input VAT credit.

However, the denial of an input VAT credit for transactions that should be taxed in conformity with the inherent logic of VAT is always only a second-best solution. As emphasized already above,[289] technical developments and academic discussions should therefore be carefully monitored by the legislator and also from a constitutional viewpoint.

Moreover, it might be recommendable and indeed consistent to grant an input VAT credit insofar as the relevant exemption can additionally be justified for reasons of international tax competition. This aspect is of special relevance for the financial services industry. Here, an implicit input VAT burden can constitute a significant obstacle for European financial institutions and put them as a competitive disadvantage in their home market vis-à-vis financial institutions established in third countries (import bias),[290] since the VAT rates in EU Member States and thus input VAT are often

286. Likewise Cnossen 1988 (n. 66 above), 399, 405, regarding the exemption for rental charges; Ruppe 1995 (n. 63 above), 457, 464. See also in more general terms D. M. Newbery, *On the Desirability of Input Taxation*, 20 Econ. Lett. 267 et seq. (1986), who discusses the desirability of input taxes when taxation of final goods is not possible. For a different opinion, see Heidemann (n. 61 above), 174 et seq.
287. As authorized by Art. 137 (1) (d) of the EU VAT Directive, and provided that the supplier has made use of that option.
288. For a different opinion, see Hoffsümmer (n. 74 above), 147; Crawford et al. (n. 25 above), 275, 304, who give too much weight to administrative concerns, though.
289. See above at §2.04[F].
290. Cf. Bird & Gendron (n. 16 above), 99.

comparatively high.[291] This is particularly true with respect to competitors from countries that do not as yet levy any VAT on input supplies of services (e.g., the United States). Insofar as EU-based customers view such third-country supplies as a viable alternative, zero-rating could therefore not be objected to.

291. Likewise Kirchhof (n. 122 above), § 11 paras. 58 et seq.; Heidemann (n. 61 above), 36 et seq.

Comments: The EU Perspective on VAT Exemptions

Richard Lyal*

I INTRODUCTION

It would be difficult to argue that the provisions of EU VAT legislation on exemptions are wholly satisfactory. They are probably the biggest single source of disputes and litigation, and it is at least questionable whether the difficulty to which they give rise is justified by any benefit.

It is equally difficult to find much ground for disagreement with what Professor Englisch has said in his paper.[1] It may nevertheless be useful to add a few words of criticism of the existing legislation, offer some historical background and finally make some specific comments on a few aspects of the paper.

[A] The Exemptions

There are essentially two categories of exemptions in the EU legislation:

- the first, formerly contained in Article 13(A) of the Sixth Directive[2] and now mainly in Article 132 of the EU VAT Directive,[3] are said to be necessary in the public interest;[4]

* The views expressed are personal to the author and should not be attributed to anyone else, least of all the European Commission.

1. J. Englisch, 'The EU Perspective on VAT Exemptions', Ch. 2 in this volume.
2. Sixth Council Directive 77/388/EEC of 17 May 1977 on the harmonization of the laws of the Member States relating to turnover taxes - Common system of value added tax: uniform basis of assessment, OJ L145/1 of 1977.
3. Council Directive 2006/112/EC of 28 November 2006 on the common system of value added tax, OJ L347/1 of 2006 (Hereafter 'EU VAT Directive').
4. Quite aside from academic commentary, that may be inferred from the rubric of Article 13(A) and from the chapter heading under which Article 132 falls.

- the second, laid down in Article 13(B) of the Sixth Directive and now in Article 135 of the EU VAT Directive, resist such simple attribution. There is no very obvious explanation for them other than a perceived difficulty in determining the taxable amount.

In relation to the first category, it seems logical to argue that if these exemptions are truly necessary in the public interest, then they should be zero-rated or taxed at a reduced rate. As matters stand, they bear a certain proportion of VAT, but there is no way of knowing what that proportion is. Even worse, the proportion will almost certainly vary from one service provider to another, depending in particular on the taxpayer's degree of vertical and horizontal integration. That has obvious negative consequences for neutrality and competition.

Equally, if it is true that the second category of exemptions was prompted by despair, by inability to find an acceptable way of determining the taxable amount, then there is no very good justification for maintaining that treatment. Nowadays, more than thirty years after the adoption of the Sixth Directive, it should be possible to find a way of taxing most of the services concerned; there is in any event no reason to relieve them of any tax burden. A nuance here: it is possible that insurance and gambling services are exceptions to this rather broad-brush approach. One contemporary justification for exemption of those activities was that they would be better dealt with by separate, specific tax schemes.

Two aspects of this debate merit further reflection: the very existence of exemptions and the inability to recover input tax.

Why should these exemptions exist in the first place? The public interest rationale has a certain obvious appeal, but it does not necessarily stand up to closer examination. It is based presumably on the idea that it is desirable to relieve the tax burden on items to which everyone should have access. But in the existing system, in which exemption is not accompanied by recovery of input tax, there *is* a more or less large tax burden on these services which should, according to this rationale, be spared taxation because they are essential. And, as already noted, that tax burden is not uniform. So there is some tax relief, but no one can know how much.

Perhaps more importantly, this relief is not targeted – the rich benefit as much as the poor: indeed, probably more. Tax exemption for golf club memberships and for private health care is not necessarily the most effective way of mitigating the presumed regressive effect of VAT. In any event, if that regressive effect is seen as a problem that should be mitigated, the answer is not to be sought in modulation of the VAT system. On the contrary, that cannot be done in an efficient or effective manner. By its nature, a consumption tax does not take into account the contributive capacity of consumers. Instead, any effort to limit the impact of taxation on the poor should be made through the direct tax system, since this is the framework in which a link can be made between income or wealth and taxation. The main consequence of VAT exemptions is to complicate the system and create incentives for people to manipulate it. And, of course, to distort the price mechanism.

The argument from despair – that is to say, inability to determine the taxable amount in relation to financial services and insurance – is not so immediately attractive, but it does have a certain common-sense appeal. After all, if there is no way of determining the taxable amount, then there is no way to charge tax, and exemption may appear to be the only option. The question is, though, just to what extent can this be justified? If this is a consumption tax, is it really not possible to identify what people are consuming? That is to say, can we not identify the real 'price' or 'consideration' element even in complex transactions? Where the provision of financial services is paid for by way of a commission, there would seem to be no difficulty. More generally, it should be possible to determine the amount of money that remunerates the service provided and does not correspond to some other element of the transaction (mutualization of loss in insurance, the time value of money in lending transactions, for example).

Some years ago a study was carried out for the Commission on a possible solution for the taxation of services remunerated by the margin retained by the taxpayer (the 1996 TCA-ADD report, available on the website of the Commission's Directorate General for Taxation and Customs Union). In relation to loans, the taxable amount would be the difference between the interest charged by the financial institution and the short-term inter-bank interest rate, taken to be a proxy for a rate which includes no risk or service element. Despite its attraction, such an approach has not been the object of any proposal by the Commission.

One objection is that in many cases the method of calculating the taxable amount will not permit identification of that amount transaction by transaction (Case C-38/93 *H. J. Glawe Spiel- und Unterhaltungsgeräte Aufstellungsgesellschaft mbH & Co. KG v. Finanzamt Hamburg-Barmbek-Uhlenhorst* [1994] ECR I-01679, in which the method adopted in order to determine the taxable amount was workable only over a more or less large number of transactions taken together). That may be an important objection where services supplied to business (so-called 'B2B' transactions) are concerned, since economic operators need to know the amount of tax that they are entitled to deduct, but it is difficult to see any difficulty in dealings with consumers ('B2C' transactions), since they have no interest in knowing the precise amount of tax. And even in relation to B2B supplies there must be ways of resolving the problem for the customer of identifying his input tax. One possible, even elegant, method is that applied in New Zealand, of zero-rating. If limited to B2B transactions, this could ensure VAT neutrality in the chain of supply without affecting the tax burden on the ultimate consumer. Such a method does, of course, bring with it the need to ensure that the recipients of zero-rated services are themselves taxable persons, but that does not seem unduly difficult.

Accordingly, Professor Englisch's suggestion that these exemptions may be justified on the basis that no consumption takes place is unsound. There is indeed consumption in the case of financial services and insurance. For example, the interest charged by a bank loan does not simply represent the time value of money; it incorporates an amount which remunerates the service provided by the bank, and that service is consumed by the customer. More precisely, there is direct consumption in the B2C situation; there is a service which is incorporated in downstream consumption in the B2B context. What is necessary is to distinguish the consumption from the non-consumption element of these transactions.

As for recovery of input tax, the need for that, or its desirability, may depend on what the justification for the exemption is. As already noted, if the purpose of exemption is to relieve consumers of the tax burden on services to which it is thought desirable that people should have access irrespective of their means, then there should be recovery. That is to say, those services should be zero-rated, which would correspond to what an innocent bystander might understand exemption to mean.

Conversely, if the reason for exemption is the inability of taxpayers and tax authorities to ascertain the taxable amount, then there is surely an argument for letting the tax lie where it falls. The fact that it is difficult to tax output is not a reason for repaying input tax. There is no need to relieve consumers of a tax burden. For the rest, if some commentators were right to say that non-consumption was the basis for the exemptions contained in Article 135, then there would be a downstream controversy to resolve. On the one hand, it could be argued that there should be recovery of input tax, since otherwise there would be taxation of something that in reality lies outside the object of the tax. On the other, it could be argued that the situation is the same as any other out-of-scope activity and that there should therefore be no recovery. In a sense, there has been consumption of the inputs supplied to the taxpayer. They have not been used for the purposes of the taxpayer's taxable transactions and the right to recover thus does not arise.

That is criticism of the present system. In a discussion of this kind it is necessary to distinguish between the analysis of what the system should be (or what the justification of the existing exemptions should be) and what the system actually is; that is to say, how these exemptions came into existence.

[B] Historical Background

As a preliminary point, it should be recalled that VAT harmonization in the Community was a very different process from the invention of a new system of indirect taxation. The starting point was the need to minimize tax barriers to the internal market, in a situation where half of the Member States applied cumulative cascade systems of indirect taxation on goods. It was above all the extreme difficulty, in those circumstances, of calculating border tax adjustments that gave rise to the need for another approach. This was not the situation of a State deciding what its optimum tax system should be (and thus, for example, rejecting a cascade system on the ground of its distortive effects on domestic business). On the contrary, the move towards a common system was motivated by the desire to facilitate cross-border trade.[5]

From the start, the Commission had realized the importance of a common and limited set of VAT exemptions if tax frontiers were to be eliminated. The need for this

5. See the preamble to the First Council Directive 67/227/EEC of 11 April 1967 on the harmonization of legislation of Member States concerning turnover taxes, OJ 71/1301 of 1967 (English Special Edition 1967/14).

was recognized in the Neumark report[6] in 1962, which drew attention to the distortive effect of exemptions while recognizing that they could be desirable in relation to items of prime necessity.

These considerations became all the more important once the decision was taken to incorporate VAT as an important part of the funding of the European Community – the so-called VAT own resource.[7] Since exempt transactions are excluded from the tax base for the purpose of calculating own resources, variations in the scope of exemptions between Member States would affect the contribution of each State to the Community budget.[8]

The Second VAT Directive[9] allowed Member States to establish exemptions more or less freely. Article 10(3) provided that 'each Member State may, subject to the consultations mentioned in Article 16 [that is to say, consultation of what is now called the VAT Committee], determine the other exemptions which it considers necessary'.[10] Nevertheless, the explanatory memorandum which accompanied the proposal for the Directive[11] pointed out the need to limit the number of exemptions as much as possible. In order to achieve a pure and neutral system, the scope of the tax should be completely general, covering all economic activities. Consultation of the VAT Committee was intended to prevent excessive diversity.

The Sixth Directive abolished that freedom for the Member States and established a common set of exemptions. It could have been more rigorous but, to a large extent, took over the exemptions which were in general use in the Member States. In the explanatory memorandum to its proposal,[12] the Commission stated:

> The list of exemptions has been drawn up having regard (i) to the exemptions already existing in the various Member States and (ii) the need to keep the number of exemptions as small as possible. This need reflects a concern to keep exemptions to the minimum in a general system of taxation of consumption, but also reflects a desire to avoid the inconveniences which such exemptions cause, mainly by reason of the fact that, unless the transaction exempted becomes part of an international trading operation, taxes paid on inputs will not be deductible.

6. The EEC Reports on Tax Harmonization – The Report of the Fiscal and Financial Committee and the Report of the Sub-Groups A, B and C (Amsterdam: IBFD Publications, 1963) (unofficial English-language version).
7. Council Decision 70/243/ECSC, EEC, Euratom of 21 April 1970 on the replacement of financial contributions from Member States by the Communities' own resources, OJ L94/19 of 1970 (English Special Edition 1970(I)/.224).
8. Curiously, this aspect is the only one mentioned in the preamble to the present EU VAT Directive, according to which: 'A common list of exemptions should be drawn up so that the Communities' own resources may be collected in a uniform manner in all the Member States' (recital 35, reproducing the 11th recital in the preamble to the Sixth Directive).
9. Second Council Directive 67/228/EEC of 11 April 1967 on the harmonisation of legislation of Member States concerning turnover taxes – Structure and procedures for application of the common system of value added tax, OJ 71/1303 of 1967 (English Special Edition 1967/16).
10. 'Other' in relation to the exemptions provided for in Article 10(1) and (2) – exported goods and the provision of services in relation to such goods, possible exemption of services in relation to imports of goods.
11. Document IV/COM(65) 144 final.
12. Document COM(73) 950.

It is likely that more stringent limitation of the scope of exemptions was not a political priority: there were already several controversial issues on which it was difficult to attain the agreement of Member States (agriculture; small- and medium-sized undertakings; zero-rates; and transactions in land, to name only a few), and the Commission can be forgiven for not seeking to be over-ambitious. Nevertheless, it was a lost opportunity, and one that is not going to be repeated. That is all the more true inasmuch as it was clearly recognized that there should be a common and narrowly limited set of exemptions. In the event, we are left with a *common* set, but one which is not narrowly limited. It is probably fair to say, however, that there was less awareness of the negative effects of exemptions in the mid-1970s, and in practical terms those effects were perhaps less visible at the time – many of the suppliers of exempt services were vertically and sometimes horizontally integrated.

The reason for saying that the opportunity will not be repeated lies of course in the difficulty that would be faced in seeking to make changes now. As an indication of that difficulty, it may be noted that the Commission proposed the elimination of the postal services exemption in 2003.[13] It is generally accepted, and for that matter obvious, that the exemption is obsolete, but there has been no progress in amending the Directive to eliminate it. It may also be recalled that in the proposal for the Sixth Directive the Commission did make an effort to limit the scope of the exemption relating to immovable property; even that rather timid proposal was unsuccessful.

A truly comprehensive analysis of the reasoning lying behind the exemptions contained in the Sixth Directive would require research into the grounds relied on by the Member States in establishing their exemptions during the period from 1967 to 1975 (and from the mid-1950s onwards in the case of France). That is a rather larger task than has been feasible for the purposes of the present remarks.

In relation to the non-recovery of input tax, it should be borne in mind that the Neumark report – and the Commission's original proposal for the First VAT Directive – proposed a VAT system which included the wholesale but not the retail stage, essentially because it was thought that small retailers were incapable of operating the VAT system. So at least in relation to B2C transactions (including in general the services exempted by Article 132 of the EU VAT Directive), the tax would have been final at the previous stage. The result would thus have been incorporation of input tax in the retail price, whether or not Member States applied a separate retail sales tax as envisaged at the time. In that context, there would have been nothing unusual about the fact that exempt supplies to consumers carried an implicit and variable VAT burden.

In the explanatory memorandum to the Commission's proposal for the Second Directive, non-recovery of input tax in relation to exempt transactions was said (by the Member States) to be justified by 'administrative difficulty', consisting essentially in the fact that there would be taxpayers who were consistently due refunds of tax

13. *Proposal for a Council Directive amending Directive 77/388/EEC as regards value added tax on services provided in the postal sector*, COM(2003) 234 final. See also the opinions of the Economic and Social Committee, OJ C80/135 of 2004, and of the European Parliament, OJ C102E/645 of 2004.

('repayment taxpayers', as they are called in the United Kingdom). The tax authorities would have to set up a special service to check and pay refunds. Moreover, repayment would be inconsistent with the principle of a general tax applicable to all consumption, and would have to be funded by an increase in the rate of tax. None of these objections is particularly convincing, and it may be thought that the real reason was reluctance to give up tax revenue.

Another contemporary explanation for the non-recovery of input tax is the theory, widely held at the time, that there must be enough taxation of output to cover the deductible input tax. That was the main reason advanced for seeking to abolish zero-rates at the time of the Sixth Directive (and it is still advanced by people who regard zero-rates as a form of State aid, distinguishable from other reduced rates). Such an approach is to be seen in the fifth recital to the Second Directive, and survives in Article 99(2) of the EU VAT Directive. It perhaps reflects the notion of a 'value added' tax rather than a consumption tax with a fractionated collection system.

This last point well illustrates an important aspect of the problem: the situation today is at least in part the result of debate and compromise between people holding a range of ideas based on unspoken and conflicting premises.

[C] Specific Comments

Finally, a few specific comments on aspects of Professor Englisch's paper may be useful.

Professor Englisch considers that the threshold for tax liability on the part of small- and medium enterprises (SMEs) is a form of exemption and should be analysed from the same perspective.

However, the existence of a threshold is a different phenomenon from that of exemption and should not be discussed on the same footing. It is a solution of facility, aimed at reducing administrative expense for both taxpayers and tax authorities. Indeed, to some extent it may be thought of as a vestige of the original idea that VAT should operate only as far as the wholesale stage. The result is some under-taxation of B2C transactions, but it probably has negligible impact on B2B operations.

Professor Englisch suggests that there may be a problem of international tax competition if exemption of financial services is eliminated. He fears that suppliers of services within the Union could be placed at a disadvantage in relation to foreign suppliers who could provide services free of tax. However, as he implicitly acknowledges, there is no reason for any competitive disadvantage to arise in relation to B2B transactions once the place of supply is at the place of business of the *customer* (who is obliged to account for tax under a reverse charge).[14] There would be no scope for the acquisition by businesses of services free of VAT from offshore suppliers. It is true that there would be scope for tax-free purchases by consumers, but it is not clear how great the competitive problem would be. One may be sceptical as to the size of the potential

14. Article 44 of the EU VAT Directive as amended by Directive 2008/8/EC of 12 February 2008 amending Directive 2006/112/EC as regards the place of supply of services, OJ 44/11 of 2008 (EU VAT Directive).

market for consumer financial services or insurance provided from abroad by persons without a permanent establishment in the EU.

Professor Englisch is perhaps a little too severe in his strictures regarding the 'strict interpretation' of exemptions by the CJEU. Attention should be directed to what the CJEU does, not what it says. It does indeed state fairly systematically that 'the terms used to specify the exemptions in Article 13 of the Sixth Directive are to be interpreted strictly since they constitute exceptions to the general principle that VAT is to be levied on all goods and services supplied for consideration by a taxable person'. However, 'strict' does not necessarily mean restrictive or narrow.[15] The CJEU typically goes on to state that:

> Nevertheless, the interpretation of those terms must be consistent with the objectives pursued by those exemptions and comply with the requirements of the principle of fiscal neutrality inherent in the common system of VAT. Thus, the requirement of strict interpretation does not mean that the terms used to specify the exemptions referred to in Article 13 should be construed in such a way as to deprive the exemptions of their intended effect.[16]

The essential rule is thus that exemptions must not be extended beyond their natural scope, having regard to the function they perform in the VAT system. The CJEU's statement is simply a reminder that exemptions should be limited as much as possible (which, after all, has been one of the basic ideas since the 1960s), and in particular that application by analogy is not permissible. For the rest, as Professor Englisch acknowledges, the CJEU makes a serious effort to understand the intended scope of exemptions, using all the familiar tools of interpretation.

It should also be borne in mind that in the cases which come before the CJEU, the debate almost always concerns attempts to extend exemption to services which are in reality an input to an exempted service. It seems legitimate, in such cases, to speak of strict interpretation.

II CONCLUSION

As indicated at the outset, it is hard to disagree with Professor Englisch, in particular with his conclusion that the exemptions are an unnecessary evil. In an ideal system, the services covered by the exemptions in Article 132 of the EU VAT Directive should at most be taxed at a reduced rate (subject always to the more general objection to reduced rates which flows from the view that tax differentiation should take place in the direct tax system and not in the taxation of goods and services). The exemptions in Article 135 should not exist, and the services in question should be taxed.

15. See the Opinion of Advocate General Sharpston in Case C-407/07 *Stichting Centraal Begeleidingsorgaan voor de Intercollegiale Toetsing v. Staatssecretaris van Financiën* [2008] ECR I-9615, para. [14].
16. See, most recently, the judgment in Case C-262/08 *CopyGene A/S v. Skatteministeriet* [2010] ECR I-5053, para. [26].

Part II

Exemptions for Public Services and Merit Products

CHAPTER 3

VAT Treatment of Public-Sector Bodies: The Canadian Model

Pierre-Pascal Gendron*

§3.01 INTRODUCTION

The goods and services supplied by the sector that consists of government entities, public-sector bodies, non-profit organizations, charitable organizations (hereafter collectively referred to as the *PNC* sector) continue to elude the best practice under the value added tax (VAT): full taxation of goods and services supplied by the PNC sector, with credit for tax paid on purchases made in order to render the supplies. Although there are very few genuine conceptual problems preventing the full taxation of such supplies under the VAT, some roadblocks remain in the way. Often, they come in the form of policy concerns revolving around social objectives and income distribution. Those explain to a large extent the exceptional (and exceptionally complex) treatment of PNC supplies under the VAT in many countries. Complexity often arises because exemptions may be restricted to particular items (goods and services), or apply to supplies rendered by certain types of entities, or a combination of both. Other times, obstacles come in the form of political inertia and barriers.

While the consequences of the VAT-exempt treatment of the supplies made by the PNC sector are well understood at the theoretical level, there has been little

* I am grateful for helpful comments from two anonymous referees, Rebecca Millar, and Rita de la Feria. For an opportunity to first articulate some of the ideas contained in this paper, I am grateful to Patrice Pillet and participants at the Fiscalis Seminar on *The VAT Treatment of Bodies Governed by Public Law and of Subsidies: Issues and Prospects*, Florence, Italy, 30 November–2 December 2009. Of course, I am solely responsible for the contents of this paper and any errors. An earlier version of this paper was also available as an Oxford University Centre for Business Taxation Working Paper: 'VAT Treatment of Public Sector Bodies: The Canadian Model' (No. 10/17), available at www.sbs.ox.ac.uk/centres/tax/Documents/working_papers/WP1017.pdf.

quantification of its economic effects. They are believed to be quite important when taken together.[1] Such effects includes distortions, compliance costs, administrative costs, and the cost savings from using tax or expenditure policy instruments that are better suited than the VAT to achieve distributional and other social objectives. In aggregate, the distortions from the exempt treatment of the PNC sector are likely to be significant, especially in countries where the PNC sector accounts for an important proportion of the gross domestic product.

This chapter examines in some detail one alternative to the pure exemption model for the PNC sector. Under Canada's VATs, most supplies made by PNC bodies are exempt but such bodies are usually eligible for a rebate of VAT paid or owed on expenses incurred to make such exempt supplies. This systematic rebate system is hereinafter termed the *Canadian Model*. It is argued that the Canadian Model would be a highly desirable alternative to the current EU VAT treatment of public service bodies, a situation that is widely perceived as being deeply unsatisfactory.[2] As an alternative, the Canadian model would seem to be far more feasible than the full taxation of the PNC sector or its variants as practiced in New Zealand or, to a lesser extent, in Australia.

The chapter is organized as follows. The next (first) section provides a synthetic overview of VATs in Canada – the GST/HST and QST system – and the basic VAT treatment of the PNC sector. The second section describes the treatment of government-to-government transactions under Canadian VATs. The third describes the Canadian rebate model in some detail and its application, considering practical issues such as federal-provincial variations and the treatment of grants and subsidies. The fourth section reviews the tax expenditures associated with the rebate approach as used in Canada. The fifth section provides an overview of alternative systems other than the Canadian model. The last section benchmarks the Canadian system against others and suggests that it constitutes a viable and realistic option for reform of the EU VAT treatment of the PNC sector.

§3.02 OVERVIEW OF VATS IN CANADA

This section provides a brief overview of VATs in Canada and then describes the VAT treatment of the public-sector bodies.[3] This chapter refers to the sector that incorporates the public sector and governments, the non-profit sector, and the charitable sector as the PNC sector. The term Public Service Bodies is used in Canada in a more restrictive sense so the convention to use PNC is followed to avoid confusion and be

1. See P.-P. Gendron, *How Should the U.S. Treat Government Entities, Nonprofit Organizations, and other Tax-Exempt Bodies under a VAT?*, 63 Tax L. Rev. 477 (2010). An illuminating commentary on that article is provided by M. Aujean, *Commentary*, 63 Tax L. Rev. 509 (2010).
2. R. de la Feria, *The EU VAT Treatment of Public Sector Bodies: Slowly Moving in the Wrong Direction*, 37 Intertax 148 (2009).
3. This section draws on R.M. Bird & P.-P. Gendron, *Sales Taxes in Canada: The GST-HST-QST-RST 'System'*, 63 Tax L. Rev. 517 (2010).

inclusive as many of the issues concerning the VAT treatment are similar across the three component sectors.

[A] GST/HST System in General

Three VAT systems are currently in operation in Canada: the federal goods and services tax (GST), the harmonized sales tax (HST) - operated jointly with the GST in the provinces of: British Columbia;[4] Ontario; New Brunswick; Nova Scotia; and Newfoundland and Labrador, collectively referred to as the five *participating provinces* - and the Québec sales tax (QST) in operation in the Province of Québec. The GST applies in all ten provinces and three territories at a rate of 5%. The HST (normally referred to as *GST/HST* in government literature) is a joint federal-provincial VAT that applies at various combined rates, as follows: 12% (5% federal GST plus 7% provincial component) in British Columbia; 13% (5% federal GST plus 8% provincial component) in Ontario, New Brunswick, and Newfoundland and Labrador; and 15% (5% federal GST plus 10% provincial component) in Nova Scotia. Finally, the QST is a dual VAT that applies in Québec at a rate of 8.5% on the GST-inclusive price.[5] The intended base of all three taxes consists of domestic consumption, whether produced locally or imported, although place of supply rules apply in the case of services.

In sum, Canada is the only federal OECD country - other than the US - in which subnational governments have the choice of whether or not to impose their own VATs. There are six provinces out of ten with their own VAT at the moment. Table 1 provides a snapshot of the sales tax systems Canadian, including the type of tax and rate in each province, as well as its yield as a percentage of total tax revenues. It is important to note that the Province of Alberta and the three territories (Yukon, Northwest Territories, Nunavut) do not have provincial or territorial sales taxes so only the GST applies in those jurisdictions.

4. This information was correct at the time of writing. However, the government of British Columbia is in the process of replacing the HST with the PST (a retail sales tax similar to the one that preceded the HST) by 1 April 2013. I will ask readers to bear this in mind with subsequent references to British Columbia in this paper.
5. This information was correct at the time of writing. However, the government of Québec will be harmonizing the QST to the HST effective 1 January 2013. See www.finances.gouv.qc.ca/documents/bulletins/en/BULEN_2012-4-a-b.pdf. I will ask readers to bear this in mind with subsequent references to Québec in this chapter.

Table 3.1 Sales Taxes in Canada, July 2010

Jurisdiction	***Name of Tax***	***Type of Tax***	***Rate (%)***	***Administration***	***Comments***
Canada	GST/HST	VAT	5 / 12,/ 13, 15	Federal except in Québec, where it is provincial	GST rate (federal) is 5% and applied throughout the country; the federal government also administers a provincial sales tax rate of 7% in one HST province (sum is 12%), 8% in three HST provinces (sum is 13%), and 10% in one HST province (sum is 15%)
Newfoundland and Labrador	HST	VAT	8	Federal	HST revenues collected in the HST provinces are distributed to provinces based on estimated taxable consumption
Nova Scotia	HST	VAT	10	Federal	Same as for Newfoundland and Labrador
New Brunswick	HST	VAT	8	Federal	Same as for Newfoundland and Labrador
Prince Edward Island	PST	RST	10	Provincial	Applied to retail sales price including GST
Québec	QST (TVQ)	VAT	8.5	Provincial	Applied to GST base plus GST
Ontario	HST	VAT	13	Federal	Same as for Newfoundland and Labrador
Manitoba	PST	RST	7	Provincial	Applied to retail sales price (excluding GST)

Jurisdiction	*Name of Tax*	*Type of Tax*	*Rate (%)*	*Administration*	*Comments*
Saskatchewan	PST	RST	5	Provincial	Same as Manitoba
British Columbia	HST	VAT	12	Federal	Same as for Newfoundland and Labrador

Source: Updated version of Table 1 in Bird & Gendron (n. 3), 519.

Note: The base of the Québec Sales Tax (QST or TVQ, *Taxe de vente du Québec*) differs slightly from that of the GST. Moreover, although the base of the provincial HSTs is the same as that of the GST, each province can alter the effective base by rebating its tax. Each Retail Sales Tax (RST) province has its own tax base, generally with considerable taxation of business inputs and with limited coverage of services. These taxes are not coordinated in any way with each other or with the federal GST.

In sum, the four principal components of the Canadian sales tax system consist today of:

- the federal VAT introduced in 1991 – the Goods and Services Tax (GST);
- the unique provincial VAT introduced in 1991 in the province of Québec – the Québec Sales Tax (QST), a dual VAT;
- the extension of the GST in 1997 to three small eastern provinces – the Harmonized Sales Tax (HST);[6]
- the extension of the GST on 1 July 2010 to two large provinces (Ontario; British Columbia) – the Harmonized Sales Tax (HST); and
- the provincial sales tax that continues to exist in most other provinces – the retail sales tax (RST).[7]

[B] Exemptions in the PNC Sector

The majority of the goods and services sold and consumed in Canada are subject to and within the scope of the GST/HST. There are about ten major statutory exemptions under the GST/HST,[8] many of which depend on the satisfaction of numerous detailed conditions and criteria. Like many VAT regimes around the world, the GST/HST features statutory exemptions in the areas of: real property; health services; education services; daycare and personal care services; legal aid services; supplies made by charitable organizations; public-sector bodies; financial services; and ferries, toll roads, and toll bridges.

Under the GST/HST, taxable supplies are goods and services that are supplied in the course of a commercial activity and are subject to GST/HST, including zero-rated supplies. The latter are supplies that are taxable at a rate of 0%. Exempt supplies are supplies of goods and services that are not subject to GST/HST. A registrant cannot claim input tax credits for the GST/HST paid on expenses incurred to make such supplies. Public Service Bodies (PSB) may be eligible to claim a full or partial GST/HST

6. Strictly speaking, the terminology sometimes used in Canada, especially at the federal level, is not GST (for federal) and HST (for provincial) as we use those terms here but rather CVAT (for Canada-VAT, not the Compensating VAT) for the federal portion of the tax that applies in all provinces) and PVAT (Provincial-VAT) for the portion of the tax that applies on property or services supplied in or brought into a participating province. The official name of the (combined) federal-provincial tax is the GST/HST, as used in the text below. It is also common in Canada to refer to all three varieties of subnational sales taxes simply as Provincial Sales Taxes (PSTs): for example, see the discussion in K. Treff & D.B. Perry, *2007 Finances of the Nation*, Ch 5 (Canadian Tax Foundation, 2008). This treatment is essentially correct: it makes almost no difference to the country as a whole whether any particular province chooses to impose its sales tax in the form of VAT or an RST. It may, however, make a considerable difference to the province in question. Along the same lines, provincial governments usually refer to their sales tax (regardless of how it is characterized in this paper) simply as a PST (provincial sales tax) rather than an RST (retail sales tax) or a VAT (HST or QST, as the case may be): the RST terminology is used here to clarify.
7. Again, the province of Alberta and the three northern territories (Yukon, Northwest Territories, Nunavut) have no sales tax, although the GST applies in those jurisdictions.
8. See *Excise Tax Act* (hereinafter 'The Act'), RSC 1985, Ch. E-15, Schedule V.

rebate for the tax paid or payable to make exempt supplies. PSB means a non-profit organization, a charity, a municipality, a school authority, a hospital authority, a public college or a university.[9] Commercial activity means any business or adventure or concern in the nature of trade carried on by certain persons, but does not include the making of exempt supplies or any business or adventure or concern in the nature of trade carried on without a reasonable expectation of profit by an individual, a personal trust, or a partnership where all of the members are individuals.

Persons are required to register for GST/HST if they provide taxable supplies in Canada and are not small suppliers. A business that is not a PSB is considered a small supplier if its total revenues from taxable supplies from all its activities are CAD 30,000 or less per year. This is a fairly low threshold by international standards. A PSB is considered a small supplier if its total revenues from taxable supplies from all its activities are CAD 50,000 or less per year. A gross revenue threshold of CAD 250,000 also applies to charities and public institutions. A non-profit organization (NPO) that is a small supplier may elect to register voluntarily provided that it is engaged in commercial activity in Canada. An NPO that made only exempt supplies would be deemed not to be engaged in commercial activity and would therefore not be allowed to register. While a charity that makes taxable supplies may register as a small supplier, most supplies made by charities are exempt. For that reason, a charity that makes exclusively exempt supplies is not allowed to register and is therefore exempt by default. Even though such a charity cannot claim input tax credits for tax paid or owed on purchases, it is eligible to claim a PSB rebate of GST/HST paid on eligible expenses. In other words, a non-registrant PSB can never claim input tax credits but may be eligible for a rebate. Similar rules apply to municipalities and the single entity model is used for registration purposes. Municipal boards, commissions and departments that are legally part of a municipality cannot register separately.

From an overall system perspective, the majority of the goods and services supplied by the PNC sector in Canada are exempt, although some are taxable and some are zero-rated. Taxes incurred by PNC entities on any purchases made to deliver taxable or zero-rated supplies (commercial activity) are fully creditable. There are specific exemptions for hospital and clinical care, medical and dental services, public and private nursing home services, educational and social welfare agencies, recreational public-sector programs for youth, municipal services and most supplies made by charitable organizations. In dealing with exempt supplies, the GST/HST and QST systems depart from the pure exemption model by granting rebates of some or all of the tax paid on the inputs purchased to make exempt supplies. These rebates are granted ex post and at variable factors, where factors are a fraction of the tax paid or owed that is rebated. Interestingly, medical devices and prescriptions drugs – which may also be supplied by exempt organizations – are actually zero-rated. In situations where PNC entities supply those, zero-rating clashes with the sector's exempt treatment and results in increased complexity. The system is described in more detail in the sections that follow.

---

9. Canada Revenue Agency, *GST/HST Public Service Bodies' Rebate*, 4 (Government of Canada 2010), www.cra-arc.gc.ca/E/pub/gp/rc4034/rc4034-11-10e.pdf (accessed 18 May 2012).

§3.03 TREATMENT OF GOVERNMENTS IN THE CANADIAN SYSTEM

This section reviews the portion of the activities of the PNC sector which consists of government-to-government (G2G) transactions.[10] Such transactions are also special in Canada since the design of the GST in respect of their treatment has been influenced by a long history of federal-provincial relations.

Under Canada's constitution, federal and provincial governments cannot tax each other so the federal GST could not be applied to sales to provincial governments. However, the governments of the HST provinces, like the federal government, have agreed to pay GST/HST on their taxable purchases in order to simplify the administration of the tax by vendors. Sales to other provinces are not taxable if properly certified, since suppliers are entitled to claim input tax credits (ITCs) on all supplies made to provincial or territorial governments, whether or not GST/HST is collected. Thus, such sales are in effect zero-rated.[11] These rules do not apply to provincial public-sector enterprises (Crown corporations) such as large electricity suppliers, so these companies are both responsible for collecting the tax on their supplies and able to claim refunds of taxes paid on their inputs. In other words, they are treated like any other business. In principle, the important public-sector institutions included in the so-called MASH[12] sector were, as agents of the provinces, exempt from charging federal GST on sales (unless they sold taxable goods). On the other hand, unlike the provincial governments, these institutions were subject to tax on business inputs. However, the federal government decided to provide a partial refund of taxes on inputs purchased by the MASH sector in order to keep these bodies in more or less same relative position as they had previously been under the manufacturers' sales tax (the GST's predecessor tax, which was embedded in the prices of their inputs). Although the refunds varied by type of provincial body, on average they amounted to roughly two-thirds of input taxes paid by the sector.[13]

The federal government of Canada is considered a single entity for GST/HST purposes, and includes all departments, branches, corporations and agencies. The federal government pays GST/HST on its purchases, and charges GST/HST on its taxable supplies. Municipalities are subject to the same treatment with the key difference that many supplies of goods and services by municipalities and para-municipal organizations are exempt.

10. This section draws on Gendron (n. 1 above), and Bird & Gendron (n. 3 above).
11. Although all governments are subject to GST/HST on taxable supplies, all departments and agencies are registered as one entity and hence supplies within any government (broadly defined) are not taxable. In addition, certain supplies are specifically exempted, including most registration, information provision, and licensing activity as well as homemaker services provided in residences, garbage collection, and law enforcement and fire protection.
12. Municipal, academic, schools, and hospitals.
13. Given the huge and varied collection of VAT registrants in Canada lumped together as 'non-profits', their 50% rebate seems more likely to be a compromise between 0% and 100% than an estimate based on any careful study. Interestingly, is shown in Table 4 below, the same (arbitrary) rate is currently applied in all other Canadian VATs, although most apply different rebates in other sectors.

Special arrangements exist with respect to the treatment of sales or supplies to provincial and territorial governments under the GST/HST. The governments of the five participating HST provinces (British Columbia; Ontario; New Brunswick; Nova Scotia; Newfoundland and Labrador) have agreed to pay GST/HST on their taxable purchases. Also, all government departments and agencies in the Province of Prince Edward Island and the territory of Nunavut (which has no territorial sales tax) pay GST/HST on their taxable purchases. The remaining provincial and territorial governments (see Table 3.1), however, do not pay GST/HST on their taxable purchases subject to the provision of certification that purchases are made with Crown (government) funds. Government authorities eligible under this arrangement include all departments or ministries, and some of their Crown corporations, boards, commissions and agencies. Businesses that make supplies to the remaining governments do not charge GST/HST but they are entitled to input tax credits for any GST/HST paid on expenses incurred to make those supplies. The supplies are effectively zero-rated in that case.

Under a reciprocal federal-Québec tax agreement, the federal government, its corporations and agencies are generally not required to pay QST on their purchases which are effectively zero-rated. Agencies not covered by the agreement must pay QST. Québec government corporations and agencies listed in the agreement are not required to pay GST (or the QST) on their purchases. The Québec government, its corporations, agencies and agents are required to collect GST and QST on their taxable sales, unless those are specifically zero-rated. Similar to the federal system, the Québec government authority must deliver a certification that purchases have been made with public funds.

The incorporation of the largest possible fraction of government activity in the scope of the GST/HST is important in four important respects: simplicity, accountability, transparency and VAT mechanics.[14] Bringing governments into the tax simplifies administration considerably and avoids the need to manage multiple exemptions. Accountability and transparency are also enhanced because governments appear to stakeholders as being part of the system as opposed to lying at its margins. Finally, VAT mechanics are preserved as the VAT chain is kept intact all the way to the end. Multiple exemptions at this level have impacts that are so complex that it is almost impossible to assess with certainty which parties benefit from them.

§3.04 THE CANADIAN PUBLIC SERVICES BODY REBATE

The GST/HST is an integrated federal-provincial sales tax in the sense that both the federal and provincial components are applied on the same base by the same administration at the same time. There are some deviations from this harmonization ideal though. One important instance arises with the GST/HST rebate system in relation to the PNC sector.

14. The first three were also noted by R.F. van Brederode, *Systems of General Sales Taxation: Theory, Policy and Practice*, 202 (Wolters Kluwer 2009).

[A] Rebates in General

As part of the gradual harmonization process between the federal GST and provincial sales taxes over time, a variety of VAT rebates have come to be granted in sectors such as PNC and real property (new housing), and for specific goods such as books. Thus, even if the statutory rates of the federal and provincial taxes were identical, the effective rates of the provincial components of this integrated sales tax imposed on different activities would not necessarily be the same as those of the federal component, nor entirely identical in all the HST provinces. The reason is simply because the rebates that characterize the Canadian VAT system do not always apply in the same way in different provinces. The GST/HST and QST systems have featured rebates from their inception to achieve certain socio-economic objectives while recognizing the problems and burdens a pure exemption causes.[15]

[B] Rebates on PNC Bodies

Under the GST/HST system, PNC bodies fall within the scope of the GST/HST but many of their supplies are treated as exempt, with a fraction of the GST/HST paid on purchases rebated following the filing and processing of a rebate application. The same goes under the QST system. General rules that apply to registration of PNC bodies under the GST/HST system are described next.

PNC bodies that make exempt supplies exclusively cannot register for GST/HST. They can, however, claim a public service bodies' rebate for GST/HST paid on eligible expenses. PNC bodies that make taxable supplies have to register unless their supplies amount to less than CAD 50,000 per annum. A body with supplies below that amount is considered a small supplier and does not have to register, although it may do so voluntarily. A small supplier does not collect GST/HST on supplies and cannot receive GST/HST input tax credits on purchases. It may, however, claim a public service bodies' rebate for GST/HST paid on eligible expenses. This is developed further below.

A public services bodies' rebate is available if an organization falls into either one of the following categories:[16] (i) public institution; (ii) public service body [PSB]; (iii) qualifying non-profit organization [qualifying NPO]; (iv) selected public service body; or (v) First Nation or Inuit Government [self-government refund]. Here, public institution means a registered charity for income tax purposes that is also a school authority, a hospital authority, a public college or a university. A qualifying NPO means an NPO that receives at least 40% of its total revenue in government funding. A PSB may be a non-profit organization, a charity, a municipality, a school authority, a hospital authority, a public college or a university. A *selected* public service body may be a: school authority, university or public college that is operated other than for profit; a hospital authority; a municipality; a facility operator; or an external supplier. The rebate program in the first three cases is called the *GST/HST Public Service Bodies'*

15. Rebates that apply in areas outside the PNC sector are described in Bird & Gendron (n. 3 above), 550.
16. Canada Revenue Agency (n. 9 above).

Rebate, and the last is called *GST Self-Government Refund*. A First Nation or Inuit Government is also eligible provided that it has entered into an agreement with the Government of Canada that provides for a 100% refund of GST for goods and services acquired for self-government activities. Municipalities,[17] charities[18] and non-profit organizations[19] are collectively important and all feature their own set of rules. They include a list of goods and services that are exempt. Table 3.2 lists the supplies of municipalities, charities and non-profit organizations that are exempt. Subject to some minor exceptions, all GST/HST paid on purchases to make the supplies listed in the table are eligible for the public service bodies' rebate.

In principle, supplies not listed as exempt are taxable, either at positive rates (5% or 12% or 13%), or at the zero-rate. In order to appreciate the limits of the exemption of the PNC sector, it is highly instructive to list goods and services that are taxable when made by municipalities, charities and non-profit organizations. Table 3.3 lists such supplies. Many goods and services are taxable. In addition, goods and services exported by a charity or public institution entitle the organization to claim a rebate of 100% of the GST/HST paid. Similarly, municipalities in non-participating (non-HST) provinces can claim the provincial part of the HST when they buy goods in a participating (HST) province but consume the goods outside the participating provinces. In this system, organizations that make a combination of taxable and exempt supplies must allocate GST/HST paid to taxable and exempt activities. They are entitled to input tax credits on GST/HST paid on the portion of purchases allocated to taxable supplies, just like any other business. They are also entitled to a public service body rebate of the GST/HST paid on the portion of purchases allocated to exempt supplies. Two factors mitigate the difficulties generally associated with input tax allocations. First, since most supplies made by charities in practice are exempt, allocations are rarely needed for charities. Second, taxable supplies include potentially important ones from the point of view of transactions values. Examples of the latter include supplies of real property and personal capital property. In situations where taxable and exempt supplies are made by a PNC body, segregating purchases, tracking tax, and allocating GST/HST to such transactions is relatively straightforward when compared to other purchases.

17. Canada Revenue Agency, *GST/HST Information for Municipalities* (Government of Canada 2010), www.cra-arc.gc.ca/E/pub/gp/rc4049/rc4049-10e.pdf (accessed 18 May 2012).
18. Canada Revenue Agency, *Basic GST/HST Guidelines for Charities*, GST/HST Info Sheet GI-067 (Government of Canada 2011), www.cra-arc.gc.ca/E/pub/gi/gi-067/gi-067-e.pdf (accessed 18 May 2012); Canada Revenue Agency, *GST/HST Information for Charities* (Government of Canada 2010) www.cra-arc.gc.ca/E/pub/gp/rc4082/rc4082-10e.pdf (accessed 18 May 2012).
19. Canada Revenue Agency, *GST/HST Information for Non-Profit Organizations* (Government of Canada 2010), www.cra-arc.gc.ca/E/pub/gp/rc4081/rc4081-10e.pdf (accessed 18 May 2012).

Table 3.2 Supplies that Are Exempt[a] when Made by Municipalities, Charities or Non-profit Organizations

Municipalities[b]	*Charities*	*Non-Profit Organizations*
Library services	Most services	Admission to a place of amusement*
Registration, licences, and permits	Supplies of used or donated goods	Admission to athletic events*
Law enforcement and fire protection services	Short-term residential accommodation	Free supplies*
Residential services	Meals-on-wheels programs	Fund-raising activities*
Garbage collection	Parking space rentals	Gambling activities or events*
Municipal water distribution, sewerage, or drainage systems	Facility rentals (for events, for example)	Goods and services sold for direct cost*
Water (except bottled)	Catering services for private functions	Memberships*
Municipal transit services	Other exemptions[c]	Public libraries
Inter- and intra-municipal supplies		Recreational programs*
Ferry, road, and bridge tolls		Relief of poverty, suffering, or distress*
Admission to a place of amusement		
Amateur performances and events		
Recreational programs		
Relief of poverty, suffering, or distress		
Homemaker services		
Charitable events by a public institution		

Source: Author's compilation based on sources referenced in notes 17, 18 and 19.

Notes:

a Some exemptions are granted subject to de minimis rules.
b Other exempt services include: installing, replacing, repairing, and removing street or road signs, barriers, street or traffic lights, or any similar property; removing snow, ice, or water; removing, cutting, pruning, treating, or planting vegetation; repairing or maintaining roads, streets, sidewalks, or similar or adjacent property; or installing accesses or egresses.
c See items marked with an asterisk (*) in Non-profit Organizations column.

Table 3.3 Supplies that Are Taxable[a] when Made by Municipalities, Charities or Non-profit Organizations

Municipalities	*Charities*	*Non-profit Organizations*
Real property	Supplies of certain personal property	Registration for conferences, seminars, and trade shows
Personal property and personal capital property	New goods bought, manufactured, or produced for resale	Theatre subscriptions
Telecommunications services, electricity, and natural gas	Sales and leases of real property	Books and periodicals subscriptions
Municipal services provided on a fee-for-service basis	Admission to a place of amusement	Mailing list sales
End-user licences to remove forestry or fishery products	Some memberships that confer benefits	Advertising services
Services for testing and certifying property	Services of performing artists	Restaurant meals
Supplies of property or service made by a public institution or charity that is a municipality	Lottery tickets if sold for a provincial lottery corporation	Short-term rental accommodations
	Restaurant operations	Banquet facilities
	Professional theatre subscriptions	Club memberships

Source: Author's compilation based on sources referenced in notes 17, 18 and 19.

Note:

a Goods taxable at a rate of 0% (zero-rated) include: prescription drugs and dispensing fees; certain medical devices; basic groceries; most agriculture and fishery products; and exports.

Rebate factors vary by province and type of supplier, although the GST component (the federal component of GST/HST in participating provinces) is the same throughout Canada. Rebate factors are effectively rebate rates as they represent the fraction of GST/HST paid on purchases made to produce exempt supplies that is refunded to PNC bodies. Table 3.4 and shows rebate factors for the GST, HST and the QST for PNC bodies by type of supplier.

Certain supplies by PNC bodies are also eligible for special rebates as follows. First, books give rise to a 100% rebate of GST/HST, federal component only. Second, as noted earlier, goods and services exported by a registered charity or public institution give rise to a 100% rebate of GST/HST, both federal and provincial components; third, self-government refunds amount to 100% of tax paid; and finally, eligible facility operators or external suppliers obtain a rebate of 83% of GST/HST, federal component only.

Table 3.4 GST/HST and QST Rebate Factors (%) in PNC Sector, Canada, July 2010

Type of Organization	*GST*	*HST British Columbia*	*HST Ontario*	*HST New Brunswick*	*HST Newfoundland*	*HST Nova Scotia*	*QST Québec*
Municipality	100	75	78	57.14	0	57.14	0
Hospital authority, facility operator, or external supplier	83[b]	58	87	0[c]	0	83	51.5
School authority	68	87	93	0[c]	0	68	47
University or public college[a]	67	75	78	0	0	67	47
Charity or public institution	50	57	82	50	50	50	50
Qualifying non-profit organization	50	57	82	50[d]	50[d]	50[d]	50

Sources: KPMG, Tax Facts 2010–2011 (Canada: KPMG LLP), 204; Gendron (n. 1 above), 498; Canada Revenue Agency (n. 9 above).

Notes:

a Includes affiliated colleges or research institutes under the GST.
b Health care rebate applies to charities, non-profit organization and public institutions that render services similar to those usually rendered by hospitals.
c In New Brunswick, hospital and school authorities that are part of the provincial government pay HST on their purchases, but the full amount of HST (100% of the provincial component) is rebated to them.
d NPO qualifies for 50% rebate of provincial part of HST if it is not a selected Public Service Body.

Rebates are funded out of general government revenues. Interestingly, even though the GST/HST is a joint system, HST provinces do exert some control over their tax base – on the side of base expansion – by deviating from GST rebate rates for some components. GST rebates have been enhanced over time, most notably in the case of municipalities. The rebate factor rose from 57.14% of the tax paid on purchases to 100% in 2004. The rebate applies to the GST and the federal portion of the HST. It is interesting to note that the rebate rate for the provincial portion of the HST has remained at the old rate, and it is actually zero in Newfoundland and Labrador. One year later, the federal government extended the 83% GST rebate factor for hospitals to eligible charities, non-profit organizations and public institutions that render services similar to those usually rendered by hospitals. Rebates are most generous for the federal portion of the HST, but much less so for the provincial portion outside the Province of Nova Scotia. Overall, Nova Scotia has harmonized its rebate factors to the GST the most. QST rebates, which apply to the Province of Québec are less generous than GST rebates but more so than those in New Brunswick and Newfoundland and Labrador. Initial rebate factors – which have, on average, increased since 1991 – were initially set then to ensure that the average sectoral tax burden would not increase when the GST replaced the manufacturer's sales tax.

The rebate system only mimics zero-rating in two cases: first, regarding the GST municipalities pay on purchases, or the federal portion of the HST municipalities pay in the participating provinces, and second, with respect to the provincial component of HST paid on purchases by government-run hospitals and schools in New Brunswick. All eligible bodies must file the same tax return form to receive their *GST/HST Public Service Bodies' Rebate*, whether they are municipalities subject to the 100% GST rebate or any other type of eligible body to the rebate. Thus, no eligible PNC body handles GST/HST like an ordinary commercial business would. In an effort to alleviate compliance costs, however, the authorities allow charities to use special simplified tax calculation methods. The tradition of having different rebate rates for federal and provincial components continues with British Columbia and Ontario now in the system.

A system with fixed rebate rates appears, at first glance, quite simple and predictable for registrants. It may be the latter, but certainly not the former due to the heterogeneous treatment of entity and supplier types and actual supplies. Rebate rates do indeed vary by type of supplier, by the place where supplies are made, and by type of good or service supplied. As a result, there is non-neutral treatment of similar supplies made by different types of suppliers in different provinces. The varying rates may also create incentives to choose certain organizational forms over others to deliver certain goods and services over others. Another source of non-neutrality is the fact that the treatment of some supplies approximates zero-rating (when rebate rates are close to 100%) for some suppliers but not for others. Finally, businesses that operate in several provinces (e.g., New Brunswick and Québec) must fill two rebate claim forms that feature three sets of calculations.

In spite of the fact that the GST and QST are relatively well harmonized, the Québec rebate system is far less generous on average. Different rates for the same supplier-activity combinations introduce additional compliance costs. Under the

Québec system, the apparently equal - featuring 50% rebate rates in both cases - treatment of charitable and non-profit organizations effectively penalizes charitable organizations, since most of the supplies they make are exempt while most supplies made by non-profit organizations are taxable. As a consequence, non-profit organizations recover a larger fraction of the total QST paid on inputs than charities do. Beyond non-neutralities, the problem of the Canadian system is its failure to make a choice between full taxation and zero-rating of the PNC sector, even though it has already moved part of the way towards either goal in some cases. The Canadian system is stuck, in some way, since full zero-rating is unrealistic from a revenue perspective and inappropriate as an overall policy standpoint as it would fail to tax the consumption of the outputs of the PNC sector and therefore create its own non-neutralities. Calls have been made by experts in the Canadian business press to have the Canadian GST follow Australia and New Zealand in treating bodies in the PNC sector in the same manner as private-sector organizations.[20] Their plea remains unanswered to this day and there is no evidence that Finance Canada - the federal government department responsible for tax policy - is considering this now.

In closing, it should be noted that the GST/HST and QST systems operate independently of provincial RSTs, without any coordination. Services are usually not an issue since the vast majority of services are non-taxable under RSTs, but certainly many goods purchased and sold by PNC entities would be subject to RST unless specifically exempt by law.

[C] Treatment of Grants, Subsidies and Government Funding

It has been argued for the first time, and over a decade ago, that the correct treatment of grants or subsidies is to add them to the price of the good or service to arrive at the consideration for VAT purposes as they can be linked directly to supply.[21] Table 3.5 summarizes the correct treatment under various situations, including those where grants or subsidies are awarded. The shaded cell represents the situation of interest here, where an adjustment should be made for grants or subsidies directly linked to supply.

20. I. David & S. Poddar, *Now Fix Rest of GST*, National Post [Toronto], 6 February 2004, FP15.
21. M. Aujean, P. Jenkins & S. Poddar, *A New Approach to Public Sector Bodies*, 10 Intl. VAT Monit. 144 (1999).

Table 3.5 Requirements for Equal Treatment under Full Taxation

Criterion	*Taxation of Private Goods*	*Taxation of Public Goods*
Economic neutrality	Same treatment of supplies made by private businesses and PNC bodies	Apply to any consideration charged for supplies
Consideration	Apply VAT on amounts charged as consideration (price and grants directly linked to supply)	Supplies made for nil consideration call for zero tax (effectively zero-rating)
Input tax credit	Full (once supplies become taxable)	Full
Revenue loss	None	None if government collecting VAT is the one making the supply
Distortion of competition	None	None since public goods are supplied by private-sector businesses

Source: Gendron (n. 1 above), 485.

Private goods supplied by PNC entities without any grants are treated the same way as private goods supplied by the private sector: VAT applies to the full amount of consideration. In the case where grants are linked directly to the supply of private goods by PNC entities, the grant amounts must be taken as consideration. In practice, this means that grants and subsidies are included in taxable sales, as the following discussion of Canadian rules shows.

This treatment of grants avoids a distortion of competition between the private and public sectors as PNC grants linked to supply are used to equalize the full consideration for VAT purposes. With that adjustment, private and public-sector bodies rest on an equal footing for VAT purposes. Left unchecked, such a distortion would favour the public sector when grants would allow public-sector bodies to charge a lower output price than private-sector suppliers. This would amplify the advantage of public-sector bodies from not having to charge VAT while similar private-sector suppliers would have to. This advantage is clearly proportional to VAT rates and hence perceived to be serious in the EU due to high rates relative to countries such as Australia, Canada, Japan, New Zealand, Singapore and South Africa.

EU discussions have tended to focus on a narrow definition of distortion of competition: the advantage that may accrue to public-sector bodies from not having to charge VAT to users or consumers, while private-sector bodies making similar supplies have to. Again, the improper treatment of grants and subsidies – being left out of the calculation of consideration when they are directly linked to supply – has the potential to impede competition much more. This can be especially damaging if the entire system penalizes the development of outsourcing, which appears to be the case in the EU. Those layers of implicit support for public-sector bodies also appear to impose significant compliance costs on the private sector. Overall, this negates many of the cost advantages of outsourcing services, in favour of expenditures on tax planning to achieve a certain tax status or treatment of transactions.

The general rule for the treatment of grants and subsidies under the GST/HST is that '[I]f it is established that a supply takes place in return for a transfer payment, the payment may be regarded by the Department[22] as "consideration" for a supply. The amount of the transfer payment must then be used to calculate any Goods and Services Tax (GST) payable.'[23] For example, if a person receives a CAD 100,000 transfer payment from a grantor to set up a training program and arranges to train employees of the grantor's company, the payment will be regarded as consideration for the supply of training services to the grantor. The recipient of the payment must therefore collect the tax from the grantor. There are two tests for the tax to be payable. To determine whether a transfer payment is consideration for supply, it must first be established whether the recipient has or will make a supply as a result of having received the payment. If that is the case, then one must then determine whether there is a direct link between the transfer payment and the supply. There are several exclusions from this general rule. For instance, the following transfers are not considered to be consideration for supply: transfers that constitute charitable donations made in exchange for an income tax receipt; transfer payments by governments and public service bodies made in the public interest rather than for the direct benefit of the body itself; and transfers that form part of ongoing program of financial support.

The rules for the Canadian PNC sector may be summarized as follows. In the case of municipalities, transfer payments made or received in the public interest or for charitable purposes do not give rise to GST/HST either way (as above). If, however, there is a direct link between a transfer payment made by the grantor and a taxable supply made by the recipient of the payment, the transfer payment may be taxable and thus GST/HST may need to be collected on the amount. The tax treatment of transfer payments is determined by the Canada Revenue Agency on a case-by-case basis.[24] Rules for charities and non-profit organizations in respect of donations, grants and subsidies are similar to those that apply to municipalities. Transfer payments are not taxable unless there is a link between the payment and a supply. Sponsorships are usually not taxable but sponsorship payments used mainly (over 50%) to fund advertising expenses, for example, would be deemed to constitute such expenses and hence be taxable.[25] Again, this is assessed on a case-by-case basis by the tax authority.

There is also a government funding test for non-profit organizations. This refers to an amount of money (including a forgivable loan that is easily identifiable) that that is either used to support the non-profit organization's objectives but not to pay for goods or services supplied by the organization or the grantor, or for an exempt sale of

22. *Department* refers to the Canada Revenue Agency, the federal tax administration in Canada.
23. Canada Revenue Agency, *Goods and Services Tax Treatment of Grants and Subsidies*, GST/HST Technical Information Bulletin B-067 (Government of Canada 1992), www.cra-arc.gc.ca/E/pub/gm/b-067/b-067-e.html (accessed 18 May 2012).
24. Canada Revenue Agency (n. 17 above), 24.
25. Canada Revenue Agency, *GST/HST Information for Charities* (n. 18 above), 9; Canada Revenue Agency (n. 19 above), 10.

goods and services made by the organization but not for the use or consumption of the granter. A non-profit organization is said to be qualifying when its percentage of government funding for a given fiscal year is at least 40% of revenue.[26] For example, according to Table 3.4, a qualifying non-profit organization can claim 50% of the GST or the federal portion of HST. It can also claim 50% of the provincial part of the HST if it is not also a selected public service body.

In closing, it should be noted that recent case law has eschewed the policy guidelines of the GST/HST Technical Information Bulletin B-067 in favour of the use of fundamental contractual and statutory principles. A recent case[27] involved the City of Calgary and the Province of Alberta which entered into a series of agreements under which the province funded most of the capital costs of various public transit facilities and rolling stock that the city purchased or built. The Tax Court of Canada (TCC) ruled that the payments by the province were consideration for a taxable supply of a service made by the city to the province even though the city used the equipment to render exempt supplies. The decision meant that the city was entitled to claim input tax credits for the full recovery of the GST paid on the assets' input costs. The decision disregarded the various tests provided in The Act.[28] If this trend continues, there should be a serious revisiting of the proper treatment of grants and subsidies in Canada. In the interim, this case could complicate the characterizations of transactions.

§3.05 TAX EXPENDITURES ON CANADIAN VAT RELIEF

This section discusses tax expenditures on the Canadian rebate model within and outside the PNC sector, and presents estimates. Other VAT relief measures such as exemptions and non-export zero-rating are also shown for comparative purposes. Such estimates are quite illuminating, not so much in terms of large amounts of revenue foregone - which is fully expected - but rather for what they suggest about the importance of the economic distortions due to the exemption in the PNC sector. From the point of view of the overall efficiency of the VAT - including traditional measures of economic efficiency as well as compliance and administrative costs - operating a VAT where the PNC sector is fully taxable[29] is not equivalent to operating a VAT where the PNC sector is fully exempt but the VAT on purchases is returned in varying amounts to different organizations for different supplies, even with generous recoveries (say, over two-thirds of VAT paid). Obviously, the overall efficiency cost per dollar of revenue is higher under the latter scenario since the VAT fails to reach the intended VAT base: final consumption including, in practice, purchases by all non-registered persons. This means that most of the last component of value added is missed, where it is assumed that some VAT on inputs may end up being shifted forward in higher output prices. Given that many of the supplies of the PNC sector are income elastic, this last component is not trivial.

26. Canada Revenue Agency (n. 9 above), 17.
27. *City of Calgary* (2009, TCC 272).
28. P. Mitchell, *GST Policy on Grants and Subsidies*, 17 Can. Tax Highlights 9 (2009).
29. See the discussion of New Zealand in the next section.

Table 3.6 shows estimated GST tax expenditures as a percentage of GST revenues for various rebates, exemptions and zero-ratings.[30] Data are presented for two years (2005 and 2008) since the GST rate fell from 7% in 2005 to ultimately 5% for part of the fiscal year ending in 2008. There was a transitional rate of 6% in between. This fact explains the drop in tax expenditures from 2005 to 2008. All monetary figures are expressed in millions of current Canadian dollars, and the base used to calculate the percentage figures is the net GST collected during the year. The figures are only estimates, and as such, cannot be added up meaningfully.

It is striking that tax expenditures on the zero-rating of basic groceries exceeds any one of the other line items. The definition of basic groceries is evidently broad. Tax expenditures on rebates and exemptions for items outside the PNC sector are shown for comparative purposes only. The top three rebate items, in decreasing order, were municipalities, education and hospitals, with tax expenditures on municipalities' rebates more than twice as large as the second largest component. Tax expenditures on exemptions are not so directly interpreted. Their estimates reflect the revenues that would be collected if the supplies were taxed but input tax credits were allowed for taxable purchases by suppliers. The top three exemption items, in decreasing order, were health care, education and municipalities.

Three remarks about these numbers are in order: first, there is less dispersion in exemptions than rebates and the top three items are of the same order of magnitude and fairly close. Second, health care exemptions rank higher than hospital rebates because the former also reflects the delivery of health care by non-hospital institutions and centres, and non-profit and charitable organizations. Finally, tax expenditures on rebates are more important than the (loosely) corresponding expenditures on exemptions. Again, rebates have a direct impact on revenues since effectively transform the exemption of PNC bodies into a partial zero-rating system. A genuine zero-rating system for PNC bodies has been touted before; it is clear from the top half of the table that such a system would sacrifice significantly more revenue than is shown in the table. In terms of Table 3.4, that would make rebate rates in the leftmost equal to 100% throughout. The additional revenue loss would also affect provinces with VATs if those were to increase rebate rates on the provincial portion of the HST or on the QST.

Table 3.6. Estimated GST Tax Expenditures, CAD millions (% of GST Revenues), 2008

Item	*2005*	*2008*
Rebates		
Charities	295(0.09)	255(0.08)
Non-profit organizations	75(0.02)	60(0.02)
Education	805(2.43)	675(2.02)

30. The data are drawn from R.M. Bird, *The GST in Canada: Plus ça change, plus c'est la même chose?*, 63 Bull. Intl. Tax. 414 (2009). The chapter should be consulted for additional details such as data notes, caveats and original primary data sources.

Item	*2005*	*2008*
Hospitals	515 (1.56)	435(1.30)
Municipalities	1,730 (5.23)	1,520(4.55)
Housing	960 (2.90)	815(2.44)
Tourists	80 (0.02)	10(0.00)
Exemptions		
Child care	155 (0.47)	130(0.39)
Education	555 (1.68)	460(1.38)
Health care	585 (1.77)	490(1.47)
Municipalities	430 (1.30)	365(1.09)
Legal aid	25 (0.01)	25(0.01)
Housing	1,375 (4.16)	1,150(3.44)
Road tolls, bridges, ferries	25 (0.01)	25(0.01)
Zero-rating		
Basic groceries	3,920(11.86)	3,200(9.58)
Drugs and medical devices	920 (2.78)	785(2.35)

Source: Bird (n 30 above), 418.

To conclude, the GST system relies on extensive tax relief using rebates, exemptions, and zero-rating. This adds up to substantial relief indeed and significant foregone revenues. This problem could be mitigated if grants and subsidies were cut. How much is not known as sufficiently detailed grant and subsidy figures are unavailable. Based on 2007–2008 fiscal statistics, total GST foregone as a result of broadly defined GST relief (including minor items not included in the table) added up to at least CAD 16 billion while the GST's net revenue yield was about CAD 29.9 billion. This means that that all forms of relief amounted to over half (53.5%) of actual GST collections. On the bright side, the system provides a very clear path to increasing revenues; either: reduce rebate rates on PNC bodies (the indirect and less visible approach); convert exempt goods and services into taxable good and services (the direct and visible approach); or convert zero-rated items into taxable items (the politically reckless approach). In relation to the last possibility, it should be noted that the federal income tax return features a refundable GST tax credit that is meant to compensate low-income households for some of the GST paid. The credit is proportional to the number of dependents and is clawed back with rising household income. Claiming it requires filing a federal tax return, something not all low-income individuals or households necessarily do or wish to do.

§3.06 OVERVIEW OF OTHER SYSTEMS

This section presents a brief overview of the notable alternative treatments of public-sector bodies that have been used in practice in jurisdictions other than Canada. It does not review those models in great detail as they have been discussed extensively and recently in the literature.[31] The discussion of the treatment of PNC bodies in Australia and New Zealand is very brief since, as argued below, the central question in the remainder of the paper concerns the suitability of the Canadian model to the EU.[32]

[A] Australia

All activities of public bodies and non-profit organizations (the 'PN' of PNC) are within the scope of the GST. Two important features of the system as it applies to the PN sector are worth noting. First, there is no exemption system applying specifically to supplies by PN bodies. Second, expenditure budgets approved by Parliament for such bodies are not, unlike the case of New Zealand (see below), viewed as consideration for the supply of public administration or other functions of the body.

Examples of supplies made by a non-profit organization that will be taxable under GST include: entry to an event such as a show, concert or exhibition; hiring out rooms or equipment for a fee; providing membership to an organization; or selling items such as books, clothing and most food items. Most education, child care and health services are zero-rated (*GST-free*). Some transactions remain exempt (*input taxed*) however. An example would include the supply of food and beverages provided at school tuck shops run by non-profit organizations.

A few special rules apply to charities (the 'C' of PNC), gift-deductible entities and government schools. The following goods and services are zero-rated when supplied by charities, gift-deductible entities or government schools: sales of donated second-hand goods; raffles and bingos; and non-commercial sales of goods and services (including accommodation). Sales by such entities will be zero-rated when deemed non-commercial. This determination requires that the amount charged by the organization for the good or service be either less than 50% (75% for accommodation) of the market value, or less than 75% of the amount the organization paid to acquire the good or service. A charity, gift-deductible entity or government school may also elect to make its sales at a fund-raising event exempt if the event does not recur regularly. This would effectively relieve the organization of the obligation to collect GST on the supplies, calculating GST on supplies and purchases, filing GST returns and making payments. As an additional measure to relieve the compliance burden, non-profit organizations that are members of the same non-profit association can elect to form a GST group if they make many sales and purchases among themselves. With group treatment, the members do not have to pay GST on group transactions and, of course, no credits can be claimed. Activities eligible for the exemption election would include shows, dinners and performances, events where all goods except alcohol and tobacco are sold for AUD 20 or less, and approved fund-raising events. Supplies made at

31. See, for example, Gendron (n. 1 above), 492, on which the overviews that follow draw; van Brederode (n. 14 above), 194; M. Aujean, *Application of VAT to public Bodies: The EU VAT System, Current Issues and Proposals*, in *VAT in Africa*, 71 (R. Krever ed., Pretoria University Law Press 2008); and A. Schenk & O. Oldman, *Value Added Tax: A Comparative Approach*, 285 (Cambridge University Press 2007).
32. Furthermore, R. Millar, 'Smoke and Mirrors: Applying the Full Taxation Model to Government under the Australian and New Zealand GST Laws', Ch. 4 in this volume, presents a highly detailed discussion of the functioning of the systems in Australia and New Zealand.

regularly occurring events (fifteen times per year or more) will be automatically taxable.

[B] New Zealand

The base of New Zealand's VAT (GST) is probably the broadest in operation today. The treatment of the PNC sector contributes to this state of affairs. As in the case of Australia, New Zealand's GST distinguishes itself from other VATs around the world by treating entities in the PNC sector as suppliers to both the private and the public sector.[33] This treatment means that goods and services provided by the PNC sector are taxable. Fees and charges are used to measure the value of supplies to the private sector. Following a unique model, and unlike Australia, supplies to the government are measured by the corresponding parliamentary budget appropriations. Generally speaking, PNC bodies add VAT to their invoices and obtain credit for the VAT paid on purchases from private *or* PNC sector suppliers. This simple and neutral treatment effectively eliminates the numerous non-neutralities encountered when PNC supplies are exempt while similar private-sector supplies are taxable.

There are further differences with Australia, however. The New Zealand system allows for even fewer zero-ratings and optional exemptions. Going further than Australia and Canada, the New Zealand GST taxes the 'untouchables' such as food, children's clothing, and books and medicine.[34] There remain some concessions under the New Zealand system, however. For example, non-profits funded by donations effectively receive zero-rated treatment. More importantly, administrative concessions are granted to non-profit organizations as a means of facilitating compliance rather than as a matter of tax policy. Those concessions relate to accounting methods, registration thresholds and group taxation. A desirable feature of such concessions is that they do not fundamentally undermine the functioning of the VAT.

[C] European Union

In the EU, so-called public bodies are governed by public law and are within the scope of the VAT for the integrality of their economic activities.[35] In principle, supplies by public bodies are taxable but then public bodies that engage in transactions in their role as public authorities are non-taxable persons placed outside the scope of the VAT.[36] An

---

33. Schenk & Oldman (n. 31 above), 289.
34. 'Untouchables' are, in the mind of the public, what should just not be taxed. See D. White, *The Serious Research Gap on VAT/GST: A New Zealand Perspective after 20 Years of GST*, 18 Intl. VAT Monit. 343 (2007). There are obviously other differences between the Australian and New Zealand regimes but they are not essential to this exposition and are therefore omitted here.
35. This subsection draws on Gendron (n. 1 above). A recent paper by de la Feria (n. 2 above) provides a critical assessment of the EU VAT, including a discussion of EU refund schemes. I thank Michel Aujean for pointing me to an earlier version of that paper.
36. Council Directive 2006/112/EC of 28 November 2006 on the common system of value added tax, Art. 13, OJ L/347/1 of 2006, 12 ('EU VAT Directive').

example would be a local government that collects refuse. Such entities do not charge VAT on their supplies and they cannot obtain credit for VAT paid on their purchases. This is subject to exceptions. The convoluted decision-tree nature of the problem is highlighted in the following passage: 'Overall, the VAT treatment of public-sector bodies is dependent on the answers given to two fundamental questions: Is the transaction taxable or non-taxable, and, if it is taxable, is it exempt or not exempt?'[37] To complicate matters further, exempt status features derogation for taxation, while taxable (with 'not negligible' supplies) status allows for derogation for exemption. Moreover, some services are exempt in the EU. Important examples include: public postal services, hospital and medical care, education and university education, and activities of charitable organizations.[38] This list also contains the major exempt supplies made by public bodies under Canada's GST/HST system, except for postal services, which are taxable in Canada. In fact, their presence in this list points to a problem: the fact that potential competition from private-sector providers exists in several of those areas.

One of the notable results of the system sketched above is that public bodies often need to compute complicated input VAT apportionments and may still end up bearing a significant amount of unrelieved input VAT. In response to this reality, authorities in some EU Member States including Denmark, Finland, the Netherlands, Sweden and the United Kingdom have established systems to compensate public bodies for the input VAT paid to make exempt or non-taxable supplies.[39] Just outside the EU, Norway also features such a system. Those refund systems are run outside the VAT framework and may be funded out of general revenues or by subnational governments directly (so-called self-funded in the latter case). On the surface, those refund systems are indeed similar to the Canadian rebate model. In contrast to the latter model, the application of EU refunds is not universal and far less uniform and certain, as is illustrated next.

A specific example of the lack of uniformity of EU VAT refund schemes is provided by refuse collection services.[40] Such schemes are general and apply to non-taxable or exempt activities of local governments. Norway, even though it is not a Member State, is added for comparative purposes. Table 3.7 summarizes the key characteristics of the schemes in operation to compensate European suppliers of refuse services for the VAT paid on inputs to ostensibly level the playing field between government and private-sector supplies. Individual refund rates are unavailable but they are known to vary by activity, and it is suspected that they are beneath 100%. As it should, the Netherlands provides refunds for the VAT incurred in the Netherlands or in other EU Member States, while none of the other refund schemes covers the VAT paid to other EU Member States.[41] The United Kingdom's refund scheme is the only one

37. de la Feria (n. 2 above), 149.
38. EU VAT Directive (n. 36 above), Art. 132.
39. Aujean (n. 1 above), 514.
40. Gendron (n. 1 above), 501. Additional details are provided by M.C. Wassenaar & R.H.J.M. Gradus, *Contracting Out: The Importance of a Solution for the VAT Distortion*, 50 Cesifo Econ. Stud. 377 (2004).
41. Netherlands: Turnover Tax Act of 18 June 1968 wrk art G (1968).

that is funded by the central government. All the others create vertical imbalances by forcing local authorities to contribute the majority of the cost of the refunds by bearing offsetting reductions in grants from the central or federal government. Increased VAT receipts appear to have been insufficient to pay fully for the refund schemes. In situations of imbalance, central governments may benefit from net revenue windfalls while local public bodies are left to pay the bills and may need to increase local property taxes, fees, and other levies to make up for the shortfall.

Table 3.7 Input VAT Compensation on Public-Sector Services in Europe

Country	*Compensation scheme*[a]	*Suppliers*	*Funding of scheme*
Denmark	VAT refund, taxable activity (refuse collection)	Counties, municipalities, inter-authority companies	Municipalities fund a 'VAT Compensation Fund'
Finland	VAT refund	Municipalities, municipal federations	Municipalities fund the refund scheme
Netherlands	VAT refund	Municipalities, provinces	Through reduction in grants[b]
Norway	VAT refund, taxable activities (postal services, refuse collection, etc.)	Local governments	Through reduction in general grant to municipalities[b]
Sweden	VAT refund	Municipalities, country councils	Municipalities and country councils fund the refund scheme
United Kingdom	VAT refund	Local and police authorities	Central government revenues, no contribution by local authorities

Source: Gendron (n. 1 above), 502.

Notes:

a Further details, including exceptions and exclusions, are provided by Wassenaar & Gradus (n 40 above).
b Additional VAT receipts from increased contracting out are added to the fund, but that does not cover the drop in grants).

The above example is slightly dated today, but fortunately refund schemes have recently reappeared in EU discussions and research activity, more recently under the heading of partial exemption.[42] The next section addresses criticisms of such schemes in some detail.

§3.07 BENCHMARKING SYSTEMS AND LESSONS FOR THE EU

This section presents a high-level comparison of the alternative systems currently in use worldwide. It then proceeds to evaluate the strengths and weaknesses of the Canadian model with an eye to its applicability in the EU context.

[A] A High-Level Comparison

The Australian–New Zealand system comes closest to the theoretical ideal of full taxation of the PNC sector. It does so in a relatively clean way while relying on a few administrative accommodations for entities that would otherwise incur disproportionate compliance costs. It is by far the simplest of all alternatives considered here. The New Zealand treatment of the PNC sector, in particular, receives support in the comparative sales taxation literature.[43] The Australian model appears to be somewhat more complex.

The Canadian system occupies an interesting middle ground with a broad (but incomplete) exemption that is partly offset by rebates that can be quite generous in some cases. While GST/HST rebate rates have been relatively stable, they have slowly become more generous with the passage of time. The Canadian system is not simple, however, and therefore imposes compliance and administrative costs which would exceed those under full taxation. That is because PNC bodies get special VAT treatment which differs from that received by other persons. Conceptually, this dual (exempt public sector versus taxable private sector) system is more complex than the Australia–New Zealand model. In practice, however, many outputs are taxable (as shown in an earlier section) and the uniform application of the Canadian public service bodies' rebate system across the entire country (including all provinces and territories) does tend to undo some of the complexity.

The EU system lies at the other extreme from the New Zealand model. The complexity of its treatment of public service bodies appears to even surpass that of the Canadian system by a wide margin. It suffers from many well-documented - although hard to quantify - economic non-neutralities, arbitrariness and proneness to litigation. One problem less frequently mentioned but noted in the financial and trade press from time to time is this: the EU VAT system is a fount of professional fees for tax advisors and consultants in the VAT planning and recovery businesses. Taking a broad view of efficiency forces one to consider those compliance costs. In turn, aggressive planning entails higher administrative and legal costs. All of this is heaped on top of efficiency losses due to distortions.

42. R. de la Feria, *Partial-Exemption Policy in the United Kingdom*, 21 Intl. VAT Monit. 119 (2010).
43. van Brederode (n. 14 above), 202.

In practice, things are of course not that clear-cut and there is much more to consider. As a way of avoiding this messy exercise, as well as to set up the next subsection, Table 3.8 presents a subjective evaluation of the four alternative VAT models for the PNC sector. The criteria are arbitrarily selected and restrictive. They include: administrability, simplicity, efficiency, predictability and base autonomy. *High* stands for very good while *Low* stands for poor.

Table 3.8 Evaluation of VAT Models for the PNC Sector

Criterion/ Country	*Australia*	*New Zealand*	*Canada*	*EU*
Administrability	High	High	High	Medium
Simplicity	Medium	High	Medium	Low
Efficiency	Medium	High	Medium	Low
Predictability	High	High	High	Low
Base autonomy	Not applicable	Not applicable	Medium	Medium

The New Zealand model comes close to the ideal of full taxation and thus ranks highest against all criteria, with Australia a close second. Base autonomy is irrelevant to both countries: New Zealand is a unitary country, while GST revenues in Australia are distributed to states and territories based on a formulary approach. In both cases, compliance and administrative costs are unlikely to be trivial, but would be lower than under the Canadian or EU models. Predictability is an important consideration and relates to the comparison of economic outcomes with legislative intent. Simpler systems tend to be more predictable. Both Canada and EU countries can influence the base using rebate systems.

[B] Canada and EU: Refund (Rebate) Schemes Reconsidered

Various commentators seem near-unanimous in their assessment that national refund schemes in the EU have not worked too well and that they do not, in their current form, present a solution to the problem. This situation calls for deeper reforms,[44] possibly including genuine VAT harmonization of the kind Canadian provinces and the federal government have been engaged in since 1991. The reasons for these negative views are numerous. National refund schemes introduce several new distortions, inequities, asymmetric treatment of states and hence some forms of discrimination, with some schemes seen as constituting illegal state aid. In addition, in most cases the schemes are disconnected from the VAT system as they involve budget expenditures that fall outside the VAT systems.

44. M. Aujean, *Le système de TVA et le marché unique européen*, 49 Reflets & perspectives de la vie économique 91, 101 (2010); Aujean (n. 1 above), 515; de la Feria (n. 42 above), 123; de la Feria (n. 2 above), 162.

The most obvious way out of this quagmire is to move to the full taxation of the PNC sector in all EU Member States. This proposal – with a variant featuring an option to collect tax – has been made in the eventuality that the United States would adopt a stand-alone federal VAT.[45] Is a move to full taxation a likely outcome for the EU, given the history and the current context and decision-making rules? The answer must be an unqualified no.

The second way is to rationally analyse the case for exemption using criteria such as effectiveness, economic (efficiency plus compliance plus administration) costs and other distortions (competition, market structure, organizational form, etc.). This is a conceptually correct approach that would nevertheless consume immense resources only to conclude, years later, that the case for the exemption of the PNC sector no longer exists. This approach is perhaps more likely than a brutal move to full taxation, but it would be pointless. In the meantime, converting some presently exempt supplies into taxable ones and/or providing options to tax could nibble at some inefficiencies and inequities without solving the overall problem.

The third way would be to consider the Canadian rebate model for possible adoption and (necessarily) adaptation to EU circumstances. This idea, beyond the mere consideration stage, faces several objections that have been expressed in conference commentaries and elsewhere.[46] First, the Canadian model does not address the subsidization and price controls that prevail with public-sector bodies and does not resolve the issues that lie beyond the *bookkeeping* aspects of things: outsourcing, avoidance (such as using shell companies from which to rent services), and input VAT allocations. Second, it does not provide a sufficient departure from existing national refund schemes to be a worthwhile intermediate step towards full taxation. Those are important objections and they are addressed separately next.

When compared with the current EU system featuring some selective national rebate schemes, it is correct to say that the Canadian rebate model does not fully eliminate the problems noted above and which are associated with exemptions in general.[47] Only full taxation would do that. On the other hand, direct subsidization of the PNC sector is an issue that goes beyond the VAT system. In Canada, subsidy numbers are not even known. In an ideal world, it would be ideal to subsidize – only when absolutely necessary – PNC bodies directly and completely outside the VAT system. Contexts also differ as the price controls in the PNC sector in Canada are much less important than in the EU. One can surmise that the Canadian model mitigates many of the distortions from the exemption (especially the penalty on outsourcing that comes from the incentive to self-supply) given the high rebate factors in place in some major sectors (see Table 3.4). The bookkeeping aspects arise because many VAT versus expenditure policy permutations are possible: increase rebates to 100% and cut subsidies commensurately; reduce rebates to zero (pure exemption) and increase subsidies commensurately; zero-rate and cut subsidies commensurately, and so on. In practice, those are political choices. One can surmise that the Canadian system, in this respect, is less distorting

45. Gendron (n. 1 above), 506, with support from Aujean (n. 1 above), 516.
46. Aujean (n. 1 above), 516.
47. The various economic effects of exemptions are reviewed in Gendron (n. 1 above), 489.

than the EU system because it is less complex and the fixed rebate factors provide it with a degree of predictability and stability.

It is fair to say that the dual Canadian system (public sector exempt with rebates versus taxable private sector) violates VAT logic, just like the EU system does. At the same time, however, the Canadian rebate system departs significantly from EU rebate schemes in two respects. First, the mechanics: the uniformity of the rebate factors and application rules as per federal-provincial harmonization arrangements removes much discretion for provinces, aside from rebate factors on the provincial (only) portion of harmonized taxes. To transpose this to the EU context would require giving some latitude to states with respect to rebate factors, but those could be negotiated subject to binding floors, just as in the case of VAT rates. Second, the process: the Canadian rebate system came about during federal-provincial harmonization negotiations which involved federal compensation paid to some provinces for revenue losses. In principle, even if one accepts that the Canadian rebate system is not a satisfactory intermediate step for full taxation, considering the model may provide an outstanding opportunity to harmonize VAT regimes throughout the EU - at least in one important dimension - perhaps using national refund schemes as a point of departure. To say that outsourcing in the EU is insufficient to justify the generalization of rebates à la Canada is akin to saying that the market that is being impeded will have to improve on its own before one removes the tax penalty that is impeding its growth in the first place. It is not a good argument to delay the realization of efficiency gains.

[C] Lessons for the EU

The compliance and administrative burdens of the Canadian model are not trivial. But the application of such a system in an EU context could probably lower those costs from their current levels by improving predictability, and dispensing with notions or tests such as distortion of competition, delivery as public authorities, out of scope supplies, and so forth. In its present form, the Canadian system relies on a very significant amount of relief and hence sacrifices significant revenue. Ultimately, the rebate model has been too gradualist and has tended to converge towards the wrong system because its partial or full zero-rating is too generous a treatment for the PNC sector, conceptually speaking. It certainly appears to achieve a number of socio-economic objectives but does so at a cost. Full zero-rating would end up creating new non-neutralities by favouring outputs of PNC sector activities as opposed to others. Moreover, given that the income elasticity of much of the outputs of the sector (e.g., education, health, municipal infrastructure) exceeds one, the rebate model may end up sacrificing growing amounts of revenue over time. This problem could be mitigated provided that subsidies are also cut but this is a much harder result to guarantee as subsidies are far less transparent than the rebate system and are far more open to political manipulation. Again, the correct VAT treatment of the outputs of the PNC sector is full taxation, full stop.

Given the existing expenditure framework in Canada (transfers, equalization, etc.), the Canadian model could of course be improved by making all the outputs of the

PNC sector taxable and using expenditure policies to replicate some of the targeted forms of relief (only if politically or practically - in the case of some charities, for example - necessary) as well as the income tax system to provide GST relief to low-income households. There does not seem to be any appetite for such reforms in Canada at the moment, although one should note that the increasing harmonization of the sales tax field would seem to be setting the stage for such reforms to take place in the next five years. That is especially likely if the provinces that will still operate retail sales taxes after 1 July 2010 (Saskatchewan; Manitoba; Prince Edward Island) finally join in by harmonizing their retail sales taxes with the federal GST.[48]

Whether the Canadian model should be used elsewhere ultimately depends on the particular context. As noted elsewhere, a country considering the adoption of a VAT would do well by getting the design right and applying full taxation to the PNC sector from inception.[49] This is an easy case compared to situations where an existing system is flawed but hard to reform for a number of reasons; the EU VAT provides a good example of this situation. At this point, it is useful to consider the suggestion to apply the cost-benefit criterion when addressing concessional exemptions.[50] From the perspective of both the EU and Canadian models, it is not known whether concessional exemptions achieve clear objectives at a reasonable cost. One could guess that they do not. The earlier discussion of tax expenditures under the Canadian system provides a rough indication of the magnitude of concessions, though, but is not informative as to their effectiveness. The legal and collateral costs of both systems are also hard to measure, although one may presume that they are higher in the EU due to the lack of structure of rebates (when compared to the Canadian system with fixed rebate factors), and its considerable complexity and attendant litigation.

Again, the ideal solution for the EU would be simple: bring the entire PNC sector under VAT along the lines of the Australian–New Zealand model. Although it lies far beyond the scope of this chapter, a full cost-benefit analysis that incorporated all compliance and administrative costs (in addition to cost-benefit considerations) would probably support that notion. Given the history of policy-making and rules that govern decision-making in the EU, the New Zealand (and even Australian) model seems too radical a surgery to contemplate as a fix for the exemptions of the PNC sector in the EU. The other extreme - leaving the EU system as it is - is undesirable and has given rise to plentiful criticism and calls for change.

As a practical compromise, a variant of the Canadian rebate model suitably adapted to EU conditions is worthy of serious consideration for EU Member States. Based on available evidence and the foregoing discussion, it appears reasonable to suppose that the Canadian rebate model outperforms the EU model on the basis of the cost-benefit criterion. Perhaps the Canadian model could constitute the first step in breaking the EU VAT impasse in the PNC sector.

48. While this was correct at time of writing, see the forthcoming changes in British Columbia (n. 4 above) and Québec (n. 5 above). Prince Edward Island will also join The HST in 2013.
49. This point was made in the case of a potential US VAT by Gendron (n. 1 above), 508.
50. R. de la Feria & R. Krever, 'Ending VAT Exemptions: Learning from Experience, Towards a Post-Modern VAT', Ch. 1 in this volume.

CHAPTER 4

Smoke and Mirrors: Applying the Full Taxation Model to Government under the Australian and New Zealand GST Laws

Rebecca Millar*

§4.01 INTRODUCTION

The VAT treatment of government under the EU VAT Directive[1] will be well known to most readers of this volume. Article 13(1) excludes many government activities from the tax base by providing that government authorities (national, regional, and local) 'shall not be regarded as taxable persons in respect of the activities or transactions in which they engage as public authorities, even where they collect dues, fees, contributions or payments in connection with those activities or transactions.' The exclusion also applies to 'other bodies governed by public law', in respect of which Article 13(2) specifies a wide range of exempt activities that may be regarded as activities in which those bodies engage as public authorities.[2,3] The exclusion of government activities is subject to two exceptions:

* I am grateful to Erik Larsen (Norwegian Ministry of Finance) for alerting me to the case law regarding the Norwegian rebate schemes and providing me with links to the relevant materials. Thanks also to Christophe Waerzeggers (Consulting Counsel, Legal Department, International Monetary Fund) for assisting me by explaining the EU financing arrangements, providing links to associated information, and for acting as a sounding board and assisting with proofing. All errors are, of course, entirely of my own making. This paper describes the Australian and New Zealand GST laws at 1 July 2011.

1. Council Directive 2006/112/EC of 28 November 2006 on the common system of value added tax, OJ L347/1–118 of 2006 ('EU VAT Directive').
2. The list covers a fairly extensive range of exemptions, including those available under transitional derogations: EU VAT Directive, Article 13(2) lists 'Articles 132, 135, 136 and 371, Articles 374 to 377, Article 378(2), Article 379(2) or Articles 380 to 390b'.
3. Throughout this paper, the word 'government' is used as a generic term to cover government authorities and other bodies covered by public law, however they might be categorized by particular countries.

- activities or transactions in respect of which the exclusion of government 'would lead to significant distortions of competition'; and
- activities specified in Annex I of the Directive, which are generally commercial activities of government, unless they are carried out on a very small scale.[4]

Article 13 gives rise to complex legal issues: What is a government authority? What is an 'other body governed by public law'? When does a public authority engage in a transaction as a public authority? What is a significant distortion of competition and when would such a distortion arise if government activities or transactions were excluded from the VAT system? What are the boundaries of each of the matters specified in Annex I and how small is 'very small scale'? Excluding government from the concept of a taxable person is effectively equivalent to exemption and even if these legal complexities could be resolved, government entities would still face all the same negative consequences of exemption that are faced by other entities making exempt supplies. Indeed, using exclusions from the concept of taxable person to effect the exemption exacerbates these problems by adding to the compliance burden of government, because it complicates the way in which the affected entities are required to determine their deductible input tax.

As with other exemptions discussed in this book, the EU VAT treatment of government has come under scrutiny as an area for reform. In their seminal 1999 article, Aujean, Jenkins, and Poddar criticize the complexity of the European approach and recommend the adoption of a full taxation model such as that used in the New Zealand GST.[5] Professor Gendron also generally favours full taxation. In his recommendations for the design of a United States VAT, he concludes that 'the case for full taxation of the PNC sector is strong' and states that:

> [T]he Australian-New Zealand model emerges as the best alternative to the exempt treatment of PNC sector supplies. Under this model, essentially all the goods and services supplied by PNC bodies are within the scope of the VAT and treated like any supplies from the private sector.[6]

---

4. The Annex specifies the exceptions by reference to different criteria. It includes exceptions for particular supplies (new goods manufactured for sale; telecommunications services; water, gas, electricity and thermal energy; transport of passengers or goods; port and airport services; warehousing; the organization of trade fairs and exhibitions, and the running of staff shops, cooperatives, industrial canteens, and similar institutions), for activities carried out by specified types of person (commercial publicity bodies; travel agents; and commercial activities of radio and television bodies, not including their non-commercial activities), and for certain transactions of agricultural intervention agencies: EU VAT Directive, Annex I.
5. M. Aujean, P. Jenkins & S. Poddar, *A New Approach to Public Sector Bodies*, 10 Intl VAT Monit. 144 (1999).
6. P.-P. Gendron, *How Should the United States Treat Government Entities, Nonprofit Organizations, and Other Tax-Exempt Bodies Under a VAT?*, 63 Tax L. Rev. 477–508, 507–508 (2010). The acronym PNC, which appears in the quoted passages, refers to the wider sector (public sector bodies, non-profit entities and charities) addressed in Gendron's paper.

As alternatives, he recommends either the Canadian rebate system (explained in Chapter 3 of this book) or 'at the very least' the taxation of all specific fees charged by government.[7] In some senses, these two recommendations go to different aspects of the issue. The rebate approach merely relieves government from the problems created by input tax credit denials by effectively zero-rating government activities. The taxation of specific fees goes more to expanding the tax base; it has an impact on input tax recovery only if the law is designed in a way that links input tax recovery to the making of taxable supplies, but while this is a common design feature of VAT laws, it is neither universally nor necessarily so.[8]

While reiterating support for the New Zealand model in *VAT in Developing and Transitional Countries*, Bird and Gendron recognize that some countries may lack the administrative capacity to implement the full taxation approach, or may simply be unwilling to do so.[9] Reversing the order of Professor Gendron's earlier preferences, they recommend that such countries should start by taxing user fees and then gradually move towards a Canadian rebate approach.[10]

In contrast, Ebrill et al. the authors of *The Modern VAT*, appear less committed to the full taxation approach, noting that from a revenue perspective there is little difference between full taxation and exemption since 'any revenue that the government collects by denying the recovery of input tax on purchase[s] by public bodies is exactly offset by an increased cost to the government of financing those bodies' activities'.[11] Nonetheless, they note that non-revenue reasons favouring the full taxation of government are the same as those that apply to any other entity: preventing the distortion of production decisions (driven by cost minimization rather than profit maximization), the complexities of partial exemption, the bias to self-supply, and classification disputes.[12] They conclude that such distortions are reduced by the Canadian rebate system but can be more systematically addressed by adopting the New Zealand full taxation model, which preserves the VAT chain by taxing all transactions.[13]

Despite their differences, the EU VAT and the Australian and New Zealand GSTs have common origins and share many similar design features. If full taxation is possible in Australia and New Zealand, it is possible in the EU; if complexities have

7. P.-P. Gendron, *Value-Added Tax Treatment of Public Sector Bodies and Non-Profit Organizations: A Developing Country Perspective* (International Tax Program Papers 2005), TP Paper 0514.
8. Australia and Switzerland both link input tax recovery to the carrying on of an economic activity, then deny credits for inputs that are private or domestic or that relate to making exempt supplies: A New Tax System (Goods and Services Tax) Act 1999 (Australia) ('GST Act 1999 (Aus)'), Div.11 & 15; Federal Law with regard to Value Added Tax (Switzerland), Articles 28 & 29 (unofficial translation, www.deloitte.com/assets/Dcom-Switzerland/Local%20 Assets/Documents/EN/Tax/VAT/ch_en_Swiss%20VAT%20Law.pdf).
9. R.M. Bird & P.-P. Gendron, *VAT in Developing and Transitional Countries*, 89–97 (Cambridge University Press 2007).
10. *Ibid.*, 97.
11. L. Ebrill et al., *The Modern VAT*, 92 (International Monetary Fund 2001).
12. *Ibid.* A bias to import services will also be present if the law does not effectively ensure that imported services are taxed.
13. Ebrill et al. (n. 11 above), 93.

arisen there, it is highly likely that they would also arise if the EU were to adopt the full taxation model. Given these similarities and the widespread support for the approach to the public sector adopted in Australia and New Zealand, it is worthwhile considering exactly how those models actually work in practice and evaluating them against the two separate streams of reasoning that underpin support for the full taxation model:

- removing the problems created by exemption (for government) and more generally preserving the VAT chain (for both government and business); and
- expanding the tax base.

The full taxation model is frequently discussed as if the solution to one of these problems necessarily implies a solution to the other but this is not necessarily the case, as closer scrutiny of the Australian and New Zealand approaches to the full taxation models reveals. While the New Zealand GST law aims to do both, the 'full' taxation model followed in the Australian GST law addresses the problems of exemption while consciously disavowing any attempt to expand the tax base and in fact contracting it. While it is true that both countries' laws are probably simpler for government than the European VAT, it would be wrong to conclude that they are without problems, and equally wrong to conclude that in practice all government activities are effectively included in the VAT chain. In addition to intentional exclusions from the tax base, court decisions have had an impact on the operation of the full taxation model in both countries.

§4.02 THE VAT TAX BASE

For the purposes of this paper, I take the intended tax base of a VAT to be final private consumption expenditure, established on a destination basis.[14] This is essentially consistent with the design features of most modern VATs, in which public (collective) consumption expenditure is not included in the tax base.[15] For example, the Explanatory Memorandum to the bill that introduced the Australian GST Act states:

> The GST is a broad based indirect tax introduced by the Government to replace the wholesales sales tax and a number of State indirect taxes. Broadly speaking, the GST is a tax on *private consumption* in Australia. The GST taxes the consumption

14. I therefore explicitly disavow the view that a VAT should be benchmarked against a comprehensive expenditure tax under which all outgoings that are not savings (including all taxes, donations and redistributions) form part of the tax base.
15. 'Collective consumption refers to services provided simultaneously to all members of the community or to all members of a particular section of the community, such as all households living in a particular region. Collective services are automatically acquired and consumed by all members of the community, or group of households in question, without any action on their part. Typical examples are public administration and the provision of security, either at a national or local level. Collective services are the "public goods" of economic theory. By their nature, collective services cannot be sold to individuals on the market, and they are financed by government units out of taxation or other incomes.' D. Trewin, Australian Statistician, *Australian System of National Accounts: Concepts, Sources and Methods*, 451 (Australian Bureau of Statistics 2000).

> of most goods, services and anything else in Australia, including things that are imported. Generally the GST will not apply to consumption *outside Australia*, which is why the GST does not apply to exports.[16](Emphasis added.)

This is consistent with the recommendations of the commentators mentioned in the introduction. Ebrill et al. note that 'the proper treatment of services provided by the public sector either free of charge to the final user—defence and other classic public goods fall into this category—or more generally on a not-for-profit basis' is contentious.[17] Their subsequent discussion, however, does not suggest charging VAT on income tax, for example, or on other means by which consumers pay for collective consumption. The outer limit of their recommendations is that all government user charges and all subsidies tied to production should be taxed, though they note that taxing subsidies paid by the government that is collecting the tax will raise no net revenue.[18] Moreover, in using the C-efficiency ratio as 'the benchmark of a uniform tax on all consumption',[19] they measure the performance of VATs by reference to private consumption.[20]

Similarly, in discussing future refinements of its variation on the C-efficiency ratio – the VAT Revenue Ratio (VRR) – the OECD states that 'collective consumption expenditure ... is by its nature outside the scope of VAT' and so does not form part of the potential tax base against which actual performance of a VAT should be measured.[21]

Aujean et al. also address this issue. They consider the activities of government in three categories:[22]

(1) *Redistributions*, in respect of which they note that no value is created (nothing is produced) even though input tax is incurred in administering the redistributions.
(2) *The provision of public goods*, in which they include both collectively consumed goods and those 'merit' goods such as health and education that benefit individuals but are frequently supplied by government without an

16. Explanatory Memorandum to A New Tax System (Goods and Services Tax) Bill 1998, Ch 1, Executive Summary.
17. Ebrill et al. (n. 11 above), 91.
18. *Ibid.*, 93.
19. *Ibid.*, 41.
20. *Ibid.*, 41, fn. 45. It is true that they note a key reason for doing this is because there is only accurate data available for private consumption, but their discussion of taxing public consumption in Ch 8 never reaches the point of recommending that it should be subject to VAT.
21. OECD, *Consumption Tax Trends 2010: VAT/GST and Excise Rates, Trends and Administration Issues*, 107 (OECD Publishing 2011). Oddly, the OECD goes on to recommend removing from the calculation of the potential tax base only the value added by government (salaries, wages, and depreciation), treating the other expenditures of government as part of the consumption tax base. This approach effectively presumes the European approach to delineating the tax base and ignores the fact noted by Ebrill et al. (n. 11 above), that the VAT/GST collected from those supplying goods or services to government is necessarily matched by the corresponding government outlay to acquire those goods or services, thus in fact having no net effect on revenue.
22. Aujean et al. (n. 5 above), 144.

explicit fee, at less than cost price, or at less than the market price charged for comparable goods or services by the private sector.[23]

(3) *The provision of goods and services similar to those supplied by the private sector*, which covers what might be loosely described as the commercial activities of government.

Implicitly accepting that redistributions do not form part of the tax base, they note that most of the problems relating to the VAT treatment of government arise in the context of the provision of public goods. In particular, they note that because VATs operate as multi-stage transaction taxes, charged on the consideration paid for supplies of goods and services, the real problems that prevent the full taxation of government are the concept of consideration and the requirement that the consideration be linked to the making of a supply.[24] Their proposed solution involves the following elements:[25]

- governments should be thought of as suppliers, rather than as consumers, and their activities should be on the same footing as the economic activities of the private sector;
- all inputs of the public sector should be treated as relating to the activities they carry on and 'as ultimately leading to a supply of some sort';[26]
- since input tax incurred by government relates to its supplies, all such input tax should be creditable unless it relates to the making of an exempt supply;
- the scope of the concept of consideration should be broadened 'on a scale which would range from inclusion only of explicit fees charged for services, to all funding sources, including taxation revenues'.[27]

At the extreme end of this last point, taxing taxation revenues (e.g., charging VAT on income tax) would clearly include collective consumption in the tax base. However, when they come to consider just how far the concept of consideration should be expanded, they effectively exclude most payments for collective consumption, recommending that the concept of consideration should encompass the following:[28]

- explicit fees (amounts charged for identifiable supplies);
- subsidies and grants, whether or not directly linked to supplies; and
- mandatory levies that give 'reasonably clear benefits' to those paying the levies.

The first and third of these points relate to the treatment of government revenue and therefore to the expansion of the tax base and, to the extent the payer is a registered business, preserving the VAT chain. The second has mixed perspectives: that of

23. The subsidization of merit goods can be thought of as collectively consumed private consumption.
24. Aujean et al. (n. 5 above), 146.
25. *Ibid.*
26. *Ibid.*
27. *Ibid.*
28. *Ibid.*, 147.

government (the payer) and business (the payee).[29] From the government perspective, Aujean et al. leave open the possibility of taxing subsidies and grants only where there is a link to the making of supplies, provided that the exclusion of more general grants does not affect the deductibility of government input tax. Their concern is to ensure that input tax incurred on goods and services acquired by government in carrying on the activity of paying grants and subsidies should not be seen as linked to exempt or out-of-scope activities. But in VAT design, expenditure is 'consideration' rather than a supply, so treating a general grant as consideration for a taxable supply by the payee does not actually solve the government input tax problem. A solution must still be found to ensure that input tax included in expenditure on inputs that relate to other expenditure (the making of general grants not linked to supplies) is deductible. The business perspective is seen in the conclusion reached by Aujean et al.: since, irrespective of whether they are linked to the price of supplies, the full taxation of grants has no effect on VAT revenues because the output tax of the payee is creditable input tax for the payer, the inclusion of all grants and subsidies is preferable because it simplifies compliance by removing the need to establish whether there is a sufficient link between the grant/subsidy and a supply.[30]

In contrast, Aujean et al. conclude that 'fines, penalties, general taxes such as income tax and "labelled" levies not linked to a supply' should not be treated as consideration for supplies.[31] When combined with their recommendation to treat the provision of public goods as a taxable supply made in the course of an economic activity, these exclusions would have the effect that VAT/GST would be charged on supplies of public goods only if a specific fee is charged. Since most collective consumption would be supplied for no consideration (taxes being excluded from the definition of consideration), government would have no output tax but a full refund of input tax.[32] In other words, this model of full taxation effectively zero-rates the non-commercial activities of government. In the case of merit goods supplied for less than the private sector price, VAT/GST would be charged only to the extent of any payment made. That part of individual consumption that is collectively funded would again be zero-rated. The one exception Aujean et al. make is to allow for the possibility of treating local taxes as consideration for supplies in order to simplify administration.[33]

Turning to Europe, in a study prepared for the European Commission, Copenhagen Economics note that the full taxation model could be designed to tax supplies funded from taxation or similar sources, but they choose not to focus on such a model because 'a shift towards taxation of supplies with no consideration would be a

29. Implicitly, grants and subsidies to consumers are never consideration for a taxable supply because consumers are not carrying on an economic activity.
30. Aujean et al. (n. 5 above), 147.
31. *Ibid.*
32. Of course, this would not be the case if the law deemed supplies for no consideration to have a taxable value: cf EU VAT Directive, Article 26. Such an approach is not followed in the Australian and New Zealand GST laws, except in the case of supplies to associates.
33. Whether it does in fact simplify administration in practice is another question.

fundamental change in the entire EU VAT system'.[34] The same could be said for all modern VATs, since their fundamental design feature is that they are multi-stage transaction taxes in which VAT is charged on supplies made for consideration and the amount of tax payable is calculated by reference to the amount of that consideration.

The widespread support of commentators for the full taxation approach is clearly based on a presumption that most, if not all, collective consumption should not form part of the tax base for VAT. As will be seen, this is consistent with the Australian law, which taxes only private consumption, and the New Zealand law, which taxes private consumption and only that part of private expenditure on collective consumption that is provided by local government.[35] It is also an essentially logical approach. Where the government charging the VAT is the government providing the collective consumption, it is somewhat futile to charge VAT on the other main source of revenue (income taxes) since this is no different from simply increasing the rate of income tax. Such an approach would also raise more revenue than intended unless the imposition of VAT on income tax was accompanied by a decrease in the rate of one or other, or both, of the two taxes, accommodating the very different policy designs of the two taxes in the process. In the end, such moves would simply alter the balance between the two types of tax. There is no obvious logic to grossing up income tax for VAT to give the appearance that collective consumption is being taxed if all that happens is the rates of each tax are re-adjusted to achieve the same net tax effect on individuals. The difficulty of explaining the policy to voters might also be a powerful reason not to expand the notion of consideration this far.

Where the government charging the VAT is not the government providing the collective consumption, different issues arise. As noted, Aujean et al. allow for the possibility of applying VAT to local taxes in order to simplify administration, as is done in New Zealand. However, complex constitutional and political issues may arise in this respect, particularly in federal nations. When different levels of government are involved, the full inclusion of government in a value added tax regime can result in the shifting of revenue between those governments. Where that is compensated for in grants by the taxing government to the taxed government, the appearance of taxing

34. Copenhagen Economics, *VAT in the Public Sector and Exemptions in the Public Interest*, Final Report for TAXUD/2009/DE/316, 2 March 2011. They also choose not to consider the approach because it 'would lead to types of costs to the private and public sectors which we are not able to quantify within the scope of this analysis'. Note that this chapter was written in 2010, before the Copenhagen Economics report was released. Although some references to the report have been added prior to publication of this chapter, a full analysis of that report has not been undertaken.

35. A very rough estimate of the size of local government and central government in New Zealand is revealed from their comparative revenue: on 2009 figures, total local government revenue was NZD 6.3 billion while total central government revenue was NZD 79.9 billion. Figures are in New Zealand dollars and are taken from the Ministry of Internal Affairs (New Zealand), www.localcouncils.govt.nz/LGIP.nsf/wpg_URL/About-Local-Government-Local-Government-Statistical-Overview-Index (data collected 11 October 2010, this version no longer available online) and The Treasury, *Summary Statement of Financial Performance for the year ended 30 June 2009*, www.treasury.govt.nz/government/financialstatements/yearend/jun09summary/02.htm.

disguises the reality that no net revenue is collected. In such cases, the generally observed approach of not taxing other taxes is probably preferable.[36]

§4.03 THE ANTIPODEAN 'FULL' TAXATION MODELS

Under both the Australian and New Zealand GSTs, the treatment of government can be summarized as follows:

- (mostly) only privately consumed goods are taxed;
- collectively consumed goods are (mostly) not taxed; and
- privately consumed collective consumption - i.e. private consumption subsidized by government - is (mostly) not taxed.

The words 'mostly' appear in brackets since collectively consumed goods supplied by local government are taxed in New Zealand but not in Australia. However, in both countries, but more so in Australia, not all payments by private consumers for government-provided consumption are taxed. In New Zealand, the exclusions are the result of case law. In Australia, there is a much more widespread excision from the tax base of the non-commercial activities of government and of some competing areas of private sector activity. The following sections outline how these 'full' taxation models work in practice.

[A] New Zealand

The treatment of government under the New Zealand GST reflects its system of public sector financial management, which applies modern financial management techniques to the public sector.[37] Government activities are accounted for on an accruals basis using generally accepted accounting principles, under which government departments account for their 'inputs' and 'outputs', defined as follows:

> ***Inputs*** are the resources (such as capital, personnel, accommodation, equipment, information and time) used to produce goods and services. For example, the salaries of a police officer or policy adviser, and the purchase and maintenance of motor vehicles, are 'inputs' into the production of 'outputs'.
>
> ***Outputs*** are the goods and services purchased by Ministers from public and private sector producers. Outputs may include the supply of policy advice, enforcement of

36. It is important to note that this discussion is referring to general taxes charged without any link to a particular supply made to the payer. It is not referring to situations where the consideration provided for a supply is calculated to include reimbursements to the supplier for other taxes. When a supplier incurs a liability for customs duty and excise tax in relation to an import and on-supply of goods, and charges a price on the sale of those goods that includes the passing on of the customs duty and excise tax, VAT/GST should be charged on the full consideration, including those duties and taxes.
37. Inland Revenue, 4 *Tax Information Bulletin* 7 (1992); Public Finance Act 1989 (NZ).

> regulations such as speed limits, provision of a range of other services, negotiation and management of contracts, and administration of benefits.[38]

This is translated in the GST law to an approach in which many, but not all, flows of government money are treated as consideration for supplies. In common with most developed country VATs, the legal design of the New Zealand GST is that of a multi-stage transaction tax. GST is charged on all supplies of goods and services made in New Zealand by a registered person in the course or furtherance of a taxable activity carried on by that person, unless the supply is exempt.[39] The amount of tax charged is either 15% or 0% of the value of the supply.[40] To encompass government activities within these legal parameters, and to marry it with public sector accounting, the normal concepts of 'supply of goods', 'supply of services', 'person', 'taxable activity', and 'value' must be expanded to encompass the activities of government and the revenue generated by those activities. The law achieves this through a series of specific provisions dealing with public authorities (essentially the central government), local authorities (local government), and government grants and subsidies.[41] A basic description of how the provisions work follows.

[1] Central Government

[a] Public Authorities

A 'public authority' is included in the definition of a 'person'[42] and the activities carried on by public authorities are considered to be 'taxable activities'.[43] The term 'public authority' is defined to mean:

> all instruments of the Crown in respect of the Government of New Zealand, whether departments, Crown entities, State enterprises, or other instruments; and includes offices of Parliament, the Parliamentary Service, and the Office of the Clerk of the House of Representatives; but does not include the Governor-General, members of the Executive Council, Ministers of the Crown, or members of Parliament.[44]

Public authorities are 'deemed to supply goods and services where, within the meaning of the Public Finance Act 1989, any amount is brought to charge by the public authority

38. The Treasury (New Zealand), *Putting it Together: An Explanatory Guide to the New Zealand Public Sector Financial Management Sector*, 13 (Treasury Publication 1996).
39. Goods and Services Tax Act 1985 (New Zealand) ('GST Act 1985 (NZ)'), s. 8(1).
40. *Ibid.*
41. Note that New Zealand is a constitutional monarchy with a unitary structure and a unicameral parliament. Taxes are levied by or under Acts of Parliament, which are passed by a simple majority of the House of Representatives and signed into effect by the Head of State (the Queen), or by her representative in New Zealand, the Governor-General. The Crown may not levy taxes, raise loans or spend public money except by or under an Act of Parliament: Constitution Act 1986 (New Zealand), s. 22.
42. GST Act 1985 (NZ), s. 2.
43. GST Act 1985 (NZ), s. 6(1)(b).
44. GST Act 1985 (NZ), s. 2.

as revenue from the Crown for the supply of outputs'.[45] GST is charged on the value of the deemed supply, which is the amount brought to charge as revenue from the Crown,[46] and is accounted for in the tax period in which the revenue is brought to account.[47] Public authorities may therefore be registered for GST, and will generally be required to be registered since most will exceed the NZD 60,000 registration threshold.[48]

'Revenue from the Crown' is defined so that it excludes from the amount brought to charge:

- the GST chargeable on the supply of the outputs;
- revenue collected as agent for the Crown; and
- revenue received from another public authority.[49]

Each of these exclusions requires explanation. Applying the deemed supply mechanism to all outputs means that public authorities require funding on a GST-inclusive basis. However, since the Crown cannot raise money from itself, GST-inclusive accounting does not give a meaningful reflection of government activities[50] which is why revenue from the Crown is defined as a GST-exclusive amount. A department needing revenue from the Crown of NZD 1 million will need to receive NZD 1.15 million in order to pay the GST on the deemed supply. To make up the shortfall, in addition to drawing down the GST-exclusive revenue authorized by an appropriation, public authorities can draw down an amount for GST without the need for an appropriation.[51]

In addition to its departmental activities, a department may also conduct 'non-departmental activities', receiving revenues and incurring expenditure on behalf of the Crown, rather than in its own right. Taxes, duties and fines collected by a

45. GST Act 1985 (NZ), s. 5(6).
46. GST Act 1985 (NZ), ss. 8 & 10(10).
47. GST Act 1985 (NZ), s. 9(7).
48. GST Act 1985 (NZ), s. 51.
49. GST Act 1985 (NZ), s. 2.
50. The Treasury (NZ) (n. 38 above), 18.
51. An appropriation is essentially an authority to spend public money, granted under an annual Appropriation Act. The Treasury notes that 'Appropriation amounts generally exclude goods and services tax (GST) – this reflects the fact that GST is not generally an expense to the Crown and is consistent with the basis on which fiscal forecasts and financial statements are presented. Section 6 provides authority for the actual payment of GST.': The Treasury (New Zealand), A Guide to the Public Finance Act (Wellington: Treasury Publication, 2005), 18. The legislative reference is to the Public Finance Act 1989, s. 6, headed 'Authority to spend public money', which states that 'Public money may be spent, without further authority than this section, for the purpose of—

    (a) meeting expenses or capital expenditure incurred in accordance with an appropriation or other authority by or under an Act; and
    (b) the payment of goods and services tax in relation to those expenses or capital expenditure ...'

government department are examples of non-departmental revenues, while the payment of subsidies, grants, and other transfer payments are examples of non-departmental expenditures.[52] Non-departmental revenue is excluded from 'revenue from the Crown' but the relevant department is nonetheless responsible for accounting for its non-departmental activities. A department may therefore be required to have two GST registrations: one in its own right and the other as a branch of the Crown.[53]

Finally, revenue from other public authorities is excluded from the definition of 'revenue from the Crown' in order to prevent double taxation, since the receipt of such monies will generally be consideration for supplies under other provisions of the Act, either because they fall under the normal concepts of a supply of goods or services or because they are taxed under the grants and subsidies rules.

[b] Grants and Subsidies

Payments of grants or subsidies 'on behalf of the Crown or by a public authority' in relation to a person's taxable activity are treated as being consideration for a supply made by the person in the course of its taxable activity.[54] This applies even if the grant or subsidy is paid to a non-profit body. Ordinarily, an unconditional gift is not treated as consideration for a supply because it is merely a transfer payment[55] but when the payment is made by the Crown or a public authority, it is treated as if it were not an unconditional gift or payment.[56]

[c] Effect on the Tax Base

The definition of 'public authority' means that each part of the government is treated as a separate person, even though legally a government is a single entity. In contrast, the Canadian GST treats each Government (whether of Canada or of a Province or Territory) as a single person, reflecting the true legal position.[57] The New Zealand approach means that both revenue from the Crown and grants from one public authority to another are treated as consideration for taxable supplies, but the effect is merely to tax and credit at each level of the chain of government activity without raising any net revenue. When the single person treatment is reflected in a GST law, nothing happens when revenue is appropriated to, and grants are made between, different levels of that single person because a person cannot make a supply to itself. The fact that New Zealand applies (and credits) GST on interactions between the different levels of the single entity does not change the fact that no revenue is raised from these intra-person flows of money: government remains 'inside the ring' of

52. The Treasury (NZ) (n. 51 above), 64.
53. Treasury Circular 2005/11, *Guidance on GST for Non-Departmental Operations*, 14 July 2005 (Treasury Publication 2005), 6, para 20.
54. GST Act 1985 (NZ), s. 5(6D).
55. GST Act 1985 (NZ), s. 2, definition of 'consideration'.
56. GST Act 1985 (NZ), s. 2, definition of 'unconditional gift'.
57. See P.-P. Gendron, 'VAT Treatment of Public Sector Bodies: The Canadian Model', Ch. 3 in this volume.

taxable businesses at all times.[58] Just as business-to-business (B2B) supplies between registered persons raise no net revenue, so too government-to-government (G2G) supplies raise no net revenue (except, in either case, to the extent that the purchaser is making exempt supplies). Full taxation of G2G supplies preserves the tax chain but mostly results in the circulation of 'tax' within the government. Moreover, since government is fully taxable, when a public authority acquires goods or services from a registered person, the GST paid by the supplier gives rise to an input tax credit for the public authority. Taxable B2G, G2B, G2G and B2B supplies all raise no net revenue unless they are inputs to exempt supplies. Real revenue is raised only when there is a business-to-consumer (B2C) or government-to-consumer (G2C) supply.[59]

Like the tax on G2G transactions, taxing subsidies paid by central government also raises no net revenue. Because public authorities can claim input tax credits for taxed inputs, the payment of a subsidy to a taxable person results in a payment of output tax by that person and a corresponding deduction of input tax for the public authority making the payment. Government remains effectively zero-rated. It is interesting to note, however, that although the New Zealand GST law allows taxpayers to increase the price of their supplies when the rate of GST or the tax status of a supply is altered, the law specifies that a public authority is not required to increase the amount of a grant or subsidy.[60] In such cases, the person receiving the grant or subsidy must simply accept an effectively lower rate of subsidy until such time, if any, as the public authority agrees to an increase. Given the recent increase of the GST rate from 12.5% to 15%, this will have been an issue for public and local authorities and other registered persons receiving grants and subsidies in 2011.

It should also be noted that case law has the effect that not all outgoings paid by government are treated as consideration for taxable supplies, even if they are economically equivalent to subsidies. It is beyond the scope of this paper to analyse the case law in detail, but the following excerpt from an interpretation statement issued by the New Zealand Inland Revenue sets out the basic principles emerging from the case law, which relate to the basic issues of the notions of supply, consideration, and the link between them that must be established in order to identify a taxable supply. These principles should have a ring of familiarity about them to many European VAT practitioners:[61]

---

58. 'Within the ring' of taxable businesses, all output tax paid by suppliers becomes the deductible input tax of recipients, which means that transactions 'within the ring' are effectively tax free. The concept of the ring of taxable businesses is discussed in S. Cnossen, *VAT Treatment of Immovable Property,* in *Tax Law Design and Drafting,* 231–245, 233–234 (vol. 1, V. Thuronyi ed., International Monetary Fund 1996) and S. Cnossen, *A VAT Primer for Economists, Lawyers, and Accountants,* 54 Tax Notes Intl. 319 (2009). It is also discussed in R. Millar, 'VAT and Immovable Property: Full Taxation Models and the Treatment of Capital Gains on Owner-Occupied Residences', Ch 8, this volume.
59. For the purposes of simplicity, in this chapter I use the term 'consumer' and the letter 'C' in B2C, G2C, and similar acronyms, to refer to any person to the extent that the person cannot claim a credit/deduction for input tax incurred on its purchases. This is despite the fact that in Ch 8, addressing a very different issue, I treat exempt suppliers as businesses making 'input taxed' supplies, rather than as consumers.
60. GST Act 1985 (NZ), s. 78(2).
61. Note that, despite the reference to 'enforceable reciprocal obligations', it is unlikely that a case such as Case C-498/99, *Town & County Factors Ltd v. Commissioners of Customs and Excise* OJ

> Underpinning all transactions where a payment is within the definition of consideration for a supply is the requirement there are enforceable reciprocal obligations between the parties. Earlier cases... emphasised the broad nature of the definition yet more recently attempts to use a broad linkage have been rejected by the courts. All transactions where a payment is consideration for a supply must be based upon a platform of reciprocal obligations...
>
> In order to determine when a payment is 'sufficiently connected' to a supply to be consideration for that supply, the following principles can be drawn from the cases:
>
> - It is the legal nature of the transaction that will define the nexus between the payment and any supply: *Chatham Islands Enterprise Trust.*
> - For a payment to be consideration for a supply there must first be an identifiable supply: *NZ Refining* and *Chatham Islands Enterprise Trust.*
> - The concept of supply is active; to supply is to furnish or provide: *Databank.*
> - For a payment to be consideration there must be a sufficient connection between the payment and a supply of goods or services: *NZ Refining.*
> - Tenuous or unrealistic connections between the payment and supply will not be sufficient: *Suzuki* (HC).
> - A sufficient connection involves legally enforceable reciprocal obligations between the payer and payee: *Chatham Islands Enterprise Trust, New Zealand Refining* and *Suzuki.*
> - Conditions that must be fulfilled to receive payment do not, without more, evidence a supply: *NZ Refining.*
> - An expectation that the recipient of the payment would carry out a certain activity is not enough for a payment to be in respect of or for the inducement of a supply. It is not sufficient that the person who receives the payment carries out some activity that has the effect of benefiting either the person making the payment or some other person. See *Chatham Islands Enterprise Trust.*
> - A supply will only be liable to tax if it is made in the course or furtherance of a taxable activity: *Chatham Islands Enterprise Trust.*[62]

The two cases most frequently mentioned in this list involved payments by central government. In the *New Zealand Refining* case,[63] a series of payments totalling NZD 83 million were made. In each case, the payment would only be made if the refinery fulfilled the condition to receive it, which was that it had remained in operation. It was under no legal obligation to remain in operation and the government's only recourse if the refinery did close down was to withhold the payment. The Court held that this relationship lacked the necessary reciprocity to be a supply for consideration. Similarly, in the *Chatham Islands Enterprise Trust* case, the central government settled NZD 8 million on a trust to be used for the benefit of the self-government of the people of the Chatham Islands. The Court held that this did not constitute consideration for a supply. The expectation that the trust would use the funds to set up companies to run key

C/47 of 2000 would be decided any differently in New Zealand. The excerpt, which in any case represents only the views of Inland Revenue, must be read in the context of the cases to which they refer, none of which addressed a similar issue.

62. Inland Revenue (New Zealand), 'GST Treatment of Court Awards and Out of Court Settlements', Interpretation statement IS3387 issued by Adjudication & Rulings, September 2002, 12–13.
63. *Commissioner of Inland Revenue v. New Zealand Refining Co Ltd* (1997) 18 NZTC 13,187.

activities on the Chatham Islands did not amount to a supply, either to the government or to the people of the Chatham Islands. Nor was the payment of the funds into the trust consideration for the trustee entering into the trust obligations in relation to the payment.

Since no net revenue is raised by central government subsidies, it does not much matter whether such payments are taxed so long as the parties involved know from the outset what the position will be. Full taxation is merely smoke and mirrors. If the government intends the amount it pays to be taxable, it will pay an amount that includes tax; if it does not, it will not. Problems only arise when one party thought it had paid, or been paid, a subsidy amount that was grossed up for tax but the other party disputes that position. This consequence was not lost on the judges in the *Chatham Islands Enterprise Trust* case, all of whom criticized the Commissioner of Inland Revenue for running the case. In the High Court, Herron J made the following comments:

> [I]t seems to me there is a convincing argument that the negotiations proceeded on the basis that they were to be exclusive of GST, but I am not asked to decide that issue which is an issue between Government and the Chatham Islands Enterprise Trust... if the outcome of this case is such that the NZD 8 million is reduced by the incidence of goods and services tax, then I have no hesitation in saying that it runs counter to what I perceive was the understanding of the parties... if tax is payable on this sum then there must be a strong case in equity...to have the deduction made good.[64]

All three judges in the Court of Appeal endorsed this statement, the most strongly worded comment coming from Justice Tipping who said:

> This litigation must have cost a lot in terms of time, money and worry. It is not as if this was a straightforward and clear case of liability for GST. Even if it had been, the utility of the Commissioner claiming GST on behalf of the Crown would have been questionable when the Crown would clearly have had a strong moral responsibility to pay the amount collected back to the Trust, plus, I suppose, an additional 12 1/2% on the top up payment. The Commissioner's responsibility to collect tax on behalf of the Crown must surely carry with it a responsibility to exercise a measure of discretion, the more so when the claim made is dubious and, when viewed in its wider context, of little or no practical utility.[65]

Since GST on subsidies is a wash, one of the most effective ways of dealing with such issues would be to provide that a payment by government is taxable if government says that it is taxable, either in the law under which the payment is made, in the agreement under which it is made, or in some other document or law that is binding on both payer and payee.

In the description thus far, we have seen that the New Zealand GST preserves the VAT chain in intra-government activities, and in interactions between government and

64. *Chatham Islands Enterprise Trust v. Commissioner of Inland Revenue* (1998) 18 NZTC 13,817, 13,820.
65. *Chatham Islands Enterprise Trust v. Commissioner of Inland Revenue* (1999) 19 NZTC 15,075, para. 34.

registered persons, but without altering the tax base. Its effect on the tax base becomes apparent only when we consider supplies made by central government to consumers (i.e. by looking at government revenues rather than government expenditures). The provision of collectively consumed public goods by central government out of tax revenues without any direct charge to individuals is not taxed. Central government taxes are not also themselves treated as consideration for taxable supplies: there is no GST on GST, and no GST on income tax. Similarly, as already noted, where government subsidizes private consumption, no GST is collected on that part of the consumption that is funded by the subsidy. The concept of consideration means that private consumption provided or subsidized by government can only be taxed to the extent of any amount paid by the consumers. Where government supplies goods or services to particular consumers:

- if the consumer pays no consideration, there is no GST;
- if the consumer pays the market price, GST is charged accordingly;
- if government subsidizes the supply, GST is only collected on the amount paid by the consumer.

However, the case law discussed above has an impact on the application of the GST law to supplies that are subsidized by government. As an example, consider the education sector, which is 'fully taxed' under the New Zealand GST. Both state and private schools receive government funding and are treated as making taxable supplies on receipt of that funding, but as noted earlier, no net revenue is raised when central government subsidizes schools since the output tax of the school is paid back to the government paying the subsidy. As with all other areas of central government activity, GST revenue is only collected if payments are made by consumers.

If parents enrol their children in private schools, the fees charged by the school are subject to GST.[66] If parents enrol their children in state schools, to the extent that there is no fee, there will be no GST. However, since the New Zealand law is clearly designed to tax private consumption expenditure, one would expect that if consumers do pay fees to state schools, GST would apply. This is not the case. At public sector primary and secondary schools, including both state schools and private schools that are 'integrated' with the state school system, education is free. Many such schools nonetheless levy fees on the parents of their students. The fees fall into three classes:

- Enrolment fees for integrated schools.
- General fees to help cover costs.
- Activity fees for class trips, materials, attendance at particular events, etc.

In light of the cases cited earlier, and others directly addressing education, a Public Ruling has been issued to outline Inland Revenue's view of the circumstances in which such fees will be subject to GST:

66. Education is both free and compulsory and the school system includes two types of publicly funded school – state schools and integrated schools – as well as private schools, which receive some state funding but are also funded by fees.

- *Enrolment fees* for integrated schools are taxable: 'Attendance dues paid to the proprietors of integrated schools are subject to GST, being payments to secure the enrolment of a pupil in a school for which the proprietors provide the buildings and ensure the special character [of the school]: *Turakina Maori Girls College Board of Trustees v. CIR* (1993) 15 NZTC 10,032'.[67]
- *General fees* contributed to a fund to cover a school's costs are not subject to GST, whether the school is a state school or an integrated school. This is because the students have a statutory right to be provided with education and the schools have a statutory obligation to provide that education free of charge.[68] This GST treatment is consistent with the views of the Ministry of Education that 'whatever terms are used to describe such payments, they are in fact donations and cannot be made compulsory'.[69]
- *Activity fees* are only taxable if they meet the requirement of being consideration for a supply that is not linked to the education services which students are statutorily entitled to receive for free and if 'the supply is conditional on payment being made for such services'.[70] To explain what this means, the ruling gives a series of examples which make somewhat esoteric distinctions. For example, where students are asked to pay for materials used in a clothing class, no GST is chargeable unless the student elects to take ownership of the resulting clothing.[71] Photocopying charges for materials used in class are not taxable but 'if a student chooses to purchase a photocopy of an optional workbook or magazine produced by students that the student may retain, the payment made would be consideration for the supply of that item and GST would be chargeable on the payment'.[72] Fees for food and transport associated with field trips and school camping trips are subject to GST because 'the supply of transport is not integral to the supply of education'.[73] The same is presumably true of food. The fact that payment is waived for some students does not alter these conclusions.[74] The sale by a school of workbooks, textbooks and attendance at school plays is taxable.[75]

These conclusions have their foundation in the statutory regime that regulates the provision of education and is informed by the views of the Ministry of Education about what kinds of payments state and integrated schools may request/require students to pay in the context of their entitlement to free education. The result is a somewhat complex web of decisions to be made by the school and a clear distortion from the

67. Commissioner of Inland Revenue, 'Public Ruling BR PUB 09/01 Payments Made by Parents or Guardians of Students to State Schools - GST Treatment', 23 March 2009, 3.
68. *Ibid.*, 1.
69. *Ibid.*, citing Circular 1998/25 issued by the Ministry of Education.
70. *Ibid.*, 1.
71. Commissioner of Inland Revenue (n. 67 above), 16, Example 2.
72. *Ibid.*, 16, Example 3.
73. *Ibid.*, 16, Example 4.
74. *Ibid.*, 16–17, Example 5.
75. Commissioner of Inland Revenue (n. 67 above), 17, Examples 6 & 7.

intended tax base, which was presumably intended to cover all such payments. The non-taxation of some consumer contributions to publicly provided education also exacerbates the lack of neutrality with privately funded education. As noted, central government subsidization of privately consumed goods is effectively zero-rated under the New Zealand full taxation model. This means that the New Zealand GST is not neutral when it comes to goods and services supplied by government in competition with the private sector at reduced prices or for free. Aujean et al. argue that this treatment is neutral because VAT is charged at the same rate on supplies provided by the public and private sector: it is just that in the public sector applying the tax rate to zero consideration means that there is no tax impost on publicly provided merit goods. There is, however, a change in relative prices, which is clearly a matter of political concern, if not also of neutrality.

However, the context of the New Zealand education system gives a better understanding of the minimal extent of this distortion in practice: 97% of children attend schools that are largely funded by central government – 87% at state schools and 10% at integrated schools. Only 3% of children attend private schools,[76] which are themselves partly subsidized by government. Any difference in tax effect is more than likely considered not only acceptable but also desirable in the context of the social ethos reflected in New Zealand's education regime and in the widespread reliance on public sector education.

[2] Local Government

Unlike central government, local government is treated like any other business. The term 'local authority' is defined to include bodies designated as such under the Local Government Act 2002 as well as a number of other specified entities.[77] A 'local authority' is included in the definition of a 'person'[78] and the activities carried on by local authorities are considered to be 'taxable activities'.[79] Rates (which are essentially a property tax charged to landowners in a local authority area) are treated as being consideration for a supply by the local authority to the person paying the rates.[80, 81]

As with public authorities, local authorities are subject to financial management requirements, including the requirement to comply with generally accepted accounting standards.[82] Rates are the primary funding source for local government in New Zealand. They are used to fund both collective and individual consumption and the

76. Professor Tom Nicholson, *Private or Public?*, North and South, 98–99 (July 2000).
77. GST Act 1985 (NZ), s. 2.
78. GST Act 1985 (NZ), s. 2.
79. GST Act 1985 (NZ), s. 6(1)(b).
80. GST Act 1985 (NZ), s. 5(7). There are also provisions treating a local authority as making a supply when it is paid a financial contribution as a condition of a resource consent, or when it receives a development contribution, and zero-rating that supply to the extent that the consideration given for it is land: GST Act 1985 (NZ), ss. 5(7B) & 11B(1B). These and other provisions that are unnecessary for the purpose of illustration are not discussed in this paper.
81. Rates are charged by local authorities in accordance with the Local Government (Rating) Act 2002.
82. Local Government Act 2002, Part 5, Subpart 2.

amount charged to a particular taxpayer does not necessarily reflect the extent to which that taxpayer uses any or all of the services provided by local authorities. This lack of clear connection between the supplies made by local authorities and the rates paid by landowners is the reason why the GST law specifies that rates are to be treated as consideration for supplies. Without that provision, rates might not have been taxed.

Other local authority revenue sources include:

- User charges: fees and charges for the provision of goods and services, as well as licence fees and permit charges. These clearly amount to consideration for supplies and can therefore be subject to GST under normal rules.
- Central government grants and subsidies: these are subject to GST under the rules discussed in the previous section, which means that the amount of the grant must be effectively grossed up for GST.
- Fines and penalties, such as the fines collected for parking infringements: these are not subject to GST, since they are imposed as punishment, rather than as consideration for supplies.

In the year ending 30 June 2009, rates made up 61.1% of local government operating income.[83] The remaining income came from sales of goods and services (16.43%), grants and subsidies (10.96%), regulatory fees, fines, and penalties (6.73%), and investments (4.78%).[84] Close to 80% of local government revenue thus results in a GST impost on consumers. On the spending side, a significant amount of local government spending relates to collective consumption. The largest item in 2009 was roads, which accounted for 17% of all local government spending.[85]

Because central and local government are different entities, the effect of full taxation on local government is different from its effect on central government. GST payable by local authorities on their outputs is not revenue collected by those local governments. Moreover, input tax claimable by them on their inputs is not a repayment of revenue they have collected. Local government, unlike central government, is effectively in the same position as any other business. Any interactions between local government and registered businesses raise no net central government revenue, unless exempt supplies are involved. The GST payable on a taxable local-government-to-business (LG2B) supply is creditable to the business customer; the GST payable on a taxable B2LG supply is creditable to the local government. However, just as a taxable B2C supply imposes a burden on consumers, so too does a taxable LG2C supply.

83. Ministry of Internal Affairs (New Zealand), www.localcouncils.govt.nz/LGIP.nsf/wpg_URL/About-Local-Government-Local-Government-Statistical-Overview-Index (data collected 11 October 2010, this version no longer available online). Total local government income was NZD 6.3 billion, while spending for the same period was NZD 6.7 billion. Both figures exclude GST.
84. *Ibid.*
85. Other items included council support services (15%), planning and regulation (9%), recreation and sport (9%), transport (9%), waste water (9%), water supply (6%), culture (6%), property (5%), solid waste/refuse (4%), environmental protection (4%), governance (3%), community development (2%), economic development (2%), emergency management (1%), other activities (1%): Ministry of Internal Affairs (New Zealand) (n. 83 above).

Thus, as with central government, full taxation of local government results in a tax burden on consumers in proportion to the amount they pay to the local authority for their supplies. However, unlike central government, which does not gross up its other taxes for GST, the taxes (rates) collected by local government *are* grossed up for GST, which means that both individual and collective consumption financed by local government are taxed, except to the extent that they are subsidized by central government.[86]

[3] A Simple Illustration

Figures 4.1 and 4.2 illustrate the New Zealand treatment of central and local government through a simple example. Figure 4.1 shows the transactions or 'deemed' transactions, with the solid lines representing the supplies and the dashed lines representing the 'consideration' for the supplies. Figure 4.2 illustrates the tax effect of the transactions. In this diagram, the dashed lines represent payments of tax that are credited and therefore give rise to no net revenue, while the solid lines represent the tax included in consumer spending, including spending on local government rates. The GST rate is 12.5%, as it was in New Zealand until recently.

Figure 4.1: Tax Treatment of Government Transactions (New Zealand GST)

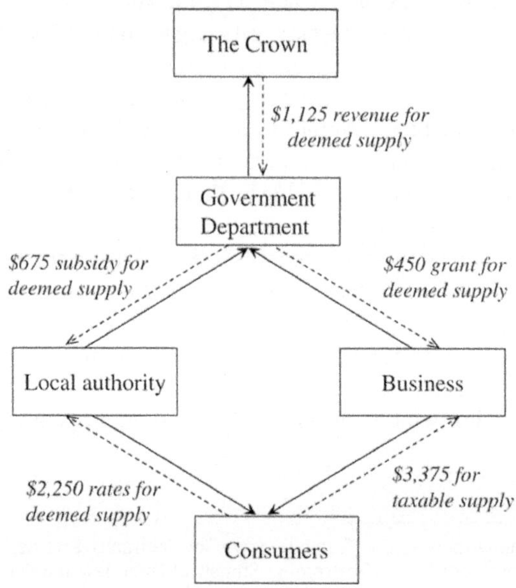

86. Moreover, since some (but not all) rates are taxes rather than user charges, including rates in the GST net could be viewed as a shifting of tax revenue from local government to central government.

Figure 4.2: Tax Flows on Government Transactions (New Zealand GST)

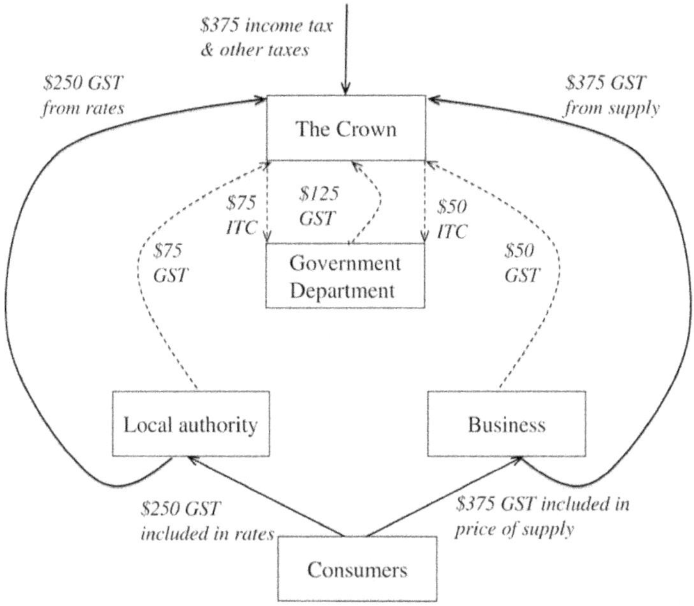

(1) Revenue from the Crown is brought to account by a government department. For the purposes of illustration, presume that the department's budget requires it to receive NZD 1,000, for which it must draw down an additional 12.5% for GST to make a total payment of NZD 1,125. Because the government department is deemed to make a supply, the Crown gives the department NZD 1,125 but receives back NZD 125 as GST. The Crown's outgoing is therefore NZD 1,000 and the department's revenue is NZD 1,000. No net GST revenue is collected because this is, after all, simply an intra-government transfer of previously collected tax or other revenue, as part of the process of spending that tax revenue.

(2) The government department spends part of its NZD 1,000 revenue by making a grant to a local authority. The local authority needs NZD 600 funding, which is grossed up to NZD 675 to cover GST. The local authority is deemed to make a taxable supply and pays NZD 75 GST to the Crown. As the recipient of that supply, the government department receives an input tax credit for that NZD 75. The Crown therefore receives no net GST revenue, while the department spends NZD 600 and the local authority receives NZD 600 revenue.

(3) The government department spends the remainder of its NZD 1,000 revenue by making a grant to a business in respect of its taxable activity. The business needs NZD 400 funding, which is grossed up to NZD 450 to cover GST. The business is deemed to make a taxable supply and pays NZD 50 GST to the Crown. As the recipient of the deemed supply, the government department receives an input tax credit for the NZD 50. The Crown receives no net GST revenue, while the department spends NZD 400 and the business receives NZD 400 revenue.

(4) The local authority charges rates of NZD 2,250, including GST, to a landowner ('the consumer') in its area. The rates are deemed to be consideration for a supply and the local authority pays NZD 250 to the Crown. The Crown raises NZD 250 because the consumer is not entitled to an input tax credit. The GST included in the rates therefore becomes a tax burden on the consumer, who is financing both individual and collective consumption.[87]

(5) The business makes a taxable supply to the consumer for a price of NZD 3,375, including GST. From this amount, the business pays NZD 375 GST to the Crown. The Crown raises NZD 375 revenue, which was included in the price charged by the business to the consumer for the supply and was therefore a burden on the individual consumption of the consumer.

(6) Finally, since this particular government is funding all of its expenditure through taxes and has raised only NZD 625 from GST, a further NZD 375 is raised through other tax sources, primarily income tax.[88]

Note that the business and the local authority have two sources of income: government grants and money received from the consumer for supplies. Although both are treated as consideration for a supply, GST is only a burden on the amounts received from the consumer, because the GST paid on the supplies that the business and the local authority are deemed to make in return for the grants is refunded as input tax credits to the department paying the grant.

[B] Australia

The Australian GST treatment of government differs from the New Zealand treatment in a number of ways. In particular, the following differences are significant:

(1) Rather than 'taxing and crediting' all flows of money through the different levels of government, Australia uses an exemption with credit approach (referred to as 'GST-free'). There are no deemed supplies on receipt of revenue from the Crown and government grants and subsidies are not taxable unless they constitute consideration for an actual supply.

87. If the rates were inputs to a taxable activity, the GST would be creditable and no net GST revenue would be raised.

88. Obviously, this is not an accurate representation of the actual balance between income tax and GST, the former being in reality the more significant source of central government tax revenue.

(2) Collective consumption of public goods is not taxed: federal, state and local taxes are not subject to GST.[89]
(3) Some specific fees charged by government are subject to GST but many others are excluded from the tax base: the basic principle is that the non-commercial activities of government are not taxed.
(4) Australia addresses the neutrality problem that comes with applying full taxation to government-funded or -subsidized merit goods by extending GST-free treatment to two key areas: health and education.

Some of these differences reflect the different political structures of Australia and New Zealand. Australia is a federation – the Commonwealth of Australia – consisting of six states and two main territories. The Commonwealth, States, and Territories each have their own parliaments and governments.[90] The relationship between the Commonwealth and the States is governed by the Constitution of Australia, which includes provisions relating to taxation powers that necessarily have an impact on the design of taxation laws. Other differences reflect different approaches taken by Australia to the tax policy design of the GST law.

[1] Government as a Taxable Person

Government is included in the GST net through the concept of an 'enterprise' – the Australian equivalent to the concept of economic activity – which includes all activities carried on by 'the Commonwealth, a State or a Territory, or by a body corporate, or corporation sole, established for a public purpose by or under a law of the Commonwealth, a State or a Territory'.[91] A body politic (i.e. the Commonwealth, a State or a Territory) is defined to be an 'entity', the term used where other VAT/GST laws use the term 'person'. Bodies corporate and corporations sole are also entities. Although parts of a body politic are not separate entities, the Australian GST follows the New Zealand, rather than the Canadian approach, to the activities of sub-parts of government. This is achieved through the concept of a 'government entity', which is defined to include:

- a Commonwealth, State, or Territory department;
- a department of the Parliament;
- an executive or statutory agency; and
- an organization that is not an entity but can be separately identified by the nature of its activities or by its location if the organization is established by the Commonwealth, a State, or a Territory to carry on an enterprise or established by law for a public purpose.

89. As noted (n. 36 above), this does not mean that taxes included in the price of a specific supply are excluded from the tax base.
90. The Commonwealth and the States are constitutional monarchies. Queen Elizabeth II is the Head of State of the Commonwealth and of the States, each of which is a sovereign entity. The Queen is represented in Australia by the Governor-General and in each State by the State Governor.
91. GST Act 1999 (Aus), s. 9-20.

Although not treated as separate entities, government entities can effectively act as if they are separate entities because 'Parts of the Commonwealth, a State or a Territory may register even if they are not separate legal entities. Once registered, they may become liable for GST and entitled to input tax credits.'[92] Within a particular body politic, all government entities are treated as associates of each other.[93]

A wider term, 'government-related entity' is also defined. It includes all government entities and also local government as well as organizations established by the Commonwealth, State, or Territory to carry on an enterprise, or established by law for a public purpose, where the organizations are not included in the narrower concept of a government entity because they are in fact separate entities (e.g., government corporations). In the following passages, unless otherwise specified, the term 'government' is used to refer to all kinds of government-related entity.

[2] Treatment of Government Spending

The basic rule in Australia is that a supply is a taxable supply if it is made for consideration in the course or furtherance of an enterprise carried on by a supplier who is registered or required to be registered. The supply must also be connected with Australia and not be 'GST-free' (exempt with credit) or 'input taxed' (exempt without credit).[94] The key issue in determining whether supplies made by or to government are taxable supplies is the need for consideration.

Government funding is largely outside the scope of the GST law. In relation to the funding of government, the Australia law partially aims to achieve the opposite of the New Zealand law. Rather than 'deemed supply' rules to turn Crown funding or transfer payments between different parts or levels of government into consideration for taxable supplies, the law provides that 'a payment made by a government related entity to another government related entity is not the provision of consideration if the payment is specifically covered by an appropriation under an Australian law'.[95] There are also no special rules for grants or subsidies, which means that their treatment falls to be determined by considering whether they are in fact consideration for a supply. In essence, this involves the same kinds of questions faced in European VAT and under the New Zealand GST: is there a relationship of reciprocity such that the payment can

92. GST Act 1999 (Aus), s. 149-1, which is an explanatory section introducing Division 149. Although government entities may be registered, they cannot be required to be registered; nor can they be required to cancel their registration: GST Act 1999 (Aus), ss 149-10 & 149-20. This addresses constitutional constraints by making compliance with the law voluntary for governments. In practice they are registered.
93. GST Act 1999 (Aus), ss 72-95 & 72-100. This has the effect that if a government entity makes a supply for no consideration or for less than the market price to another government entity within the same government, and if the recipient will use the supply to make 'input taxed' supplies, the market value must be used in working out the GST payable on the supply.
94. GST Act 1999 (Aus), s. 9-5.
95. GST Act 1999 (Aus), s. 9-15(3)(c).

be seen as consideration for a supply, or is it merely a transfer payment? As a result, grants and subsidies that are not linked to a particular supply are generally not taxed.[96]

The result is that there is no pretence that government entities are making supplies to each other and to the Crown, and no pretence that registered entities are making supplies to government when they receive subsidies and grants. Despite this, the effective zero-rating of government that is achieved in New Zealand by linking input tax incurred by public authorities to the making of deemed taxable supplies to the Crown (or to other public authorities) is achieved in Australia without the need for such a link. Where government incurs input tax acquiring real, as opposed to deemed, taxable supplies (i.e. in a B2G supply of goods or services) the input tax is creditable under the normal input tax credit entitlement rules that apply to all registered persons. Under these rules, a credit is allowed for any input tax incurred in carrying on an enterprise, unless it relates to the making of an input taxed (exempt) supply, such as a financial supply or a lease of residential property.[97] Input tax credits are also denied for acquisitions or imports that are private or domestic in nature but this is merely another way of saying that the acquisition or import is not made in carrying on an enterprise. Since the activities of government are defined to be an enterprise, government activities are, by their nature, not private or domestic. This is consistent with the recommendations of Aujean et al.

As in New Zealand, there has been case law on government subsidies. The first case focussed on the treatment of a subsidy in the hands of the payee. In *TT-Line Company Pty Ltd v. Federal Commissioner of Taxation*,[98] a Tasmanian government-related entity (TT-Line) operated a ferry service carrying passengers and vehicles across the Bass Strait between Victoria and Tasmania. The Commonwealth established a scheme to subsidize the cost of transporting vehicles across Bass Strait by paying a rebate that was intended to equalize the cost of a driver travelling across on the ferry with the cost of driving an equivalent distance on a highway. Rebates would be paid irrespective of whether the transport was provided by a private sector ferry operator or a government-related entity. TT-line discounted the fares charged to passengers eligible for the rebate and was reimbursed on a monthly basis by the Commonwealth Department of Transport and Regional Services. A case was argued in respect of the transport of a single passenger and his vehicle, for which the passenger paid NZD 574 and the Commonwealth subsequently paid TT-Line a NZD 336 rebate. TT-line argued that it should not be required to remit GST out of the NZD 336 received from the Commonwealth because it was not consideration for the transport supplied to the passenger. Alternatively, it argued that the payment was specifically excluded from the tax base because it was a payment made by one government-related entity to another

96. Commissioner of Taxation, 'GSTR 2000/11 Goods and services tax: grants of financial assistance', 12 May 2000, is a public ruling outlining the Commissioner's view of the criteria to be applied in making this decision. [Note that this ruling was withdrawn on 30 May 2012 – 11 months after the completion of this chapter. It was replaced by 'GSTR 2012/2 Goods and services tax: financial assistance payments'. The new ruling takes account of the recent Australian case law discussed in this chapter.]
97. GST Act 1999 (Aus), Divisions 11 and 15.
98. *TT-Line Company Pty Ltd v. FCT* (2009) 181 FCR 400; [2009] FCAFC 178 ('the TT-Line case').

and was specifically covered by an appropriation. On appeal to the Full Federal Court both arguments were rejected. It was concluded that the payments were third party consideration for the transport services supplied to eligible passengers.

In respect of the intended scope of the exclusion of appropriations from the tax base, two judges held that this must be understood in the context of an underlying GST policy of equal treatment between government and the private sector. Where a payment under an appropriation could be made either to a government supplier or to a private sector supplier, both should be treated in the same way. Thus, the exclusion of appropriations from the tax base could not apply to the receipt of a rebate by TT-Line (a government supplier) if it would be treated as consideration for a taxable supply when received by a private sector supplier. Had the terms of the scheme been such that the rebate would only be paid to government suppliers, 'the potentiality for discrimination between government related and non-government entities [would] not exist'.[99] The law was not intended to 'discriminate in favour of the government related entity'.[100] The reasoning of the third judge was slightly different, linking the conclusion on the appropriation issue with the conclusion on the third party consideration issue:

> The object of the [exclusion of appropriations] is to ensure that there will be no GST where the purpose of the relevant appropriation is to provide funds to a government related entity. To satisfy the provision, it must be clear that the appropriation is for the benefit of a government related entity ... [In this case] the appropriation is to provide a benefit to eligible passengers in respect of the carriage of eligible passenger vehicles. It was [the passenger] who received the benefit of the rebate, not TT-Line. TT-Line was no more than a conduit for the providing of the rebate to [the passenger]. The payment was not a payment by one government related entity to another in the relevant sense whether or not it was specifically covered by the appropriation under the Appropriation Act.[101]

This result is obviously correct. In European terms, the subsidy was directly linked to the price of the supply and therefore should be included in the taxable value of that supply.[102] The decision, however, focussed only on the tax position of the entity to which the rebates were paid. The effect of the payment of the subsidies was not considered from the perspective of the Commonwealth entity that paid the rebates. A subsequent case did directly address this issue but in relation to a different subsidy scheme. In *FCT v. Secretary of the Department of Transport (Victoria)*,[103] the Victorian Department of Transport (DOT) ran a subsidy scheme, the Multi Purpose Taxi Program ('MPTP'), under which DOT paid 50% of the price of taxi transport for disabled residents who were unable to use public transport. The issue in this case was not whether the taxi drivers must remit GST on the full amount received but whether DOT was entitled to an input tax credit in respect of its payment. In other words, was the subsidy 'third party consideration' for a supply by the taxi driver to the passenger or

99. *Ibid.*, [2009] FCAFC 178, para. 62 per Edmonds J.
100. *Ibid.*
101. *Ibid.*, [2009] FCAFC 178, para. 24 per Emmett J.
102. Cf. EU VAT Directive, Art.73.
103. *Commissioner of Taxation v. Secretary of the Department of Transport (Victoria)* [2010] FCAFC 84 ('the Victorian Department of Transport case').

were there two supplies: one to the passenger and another to DOT? The Court ruled that there were two supplies and that DOT was entitled to an input tax credit.

The decision turned on the particular details of the scheme, which was implemented by DOT in carrying out its obligations under Victorian state legislation.[104] In particular, it was considered significant that eligible users of the scheme were issued with smart cards, which the driver was obliged by law to accept. The smart card was swiped at the beginning and end of each journey. This had the effect of creating an entitlement for the driver to be paid by DOT and reducing the passenger's liability to the difference between the full fare and the subsidy to be paid by DOT. This was reflected in the invoices generated by the electronic funds transfer point of sale (EFTPOS) equipment, which every taxi was required to have as a condition of its DOT-issued licence. Two invoices were printed: one showing the amount paid by the passenger and the GST payable out of that amount; the other showing the amount payable by DOT and the GST payable out of that amount.

One judge dissented, arguing that the payment was essentially a government transfer payment designed to give effect to a social welfare policy and it was not 'at all unnatural that a government department would make such a payment - even bind itself to do so in defined circumstances - without acquiring anything in return'.[105] The Commissioner of Taxation has, however, accepted the decision and is not appealing. In a Decision Impact Statement on the case, he indicates his intention to reconsider his previous views and states the following:

> In the interim, and subject to the necessary qualification that all factual circumstances need to be taken into account, the ATO accepts that a supply to the paying agency for which the subsidy is consideration occurs if:
>
> - subsidy payments are made to an entity (the supplier) by a government department or agency (the agency) in circumstances where the supplier supplies goods or services to a third party;
> - the supplier obtains, before each individual supply of goods or services is made by the supplier to the third party, advance authorisation from the agency that the agency would make the payment to the supplier if the goods or services are supplied; and
> - the supply by the supplier to the third party promotes the objects or functions of the agency.[106]

Whether this decision lacks neutrality depends on the perspective taken. The decision is consistent with the treatment that would have applied had DOT in-sourced the provision of the transport and directly supplied transport for disabled residents, though the likelihood of that occurring might seem distant. As a result, the case diminishes the incentive to in-source such social services. On the other hand, if the subsidy had been delivered by paying it directly to the disabled person, that person would then have had to pay the full taxi fare and would generally not have been entitled to an input tax credit. That would result in the tax fraction of Victorian government subsidies being

104. Transport Act 1983 (Victoria).
105. *Secretary of the Department of Transport (Victoria)* (n. 103 above), para. 82, per Jessup J.
106. Decision Impact Statement LIT/ICD/VID 845 of 2009, issued on 15 February 2011.

directed to the Commonwealth GST revenue pool for redistribution to the States and Territories according to a formula that does not simply reflect consumption expenditure in each location. The decision of the Court prevents that circulation of revenue between different levels of government, but only if subsidies are paid to the supplier rather than the consumer. As a result, there is an incentive for government-related entities to structure their subsidy payments in a way that ensures they will receive input tax credits because one method (a subsidy paid to the consumer) will result in the imposition of GST on collectively consumed private consumption – the merit good of providing a viable means of transport for disabled persons – while the other method (a subsidy paid to the supplier) will not.

[3] Treatment of Supplies by Government

It is in the treatment of supplies made by, rather than to, government that the effects on the tax base can be seen. Until recently, Australia adopted an interesting, possibly unique, technique for dealing with taxes and user charges. The law provided that '[t]he payment of any Australian tax, fee or charge (other than the GST)' is treated as consideration for a supply made by the person receiving the payment to the person making the payment.[107] Taking this provision in isolation, it might be thought that Australia was 'taxing' collective consumption, with all taxes, fees and charges being grossed up for GST. However, the law went on to provide that any tax, fee or charge specified in a legislative instrument issued by the Treasurer would not be treated as consideration for a supply. The Treasurer's determinations under this provision were extensive and were regularly updated. One of the more recent versions, issued on 1 July 2010,[108] ran to 675 pages and excluded from the tax base:

- Commonwealth government taxes, including income tax, fringe benefits tax, Medicare levy, and other indirect taxes (Luxury Car Tax, Wine Equalisation Tax, Excise Tax);
- a range of State taxes, including taxes on gambling;
- local government rates, including water and waste disposal rates;
- user charges, including State and Territory fees to search a register of births, deaths and marriages; filing fees for courts and Tribunals; driver's and rider's licence fees and driving test fees.

Thus, while the law itself gave the impression that the tax base included all government-provided collective and private consumption, the determination made it clear that this was not the case. The underlying logic of the exclusions was explained in the Explanatory Statement to the Determination:

107. GST Act 1999 (Aus), s. 81-5(1). The 'connected with Australia' requirement did not need to be established for the supply to be taxable.
108. A New Tax System (Goods and Services Tax) (Exempt Taxes, Fees and Charges) Determination 2010 (No. 2).

> An Australian tax, fee or charge may be listed on the Determination in accordance with the following principles:
>
> - taxes that are in the nature of a compulsory impost for general purposes and compulsory charges by the way of fines or penalties will be exempt from GST
> - regulatory charges that do not relate to particular goods or services will be exempt from GST, including—
>   - fees and charges levied on specific industries and used to finance particular regulatory or other activities in the government sector; and
>   - licences, permits and certifications that are required by government prior to undertaking a general activity.

Unlike the New Zealand position, this is a long way from the recommendations of Aujean et al. and Gendron that all specific charges made by government should be taxed. Nonetheless, it is entirely consistent with the original Australian design intentions for the tax, as stated in the ANTS White Paper which outlined plans for the introduction of GST to Australia:

> The non-commercial activities of government will be outside the scope of the GST. For example, appropriations for general government activities will not be taxable, nor will grants from one level of government to another, as neither constitutes consideration for a supply. Fines, penalties and taxes are not usually commercial transactions. The range of taxes and charges that will not be subject to the GST is extensive and will include taxes and charges levied at all levels of government.[109]

Recent changes to the Australian law reaffirm that that the Australian GST is intended to tax only the commercial activities of government and to effectively zero-rate non-commercial activities. Under the new approach, the original design outlined above has been effectively reversed: instead of including everything in the law and then excluding non-commercial activities by determination, the law now excludes most non-commercial activities by providing that:

- the payment of a tax (however described) is not consideration for a supply;[110]
- the payment of a fee or charge (however described) 'imposed under an Australian law and payable to an Australian government agency' is not consideration for a supply if:
  - it is for or relates to the 'provision, retention, or amendment, under an Australian law, of a permission, exemption, authority or licence (however described)'; or
  - it is paid to a government agency for recording, copying, modifying, allowing access to, receiving, processing, or searching for information.[111]

Regulations may reverse the exclusions (by providing that a particular tax, fee or charge will be treated as consideration for a supply by government to the payer) or add

109. P. Costello, Treasurer of the Commonwealth of Australia, *Tax Reform: Not a New Tax, A New Tax System (The Howard Government's Plan for a New Tax System)* (AGPS 1998), 93 ('the ANTS White Paper').
110. GST Act 1999 (Aus), s. 81-5 (applicable from 27 June 2011).
111. GST Act 1999 (Aus), s. 81-10 (applicable from 27 June 2011).

to them (by providing that other fees or charges are also not consideration for a supply). The Explanatory Memorandum to the bill that made these changes reiterated the basic principles on which it should be determined whether particular government fees or charges should be included in the tax base.[112] New regulations give effect to those principles by specifying that the following fees or charges will be taxable: parking fees, road tolls, fees for hire or use of a facility (not including entry to a national park), fees to use waste disposal facilities, fees for pre-lodgement advice relating to licences, permits and certifications if it is not compulsory to seek the advice, and a fee for the provision of information if the information is not required to be provided under an Australian law.

It is important to be clear that these changes altered the technical design of the law but not the underlying principles to which it gives effect. Under both the old and new rules, the effect of the law was intended to be the same: in Australia, collective consumption of public goods provided by government is not subject to GST and a considerable amount of government-provided private consumption is also not subject to GST.[113]

[4] Government Subsidized Merit Goods

A further difference between the Australian and New Zealand models is the treatment of government-funded merit goods. Australia addresses the neutrality problem that comes with full taxation by extending GST-free treatment to key areas in which government supplies individual consumption for free, or at less than market value, in competition with the private sector. Education and health care are therefore GST-free. The ANTS White Paper had this to say about the health sector:

> The health sector in Australia has significant government involvement through direct subsidy and regulation. Many health services are provided to patients free of any direct charge or by means of a co-payment that is a fraction of the total cost of providing the service.
>
> Applying taxes to health care would place the private health sector, with its heavier reliance on direct fees, at a competitive disadvantage with the public health system.
>
> For this reason, most medical and hospital care services and health insurance will be *GST-free.*[114]

It went on to say:

> Like health and medical care, education receives significant government assistance. Public primary and secondary education is provided free of charge and significant

112. Explanatory Memorandum to *Tax Laws Amendment (2011 Measures No. 2) Bill 2011*, Ch 4.
113. Note that since this paper was completed, the Commissioner of Taxation has issued a number of opinions suggesting that in his view the effect of the law has changed and treating as consideration for a taxable supply a payment that was previously listed as exempt. See, for example, the difference between ATO ID 2012/21 'GST and Division 81 of the GST Act: fee imposed before 1 July 2012 that was specified in the final Determination' and ATO ID 2012/22 'Goods and Services Tax: GST and Division 81 of the GST Act: judicial system daily hearing fee imposed after 30 June 2012'. Whether the Commissioner's view is accurate has yet to be tested.
114. The ANTS White Paper (n. 109 above), 93.

assistance is given to private schools and tertiary and vocational education. Applying the GST to education would discriminate against private providers.

Most educational services will therefore be *GST-free*.[115]

Thus, Australia has chosen to reduce its revenue base in order to fully include government in the GST regime but retain neutrality between public and private sector supplies of goods or services. It has done so, however, in a manner that avoids the problems that come with the European exemption of the government, health, and education sectors because it treats all government activity as commercial activities and allows full input tax credits, including for inputs that relate to supplies made for no consideration or to the community at large, under the same input tax credit rules that apply to the private sector.

[5] Why Has Australia Adopted this Approach?

Australia's federal structure explains why it chose to adopt the GST-free approach rather than to follow the New Zealand deemed supply model. If revenue from the Crown and grants by one part of government to another were deemed to be consideration for taxable supplies, the result would be a redistribution of revenue from one government to another. In New Zealand, the GST charged on intra-government revenue flows goes back to the government doing the spending, with no net effect on revenue. By way of contrast, consider the situation if a New South Wales (NSW) government department were inserted into the fact situation illustrated in Figure 4.2. If the New Zealand approach were applied in Australia, the following consequences would follow:

(1) Revenue brought to account by a NSW government department from the Crown would be subject to GST, which would be paid to the Commonwealth. As a result, 1/11th (the tax fraction) of all NSW spending would be redirected to the Commonwealth. Although the Commonwealth redistributes most of the GST revenue to the States and Territories, NSW would not be fully compensated for the tax on its spending because it is a net donor to other States and Territories under the revenue distribution formula.[116]

(2) As in New Zealand, grants by a NSW government department to a local government and a business would give rise to no net effect for either the Commonwealth or the State because the output tax paid by the local government and the business would give rise to an input tax credit for the department.

(3) Taxing local authority rates would also give rise to a redistribution from local government to the Commonwealth. Given that one part of the tax reform agreement between the Commonwealth and the States involved the transfer of responsibility for funding local government from the Commonwealth to

115. *Ibid.*, 94.

116. In addition, part of the GST revenue is paid to the Australian Taxation Office to cover its costs of collection.

the States, this would obviously be difficult to justify politically.[117] On the other hand, since this output tax is intended to be a burden on consumers, rates could be subject to GST so long as local authorities were able to pass on the full effect to consumers and did not require top-up payments from the State government.

(4) The taxable supply by the business to the consumer would (appropriately) raise GST revenue for the Commonwealth, which would then be redistributed to the States and Territories.

The critical stumbling block is clearly the first step, in which the tax fraction of NSW government spending ends up in the hands of the Commonwealth. The Australian exclusion of payments specifically covered by an appropriation prevents this from happening. At the same time, it prevents the tax fraction of Commonwealth spending being diverted into the GST revenue and distributed to the States and Territories.

The federal structure also explains why it is important to give input tax credits to government. In common with the constitutions of many federal nations, the Australian constitution prohibits the Commonwealth imposing taxes on State property.[118] However, since the GST law was introduced as part of a tax reform agreement under which the States and Territories abandoned some of their existing tax base in exchange for a share of the Commonwealth GST revenues,[119] the States are desirous of working around this constitutional prohibition in order to make the tax work. This is achieved with more smoke and mirrors. The Commonwealth GST imposition laws state:[120]

5. Act does not impose a tax on property of a State

(1) This Act does not impose a tax on property of any kind belonging to a State.

(2) *Property of any kind belonging to a State* has the same meaning as in section 114 of the Constitution.

At the same time, State legislation allows State government entities to proceed as if GST applied. The New South Wales law states:[121]

117. Costello (n. 109 above), 25–26 and 84–85.

118. Commonwealth of Australia Constitution Act, s. 114.

119. Council of Australian Governments, *Intergovernmental Agreement on The Reform of Commonwealth-State Financial Relations* (1999), entered into by the Federal Government (the Commonwealth of Australia), the six Australian States (New South Wales, Queensland, Victoria, South Australia, Tasmania, and Western Australia), and the two main territories (the Northern Territory and the Australian Capital Territory) (hereafter 'the Intergovernmental Agreement'). For the current agreement, see Council of Australian Governments, *Intergovernmental Agreement (IGA) on Federal Financial Relations* (2009).

120. See section 5 in each of the GST imposition laws. For unrelated constitutional reasons, it takes six GST imposition laws to impose the GST that is described in the GST Act 1999: A New Tax System (Goods and Services Tax Imposition–General) Act 1999, A New Tax System (Goods and Services Tax Imposition–Customs) Act 1999, A New Tax System (Goods and Services Tax Imposition–Excise) Act 1999, A New Tax System (Goods and Services Tax Imposition (Recipients)–General) 2005, A New Tax System (Goods and Services Tax Imposition (Recipients)–Customs) 2005, and A New Tax System (Goods and Services Tax Imposition (Recipients)–Excise) 2005.

121. Intergovernmental Agreement Implementation (GST) Act 2000 (New South Wales), s. 5.

5. Payment of GST equivalents by State entities
A State entity may pay to the Commissioner of Taxation amounts representing amounts that would have been payable for GST if:

(a) the imposition of that GST were not prevented by section 114 of the Commonwealth Constitution, and
(b) section 5 of each of the GST Imposition Acts had not been enacted,

and may do things of a kind that it would be necessary or expedient for it to do if it were liable for that GST.

Thus, the Commonwealth laws say that they do not tax State property and the State laws say that State entities may pretend that they do, and may act accordingly. Given the input tax credit rules, the overall effect is that the GST law does indeed not tax property of a State, since any tax imposed on a supply to a State entity is creditable, while any tax imposed on a supply by a State entity is paid by the customer by being included in the price of the supply. Not imposing GST on consideration charged for non-commercial supplies by government further ensures that there is no appearance of State revenue being diverted to the Commonwealth.

If Figures 4.1 and 4.2 were adapted to show the effect of Australian GST, there would be little to show. The only supply for consideration is the supply by the business to the consumer. Everything else effectively disappears from the GST net. The churning of GST through the various levels of government disappears without losing the benefits of including government in the full taxation regime. The total revenue raised is, of course, also different because New Zealand taxes local government-provided collective consumption and most government-provided private consumption but Australia does neither.

§4.04 REFORMING THE EU APPROACH

Should the European VAT treatment of government be reformed, and if so, how? Although it is beyond the scope of this chapter to consider this issue in any detail, some preliminary thoughts are nonetheless offered. A full answer would require the considered opinion of someone more experienced in the operation of European VAT laws.

[A] The 'Canadian' Rebate System?

Professor Gendron suggests that the full taxation approach might be too difficult and recommends the Canadian rebate approach as an alternative.[122] A good deal of the complexity that leads Canada to favour rebates comes from its complex mix of federal and provincial taxes, a mix that might well be more complex than the divergent approaches to the EU VAT Directive that are evident in Europe. The underlying legal structures in operation in Canada are frequently disguised by the language in which the Canadian consumption tax arrangements are discussed. From the perspective of legal

122. Gendron (n. 57 above).

structure, Canada's ten provinces and three territories can be categorized into two groups, each with two sub-groups, as shown in Table 4.1.

Table 4.1 Subgroups of Canadian VAT laws as at 1 July 2010[123]

Single Law Provinces/Territories		*Double Law Provinces*	
GST Only	*GST/HST*	*GST/RST*	*GST/QST*
Alberta Northwest Territories Nunavut The Yukon Territory	Newfoundland and Labrador New Brunswick Nova Scotia Ontario British Columbia	Prince Edward Island Manitoba Saskatchewan	Quebec

In the single law provinces and territories, tax is imposed under a single federal law: the Excise Tax 1985 ('the ETA'):[124]

(1) GST only: In Alberta and the three territories, the ETA imposes the 5% Canadian GST (the CVAT). This is a federal tax, the revenue from which the federal government is entitled to retain for itself.
(2) GST/HST: In the provinces participating in the 'harmonized' sales tax, the ETA imposes a single tax at a rate of that differs between provinces. The rates range from 12% to 15%. Part of the revenue collected from this tax is redistributed to the participating provinces in accordance with agreements entered into between the federal government and each provincial government. Although the tax is always discussed as consisting of separate elements – a 5% federal GST or CVAT and a 7% to 10% provincial Sales Tax (the PVAT) – the amount of revenue distributed to each province is calculated under agreed formulae, and does not depend on an exact determination of how much net revenue is collected from a particular province.[125]

In the double law provinces, separate federal and provincial consumption tax laws apply.

123. In addition, a First Nations Tax replaces the federal element of the GST in some First Nations reserves: First Nations Goods and Services Tax Act, S.C. 2003, c. 15, s. 67. [Note that since this paper was written, British Columbia has withdrawn from the GST/HST regime.]
124. Excise Tax Act, R.S.C 1985, c. E-15. Part IX of the Act deals with goods and services tax.
125. The disconnect between revenue raised and revenue distributed is noted in R.M. Bird & P.-P. Gendron, *VATs in Federal States: International Experience and Emerging Possibilities*, 55 International Bulletin of Fiscal Documentation 293–309 (2001). For an example of the formulae used to estimate the revenue raised in a particular province, see Annexure A to the *Comprehensive Integrated Tax Coordination Agreement Between The Government of Canada and The Government of Ontario*, www.fin.gov.on.ca/en/publications/2009/citca.html, which deals with revenue allocation and sets out the calculations required to determine the amount of revenue to be allocated to Ontario.

(3) GST/RST: In three provinces, the ETA imposes the 5% federal GST and a separate provincial law imposes a retail sales tax, with each government entitled to retain the revenue from its own tax.
(4) GST/QST: In one province (Quebec), there are dual VATs, one imposed under a federal law (the 5% GST) and the other imposed under a provincial law (the Quebec Sales Tax, or QST).[126] As Gendron notes in his paper, this is the only province in which one tax is included in the tax base of the other (the QST applies to GST-inclusive prices). Both are collected by the Quebec Revenue authority and it is presumed that the GST revenue is either actually or notionally redistributed to the federal Government.

The agreements, the law and the language in which the harmonized sales tax arrangements are discussed reflect the political decision to respect the independent taxing power of the provinces, allowing them to specify variations in the tax base and rate for the provincial element of this federally-imposed tax. Quebec is, however, the only province in which one government has been delegated to collect a tax imposed by another government's law. In the HST provinces, it is the legal imposition of the tax that has been delegated. The ETA nonetheless imposes the GST/HST (CVAT/PVAT) in accordance with the agreements with each province, reflecting the provincial decisions about rate and base in the federal law. From a legal perspective, however, the participating provinces have essentially given up exercising their right to directly impose and collect sales taxes in exchange for a share of the GST/HST revenue collected by the federal government.

Although Australia is also a federation, its situation is different. The early rhetoric that the Australian GST was a State tax being collected by the federal Government on behalf of the States has been largely dropped in favour of an acknowledgement of the legal reality. The Australian GST is a single federal tax, imposed at a single rate and on a common base throughout the whole of Australia by laws of the Commonwealth of Australia. The Commonwealth's Consolidated Financial Statements recognize the GST revenue as Commonwealth revenue and report the distribution of that revenue to the States and Territories as Commonwealth grants.[127] As with the Canadian HST/GST, the Australian States and Territories ceased to exercise some of their taxing powers in exchange for a share of the federally imposed and collected GST revenue. Through the Council of Australian Governments (COAG), they have an ongoing say in GST policy, and any changes to the rate or the base must be unanimously agreed to by all States and Territories. However, unlike the Canadian position, this process does not involve separate and independent agreements between the Commonwealth and each State or Territory and does not encompass variations to the tax rate or base from one State/Territory to another.[128]

126. *Loi sur la Taxe de vente du Québec*, L.R.Q. c. T-0.1 (An Act Respecting the Québec Sales Tax, R.S.Q. c. T-0.1).
127. The Hon Lindsay Tanner MP, Minister for Finance and Deregulation, *Media Release 01/2007 Consolidated Financial Statements 2006-07*, 20 December 2007.
128. Council of Australian Governments (n. 119 above).

If we look at the legal structure of VAT in Europe, it is clear that none of the systems in place in Canada, Australia or New Zealand provides an exact analogy for the European experience. The EU VAT Directive does not directly impose tax in Member States and must instead be implemented by domestic legislation:

- The equivalent of the Australian situation would be a tax directly imposed by the European Union at a single, common rate throughout Europe, with the revenue distributed back to the Member States.
- The equivalent of the Canadian GST/HST provinces would be similar, but with rate and base variation allowed to each Member State. These variations would have to be reflected in territorial variations in the European law, which would be administered centrally, at European expense.
- The equivalent of the Quebec situation would involve a single European law imposing tax in every Member State, alongside separate national VATs, with the revenue authorities from each Member State collecting both taxes together and distributing the European share back to the EU.[129]
- The equivalent of the New Zealand situation would require Europe to be a single country.

Not only do none of these comparisons reflect the actual situation, they are also unlikely to do so at any stage in the near future. From a VAT perspective, the current European situation can be most closely conceptualized as a reverse of the situation in Australia and the Canadian GST/HST provinces. Each of the Member States imposes a VAT under its own law. Although the design of the law is constrained by the requirements of the EU VAT Directive, subject to the discretions allowed to Member States under the Directive and to derogations granted to the Member State, each Member State is an independent nation raising its own revenue, under its own law.

Just as, in Australia, and in Canada for the participating provinces, a proportion of the VAT collected is 'redistributed' to the states/provinces, in each Member State a proportion of the VAT revenue is then 'redistributed' to the European Union.[130] Moreover, the similarities do not end there, because the revenue distributed to the Union is not a direct proportion of the actual revenue collected, but an amount calculated according to a formula. Member States make calculations in accordance with Council Regulations[131] to get to a common tax base, which is 'a theoretical construct that compensates for the fact that neither the VAT rates nor the list of goods

129. This corresponds to a recent proposal of the Commission to introduce an EU VAT at a low rate (1–2%), to be collected by the Member States: Commission Staff Working Document, 'Technical Annexes, Accompanying Document to the Communication from the Commission to the European Parliament, the Council, the European Economic and Social Committee, the Committee of the Regions and the National Parliaments The EU Budget Review COM(2010) 700 final', SEC(2010) 7000 final, Section 11.5, 34–35. It is presumed that the EU VAT would not form part of the tax base for the Member States' VATs (cf. the tax base of QST, which does include the Canadian GST).
130. The VAT-based resource is one of three sources of revenue for the Union.
131. Primarily Council Regulation (EEC, EURATOM) No 1553/89 of 29 May 1989 on the definitive uniform arrangements for the collection of own resources accruing from value added tax, OJ L155/9–13 of 1989.

and services covered by VAT are harmonised at EU level'.[132] The common tax base is also limited by reference to gross national income (GNI). A uniform rate of call is applied to this base to determine how much each Member State must contribute to the Union. Whereas the proportion of GST/HST that is distributed to the Canadian provinces is significant, and almost all of the Australian GST is redistributed to the States and Territories, the percentage of VAT revenue that must be given to the European Union is very low. The uniform rate of call is 0.30% for all Member States, but is reduced to 0.225% for Austria, to 0.15% for Germany, and to 0.10% for Sweden for the period 2007–2013.[133]

The rebate approach suggested by Gendron is one way of addressing the problems created by exemption without expanding the tax base and in fact a number of European countries already do pay VAT rebates to government. For example, under the United Kingdom VAT law, input tax incurred by certain public bodies will be refunded so long as it does not relate to a business carried on by the body.[134] A similar approach is taken in the Netherlands.[135] Other EU Member States also offer such rebate schemes, some targeted more widely than others.[136] Rebates are therefore nothing new in Europe; it is just that they are not a formal feature of the VAT regime.

While rebates can reduce the impact of the exclusion of government, they suffer from a number of problems. They lack transparency; they are generally paid in lump sums on an intermittent basis, rather than immediately on the VAT return; they require separate compliance and administration regimes; to the extent that only some of the input taxed incurred is rebated, they are an incomplete solution. A cautionary note that might also be important for Member States paying rebates to public bodies is the prohibition on state aid.[137] Though not a member of the EU, Norway is a member of the European Free Trade Association (EFTA) and therefore part of the European Economic Area (EEA). Norway is therefore a participant in the European single market and is subject to a prohibition on state aid.[138] In 2007, the EFTA Surveillance Authority issued a decision in relation to a complaint about the Norwegian VAT Compensation Act.[139,140] Under that Act, public bodies were entitled to receive refunds for the VAT

132. ec.europa.eu/budget/budget_detail/revenue_detail en.htm (data collected 8 October 2010, this version no longer available online).
133. *Ibid.*
134. Value Added Tax Act 1994, s.33
135. Article 3 of the Law of 27 June 2002 on the VAT Compensation Fund (*Wet van 27 juni 2002, houdende de Wet op het BTW-compensatiefonds*) rebates input tax to public bodies on goods and services purchased or imported for purposes 'other than carrying on an enterprise'.
136. In addition to the Dutch and British schemes, the EFTA decision discussed later in this section (see n. 140 below) notes the existence of such schemes in Sweden, Denmark, Finland, France, Luxembourg, Austria, and Portugal.
137. See Articles 107, 108 and 109 of the Treaty on the Functioning of the European Union (TFEU).
138. Article 6(1) of the EEA Agreement states: 'Save as otherwise provided in this Agreement, any aid granted by EC Member States, EFTA States or through State resources in any form whatsoever which distorts or threatens to distort competition by favouring certain undertakings or the production of certain goods shall, in so far as it affects trade between Contracting Parties, be incompatible with the functioning of this Agreement.': Agreement on the European Economic Area, OJ L1/3 of 1994.
139. Act No. 108 of 12 December 2003 on VAT compensation to local and regional authorities (*Lov om kompensasjon av merverdiavgift for kommuner, fylkeskommuner mv*).

they incurred when acquiring goods and services. One of the reasons for introducing the scheme was to counteract the incentive to in-source services (eg., by employing cleaners directly rather than subcontracting to a specialist cleaning business). However, the right to refunds of VAT granted to public bodies under the VAT Compensation Act was unlimited, and public bodies were able to claim refunds of VAT when they carried out activities in competition with the private sector, even if the public sector activities were exempt. The VAT compensation scheme gave the appearance of effectively zero-rating public bodies, giving them an advantage over their exempt private sector competitors. The particular activity of concern in the case was the supply 'by particular municipal schools, which provide specialised services to the offshore sector in competition with [exempt private sector education suppliers]'.

The EFTA Surveillance Authority concluded that the payment of refunds to public authorities did constitute state aid to the extent that the VAT refunds related to exempt activities carried on by the public bodies in competition with the private sector. The authority considered it irrelevant that since the public bodies were publicly funded, the refunding of the VAT was economically no different from giving a higher level of public funding in the first place, to cover the input tax that would be incurred by the body.[141] As a result of the decision, Norway could not simply fund public bodies on a VAT-exclusive basis and later refund to them the VAT they incurred. Instead, at least to the extent that public bodies carry out exempt activities in competition with the private sector, it must fund them on a VAT-inclusive basis, something that will obviously be less exact than the measures that had been in place under the VAT compensation scheme. Clearly, such considerations mean that any widespread adoption of the Canadian rebate model throughout Europe could be fraught with the same difficulties that the current exemption regimes already bring.

[B] A 'Full' Taxation Model?

There is really no obvious reason why full taxation cannot be adopted in Europe: the only question is how far that process should go. Should it extend only to alleviating the problems of exemption or should it also extend the tax base to include all private consumption expenditure and possibly some aspects of collective consumption expenditure?

A full taxation model can achieve the same results as a well-designed rebate system without necessarily expanding the tax base, with significant benefits in terms of integration with the VAT regime. The net effect of the United Kingdom rebate scheme

140. The EFTA Surveillance Authority Decision No. 155/07/COL of 3 May 2007 on State aid granted in connection with Article 3 of the Norwegian Act on compensation for value added tax (VAT), OJ L249/35-36 of 2008.

141. In defence of the scheme, Norway had noted that its introduction was accompanied by a reduction in funding to public bodies. The rebates were therefore merely an alternative way of delivering government funding. In addition to ruling that this was irrelevant to the question of whether the rebates constituted state aid, the authority noted its understanding that 'each municipality does not get a reduction in the state transfer exactly corresponding to the exact VAT compensation it receives': *ibid.*, 10.

is similar to the effect of the Australian GST law. The United Kingdom refunds the input tax incurred on excluded government activities, thereby effectively zero-rating collective consumption. Where public authorities carry on a business, they are subject to the same rules as other registered persons. If they make taxable supplies, they will be entitled to input tax credits, even if those supplies are made at subsidized prices. If they make exempt supplies, they will not be entitled to input tax credits. Australia achieves the same result simply by treating the activity of being a government entity as an economic activity and then subjecting government to the same basic rules as all other businesses. Importantly, these rules include giving input tax credits for all inputs other than those that relate to making exempt supplies.

While the United Kingdom rebate approach is, at least on the surface, comparatively simple because of its breadth, it nonetheless still requires public bodies to separately identify their 'business' and 'non-business' activities, something that the Australian approach does not require. Moreover, because the non-business activities of government are still 'out-of-scope', the system remains complex if the refunds must be applied for under a separate regime, rather than being administered as if they were no different from input tax deductions.

If the main aim of adopting full taxation in Europe would be to ensure input tax recovery on non-exempt government activities, there is no reason why that should be achieved in the same way by each country. In particular, given that each Member State enacts its own separate VAT law, it would be perfectly feasible for the treatment of intra-government spending flows, grants, and subsidies to be dealt with differently by different Member States, so long as the tax effect for government (and business) activity was purely domestic. The treatment of transnational subsidies and grants would need to be addressed but it should be perfectly feasible for some states to adopt the New Zealand approach and others to adopt the Australian approach, since the net effect is similar for them both.

In the end, however, the treatment of government cannot be separated from a wider review of the entire VAT system. The input tax credit rules, the use of partial apportionment formulae, the exemption of merit goods and a wide range of other goods: all of these impact on the treatment of government, and vice versa. The real stumbling blocks to a more full inclusion of government in the European VAT are the other exemptions in the Directive. So long as there are broad exemptions (and variations in exemptions) for education, health, immovable property, and other items, the VAT treatment of government will need to be designed to ensure neutrality between government and private sector providers of such goods and services. The Australian approach of ignoring revenue flows within government and also ignoring grants and subsidies that are not linked to the price of a supply would probably be more effective in the context of a regime that includes such exemptions. Certainly, it is closer to the existing framework of the EU VAT Directive. It is also preferable to the New Zealand 'deemed supply' approach if revenue formulae continue to be used to calculate the input tax credits of government entities. Consider, for example, a government school that receives funding from a government education department and uses the funding to supply exempt education services for free or at considerably less than market value. If the school is treated as making a taxable supply in return for the government funding, as it would be in New Zealand, the use of a revenue formula to calculate its input tax credit entitlement would effectively zero-rate the education because the combination of the 'consideration' for the deemed taxable supply and the lack of consideration for the exempt supplies would distort the formula. The Australian approach that treats the grant as merely a transfer payment not linked to the price of a supply would clearly be better in such circumstances.

CHAPTER 5

Comparing the Treatment of Charities under Value Added Taxes and Retail Sales Taxes

Walter Hellerstein*

§5.01 INTRODUCTION

This paper compares the treatment of charities under value added taxes (VATs) and retail sales taxes (RSTs) from both a normative and descriptive perspective. A comparative analysis of the treatment of the charitable sector under two different consumption tax regimes yields some interesting insights about the nature of both regimes, the operation of the charitable exemption, and the relationship between consumption taxation and the charitable sector.[1]

* I am extremely grateful to Julia Titolo for her valuable research assistance in connection with this paper, and, in particular, with the preparation of the paper's appendix. I am also grateful to Edith Brashares, Harley Duncan, Paul Heald and Jon Sedon for comments on an earlier draft of this paper. Errors or omissions are mine alone.

1. The comparative focus of this paper in a volume devoted to VAT exemptions may warrant a brief preliminary explanation or, perhaps, confession. Although I have devoted increasing attention to VATs in recent years, see, e.g., M. Keen & W. Hellerstein, *Interjurisdictional Issues in the Design of a VAT*, 63 Tax L. Rev. 359–408 (2010); W. Hellerstein & H. Duncan, *VAT Exemptions: Principles and Practice*, 128 Tax Notes 989–999 (2010), the lion's share of my work on consumption taxation has been devoted to the American subnational RST. See, e.g., J. R. Hellerstein & W. Hellerstein, *State Taxation* (vol. II, 3d ed., 2012 rev., Warren, Gorham & Lamont 2010), including eight chapters devoted to US subnational RST; W. Hellerstein & J.A. Swain, *Streamlined Sales and Use Tax* (Warren, Gorham & Lamont 2009). Accordingly, while undertaking a comparative analysis of the VAT and the RST treatment of charities is justified by the intrinsic interest of the inquiry, it confers the additional benefit of allowing me to respect the admonition to 'write what you know'.

§5.02 COMPARING THE TREATMENT OF CHARITIES UNDER AN IDEAL VAT AND AN IDEAL RST

[A] The Equivalence between an Ideal VAT and an Ideal RST

There is general agreement, at least among academic observers, that an ideal VAT and an ideal RST would (at the end of the day) tax supplies or sales in the same appropriate way, namely, imposing a uniform levy on final consumption.[2] Accordingly, under an ideal VAT or RST, all sales to final consumers would be taxed and businesses would not bear any economic burden from the tax, other than the burden of complying with tax administration. In short, '[t]he "pure" versions of the RST ... and the VAT are ... equivalent ...'.[3] This equivalence may be illustrated by a simple example.[4]

Let us assume that a 10% VAT is applied to the production and sale of notepads. We further assume that a tree farmer, who makes no purchases,[5] harvests trees and sells them to a paper mill for USD 100, plus a USD 10 VAT; the paper mill, in turn, produces paper that it sells to a printer for USD 150, plus a USD 15 VAT against which it credits the USD 10 VAT it paid, remitting the USD 5 balance to the government; the printer, in turn, binds and colours the paper, selling it to the retailer for USD 300 plus a USD 30 VAT against which it credits the USD 15 VAT it paid, remitting the USD 15 balance to the government; and the retailer sells the notepads to consumers for USD 500 plus a USD 50 VAT against which it credits the USD 30 VAT it paid, remitting the USD 20 balance to the government.

Now assume, alternatively, that a 10% RST is applied to the production and sale of notepads under the same economic assumptions that governed the VAT transactions described in the preceding paragraph. The tree farmer harvests trees and sells them to a paper mill for USD 100, charging no tax because he receives a 'resale certificate' from the paper mill.[6] The paper mill, in turn, produces paper that it sells to a printer for USD 150, again charging no tax because it receives a resale certificate from the printer. The

---

2. See, e.g., Organisation for Economic Cooperation and Development, *OECD International VAT/GST Guidelines: Draft Guidelines on Neutrality* (OECD, December 2010), 4, available at www.oecd.org/topic/0,3699,en_2649_33739_1_1_1_1_37427,00.html ('VAT is a tax on consumption, paid, ultimately by final consumers, and collected by businesses'); C.E. McLure Jr. & W. Hellerstein, *Congressional Intervention in State Taxation: A Normative Analysis of Three Proposals*, 31 St. Tax Notes 721–735, 727 (2004) ('A neutral system of sales taxation would follow these ... tenets: (a) all sales to consumers would be taxed uniformly; (b) all sales to businesses would be exempt....').
3. M. Gillis, P. Mieszkowsi & G. R. Zodrow, *Indirect Consumption Taxes: Common Issues and Differences among Alternative Approaches*, 51 Tax Law Rev. 725–774, 754 (1996).
4. The example draws freely from Hellerstein & Duncan (n. 1 above), 989–990.
5. This unrealistic (but harmless) assumption simply allows us to start the VAT chain with the tree farmer's sale rather than further 'upstream' in the economic process (i.e., suppliers who sell to the tree farmer). We also assume unrealistically (but harmlessly) that the transactions described are the only transactions in which the various economic actors engage, thereby limiting the output tax and input tax credits to those generated by those transactions.
6. A supplier, who generally must charge RST on taxable items, is relieved of this obligation if he receives a resale certificate from the purchaser, which indicates that the item is purchased for resale. Under these circumstances, the sale is exempt from tax. See generally Hellerstein & Hellerstein (n. 1 above), para. 14.02.

printer, in turn, binds and colours the paper, selling it to the retailer for USD 300, again charging no tax because it receives a resale certificate from the retailer. Finally, the retailer sells the notepads to consumers for USD 500 plus a USD 50 RST, which it remits to the government.

The equivalence between these two sets of transactions is reflected in Tables 5.1 and 5.2, which are hardly original.[7]

Table 5.1 Ideal VAT (10%)

	Purchases	*Sales*	*Output Tax*	*Input Tax Credit*	*Net VAT Liability*
Tree Farmer	USD 0	USD 100	USD 10	USD 0	USD 10
Paper Mill	USD 100	USD 150	USD 15	USD 10	USD 5
Printer	USD 150	USD 300	USD 30	USD 15	USD 15
Retailer	USD 300	USD 500	USD 50	USD 30	USD 20
Total					USD 50

Table 5.2 Ideal RST (10%)

	Purchases	*Sales*	*Output (Sales) Tax*	*Input Tax Credit*	*Sales Tax Liability*
Tree Farmer	USD 0	USD 100	USD 0 (exempt sale for resale)	Not Applicable	USD 0
Paper Mill	USD 100	USD 150	USD 0 (exempt sale for resale)	Not Applicable	USD 0
Printer	USD 150	USD 300	USD 0 (exempt sale for resale)	Not Applicable	USD 0
Retailer	USD 300	USD 500	USD 50	Not Applicable	USD 50
Total					USD 50

[B] An Ideal VAT or RST Should Not Be Modified for Charities

Beyond the general agreement as to the economic equivalence of an ideal VAT and an ideal RST, there also appears to be an academic consensus that one should not modify the ideal VAT or RST regime to deal with the perceived 'problem' of charities. The

7. See, e.g., S. Cnossen, *A VAT Primer for Lawyers, Economists, and Accountants*, 55 Tax Notes Intl. 319–332, 321 (2009) (table demonstrating equivalence of taxation between various forms of consumption tax, including VAT and RST).

problem, of course, is that charities engage in activities, or produce goods and services, that government wishes to encourage. Saddling charities, or their beneficiaries, with a consumption tax burden, would appear to undermine the policy of encouraging charitable activities. Accordingly, it may be logical to conclude that removing the VAT or RST burden from essential or desirable goods and services reduces the cost of such supplies and makes them more accessible to those who otherwise might be unable to enjoy them.[8]

The difficulty of addressing this problem through a modification of the VAT or RST is that the 'cure' may be worse than the 'disease'. Thus, however the VAT or RST is modified – by exempting supplies made to or by charities, through lowering (or zeroing) the rates on such supplies, or by means of some other adjustment to the structure of the tax – these modifications are likely to raise a series of fundamental concerns regarding their impact on the underlying tax regime. These include:

- undermining economic neutrality by distorting input choices, creating an incentive to self-supply, and frustrating the destination principle;
- producing negative revenue consequences;
- fostering 'exemption' or 'rate reduction' creep; and
- adding considerably to the complexity of tax administration.[9]

As a result of these concerns, 'best practices' for charities under a VAT or an RST would counsel against special treatment within the tax regime itself and would look to other remedies for the perceived malady of imposing a tax burden on charities, such as direct subsidies. As Pierre-Pascal Gendron put it succinctly for the VAT, this means 'full taxation of goods and services supplied by the [charitable] sector, with credit for tax paid on purchases made in order to render the supplies'.[10] Under an ideal RST, this would mean full taxation of the final sale with sale-for-resale exemptions, or zero-rating, of all sales prior to the final sale. The solution to the problem of charities (as Alan Tait concluded) lies outside the VAT regime: 'If governments wish to help

8. L. Ebrill et al., *The Modern VAT*, 85, 91 (International Monetary Fund 2001); Hellerstein & Duncan (n. 1 above), 997; J.L. Mikesell, *State Retail Sales Tax Treatment of Nonprofits*, 52 St. Tax Notes 721–731, 723 (2009); A. Schenk & O. Oldman, *Value Added Tax: A Comparative Approach*, 282–283 (Cambridge University Press 2007).

9. Ebrill et al. (n. 8 above), 83–100; Hellerstein & Duncan (n. 1 above), 991–995, 997–998; Mikesell (n. 8 above), 723–724; Schenk & Oldman (n. 8 above), 282–298.

10. P.-P. Gendron, *How Should the United States Treat Government Entities, Nonprofit Organizations, and Other Tax-Exempt Bodies under a VAT?*, 63 Tax L. Rev. 477–508, 477 (2010). Gendron's observations are addressed to the 'PNC' sector, which encompasses ***P***ublic, **N**on-profit, and **C**haritable entities, although this paper addresses only the '*C*' segment of the sector. Accordingly, the quotations from his observations in the text and in the ensuing discussion substitute '[charitable]' for his original use of 'PNC'. See also M. Aujean, P. Jenkins & S. Poddar, *A New Approach to Public Sector Bodies*, 10 Intl. VAT Monit. 144–149 (1999); M. Aujean, *Commentary*, 63 Tax L. Rev. 509–516, 509 (2010) ('Let's apply the VAT in full to the PNC sector!'); A.A. Tait, *Value Added Tax: International Practice and Problems*, 79 (International Monetary Fund 1988) ('In general, for all these 'merit' goods and services, common sense suggests that as far as possible, they should be treated under the usual VAT regulations.').

particular households, transfers should be made through the budget.'[11] The same point can be made for the RST: 'The presumption is against all exemptions and exclusions except those necessary to define the tax base',[12] and the ideal solution to the problem of charities lies outside the RST system.

At least one VAT regime has, in fact, approximated 'best practices' in its approaches to charities. New Zealand's Goods and Services Tax (GST) is widely recognized as having the broadest VAT base in operation today.[13] Under New Zealand's GST, charities are generally treated like other taxable entities, charging VAT on their supplies and taking credit for the VAT paid on their purchases. As Gendron observes, '[t]his simple and neutral treatment effectively solves the numerous non-neutralities encountered when [charitable] supplies are exempt while similar private sector supplies are taxable'.[14]

§5.03 COMPARING THE TREATMENT OF CHARITIES WITHIN VATS AND RSTS

[A] Alternatives under an Otherwise Ideal VAT or RST Modified Only for Treatment of Charities

When we venture outside the hallowed halls of academia, and the VAT utopia of New Zealand, we confront the reality that real rather than ideal VAT and RST regimes *do* attempt to address the problem raised by taxation of charities by modifying the tax regime from the ideal norm described above. Assuming, for the moment, that these regimes remain 'ideal' except for their 'misguided' effort to modify the general rules of taxation to assist charities or the activities they support, they can do so in essentially two ways: (1) by modifying the treatment of the *charities' purchases* by zero-rating them or exempting them without input tax credit and/or (2) by modifying the treatment of the *charities' sales* by zero-rating them or exempting them without input tax credit.[15]

These options may be illustrated by assuming, in our earlier example of an ideal VAT and RST,[16] that the retailer of notepads is a charitable organization (e.g., a hospital that sells notepads at the hospital gift shop).[17] Under the modified example,

11. Tait (n. 10 above), 79.
12. Mikesell (n. 8 above), 729.
13. Gendron (n. 10 above), 493; Schenk & Oldman (n. 8 above), 69.
14. Gendron (n. 10 above), 494.
15. See Gendron (n. 10 above), 480. The distinction between zero-rating and exempting without input tax credit technically has no relevance to the ideal RST, because in the ideal RST there is no tax on inputs, due to the sale-for-resale exemption.
16. See §5.02[A] above, Tables 5.1 and 5.2.
17. One may quibble with the choice of example, because the charity is arguably engaging in a 'non-charitable' function (selling notepads), even if the proceeds support the charitable function. However, the choice reflected a deliberate effort to facilitate the VAT/RST comparison. Because the US RST, which is the principal focus of our VAT/RST comparison, generally does not tax services, see §5.03[B][1], it is important to use an example (the sale of goods) that allows for a meaningful comparison. The principles at issue remain the same regardless of the

when the charitable retailer purchases the notepads for USD 300 from the printer, who paid a USD 15 VAT on its USD 150 purchase of the paper from the paper mill, the VAT regime may:

- treat the supply as taxable, in which case the printer must charge the charity USD 30 VAT, but will receive a USD 15 input tax credit for the VAT paid;
- zero-rate the supply, in which case the printer will not charge the charity any VAT, but will receive a USD 15 input tax credit (or refund) for the VAT paid; or
- exempt the supply, in which case the printer will not charge the charity any VAT, but will receive no input tax credit (or refund) for the VAT paid.

When the charity sells the notepads at the hospital gift shop for USD 500, the VAT regime may:

- treat the supply as taxable, in which case the charity must charge the purchasers USD 50 VAT, but will receive a USD 30 input tax credit if its purchases were taxable;
- zero-rate the supply, in which case the charity will not charge the purchasers any VAT, but will receive a USD 30 input tax credit (or refund) if its purchases were taxable; or
- exempt the supply, in which case the charity will not charge the purchasers any VAT, but will receive no input tax credit (or refund) for the USD 30 VAT it may have paid to the printer.

These alternatives are reflected in Table 5.3.[18]

---

choice of the example. One could substitute the hospital's sale of prescription drugs (clearly within its 'charitable function'), and the analysis would not change. The choice of notepads was driven by the use of notepads (rather than prescription drugs) in the previous examples.

18. This table (and the accompanying discussion) ignores two additional complicating factors – namely, the fact that charities may be completely 'outside the scope' of VAT and that some supplies may be mixed. The discussion assumes that charities are within the scope of VAT and that there are no mixed supplies (i.e., they all will be treated in the same way, taxable, taxable but zero-rated, or exempt without input tax credit). In addition, the table reflects only the legal consequences of modifying the VAT for charities' purchases and sales. It does not consider the economic burden that charities or their customers may bear from increased prices attributable to irrecoverable VAT paid by charities or their suppliers on their inputs when their supplies associated with such inputs are exempt and limit the suppliers' right to input tax credits. See §5.02[C][1] for discussion of this issue.

Table 5.3 Alternative Treatment of Charities under an Otherwise Ideal VAT (10%)

	Purchases	*Sales*	*Output Tax*	*Input Tax Credit*	*Net VAT Liability*
Tree Farmer	USD 0	USD 100	USD 10	USD 0	USD 10
Paper Mill	USD 100	USD 150	USD 15	USD 10	USD 5
Printer	USD 150	USD 300	USD 30 (taxable)	USD 15	USD 15
			USD 0 (zero-rated)	USD 15	USD 0
			USD 0 (exempt)	USD 0	USD 15
Charity	USD 300	USD 500	USD 50 (taxable)	USD 30/ USD 0/ USD 0[a]	USD 20/ USD 50/ USD 50[b]
			USD 0 (zero-rated)	USD 30/ USD 0/ USD 0	USD 0/ USD 0/ USD 0
			USD 0 (exempt)	USD 0/ USD 0/ USD 0	USD 30/ USD 0/ USD 0
Total					?[c]

a The three input tax credit alternatives in each of the three subdivisions of this row reflect the result of the specified treatment of the charity's supplies under the output tax (taxable, zero rated, or exempt) in light of the specified treatment of the charity's purchases from the printer under the input tax (taxable, zero-rated, or exempt). Thus, if the charity's supplies of notepads are taxable or zero-rated under the output tax (first two subdivisions), it receives a USD 30 input tax credit if its purchases were taxable and USD 0 input tax credit if its purchases were zero-rated or exempt; hence USD 30/USD 0/USD 0. If the charity's supplies of notepads are exempt under the output tax (third subdivision), it receives no input tax credit regardless of the treatment of its purchases; hence USD 0/USD 0/USD 0.

b The three net VAT liability alternatives in each of the three subdivisions of this row reflect the result of the specified treatment of the charity's supplies under the output tax (taxable, zero-rated, or exempt) and its right to an input tax credit based on the specified treatment of its purchases from the printer. Thus, if the charity's supplies of notepads are taxable under the output tax (first subdivision), its net VAT liability is USD 20 if its purchases were taxable (USD 50 output tax less USD 30 input tax) and USD 50 if its purchases were zero-rated or exempt (USD 50 output tax less USD 0 input tax); hence USD 20/USD 50/USD 50. If the charity's supplies of notepads are zero-rated under the output tax (second subdivision), its net VAT liability is USD 0 if its purchases were taxable (USD 0 output tax less USD 30 input tax plus USD 30 refund), and USD 0 if its purchases were zero-rated or exempt (USD 0 output tax less USD 0 input tax); hence USD 0/USD 0/USD 0. Finally, if the charity's supplies of notepads are exempt under the output tax (third subdivision), its net VAT liability is USD 30 if its purchases were taxable (USD 0 output tax plus USD 30 irrecoverable input tax) and USD 0 if its purchases were zero-rated or exempt (USD 0 output tax less USD 0 input tax); hence USD 30/USD 0/USD 0.

c The range of possibilities for the aggregate VAT that the government actually receives (after refunds) is illustrated by the Table 5.4.

Table 5.4 Alternative Amount of VAT Received by Government

	Taxable/ Taxable	*Taxable/ Zero-rated*	*Taxable/ Exempt*	*Zero-Rated/ Taxable*	*Zero-Rated/ Zero-Rated*	*Zero-Rated/ Exempt*	*Exempt/ Taxable*	*Exempt/ Zero-Rated*	*Exempt/ Exempt*
Tree Farmer	USD 10	USD 10	USD 10	USD 10	USD 10	USD 10	USD 10	USD 10	USD 10
Paper Mill	USD 5	USD 5	USD 5	USD 5	USD 5	USD 5	USD 5	USD 5	USD 5
Printer	USD 15	USD 15	USD 15	USD -15	USD -15	USD -15	USD 0	USD 0	USD 0
Charity	USD 20	USD -30	USD 0	USD 50	USD 0	USD 0	USD 50	USD 0	USD 0
Total	**USD 50**	**USD 0**	**USD 30**	**USD 50**	**USD 0**	**USD 0**	**USD 65**	**USD 15**	**USD 15**

The designation in the first row (e.g., Taxable/Taxable, Taxable/Exempt) represents, first, the treatment of the sale by the printer, and, second, the treatment of the sale by the charity (so, for example, Taxable/Exempt indicates that the printer's sale to the charity is taxable and the charity's sale to the purchaser is exempt).

Under an otherwise ideal RST, the effort to support charities within the framework of the tax regime is actually quite simple, at least by comparison to analogous efforts under a VAT. Under an ideal RST, there is, in principle, only a single stage at which one would contemplate modifying the tax treatment for charities, because all earlier stages of the economic process would involve exempt (zero-rated) sales for resale, and there is no problem of irrecoverable input tax. The solution within the ideal RST regime would thus be to exempt or zero-rate the final sale to consumers, which would have the effect of relieving the charities' supplies of any RST burden.[19]

This approach is reflected in Table 5.5, where exempting the charity's sale would result in no tax burden.

Table 5.5 Alternative Treatment of Charities under an Otherwise Ideal RST (10%)

	Purchases	*Sales*	*Output (Sales) Tax*	*Input Tax Credit*	*Sales Tax Liability*
Tree Farmer	USD 0	USD 100	USD 0 (exempt sale for resale)	Not Applicable	USD 0
Paper Mill	USD 100	USD 150	USD 0 (exempt sale for resale)	Not Applicable	USD 0
Printer	USD 150	USD 300	USD 0 (exempt sale for resale)	Not Applicable	USD 0
Charity	USD 300	USD 500	USD 50 (taxable)	Not Applicable	USD 50
			USD 0 (exempt) [zero-rated]	Not Applicable	USD 0
Total					?

[B] The US RST Compared to an Ideal RST

When we turn from the question of how VATs and RSTs might be modified to accommodate charities to the question of how such regimes have in fact been modified to accommodate charities, we find some interesting points of comparison and contrast.[20] But before we can do that, we must relax our academic assumptions a bit further and look at the reality of the RST that is the focus of our actual comparison – the

19. Recall that the distinction between zero-rating and exempting without input tax credit technically has no relevance to the ideal RST, because there is no tax on inputs, due to the sale-for-resale exemption (see n. 15 above). In other words, under an ideal RST, an exemption is equivalent in VAT terminology to zero-rating or exempting with input tax credit. But see §5.02[B] for the implications of exemption under a less-than-ideal RST.
20. See §5.03[C].

US subnational RST (US RST)[21] - rather than an ideal RST (as modified to assist charities).

The actual US RST is a far cry from an ideal RST in two fundamental respects. First, the US RST applies generally only to goods; its application to services is quite limited.[22] Consequently, most supplies provided by charities are not taxable because they lie outside the scope of the US RST. Second, a very substantial proportion of business purchases is in fact subject to US RST, i.e., it is not exempt or zero-rated under a sale-for-resale exemption.[23] Indeed, according to most estimates business purchases constitute roughly 40% of the US RST base, i.e., 40% of the US RST is irrecoverable.[24]

So, how does this affect the treatment of charities? It does so in ways that, somewhat ironically, make the US RST problem more analogous to the problem confronting existing VAT regimes in many countries. First, because charities are engaged primarily in selling services, they will - in the absence of any special rules governing their purchases - be required to pay sales tax on their purchases of goods, because they will not be able to claim a resale exemption. They are deemed to be 'using' goods in the course of selling services rather than reselling goods. Hence there will be embedded irrecoverable RST in the price of what they sell.

[1] Treatment of Charities under US RST with No Special Rules

The US RST treatment may be illustrated by returning to our example of the charity hospital that buys notepads from the printer.[25] However, now assume that, instead of reselling the notepads in the hospital gift shop, the hospital uses the notepads in its own operations. In this case, the hospital would pay sales tax to the printer on the taxable purchase but would collect no sales tax on its out-of-scope supply of services. In short, in the absence of any special rules applicable to charities, a US charitable supplier is in many respects treated like an entity making exempt supplies under VAT, paying irrecoverable tax on its purchases (of goods) but making non-taxable (out-of-scope) supplies of services. This state of affairs is reflected in Table 5.6.

---

21. There is no 'US subnational RST' (US RST) as such. However, 45 states and the District of Columbia have retail sales taxes that share many common features. See generally Hellerstein & Hellerstein (n. 1 above). For purposes of the exposition of the comparison between VATs and RSTs, the US RST may fairly be characterized as a generic levy. We address differences between different states' approaches to the taxation of charities under their particular RSTs in §5.02[C][2] and in the Appendix to this chapter.
22. Hellerstein & Hellerstein (n. 1 above), para. 12.05.
23. Hellerstein & Hellerstein (n. 1 above), para. 12.01
24. R. Cline et al., *Sales Taxation of Business Inputs: Existing Tax Distortions and the Consequence of Extending the Sales Tax to Business Services*, 35 St. Tax Notes 457–470 (2005); R. Ring, *Consumers' Share and Producers' Share of the General Sales Tax*, 52 Natl. Tax J. 79–90 (1999); R. Ring, *The Proportion of Consumers' and Producers' Goods in the General Sales Tax*, 42 Natl. Tax J. 167–179 (1989). This does not mean, of course, that the economic burden of the tax is not passed on, at least in part, depending on supply and demand for the supplies in question.
25. See §5.03[A], Table 5.5.

Table 5.6 Treatment of Charities under the US RST (10%) With No Special Treatment

	Purchases	*Sales*	*Output (Sales) Tax*	*Input Tax Credit*	*Sales Tax Liability*
Tree Farmer	USD 0	USD 100	USD 0 (exempt sale for resale)	Not Applicable	USD 0
Paper Mill	USD 100	USD 150	USD 0 (exempt sale for resale)	Not Applicable	USD 0
Printer	USD 150	USD 300	USD 30	Not Applicable	USD 30
Charity	USD 300	USD 500	USD 0 (out-of-scope) [services]	Not Applicable	USD 0
Total					USD 30

Second, even if a charity were in a position to claim a resale exemption – for example, the Girl Scouts' purchase of Girl Scout cookies for resale to support the Girl Scouts' activities – whatever it purchases from another business is likely to contain a fair portion of embedded or irrecoverable RST in the price that businesses, who themselves were required to absorb the RST because of the narrow resale exemption, now pass on to the charity.

[2] Treatment of Charities under US RST with Special Rules

When, however, the US RST is modified, as it frequently is,[26] to exempt (or zero-rate[27]) charities' purchases or sales, in addition to those that would be non-taxable under general principles as sales for resale (goods) or outside the scope of the RST (services), the alternatives under the RST broadly resemble those reflected in many VAT regimes. Thus, to return to our earlier example involving a charitable hospital's purchase of notepads from a printer for USD 300, the RST regime may:

- treat the sale as taxable, if the hospital were not reselling the notepads as such, in which case the hospital must pay a USD 30 RST;
- treat the sale as exempt, because the notebooks were purchased for resale (say, in the hospital gift shop); or
- treat the sale as exempt, because it generally treats sales to charitable organizations as exempt.

26. See §5.03[C][2] and Appendix.
27. See n. 15 above.

If the hospital sells services, but not notepads, the RST regime will normally treat the sales as outside the scope of the RST. If the hospital sells the notepads at the hospital gift shop for USD 500, the RST regime may:

- treat the sale as taxable, in which case the hospital must collect an RST of USD 50; or
- treat the sale as exempt, because it generally treats sales by charitable organizations as exempt.

These alternatives are reflected in Table 5.7.

Table 5.7 Alternative Treatment of Charities under the US RST (10% RST)

	Purchases	*Sales*	*Output (Sales) Tax*	*Input Tax Credit*	*Sales Tax Liability*
Tree Farmer	USD 0	USD 100	USD 0 (exempt sale for resale)	Not Applicable	USD 0
Paper Mill	USD 100	USD 150	USD 0 (exempt sale for resale)	Not Applicable	USD 0
Printer	USD 150	USD 300	USD 30 (taxable)	Not Applicable	USD 30
			USD 0 (exempt, resale)	Not Applicable	USD 0
			USD 0 (exempt, charity)	Not Applicable	USD 0
Charity	USD 300	USD 500 (services)	USD 0 (outside scope)	Not Applicable	USD 0
		USD 500 (notepads)	USD 50 (taxable)	Not Applicable	USD 50
		USD 500 (notepads)	USD 0 (exempt, charity)	Not Applicable	USD 0
Total					?

[C] Actual Experience of Modifying VATs or RSTs to Provide Alternative Treatment of Charities

[1] Treatment in Practice of Charities under VATs

Most VAT regimes treat charities as exempt, imposing no tax on their sales but taxing their purchases without credit or refund for taxes paid. 'In the prevalent situation around the world, [charitable] purchases are taxable but supplies are exempt so tax gets paid on the value added up to and including purchases by the [charitable] entity.'[28] The OECD lists 'charitable work' as a 'standard exemption',[29] and notes that 'all OECD countries (with the exceptions of New Zealand and Turkey) exempt a number of specific sectors considered essential for social reasons' including 'charities'.[30]

Needless to say, the precise treatment of charities within individual VAT regimes varies from country to country. Although the EU's VAT Directive no longer explicitly recognizes an exemption for charities as such,[31] the current VAT Directive's provision for '[e]xemptions for certain activities in the public interest'[32] broadly authorizes exemptions for activities that are regarded as charitable by Member States.[33] As the large (and ever growing) body of case law emerging from the European Court of Justice and national tribunals reveals, however, once a decision has been made to exempt charities, one inevitably encounters a host of line-drawing problems as to what constitutes a 'charity' for exemption purposes.[34] Moreover, the EU charitable exemption regime illustrates the pitfalls to which we have already alluded[35] of seeking to support the activities of charities through a VAT exemption. As former EU Commissioner for Taxes and Customs, László Kovács, observed, the Achilles' heel of this regime is that '[c]harities ... are unable to obtain a refund of the input VAT they are charged by their various suppliers' with the 'result ... that their costs are increased by this non-recoverable amount of VAT'.[36] As he further recognized, this produces the perverse result of directly undermining the exemptions' goal of reducing the cost of charitable activities, and it leads to distortion of economic decision-making as well.[37]

Even though most VAT regimes employ exemptions when they seek to address the problem of charities within the structure of the tax system, some countries have adopted other approaches that may better serve the objective of assisting charitable

28. Gendron (n. 10 above), 481.
29. Organisation for Economic Cooperation and Development, *Consumption Tax Trends 2010*, 81 (OECD 2011).
30. OECD (n. 29 above), 76.
31. For many years, the EU's Sixth Directive governing Member States' VATs provided an exemption for 'the supply of services and goods closely linked to welfare and social security work, including those supplied ... by other organizations recognised as *charitable* by the Member State concerned'. Sixth Council Directive 77/388/EEC of 17 May 1977 on the harmonization of the laws of the Member States relating to turnover taxes – common system of value added tax; uniform basis of assessment, OJ L145/1 Art. 13(A)(1)(g) (emphasis supplied). The current EU VAT Directive revised the last clause to read 'by other bodies recognised by the Member State concerned as being devoted to social wellbeing'. Council Directive 2006/112/EC of 28 November 2006 on the common system of value added tax, OJ L347/1 Art. 132(1)(g) (Hereafter 'EU VAT Directive').
32. Recast Sixth Directive (n. 31 above), tit. IX, Ch. 2.
33. Schenk & Oldman (n. 8 above), 297–298.
34. See, e.g., Schenk & Oldman (n. 8 above), 290–298 (describing cases).
35. See §5.02[B].
36. L. Kovács, *VAT for Charities – State of Play and Plans for the Future*, 1, presentation at International Philanthropy Conference, 15 September 2005, Brussels, Belgium, available at www.eccvat.org/conferences/2005/09/presentations/kovacs.pdf.This result is illustrated in §5.03[A], Table 5.3, by the charity's purchase of notepads for USD 300 from the printer, which attracts a USD 30 VAT paid by the charity, but the denial of an input tax credit if the charity's supplies are exempt.
37. Kovács (n. 36 above), 2.

undertakings and be less inconsistent with the normative principles that ought to govern a VAT. One alternative that more fully supports the charitable sector is to zero-rate rather than exempt the charity's supplies. Under this approach, there is no irrecoverable VAT associated with the charitable activity.[38] Although there are still negative revenue effects - indeed, they are greater than those created by exemption, because the taxing authority does not retain any irrecoverable VAT - there is less interference with economic neutrality as compared to the use of an exemption. Broad zero-rating of charities thus permits VAT regimes to accomplish two objectives at once: inclusion of the charitable sector within the tax structure and provision of tax relief to the charitable sector. The Australian GST 'comes closest to the ideal of full taxation of the [charitable] sector'[39] along with zero-rating of 'noncommercial sales of goods and services'.[40]

Another alternative to the prevailing approach of simply exempting charities from VAT is the Canadian approach of providing rebates to charities (as well as to other exempt bodies).[41] In substance, this may be viewed as a variant on zero-rating, although, at least in the Canadian case, with less than a full credit for input tax. Under Canada's GST (and harmonized sales tax (HST)[42]), most supplies made by charitable organizations are exempt, but 50% of the GST/HST paid by charities is rebated. The Canadian regime for charities thus represents a 'middle ground'[43] between exemption with no input credit and full zero-rating. Although the split-the-baby approach may seem like a simple, if somewhat arbitrary, compromise between the two extremes of no input tax credit and full zero-rating, it should come as no surprise that 'the system is not simple'.[44]

[2] Treatment in Practice of Charities under the US RST

How have the US states responded to the problem of taxing (or not taxing) charities under their RSTs? They have done so in the way that states have responded to many

38. This result is illustrated in §5.03[A], Table 5.3, by the charity's purchase of notepads for USD 300 from the printer, which attracts a USD 30 VAT paid by the charity, but provision of a USD 30 input tax credit (or refund) upon the zero-rating of its supplies.
39. Gendron (n. 10 above), 503.
40. Gendron (n. 10 above), 493. For these purposes, non-commercial means that the amount charged by the charitable organization for its goods or services must be either less than 50% of their market value or less than 75% of the amount the charitable organization paid to acquire the goods or services.
41. Gendron describes the Canadian system in detail (n. 10 above), 494–500, and the ensuing discussion relies on this description, although modified to focus exclusively on the charitable sector. As noted earlier (n. 10 above), Gendron focuses on the entire PNC sector.
42. The HST is the provincial-level tax that is harmonized with the national GST in a number of Canadian provinces.
43. Gendron (n. 10 above), 503.
44. *Ibid.* Analogous refund schemes have been enacted by some EU Member States to compensate public bodies for VAT input taxes, but they usually operate outside of the VAT regime. Gendron (n. 10 above), 501. R. de la Feria, *The EU VAT Treatment of Public Sector Bodies: Slowly Moving in the Wrong Direction*, 37 Intertax 148–165, 161–162 (2009). These refund schemes are superficially 'similar to the Canadian rebate model', but '[t]heir application in the EU is far less uniform, widespread, and certain ...' Gendron (n. 10 above), 501.

problems, each it in its own idiosyncratic manner,[45] although one can make some generalizations.

First, with regard to sales *to* charities, more than half of the 45 states (and the District of Columbia) with RSTs have attempted to relieve charities of the burden of paying sales tax (which they would otherwise have to pay because they would not normally qualify for a resale exemption) by exempting (zero-rating) their purchases.[46]

At the same time, while less than half the states generally tax sales to charities, even those states usually provide for some exemptions (e.g., the American Cancer Society or the Girl Scouts), although the extent of such specified exemptions varies from state to state.[47] In addition, of course, there are the same types of line-drawing problems under the US RSTs that the EU and other VAT regimes have confronted in delineating the precise scope of the charitable exemption, however defined.[48]

Second, with regard to sales *by* charities, less than one-third of the states broadly exempt or zero-rate their sales, with the usual state-by-state variations and exceptions as to which organizations qualify for the sales exemption.[49] However, to conclude from this statement that states therefore generally subject charities' sales to RST paints a misleading picture of the actual treatment of such sales. While sales by charitable institutions' gift shops may normally be taxable, the overwhelming proportion of charities sales will, as noted earlier, fall 'outside the scope' of the RST, because they constitute non-taxable sales of services (e.g., the services of a charitable hospital, homeless shelter, or day care centre). Furthermore, returning to our Girl Scout Cookie example, even such sales may be exempt or zero-rated, because they will be treated as 'occasional sales', which likewise fall outside the scope of RST.[50]

---

45. Justice Brandeis once famously compared each state to a 'laboratory' of democracy that could experiment with original and individualized solutions to economic and social problems. See *New Ice Co. v. Liebman*, 285 U.S. 262, 311 (1932) (Brandeis, J., dissenting) ('It is one of the happy incidents of the federal system that a single courageous state may, if its citizens choose, serve as a laboratory; and try novel social and economic experiments without risk to the rest of the country.').
46. See the Appendix to this paper (indicating state-by-state treatment of purchases by charitable organizations); see Mikesell (n. 8 above) (including similar charts on non-profits generally, including charities); J.L. Mikesell, *Sales Taxation of Nonprofit Organizations: Purchases and Sales*, in *Sales Taxation: Critical Issues in Policy and Administration*, 121–130 (W.F. Fox ed., Praeger Publishers 1992) (state-by-state charts indicating taxability of sales to charities and sales by non-profit organizations generally, including charities); Research Institute of America (RIA), *All States Tax Guide*, para. 255 (state-by-state chart indicating taxability of sales to non-profit organizations generally, including charities), available at www.checkpoint.thomsonreuters.com (visited on 30 July 2012). One indication of the difficulty of accurately describing precisely how each state treats purchases and sales by charities is that each of these charts differs from one another in particular details, although they generally reflect the same overall picture.
47. See Appendix and sources cited above (n. 46).
48. See the Appendix to this chapter (summarizing state-by-state definitions of charities qualifying for exemptions).
49. See Appendix and sources cited above (n. 46).
50. As Professor John Mikesell has observed:

> State practice has traditionally been to exempt charitable … institutions on casual sales or periodic fundraising events like rummage sales, fish fries, bean suppers, and other regional favorites, or sales of seasonal fundraising items. Laws usually extend the normal casual sales exemption, specifying, for instance, the maximum number of days

Finally, when we come to policy concerns, assuming that a state has rejected the general advice of eschewing 'all exemptions and exclusions except those necessary to define the tax base',[51] as all states have, the question becomes how can states best accommodate charities within their RST regimes without violating normative criteria of consumption taxation and how well have the states measured up to these guidelines. Table 5.7[52] reveals the key issues: first, whether the charity's purchases should be exempt apart from non-taxability based on general features of the RST, namely, the sale-for-resale exemption; second, whether the charity's sales should be exempt apart from non-taxability based on general features of the RST, namely, limiting the tax base to the sale of goods with the sale of services being outside the scope. There does not appear to be any policy basis for *taxing* charitable purchases or sales when comparable purchases or sales not involving charities would be exempt (whether effectively zero-rated or outside the scope of the RST).

Professor John Mikesell has articulated the guiding principles for exempting charities under the US RST.[53] First, RST exemptions for sales by charities should focus on the customer of the charity's goods and services, or on goods and services themselves, *not* on the organization selling the goods and services. Accordingly, if both charitable and private organizations sell a particular good or service, taxability should depend on the nature of the buyer or the nature of the product, not the nature of the seller. Charitable exemptions for sales under the US RST plainly flunk this test because they are almost all based on the nature of the selling organization and not on the nature of the organization's customer. As Mikesell bluntly concludes, the organizational focus of the charitable exemption 'has typically been embodied in sales tax policy' but '[i]t makes no sense'.[54]

Second, charitable organizations are producers of goods or services and should not be treated as if they were final consumers of the inputs they purchase, lest their input tax become 'a concealed (and potentially pyramided) tax burden on the customers for whom they provide services'.[55] The difficulty with this principle, as Mikesell recognizes, is that it is applicable to *all* purchases by intermediate purchasers, not just 'charitable' purchasers. Under a normatively sound RST, of course, the problem would not exist.[56] But under the US RST it is a fundamental 'design' feature (and problem).[57] Under the US RST, service providers generally must absorb (or pass

for the sale, the maximum number of events during the year, a ceiling on the price of items being sold, or the total sales volume permitted.

Mikesell, 'Sales Taxation of Nonprofit Organizations: Purchases and Sales' (n. 46 above), 126. See also Appendix.

51. Mikesell (n. 8 above), 729; see generally §5.02[B].
52. See §5.03[B][2].
53. Mikesell (n. 8 above), 729. Mikesell addresses non-profit organizations generally (including charitable organizations), although our exposition of these principles in the text is limited to charities.
54. Mikesell (n. 8 above), 730.
55. *Ibid.*
56. See §5.02[A].
57. See §5.03[B].

on) the RST they pay, because they are not entitled to a resale exemption.[58] There is no reason as a matter of principle why one would resolve this problem *only* for charitable purchasers.

There is, however, a charity-specific case to be made for exempting (or zero-rating) sales to charities when the charities' own sales are explicitly exempted (zero-rated) on policy grounds.[59] As Mikesell observes: 'It is a policy travesty to deem the customers of a non-profit organization worthy of exemption when the organization makes sales to them and then to try to recoup lost revenue by taxing inputs purchased by that organization.'[60] The US RST does not fare quite as badly when judged by policy norms governing charities' purchases as it does with respect to policy norms governing charities' sales, because a large number of states do exempt charities on their purchases, and the scope of a charity's exempt sales, when made in a state that does not exempt its purchases, has somewhat limited economic significance. Nevertheless, US RST treatment of charitable purchases from a policy standpoint leaves much to be desired.

§5.04 CONCLUSION

If the foregoing discussion has accomplished nothing else, it has revealed that many of the problems created by the charitable exemption under the VAT likewise exist under the RST, including concerns of competitive neutrality, revenue losses and administrative complexity.[61] Accordingly, we end where we began. A good VAT resembles a good RST. The theoretically sound approach to the charitable sector under both regimes is for the consumption tax to treat that sector substantially as it treats other suppliers. Ideally, assistance for the charitable sector should be provided outside of the structure of tax regime itself. Moreover, insofar as the problem of the charitable sector is addressed within the structure of the VAT or RST, the best approach is to eliminate the tax burden on *both* the charity's purchases *and* its sales to ensure that the objects of the charitable exemption are not directly or indirectly burdened by the tax.

58. See §5.03[B][1].
59. At the risk of repeating the same point too often, but, perhaps, one worth taking on the assumption that the average reader of this paper will not be familiar with American consumption tax 'exceptionalism', it is important to keep in mind that we are almost invariably talking about an exemption of a charitable organization's sale of goods, because its services would not ordinarily be taxable to begin with, due to the limited scope of the RST.
60. Mikesell (n. 8 above), 730.
61. For a full appreciation of the last point with regard to the US RST, see the Appendix to this chapter.

APPENDIX: STATE TREATMENT OF CHARITIES UNDER US SUBNATIONAL RST

Overview. In the 'Charity' column, which characterizes the state's approach to defining a charity, the term 'list' means that the state enumerates organizations eligible for a charitable purchase or sales exemption; the term '501(c)(3)' means that the state definition of charity is linked to the federal definition of a charitable organization in federal Internal Revenue Code (IRC) § 501(c)(3), described more fully below in note iii; and the term 'State Definition' means that the state has its own definition of a charity. In the 'Sales to Charity' and 'Sales by Charity' columns, the description seeks to capture the general treatment of the sales as exempt or taxable. Readers should keep in mind that 'exempt' in this context effectively means 'zero-rated' but without any credit for input taxes, because such credits do not exist under an RST. For each state, citations are provided for both the definition of the charity (which may be briefly described) and the treatment of the charity's sales and purchases as described in the chart.

State	*Charity*	*Sales to Charity*	*Sales by Charity*
Alabama	List[i]	Taxable, with specified exemptions	Taxable, with specified exemptions
Alaska[ii]			
Arizona	501(c)(3)[iii]	Taxable, unless specifically exempted	Exempt
Arkansas	State Definition[iv]	Taxable, unless specifically exempted	Exempt unless made for profit or made in competition with a sales-for-profit business
California	State Definition[v]	Taxable, except for items to be donated by the charity	Exempt under stated conditions
Colorado	State Definition[vi]	Exempt	Taxable, unless for fundraising with USD 25,000 limit
Connecticut	501(a)[vii] and 501(c)(3)	Exempt	Taxable, except for charity events 5 days per year
Delaware[viii]			
Dist. of Columbia	State Definition[ix]	Exempt	Taxable, if sales regular
Florida	501(c)(3)[x]	Exempt	Taxable
Georgia	List[xi]	Taxable, with specified exemptions	Taxable, with specified exemptions
Hawaii	State Definition[xii]	Taxable	Exempt
Idaho	List[xiii]	Taxable, with specified exemptions	Taxable, with specified exemptions
Illinois	State Definition[xiv]	Exempt	Taxable, except sales to own members or that do not compete with retailers
Indiana	State Definition[xv]	Exempt	Taxable, except for sales made for 30 days or less per year

State	*Charity*	*Sales to Charity*	*Sales by Charity*
Iowa	State Definition[xvi]	Taxable, with specified exemptions	Exempt
Kansas	501(c)(3)[xvii]	Taxable, with specified exemptions	Taxable, if regular
Kentucky	501(c)(3)[xviii]	Exempt	Taxable
Louisiana	State Definition[xix]	Taxable, with limited exemptions	Taxable, with limited exemptions
Maine	State Definition[xx,]	Taxable, with specified exemptions	Taxable, except for fundraiser sales
Maryland	State Definition[xxi]	Taxable, with specified exemptions	Taxable, with limited exemptions
Massachusetts	501(c)(3)[xxii]	Exempt	Taxable, unless isolated
Michigan	State Definition[xxiii]	Exempt	Taxable, unless less than USD 5,000 per year
Minnesota	State Definition[xxiv]	Exempt	Taxable, except for fundraiser sales
Mississippi	List[xxv]	Taxable, with specified exemptions	Taxable, with specified exemptions
Missouri	State Definition[xxvi]	Exempt	Exempt
Montana[xxvii]			
Nebraska	State Definition[xxviii]	Taxable, with specified exemptions	Taxable, except for limited portion of fundraiser sales
Nevada	State Definition[xxix]	Exempt	Exempt
New Hampshire[xxx]			
New Jersey	State Definition[xxxi]	Exempt	Exempt
New Mexico	501(c)(3)[xxxii]	Taxable for sales of services; exempt for sales of tangible personal property for ordinary use	Exempt
New York	State Definition[xxxiii]	Exempt	Exempt, except for certain retail sales

State	*Charity*	*Sales to Charity*	*Sales by Charity*
North Carolina	501(c)(3)[xxxiv]	Taxable, but refunds provided	Taxable, unless proceeds go to state or for annual fundraiser
North Dakota	State Definition[xxxv]	Taxable, with extremely limited exemptions	Taxable, with limited USD 5,000 exemption
Ohio	State Definition[xxxvi]	Exempt	Taxable, except for sales made for 6 days or less per year
Oklahoma	List[xxxvii]	Taxable, with specified exemptions	Taxable, with specified exemptions
Oregon[xxxviii]			
Pennsylvania	State Definition[xxxix]	Exempt	Taxable, with limited exemptions
Rhode Island	State Definition[xl]	Exempt	Taxable, after two events lasting more than 6 days
South Carolina	State Definition[xli]	Taxable	Exempt
South Dakota	501(c)(3)[xlii]	Exempt	Taxable, with limited exemptions
Tennessee	501(c)(3)[xliii]	Exempt, except for items to be resold in occasional sale	Taxable, unless occasional
Texas	501(c)(3)[xliv]	Exempt	Taxable, except for sales for USD 5,000 or less at two annual one-day auctions
Utah	501(c)(3)[xlv]	Exempt	Exempt
Vermont	501(c)(3)[xlvi]	Exempt	Taxable, unless the prior year's sales were less than USD 20,000
Virginia	501(c)(3)[xlvii]	Exempt	Exempt
Washington	State Definition[xlviii]	Taxable	Taxable, except sales for fundraising activities

State	Charity	Sales to Charity	Sales by Charity
West Virginia	State Definition[xlix]	Exempt	Taxable, except for occasional sales for fundraising
Wisconsin	State Definition[l]	Exempt	Taxable, with limited exemptions
Wyoming	State Definition[li]	Exempt	Taxable, except for occasional sales for fundraising

i. The state enumerates all organizations eligible for exemption in a list, e.g., American Cancer Society, Habitat for Humanity, Red Cross. Ala. Admin. Code r. 810-6-3-.03; Ala. Admin. Code r. 810-6-3-.07.05.

ii. Alaska does not have a state sales tax, but some local jurisdictions impose a local sales tax. Alaska Department of Revenue: Tax Division, <www.tax.alaska.gov/programs/programs/index.aspx?10002> (last visited 30 July 2012).

iii. The state defines charity for RST purposes by reference to Section 501(c)(3) of the federal Internal Revenue Code (IRC). Ariz. Admin. Code R15-5-182. The IRC is the main body of federal statutory tax law in the United States, which many states incorporate by reference for state personal and corporate income tax purposes. IRC § 501(c)(3) provides a description of organizations that are exempt from taxes on their own income and that generally are eligible for tax-deductible charitable contributions from others under IRC § 170. Such organizations must be 'organized and operated exclusively for religious, charitable, scientific, testing for public safety, literary, or educational purposes, or to foster national or international amateur sports competition..., or for the prevention of cruelty to children or animals'. The earnings of these organizations must not benefit any shareholder or individual, and the organizations must not attempt to influence legislation or intervene in any political campaign on behalf of any candidate for public office.

iv. A 'charitable organization' is an organization whose purpose is benevolent, philanthropic, patriotic or eleemosynary and whose function if performed, and not performed by a private party, would have to be performed at public expense. Ark. Code Ann. § 26-51-402(2); Ark. Regs. §§ GR-37(E)(6), GR-39.

v. Under Cal. Code Regs. tit. 18, § 1570, sales by 'charitable' organizations are exempt if:

- the organization is formed and operated for charitable purposes and qualifies for the 'welfare exemption' from property tax under Cal. Rev. & Tax. Code § 214;
- the organization is engaged in the relief of poverty and distress;
- the organization's sales or donations are made principally as a matter of assistance to buyers or donees in distressed financial condition; and
- the property sold or donated was made, prepared, assembled or manufactured by the organization.

vi. The state definition is virtually identical to the definition of charitable organization under IRC § 501(c)(3) (described in note iii of this appendix). Colo. Rev. Stat. §§ 39-26-102(2.5), 39-26-713(2)(d), 39-26-718(1)(b).

vii. IRC § 501(a) provides that certain qualified pension plans are exempt from federal income taxation; IRC § 501(c)(3) organizations are described in note iii of this appendix. Conn. Gen. Stat. §§ 12-412(5), 12-412(8), 12-412(94).

viii. There are no state or local retail sales taxes in Delaware. Instead, Delaware imposes license and gross receipts taxes on the sale of most goods and services. These fees are imposed on the seller or service provider and may not be passed on to the consumer as separately stated additions to the sales price. Delaware Division of Revenue, <revenue.delaware.gov/services/Business_Tax/Exemptions.shtml> (last visited 30 July 2012).

ix. 'Semipublic' institutions qualifying for exemption are defined as any corporation, community chest, fund or foundation, organized exclusively for religious, scientific or charitable purposes, if no part of the net earnings benefits any private shareholder or individual. D.C. Code Ann. §§ 47-2001(r), 47-2005(3), 47-2005(7) § 47-2201(j).

x. The state defines charity for RST purposes by reference to IRC § 501(c)(3) (described in note iii of this appendix). Fla. Stat. § 212.08(7)(p).

xi. The state enumerates all organizations eligible for exemption in a list, e.g., American Cancer Society, Habitat for Humanity, Red Cross. Ga. Comp. R. & Regs. § 560-12-2-.22.

xii. Corporations, associations, trusts or societies organized and operated exclusively for religious, charitable, scientific, or educational purposes qualify for the applicable exemption. Haw. Rev. Stat. §§ 237-23(a)(3)-(5)), 237-23(b). Hawaii's 'sales' tax is a 'general excise tax', a business privilege tax that is imposed on the gross receipts of virtually any economic activity carried on in the state. It therefore is distinguishable from the typical state RST.

xiii. The state enumerates all organizations eligible for exemption in a list, e.g., American Cancer Society, American Diabetes Association, Easter Seals. Idaho Code § 63-36220(1); Idaho Admin. Rules § 35.01.02.085.

xiv. The state definition is virtually identical to the definition of charitable organization under IRC § 501(c)(3) (described in note iii of this appendix). Ill. Comp. Stat. §§ 120/2-5(9) to 120/2-5(11); 86 Ill. Admin. Code §§ 130.2005(a)(2) to 130.2005(a)(4), 140.125(h)(5).

xv. The state definition is similar to the definition of charitable organization under IRC § 501(c)(3) (described in note iii of this appendix). Ind. Code §§ 6-2.5-5-21(b)(1), 6-2.5-5-25, 6-2.5-5-26.

xvi. The state definition is similar to (and makes reference to) the definition of charitable organization under IRC § 501(c)(3) (described in note iii of this appendix). Iowa Code § 423.3(78); Iowa Admin. Code § 701—17.1(6) (422, 423).

xvii. The organization must be a charitable organization under IRC § 501(c)(3) (described in note iii of this appendix) and be listed in the statute. Kan. Stat. Ann. § 79-3606(vv); Kan. Admin. Reg. § 92-19-67.

xviii. The state defines charity for RST purposes by reference to IRC § 501(c)(3) (described in note iii of this appendix). Ky. Rev. Stat. Ann. §139.495.

xix. The state has a limited definition of a charitable organization which must be a charitable organization under IRC § 501(c)(3) (described in note iii of this appendix) and must devote at least 75% of its annual revenue to job training or related community services for people with workplace disadvantages. La. Rev. Stat. Ann. §§ 47:301, 47:301(8)(f).

xx. In addition to qualifying as an exempt organization under IRC § 501(c), the organization must be listed in the Maine statute as qualifying for exemption. Me. Rev. Stat. Ann. tit. 36, §§ 1752(7-C) 1760(c).

xxi. The organization must qualify under IRC § 501(c)(3) (described in note iii of this appendix) and meet additional state requirements. Md. Code Ann. (Tax-Gen.) § 11-204(a)(3).

xxii. The organization must qualify under IRC § 501(c)(3) (described in note iii of this appendix). Mass. Gen. Laws Ch. 64H, § 6(e).

xxiii. The organization must qualify under IRC § 501(c)(3) (described in note iii of this appendix) and meet additional state requirements. Mich. Comp. Laws Ann. §§ 205.54o, 205.54q.; Mich. Admin. Code r. 205.140(2).

xxiv. The state has its own, independent definition of a charitable organization. Minn. Stat. §§ 297A.70(subd. 1), 297A.70(subd. 4)(a), 297A.70(subd. 13); Minn. R. § 8130.6200, subp. 2a.

xxv. The state enumerates all organizations eligible for exemption in a list, e.g., Girl Scouts, National Muscular Dystrophy Association, Salvation Army. Miss. Code Ann. § 27-65-111.

xxvi. A charitable organization must benefit the common good and welfare while relieving government of a financial burden it would otherwise have to bear. Mo. Rev. Stat. § 144.030(2)(19); 12 Mo. Code Regs. § 10-110.955(2)(B).

xxvii. Montana has no general sales tax.

xxviii. There is no exemption for charitable organizations unless falling within specified categories, and the exemption is limited almost entirely to purchases of such organizations. Neb. Admin. R. & Regs. § 1-090.01.

xxix. The organization must advance a public purpose, provide a portion of its services below cost, benefit a substantial class of charitable recipients and relieve government of a burden, among other requirements. Nev. Rev. Stat. §§ 372.326, 372.3261.

xxx. New Hampshire does not have a general sales tax.

xxxi. The term 'charitable' is used in its 'generally accepted legal sense' and includes relief to the poor, lessening the burdens of government, and combating community deterioration. N.J. Rev. Stat. § 54:32B9; N.J. Admin. Code §§ 18:24-8.1, 18:24-9.7.

xxxii. The state defines charity for RST purposes by reference to IRC § 501(c)(3) (described in note iii of this appendix). New Mexico's 'sales' tax takes the form of a gross receipts tax on the business, and, while it has some features of an RST, includes a much broader range of services than most RSTs. N.M. Stat. Ann. § 7-9-29, 7-9-60. Hence the failure to exempt a charity's purchases of services is significant.

xxxiii. The state definition of a charitable organization closely resembles IRC § 501(c)(3) (described in note iii of this appendix). N.Y. Tax Law §§ 1116(a)(4), 1116(b); N.Y. Comp. Codes R. & Regs. tit. 20, § 529.7.

xxxiv. The state defines charity for RST purposes by reference to IRC § 501(c)(3) (described in note iii of this appendix). N.C. Gen. Stat. §§ 105-164.13(34), 105-164.13(35), 105-164.14(b).

xxxv. The state does not define a charity but uses the terms 'charitable activities', 'charitable purposes', and 'charitable organizations'. N.D. Cent. Code § 57-39.2-04(4).

xxxvi. The organization must qualify under IRC § 501(c)(3) (described in note iii of this appendix) and meet additional state requirements. Ohio Rev. Code Ann. §§ 5739.02(B)(9). 5739.02(B)(12).

xxxvii. The state enumerates all organizations eligible for exemption in a list, e.g., Boy Scouts, Girl Scouts, Oklahoma City National Museum. Okla. Stat. tit. 68, § 1356; Okla. Admin. Code § 710:65-19-44.

xxxviii. Oregon has no general sales tax.

xxxix. A charitable organization must (1) advance a charitable purpose (2) be free from private profit motive (3) render gratuitously a substantial portion of its services (4) benefit a substantial and indefinite class of persons who are legitimate subjects of charity, and (5) must relieve the government of some of its burden. Pa. Stat. Ann. 10, §§ 371-85; 61 Pa. Code § 32.21(c).

xl. The statute simply exempts organizations 'operated exclusively for … charitable purposes'. R.I. Gen. Laws §§ 44-18-20(g), 44-18-30(5); R.I. Reg. SU 07-48.

xli. Organizations whose property and whose net proceeds are used exclusively for charitable purposes qualify for the exemption. S.C. Code Ann. §§ 12-36-2120(41), 12-37-220(a)(4).

xlii. A charity is an organization that devotes its resources exclusively to the relief of the poor, distressed or underprivileged, and has been recognized as an exempt organization under IRC § 501(c)(3) (described in note iii of this appendix). S.D. Codified Laws §§ 10-45-10, 10-45-13.1

xliii. The state defines charity by reference to IRC § 501(c)(3) (described in note iii of this appendix), and specifies additional qualifying organizations under state law. Tenn. Code Ann. § 67-6-322(c); Tenn. Comp. R. & Regs. § 1320-5.51(2).

xliv. The state defines charity by reference to IRC § 501(c)(3) (described in note iii of this appendix). Tex. Tax Code Ann. §§151.310(a), 151.310(c).

xlv. The state defines charity by reference to IRC § 501(c)(3) (described in note iii of this appendix). Utah Code Ann. § 59-12-104(8); Utah Admin. R. 865-19S-43(A).

xlvi. The state defines charity by reference to IRC § 501(c)(3) (described in note iii of this appendix). Vt. Stat. Ann. tit. 32, § 9743(3); Vt. Code Rules § 1.9743.

xlvii. The state defines charity by reference to IRC § 501(c)(3) (described in note iii of this appendix). Va. Code Ann. §58.1-609.11.

xlviii. There is no specific definition of charitable organization, as non-profits generally are subject to tax on their purchases and sales, although organizations engaging in specified 'charitable' activities may be exempt on their fundraising activities. Wash. Admin. Code § 458-20-169.

xlix. Qualifying charitable organizations must be exempt under IRC § 501(c)(3) (described in note iii of this appendix) and meet additional state requirements. W. Va. Code §§ 11-15-9(a)(6), 11-15-9(a)(14).

l. State definition of charitable organization closely resembles definition in IRC § 501(c)(3) (described in note iii of this appendix). Wis. Stat. §§ 77.54(7m), 77.54(9a)(f).

li. State definition of charitable organizations includes IRC § 501(c)(3) organizations (described in note iii of this appendix) as well as other organizations meeting similar criteria under state law. IRC Wyo. Stat. § 39-15-105(a)(iv); Wyo. Rules Dept. Rev. Ch. 2, § 9(c).

Part III

Exemptions for Gambling

CHAPTER 6

VAT on Gambling

Yoram Margalioth*

§6.01 INTRODUCTION

This chapter addresses the VAT treatment of providers of gambling, lotteries and other games of chance. I will use the term 'gambling' to include lotteries and all other games of chance; the term 'bets' to include all forms of consideration paid to participate in the gambling activity; and the term 'casino' in reference to all providers of gambling services.

The paper is dual purposed. It provides a tax policy analysis of how VAT should be applied to gambling as well as some description of the Israeli VAT system that is otherwise nearly unavailable in English.[1]

Under a credit-invoice VAT method, the casino remits (receives) to (from) the government the difference between the tax on the price the customer is charged and the tax on business inputs.[2] Payments to winners are cash outlays taken by the business in order to generate sales. In VAT jargon, they could be referred to as business inputs.[3] Imposing a value added tax on the sale of lottery tickets, without accounting for the

* I would like to thank Tomer Blumkin and Jacob Nussim for helpful discussions while drafting the paper, Liat Tennenholtz for research assistance, two anonymous referees for very helpful comments, and Rick Krever, Alan Schenk and Howell Zee for very helpful discussions during and after the conference.

1. There is one other source that provides some description of the Israeli VAT system in English and that is D. Gliksberg, *Israel's Value Added Tax Law*, 7 International VAT Monitor 2 (1992).
2. If the purchase of an investment good is treated like any other business input, VAT taxes consumption. This is the leading VAT form and the one assumed to hold in this paper. The analysis in this paper does not rely on this assumption, but making it simplifies the presentation of the arguments.
3. This may not be an accurate terminology if we view gambling as a pooling of intermediary services, a view that will be discussed below. The fundamentals – that is, acknowledgment of the need to subtract the winnings paid out from the casino's VAT basis – are the same under both views.

cash paid out to winners, taxes the casino on its turnover instead of on the value it added.[4]

To clarify this, assume the following simple example of a lottery. The casino sells 30 tickets ('bets') at USD 10 each, for a total of USD 300.[5] Ten tickets turn out to be winning bets and the casino pays USD 15 to each winning ticket holder, for a total of USD 150. Thus, the value added by the casino is USD 150, as this is the difference between the sales and the business inputs, which, for the sake of simplicity, are assumed to consist only of the amounts paid out to the winners. Assuming a 10% tax rate, the VAT remitted should be USD 15.

Under the standard credit-invoice VAT method, USD 300 is taxed as 'sales' upon the placement of the bets, the purchase of the lottery tickets in our example. Assuming for ease of presentation that the tax is fully shifted to the price, then each of the 30 tickets will be sold for USD 10+USD 1 tax, for a total of USD 330. No tax is imposed when the winnings are paid out. Hence, the casino will remit USD 30 to the tax authority: USD 30 represents 20% of the USD 150 added value; that is, the casino in this example would pay 20% instead of the statutory 10% VAT rate. Moreover, in our example, the effective VAT tax rate would depend on the sales-prize payout ratio. If, for example, the casino paid only USD 12 to each winning ticket holder, the casino's added value would have been USD 180, and the effective tax rate would have been 16.6.%.

Taxing the casino only on its added value, using the credit-invoice VAT method, would require casinos to report the bets as outputs and the winnings paid out as inputs on a transaction-by-transaction basis. Traditionally this was regarded as too administratively costly, leading to widespread exemption. Exemption of gambling is indeed the default rule under the EU VAT Directive.[6]

Modern VAT laws, as can be found in Australia, New Zealand and a few other countries, generally adopted the margin method and tax casinos accordingly.[7] In our running example, this would result in VAT revenue of USD 15.

Dr Harry Grubert and Professor Rick Krever suggested viewing the casino as providing pooling services, intermediating between individuals who wish to bet: some of them turn out to be winners, whereas the rest turn out to be losers. The losers according to such an analysis are transferring money to the winners, and the casino gets to keep its consideration for the intermediary services it provided (USD 150 in our example). So whether we refer to the winnings paid out as being the casino's business

4. See A. Schenk & O. Oldman, *Value Added Tax: A Comparative Approach*, 301–304 (Cambridge University Press 2007).
5. I use dollar signs instead of Israeli Shekels in order to make it easier for the reader to concentrate on the substance of my argument without being distracted by the use of a less familiar currency.
6. See Article 13 of the Council Directive 2006/112/EC of 28 November 2006 on the common system of value added tax, OJ L347/1–118 ('EU VAT Directive').
7. See A. Schenk, *Gambling and Lotteries*, in *VAT in Africa*, 47–70 (R. Krever ed., Pretoria University Press 2008). Countries, however, including countries that adopted the margin system with regard to taxation of casinos, often supplement the VAT with a separate excise tax on gambling.

inputs or not, the casino would pay VAT only on the value it created, which is the difference between the bets and the winnings.[8]

However, according to Grubert and Krever, if one adopts a 'broad view' of consumption, the full price of the bet – that is, the gross amount, USD 300 in our example – provides utility to the gamblers, who derive pleasure from the game per se; hence, the gross amount should be taxed. This, they suggest, could be done by supplementing the VAT (that will be calculated under the margin method) with a separate excise tax on gambling, as countries often do.

So which of the alternative methods gets it right? There seems to be no scholarly argument that supports exemption, which is the traditional VAT method; but should we tax the gross amount, USD 300 in our example, or the margin, the USD 150? Should we tax the gross amount by not allowing a credit for the winnings paid out, or should we use a combination of the margin method VAT and a supplemental excise tax to get to that result? Should we reach the same result as the margin method in a different way, that is, by viewing the winnings paid out as business inputs? To what extent does our analysis depend on whether we adopt a 'broad' or a 'narrow' view of consumption?

In section §6.02, I will discuss these questions which boil down to one question: what should be the tax base? The way I analyse gambling does not require us to choose between a narrow and a broad view of consumption, and makes clear that the proper tax base is the margin.[9]

Section §6.03 briefly discusses three possible methods of taxing casinos only on the value they have added; namely, on the margin. The first method is practiced in Israel with regard to lotteries, which is currently the only form of legal gambling. VAT is imposed on illegal gambling in Israel. However, no credit is provided for business inputs that are directly related to the illegal nature of the activity. Therefore, I consider two other methods to be plausible interpretations of Israel's VAT law that could be considered if gambling ever becomes legal in Israel.

Now that the proper tax base is known (the margin), we still need to know what would be the optimal tax rate. Should it be equal, higher or lower than the standard VAT rate applied to all, or most, other goods and services? Section §6.04 discusses what considerations should be taken into account and traded off against each other when deciding the question of what is the optimal tax rate on gambling. Section §6.05 describes how Israel imposes its VAT on gambling. Finally, I conclude.

§6.02 THE TAX BASE

Unlike other financial services that involve investment and may therefore create a surplus (hence having a positive net present value), gambling does not create any

8. This view was also held by one of the two anonymous referees, who thought that gambling was no different from playing on the stock market. The casino, like the stock market broker, should be taxed only on the service it provided. The money transfers between losers and winners should not be taxed, and this could be achieved under a tax credit-invoice type of VAT by applying a reverse charge to the payouts.
9. I would like to thank Howell Zee for suggesting this solution to me.

surplus. The total amount of money paid for bets does not generate any additional money. Some of it is simply taken by the casino and whatever is left is distributed back to the gamblers.

The casino operates according to a formula. A fixed percentage of the sales are paid out to winners. Gamblers know it. They know that when they are placing the bet they are actually losing money as their expected payoff is lower than the price of the ticket (the bet). They are, however, willing to do it because they derive pleasure (ie., utility) from participating in the game. It is a form of entertainment. They pay for the ability to dream, for a short while, until the outcome of the bet becomes known. They also know that the ticket they have purchased is not worth zero. It is worth a fraction of what they paid for it, but it still has some positive value as it reflects the expected gain. In the example I was using, each ticket was 'worth' USD 5 upon purchase, because half of the amount collected in bets would be distributed back to the gamblers as winnings. So, in fact, every gambler 'lost' USD 5 upon the purchase of the ticket, but was willing to do so because it also purchased the pleasure of playing the game. This is similar to any other payment for entertainment services.

Looking at the gamblers as a group on the one side and on the casino on the other side, it becomes clear that both parties understand that the gamblers pay the casino (by placing a bet) a consideration in the amount of the difference between the bet (the face value of the ticket) and the expected gain that it represents which is only a fraction of the amount of the bet. The gamblers are willing to do that because they derive pleasure from playing the game. It is a form of entertainment. This is what they consume, and this is also the casino's profit.[10] The difference between the face value of all tickets sold, USD 300 in our example, and their expected gain, USD 150 in our example, is what was really paid to the casino in consideration for the entertainment it provided. Each specific gambler in my example, when purchasing a ticket for USD 10, did not really pay USD 10, because the value of the ticket he purchased was still USD 5 reflecting the expected amount that the casino was liable to pay him. So the casino received only USD 5 because it was liable to pay back USD 5 (on average) to each of the gamblers. Before the outcome of the bet became known, the value of this liability of the casino to each gambler was USD 5: the net present value of their tickets. The gambler therefore paid the casino only USD 5 and this was paid for entertainment; that is, the thrill of participating in the game, sold to him by the casino.[11]

10. The casino's profit is actually lower because it has additional expenses that I ignore in order to make the argument clear. For VAT purposes, the casino would receive credit for the tax paid on its business inputs.
11. Determining the consumption value for a specific gambler would require acknowledging that a specific gambler may not necessarily lose the expected amount. For income tax purposes we may want to consider viewing the cost of gambling as having two separate components: (i) the expected cost which is the gambler's consumption; (ii) the difference between the expected loss and the actual outcome, which is an 'investment' variation that could be positive or negative. See D. Shaviro, *The Man Who Lost Too Much:* Zarin *v.* Commissioner *and the Measurement of Taxable Consumption*', 45 Tax L. Rev. 215, 231–232 (1990) (suggesting this analysis as a thought experience, but supporting the existing law that views the actual cost as representing the consumption value). This separation is irrelevant for VAT policy analysis. The business, namely the casino, is the one being taxed. The casino's actual profit is equal to the expected profit due to the law of large numbers and to the fact that casinos limit the

There is no need to distinguish between winners and losers because when they buy the ticket, everyone is equal. By being willing to accept a ticket that is worth less than what they paid, in the sense that it reflects an expected payout that is lower than what the ticket costs, they are paying the casino for providing them some form of entertainment. It is this transaction that should be taxed under the VAT and it is equal to the difference between what the casino collects (the total consideration paid for bets) less the winnings paid out. This is what the casino was paid by gamblers in consideration for the entertainment value it provided them with. This is also their consumption, and therefore, by using the margin system, the VAT functions as a tax on consumption.

§6.03 WAYS OF IMPOSING THE VAT ON THE PROPER TAX BASE

Viewing winnings paid out as the casino's business inputs does not allow us to tax the casino on the proper tax base (the 'margin') under the standard credit-invoice method, because no tax was paid on those business inputs. Hence, the credit-invoice method results in taxing the casino on its gross sales. One simple solution to the problem would be to use an accounts-based VAT system such as the subtraction or addition VAT method, as is demonstrated below using our running example.

The firm computes its value added by adding up the value of all factors of production, such as labour and profits, as well as interest and rent if the latter two were not subject to VAT. In our example, no wages were paid; hence, the casino had USD 300 income from sales minus USD 150 in costs, leading to a profit of USD 150. Under an addition-method VAT, it would be subject to 10% VAT and pay USD 15 in tax, an effective tax rate of 10%. Formally, gambling transactions will not be subject to VAT, however, because VAT is paid (albeit, under a different method), the VAT will be reflected in the price, according to the relative elasticities of supply and demand for gambling.

[A] Legal Interpretations That Would Plausibly Allow Accounting for Winnings Paid Out under Traditional VAT Law

[1] The 'Bad Debts' Mechanism: An Ex-Post Approach

We saw that the tax imposed upon the placement of the bets, that is, the purchase of the lottery tickets in our example, resulted in an overpayment of tax by the service provider, similar to that created when a seller reports sales on an invoice method and remits VAT but the buyer fails to pay. The tax overpayment becomes evident when the winnings are paid out. At that time, the casino may be allowed to issue a self-issued

---

maximum amount of a bet that can be placed by a single gambler. The tax is therefore imposed on the consumption of gamblers as a group, which is equal to their expected loss (as a group) and is equal to the casino's gain (expected and actual).

invoice and use it as a credit to offset its VAT liability on the sales of lottery tickets or any other services it provided or goods that it sold.

[2] The Probability Based Method: An Ex Ante Approach

The casino operates according to a formula. A fixed percentage of the sales are paid out to winners. This is guaranteed in the case of lotteries, but is essentially the same, due to the law of large numbers, in all other forms of gambling services provided by a professional casino.[12] The casino's profit is assured, even though it will lose money to some of the gamblers. Hence, it can calculate, with reasonable accuracy, its value added at the time the tickets are sold, even though the winners were not yet determined. Under this *ex ante* approach, the casino will be allowed to issue a self-issued invoice and use it as a credit to offset its VAT liability on sales of lottery tickets or any other services it provided or goods that it sold, even before the winners are determined.

§6.04 THE TAX RATE

In theory, perfectly functioning competitive markets allocate resources efficiently through the mechanism of prices. In reality, markets are not perfectly competitive, and government intervention can sometimes correct market inefficiencies, often through the tax and transfer system, when this is the most cost effective tool. The primary examples are the solution to the free riding problem in the finance of public goods,[13] and the provision of tax incentives to affect positive or negative externalities, such as promoting innovation and discouraging pollution.

Efficiency is inadequate as a normative standard because it does not tell us how to rank alternative allocations of resources. To do so, we need to know what society's explicit value judgements are. There is a trade-off between efficiency and distributive justice (equity). Accounting for both is conventionally done by postulating a social welfare function. The government uses the tax and transfer system to maximize society's social welfare function; that is, to correct market inefficiencies and to redistribute income.

---

12. To eliminate the extremely low probability of an amazingly lucky gambler wiping out the casino, casinos limit the maximum amount of a bet that can be placed by a single gambler. See N. Taleb, *The Black Swan: The Impact of the Highly Improbable*, 312 (Random House 2007).
13. Public goods are non-rival and non-excludable. Their non-rivalry means that the marginal cost is zero; hence, the efficient price is zero. Their non-excludability creates an incentive for people to free ride, namely, to enjoy the benefits while letting others pay for them. Financing public goods (which does not preclude their private production) is the most basic function of society. Public goods such as security and some form of law and order were always the core of any form of large-scale society, be it a tribe or a kingdom. One could say that the need to have a tax system (coercive payment mechanism) to solve the free riding problem is the most fundamental element in the formation of society.

Tax policy literature assumes that for redistribution purposes, the only relevant differences between individuals lie in their innate earning abilities.[14] Earning ability is assumed to be private information, unobservable by the government. Therefore, the government cannot directly tax people according to their abilities. Instead, the government taxes observable characteristics, such as income and consumption, which relate to unobserved ability.[15]

In their seminal paper of 1976, Atkinson and Stiglitz concluded that taxing consumption, as is done by VAT, for example, is redundant in the presence of an optimal income tax system.[16] The Atkinson-Stiglitz result relies on an assumption known as separability. According to this assumption, variation in consumption across households is assumed to stem only from differences in their earned incomes, hence a policymaker that already employs an income tax - namely, measures individuals' earned income - cannot gain any additional information on individuals' earning abilities from looking at their consumption patterns.[17] Imposing differential consumption tax rates would introduce wedges between consumer (after-tax) and producer (pre-tax) price ratios of consumption goods, thereby adding a second kind of distortion on top of the already existing work/leisure distortions created by the income tax.

However, taking into account the high administrative costs of taxation in the real world, and especially the prevalence of tax evasion, introducing VAT alongside an income tax to collect at least part of the tax revenue would be optimal.[18]

Imposing a uniform rate VAT does not violate the Atkinson-Stiglitz result, and may be an optimal supplement to an income tax due to administrative costs and tax evasion considerations, because a uniform tax on consumption is simply another way of taxing income. It is only a differential rate VAT, which I am about to discuss as potentially warranted in the context of gambling, that violates the Atkinson-Stiglitz result.

A potential justification for differential VAT on gambling that would not be subject to the Atkinson-Stiglitz criticism would be one that relaxes their assumption that there is only one source of heterogeneity across individuals, or the assumption of separability. In the context of gambling, we know that poor people tend to spend a larger percentage of their income on gambling than non poor people. This tendency, if correlated with income, provides no additional information. However, if we assume that there is a negative correlation between the taste for gambling and earning ability, this could call for differential commodity taxation (such as VAT on gambling) on distributive grounds. The intuition is that individuals with low earning ability are more

14. J. Mirrlees, *An Exploration in the Theory of Optimum Income Taxation*, 38 Rev. Econ. Stud. 175 (1971).
15. See D. Shaviro, *Symposium on Wealth Taxes Part I: Commentary Inequality, Wealth, and Endowment*, 53 Tax L. Rev. 397 (2000): (exploring the shortcomings of the various proxies used, and explaining what policymakers should really be looking for).
16. A. Atkinson & J. Stiglitz, *The Design of Tax Structure: Direct versus Indirect Taxation*, 6 J. Pub. Econ. 55 (1976).
17. For a more elaborate, yet straightforward, explanation, see T. Blumkin & Y. Margalioth, *On the Limits of Redistributive Taxation: Establishing a Case for Equity Informed Legal Rules*, 25 Va Tax Rev. 1 (2005).
18. B. Salanié, *The Economics of Taxation*, 119 (Economica 2002).

likely to find it difficult to comprehend how slim their chances of winning are, whereas individuals that possess higher earning skills are more likely to accurately assess the extremely low probability and act accordingly. In order to be relied upon, in the design of the tax system, this intuition must be supported empirically.

Gambling could serve as an indicator good, providing the benefit of 'tagging' as in Akerlof.[19] It is observable behaviour that is negatively correlated with unobserved innate ability; relying on it may enhance redistribution. It should be noted that this would justify a *lower* VAT rate on gambling.

The tagging argument could justify exemption of gambling, which is quite a prevalent practice being at the core of the traditional VAT system, and is conventionally justified on 'difficulty to tax' grounds. As for efficiency justifications for differential VAT, the Ramsey inverse elasticity rule immediately comes to mind.[20] Assuming that gambling is addictive, as is often assumed, its demand is relatively inelastic, which may justify a higher tax rate. Clearly, if gambling is disproportionally consumed by lower-ability consumers, equity considerations discussed above point in the opposite direction and call for a lower tax rate.

Acts or goods that complement leisure (eg., ski boots) should be taxed, whereas acts or goods that are leisure substitutes (eg., working boots) should be subsidized.[21] A differential commodity tax might be levied if gambling is thought to be complementary to leisure.

Gambling activity may involve various positive and negative externalities, depending on the specific circumstances. Casinos often attract tourists, thereby increasing employment in the region and providing the government with income from foreigners. In that case, a low rate, or exemption, may be warranted, depending on the elasticity of international demand. It could also help peripheral areas of a country to attract consumers who reside in the country's core and wealthier areas, thus distributing income more equally across the country. On the other hand, under some circumstances, gambling may be associated with criminal activity (either in the context of running the business or as a result of a desperate need for cash experienced by unlucky gamblers), or with maltreatment of children and spouses by addicted gamblers[22] – justifying higher rates as a form of Pigouvian taxation.

Alternatively,[23] assuming we could distinguish between harmful (addiction-led) forms of gambling and non-harmful (entertainment-led) gambling, we would impose

19. G. Akerlof, *The Economics of Tagging as Applied to the Optimal Income Tax*, 68 Am. Econ. Rev. 8 (1978).
20. F. Ramsey, *A Contribution to the Theory of Taxation*, 37 Econ J. 47 (1927).
21. See W.J. Corlett & D.C. Hague, *Complementarity and the Excess Burden of Taxation*, 21 Rev. Econ. Stud. 21 (1953–1954) (arguing that individuals with a higher ability to earn can work less to obtain a given amount of consumption, hence by taxing leisure, the government is indirectly taxing ability).
22. When the potential addicted gamblers are minors, paternalism may justify government intervention as well. Some may apply the paternalism argument even in the case of adults. I am not sure that this is appropriate in the context of gambling. People should generally be allowed to engage in whatever gives them pleasure, in the absence of negative externalities. See O. Grosskopf, *Paternalism, Public Policy and the Governmental Monopoly over Gambling*, 7 Hamishpat 9 (2002) (arguing against paternalism).
23. As suggested to me by one of the two anonymous referees to this paper.

an externality internalizing excise tax on the former, and exemption on the latter. We would then impose a VAT on the excise-inclusive lottery price to treat gambling activities on par with the consumption of other goods and services.

§6.05 HOW DOES ISRAEL IMPOSE ITS VAT ON GAMBLING?

[A] Discrimination between Legal and Illegal Gambling

According to European Court of Justice case law, if Member States choose to tax gambling transactions, they must determine the tax base according to the basic principles of EU VAT set by the VAT Directive. This was interpreted to exclude from the tax base the winnings paid out to successful gamblers.[24] Moreover, Member States that choose to tax gambling transactions have to apply the tax across the board, and, in particular, are not allowed to discriminate between legal and illegal gambling activities.[25] Israel is not a member of the EU and, in fact, violates these two principles. Israel does not exempt gambling. It does not exclude from the tax base the winnings paid out to successful gamblers, and it taxes legal and illegal gambling differently.

The significant difference between the effective VAT rates imposed on legal and illegal activities is the result of the following factors. First, the only providers of legal gambling services in Israel are government-related institutions. Israel uses the credit-invoice VAT method with regard to all firms, except for non-profit organizations and financial institutions (banks and insurance companies), which are taxed under a VAT addition method. Illegal gambling activity is taxed under a credit-invoice VAT method, not because it is illegal, but simply because it is not run by a non-profit organization or a financial institution.

Second, tax on non-profit organizations is levied only on the wages paid to their employees, as profit, by definition, is not supposed to exist. The VAT rate under this method, however, is half of the standard VAT rate - currently 8% instead of 16%.

Third, when computing the VAT liability of illegal gambling businesses, no credit is provided for business inputs that are directly related to the illegal nature of the activity. There is a similar principle in the computation of taxable income for income tax purposes. Illegal expenses cannot be deducted. As a result, VAT paid on business inputs such as rent may be credited but winnings paid out to successful gamblers cannot, as they fall under the category of business outputs that are directly related to the illegal nature of the business.

In reality, the following factor is likely to be the most significant in discriminating between the effective tax rate paid on legal and on illegal gambling transactions. Illegal businesses do not tend to report their true sales to the tax authorities, and often do not

---

24. Case C-38/93, *H. J. Glawe Spiel- und Unterhaltungsgeräte Aufstellungsgesellschaft mbH & Co KG v. Finanzamt Hamburg-Barmbek-Uhlenhorst* [1994] ECR I-1679 ('The consideration actually received by the operator in return for making the machines available consists only of the proportion of the stakes which he can actually take for himself.')
25. See, e.g., Case C-283/95, *Karlheinz Fischer v. Finanzamt Donaueschingen* [1998] ECR I-3369; Joined Cases C-453/02 and C-462/02, *Finanzamt Gladbeck v. Edith Linneweber and Finanzamt Herne-West v. Savvas Akritidis* [2005] ECR I-1131.

register or file a report at all. As a result, VAT is imposed on illegal gambling activity only following a police raid. Until recently, tax was imposed only rarely because employees of the tax authorities in Israel generally object to taking part in police raids. They do not want to deal with non-tax criminals, and are reluctant to work at night, which is when most of such raids take place.

In those rare cases when the tax is imposed, it is calculated in a very inaccurate manner because the tax base comprises only sales that happen to be recorded in books found during the raid, or in bank and credit card records that were somehow traced to the gambling activity.

Finally, gambling is a predicate offence under the Israeli Money Laundering Prohibition law, which allows the confiscation of all captured money and property related to the illegal activity. The government is better off taking 100% of the money confiscated under that law when the gambling offence can be proved in court, rather than taking only a fraction of it in the form of taxes. Even in those cases where the amount of money captured is lower than the tax liability, the government is still in a better position with this option over trying to recoup tax owing from criminals who are highly unlikely to pay the tax.

[B] More Detailed Description

[1] The Legal Sector

Legal gambling in Israel is run by two government-controlled monopolies: Mifal HaPayis, which offers about seven different types of lotteries, and HaMoaatza LeHesder HaHimurim Basport, which enables betting on sports events.[26] In 2008, Mifal HaPayis reported an income from sales of Israeli shekels (IS) 3.9 billion and distributed winnings in the amount of IS 2.4 billion. It contributed about IS 775 million to the finance of public goods in 2008. In 2008, HaMoaatza LeHesder HaHimurim Basport reported an income from sales of IS 1.6 billion and distributed winnings in the amount of IS 942 million.[27] By law, it is required to distribute at least 42% of its sales in the form of winnings. In addition, around 15% of the sales are required to cover all other business expenses. The remainder, which was about IS 3 billion over the past decade, is used to finance public sport facilities and support local sports teams (mostly soccer and basketball).[28]

Both monopolies are registered as non-profit organizations, paying VAT according to section 4 of the Israeli VAT law. The transactions are exempt and the organization cannot get credit for VAT it paid on its business inputs. VAT is imposed on wages paid by the organization to its employees. Imposing the tax only on wages is justified because the organization is not supposed to make any profit and money that is contributed to finance public goods is similar to the government's tax revenue, hence

26. As of 2008, selling to minors is a criminal offence.
27. portal.knesset.gov.il/Com2ksafim/he-IL/Messages/news_7939.htm.
28. www.winner.co.il/.

should not be subject to tax. The tax rate is half the rate imposed on for-profit businesses, currently, 8% instead of 16%.

[2] The Illegal Sector

There are no official estimates of the size of the illegal gambling market, but unofficially, it is estimated to be about three times the size of the legal market. Gambling activities are subject to VAT in accordance with section 2 of the Israeli VAT law like any other for-profit business (which is not a financial institution). Therefore, those involved in such activities must become registered dealers for VAT purposes ('dealers'), report their specific occupation (gambling activities) to the Israeli VAT authorities, file accurate periodic reports as required by law, and pay the obligatory VAT (16% to date).

Those who do not comply with the VAT law and regulations face criminal prosecution. The Israeli police and tax authorities have been enforcing a firm economic policy targeted at obtaining all funds owed to the state; they aspire to possess assets attained illegally, and to impose taxes on Israeli crime families and organizations.[29]

Because tax authority employees were reluctant to work at night and feared physical retaliation from crime families, a special unit of 30 tax inspectors, police officers and money laundering prohibition officers, was recently formed. These officers were all offered special insurance coverage for possible injuries resulting from contact with the crime families.[30]

Recently, in an operation led by this unit and other officers from the investigation and intelligence units of the Israeli police force, hundreds of Israeli felons and their families were required to submit tax reports and declarations of capital.[31]

The operation took place early in the morning on 5 January 2010. Tax authority employees, together with policemen from all the police districts and the national police unit, arrived at the homes of the felons, and served them with demands for tax reports and declarations of capital. These demands were served after much preparation, which included mapping suspects involved or suspected of being related to criminal offences, including gambling.[32]

Though this operation was an important milestone in the enforcement system, it is only one part of the general effort to broaden the circle of tax-paying felons, while avoiding situations in which the felons are 'rewarded' for their illegal activities. Those who were required to submit tax reports and have not done so are committing a

29. www.calcalist.co.il/local/articles/0,7340,L-3385211,00.html.
30. www.globes.co.il/news/article.aspx?did=1000503843; www.globes.co.il/news/article.aspx?did=1000480426; www.globes.co.il/news/article.aspx?did=1000535410; www.news1.co.il/Archive/001-D-217347-00.html?tag=10-09-20; www.globes.co.il/news/article.aspx?did=1000520236.
31. www.globes.co.il/news/article.aspx?did=1000528096.
32. www.news1.co.il/Archive/001-D-225823-00.html?tag=14-36-54; www.calcalist.co.il/local/articles/0,7340,L-3385211,00.html.

criminal offence in accordance with section 216 of the Israeli tax ordinance, and will be criminally charged.[33]

The fact that the dealers' activities are illegal increases the burden of proof and makes expense deductions more difficult to report. As mentioned above, when illegal activities (such as gambling businesses) are exposed, the VAT authorities attempt to find documentation of taxable transactions and income, in order to quantify the VAT due. Methods used for these purposes often include documentation held in the businesses themselves; documentation from the businesses' banks, such as transfer logs, etc.; documentation from credit companies; or documentation from other companies through which the business processed payments, such as PayPal and others. Using this documentation, the VAT-owing transactions are assessed and VAT is imposed accordingly.

Expenses directly related to the illegal gambling activities may not be deducted. Other expenses, such as rent for facilities used in other aspects of the business, are generally deductable. However, the burden of proof regarding allowed expense deductions is on those assessed (rather than on the tax authorities, even if they find relevant documentation), thus making it more difficult for the dealers to decrease their VAT liability.

The authorities may seize property attained criminally, or used for criminal purposes.[34] This was done in the case of gambling ships in Eilat. When the gambling activity on these ships was exposed, the VAT authorities and other Israeli authorities pressed legal charges. Eventually, the ships were confiscated and are currently in the possession of the state treasury.

[C] Analysis

Taxing illegal gambling is so inaccurate, due to the lack of credible documentation, that the details of VAT calculation are relatively unimportant. In principle, it should be taxed, and that is indeed the current policy. If we assume that much of the sales were not documented, disallowing credit for business inputs that are related to the illegal activity may bring us closer to taxing illegal activity at effective standard rates than allowing it would.

Taxing legal gambling activity under the addition method makes sense as it solves the difficulty of accounting for the winnings as business inputs under a credit-invoice method. Imposing only half the standard rate is more difficult to justify. The fact that the business is run by a non-profit organization may justify exemption from income tax, but the character of the business and the fact that it uses its 'profits' to finance public goods cannot justify a reduced VAT rate. As discussed in section §6.03 above, the VAT rate on gambling should be determined according to the correlation between gambling and earning ability and the existence of externalities. The expected increase in administrative and compliance costs due to a switch from uniform to

33. www.calcalist.co.il/local/articles/0,7340,L-3385211,00.html; www.news1.co.il/Archive/001-D-225823-00.html?tag=14-36-54.
34. Articles 3 and 21 of the Israeli Money Laundering Prohibition Law.

differential VAT tax rates should also be taken into account in the cost-benefit analysis. The rate should then be applied to providers of gambling services whether for profit or not.

§6.06 CONCLUSION

Applying the standard credit-invoice VAT method would result in taxing the casino on its gross sales (of bets). Traditional VAT systems tend to exempt gambling as accurately calculating the tax base is thought to be too complicated. Modern VAT systems tax gambling using the margin method, that is, taxing casinos only on the difference between sales and winnings paid out. Some of these countries, however, impose a supplemental excise tax on gambling.

As explained in section §6.02 above, the proper tax base is that reached by the margin method, as it taxes the casino on the value it added and taxes the gamblers on their true consumption, which is what they paid for the pleasure of playing the game.

Interpreting the law of traditional VAT systems to reach the result of taxing only the margin – that is, not taxing the gross sales – is not trivial. It could be reached by using accounts VAT methods such as the addition or subtraction methods. However, under a credit-invoice method one would have to come up with some creative interpretation to reach the correct result. I suggest allowing the casino to issue a self-invoice – either before or after the winnings are determined, relying on an analogy to the 'bad debts' scenario in the latter case, and on the logic of probability in the former.

The optimal tax rate would depend on a cost-benefit analysis accounting for administrative and compliance costs; positive and negative externalities related to gambling; as well as equity considerations in case a correlation between gambling and innate earning ability is found to exist.

If obtaining the data necessary to compute the optimal tax rate is too costly, applying VAT to the margin, as is done under modern VAT systems and as could be done in traditional VAT system using legal interpretation along the lines I have suggested in this paper, is warranted.

Israel happens to get it right. Not because of a proper design of the system, but rather by chance.[35] It just happens to tax legal gambling under the addition method. This is not because it wishes to tax gambling on the margin, but rather because legal gambling is run only by non-profit organizations and this is the method used to tax non-profit organizations under the Israeli VAT system. Israel taxes illegal gambling on their gross sales. Again, this is not because it wishes to reach an effective rate that is close to the rate achieved when taxing legal income using the margin method (accounting for the fact that only part of the activity is revealed), but rather because it has a non-tax legal rule, based on criminal law principles, according to which expenses that are directly related to illegal activity should not be deducted for tax purposes.

35. As may be appropriate in a symbolic sense in this context of gambling.

Comments: VAT on Gambling

Alan Schenk

I INTRODUCTION

It is difficult to find an English language translation of the taxation of gambling in Israel. In his paper, Professor Margalioth provides an informative explanation and analysis of the atypical Israeli treatment of legal and illegal gambling activities. He also applies an economic analysis to explain why a country may impose a higher or lower than standard VAT rate on gambling services. We agree that the margin method used to tax these services may be appropriate, at least for some gambling services, although we use different rationales to reach that conclusion. I think that many of our differences relate to the value of the taxable services.

Professor Margalioth suggests that the addition or subtraction method of calculating periodic VAT liability would reach the correct result. Alternatively, he fits gambling into a credit-invoice VAT with 'self invoices' that give casinos credits for winnings paid to consumers. I prefer to rely on the credit-invoice method, and explain why the value of gambling supplies can be defined as the margin between bets received and winnings paid out. In this commentary, except as noted, I refer to all games of chance as gambling, and to all operators as casinos.

Most countries require registered businesses to calculate their periodic VAT liability under the credit-invoice method. Those countries either exempt gambling or tax gambling services under a 'margin' system. Countries that have adopted a 'Modern VAT'[1] typically define the value of gambling services under the margin method – the spread between bets received and winnings paid out. I agree that this approach represents an administrable way to tax this sector. In fact, I discuss and implicitly support this approach in my co-authored VAT treatise.[2] In this commentary, I refer to

1. See, the broader-based VAT discussed in L. Ebrill et al., *The Modern VAT* (International Monetary Fund 2002).
2. A. Schenk & O. Oldman, *Value Added Tax: A Comparative Approach*, Ch 10(II) (Cambridge University Press 2007).

some support for the taxation of more than the 'margin' from some gambling services.[3] Nevertheless, I conclude that taxing more than the margin is not practical, and depending upon the value of the entertainment services a casino renders to gamblers, it may be inappropriate for many types of gambling services.

II VARIOUS APPROACHES EMPLOYED TO TAX GAMBLING SERVICES

As discussed above, most countries either exempt gambling services or tax the margin. The Member States in the European Union, as mandated by the EU VAT Directive, exempt most or all gambling activities.[4] A Member State can opt to tax gambling. Some States, like the Netherlands, tax online gambling by domestic and foreign suppliers.[5] Professor Margalioth opposes an exemption for this sector. I agree.

Some 'Modern VATs', including those of South Africa, Botswana, and Singapore, tax gambling under a margin system.[6] The details vary. Some countries impose just excises on gambling, and some both tax the margin from gambling activities and impose separate excises on the same services. Finally, Israel has an atypical approach to the taxation of gambling.

III VALUE OF TAXABLE GAMBLING SERVICES

[A] Credit-Invoice VATs

A VAT imposed on final consumption ideally should be imposed on the value of all goods and services supplied to final consumers, unless there are political or administrative reasons to provide other treatment.[7] This approach simplifies administration and compliance costs, and maximizes the revenue.

3. Council Directive 2006/112/EC of 28 November 2006 on the common system of value added tax, OJ L347/1 of 2006 (EU VAT Directive). Art. 73 of the EU VAT Directive defines the taxable amount, subject to exceptions in Arts 74 to 77, as including 'everything which constitutes consideration obtained or to be obtained by the supplier, in return for the supply, from the customer or a third party, including subsidies directly linked to the price of the supply'. VAT may be imposed on more than the margin by defining the value of the consideration subject to output tax as gross bets, without adjustment for winnings paid out.
4. While it generally has been assumed that a Member was required to either tax or to exempt all gambling, a recent Opinion of an Advocate General of the CJEU (not a binding judgment) indicates that a Member can exempt some, but not all gambling services. See the Opinion of Mr Advocate General Bot in Case C-58/09, *Leo-Libera GmbH v. Finanzamt Buchholz in der Nordheide* [2010] ECR I-5189, opining that Art. 135(1)(i) of the EU VAT Directive (n. 3 above) permits Member States to exempt racing from VAT, while excluding other forms of gambling from the exemption. But see, Schenk & Oldman (n. 2 above), at Ch 10(II).
5. See, R. van der Paart, *Taxation of Internet Gaming and Gambling in the European Union*, 10 ERA-Forum 525–531 (2009).
6. New Zealand treats the sales of lottery tickets as supplies of gambling services, and allows the lottery operator to reduce those supplies by the amount of unsold tickets.
7. VAT systems typically provide exceptions to this rule. For example, to reduce administration and compliance costs, VATs typically exclude small businesses that add very little value added.

The credit-invoice VAT, used almost universally around the world, is a transaction-based, 'tax-against-a-tax' system. It attempts to tax the full ***value*** of goods and services supplied to final consumers, but not more. The tax authorities rely on VAT invoices as an audit tool to verify that tax listed on VAT invoices is reported as output by registered sellers and that only tax on VAT invoices is claimed as credits by registered purchasers. Registered businesses demand VAT invoices from their registered suppliers in order to claim credit for the tax charged on those purchases. As a result, under the almost universal practice, a registered person generally must report tax on the ***value*** of taxable supplies (output tax), and can claim credits against that output tax only for tax (listed on VAT invoices) that was paid on purchases from other registered persons (input tax credits). The tax embedded in purchases from unregistered persons (such as final consumers and exempt small businesses that cannot issue VAT invoices) is not creditable. Those purchases are taxed in full at the next stage when the registered person makes a supply that includes this input. For these transactions, tax will be imposed on more than the full value of taxable outputs. In the following example, assume that a 9.0909% VAT is imposed on tax-inclusive bets. Assume that total bets are USD 110,000, purchases from registered businesses are USD 8,000 plus USD 800 VAT and total winnings paid out are USD 49,500. With a pure credit-invoice VAT that denies credits for inputs from consumers, assuming that gross bets can be identified, the tax on gambling services is USD 9,200, calculated as follows:

Output tax
USD 110,000 gross bets x 9.0909% USD 10,000
Input tax
Tax on USD 8,000 purchases from registered persons (800)
No-tax credit for USD 49,500 winnings paid out to gamblers 0000
Net VAT liability for period USD 9,200

If gambling services were taxed under a margin system that defines the *value* of taxable output as gross bets less winnings paid out, the casino's net VAT liability for the period under a credit-invoice VAT would be USD 4,700, calculated as follows:

Output tax
USD 60,500 net bets (gross bets less winnings) x 9.0909%USD 5,500[8]
Input tax
Tax on USD 8,000 purchases from registered persons (800)
Net VAT liability for the period USD 4,700

As discussed above, output tax under a credit-invoice VAT is the tax imposed on the *value* of taxable supplies. The *value* of taxable supplies generally is the price charged (gross bets in the case of gambling), unless –

For political and other reasons, VATs also may include exemptions for items such as food and health care that represent a large portion of the budget of low-income households.

8. In practice, the bets and winnings paid would have to be calculated inclusive of VAT; that is, they would be USD 110,000 less USD 49,500, or USD 60,500.

(a) the price charged is not an arm's length price (such as sales that may occur between related persons);
(b) the price is not the value of the supply; or
(c) taxing the price is impractical.

Neither Professor Margalioth nor I claim that the prices charged for gambling (gross bets) are not arm's length prices. I therefore limit the following analysis to items listed in (b) and (c).

[B] Calculation of Value of Gambling Services

A deposit-taking financial institution engages in intermediation to the extent that it takes deposits and makes loans. It therefore is reasonable to limit the taxation of those services to the value of the intermediation services rendered.[9] The taxation of the value of intermediation services rendered by a casualty insurance company (rather than the premium charged) may be justified because the company is serving as a classic intermediary in spreading the insured's risk of loss from insured property. The pooling rationale for the taxation of intermediation services using the margin method therefore is justifiable for casualty insurance and many services rendered by financial institutions.[10]

Is a casino rendering (a) an entertainment service measured by the full consideration (bets) received, or (b) a 'pooling' or 'intermediation' service for the gamblers, represented by the spread between what is received by the casino and what they pay out to the winners, or (c) a taxable service of some other amount?

What is the service rendered to a gambler? There are many definitions. According to BusinessDictionary.com, betting or gambling 'must result either in a gain or a loss. Gambling is neither risk taking in the sense of speculation (assumption of substantial short-term risk) nor investing (acquiring property or assets for securing long-term capital gains). It also differs from insurance which may reduce or eliminate the risk of loss but offers no legitimate chance of gain.' Thus, the taxation of insurance (and many other intermediation services) under a VAT may not serve as the best guide to determine how to tax gambling. It also is not clear, as Professor Margalioth explains, that the entertainment value (utility) of gambling services can be measured precisely by the gross bets placed or by the margin of bets less winnings paid.

Can we resolve the differences between Professor Margalioth and me by treating my view as a broader view of the value of taxable consumption (no credit for inputs

9. See Schenk & Oldman (n. 2 above), at Ch 10(III). A service rendered by a financial institution in exchanging one currency for another is an intermediation service under item (b). In the EU, the *value* of that service has been held to be equal to the value of the intermediation service rendered. See, Case C-172/96, *Customs and Excise Commissioners v. First National Bank of Chicago* [1998] ECR I-4387.

10. Countries, such as New Zealand, that tax casualty insurance do not define the value of taxable services as the margin of premiums less claims paid. Rather, they impose output tax on the premiums charged, and allow input credits for claims paid out. See New Zealand Goods and Services Tax Act 1985, No. 141, §§8(1) & 20(3)(d).

acquired from unregistered persons) and Professor Margalioth's view as a narrower view of that value (the output subject to tax is equal to the spread between bets placed and winnings paid out)?[11] I do not think this description of a broader or narrower view of value captures our differences.

In part, Professor Margalioth justifies the taxation of the margin under Modern VATs on the theory that the utility (value) of the entertainment obtained from participating in a game of chance is only a fraction of the amount of the bet (the purchase price for the service). I am not an economist, but the commentators discussed by Professor Margalioth are not in agreement on how to measure the utility of the entertainment services rendered to gamblers; that is, whether it should be based on the wagers placed or on the net amount of the bets placed less winnings paid out.

The European Court of Justice, in the *First National Bank* case,[12] identified the value of a bank's currency exchange transactions (the value of the supply) as the spread between the rates to buy and sell the currency. The same rationale can be applied to treat the value of gambling services as the spread between the bets received and the winnings paid out. This rationale avoids the need for casinos to depart from the credit-invoice method of calculating periodic VAT liability that applies to other industries and to other kinds of supplies by casinos. It also avoids the need for casinos to issue a 'self invoice' to support a credit for the winnings paid out.

[C] Addition Method VATs

According to Professor Margalioth, the credit-invoice method does not reach the correct tax base for gambling services if input credits are denied for winnings paid out. He suggests, instead, the possible use of the addition method of calculating a casino's periodic VAT liability, and assumes that payments to winners would be deductible in calculating profit under the addition method. I do not find reliance on this method persuasive. The tax base, under the addition method, requires a special definition of profits.[13] Charles E. McLure, Jr criticizes a definition of profit that allows a reduction in the tax base for purchases that were not subject to tax – he was discussing a subtraction method VAT but he notes that the same rationale applies to the addition method.[14] Applying McLure's rationale to gambling, payments to unregistered gamblers would not be deductible in calculating the addition method base for VAT purposes. Thus, the addition method of calculating VAT liability does not independently support the reliance on the margin method to measure the value of taxable gambling services.

11. This difference is discussed in Professor Margalioth's paper as the Grubert and Krever approach; that is, under the broader view, the full price of the bet can be taxed because the utility may be that amount.
12. See *First National Bank* (n. 9 above).
13. C.S. Sullivan, *Tax on Value Added*, 8, 24 (New York: Columbia University Press, 1965).
14. See C. McLure Jr., *The Value-Added Tax: Key to Deficit Reduction?*, 75, 96 (American Enterprise Institute for Public Policy Research, 1987).

[D] Practicality of Taxing Gross Bets?

In my analysis, assuming that (1) gross bets are priced at arm's length; (2) gambling is not analogous to many intermediation services; and (3) according to some commentators, the value of at least some gambling services could be measured by more than the 'margin,' we are left with another question. Is it practical to tax the price charged (gross bets)? As Margalioth points out, a major rationale for the exemption of gambling services under the European VAT harmonization rules was the practical difficulty of taxing that sector. For table games and possibly for slot machines, the bets and winnings may be intermingled. If so, it is impractical to calculate and tax gross bets. It is practical to determine gross bets in lotteries and it may be practical to identify gross bets placed in internet games of chance. In my view, the margin system adopted in the *First National Bank* case may be a reasonable compromise for casino operations. In fact, to fit gambling into a credit-invoice system, the default rule should be to measure the value of taxable casino gambling (the amount subject to output tax) by the margin between gross bets and winnings paid out, even if the entertainment value of some gambling services exceeds that margin.

IV ISRAELI TAXATION OF GAMBLING SERVICES

Professor Margalioth evaluates the Israeli VAT on how well it performs in taxing value added by operators and taxing gamblers uniformly on the gambling services they receive. Whether the Israeli approach is successful or fails to achieve these goals, in Professor Margalioth's view, the theoretical foundation for taxing legal and illegal gambling differently is wrong. I agree.

Israel taxes only wages paid by non-profit governmental organizations[15] in connection with the rendering of legal gambling services. In contrast, Israel imposes the regular credit-invoice rules on operators conducting illegal gambling. Under those credit-invoice rules, credit is denied for tax on acquisitions from unregistered persons—the winnings paid out. Thus, Israel includes gross bets in the VAT base for illegal gambling and denies deductions for expenses directly linked to illegal activities.

V FINAL COMMENTS

Assuming that VAT is a tax on final consumption calculated under a credit-invoice method, the value of taxable gambling services may be defined as gross bets or the margin between the bets received and the winnings paid out. Both may be justifiable, depending on the value of the entertainment received for bets placed. For practical administrative reasons, even if the value of the services should be measured by gross bets, output tax should be imposed on the margin when a casino cannot separately calculate gross bets from those services.

15. In the UK, lotteries operated by government agencies and non-profit organizations are exempt from VAT.

Part IV
Exemptions for Immovable Property

CHAPTER 7

A Proposal to Improve the VAT Treatment of Housing in the European Union*

Sijbren Cnossen

§7.01 INTRODUCTION

Under a pure value added tax (VAT), rents and rental values of owner-occupied property, as well as sales, would be taxed like other goods and services with a credit for the VAT on purchases of the property. Since this is not considered feasible, best-practice VATs tax the value of new residential housing as a proxy for the present value of the VAT on the future flow of housing services. This 'pre-payment' method is also applied to other consumer durables, such as cars and household appliances. But the long-lived nature of housing makes it more likely that unanticipated changes will occur in its value, and hence in the services that it renders, which do not enter the VAT base (In addition, the VAT rate may change.).

To remedy this shortcoming, this paper proposes to apply the VAT to the increase[1] in the value of residential property each time the property is sold after the first taxable sale following construction. The VAT on the increase in used housing values should be seen as an alternative to existing distortionary transfer, registration or stamp duties,[2] not as a way to raise additional revenue. These duties resemble cascading

* This paper was originally published in 32 *Fiscal Studies* (2011): 455–481. Permission for republication is gratefully acknowledged. The paper has benefited from the report that the author (assisted by Gerhard Badenhorst) prepared for the Tax Policy Unit, National Treasury of South Africa, and the South African Revenue Service, titled *VAT, Transfer Duty, and Stamp Duty on Fixed Property* (June 2008), and from the comments by Antoine Bozio, Judith Payne, and an anonymous referee. The usual caveat applies.

1. Unless otherwise indicated, references to increases in property values should be understood to include decreases, which would involve VAT refunds.
2. Unless the context requires otherwise, references to transfer duty include registration and stamp duties levied on the same base.

types of turnover taxes whose burden increases capriciously the more often the property is sold. Also, the duties cause lock-in effects, since people will hold on to their property longer than they would have in the absence of the duties. The VAT on the increase in property values eliminates the cascading effect and mitigates the lock-in effect.

The increase in the value of exempt used residential property should be taxed upon sale (since VAT is a transactions tax) at the going rate at which newly created property is taxed. However, since sellers and buyers of exempt property are not registered for VAT purposes in respect of that property, the transfer duty collection mechanism could be retained to avoid confusion with the main VAT. One helpful feature of this approach would be that the 'new transfer duty' could continue to be linked to the property registrar's office (*cadastre*), which should keep a record of VAT payments. The new duty would resemble the tax under the margin method applied in connection with the VAT treatment of second-hand goods, such as cars. Presumably, its introduction would not require an amendment to the EU VAT Directive[3] (also referred to as the Common VAT Directive).

The paper is organized as follows. The next section describes the way in which housing and other immovable property should be taxed under a pure VAT, and how they are taxed under a best-practice VAT. Section §7.03 surveys and evaluates the various ways in which transactions in immovable property are currently taxed in the EU under the VATs, as well as under other taxes, duties and levies, which interact with the VAT. A confrontation between actual and best-practice treatment reveals a number of discrepancies, which are examined in section §7.04. Section §7.05 elucidates the main proposal of the article to include increases in used housing prices in the VAT base, and illustrates this by reference to the Dutch situation. The last section summarizes the treatment of housing and other immovable property under the VAT if the new transfer duty were adopted.

This review and evaluation of the VAT treatment of immovable property is undertaken in response to the European Commission's call for contributions dealing with the issues raised in its Green Paper on the future of VAT.[4]

§7.02 HOW SHOULD IMMOVABLE PROPERTY BE TAXED?

How should immovable property ideally be taxed under a cash-flow, tax credit type of VAT? And what concessions have to be made to a pure VAT to make it workable, i.e. to turn it into a best-practice VAT?

3. Council Directive 2006/112/EC of 28 November 2006 on the common system of value added tax, OJ L347/1-118 of 2006 ('EU VAT Directive').
4. See European Commission, '*Green Paper on the Future of VAT: Towards a Simpler, More Robust and Efficient VAT System*', Brussels, COM(2010) 695 final, as well as the accompanying European Commission Staff Working Document, '*Accompanying Document to the Green Paper on the Future of VAT: Towards a Simpler, More Robust and Efficient VAT System*', Brussels, SEC(2010) 1455 final.

[A] Treatment under a Pure VAT

It is generally agreed that VAT should be imposed on the widest possible range of goods and services that are used or consumed by businesses and individuals. Exemptions and rate differentiation violate the logic and functionality of the VAT.[5] This dictum applies also to immovable property. All transactions in property – land and buildings, residential or commercial, privately or publicly owned or leased – should be included in the VAT base and taxed at the standard rate. This rate should apply to the construction, repair and maintenance, sale, lease and owner-occupancy of new and used property. The VAT's tax credit mechanism should be relied upon to ensure that the VAT sticks only to consumer or end-use of the services provided by immovable property, not to business use.

To understand the correct VAT treatment of immovable property, it is instructive to view land and buildings as stocks that can be used for consumption or production purposes.[6] If property, such as a factory building, is used for production purposes, the services that it generates should not be subject to VAT. Normally, the value of these services will be incorporated in the price of production that, if a sale were involved, would be subject to VAT. Moreover, any VAT paid at the time of the purchase of the building should be creditable against the VAT chargeable on the products made by the factory situated on the property. If there is no VAT on sales, simply because there are no sales, a refund would be due.

Ideally, the same treatment should be accorded immovable property that generates housing services. The most attractive solution would be to register all persons, natural as well as legal, who own or buy residential property, for VAT purposes. By purchasing a dwelling, these persons would become producers (called taxable persons under VAT legislation) of housing services. In their role as producers, they would subsequently sell the housing services to consumers. These consumers could be lessees who buy the services for consideration – i.e. a rental charge – but it is also possible that the producers would put the house at their own disposal. In other words, as owner-occupiers (landlords) they would 'sell' the housing services to themselves in their role as occupier-consumers (tenants).

The VAT consequences of these events are obvious. The taxable person who buys a bundle of housing services in the form of a dwelling pays VAT on the purchase price, but, at the same time, he is entitled to a tax credit (and refund, if due) for the same amount. If he sells the housing services to a lessee, he would have to charge VAT on the amount of the rental. The lessee, being a non-taxable consumer, would not be able to pass the VAT on; he would be stuck with it just like consumers of other services and goods. Similarly, in his role as owner-occupier, the producer of housing services would 'charge' VAT on these services, whose value equals the rental value of the dwelling, rendered to himself as consumer. And like the lessor, he would have to remit

5. L. Ebrill et al., *The Modern VAT* (International Monetary Fund 2001).
6. The following paragraphs draw on S. Cnossen, *VAT Treatment of Immovable Property*, in *Tax Law Design and Drafting*, 231–245 (vol. 1, V. Thuronyi ed., International Monetary Fund 1996).

that VAT (net of any VAT on inputs, such as repair and maintenance services) to the VAT authorities. And just like the lessee, he would be stuck with the VAT on the rental value of his dwelling.

The treatment of land would not differ from the treatment of buildings. If land generates production services, as in agriculture, it should be treated in the same manner as the factory above. If it is a producer good that generates consumption services because it is used for camping or hunting purposes, for example, then the same reasoning holds as given above in respect of housing services. Feasibility considerations may dictate other solutions, but it seems incorrect to say that land should be left out of the base because it is not a consumer good. The issue is whether land generates (on balance, non-taxable) production services, or (in principle, taxable) consumption services.[7]

In sum, under a pure VAT, residential property would always be a producer good. Sales, rentals and rental values would be taxable and a credit would be available for the VAT on purchase. In fact, this pure treatment has been proposed for housing in the UK by the Mirrlees Review.[8] Presently, under the UK VAT, the construction and sale of new housing are zero-rated. To tax the current consumption of housing services, the Review proposes to replace the council tax (levied as a percentage of the estimated market value of residential properties) by a new housing services tax on rents and rental values at (eventually) the VAT rate, using the 'rating lists' – which would have to be modified and updated – compiled and maintained by the Valuation Office Agency.

The proposed housing services tax would be a surrogate VAT on the current consumption of housing services, whether supplied in rented or owner-occupied form. A shortcoming is that there would be no credit for tax on renovations that increase rental values. No doubt, as the Review makes clear, it would also be difficult to keep rental values up to date, as illustrated by the experience with the council tax and their taxation for income tax purposes elsewhere.[9] In addition, the VAT zero-rate on new housing is an invitation to tax evasion since it is tempting to misclassify building materials and services used for taxable non-business activities as zero-rated products

---

7. It is quite another matter that land is not a produced input – that its supply is fixed (except perhaps in Holland), so that taxing land ownership is taxing an economic rent. See J. Mirrlees et al., *Tax by Design: The Mirrlees Review*, Ch. 16 (Institute for Fiscal Studies 2011), available at www.ifs.org.uk/mirrleesreview (Mirrlees Review). Accordingly, the tax would be capitalized in the value of the land without any effect on economic activity. But this feature calls for a separate land or land value tax, not a VAT. Under a VAT, the tax on land would be washed out if the land is used for taxable activities by taxable persons, but not if used or owned by non-taxable persons.
8. Mirrlees Review (n. 7 above), Ch. 16.
9. The rationale for taxing rental values under the income tax runs parallel to that under a pure VAT. Rather than earning a return on his house in the market on which he would be taxed, the owner-occupier offers the return to himself as investor, which should be included in his income tax assessment. Taxing this return under the income tax as well as the VAT is not a form of double taxation, just as the application of the VAT to the consumption of a market-earned rental charge, on which income tax has been paid, is not considered double taxation. The application of both taxes arises because owner-occupied houses are an investment as well as a consumption good.

and services. Some people might also consider the taxation of rental values alien to a transactions tax, such as the VAT, which taxes actual expenditures rather than presumptive consumption.

[B] Best Practice

In all EU Member States (and OECD countries) other than the UK, new residential housing is taxed under the VAT, while rents and rental values are considered outside its scope, i.e. de facto exempt. In most countries, the registration for VAT purposes of all owner-occupiers and the annual computation of all rental values would present formidable administrative (and political) difficulties, which are not considered to be surmountable in practice. But if rental values cannot be taxed, the taxation of rental charges would appear to favour owner-occupiers over lessees.[10] In addition, the taxation of rental charges only would involve the registration of many small landlords, and complications would arise from changes in the status of dwellings from owner-occupation to rental use and vice versa.

As a second-best approach, therefore, all countries with a VAT exempt rental values and nearly all countries exempt rental charges as well. Instead, these countries tax new residential construction. But since the purchase price of a house may be taken to represent the present discounted value of its future services, by extension the VAT on the purchase price may be considered a good proxy for the discounted value of the VAT that should have been levied on the flow of housing services.[11] Thus, owners and lessors of dwellings are indirectly subject to VAT on the consumption of housing services by themselves or by lessees.

Prima facie, this is a neat result that indicates that the exemption of lessees (and landlords) and owner-occupiers does not favour housing services over the consumption of other goods and services. It debunks the notion that housing services are not taxed because their current use is exempted. But the equivalence between the VAT on newly constructed immovable property and a hypothetical VAT on the present discounted value of all future rental values or charges does not hold in the face of changing property values and, by extension, the changing value of the housing services provided by the property. In addition, changes in VAT rates put the equivalence into doubt. And the importance of all these increases in view of the long-time use of properties. Clearly, this is a shortcoming that needs to be addressed. But there is more amiss with the tax treatment of immovable property in the EU, as the following brief survey shows.

10. In this respect, the treatment of immovable property differs from the treatment of other consumer durables, such as new cars, which are taxed in full if purchased by a consumer (just like newly built residential property), but whose lease is also taxed (unlike housing rentals).
11. S. Poddar, *Taxation of Housing Under a VAT*, 63 Tax L. Rev. 443–470 (2010), contains a numerical illustration of the equivalence between a VAT on the present discounted value of rents and rental values and its 'prepayment' through a VAT on the value of newly constructed residential premises.

§7.03 HOW IS IMMOVABLE PROPERTY TAXED?

An evaluation of the EU's VAT treatment of immovable property, especially housing, requires a brief review of the agreed common rules and actual practices in the various Member States. Additional or alternative taxes, duties and levies on immovable property transfers, which interact with the VATs, also should be examined.

[A] VAT Treatment

[1] Common Rules

The Common VAT Directive provides the following rules on the treatment of immovable property (Articles refer to Council Directive, 2006):

- The supply of land is exempt (Article 135(1)(k)), except building land (Article 12(1)(b)).
- Building materials, repair, maintenance and construction services are subject to VAT (Articles 14 and 24).
- New buildings (generally, before first occupation) together with the land on which they stand, are taxable (Article 12(1)(a)). Buildings are defined as including any structure immovable to or in the ground.
- Leasing and letting of used immovable property are exempt (Article 135(1)(l)), except hotel and holiday camping accommodation, parking facilities, permanently installed equipment and machinery (immovable by destination) and the hire of safes (Article 135(2)).
- The sale of used immovable property is exempt, but taxable persons are allowed an option to be taxed (Article 137(1)(b–d)). The transfer of property as part of a going concern can be effected VAT-free (Article 19).
- Input tax on property expenditure should be adjusted over a period of 5–20 years under the capital goods scheme (CGS) when the property becomes taxable (Article 187).

[2] Practice in the Member States

Table 7.1 provides an overview of the VAT treatment of the construction, lease and sale of new and used property in the 27 Member States of the EU (column 1). Few Member States apply the standard VAT rate (column 2) without further ado. There is substantial variation in the application of the common rules (allowed under discretionary or transitional rules or by way of derogation) between Member States, mainly for historic, legal, budgetary or tax assignment reasons, and in the interaction with transfer and stamp duties. Perhaps the best way to try to get a grip on what is going on is to review the process of the creation of new buildings (starting with the treatment of building land and construction work), move on to social housing and to renovation and repair, and from there to leasing and letting, and to the sale of used property. Along the way, the major VAT aspects in the various Member States are noted.

Table 7.1. VAT Treatment of Immovable Property in the European Union, 2011

Member State	*Standard Rate*	*Construction, Repair and Maintenance*					*Leasing and Letting*	*Sale of Used Property*	*Conditions*
		Building land	*Construction work on new buildings*	*New buildings*	*Social housing*	*Renovation & repair**	*(residential / non-residential)*		**Excluding materials if lower rate applies*
(1)	(2)	(3)	(4)	(5)	(6)	(7)	(8)	(9)	(10)
Austria	20	E	20	E°	20	20	10 / $E^{\o}$	$E^{\o}$	
Belgium	21	E	6 / 12 / 21	21	6 / 12	6* / 21	E / T	$E^{\o}$	*Dwelling ≥5 yrs old
Bulgaria	20	20	20	20	20	20	E / T	E / T	
Cyprus	15	E	15	15	15	15	E	E	
Czech Rep.	20	20	20	20	10	10	$E^{\o}$	E	
Denmark	25	E	25	E°°	25	25	$E^{\o}$	$E^{\o}$	
Estonia	20	20	20	20	20	20	$E^{\o}$	$E^{\o}$	
Finland	23	E°	23	E°°	23	23	$E^{\o}$	$E^{\o}$	
France	19.6	19,6	19.6	19.6	5.5 / 19.6	5,5* / 19.6	$E^{\o}$ / T	E	*Dwellings ≥2 yrs old
Germany	19	E°	19	E°	19	19	$E^{\o}$	$E^{\o}$	
Greece	23	E	23	23	23 / E	13*/ 23	E / T	E	*Old dwellings
Hungary	25	25	25	25	25	25	$E^{\o}$	E / T	
Ireland	21	E	13.5*	13.5*	13.5	13.5*	$E^{\o}$	E	*Parking rate

Member State	*Standard Rate*	*Construction, Repair and Maintenance*					*Leasing and Letting*	*Sale of Used Property*	*Conditions*
		Building land	*Construction work on new buildings*	*New buildings*	*Social housing*	*Renovation & repair**	*(residential / non-residential)*		**Excluding materials if lower rate applies*
Italy	20	20	4* / 10	4* / 10 / 20	4 / 10	10	$E^{\emptyset}$ / T	E / T	*First dwelling
Latvia	22	E	22	22	22	22	E / T	E	
Lithuania	21	21	21	21	21	21	$E^{\emptyset}$	$E^{\emptyset}$	
Luxembourg	15	E^{o}	3* / 15	E	3* / 15	3* / 15	3 / $E^{\emptyset}$	$E^{\emptyset}$	*Principal or old dwelling
Malta	18	E	18	E	E	18	E / T	E	
Netherlands	19	19	19	19	19	6* / 19	$E^{\emptyset}$	$E^{\emptyset}$	*Painting/ plastering
Poland	23	23	23	23	8	8	E / T	E / T	
Portugal	23	E^{o}	6 / 23	E^{o}	E / 6	6 / 23	$E^{\emptyset}$ / T	$E^{\emptyset}$	
Romania	24	24	24	24	5	24	E	E	
Slovak Rep.	20	E* / 20	20	20	20	20	$E^{\emptyset}$	$E^{\emptyset}$	*If exempt
Slovenia	20	20	20	20	8.5	8.5	$E^{\emptyset}$	$E^{\emptyset}$	
Spain	18	18	4 / 8	8 / 18	4 / 8	8*/18	E / T	$E^{\emptyset}$	*Brick laying
Sweden	25	E	25	E^{oo}	25 / E	25	$E^{\emptyset}$	$E^{\emptyset}$	
United Kingdom	20	E^{o} / 20	0 / 20	0 / 20	0 / 20	5* / 20	$E^{\emptyset}$	$E^{\emptyset}$	*Isle of Man

Source: European Commission, Taxation and Customs Union, VAT Rates Applied in the Member States of the European Union as at 1 January 2011, and country legislation.

Notes: E = exempt, but E° indicates that developers can opt for taxation and E°° that developers can recover input tax if the building is sold to a taxable person; T = taxable; ø = option for taxation by taxable persons. The table does not cover all exceptions to the main rule and some information may not be complete.

[a] Building Land

Non-building land is exempt in all Member States except Italy, where its sale is exempt 'with credit' (i.e. it is zero-rated) so that taxable persons can recover input tax on improvements. In contrast to the rule prescribed by the 2006 Council Directive, which suggests that building land should be taxed, 14 Member States exempt building land along with other land (Table 7.1, column 3), although various Member States permit developers to opt for taxation so that they can recover any VAT incurred in preparing building land for construction purposes.

[b] Construction, New and Social Housing, Renovation and Repair

Construction work on new buildings (Table 7.1, column 4) is taxed in all Member States, although six apply a lower rate if the work involves residential buildings. Ireland levies a lower-than-standard-rate of 13.5% on all construction, residential and non-residential. The UK is the only Member state that zero-rates new housing. Of course, in all Member States, the VAT on construction work for new buildings, which are used for taxable purposes and for which the option of registration and taxation (if available) is being used, is washed out through the tax credit mechanism.

It might be expected that the VAT treatment of new buildings (column 5), including the distinction between residential and non-residential buildings, would follow that of construction work on new buildings, but this is not always the case. In several countries, the supply of new buildings is exempt (often because transfer duty applies), although in Finland and Sweden the exemption actually implies full taxation, because developers have to pay tax on the 'self-supply' of buildings (with credit for input tax) before they can sell them. In Denmark, the purchaser takes on responsibility for the developer's input tax under the capital goods scheme. Various Member States define reconstructed or renovated buildings as new buildings, so that they attract VAT. France and Spain tax social housing at a concessionary VAT rate (column 6), lower than the (reduced) rate applicable to new residential premises.

Understandably, renovation and repair services (column 7) are more often taxed at the standard VAT rate than social housing or new buildings, because these services can be used for residential as well as non-residential purposes (Taxation at the standard rate without regard to end-use makes evasion more difficult.). The reduced rates on renovation and repair services for old dwellings in Belgium, France, Greece, Luxembourg and the Netherlands were introduced to stimulate employment in the construction sector.

[c] Leasing and Letting

The letting of residential premises is exempt in all but two Member States (Table 7.1, column 8). Apparently, to achieve parity between 'rooms for rent' and hotel accommodation, Austria taxes lettings at 10% and Luxembourg at 3%. Leasing and letting of non-residential buildings also are exempt under the 2006 Council Directive, but 10 Member States tax them, while nearly all the other Member States allow the option of registration and taxation. Some States do not have an option to tax, but the exemption for non-residential buildings is so limited that the option would be redundant. In 10 Member States, lettings of non-residential property are usually taxable.

[d] Sales of Used Property

Sales of used residential and non-residential properties are exempt under the 2006 Council Directive. In Bulgaria, Hungary, Italy and Poland, however, the exemption is very limited and never applies to business premises. In France, property sales by a property dealer (*marchand de biens*) are taxable, but usually only on the dealer's margin.

All Member States except Greece, Italy and five new accession countries have an option to tax for non-residential property. Another four States allow an option for leasing or letting, but not for sales, while in several countries the option is only available if the purchaser or tenant has a certain level of VAT recovery. In various Member States, the wide-ranging compulsory taxation of property transactions means that there is less need for an option.

Member States are required to adjust the input tax on immovable property (and other capital goods) over a period of up to 20 years under the capital goods scheme if the property becomes taxable. Most Member States have a 10-year period, but do not apply the adjustment to building work. Finland and Ireland do not permit adjustments, but their rules for new buildings deal with many of the same situations where a capital goods scheme might otherwise be applicable.

This brief review indicates that there is probably less alignment across the EU in the treatment of immovable property than in most other areas of the common VAT. The overall picture is complex and non-transparent, although Estonia, Hungary, Lithuania and Poland (all new accession states) stand out for the limited scope of exemptions and rate differentiation for transactions in immovable property. In general, the common rules and the situation in most Member States deviate from best practice in three important respects.

(1) The sale of all used properties is in principle exempt (not just the sale of used residential property) rather than taxed, although an option for taxation is available for commercial property in many cases.
(2) Non-building land is exempt (except in Italy) rather than taxed.
(3) Increases in the value of exempt immovable property are not included in the VAT base.

An overall evaluation needs to take account of transfer, registration and stamp duties, which interact with the VATs. They are reviewed in the next subsection.

[B] Additional or Alternative Taxes

All Member States levy additional or alternative taxes on the sale and lease of new and used property. Table 7.2 provides an overview of their prevalence in the EU. Generally, revenues do not exceed 2% of total tax revenue, although Belgium, Cyprus, Greece, Italy, Luxembourg, Malta, the Netherlands, Portugal and Spain are notable exceptions. Often the revenues accrue to regional or local governments (Table 7.2, last column), complicating efforts at reform. The taxes can be a significant cost for business.

Table 7.2. Taxes on Transactions in Immovable Property in the European Union, 2010

Member State	*English name*	*National name*	*Tax base or object*	*Most common rate(s)*	*Revenue yield (2008), % of*		*Beneficiary government*
					Total tax	*GDP*	
Austria	Real estate transfer tax	Grunderwerbsteuer	Purchase price	3.5% (2% for relatives)	0.56	0.23	Central/Local
	Legal and administrative duties	Stempel- und Rechtsgebühren	Tenancy and loan agreements	Wide range of specific duties	0.70	0.29	Central
Belgium	Miscellaneous duties and taxes	Droits et taxes divers/ Diverse rechten en taksen	Deeds drawn up by notaries and banks	€50 for notaries; €2 for mortgages	0.96	0.42	Central
	Registration, mortgage and court rights	Droits d'enregistrement, d'hypothèque et de greffe / Registratie-, hypotheek- en griffierechten	Contractual value	10% (12.5% in Walloon Region)	2.20	0.97	Central/Regional
Bulgaria	Taxes on acquisition of property	Данък при придобиване на имущества по дарение и по възмезден начин	Value assessed by Municipal Council	1.3%-2.6%	1.63	0.55	Local
Cyprus	Lands and surveys fees	Τέλη που επιβάλλονται και εισπράττονται από το Τμήμα Κτηματολογίου και	Property value or amount of mortgage	3%-8%; 1% on mortgages	1.54	0.64	Central
	Stamp duty	Χωρομετρίας	Value of agreement or standard fee	0.15% -0.2% or €34.17	1.11	0.46	Central

Member State	English name	National name	Tax base or object	Most common rate(s)	Revenue yield (2008), % of		Beneficiary government
					Total tax	GDP	
Czech Republic	Immovable estate transfer tax	Daňz převodu nemovitostí	Transfer price or officially assessed value	3%	0.76	0.28	Central
	Administrative fees	Správní poplatky	Transfers and mortgage deeds	Wide range of specific duties	0.30	0.11	Central/Local
	Fee on building land betterment	Poplatek za zhodnocení stavebního pozemku	Difference in value before and after improvement	Per m^2 specified by municipality	0.00	0.00	Local
Denmark	Registration tax (stamp duty)	Afgift af tinglysning og registrering af ejerog pantrettigehder mv	Registration of ownership and mortgages	1,400 DKK + 0.6% of sale price (1.5% for mortgages)	1.04	0.50	Central
	Property release duty (derestriction tax)	Frigørelseafgift på fast ejendom	Increase in value due to change in zoning	40% on DKK 200,000 and 60% on balance	0.00	0.00	Central/Local
	Taxation of the sale of immovable property	Lov om beskatning af fortjeneste ved afståelse af fast ejendom	Sale price minus acquisition cost	Capital income tax rates	–	–	Central
Finland	Transfer tax	Variansiirtovero/ Överlåtelseskatt	Transfer price	4%	0.90	0.38	Central

Member State	*English name*	*National name*	*Tax base or object*	*Most common rate(s)*	*Revenue yield (2008), % of*		*Beneficiary government*
					Total tax	*GDP*	
France	Principal registration duties	Principaux droits d'enregistrement	Higher of price plus charges or market value	7.5%	1.24	0.53	Central/ Regional/Local
Germany	Immovable property transfer tax	Grunderwerbsteuer	Amount of consideration	3.5%	0.72	0.28	Regional
Greece	Immovable estate transfer tax	'Τέλος Χαρτοσήμων'	Contractual sale price	7%-9%	1.86	0.59	Central/Local
	Stamp duties	Φόρος μεταβίβασης	Sales, rents and loans	3%	0.87	028	Central
Hungary	Property transfer tax	Visszterhes vagyonátruházási illeték	Market value	10%	1.16	0.46	Central/Local
Ireland	Stamp duty on property	Stamp duty on property	Contractual consideration	0%-9% (over €875,000)	1.96	0.57	Central
Italy	Registration tax on property transfer	Imposta di registro	Market value or estimated rent	0.5%-15% (first house: 3%)	0.89	0.38	Central/ Regional
	Mortgage tax and land registry fee	Imposte ipotecarie e catastali	Amount of mortgage or value of property	Cadastre: 1%, mortgage: 0.5%-3%; or €168	0.35	0.15	Central/ Regional
	Stamp duty	Imposta di bollo	Deeds and documents	€14.62	0.75	0.32	Central/ Regional/Local

Member State	*English name*	*National name*	*Tax base or object*	*Most common rate(s)*	*Revenue yield (2008), % of*		*Beneficiary government*
					Total tax	*GDP*	
	Replacement tax	Imposta sostitutiva	Amount of mortgage	2%	0.44	0.19	Central
	Municipal tax on building licenses	Contributi concessioni edilizie	Amount of building cost and town planning	–	0.49	0.21	Local
Latvia	Duty for consolidation of ownership and legal liens in Land Register	Nodeva par īpašuma tiesību un ķīlas tiesību nostiprināšanu zemesgrāmatā	Property value or amount of loan agreement	2% subject to ceiling of LVL30,000	0.69	0.20	Central
Luxembourg	Registration taxes	Droits d'enregistrement	Market value	6%	5.31	1.89	Central
Malta	Duty on documents and transfers – Immovables	Taxxa fuq dokumenti u trasferimenti – immobili	Market value	3.5% (5% for non-residential property)	2.80	0.96	Central
Netherlands	Tax on legal transactions	Belastingen van rechtsverkeer	Market value	6%	2.62	1.02	Central
Poland	Tax on civil law transactions	Podatek od czynności cywilnoprawnych	Market value or amount of mortgage	2% or 0.1%	0.64	0.22	Local
	Stamp duty	Oplata skarbowa	Type of document	Specific	0.16	0.05	Local

Member State	English name	National name	Tax base or object	Most common rate(s)	Revenue yield (2008), % of		Beneficiary government
					Total tax	GDP	
Portugal	Immovable property municipal transfer tax	IMT – Imposta municipal sobre as transmissões onerosas de imóveis	Higher of contractual price or taxable value	Rural: 5% Urban: 0%-8%	1.28	0.47	Local
	Stamp duty	Imposto do selo	Higher of contractual price or taxable value	0.8%	3.01	1.10	Central
Slovenia	Real property transactions tax	Zakon o davku na promet nepremičnin	Selling price	2%	0.35	0.13	Local
Spain	Tax on capital transfers and documented legal acts	Impuesto sobre transmisiones patrimoniales y actos jurídicos documentados	Market value	6%; deeds: specific	4.46	1.65	Regional
	Tax on construction, installation and works	Impuesto sobre construcciones, instalaciones y obras	Value of construction, installation or work	2.4%-4%	0.41	0.13	Local
	Tax on the increase in the value of urban land	Impuesto sobre incremento del valor de los terrenos de naturaleza urbana	Increase in value upon sale	Up to 30%	0.36	0.13	Local

Member State	*English name*	*National name*	*Tax base or object*	*Most common rate(s)*	*Revenue yield (2008), % of*		*Beneficiary government*
					Total tax	*GDP*	
Sweden	Stamp duty	Stämpelskatt	Price of property or amount of mortgage	1.5% or 2%	0.63	0.29	Central
United Kingdom	Stamp duty land tax	Stamp duty land tax	Consideration for chargeable interest	1%-4% on sale and 1% on rent	1.04	0.39	Central

Source: European Commission: 'Taxes in Europe' database: search results, downloaded 13 April 2011. Taxes on ownership and/or use of immovable property found in all Member States are not shown. Taxes on transfers by gift or at death and some other duties and levies covered by the legislation also are not shown, but the revenues (which cannot be separated out) are included under yields. Some information may not be complete.

[1] Overview

Most of the taxes shown in Table 7.2 go by the name of transfer duty, registration duty or stamp duty. The difference between transfer duty and registration duty (as well as stamp duty in Ireland and the UK) tends to be one of name only. Both are levied on the sale price agreed to between the parties to the transaction or on the fair market value. The same applies to the lands and surveys taxes in Cyprus and the taxes on legal or civil law transactions in the Netherlands and Poland.

Various Member States prevent the simultaneous application of VAT and transfer duty. In Cyprus, Germany, the Netherlands and Spain, for instance, transfer duty does not apply if the property transaction is subject to VAT. In Belgium and Italy, registration duties are reduced if VAT applies as well. By contrast, Luxembourg subjects property to transfer tax of 6%, whether or not VAT applies. Nine Member States subject residential leases to registration tax or stamp duty. Austria, Ireland, Spain and the UK apply these taxes to leases of business premises too, which violates production efficiency. Usually, the basis of assessment is the total rents under the lease, but the UK and Ireland assess stamp duty on the annual rent.

Of particular interest are the various taxes levied on increases in property values. Denmark, for instance, imposes tax on the capital gain realized on the sale of immovable property. Although subject to income tax, the base of this tax is identical to the base under a VAT levied on the increase in the value of exempt property. Also, Denmark imposes a 'derestriction' tax on the gain in the value of property whose zoning designation changes from agricultural land to urban or cottage land, which implies permission to build on the land and hence a windfall gain. Similarly, Spain taxes the increase in the value of urban land.

The conventional stamp duties on official documents related to transactions in immovable property (and various other dutiable events) are a separate category. Although the rates, often specified by type of event, tend to be low, the duties exhibit the same cascading effects as transfer duties, at least to the extent that they cannot be regarded as a consideration for services rendered by government. As Table 7.2 shows, many Member States still are enamoured by these anachronistic nuisance levies.

[2] Evaluation

This brief overview shows that there seems to be little rhyme or reason to the transfer (or registration) and stamp duties on property transactions in the EU.[12] The duties act as cascading turnover taxes. The more often a property is sold, the more often transfer duty has to be paid. In addition, the transfer duty causes a lock-in effect, in that owners will hold on to their property longer than they would if there had been no transfer duty. In economic terms, ownership preferences and risk profiles diverge, similarly to the

12. In Italy, duplication and non-transparency have reached such proportions that the government has legislated a replacement tax (see Table 7.2), purportedly in lieu of the registration duty, stamp duty, mortgage tax, cadastral tax and the duty on official concessions for medium- and long-term loans.

case under a tax on capital gains, and residential mobility suffers. If possible, tax systems should avoid such effects; they are a deadweight loss to the economy.[13] Further, there is an element of double taxation if VAT as well as transfer duty applies –for instance, in the case of a newly built dwelling (subject to VAT) that is subsequently sold by its owner (subject to transfer duty). Surely, no case can be made for levying transfer duty on commercial property – final consumer expenditures should be taxed, not business inputs (unless externalities have to be accounted for).

This examination of the VAT treatment of immovable property and the alternative or additional duties suggests that neutrality and administrative gains might be reaped by abolishing most of the transfer, registration and stamp duties and making up for the revenue loss by extending the VAT to increases in the value of exempt properties, particularly residential properties, if and when the properties are sold. But before considering this conclusion, some other departures from best practice should be reviewed.

§7.04 ADJUSTMENTS TO THE COMMON DIRECTIVE

The VAT treatment of transactions in immovable property in the EU would benefit from an examination of best practices in Australia, New Zealand and Canada, where all immovable property, including land, is taxed apart from the sale of used residential property (and rents and rental values).[14] Conformation to best practice would require adjustments to the Common Directive in line with the wholesale review currently being undertaken by the European Commission (2010). Although not a prerequisite, the adjustments have a bearing on the taxation of increases in property values of used housing. Accordingly, they are dealt with before the main proposal of the paper is put on the table.

13. Elsewhere, the Australian States impose stamp duty on the transfer of immovable property, differentiated by state, property category (principal residences may attract reduced rates) and purchase price. There is no link between the federal VAT and the state stamp duty. A study by the Property Council of Australia concluded that the abolition of stamp duty on leases would be highly desirable: Property Council of Australia, *The Case for Abolishing Stamp Duty on Commercial Leases* (Property Council of Australia 2003). In Canada, most provinces impose land transfer taxes, often at graduated rates. New Zealand does not levy transfer or stamp duties.

14. For the taxation of land in New Zealand, see G.J. Harley,*Dilemma for GST Tax Policy Designers – Land Transactions,* in *GST in Retrospect and Prospect,* 213–241 (R. Krever & D. White eds., Thomson Reuters 2007), and for the treatment of immovable property, M. Smith,*Dilemma for GST Tax Policy Designers – Land Transactions,* in *GST in Retrospect and Prospect,* 277–308 (R. Krever & D. White eds., Thomson Reuters 2007). The Australian's GST treatment of immovable property is reviewed by M. Evans,*The Value Added Tax Treatment of Immovable Property – An Antipodean Context,* in *GST in Retrospect and Prospect,* 243–276 (R. Krever & D. White eds., Thomson Reuters 2007). The situation in both countries is compared by R. Millar, 'VAT and Immovable Property: Full Taxation Models and the Treatment of Capital Gains on Owner-Occupied Residences', Ch. 8 in this volume, who holds a view contrary to the one held in this chapter.

[A] Adopting the Tax Method

An essential difference regarding the VAT treatment of immovable property between modern and old VATs, as found in the EU, is that all transactions in immovable property are exempt under the EU's Common Directive, except newly constructed property (exemption approach), while all transactions are taxable under modern VATs, except the sale of residential premises (tax method).

Under the exemption method, prescribed in the EU's Council Directive (2006), the sale, lease and use of immovable property (residential and non-residential) are, in principle, exempt, but newly constructed buildings, as well as alterations and maintenance of the existing building stock, are taxable without credit for tax. The exemption method needs a definition of specified non-residential use, such as hotel accommodation, boarding houses, camping facilities and parking space – all of which are taxable. Furthermore, since the business use and sale of existing non-residential immovable property also are exempt, an opportunity for optional registration and payment of VAT is desirable to avoid potential discrimination and cascading of tax.

Under the tax method adopted by Australia, Canada and New Zealand, the sale and lease of all immovable property is, in principle, taxable, but residential rents (and rental values) are exempt (or outside the scope of the VAT), as is the sale of previously occupied residential property (unless sold by a taxable person). This implies that the construction, sale, lease, alteration and maintenance of all non-residential buildings are taxable. Sales of existing buildings also are taxable, unless such buildings constitute residential property. The tax method requires a definition of residential use (but not of specified non-residential use, unless taxed differentially lower or higher), but an option to register and pay VAT for commercial purposes is not necessary.

The tax method seems superior to the exemption approach on the philosophy that exceptions to the first-best VAT treatment of immovable property should be formulated restrictively. The tax method does this by including changes in non-residential property values in the VAT base (if the property is used for taxable purposes), while the exemption method does not do so if no use is made of the registration option.[15] Since the reach of the tax method is greater than the reach of the exemption method, it results in more even-handed and neutral treatment.

Neither the tax method nor the exemption approach includes increases in the value of exempt property in the VAT base, although this would be desirable on neutrality grounds. The issue is particularly important regarding used residential property, but under either the tax method or the exemption approach it would also be relevant for used non-residential property sold by exempt entities to other exempt entities.

15. Note that both methods would have the same effect if all registered persons opted for taxation of non-residential property under the exemption approach.

[B] Taxing Non-building Land

Australia, New Zealand and Canada did not want to tax land at the inception of their VAT (called the Goods and Services Tax, or GST) since this would constitute a one-off wealth tax on landowners. New Zealand achieves this by taxing land as a second-hand good. Persons registered for VAT are allowed a notional tax credit in respect of land bought from non-registered persons against the VAT on sale, which has the effect of sheltering such land from taxation.[16] Australia only taxes the margin by allowing a deduction for the acquisition price of the land. Canada taxes the sale of all land, except land held for personal use. Land acquired by a non-registered person attracts tax, but personal-use land held by an individual remains exempt as resale of used residential property. When personal-use land is sold to a registered person, it becomes taxable.

The exemption of non-building land in the EU is closely tied in with the exemption of agriculture. At the time the VATs were introduced, most States did not consider it feasible to include farming, fishing and forestry in the base. Accordingly, these sectors were exempted and various presumptive schemes were designed to enable farmers to get rid of the tax on their taxable inputs.[17] Further, farmers were given the option to register for VAT, just like businesses with a turnover below the threshold. Of course, the presumptive schemes are merely a rough-and-ready form of input tax compensation, sometimes inadequate, more often overly generous, particularly if agricultural ministries are involved in the calculation of the presumptive VAT rate or input tax credit.

Over the years, farmers' ability to comply with VAT obligations has greatly improved in most Member States. This implies that taxing agriculture on the same footing as other businesses should become the rule rather than the exception. This would open the door to the taxation of all non-building land. In various Member States most non-agricultural land is already within the ambit of the VAT. This practice could become the general rule, perhaps by following the New Zealand and Australian examples by taxing land as a second-hand good or by confining the VAT to the seller's margin.

[C] Some Further Observations

A review of the Common Directive could also be used to correct various other departures from best practice. Important among these is the widest possible application of the standard rate to building land, construction, social housing, renovation and repair. Lower-than-standard rates distort consumer choices and tend to be ill-targeted measures to help the poor, promote property ownership or boost employment in the

16. Poddar (n. 11 above).
17. These schemes enable farmers to charge VAT on their sales at a rate approximately equivalent to their average total input tax as a percentage of turnover, obviating the need for filing and payment of tax (Germany), or they provide for a presumptive tax credit to purchasers of farm output, again approximately equivalent to the VAT on farmers' inputs (the Netherlands). For more on these schemes, see S. Cnossen, *Value-Added Taxes in Central and Eastern European Countries: A Comparative Survey and Evaluation*, Ch. 9 (OECD 1998).

construction sector. For example, the benefit of reduced rates on renovation and repair services for old dwellings in various Member States (see Table 7.1) may leak away and increase tax evasion.[18] Similarly, a reduced rate for new social housing does not make much sense, since social housing is defined as housing that is partially or wholly financed by government. Accordingly, this implies that the lower rate can be replicated by an adjustment of the subsidy, which would block a potential avenue for tax evasion.

Further, adjustment periods for exempt immovable property tend to be too short in the Member States. The shorter the adjustment period, the more tempting it becomes for exempt entities to establish a taxable business that buys the property and rents it out to the exempt entity. The business would credit the VAT on the purchase of the property against the VAT on the taxable rental charges, and would transfer the property VAT-free to the exempt entity after the prescribed adjustment period expires.[19] No doubt a systematic review of the VAT treatment of immovable property in individual Member States would reveal other anomalies that should be corrected in light of best-practice rules. Such a review should also take the transfer (registration) and stamp duty regimes into consideration, as exemplified in the following section.

§7.05 IMPROVING THE VAT TREATMENT OF HOUSING

Although all best-practice VATs have capital goods schemes, which adjust the VAT incorporated in the price of exempt property when bought for taxable purposes, apparently none taxes the increase in exempt property values, which reflects the increase in the future value of building services rendered by the property. This is surprising because value increases in properties used for taxable purposes are included in the VAT base and taxed when the properties are sold to non-registered persons. This section examines the case for correcting this anomaly and illustrates the proposed solution by reference to the situation in the Netherlands. It focuses mainly on housing, although transactions in other exempt properties should be treated similarly.

[A] VAT Instead of Transfer Duty

Apart from the revenue it raises (an important consideration), the only possible rationale for levying transfer, registration or stamp duty on immovable property transactions between non-taxable persons is that the duty resembles a poorly designed surrogate VAT on the increase in rents and rental values associated with increases in property values. But if this is its rationale, the base of the transfer duty should be redefined as the difference between the selling price and the purchase price (or some proxy if information on the purchase price is not available) of immovable property

18. Ebrill et al. (n. 5 above).
19. The issue has to be reviewed in light of the VAT rebate schemes for public bodies that various Member States have introduced in recent years. For a general treatment, see P.-P. Gendron, *How Should the United States Treat Government Entities, Nonprofit Organizations, and Other Tax-Exempt Bodies under a VAT?*, 63 Tax L. Rev. 477–516 (2010).

traded between non-taxable persons. This margin, which reflects the present discounted value of the increase in anticipated future building services, should be included in the VAT base and taxed at the standard rate, at the level of either the seller or the buyer of the property through a reverse charge. Basically, all transactions in immovable property between non-taxable persons should be subject to the reformed transfer duty, including those by or between governments and non-profit organizations. Also, the increase in value should be taxed if immovable property passes on to heirs and legatees; after all, title passes on, too.

The proposed margin scheme for transactions in exempt immovable property could be incorporated in the VAT (and the transfer duty abolished) or it might continue to be called transfer duty, while retaining the tax collection procedures (for exempt persons, such as individuals and non-registered entities) currently on the transfer duty statute. Since the new transfer duty should be levied in close cooperation with the administration of the immovable property registrar's office, retention of the transfer duty mechanism for assessing and collecting the new tax probably is to be preferred. Separate collection would make it possible to cede the revenue to regional and local governments in lieu of the revenue from the old transfer, registration or stamp duties.

The exact design of the new transfer duty in individual Member States would depend on the nature of the existing transfer, registration or stamp duty regimes, but some common issues can be identified. The most important issue would be to ascertain the acquisition value of properties in order to compute the taxable margin. Most properties would have been bought many years ago, possibly even before the introduction of the VAT. Subjecting the value increases of these properties to the new duty might be viewed as a form of expropriation and would ignore the impact of the alternative taxes levied previously. The issue is akin to the taxation of land upon the introduction of the GSTs in New Zealand and Australia, and the solution might be similar: do not tax the full value (increase) when the property is sold by exempt persons to taxable persons but only the presumptively determined margin (and subsequent increases in value). As illustrated below for the Netherlands, the presumptive acquisition value can be set so that the VAT yield on the value increase realized at the time of the first transfer following the introduction of the new duty approximately equals the yield of the old transfer duty had it been retained.

The new transfer duty should be refunded if the property is sold below its acquisition value. The future value of the housing services embodied in the property has declined and so has the value of future consumption. The refund would be calculated on the difference between the selling price and the (presumptive) acquisition price, but only if VAT has been paid at the time of construction. In practice, the refund issue is unlikely to occur because, as a cash-flow tax, the VAT is based on nominal, not real, values of properties actually sold. Since the new transfer duty would only apply to transactions between non-taxable persons, any application for a refund should attract the attention of the VAT authorities, which could then check suspicious transactions. Further, much can be said for a credit against the new transfer duty for any VAT paid on major renovations that have increased the value of the property. Currently, these renovations are taxed twice, under the VAT as well as the transfer duty. On feasibility grounds, a minimum would have to be prescribed for the size of renovations (expressed, for instance, in terms of the property's value), while the eligibility for the credit should be limited to a specified period immediately preceding the sale.

The redesigned transfer duty resembles, but is not, a capital gains tax. Although the two taxes are imposed on the same base, the new transfer duty is a tax on consumption, whereas the capital gains tax is a tax on income. Tax should be imposed on both counts, just as rental values should be subject to income tax as well as VAT. But the difference is that taxable capital gains represent an ex post adjustment for past accruals of income. Ideally, income tax should be imposed as the gain accrues rather than upon realization. Accordingly, it would be appropriate to levy interest on the tax over the period during which the gain accrued. By contrast, the VAT on the increase in value added should be considered an ex ante tax on the discounted present value of anticipated future housing services. Interest or indexing arrangements would, therefore, seem inappropriate. True, the owner-occupier who sells his house has benefited from not having had to pay more VAT after he bought the dwelling, but this fortuitous result is inherent to a cash-flow consumption tax under which the VAT on durable consumer goods is prepaid rather than imposed as the services of the durable goods are consumed. Moreover, the owner would not have received a credit for the VAT paid on repair services, which maintain the value of the property. Some imperfection has to be accepted here in the interest of feasibility.

To my knowledge, the proposed margin scheme for housing is not found anywhere, perhaps because it is not considered feasible or shows too much similarity with a capital gains tax. New Zealand and Australia, however, do apply the scheme to land or increases in business property values and have done so since the introduction of the GST.[20] Similarly, as shown in section §7.03[B], Denmark and Spain tax increases in property values, albeit under separate statutes. Ebrill et al. argue that the value increase should be included in the VAT base, but do not consider it practicable for owner occupied property.[21] Cnossen and Badenhorst propose the introduction of a margin scheme for housing in South Africa in lieu of the transfer duty.[22] Also, Poddar[23] favours the taxation of increases in value of exempt immovable property, but wants to apply the scheme in full, going back to before the introduction of the VAT. Neither

20. In 2010, the Australian GST margin scheme was reviewed. See Australian Treasury, *Consultation Paper on the Review of the Margin Scheme* (Australian Treasury 2010), available at archive.treasury.gov.au/documents/1528/PDF/GST_Margin_Scheme_Review.pdf, and Australian Treasury, *Implementation of the Recommendations of Treasury's Review of the GST Margin Scheme, Discussion Paper, 10 December 2010* (Australian Treasury 2010), available at archive.treasury.gov.au/documents/1915/PDF/discussion_paper_margin_scheme.pdf.
21. Conrad (R.F. Conrad, *Commentary on S. Poddar, Taxation of Housing under a VAT,* 63 Tax L. Rev. 471–476 (2010)) believes that VAT should be levied on the selling price and that a credit should be allowed for the inflation-adjusted VAT on the purchase price, but this appears difficult to reconcile with the cash-flow nature of the VAT. For more details on this 'S-tax' ('S' for 'stock'), see R.F. Conrad & A. Grozav, *Immovable Property and VAT,* in *VAT in Africa,* 81–112 (R. Krever ed., Pretoria University Law Press 2008).
22. S. Cnossen & G. Badenhorst, *South Africa: VAT, Transfer Duty, and Stamp Duty on Fixed Property,* Report prepared for the Tax Policy Unit, National Treasury of South Africa and the South African Revenue Service (June 2008).
23. Poddar (n. 11 above).

Poddar nor Ebrill et al. consider the possibility of viewing the new transfer duty as an alternative to existing distortionary duties, rather than as a way of raising additional revenue.

[B] Application to the Netherlands

The substitution of the transfer duty by a VAT on the increase (decrease) in the value of used residential property upon sale has been proposed for the Netherlands.[24] As shown in Table 7.1, the Netherlands taxes immovable property in accordance with the Common Directive, i.e. new buildings and the land on which they stand are taxed at the standard rate of 19%, and so are repairs and renovations in general. Subsequent sales of immovable property are exempt, although registered persons can opt for full taxation. Further, property transfer duty of 6% applies when exempt property is sold. The value of the property is based on official three-year valuations.[25]

To maintain the same yield, I have proposed imposing 19% VAT on a value increase of 6/19 of the officially rated value. In practice, this could be effected by sending every owner of exempt immovable property a notification informing him that the presumptive purchase value of his property for the first time that the new duty would be levied has been estimated at 13/19 of the rated value at the time of the notification. At the time of the subsequent sale, VAT would then be paid (or refunded) on the difference between the rated value at the time of sale and the notified value. Subsequently, VAT would be levied on the difference between the rated value at the time of sale and the rated value at the time of purchase. These values would be recorded in the cadastre along with the VAT payments.

Just as under the transfer duty, renovations, which increase the value of the property, would be doubly taxed under the VAT. To mitigate this effect, I have suggested that the VAT on renovations made within, say, five years of the date of sale and involving outlays of more than, say, 10% of the rated value in the year of renovation should be made creditable against the VAT incurred on the increase in value at the time of the later sale. This rough-and-ready approach would not be perfect, but should be acceptable for expediency's sake.

The new transfer duty would have some interesting side effects. First, VAT-registered persons would probably opt more often for having their non-residential property included in the VAT base, in effect converting the exemption approach into the full tax method. This would promote equal treatment and neutrality. Second, owners of exempt property would be interested in high rated values at the time of the

24. S. Cnossen, 'Vervang overdrachtsbelasting door BTW over waardevermeerdering huis (Replace transfer duty by VAT on value increase of house)', *Me Judice* 3 (28 December 2010). Also published in *Weekblad Fiscaal Recht* 6889 (20 January 2011): 47–54.
25. These valuations are also used for income tax, municipal property tax and inheritance tax purposes. The rental value of owner-occupied property is subject to the progressive income tax, but effective rates are low, because taxable rental values are computed using lower percentages applied to rated values than would accord with arm's length rates. Since mortgage interest is fully deductible, the income tax treatment of rental values results in a sizable net subsidy to homeowners.

changeover in order to reduce their future transfer duty liability. This would be good news for municipalities, since the VAT is remitted to the national treasury, while municipal receipts would increase on account of the higher rated annual property tax. Municipalities would not benefit if the revenue from the additional VAT would be assigned to them, for which there is much to be said. After all, higher rated values would imply lower future VAT revenues. A drawback of the changeover would be that, over time, it would not be possible to maintain the initial equal-yield assumption. But the revenue shortfall could be made up by gradually restricting the deductibility of home mortgage interest for income tax purposes.

§7.06 CONCLUDING COMMENTS

The taxation of newly created residential property is a good but still second-best substitute for the exemption of rents and rental values, because the approach cannot take account of future changes in property values and the VAT rate. To remedy this defect, I propose the taxation of the difference between the selling price and the purchase price (presumptively determined) of exempt properties, net of, ideally, the cost of subsequent renovations, which are capitalized in the value of the property (and on which VAT has been paid). The VAT on the margin should replace the distortionary transfer, registration and stamp duties currently levied in the Member States.

This VAT or new transfer duty can be imposed without amending the Common VAT Directive. A beneficial side effect would be that registered persons would more often opt for having their business properties taxed under the VAT. Nevertheless, it would be advisable to replace the exemption approach (under which all immovable property is exempted, except newly created buildings) by the tax method (under which all immovable property is taxed, except used residential property). The tax method is found in countries with a modern VAT. In addition, land transactions should be taxed under a second-hand goods scheme or margin method. These measures, which require adjustments to the Common Directive, would promote equal treatment and neutrality.

If the margin scheme and the tax method would be adopted, the present and proposed application of VAT to transactions in immovable property can be summarized as follows.

(1) As at present, sales of immovable property between taxable persons are considered a 'normal transaction', i.e. VAT is imposed by the seller and a tax credit is available to the buyer.
(2) Currently, sales of immovable property by taxable persons to non-taxable persons also attract VAT (which is included in the sale price) in the normal way, although the purchaser, not being a taxable person, cannot take credit for it.
(3) Sales of immovable property by non-taxable persons to taxable persons attract VAT under the capital goods scheme, which entitles the buyer to a notional VAT credit if he opts for taxation.

(4) Sales of immovable property by non-taxable persons to other non-taxable persons should be made subject to a reformed transfer duty – i.e. a surrogate VAT – on the increase (decrease) in the value of the property.

These transactions would all be subject to VAT and no other transactions taxes would apply, but the new approach would not preclude the (annual) taxation of the ownership or use of immovable property (on benefit-received grounds), or, for that matter, the imposition of net wealth taxes, estate duties and gift taxes.

CHAPTER 8

VAT and Immovable Property: Full Taxation Models and the Treatment of Capital Gains on Owner-Occupied Residences

Rebecca Millar*

§8.01 INTRODUCTION[1]

At least some immovable property transactions continue to be treated as exempt under even the most broad-based VAT regimes.[2] In the European Union, the provisions of the

* I am grateful to Christophe Waerzeggers (Consulting Counsel, Legal Department, International Monetary Fund) for his assistance with proofing and for his guidance on the EU VAT Directive and CJEU case law, and to Marie Pallot and Scott Davidson (New Zealand Inland Revenue) for responding to my questions about the finer points of the New Zealand GST law as it applied to the hypotheticals in section §8.05 in this chapter. Any errors are nonetheless entirely my own. Thanks also to Professor Lee Burns (Sydney Law School) for reading one of the many drafts and providing encouragement to continue. Finally, I thank the anonymous referee, with whose views this paper disagrees, but whose feedback has, I hope, helped me to improve the clarity with which I have stated my position.

1. In preparing this chapter, I was acutely aware of treading on ground more commonly occupied by economists. Geoff Harley addressed a similar concern in 2006. In a paper reflecting, with twenty years' hindsight, on the treatment of land transactions in the New Zealand GST, he light-heartedly stereotyped the prejudiced views that lawyers and economists are purported to hold for each other: on tax policy matters, economists lay claim to 'the pursuit of truth, light and depth of understanding', seeing lawyers as 'unwanted interlopers in an intellectual minefield for which they are not properly equipped' and blaming them for failing to adequately give effect to tax policy; lawyers think economists don't understand law or politics, and so develop tax policy without any consideration of whether, or how, it can be effected, basing their recommendations on 'incomplete and intuitively based assumptions' that do not reflect the real world. In Harley's view, neither lawyers nor economists can reliably predict or test whether a particular policy will be effective, appropriate, or capable of implementation. Compromise in the design of tax laws is therefore inevitable, whether because the perfect policy is unworkable, too expensive, or simply too politically unpopular: G.J. Harley, *Dilemmas for GST Tax Policy Designers – Land Transactions*, in *GST in Retrospect and Prospect*, 213–241, 213–214 (R. Krever & D. White eds., Thomson Brookers 2007). In the spirit of Harley's comments, I acknowledge that I am not an economist and offer my thoughts on VAT policy from the perspective, and using the analytical framework, of an academic lawyer.
2. Throughout this chapter, when the concept of exemption is used without qualification, it refers to exemption *without* credit. Where exemption *with* credit is discussed, this is always made clear, either by qualifying the word exemption or by using the terms 'zero-rated' or 'GST-free'.

EU VAT Directive[3] leave scope for Member States to adopt significantly divergent approaches. At one extreme, a Member State could follow the minimum requirements of the Directive by taxing sales of new buildings and building land (other than occasional sales), exempting all other sales of immovable property, and exempting all leasing and letting of immovable property, other than hotel and similar accommodation, parking, leasing of fixtures, and the hire of safes.[4] At the other extreme, a Member State could add occasional sales to the tax base, and could grant taxable persons an option to tax all remaining exempt immovable property transactions (including sales, leasing, and the letting of immovable property).[5,6]

In contrast, the New Zealand and Australian goods and service tax (GST) laws are frequently cited as two examples of VAT laws that go furthest towards fully including immovable property in the tax base,[7] taxing non-residential property and the 'first sale' of new residential premises, and exempting only residential leasing and subsequent sales of residences. Renewed interest in the possibility of a VAT for the United States has reignited the debate about the proper treatment of land under a VAT, with both Satya Poddar[8] and Sijbren Cnossen[9] recommending that countries go beyond the Australian and New Zealand position to fully tax both residential leasing and resales of residential property.

For Europeans looking for alternatives to the mix of exemption, optional taxation, and mandatory taxation provided for under the EU VAT Directive, there is clearly something to be gained from examining exactly how Australia and New Zealand impose VAT on immovable property and comparing that with the proposals of Poddar, Cnossen and others. This paper examines these matters in detail, highlighting the complexity that can arise in giving effect to what appears to be a relatively straightforward tax policy design. Section §8.02 sets out the essential features of a modern VAT. Section §8.03 considers what, if anything, about immovable property might be special from a VAT perspective, making it difficult or undesirable to tax appropriately under a VAT. Section §8.04 outlines the consequences of taxing immovable property in full under a VAT, using an example that is gradually changed to illustrate the effects of different approaches. The examples illustrate how full taxation of sales of immovable property equates to non-taxation, while taxing resales of residential property with

3. Council Directive 2006/112/EC of 28 November 2006 on the common system of value added tax, OJ L347 of 2006, 1–118 ('EU VAT Directive').
4. EU VAT Directive, Articles 9(1), 12, 135(1)(j), (k), & (l), and 135(2). In addition, a sale of goods used solely for the exempt transactions would also be exempt under Article 136.
5. The Directive allows Member States to treat persons engaging in occasional transactions as taxable persons and also allows them to grant suppliers a full or limited option to tax: EU VAT Directive, Articles 12 & 137.
6. For a recent analysis of the position in Europe, see: C. Armand, G. Schellmann & R. Vermeulen, *Immovable Property and VAT—Lessons from Past Experience*, Intl. VAT Monit. 325 (2005).
7. See, for example, S. Poddar, *Treatment of Housing under VAT for the US* (February 2009), given at a conference entitled *Structuring a Federal VAT: Design & Coordination Issues* (2009); 63 Tax Law Review 443 (2010).
8. *Ibid.*
9. See S. Cnossen, 'A Proposal to Improve the VAT Treatment of Housing in the European Union', Ch 7, this volume.

deferred input tax credits (whether without indexation, as proposed by Poddar, or with, as proposed by Robert F. Conrad)[10] amounts to a capital gains tax on homeowners. The paper concludes that existing models, involving the upfront taxation of new residential property and the exemption of resales, are not merely acceptable alternatives to a full taxation ideal but are also the only approach that is consistent with the underlying design features of transaction method VATs. Given that the standard credit-invoice method VAT cannot effectively separate that part of the capital appreciation on land that is attributable to savings rather than consumption, these models provide the cleanest approach to dealing with immovable property under a VAT. Section §8.05 considers exactly how such models can be given legal effect, focussing on the Australian and New Zealand GST laws, which purportedly follow these design parameters.

A considerable part of the discussion in sections §8.04 and §8.05 focuses on the New Zealand GST treatment of immovable property, comparing it with aspects of the more complex Australian approach. In particular, the discussion highlights one critical design feature of both countries' laws, which is ignored in most comparative tax discussions. Both countries target their GST only at value added to land by persons carrying on economic activities. They exclude from the tax base any capital appreciation (or depreciation) on immovable property held by owner-occupiers, residential landlords, and mere investors – an effect that is diametrically opposed to the proposals of Poddar and Cnossen. New Zealand excludes capital gains/losses on residential property after the first sale only if the seller is not carrying on an economic activity.[11] In contrast, Australia fully excludes capital gains/losses on residential property after the first sale, as well as some value added by taxable persons, but at a cost of significant additional complexity. The New Zealand approach has the advantage of being simpler and conceptually clearer, from a legal perspective, and is probably to be preferred.

§8.02 VAT AS A TRANSACTION TAX: THE LEGAL VIEW OF VAT[12]

It is useful to take as a starting point a clear statement of the structure and purpose of a VAT, in order to develop a vision of what would be required if the tax were applied to immovable property in accordance with its normal design features. For the purposes of discussion, I take the essential legal design features of a modern, consumption-type value added tax to be the following:

10. R.F. Conrad, 'Comments on VAT and Housing', comments on a paper given by Satya Poddar at a conference entitled *Structuring a Federal VAT: Design & Coordination Issues* (2009); 63 Tax L. Rev. 471 (2010).
11. As will be illustrated later, it is important to understand this statement in light of the fact that the New Zealand concept of an economic activity (termed 'taxable activity') does not include activities to the extent that they involve making exempt supplies.
12. The notion of a 'legal view of VAT' is taken from S. Cnossen, *VAT Treatment of Immovable Property*, in *Tax Law Design and Drafting*, 231–245, 233–234 (vol. 1, V. Thuronyi ed., International Monetary Fund 1996). See also S. Cnossen, *A VAT Primer for Economists, Lawyers, and Accountants*, 54 Tax Notes Intl. 319 (2009).

(1) The economic objective is to tax consumption but that objective is subordinated to the legal form of the tax: VAT operates as a multi-stage tax on transactions.[13] It taxes the outputs of economic activities and credits the tax on inputs to those economic activities.[14] The cumulative effect of imposing VAT on transactions throughout the chain of production and distribution can be looked at from three perspectives:
    (a) for suppliers (producers): VAT taxes the 'value added' in the course of their economic activities;
    (b) for consumers: VAT taxes their expenditure on goods or services for current or future consumption;
    (c) for revenue authorities: the tax revenue collected in a particular tax period is related to the tax fraction of domestic spending on consumption in that period.
(2) The measure of the outputs and inputs of economic activities, and so also of 'value added' and 'consumption', is the expenditure incurred on those outputs and inputs.[15]
(3) VAT is charged at or near the time of each transaction[16] and the right to deduct input tax (if applicable) arises at the same time, irrespective of whether the input is capital or revenue for tax or accounting purposes.[17,18]
(4) In the case of purchases that are not immediately consumed, the price of the supply is presumed to be equal to the net present value of the future consumption

13. EU VAT Directive, Article 1; Explanatory Memorandum to the *A New Tax System (Goods and Services Tax) Bill 1998* (Aus), Chapter 1, Executive Summary; New Zealand Inland Revenue, *GST: A Review, A Government Discussion Document* (March 1999). See also Cnossen (1996) and (2009) (n. 12 above).
14. In most VATs, the right of deduction is limited to inputs to taxable outputs (or exported non-taxable outputs). See, for example, EU VAT Directive, Articles 168 & 169 and *Goods and Services Tax Act 1985* (New Zealand) ('GST Act 1985 (NZ)'), s. 3A (definition of 'input tax'). Some countries allow input tax credits/deductions on the basis of a connection with the economic activity, but deny them if there is a link to the making of exempt supplies: see, for example, *A New Tax System (Goods and Services Tax) Act 1999* (Australia) ('GST Act 1999 (Aus)'), ss. 11-15 & 15-10 and *Federal Law with regard to Value Added Tax* (Switzerland), Articles 28 & 29 (unofficial translation), http://www.deloitte.com/assets/Dcom-Switzerland/Local %20Assets /Documents/EN/Tax/VAT/ch_en_Swiss%20VAT%20Law.pdf, 25 September 2011.
15. EU VAT Directive, Article 73; GST Act 1999 (Aus), ss. 9-15, 9-70, 9-75, & s.195-1 (definition of 'consideration'); GST Act 1985 (NZ), ss. 2 (definition of 'consideration'), 8(1), & 10.
16. EU VAT Directive, Article 63. To the extent that VAT laws link the timing of tax to the time of invoice or payment, the link between time of supply and the time for paying tax is broken: EU VAT Directive, Articles 64–67; GST Act (Aus), Subdiv 29-A & Div 33; GST Act 1985 (NZ), s. 9. The close proximity between the real time of supply and the VAT accounting 'time of supply' generally remains, but only because most traded commodities are invoiced and paid for within a reasonable time of the actual supply. For a discussion of cases dealing with taxpayers' attempts to exploit this disconnect to make a gain from the tax system, see R. Millar, *Time Is of the Essence: Supplies, Grouping Schemes, and Cancelled Transactions*, 7 Journal of Australian Taxation 132–195 (2004) (Sydney Law School Research Paper No. 07/83. Available at SSRN: http://ssrn.com/abstract=711581).
17. EU VAT Directive, Article 167; GST Act 1999 (Aus), Divs 9, 11, & 15; GST Act 1985 (NZ), ss. 8 & 3A.
18. References to 'deduction' and 'deductible' should be read as equivalent to references to 'credit' and 'creditable'; the terms are interchangeable in function and countries vary as to which they use.

of the commodity.[19] The upfront allowance (or denial) of input tax deductions rests on a presumption that the purchaser will use the commodity as intended. For goods and services that are not immediately consumed, particularly capital assets, this presumption will not always hold true and for this reason VAT laws generally include rules to deal with subsequent events. Such rules modify the initial allowance or denial of input tax deductions either directly (by adjusting the amount of input tax deducted) or indirectly (by a deemed supply or acquisition mechanism).[20]

The concept of 'value added', so frequently used in the name of the tax, is simply the difference between the price of a supplier's taxed outputs and the cost of its taxed inputs.[21] All outputs and inputs are treated in the same way. Thus, a tax on 'value added' taxes both revenue and capital gains of suppliers. As this paper will show, however, in relation to appreciating assets such as land, the assertion of Conrad and Grosav that 'economists, lawyers and tax administrators are not concerned with whether a taxpayer uses the asset or merely holds it expecting a gain'[22] only holds true *after* one has decided what a taxpayer is for VAT purposes.

Any concepts of 'consumption' or 'consumption expenditure' embodied in a transaction-type VAT law are legal constructs, related to but independent from the economic concept of consumption. At its most basic, *consumers* are persons who cannot claim input tax credits and who are not required to pay output tax on any supplies they make. From a legal perspective, both small businesses who are not registered for VAT and registered persons who make exempt supplies can be thought of as consumers because they are in the same position, vis-à-vis input tax, as consumers. Alternatively, since they are in fact carrying on economic activities and making supplies, they can be more accurately described as producers whose supplies are *input taxed*, the term used in the Australian GST law to describe supplies that are exempt without credit.[23] When undeductible input tax is factored into the price of

19. Taxing the purchase of a stock is therefore equivalent to a prepayment for the future flow of services from that stock. For discussions of this prepayment concept see: L. Ebrill et al., *The Modern VAT*, 98 (International Monetary Fund 2001); M. Evans, *The Value Added Tax Treatment of Real Property*, in *GST in Retrospect and Prospect*, 243–276 (R. Krever & D. White eds., Thomson Brookers, 2007); and Cnossen (1996) and (2009) (n. 12 above).
20. Such rules can apply where there is a change in the extent to which an acquisition is used to make taxable or exempt supplies, as well as in situations where the extent of private-use changes: for example, GST Act 1999 (Aus), Div.129; GST Act 1985 (NZ), former ss. 21 to 21H (to 1 April 2011). Changes in registration status are a particular example of changes in use, and many VAT laws require input tax to be repaid for assets on hand when registration is cancelled: see, for example, GST Act 1999 (Aus), Div 138. Credits may also be allowed for tax-paid assets on hand on becoming registered: see, for example, GST Act 1999 (Aus), Div 147, which applies only for trading stock; cf. GST Act 1985 (NZ), former s. 21E (until 1 April 2011) and current s. 21B (from 1 April 2011), which are far more generous.
21. The tax on a supplier's value added is thus a tax on salaries and wages, profits (including capital gains), and other untaxed inputs.
22. Conrad & Grosav (n. 27 below), 87.
23. See GST Act 1999 (Aus), ss. 2-10 & 9-30, the definition of 'input taxed' in s. 195-1, and Chapter 3 (the exemptions), especially Div 40 (the input taxed exemptions). The term *input taxed*

outputs, those outputs are partially taxed, even though from the customer's perspective they appear to be untaxed.[24]

A VAT can be seen as ring-fencing *taxable suppliers*, who charge tax and claim input tax credits, from *consumers* and *input taxed suppliers*, who do not charge tax and cannot claim input tax credits.[25] Inside the ring, where taxable suppliers transact with taxable suppliers, no revenue is raised: tax is both paid and refunded on each transaction. It is only when a transaction involves a supply by a taxable supplier inside the ring to a consumer or input taxed supplier outside the ring that revenue is actually raised: on such transactions, the tax paid is not creditable. Transactions may also occur outside the ring. Input taxed suppliers supply to each other and to consumers. In addition, a consumer may turn out not to be an *end consumer* (someone who has no outputs) and become instead an input taxed supplier. This will occur whenever a consumer makes a supply, for example by selling second-hand goods or services. This is not problematic if the supply is made to a customer who is also outside the ring: in such cases, just as the previously taxed commodity is consumed by more than one consumer consecutively, so too the VAT burden – having formed part of the price of the goods – is shared between them by being reflected in the price of the resale. But when consumers and input taxed suppliers supply back inside the ring by making supplies to registered persons who are inside the ring, tax cascading will result. In the case of input taxed suppliers, this cascading is an accepted (and intended) feature of the tax. In the case of purchases of second-hand goods by registered persons, many VAT laws, though by no means all, have special rules to prevent this cascading.

This second-hand goods problem is particularly acute for durable assets, and more so for enduring assets such as immovable property. Both the Australian and New Zealand GST regimes for immovable property have two ways of dealing with the on-supply of such property by consumers. Through a combination of exclusions from the definition of an economic activity (effectively excluding owner-occupiers, residential landlords, and long-term investors) and the application of a form of second-hand goods treatment to purchases of real property by GST-registered persons from consumers and other input taxed suppliers,[26] they endeavour to ensure that GST is imposed only on value added by persons carrying on economic activities and not on long-term, 'private' capital gains.

---

acknowledges the intended effect of exemption without credit, which is to tax the inputs to particular commodities but not the value added by the suppliers of those commodities.

24. Hill J explained that partial taxation was the intended effect of exemption without credit, as indicated by the use of the term 'input taxation': *HP Mercantile Pty Limited v. Commissioner of Taxation* [2005] FCAFC 126. Bird and Gendron concur with this view of input taxation as partial taxation: R. Bird & P.-P. Gendron, *The VAT in Developing and Transitional Countries*, 134–135 (Cambridge University Press 2007).
25. Cnossen (1996) and (2009) (n. 12 above).
26. GST Act 1999 (Aus), Divs 66 & 75; GST Act 1985 (NZ), s. 3A(2) & (3).

§8.03 IS IMMOVABLE PROPERTY SPECIAL?

If for no other reason, immovable property is indeed special because of the near universality with which it is subject to some form of VAT exemption.[27] Something about immovable property makes countries reluctant to apply full taxation, even though it can fit easily into the transactional framework of a VAT. Immovable property seems to fit more naturally into a transaction tax than financial services. Supplies of immovable property are tangible: they are supplies of rights in rem or other supplies so closely connected with land that it is easy to analogize with goods. Immovable property (or at least the land to which it relates) doesn't move, which means that it is identifiably connected with a particular jurisdiction. Most transactions relating to immovable property do not involve intermediation, at least not in the way that makes financial services the quintessential example of difficult-to-tax commodities. Thus, most immovable property transactions can relatively easily be taxed under a transaction method VAT: they have an identifiable supplier, an identifiable recipient, an identifiable subject matter, an identifiable place of taxation, and a price that is not dependent on set-off against other transactions.

On the other hand, exactly the same comments could be made about share transactions. Consider a sale by A to B of a parcel of shares in Company C, for a price of $ 1,000. From a transaction tax point of view there is an identifiable supplier (A), an identifiable recipient (B), an identifiable subject-matter (the shares), and an identifiable and quantifiable amount of consideration ($ 1,000). Yet from a consumption tax point of view there is nothing to tax: A and B have simply exchanged one form of capital for another. In buying the shares, B has not bought a commodity for consumption but merely changed the form in which his/her capacity to consume is invested. The same is true for A, who has realized the value of the shares in money, which is but another form of storing the capacity to consume. At any particular time, A or B could use the money (or the shares) to pay for consumable commodities, on

27. Conrad and Grosav list 13 of 107 surveyed countries as engaging in 'complete' taxation of land under their VATs: R. Conrad & A. Grosav, *Real Property and VAT*, in *VAT in Africa*, 81–112, Table 1 on 96–117 (R. Krever ed., Pretoria University Law Press 2008). These claims are difficult to verify because they are not referenced to sources. It is also unclear whether the tax is effectively collected in practice. A brief review of the entries for countries with which the author is familiar (New Zealand, Australia, South Africa, and Albania) identified a number of errors that raise questions about the accuracy of the claims. Australia is listed as taxing land at the standard rate and exempting sales of new residential property. In fact, new residential property is taxed and some supplies of land are GST-free (zero-rated). New Zealand is listed as exempting all sales of residential property yet most residential property sold by taxable persons is in fact taxable. South Africa is listed as exempting commercial rents and all residential property but these supplies are taxable when made by a registered person. Albania is listed as taxing all supplies of real property at the standard rate but Article 20 of the *Value Added Tax Law (No.7928, date 27.4.1995)* exempts most supplies of land and buildings (English language version of the law at http://www.tatime.gov.al/gdt/Value_Added_Tax_(VAT).aspx, 24 September 2010). Given that over 150 countries have a VAT (*Consumption Tax Trends: VAT/GST, Excise and Environmental Taxes* (OECD 2008) ('*OECD Consumption Tax Trends*'), even if the claims were correct, the countries allegedly fully taxing land would represent a small proportion of the VATs in operation. No OECD country fully includes immoveable property in its VAT: *OECD Consumption Tax Trends*, Table 3.1.

which a tax burden could rightly be imposed, but the share transaction itself does not involve consumption. The sale of shares is a transaction involving a supply for consideration and so it looks like an appropriate subject matter for VAT, but it is not.

Other exchanges of capital are also not considered appropriate subject matters for tax. If X puts $ 1,000 cash into Bank Y (converting the money into an interest in a debt) and Y then lends the $ 1,000 to Z (thereby acquiring an interest in a debt), the initial flows of money and the subsequent repayments of that money are not subject to VAT. Similarly, if T exchanges USD 1,000 for AUD 997, neither the payment of the $ 1,000 nor the payment of the $ 997 are subject to VAT.

In each case, there may be genuine consumption, which should (if possible) be taxed. In the case of the share transaction, A and B will acquire the services of share brokers and will pay fees for other related services; in the case of the loan, Bank Y will provide financial intermediation services to X and Z; in the case of the exchange of US dollars for Australian dollars, T will be supplied with currency exchange services. But in each case, the flow of the capital has nothing to do with consumption and should effectively be excluded from the VAT net.

Apart from the problem that these intermediation services can be hard to identify and value, and hard to allocate between customers, the fact that VAT operates as a transaction tax is in itself problematic for these services. Because VAT laws tax transactions, and because they value those transactions by reference to expenditure, making no distinction between capital and revenue, they risk taxing savings and investments when they are intended to tax only consumption. This focus on expenditure can lead to the error of mistakenly presuming there is consumption whenever there is a flow of money.[28] For taxable suppliers, taxing the purchase and sale of capital assets achieves neutrality: full taxation ensures that VAT flows through the chain of production and distribution without cascading. When consumers purchase stocks, however:

- they are taxed if the payment constitutes a prepayment for future consumption; and
- they are exempt if the payment constitutes investment/savings.

Most VAT regimes avoid taxing capital payments that constitute investment or savings by excluding 'money' from the concept of a consumable commodity (i.e. from the definitions of goods and services) and by exempting (with or without credit) a range of transactions that are defined to be 'financial services'. Even those countries that do tax financial services tax financial intermediation services but do not (or ought not to) tax these flows of capital.

Similar issues arise with immovable property, but the situation is more complex because the price paid for immovable property covers consumable and unconsumable commodities. While land can be used, and improvements to land can be consumed, the

28. Those who view VAT as simply a flawed means of legislating a personal expenditure tax might well take the view that a consumption tax should tax all expenditure but this is not how VATs in fact work and most are clearly designed to tax only private consumption expenditure, which must be presumed to have been the intended tax base of the legislators.

immovable property itself is not consumed. Its value might go up or down (whether because of its use or for other reasons such as fashion, speculation, changes to land title, and the change in value of money over time) but the immovable property as a juridical concept remains: it is a right in rem in relation to a designated area of space. A person who buys immovable property is partly swapping one form of capital for another (an exempt investment activity) and partly buying consumable improvements (which should be taxed). Home ownership and the ownership of investment properties for lease are frequently intended to be (rather than incidentally being) long-term investments, in lieu of other forms of saving or investment. The notion of a second home as one's superannuation reflects a popular (if potentially misconceived) notion that buying immovable property is a sensible alternative to putting money in the bank, owning shares, or locking one's money in superannuation funds over which one has little or no control.[29] If one conceptualizes VAT as a tax on consumption, the fact that immovable property has an enduring nature means that it cannot be consumed and should not form part of the tax base.[30]

On the other hand, a flow of services from the use of land is consumed, and those services should be taxed.[31] But VAT operates as a tax on transactions, not as a direct tax on consumption. As a result, it does not readily lend itself to taxing self-supplies, particularly when those 'self-supplies' are provided by consumers to themselves. Not only is it politically difficult to impose such taxes, but to do so would add a level of complexity to the administration of the tax. If consumer-to-consumer and input-taxed-supplier-to-consumer transactions are outside the ring, it is hard to justify inventing a concept of consumer-to-self supply and then putting that supply inside the ring. While it is true that many VAT laws do include rules to deal with the application of business assets to own use, often by using a deemed supply mechanism that fosters the development of a concept of 'self-supply,' these rules are generally (but not always) aimed at reversing the effect of previous input tax credits given to suppliers who sit both inside and outside the ring, rather than at taxing self-supplies per se. As a result, they are almost always rules applicable to persons carrying on an economic activity, not to consumers.

Furthermore, since a VAT taxes consumption in advance by taxing the full price at the time of sale of a commodity that will be consumed in the future, any imposition of tax on the subsequent own use of that asset necessarily entails the need to grant an input tax credit for its acquisition, otherwise there will be double taxation. And since input tax credits are given upfront at the time of making an acquisition for the purpose of making taxable supplies, the imposition of a tax on the self-supply of services

29. See N. Ferguson, *The Ascent of Money: A Financial History of the World*, Chapter 5: 'Safe as Houses' (Penguin Press, 2008).
30. A.A. Tait, *Value Added Tax: International Practice and Problems*, 80 (International Monetary Fund 1988). Of course, the effects of natural forces might see the subject-matter of the property disappear altogether as, for example, happens if erosion or rising sea levels cause land to be submerged under water. In that case, however, there is still no 'consumption' of the property; it is simply that this particular immoveable property has turned out to be a bad investment, just as shares in a failed company are a bad investment. One can lose as well as gain when saving.
31. Ebrill et al. (n. 19 above), at 98; Cnossen (1996) and (2009) (n. 12 above); Evans (n. 19 above).

consisting of the owner-occupation of immovable property would entail moving from a practical, upfront tax to an impractical, deferred tax, a move that is likely to be as unpopular with revenue authorities as it would be with consumers.

If the enduring nature of immovable property is problematic for a VAT, a further question arises as to whether immovable property is any different from other durable commodities. Economists seem to suggest that it is not, pointing out that all purchases of capital assets can include both a consumption element and an investment element, since the asset can always be sold before it has reached the end of its useful life, thereby realizing for the purchaser the unconsumed value and transferring to the new owner the right to future consumption.[32] They point out that immovable property is also not the only asset that tends to appreciate: jewellery, artwork, antiques and other moveable property can also appreciate. But other appreciating assets are also considered problematic in a VAT and are often subject to special VAT treatment, aimed at effectively taxing only the value added by suppliers carrying on economic activities in relation to the assets.[33] Moreover, immovable property is not simply 'the durable good *par excellence*',[34] it is an *en*during asset that in some respects has more in common with shares than with tangible goods.

Finally, in addition to the problem that immovable property is not consumed, a number of other features make it difficult to deal with from a VAT perspective:[35]

- Compared with many transactions to which VAT applies, immovable property is relatively infrequently traded, and sales of immovable property are high-value transactions.
- Immovable property is the most widely held and traded appreciating asset and a purchase of immovable property is more often than not the single most significant acquisition a person will make in his/her lifetime.
- Immovable property is sold, purchased, and held by persons who would not otherwise be considered to be carrying on an economic activity for VAT purposes. A significant proportion of traded immovable property is owner-occupied residential premises, or residences that have been leased out for occupation as a residence.
- Purchases, sales, and holdings of immovable property are generally subject to other tax regimes (income tax, transfer taxes, land tax, stamp duties) and owner-occupied properties are often given tax-preferred treatment within those tax regimes.
- In some jurisdictions, the power to impose taxes on immovable property is devolved to sub-national entities (states, regions, or local governments), making the integration of land into a VAT complex or constitutionally

32. Ebrill et al. (n. 19 above), 98.
33. See for example, HMRC VAT Notice 718, *The VAT Margin Scheme and Global Accounting* (January 2010), section 10, dealing with the treatment of works of art.
34. Ebrill et al. (n. 19 above), 98.
35. Policy Advice Division, Inland Revenue (New Zealand), *GST: Accounting for Land and Other High-value Assets: A Government Discussion Document* (Inland Revenue 2009).

impossible. In such countries, the imposition of VAT on land may be a highly sensitive political issue.

Despite all of the above, the fact that immovable property is partly consumable and partly not, and that it substitutes for other forms of saving, does not mean it cannot be included in a VAT. What it does mean is that, just as models developed to tax financial intermediation services exclude the underlying capital flows and 'pure interest' from the tax base, so too any model for taxing immovable property should ensure that the tax is applied in a way that taxes only that part of the value of land that is consumable, which essentially means improvements to the land plus the cost of holding the land.[36]

§8.04 APPLYING NORMAL VAT RULES TO IMMOVABLE PROPERTY

[A] Defining Immovable Property

Having concluded that immovable property is special, I turn now to consider how it should be treated under a VAT regime. While it is traditional to devote at least a modicum of attention to the question of what is meant by 'immovable' or 'real property',[37] the initial policy choices about the scope of the tax need not depend on the precise meaning of these concepts in domestic law. In any case, the definition of a term on its own cannot tell you anything about its significance. What matters is how the term interacts with the provisions of the tax law.

Concepts of real or immovable property are property law notions concerned with rights in relation to land. By their very nature, property rights are intangible legal concepts[38] but for VAT purposes we can and do describe immovable property as tangible. In the New Zealand GST law, the term 'real property' is not a defined term, and so takes its ordinary legal meaning. In contrast, the Australian GST law defines 'real property' so broadly that it extends well beyond the domestic law meaning of real property.[39] These differences have no real significance, however, because in both countries' laws the term 'real property' is of limited relevance to delineating the tax treatment of supplies of real property. Thus, the term 'real property' is used only twice in the New Zealand GST legislation, once in the definition of *goods* and once in the definition of *supply*, where it is used in an apportionment provision that requires a single supply of real property to be treated as two separate supplies if the property includes but is not limited to a dwelling. This ensures that if a single parcel of freehold title covers both a farm and a dwelling, when the freehold title is sold the dwelling and its associated land will be treated as one supply and the remainder of the land as

36. Poddar (n. 7 above).
37. See, e.g., Bird & Gendron (n. 24 above), 82 and Poddar (n. 7 above), section 2.1.
38. Bird & Gendron (n. 24 above), 82.
39. GST Act 1999 (Aus), s. 195-1 states that real property includes '(a) any interest in or right over land, (b) a personal right to call for or be granted any interest in or right over land; or (c) a licence to occupy land or any other contractual right exercisable over or in relation to land.'

another.[40] The critical concepts for the purposes of determining whether a supply will be taxable or exempt are discussed in more detail in section §8.05[B] of this chapter.

In Australia, the main significance of the concept of real property is in the jurisdictional rules, under which supplies of real property are taxed where the underlying land is located. The defined term 'real property' is also one element in the GST-free treatment of sales of serviced apartments in retirement villages,[41] in the input taxation of sales of residential property (other than new residential property),[42] and in the margin scheme valuation rules for such sales.[43] However, the real boundaries of the exemptions for real property are found in a range of defined terms such as *residential premises, new residential premises, commercial residential premises, commercial accommodation*, and *long-term lease*, which between them delineate the boundaries of what is input taxed. These terms describe characteristics of the underlying physical structures found on the land, and of the activities carried out in those structures, but such characteristics frequently have no legal status in the relevant transactions. The significance of this disconnect between the legal transaction and the characteristics that determine the tax treatment of the transaction are discussed in more detail in section §8.05[C] of this chapter.

[B] Full Taxation of Immovable Property under a VAT

Taking the essential features of a VAT previously outlined, consider the operation of a VAT in which no supplies are exempt, all supplies made in the course of an economic activity are fully taxable, and all persons carrying on economic activities are registered for VAT.[44] When a taxable person makes a taxable supply, the VAT will become payable by the supplier at or about the time of supply. At the same time, and in relation to the same supply:

- *inside the ring*: if the recipient is a taxable person, and makes the acquisition for the purposes of its economic activity, the recipient will be entitled to a credit for the input tax and the revenue authority will collect no net tax;

40. GST Act 1985 (NZ), s. 2 and s. 5(15). It is possible that a misreading of this section may have been the source of Cnossen's assertion that 'In New Zealand, the "land element" of the purchase price of a building must be separated out from the total consideration.': see Cnossen (1996) (n. 12 above), 237. That is not, however, the purpose of the section, which aims instead to treat the residence and its associated portion of the land as exempt while taxing the remainder of the land (Until 1 April 2011, s. 5.(15) read: 'Where a dwelling is included in a supply, the supply of that dwelling is deemed to be a separate supply from the supply of any other real property included in the supply.' From 1 April 2011, the first occurring 'dwelling' is replaced with 'principal place of residence' and the second with 'residence'. The context of these changes is discussed later in this chapter.).
41. GST Act 1999 (Aus), s. 38-25(4A)(b)(ii).
42. GST Act 1999 (Aus), Subdiv 40-C.
43. GST Act 1999 (Aus), Div 75.
44. This necessarily precludes the possibility of a registration threshold, since the exclusion of small businesses is a form of exemption without credit.

- *outside the ring*: if the recipient is not a taxable person, or makes the acquisition for a private purpose (i.e. not for the purpose of its economic activity), the recipient will not be entitled to a credit for the tax paid.

There will be no tax on 'self-supplies' because such a concept makes no sense in a transaction tax. One cannot make a supply to oneself because the very notion of a transaction requires at least two parties: a supplier and a recipient.[45] For the purposes of argument, presume that there are no provisions deeming a self-supply to take place. Since all supplies are taxable and none are exempt, the only subsequent adjustments required by the purchaser will be as follows:[46]

- input tax previously deducted will have to be repaid if a taxable person acquires something for use in its economic activity but subsequently uses it for private purposes; and
- input tax should be deductible both when a taxable person uses private assets in its economic activity and when a person becomes a taxable person and intends to use previously private assets in its economic activity.

Finally, any tax-paid asset that is sold by a consumer to a taxable person should give rise to an input tax deduction equal to the tax fraction of the (untaxed) purchase price, in order to ensure that the supplier only pays VAT on its value added and to ensure that there is no cascading of the unconsumed element of any previously collected VAT (This is the imputed credit or margin scheme for second-hand goods.).

Under this extremely broad-based VAT, tax will be a burden on end consumers but not on taxable persons. The most significant unknown in this system is how the concept of economic activity is defined because it is this that defines who the consumers are. When it comes to immovable property, the way in which the boundaries of an economic activity are defined can have a significant impact on the tax base. For the purposes of illustration, this issue can be by-passed by presuming that all transactions relating to immovable property will be treated as economic activities. Immovable property would then fit into this full taxation model as follows:

- all sales of immovable property would be taxed;
- all leases of immovable property, all supplies of accommodation, and all other supplies of rights relating to the use of land would be taxed; and
- all VAT incurred on inputs to such supplies, including the acquisitions of the immovable property itself, would be deductible.

---

45. Case C-210/04, *Ministero dell'Economia e delle Finanze, Agenzia delle Entrate v. FCE Bank plc* [2006] ECR I-2803; Commissioner of Taxation, Goods and Services Tax Ruling GSTR 2006/9 *Goods and Services Tax: Supplies* (Australian Taxation Office), Proposition 7 and also Propositions 1 and 2 (on page 5).
46. I refer here to adjustments a recipient is required to make in relation to its input tax, not to adjustments relating to the supply itself, such as when there is a cancellation, alteration of the consideration, or a bad debt: compare, for example, GST Act 1999 (Aus), Divs 19 & 21 (the post-supply adjustments) and Div 129, 130, 132, and 138 (adjustments relating to input tax incurred on acquisitions).

[1] *Full Taxation of Immovable Property (Other Than Private-use Land)*

Putting privately consumed premises to one side, it seems that there is no reason why this full taxation approach should not be applied to all supplies of immovable property, including sales and leases of unimproved land, vacant land, land with commercial or industrial buildings, farm land, options to purchase or lease such property, etc. Of course, under this extremely broad-based tax, in which all supplies made in the course of an economic activity are fully taxable, the net result of including immovable property would be that no revenue would actually be collected directly from immovable property transactions. The tax chargeable would be fully creditable, either because the purchaser would be using the immovable property it had acquired to make other (different) supplies, or because the purchaser would on-supply the immovable property, for example, by way of sale, lease, sub-lease, licence to occupy, etc. The fact that no revenue will be raised from the immovable property itself makes sense because if all transactions involving immovable property are considered to be economic activities, then all suppliers and recipients are 'in the ring' and so full taxation *should* generate no revenue because immovable property never leaves the ring. The holding costs might well be factored into the price of other supplies, but that does not detract from the fact that the immovable property transactions themselves will give rise to no net tax revenue. This 'no taxation' effect of full taxation has two benefits: it ensures that immovable property transactions do not result in tax cascading and it ensures that no tax is imposed on the investment and savings elements of the transactions.

By way of illustration, consider first a series of transactions over a period of years in which passive landowners (O1 to O4) buy and sell vacant land, which is eventually purchased by a developer who builds a commercial building complex, subdivides the land title, and then sells individual units in the complex to be used as offices or shops. All transactions are fully taxable and creditable and the rate of VAT is 10%. Table 8.1 illustrates the nil revenue effect in this case.

Poddar reports that this treatment applies to non-residential land under the Canadian GST, though the Canadian Revenue Agency suggests that not all such sales are taxable.[47] With one significant difference, it also applies under the New Zealand GST, the exception being that the concept of an economic activity (in New Zealand, a 'taxable activity') does not include passive investments in land and so the mere

47. Poddar (n. 7 above). Canada Revenue Agency, *GST/HST Info Sheet GI-003 Sales of Vacant Land by Individuals* (17 August 2004), states: 'Most sales of vacant land by individuals are exempt' and gives as examples 'the sale of land that had been kept for personal use', including where the seller first subdivides the land into no more than two parts. The document notes that sales of vacant land by individuals will be taxable if the land 'is capital property that had been used primarily in a business', land sold 'in the course of a business', or 'a parcel of land created by subdividing another parcel into more than two parts'. The exemption appears in *Excise Tax Act, RSC 1985*, c E-15 (Canada), Schedule V, Part I, s. 9(2). It also extends to individuals carrying on hobby farming activities: Canada Revenue Agency, *GST/HST Info Sheet GI-002 Sales of Farmland by Individuals* (17 August 2004) because such activities are 'carried on without a reasonable expectation of profit', which prevents them falling into the 'business' exceptions to exemption: see paragraph (a) of the definition of 'commercial activity' in *Excise Tax Act, RSC 1985*, c E-15 (Canada), s. 123(1).

realization of assets held as passive investments is not a taxable supply and the purchase of an asset to hold as a passive investment is not a creditable acquisition.[48] The earlier cited assertion of Conrad and Grosav that 'economists, lawyers and tax administrators are not concerned with whether a taxpayer uses the asset or merely holds it expecting a gain'[49] is clearly not true of the New Zealand GST.

Table 8.1. Full Taxation of Vacant Land Held for Investment and then Developed

Supply/Acquisition	*Price*	*Year 1*	*Year 2*	*Year 3*	*Year 4*	*Year 5*
01 sells land to 02	550,000	50,000				
02 claims input tax credit		-50,000				
02 on-sells land to 03	660,000		60,000			
03 claims input tax credit			-60,000			
03 on-sells land to 04	880,000			80,000		
04 claims input tax credit				-80,000		
04 on-sells land to Developer	1,100,000				100,000	
Developer claims input tax credit					-100,000	
Developer builds commercial building & sells units to taxable persons	5,500,000					500,000
Purchasers claim input tax credits						-500,000
Revenue collected by tax authority:		-	-	-	-	-

Table 8.2 shows the effect of New Zealand GST on the transactions illustrated in Table 8.1, on the presumption that the vacant land had been held by passive investors since the introduction of GST to New Zealand in 1985.

48. *Newman v. Commissioner of Inland Revenue* (1995) 17 NZTC 12,097. See also: M. Smith, *GST and Real Property Transactions in New Zealand – Some Interpretative Issues*, in *GST in Retrospect and Prospect*, 277–308 (R. Krever & D. White eds., Thomson Brookers 2007). Based on the interpretation of the Canada Revenue Agency (n. 47 above), it appears likely that this is also the situation under the Canadian GST.
49. Conrad & Grosav (n. 27 above), 87.

Table 8.2. New Zealand Treatment of Vacant Land Held for Investment and then Developed

Supply/Acquisition	*Price*	*Year 1*	*Year 2*	*Year 3*	*Year 4*	*Year 5*
O1 sells land to O2	550,000					
O2 on-sells land to O3	660,000					
O3 on-sells land to O4	880,000					
O4 on-sells to Developer	1,100,000					
Developer claims second-hand goods credit					-100,000	
Developer builds commercial building & sells units to taxable persons	5,500,000					500,000
Purchasers claim input tax credits						-500,000
Revenue collected by tax authority:		-	-	-	-100,000	-

The negative amount generated by the second-hand goods credit requires some explanation. In New Zealand, if a sale of second-hand goods to a registered person is not a taxable supply, the registered person is allowed an imputed input tax credit equal to the tax fraction of the lesser of the purchase price or the market value of the goods.[50] Since real property is included in the concept of 'goods', second-hand goods can include real property.[51] Paradoxically, the second-hand goods credit, which the developer can claim despite the fact that no previous sales of the real property had been taxed, results in a loss to revenue in our example. The granting of a second-hand goods credit in the vast majority of situations where a person 'within the ring' purchases goods from 'outside the ring' gives primacy to the focus on taxing only a supplier's value added, deductibility being the GST embodiment of the principle of fiscal neutrality.[52] Applied to our example, the New Zealand second-hand goods credit ensures that the developer pays only on its value added, but in doing so it gives a credit that exceeds any previously charged VAT (since there has been none).

50. GST Act 1985, s. 3A(2) & (3).
51. New Zealand's definition of 'goods' includes both tangible and intangible property. 'Goods' means 'all kinds of personal or real property; but does not include choses in action, money or a product that is transmitted by a non-resident to a resident by means of a wire, cable, radio, optical or other electromagnetic system or by means of a similar technical system': GST Act 1985 (NZ), s.2.
52. The principle of fiscal neutrality, as elucidated by the CJEU, is an aspect of the principle of equal treatment, under which similar taxpayers, similar activities, similar commodities, and domestic and foreign commodities should be treated similarly for tax purposes. In the VAT context, the primary way in which the principle is given effect is through the input tax credit mechanism, which ensures VAT neutrality for businesses. While clearly the EU VAT Directive does not perfectly achieve these objectives, the approach to second-hand goods, and in particular to sales of land, in the Australian and New Zealand GST laws does endeavour to do so.

Harley explains this New Zealand approach to the second-hand goods credit for real property as a necessary and effective price-adjustment mechanism.[53] He also outlines how, by generating the effect illustrated in Table 8.2, some New Zealand taxpayers were able to use the second-hand goods credit as an effective transition mechanism around the time that GST was introduced, an effect that was only possible because of the exclusion of mere investment activities from the concept of an economic activity. Harley argues that this transitional benefit to taxpayers was not really a cost to revenue since the deemed input credit would be recaptured over time. This is true only if one retains the focus on the individual taxpayer, who in most cases will ultimately use the property for which the credit has been claimed to generate taxable outputs, and will eventually have paid output tax exceeding its input tax. But if one looks instead at the effect from the revenue authority's perspective, the generation of these initial input credits resulted in an unanticipated reduction in revenue in the early years, which might not have occurred if the designers of the law had been fully aware of the possibilities.

The generation of a transitional input tax credit for real property should not, however, be seen as an inappropriate design feature for a value added tax. Had the credit not been allowed, it could equally well have been said that the Government had received an undeserved windfall benefit by imposing a one-time tax on land values at the time of implementing the tax. Indeed, in modifying the New Zealand treatment of real property in its GST law, using an optional margin scheme rather than an imputed input tax credit, Australia included a transition regime, which partially shelters the pre-GST value of land from entering the tax base, at least for residential property.[54] By doing so, Australia acknowledged and accepted three functions of a second-hand goods treatment for real property: an anti-cascading function, a fiscal neutrality function, and a transitional function.[55]

As in New Zealand, the Australian GST excludes passive investments in real property from its concept of economic activity.[56] Unlike New Zealand, however, the second-hand goods treatment of real property in Australia is incomplete. The margin scheme should in theory produce the same result as a second-hand goods credit.

53. Harley (n. 1 above), 224.
54. GST Act 1999 (Aus), Div 75.
55. For a discussion of the relationship between the functions of the Australian margin scheme see: R. Millar, *Brady King:* Reliance Carpet *Bites Back*, GST News 49 (2008); reproduced in 29 *CCH Tax Week* 653 (2008).
56. At least this is the view of the Australian Commissioner of Taxation: see Miscellaneous Tax Ruling *MT 2006/1: The meaning of entity carrying on an enterprise for the purposes of entitlement to an Australian Business Number* and Goods and Services Tax Determination *GSTD 2006/6: Goods and Services Tax: Does MT 2006/1 have equal application to the meaning of 'entity' and 'enterprise' for the purposes of the A New Tax System (Goods and Services Tax) Act 1999?* Recent case law appears to be challenging this notion, but the Commissioner is determined to limit the relevance of the cases: *FCT v. Swansea Services Pty Ltd* [2009] FCA 402 (regarding long-term investments in art works) and *Touram Pty Ltd As Trustee for the GKA Family Trust and FCT* [2008] AATA 1167 (regarding land held as an investment asset). The Commissioner has issued decision impact statements on both cases, indicating his intention to limit their impact: see law.ato.gov.au/atolaw/view.htm?DocID=LIT/ICD/2008/365/00001 &PiT=99991231235958 and law.ato.gov.au/atolaw/view.htm?DocID=LIT/ICD/WAD139of 2009/00001&PiT=99991231235958.

However, since no input tax credit can be claimed by a purchaser of real property sold under the margin scheme, it is generally not used for B2B supplies of real property.[57] The Australian version of Table 8.2 would thus look different again, as illustrated in Table 8.3.

Table 8.3. Australian Treatment of Vacant Land Held for Investment and then Developed

Supply/Acquisition	*Price*	*Year 1*	*Year 2*	*Year 3*	*Year 4*	*Year 5*
01 sells land to 02	550,000					
02 on-sells land to 03	660,000					
03 on-sells land to 04	880,000					
04 on-sells land to Developer	1,100,000					
Developer builds commercial building & sells units to new owners	5,500,000					500,000
Purchasers claim input tax credits						-500,000
Revenue collected by tax authority:		-	-	-	-	-

If we compare Tables 8.1 to 8.3, putting aside the transitional effect in New Zealand, what they all have in common is that no revenue is raised: full taxation of B2B supplies of immovable property is a zero-sum game. In Table 8.1, the multi-stage nature of the tax is honoured, taxing and crediting at every step. In Tables 8.2 and 8.3, pure investment activities are outside the scope of the tax, so that the only step on which tax is applied is the 'value adding step', in which the developer builds and sells a new commercial building.

If no revenue is raised, why would full taxation be recommended? The answer, of course, is to remove the cascading effect that results from exempting B2B immovable property transactions: the objective of full taxation is to improve the neutrality of the tax rather than to raise revenue.

However, applying full taxation (with or without the exclusion of investment assets) to immovable property might be problematic in a VAT that has widespread exemptions of other commodities. The negative effects of exemption are well-established. Exemption significantly distorts the design of a VAT: exempting business-to-consumer (B2C) transactions results in under-taxation while exempting business-to-business (B2B) transactions results in tax cascading and contravenes the destination principle by imbedding domestic tax in the price of foreign consumption. Exempting the inputs to exempt supplies mitigates the negative effects for B2B supplies, and

57. The margin scheme is optional and in practice non-residential property is usually fully taxed, in which case the pre-GST value of the land enters the tax base, though this is mostly in transactions where the tax is fully creditable and so is only in theory in the base. As a result, the transitional rules in the margin scheme mainly operate to exclude the pre-GST value of land from the tax base for residential property.

for this reason, exemptions have a tendency to engender more exemptions, even though this ultimately adds to further under-taxation of B2C supplies. Thus, for example, where the agricultural sector is exempt, full taxation of land used for agriculture will place a significant input tax burden on agricultural outputs and this will create pressure to exempt agricultural land as well. Similarly, exempting the education, health, welfare, and government sectors will inevitably lead to pressure to exempt supplies of land to those sectors. If, to cater to these pressures, some supplies of land are taxable and some are exempt, the law will become complex and countries may be tempted to exempt all land, leading to over-taxation (through cascading) of virtually all commodities. This may provide some explanation for the approaches taken to exempting immovable property in Europe, since the EU VAT Directive includes a wide range of 'public interest' exemptions.[58] The fact that many (probably most) of the CJEU cases dealing with land involve supplies to these sectors speaks for itself.

Clearly, zero-rating and lower rates are preferable means of delivering these public interest exemptions because they do not create this pressure for exemption creep. It is easy for New Zealand and Australia to tax (or zero-rate) rather than exempt non-residential land because neither country has a broad list of exempt supplies. The New Zealand GST includes only two significant exemptions: residential leasing and financial services (mostly B2C).[59] Australia's exemptions are almost as limited, covering residential leases, sales of non-new residential property, and financial services.[60] Both countries fully include government and the non-profit sector in the VAT regime[61] and either fully tax or zero-rate the health, education, welfare, religious, and charitable sectors.[62] The full taxation of immovable property used as inputs by these sectors can therefore be achieved without concern for the potential negative effects of cascading.[63]

58. EU VAT Directive, Article 132.
59. GST Act 1985 (NZ), s. 14. Supplies of donated goods or services by a charity and supplies (other than the first supply) of fine metals are also exempt.
60. GST Act 1999 (Aus), Div 40. Supplies of precious metals (after the first supply, which is GST-free) and, at the election of the supplier, charitable fundraising events and school tuck-shop supplies are also exempt.
61. See R. Millar, 'Smoke and Mirrors: Applying the Full Taxation Model to Government under the Australian and New Zealand GST Laws', Ch 4, this volume.
62. Domestic zero-rating is limited in New Zealand. The following B2B supplies are zero-rated: a supply of a going concern; the first supply, by the refiner to a dealer in fine metal, of new fine metal after its refining; most financial services (suppliers must elect to zero-rate, otherwise the supply will be exempt); and, from 1 April 2011, all B2B supplies involving land. The purpose of zero-rating B2B supplies is merely to enhance neutrality rather than to alter the consumption tax base. Various emissions trading units and non-monetary consideration given for such units are also zero-rated (whether B2B or B2C): GST Act 1985 (NZ), s.11(1)(m), (ma), (n), & (o) and s. 11A(1)(q), (r), (s), (t), (u), & (v). Of course, exports and other supplies consumed outside New Zealand are zero-rated in order to apply the destination principle: GST Act 1985 (NZ), ss. 11, 11A, & 11AB. The Australian GST differs from the New Zealand GST by zero-rating a wide range of domestically supplied 'merit goods', including food and beverages for human consumption, health, education, child care, religious services, non-commercial activities of charities, water, sewerage and drainage, and cars for use by the disabled. The first supply of precious metals, the supply of a going concern, grants of land by Government, and some supplies of farmland are also GST-free: see GST Act 1999 (Aus), Div 38.
63. Residential accommodation and some sales of residential property are exempt: GST Act 1999 (Aus), Subdivs. 40-B & 40-C; GST Act 1985 (NZ), s.14(c), (ca), (cb), & (d). In Australia, some supplies of farmland and grants of land by governments are GST-free (exempt with credit): GST

[2] *Full Taxation of All Immovable Property (Including Private-use Land)*

Let us now expand our consideration of full taxation to include privately consumed premises. For the purposes of discussion, I will take private use to mean use otherwise than for the purposes of making supplies. This means that personal enjoyment of land that is owned or occupied for residential use by individuals would be private use. Although it is possible to use non-residential land for private purposes, the most prevalent private use of land will be use as a residence. Leasing a residence to another person is a supply, and so for the lessor/landlord this would not be a private use. Similarly, selling a residence is a supply and so is excluded from the notion of private use in this example.

If we retain the transaction tax nature of the tax, residences would be included in this full taxation model as follows:

- all sales of residential property would be taxed;
- all leases of residential property and other supplies of accommodation would be taxed; and
- all VAT incurred on inputs to such supplies, including the acquisitions of the property itself, would be creditable.

Table 8.4 varies the example in Table 8.1 so that it involves a series of transactions over a period of years during which a residence is bought and sold, sometimes by owner-occupiers (OO1 and OO2) and other times by residential landlords (RL1 and RL2), until it is eventually purchased by a developer who builds a block of residential units, subdivides the land title, and sells the individual units in the block to further owners, who might themselves intend to be owner-occupiers or to rent out their residences. Table 8.4 shows only the sales of the immovable property.

The effect is exactly the same as when we applied full taxation to non-residential land: no net revenue is raised from sales and purchases of the land. Just as the purchase price of vacant land was a cost element of subsequent supplies of land by the investors, here it is a cost element of the on-supplies by the owner-occupiers and residential landlords. While this might seem like an odd result, it is a consequence of the fact that everyone is 'in the ring' when it comes to sales and purchases of immovable property. It also makes sense in light of the fact that immovable property itself is not consumed.

Act 1999 (Aus), Subdivs.40-N & 40-O. Except when land is sold as part of a going concern, New Zealand traditionally did not zero-rate land transactions, but from 1 April 2011, all B2B supplies of land are zero-rated: GST Act 1985 (NZ), s.11(1)(mb), inserted by *Taxation (GST and Remedial Matters) Act 2010*. All other sales of immovable property are taxable (including land with commercial or industrial buildings, farmland, vacant land, unimproved land, and some residential property), provided that the usual requirements of taxable supplies are met.

Table 8.4. Full Taxation of Residential Land by Owner-Occupiers, Lessors, and Developers

Supply/Acquisition	*Price*	*Year 1*	*Year 2*	*Year 3*	*Year 4*	*Year 5*
OO1 sells residence to RL1	550,000	50,000				
RL1 claims input tax credit		-50,000				
RL1 on-sells residence to OO2	660,000		60,000			
OO2 claims input tax credit			-60,000			
OO2 on-sells residence to RL2	880,000			80,000		
RL2 claims input tax credit				-80,000		
RL2 on-sells residence to Developer	1,100,000				100,000	
Developer claims input tax credit					-100,000	
Developer builds block of units and sells units to further owners	5,500,000					500,000
Purchasers claim input tax credits						-500,000
Revenue collected by tax authority:		-	-	-	-	-

While the overall 'no revenue' effect of fully taxing sales of residential land might seem odd, the authors of *The Modern VAT*[64] implicitly accept that this is not only the effect of full taxation of immovable property, but also the right result. In discussing a full taxation option, they say this:

> In principle, resales should be fully taxed to the purchaser (to capture the future services to be enjoyed by the purchaser) and fully refunded to the seller (to give, in effect, a credit in relation to services taxed at purchase but not enjoyed during their ownership). Net revenue would be zero.[65]

But something does not seem quite right in the model as proposed in Table 8.4:

- Upfront input tax credits have been allowed to owner-occupiers, even though future sales might be only a distant possibility and the immediate use of the property is private use for residential accommodation by the owner.
- Although the consequences of rent are not shown in the table, the fact that the proposed full taxation model adheres to the legal view of VAT as a tax on transactions, with no notion of a deemed self-supply, means that renters are being taxed on the cost of occupying residential premises, whereas owner-occupiers are not.

64. Ebrill et al. (2001) (n. 19 above).
65. Ebrill et al. (2001) (n. 19 above), 99.

- The prepayment theory of VAT falls down because the input tax credit given to landowners means that they never effectively bear any tax. This is not simply a result of the increasing value of the property: all sales and purchases of immovable property are 'in the ring' and so landowners would be entitled to full recovery of their input tax, even if the value of the land had gone down and even though this would result in a loss to the revenue authorities.[66]

Nonetheless, this is, with one crucial difference, the proposal of Conrad and Grosav.[67] The difference is that although they propose that all sales and leases of land should be taxable, they make a distinction between taxpayers who are otherwise carrying on an economic activity and those who are not. The latter do not get the benefit of an immediate input tax credit but must instead defer the credit until the subsequent sale (if any) of the land. It is hard to see what justification there is for treating sales of residential land (or indeed of any land) differently depending on whether the supplier is *otherwise* a taxable person. More appropriate ways of determining which taxpayers should be required to defer their input tax credits can be found in existing VAT models. For example, we could exclude two types of activity from the concept of an economic activity (on the basis that neither will be carrying on a current economic activity in respect of the land) and require these groups to defer their credits:

(1) those whose immediate use of the premises will be private; and
(2) those who own land merely as a passive investment, without using it to generate income other than from a subsequent sale.

Thus, even taxable persons who are engaged in other economic activities in respect of which they are registered for VAT will be required to defer their input tax credits for land that is not part of those other economic activities and is acquired for private use or to hold as investments (provided, of course, that those investments are unrelated to the core economic activity).

Deferral for investment-only assets reflects the fact that investment does not involve engaging in economic activities that improve the land and thereby increase what is available to be consumed. The only way in which merely holding land increases its consumable value is by the effluxion of time. For both owner-occupiers and investors, deferral also reflects the practical reality that the asset might not be employed in making a taxable supply (the on-sale of the land), or indeed any supplies, for some years down the track. The relationship between any capital appreciation or depreciation on land held by such persons and their consumption of that land is difficult to identify.

For owner-occupiers, while depreciation of buildings and other improvements on the land can be attributed to consumption and should in some way be reflected in the

66. Cf. Poddar (n. 7 above).
67. Conrad & Grosav (n. 27 above), 90–95, where they set out their proposal for a 'Real Estate VAT', a variation on a previous proposal by Conrad for a Stock or S-VAT.

resale price of the land, there is no way of identifying the value of the consumption during the period of ownership simply by looking at the purchase and resale prices, which are the only prices visible to transaction-type VATs. Certainly, the capital appreciation or depreciation cannot be attributed to consumption and so should be excluded from the tax base.

Deferral of input tax credits for private-use assets is also in keeping with the approach of most VAT/GST laws, which determine input tax credits at the time of making an acquisition on the basis of the use that will be made of the asset at that time. However, practices vary in this regard and many VAT laws do not effectively deal with apportionment issues when a person acquires assets both for private and taxable use.[68] Nor are they always particularly coherent in their approach to movements in and out of the private sphere, and many VAT laws lack any effective mechanism for giving an input tax credit when a taxable person moves a wholly private-use asset into an economic activity.[69]

Table 8.5 varies Table 8.4 by deferring the credit for the owner-occupiers, but not for the residential landlords because the latter are making immediate taxable supplies of residential leases. Revenue is raised in Year 2 but repaid in Year 3, and the revenue raised in Year 5 is counterbalanced by the revenue authority's future liability to repay it in the form of input tax credits.

68. Partial apportionment formulae are usually directed only at acquisitions intended for use to make both taxable and exempt supplies, rather than those that will be used both for private and 'business' purposes: see, for example, EU VAT Directive, Articles 173–175. Because the Directive did not directly address the latter situation, a line of CJEU case law allowed taxable persons to allocate the entire asset to their business, deduct all the input tax, and then make a series of deemed supplies for applications to own use (Article 26). This led to the somewhat absurd (at least to Australian eyes) case in which Sandra Puffer was allowed to allocate her entire residence to her business and deduct all the input tax because she had a minor (11%) purpose of using part of the residence to make taxable supplies: Case C-460/07, *Sandra Puffer v. Unabhängiger Finanzsenat, Außenstelle Linz,* [2009] ECR I-03251. This followed a similar case relating to a holiday home: Case C-434/03, *Charles-Tijmens v. Staatssecretaris van Financien,* [2005] ECR I-07037. But the deemed supplies did not directly adjust the initial input tax deduction and the valuation of the deemed supplies could fall short of, or go beyond, the repayment of the appropriate percentage of the input tax. Moreover, there was clearly a significant timing benefit in the upfront deduction. The Directive was subsequently amended by Council Directive 2009/162/EU of 22 December 2009 amending various provisions of Directive 2006/112/EC on the common system of value added tax, OJ L10/14, 14–18 ('EU VAT Directive') and introducing Article 168a, which limits the allowable deduction for expenditure relating to immoveable property to the proportion used in the business and then uses the adjustment procedures (Articles 184–192) to deal with change of use, rather than the deemed self-supply rules. Member States may also apply this apportionment approach to acquisitions of goods other than immoveable property.
69. I refer here not to deductions at the time a small business becomes registered, but to private assets that are moved into business use by a taxable person. So far as I am aware, the EU VAT Directive has no rules that would allow deductions in such cases. New Zealand's previous rules did allow such adjustments and there is nothing to suggest that the recent changes altered this position: see GST Act 1985 (NZ), former ss.21E and 21F; current ss. 21 & 21G.

Table 8.5. Full Taxation of Residential Land with Input Tax Deferral for Owner-Occupiers

Supply/Acquisition	*Price*	*Year 1*	*Year 2*	*Year 3*	*Year 4*	*Year 5*
OO1 sells residence to RL1	550,000	50,000				
RL1 claims input tax credit		-50,000				
RL1 on-sells residence to OO2	660,000		60,000			
OO2 claims input tax credit				-60,000		
OO2 on-sells residence to RL2	880,000			80,000		
RL2 claims input tax credit				-80,000		
RL2 on-sells residence to Developer	1,100,000				100,000	
Developer claims input tax credit					-100,000	
Developer builds block of units and sells units to further owners	5,500,000					500,000
Owner-occupiers must defer input tax credit						
Revenue collected by tax authority:			60,000	-60,000		500,000
Future input credit:						-500,000

Whichever mechanism is chosen to determine who should be required to defer input tax credits, one should not lose sight of the fact that deferral does not, of itself, change the 'zero revenue' analysis. Deferral merely disguises the fact that no revenue is raised because at any particular point in time, the revenue authority is holding tax revenue that it will later be required to pay back through the deferred input tax credit.

Table 8.6 further varies Table 8.5 to consider how deferral works if all of the transactions are between owner-occupiers and there is no development of the residence into new residential property. Again, the total revenue raised equals the future input tax credit the revenue authority must pay. But if one focuses on the revenue authority's position in any particular year, there clearly does appear to be tax revenue being raised, even though there is always a future credit to be paid. From the perspective of both taxpayers and the revenue authority, this looks more like a capital gains tax on owner-occupiers than a VAT on sales of residential property. This is essentially the 'VAT' on resales of residential property proposed by Poddar, Cnossen, and Conrad and Grosav.

Table 8.6. Full Taxation with Input Tax Deferral when All Suppliers Are Owner-Occupiers

Supply/Acquisition	*Price*	*Year 1*	*Year 2*	*Year 3*	*Year 4*	*Year 5*
OO1 sells residence to OO2	550,000	50,000				
OO2 claims deferred input tax credit			-50,000			
OO2 on-sells residence to OO3	660,000		60,000			
OO3 claims deferred input tax credit				-60,000		
OO3 on-sells residence to OO4	880,000			80,000		
OO4 claims deferred input tax credit					-80,000	
OO4 on-sells residence to OO5	1,100,000				100,000	
OO5 claims deferred input tax credit						-100,000
OO5 on-sells residence to OO6	1,430,000					130,000
OO6 must defer input tax credit						
Revenue collected by tax authority:		50,000	10,000	20,000	20,000	30,000
Future input credit:						-130,000

Table 8.7 adds improvements to the mix. It is presumed that the increases in property values in Table 8.6 were partly due to the owner-occupiers making improvements to their properties and partly due to inflation and/or real capital gains or losses. A deferred credit is allowed for both the purchase and the improvements. None of the amounts is indexed for inflation. Again, the total revenue raised is $ 130,000, which exactly equals the input tax credit entitlement of OO6 on a future sale, but on an annual basis, tax revenue is clearly being collected.

In their 2008 paper, Conrad and Grosav suggest that no input tax credits should be allowed for improvements made to properties that are subject to deferral.[70] They do, however, propose giving those who are required to defer their input tax credit the counter-balancing benefit of indexation of the deferred credit to reflect the change in the value of money over time. It is difficult to see what justification, in terms of VAT design, there could be for denying credits for improvements. Provided that the improvements form part of the value of the property when resold (i.e. provided that they have not been completely used up, in which case they could rightly be treated as private consumption of the owner-occupier), they ought to be creditable because they are taxed as part of the price of the on-sale.

70. Conrad & Grosav (n. 27 above), 92.

Table 8.7. Full Taxation with Input Tax Deferral for Purchase and Improvements to Residences

Supply/Acquisition	*Price*	*Year 1*	*Year 2*	*Year 3*	*Year 4*	*Year 5*
OO1 sells to OO2	550,000	50,000				
Builder supplies improvements	77,000	7,000				
OO2 claims credit for improvements			-7,000			
OO2 claims credit for purchase			-50,000			
OO2 sells to OO3	660,000		60,000			
Builder supplies improvements	176,000		16,000			
OO3 claims credit for improvements				-16,000		
OO3 claims credit for purchase				-60,000		
OO3 sells to OO4	880,000			80,000		
Builder supplies improvements	165,000			15,000		
OO4 claims credit for improvements					-15,000	
OO4 claims credit for purchase					-80,000	
OO4 sells to OO5	1,100,000				100,000	
Builder supplies improvements	258,500				23,500	
OO5 claims credit for improvements						-23,500
OO5 claims credit for purchase						-100,000
OO5 sells to OO6	1,430,000					130,000
OO6 must defer input tax credit						
Revenue collected by tax authority:		57,000	19,000	19,000	28,500	6,500
Future input tax credit:						-130,000

Table 8.8. Full Taxation with Indexed Deferred Credit for Purchase and Improvements

Supply/Acquisition	*Price*	*Year 1*	*Year 2*	*Year 3*	*Year 4*	*Year 5*
OO1 sells to OO2	550,000	50,000				
Builder supplies improvements	77,000	7,000				
OO2 claims credit for improvements			-7,368			
OO2 claims credit for purchase			-52,362			
OO2 sells to OO3	660,000		60,000			
Builder supplies improvements	176,000		16,000			
OO3 claims credit for improvements				-16,842		
OO3 claims credit for purchase				-63,158		
OO3 sells to OO4	880,000			80,000		
Builder supplies improvements	165,000			15,000		
OO4 claims credit for improvements					-15,789	
OO4 claims credit for purchase					-84,211	
OO4 sells to OO5	1,100,000				100,000	
Builder supplies improvements	258,500				23,500	
OO5 claims credit for improvements						-24,737
OO5 claims credit for purchase						-105,263
OO5 sells to OO6	1,430,000					130,000
OO6 must defer input tax credit						
Revenue collected by tax authority:		57,000	16,000	15,000	23,500	-
Future input tax credit:						-130,000

Table 8.8 modifies Table 8.7 to illustrate the effects of allowing indexation. For ease of illustration, it is presumed that all sales and improvements are invoiced on the first day of the relevant year and that the rate of the appreciation of the residences is exactly the same as the underlying inflation rate (i.e. there is no real capital gain or loss). On this basis, using the figures given in Table 8.7, inflation would be running at an annual rate of 5.26%.

Now, apart from the first year in which we have given OO1 no counter-balancing input tax credit, in each year the only revenue raised is the tax paid on the improvements to the property. This is because bringing indexation into the equation removes the previous effect of deferral, which gave the appearance that revenue was being raised from the underlying land transactions.[71] What is more, the revenue raised is only $ 111,500 but there is liability in the future to pay an input tax credit of $ 130,000, which will itself be indexed.

Of course factoring in the future input tax credit gives a false impression. So long as the tax system continues to include a VAT, it might be true that the revenue collected up to a particular time is matched by a future liability, but the infrequency with which owner-occupied housing is traded means that the ability to use the tax in the meantime is a genuine benefit for the government. Moreover, the enduring nature of immovable property means that every future repayment of input tax is matched (and usually exceeded) by a corresponding liability for output tax. In any year (for the revenue authority), and on any sale (for the homeowner), so long as the price of the sale is more than the price of the purchase, there will be revenue raised (by the revenue authority) and tax to pay (for the homeowner).

One significant difference, however, is that input tax credits are *refundable* tax credits, which means that when the property market drops, homeowners who sell at a loss will be entitled to a refund of the earlier VAT paid. On the other hand, if the model is changed so that the VAT on sales is calculated on the margin (rather than on the full price, with a credit for the input tax), the future liability disappears from the mix. Poddar suggests that the input tax credit should be limited to the lesser of the earlier VAT paid (without indexation) or the output tax payable on the on-sale.[72] This would be in keeping with the European approach to second-hand goods and the Australian margin scheme for land, both of which preclude a negative result. In contrast, as noted, the New Zealand second-hand goods credit operates as a price adjustment *at the time of purchase*, rather than a deferred input credit that can be used to reduce the output tax only on a given transaction, which is the effect under a margin scheme.

Both a margin scheme model and a deferred credit model of full taxation look much like a capital gains tax from the viewpoint of both the revenue authority and the homeowner. This conception of the VAT on homeowners as a capital gains tax explains why Conrad rejects the idea of limiting the deferred input tax credit by reference to the

71. Of course, the land could appreciate more rapidly (or more slowly) than the underlying change in value of money. In years when property values rose more rapidly, the VAT revenue would exceed the tax on the improvements, whereas in years when the property market was more sluggish, the VAT revenue would be less.
72. Poddar (n. 7 above).

output tax payable. However, in commenting on concerns raised by Poddar about the consequences of imposing a VAT on consumer resales of residential property, he makes the following comment:[73]

> Mr Poddar's concern about changes in relative prices (capital gains) should not be an issue (except perhaps on distributional grounds) because the capital gain would be treated like a capital gain of any asset (such as a marketable security). That is, if the seller consumes the capital gain, then VAT would be paid; if the seller purchases another type of asset, defined as saving, then VAT would be deferred.

It is not abundantly clear whether Conrad is proposing that rollover relief should be a feature of his deferred credit model of VAT, but even if he is, it must be said that the paragraph does seem to pose some serious problems in terms of VAT design. Firstly, most VAT/GST laws do not 'defer' VAT when the proceeds of selling an asset are reinvested in another asset. In any case, if VAT is not to apply when homeowners sell in order to reinvest in other homes, when exactly are we going to collect revenue? Predominantly when old people downsize or when over-committed poor people are forced to exit the market? That would hardly seem like a politically palatable tax policy. Secondly, and more importantly, the analogy with marketable securities does not apply. No VAT would be applied to the capital gain (unadjusted or not) on the sale of a marketable security because a supply of a marketable security would be an exempt financial supply. Finally, if the seller realizes the capital gain (and indeed all of the capital) and spends the money, the supplies of the items on which the money is spent will be taxed because they are what is to be consumed. If the capital gain has also been taxed under a form of capital-gains-VAT, the consumption will be taxed twice. Realizing a gain by selling an asset is not consumption and taxing the capital gain (with or without indexation) is a tax on income, not a tax on consumption.

Conrad envisages making his proposed indexed-deferred-credit-capital-gains-VAT progressive[74] but once made progressive, the tax could no longer feasibly be conceived of as part of a value added tax, since the consumer as supplier would be unable to pass on the full tax burden in a market where some such suppliers are taxed at one rate and some at another, but all are selling in the same property market. Conrad's proposals might, as it is evident he intends them to be, constitute one way of calculating an income tax on sales of immovable property, but they are not a proper fit for a VAT that operates as a consumption tax.

Finally, in many countries, applying VAT/GST as a capital gains tax on owner-occupied housing is not a politically viable option. New Zealand, for instance, does not have a general capital gains tax, so to introduce one for the family home would seem incongruous. In Australia, indirect taxes on land, such as land taxes and stamp duties, are some of the few remaining taxes imposed by the Australian States.[75] At the Federal

73. Conrad (n. 10 above), fn. 1.
74. Conrad (n. 10 above).
75. See the website of the New South Wales Office of State Revenue at www.osr.nsw.gov.au for a description of the taxes it collects.

level, Australia does have a capital gains tax but the principal place of residence is exempt.[76] Adding GST on capital gains to this mix would simply not be acceptable. In any case, since Australia is still offering first homeowner's grants to compensate for the increase in the price of housing after the introduction of GST more than ten years ago,[77] it would seem counter-intuitive to attempt to introduce GST on resales of private homes. The appropriateness, or otherwise, of applying VAT to resales of owner-occupied land is a land tax problem, rather than a VAT problem, by which I mean that the proper tax treatment of land is more appropriately considered as part of the policy design of income and wealth taxes, in which it is easier (as Conrad proposes) to import a level of progressivity and to take account of equity, ability to pay, and other tax policy issues that go beyond the mere focus on neutrality and revenue that has made VAT such an attractive tax in the latter half of the twentieth century.

§8.05 DEVELOPING A MODEL FOR APPLYING VAT TO IMMOVABLE PROPERTY

[A] How Should Land Be Dealt with under a VAT?

If the savings element of immovable property should not be taxed under a VAT because it is not consumed, and proposals to impose what amounts to a capital-gains-VAT on resales of owner-occupied housing should be rejected, it does not follow that immovable property transactions should be exempt. Tables 8.1 to 8.4 illustrated how full taxation amounts effectively to non-taxation when all the features of a modern VAT are applied to immovable property without any deferral of input tax credits. Full taxation of non-residential immovable property is therefore an effective method of not taxing the savings element of such property.

One significant drawback, however, is that fully taxing all *transactions* relating to immovable property means that owner-occupiers are treated differently from lessees. This is not a problem for suppliers who make only taxable supplies: for both a lessee and an owner-occupier, the VAT imposed on a lease/purchase of immovable property will be creditable and the net effect will be nil. The quantum of the tax that might have to be carried between the date when the consideration for the supply is paid and the date when the revenue authority pays the refund differs for a purchaser compared with a lessee, but this is a relatively minor effect.[78] However, if some supplies (other than

76. Income Tax Assessment Act 1997 (Aus), ss.118-110.
77. Eligible purchasers are entitled to a one-off grant of up to $ 7,000 towards the purchase of their first home. The scheme has been in place since GST was introduced on 1 July 2000 and is designed to compensate new entrants to the property market for the increase in home prices caused by the imposition of GST: see www.firsthome.gov.au. Canada has a similar scheme for newly built or substantially renovated houses: see Canada Revenue Agency, *Guide RC4028 GST/HST New Housing Rebate* (updated 29 June 2010) and Canada Revenue Agency, *RC4231 GST/HST New Residential Rental Property Rebate* (updated 29 June 2010).
78. Payment does not always come first. Within the ring, larger suppliers frequently dictate terms of trade that enable them to claim an input tax credit before they have paid for the supply (an effect that is possible when payment of tax and entitlements to credits are linked to the issue of an invoice for the supply).

immovable property) are exempt under the VAT law, a lessee who makes such exempt supplies will initially appear better off than an owner-occupier but will ultimately be worse off. Although both, being *input taxed suppliers*, can be expected to pass on the cost of uncreditable input tax on immovable property used to make exempt supplies, the lessee has the benefit of spreading the input tax burden over time, thereby more effectively matching it to the timing of the supplies on which it will recover the cost of the input tax. The owner-occupier, on the other hand, can sell the asset and, depending on how the adjustment rules apply, might recover some or all of the denied input tax. These problems confirm the point made earlier, that the 'full taxation' models for land work best when combined with a VAT that has few or no exemptions.

As with input taxed suppliers, when it comes to residential property, taxing all transactions is problematic. As we have seen, taxing owner-occupiers on resales with an immediate credit is inappropriate because it ignores the current private use of the property, while taxing them on resales with a deferred credit amounts to an income tax on capital gains rather than a consumption tax, and results in VAT being charged on savings. The best option is to tax only improvements to residential immovable property and to do so on a prepayments basis, i.e. by charging tax when the improvements are made and giving no credits. This still leaves owner-occupiers and renters in a position where they appear to be treated differently. If we want to address this, rather than simply accepting it, we must either depart from the normal transaction tax nature of a VAT and tax deemed self-supplies by owner-occupiers, or exempt leases of residential property to tenants.

One example of a method that could be used to tax the flow of services from owner-occupied housing can be found in the adjustment rules that, until recently, applied under the New Zealand GST for assets purchased for dual use. If a bank acquired a building for the principal purpose of making taxable supplies, but used the building partly to supply exempt financial services, the bank would initially claim all its input tax credits and then be required to make a series of ongoing output tax adjustments throughout the time it owned the building.[79] This might give the appearance of charging GST on the imputed rent on self-supply, but the courts held that the adjustments made over time could not exceed the input tax credit that was initially claimed.[80] It must be presumed, therefore, that any continued use of the building to make exempt supplies after the credits have been repaid would not be treated as a self-supply. In any case, when the land was ultimately sold in a taxable supply, it was necessary to re-adjust the balance between the initial input tax credit and the subsequent output tax adjustments to reflect the fact that the sale altered the balance

79. This is not unlike the approach used for dealing with business/private assets in the *Sandra Puffer* case, which was criticized in n. 68. New Zealand clearly found the deemed supply approach problematic because it was replaced with an input tax apportionment approach from 1 April 2011: *Taxation (GST and Remedial Matters) Act 2010.*

80. Although case law suggests that the adjustments must be limited to the GST payable on the acquisition, Inland Revenue remained unconvinced that this position was sufficiently clear and this was one reason why they proposed changes to the law: see Policy Advice Division, Inland Revenue (New Zealand), *Options for strengthening GST neutrality in business-to-business transactions – an official's paper* (Wellington: 2008), para 8.15.

between taxable and exempt supplies. The courts held that all of the previous output tax adjustments could be reclaimed.[81] This meant that the initial appearance of an imputed rent on consumption (albeit in relation to making financial supplies) reverted back to a zero-sum game. All of the original input tax was attributed to the taxable resale of the property and none to the exempt supplies made during the period of ownership. As a result, the only real costs to the taxpayer were the cost of financing and the change in value of money over time, since the output tax adjustments were recaptured only at their face value.

Adopting such an adjustment regime to calculate imputed rent for owner-occupiers would in any case not achieve its objective. It would require first granting the homeowner a full input tax credit, which would seem somewhat pointless if the value of the services of using the land can never exceed the purchase price of the land. One might as well have adhered to the prepayments basis for collecting VAT, which is more consistent with the transaction tax nature of the tax, less prone to evasion, and achieves basically the same result.

Poddar gives an example in which he illustrates the prepayment concept to show that taxing owner-occupiers on a prepayments basis is equivalent to a tax on imputed rent. He shows that 'rents in any given period are equal to the time value of money invested in durable goods plus depreciation' and indicates that 'any decrease in value of durable goods is on account of depreciation which in turn is assumed to be on account of consumption of the consumer goods'.[82] But the example he gives involves a home that completely depreciates to nil, whereas this is not what happens in the real world.[83] Any depreciation on the dwelling is frequently overwhelmed by the appreciation of the immovable property as a whole (including both land and dwelling) so that a homeowner's partial consumption of a residence appears not to be effectively taxed. In contrast, under a simple deferred input credit model, the *appreciation* is taxed (on an incorrect presumption that it will be consumed by the purchaser), while under Conrad's indexed-deferred-credit model, the indexed capital gain/loss is attributed to consumption (unless it is reinvested).

Technically, the prepayments method for taxing owner-occupiers could be combined with the transaction basis for taxing residential leases, but just as with a tax on imputed rent, this can only be done if double taxation is avoided by giving residential landlords input tax credits when acquiring residential property (including imputed credits if the property is purchased without tax). Taxing residential landlords on resales would mean taxing the capital appreciation on the residence while held by the landlord. Given that owner-occupiers would only have borne tax on improvements to the land, rather than the full capital appreciation, a residential landlord selling in a market dominated by owner-occupier resales would be at a disadvantage and some method would need to be found for excluding part of the capital appreciation from the tax base in order to tax only any improvements made to the land. While this is not

81. *GST: Accounting for land and other high-value assets* (n. 35 above); *Options for strengthening GST neutrality* (n. 80 above).
82. Poddar (n. 7 above), 11 (both passages).
83. Poddar (n. 7 above), 12 (Table 2).

impossible, since landlords could keep records of the purchase price and the price of all improvements, something they might well be doing for capital gains tax purposes (though for the purpose of taxing the gain, rather than exempting it), it would add to the messiness of taxing such sales in the context of a tax that normally applies tax simply to the sale price. It would also be pointless for exactly the same reason that taxing imputed rent was pointless, since to put the landlord on an equal footing with an owner-occupier the output tax on resale would have to be no more than the input tax incurred in acquiring the property and in making improvements, which might then just as well have been taxed on a prepayment basis as they are for owner-occupiers.

Furthermore, it is clear that taxing owner-occupiers on a prepayments basis and renters on a transaction basis would rarely, if ever, put owner-occupiers in the same position as renters because markets do not always accurately predict changes in market prices of housing or rents. Finally, the size of real property transactions and the lifetime over which the assets can be used to make supplies mean that the scope for evasion in approaches involving either applying VAT to imputed rent or applying it to actual rent should be immediately evident.

Far from being a distortion of the proper tax base, *input taxation* is in fact the most appropriate way to deal with residential leasing and with resales of leased housing. Exemption of residential leasing ensures that both owner-occupiers and renters are taxed on a prepayments basis, with landlords acting as *input taxed suppliers* in passing on the burden of the prepaid tax to their tenants. Exemption of resales of leased housing puts owner-occupiers and lessors on an equal footing so that the savings element of the capital appreciation on both leased and owner-occupied residences does not inappropriately enter the tax base.

What then is an appropriate regime for dealing with immovable property transactions under a VAT? Ebrill et al. in *The Modern VAT*, make the following recommendations:

(1) Construction services and materials should be fully taxed;
(2) Sales of commercial properties should be fully taxed, effectively raising no revenue;
(3) Sales of new residential properties should be taxed; and
(4) Resales of owner-occupied housing should be exempt, with no credits allowed for improvements purchased by owner-occupiers.[84]

These recommendations are, however, relatively skeletal. They are silent on the mere holding of land as an investment and they say nothing about the movement of residential property into and out of the ring, making no specific recommendation on the second-hand goods treatment of land. No recommendation is made for the treatment of agricultural or vacant land, though it can be presumed from the discussions of commercial land and of agriculture that the authors would recommend full

84. Ebrill et al. (2001) (n. 19 above), 98–99.

taxation or zero-rating rather than exemption.[85] Nor is there any specific recommendation on residential leases, though the authors seem to accept exemption of leasing and the resale of leased residences as an acceptable status quo.

Poddar essentially concurs with the recommendations in *The Modern VAT*, and cites the Australian, New Zealand, and Canadian GST laws as adopting this approach, although there are significant differences in the way these countries implement these recommendations. The conclusions from section §8.04 of this chapter, also clearly favour these recommendations, provided that they are fleshed out in a way that ensures that:

- only improvements to land are taxed; and
- VAT does not operate as a tax on investment/savings.

Drafting a VAT law to implement the recommendations in *The Modern VAT* means defining a concept of 'new residential property' to delineate the boundaries between the exemption recommended for owner-occupied housing and the taxation recommended for new housing. Combining the recommended treatment for housing with the recommended treatment for other land means that a concept of a house/residence is required, and that that concept must be defined in a way that makes sense for the society in which the tax is being applied. If residential accommodation is to be exempt, it must be distinguished at one end from hotel or holiday accommodation and at the other end from long-term leasehold interests in land, which are equivalent to 'ownership'. The law must also decide the extent to which small-scale activities similar to leasing are ignored and must deal with non-standard residential arrangements.[86]

By way of examples to illustrate how these boundaries might be drawn, the following passages describe how the Australian and New Zealand GSTs deal with these issues.

[B] The New Zealand GST as an Example[87]

[1] Non-residential Land

Except as described in the following passages, all supplies of real property, including sales, leases, and other types of supply, are taxed at the standard rate under the New Zealand GST.

85. Ebrill et al. (2001) (n. 19 above), 98–99 and Chapter 9.
86. Would a student leasing an apartment and subletting some of the rooms to other students be (a) making taxable supplies, and if so (b) entitled to input tax credits for part of his/her lease payments? Would it make any difference whether the rent charged was merely an appropriate proportion of the entire rent, so that the arrangement might be seen as 'cooperative purchasing' by consumers, rather than an acquisition and on-supply by the student as head lessor? Would it make a difference whether the sub-lease was a formal or informal arrangement?
87. The chapter was prepared in 2010 and described the law as at October 2010. Changes effected by *Taxation (GST and Remedial Matters) Act 2010*, which took effect on 1 April 2011, are also noted.

[2] Exemption for Residential Accommodation

A supply of accommodation in a *dwelling* is exempt if it is made by way of hire, service occupancy agreement, or a licence to occupy,[88] with the following definitions applying:[89]

- *Hire* is defined to include 'letting on any terms, including a lease'.
- *Service occupancy agreement* is defined as 'a licence whereby a person occupies a dwelling for no consideration'.

The definitions of dwelling and commercial dwelling have recently been modified. Historically, a *dwelling* was defined as a 'building, premises, structure, or other place, or any part thereof, used predominantly as a place of residence or abode of any individual, together with any appurtenances belonging thereto and enjoyed with it; but does not include a commercial dwelling'. The words 'residence' and 'abode', and the exclusion of commercial dwellings, narrowly targeted the exemption at long-term occupation. Despite this, the New Zealand Inland Revenue was concerned to further narrow the exemption, to target it at supplies that are equivalent to owner-occupation of residential premises. As part of a package of reforms to the GST treatment of land the definition of *dwelling* was replaced with the following:[90]

> **dwelling**, for a person,—
>
> (a) means premises, as defined in section 2 of the Residential Tenancies Act 1986,—
> (i) that the person occupies, or that it can reasonably be foreseen that the person will occupy, as their principal place of residence; and
> (ii) in relation to which the person has quiet enjoyment, as that term is used in section 38 of the Residential Tenancies Act 1986; and
>
> (b) includes—
> (i) accommodation provided to a person who is occupying the same premises, or part of the same premises, as the supplier of the accommodation and who meets the requirements of paragraph (a)(i):

88. GST Act 1985 (NZ), s. 14(1)(c). In addition to accommodation in a dwelling, two related exemptions apply. The rental of leasehold land (not including the grant or sale of the leasehold land) is exempt to the extent that that land is used for the principal purpose of accommodation in a dwelling erected on that land: GST Act 1985 (NZ), s. 14(1)(ca). This applies where a lessee resides in residential premises it erects on the land and has equitable title over the premises. In such a situation, the lessor is technically only leasing the land, but from the lessee's perspective, the rent is clearly part of the cost of residing in the premises: A. McKenzie, *GST—A Practical Guide*, 305 (7th ed., CCH Kluwer Law 2002). In addition, a lease of property to be used for the principal purpose of accommodation in a dwelling by any person, other than a registered person in the course or furtherance of a taxable activity, is exempt: GST Act 1985 (NZ), s. 14(1)(cb). This deals with head- and sub-leasing arrangements: McKenzie (this n. above), 306. This exemption is subject to an option to continue treating such a supply as taxable if the lease was entered into and treated as taxable before 16 May 2000.
89. GST Act 1985 (NZ), s. 2.
90. *Taxation (GST and Remedial Matters) Act 2010*, s. 4, modifying the definitions in GST Act 1985 (NZ), s. 2(1).

(ii) any appurtenances belonging to or used with the premises; and
(c) excludes a commercial dwelling:

The previous definition of *commercial dwelling* was also modified, adding the words highlighted in italics in the definition below, thereby cementing the restriction of the exemption to dwellings used as the principal place of residence of the occupant:[91]

commercial dwelling—

(a) means—
  (i) a hotel, motel, *homestay, farmstay, bed and breakfast establishment,* inn, hostel or boardinghouse:
  (ii) a serviced apartment managed or operated by a third party for which services in addition to the supply of accommodation are provided and in relation to which a resident does not have quiet enjoyment, as that term is used in section 38 of the Residential Tenancies Act 1986:
  (iii) a convalescent home, nursing home, rest home or hospice:
  (iv) a camping ground:
  (v) premises of a similar kind to those referred to in subparagraphs (i) to (iv): and
(b) excludes—
  (i) a hospital except to the extent to which the hospital is a residential establishment:
  (ii) a dwelling situated in a retirement village or rest home if the consideration paid or payable for the supply of accommodation in the dwelling is for the right to occupy the dwelling: *(Emphasis added).*

This contrasts with the Australian approach, in which there is some debate about whether the exemption for a lease, hire or licence of *residential premises* depends on the characteristics of the premises or the use of the premises by the recipient of the supply.[92]

Continuing with New Zealand, where individuals have their place of abode outside these narrow confines, such as when they reside long-term in commercial dwellings, the supply of the accommodation is not exempt but is instead effectively subject to a lower rate. The rate is effectively 9% and applies to a supply of *domestic goods and services* in a commercial dwelling if the accommodation is supplied for more than four weeks.[93] *Domestic goods and services* are defined to mean 'the right to occupy

91. The structure of the definition has also been modified, making it clearer that what is now sub-paragraph (v) applies to all of the supplies mentioned in subparagraphs (i) to (iv).
92. Changes to the law after its initial enactment were designed to ensure that the exemption depended on physical characteristics. To achieve this, the phrase 'regardless of the term of occupation' was added to a number of the key definitions discussed in section §8.05[C] below.
93. The law is somewhat confusing, achieving the lower rate by defining the value of the supply to be 60% of what would have been the value of the supply if the rate had been 9% and then applying the standard rate to that value. The value is normally the total consideration minus the tax payable and the relevant section presumes that the benefit of the lower rate is passed on. Thus, a supply of domestic goods and services in a commercial dwelling that would normally cost $ 115 should cost $ 109 if supplied for more than 4 weeks. Applying the formula: if the price is $ 109, the value would have been $ 100 if the rate had been 9%; 60% of $ 100 is $ 60; applying the standard rate to this value, the GST is $ 60 × 15% = $ 9: GST Act 1985 (NZ), s.10(2) & (6). Quite why the law doesn't simply say that the rate is 9% is not clear.

the whole or part of any commercial dwelling' and include (if provided as part of the right to occupy) cleaning, maintenance, electricity, gas, air-conditioning, heating, and telephone, television, radio or other similar chattels.[94]

If the domestic goods and services are supplied in a *residential establishment* (a commercial dwelling in which 70% or more of the residents to whom domestic goods and services are supplied reside for four weeks or more) the entire supply is taxable at the lower rate (including the first four weeks); otherwise, the lower rate applies only to the period after the first four weeks.[95]

[3] Exemption for Sales of Residential Property

New Zealand does not use a distinction between new and old residential property to target its GST at improvements to land. The only specified exemption for sales of real property applies when a registered person sells, in the course or furtherance of a taxable activity, a dwelling which that person has, for five years or more before the date of the supply, used exclusively to make exempt supplies of accommodation.[96] In all other cases, if a taxable person sells immovable property and the supply otherwise falls within the definition of a taxable supply, the supply will be taxable.

The requirements of a taxable supply are that it is:

- made in New Zealand;
- by a registered person;
- in the course or furtherance of a taxable activity carried on by that person; and
- is not an exempt supply.[97]

A *taxable activity* is defined as an activity that is 'carried on continuously or regularly by any person' and involves 'the supply of goods and services to any other person for

94. GST Act 1985 (NZ), s. 2.
95. The definition of *residential establishment* includes hospitals, if 'used to provide domestic goods and services in a way similar to any such residential establishment': GST Act 1985 (NZ), s. 2.
96. GST Act 1985 (NZ), s. 14(1)(d). The exemption also applies to a supply of the reversionary interest in a fee simple estate of leasehold land (For those unfamiliar with common law terminology, this is the underlying interest held by a landowner in respect of land over which a lease has been granted. When land is sold subject to a lease it is the reversionary interest that is being For property developers who temporarily rent out new dwellings, the five year rule will not necessarily apply because the New Zealand courts have held that a property which is leased out while it is being actively marketed for sale is being concurrently used both for making a taxable supply (the subsequent sale) and for making exempt supplies (the lease). During this period of concurrent use, the property is not being used *exclusively* for exempt supplies of accommodation and so the five year period does not begin to run.
97. GST Act 1985 (NZ), s. 2 definition of 'taxable supply' and s. 8(1) imposing tax on taxable supplies by reference to the value of the supply. The reverse charged 'taxable supplies' in s. 8(4B) and (4C) are not relevant because they apply only to services.

a consideration'.[98] The requirement for 'continuous or regular' activity is the source of the exclusion of activities that are merely investments in land. The definition also specifically excludes from the concept of taxable activity 'any activity to the extent to which the activity involves making exempt supplies'.[99] This means that supplying accommodation in a dwelling is neither a taxable supply nor a supply made in the course or furtherance of a taxable activity. As a result, the supply of land used only to carry out that activity is itself exempt (irrespective of the five year rule) because the asset is not used in a taxable activity carried on by the seller.

Thus, in addition to the specific exemption for the sale of a dwelling that the seller has supplied exclusively for exempt accommodation for at least five years prior to its sale, the following sales of real property are effectively exempt because they are not considered to be made in the course or furtherance of a taxable activity:

- the sale of a dwelling owned by person who has used the dwelling only to make exempt supplies of accommodation;
- the sale of land held only for investment purposes and not used in carrying on a taxable activity;
- the sale of a weekender, bach,[100] or holiday home owned by a person for private use;
- the sale of a dwelling by an owner-occupier, including the sale of a new or substantially renovated dwelling built by the owner-occupier.

If a registered person buys an existing dwelling, claims a second-hand goods credit and uses it as a place from which to run its business, without changing the character of the property so that it is no longer a dwelling, a resale of the property will be a taxable supply even though the dwelling is not new and even though it still has the character of a dwelling. Since the vast majority of homes and apartments traded on the market are existing buildings being sold by persons whose dwelling is not part of a taxable activity, there is little capacity for a taxable person who purchases such a property for business use and then sells it back into the residential market to recover the tax liability by passing it on to purchasers in an above-market price. The granting of the second-hand goods input tax credit effectively refunds, in advance, that part of the GST payable on the subsequent supply that is attributable to the purchase price, thereby ensuring that the supplier only pays tax on its 'value added'. This approach does, however, tax the capital appreciation while the property is held by the registered

98. GST Act 1985 (NZ), s. 6. The definition specifically includes activities 'carried on in the form of a business, trade, manufacture, profession, vocation, association, or club', the activities of public authorities and local authorities, and activities undertaken at the beginning and ending (including prematurely) of taxable activities, and excludes private hobbies and recreational activities, employment and similar activities: GST Act 1985 (NZ), s. 6(1) to (3).
99. GST Act 1985 (NZ), s. 6(3)(d).
100. 'Bach' (pronounced 'batch') is a New Zealand word meaning 'a weekend cottage or house, usually at the beach' or a 'shack': *Macquarie Dictionary Online* (Macmillan Publishers Australia 2010).

person (because the appreciation is part of the 'value added') even where, as in the postulated situation, the registered person does not make any improvements to the land in the course of its taxable activity. In such cases, the registered person is in no different position (with respect to the appreciation) than an owner-occupier or investor and it is not clear what policy reason there is for taking a different approach, other than simplification or a blanket rule that all gains made in the course of a taxable activity should be taxed irrespective of whether they are the result of improvements.[101]

To take an example, consider a series of transactions in which a residence moves in and out of the ring, as illustrated in Table 8.9. One owner-occupier sells to another (OO1 to OO2) and the transaction is out of scope. The new homeowner sells to a taxable person (TP1) and again the transaction is out of scope. TP1 uses the residence as a place of business and so is entitled to an immediate second-hand goods input tax credit. TP1 then sells the residence to a residential landlord (RL1) but this time the supply is a taxable supply. RL1 is not entitled to an input tax credit because it uses the residence to supply exempt accommodation in a dwelling. After using the residence only for exempt leasing, RL1 sells the residence to a property developer. This transaction is out of scope because RL1's exempt leasing activities are excluded from the concept of a taxable activity. Because the supply by RL1 to the developer is not taxable, the developer is entitled to a second-hand goods input tax credit. The developer builds a block of units, undertakes a unit title conversion and makes taxable supplies by selling the individual units to further owner-occupiers and residential lessors, none of whom is entitled to an input tax credit. At various stages, builders supply goods and services that constitute improvements to the property.

101. Previously, this result could be avoided where, before selling the property, the person returned it to 'residential use' by leasing it out in an exempt supply of accommodation in a dwelling. In such a case, the supplier could make a one-off adjustment to reflect the transfer of the property to a use wholly to make exempt supplies. The adjustment was achieved by making an output tax adjustment for a deemed supply, which was valued at the *lesser* of the cost of the property to the supplier or the market value. After making such an adjustment, a subsequent supply of the dwelling was not a taxable supply: see GST Act 1985 (NZ) (prior to 1 April 2011), s. 5(16), (17), & (18), & ss. 10(8), & 21(1). For supplies made on or after 1 April 2011, the key provision allowing this treatment, s. 5(17), has been repealed, s.10(8) has been correspondingly amended, and s. 21(1) has been completely replaced as part of a new approach to input tax credits, which abandons the deemed supply mechanism in favour of initial apportionment followed by adjustments to reflect actual use (an approach that adopts and modifies the Australian rules). The previous ability to avoid tax on part of the capital appreciation in this way might, on the face of it, seem inconsistent with the five year rule, under which a sale of a dwelling is exempt only if the supplier has rented it out in an exempt supply of a dwelling for at least the last five years. However, so long as there was no avoidance, there was nothing to prevent this effect unless the sale of the property was a taxable activity in its own right, which would be unlikely on the facts postulated. A property developer would most likely not have been able to successfully use this option to avoid the five year rule.

Table 8.9. New Zealand Treatment of Land Moving In and Out of the Ring

Supply/Acquisition	*Price*	*Year 1*	*Year 2*	*Year 3*	*Year 4*	*Year 5*
OO1 sells to OO2	550,000					
Builder supplies improvements	77,000	7,000				
OO2 sells to TP1	660,000					
TP1 claims second-hand goods credit			-60,000			
Builder supplies improvements	176,000		16,000			
TP1 claims input tax credit			-16,000			
TP1 sells to RL1	880,000			80,000		
Builder supplies improvements	165,000			15,000		
RL1 sells to Developer	1,100,000					
Developer claims second-hand goods credit					-100,000	
Developer sells to new owner-occupiers	5,500,000					500,000
Revenue collected by tax authority:		7,000	-60,000	95,000	-100,000	500,000

Over the five years, the total revenue raised ($ 442,000) is equal to the tax fraction of the sum of:

- the capital appreciation during the period of ownership by the two taxable persons (TP1 and the developer), which includes the value of the improvements; and
- the price of the improvements supplied to the two non-taxable persons (OO2 and RL1).

In contrast, under the law as it applied until 2011, if, prior to selling the residence to RL1, TP1 had commenced leasing the residence out in an exempt supply of accommodation in a dwelling, instead of having $ 80,000 output tax (the tax fraction of the price of the sale to RL1), TP1 would make an output tax adjustment of $ 76,000 (the cost to it of the premises plus the improvements) at the time it commenced the leasing.[102] The on-sale by RL1 would then be exempt because the residence would be an asset of its exempt activity. In that case, the total revenue raised would be $ 438,000, which would be equal to the tax fraction of the sum of:

102. Provided, or course, that this did not constitute tax avoidance.

- the capital appreciation during the period of ownership by the developer, including the value of the improvements made during the period of ownership; and
- the price of the improvements supplied by builders to the two non-taxable persons (OO2 and RL1) and to TP1.

Thus, while the New Zealand treatment of residential property does in some senses follow the recommendations in *The Modern VAT*, it varies from them in significant ways. Rather than focussing on whether residential premises are 'new' or 'old', it targets the objective of taxing improvements to land through its definition of taxable activity. However, in doing so it sometimes taxes not only consumable improvements to land, but also the savings element of land. Indeed, there is nothing to suggest that the designers of the New Zealand GST had any intention to exclude capital appreciation (and therefore savings) from the tax base. The fact that the law often does so is more a consequence of, rather than the intention behind, the design features of the tax. It seems more likely that the focus of the drafters was to tax all value added during the period of ownership by registered persons, irrespective of the nature of the commodity and irrespective of whether part of that value added was simply capital appreciation rather than a reflection of improvements to the land.[103]

The permanent sheltering of the capital gain (or loss) during the period of time when land is held for private purposes, by residential landlords, and by long-term investors, is the exact opposite of what Conrad, Cnossen, and others recommend, but sheltering from tax the capital gain in the hands of consumers does solve a number of problems. It ensures that the return of the invested capital, and that part of the gain that reflects the investment/savings function of holding land, are not taxed, without requiring every homeowner to keep complex records of their expenses and a running balance account of improvements to their properties. At least in theory, it also presumably relieves some of the upward pressure on property prices that would be generated by including such capital gains in the VAT base. It shelters the government from exposure to negative revenue effects when, as they sometimes do, property values fall. Similarly, to the extent that the non taxation of the capital gain is reflected in the price of land, it reduces the costs of holding rental property and so, in theory at least, it ought to reduce rents. Whether or not it encourages homeownership, it gives the impression to taxpayers that it does and so is politically attractive.

103. The original plan was to exempt land from the New Zealand GST because it cannot be consumed, but it was decided that the apportionment required to separate consumable improvements from unconsumable land would add unnecessary complexity to the law when full taxation would be much more practical. It is clear from subsequent Inland Revenue publications that the drafters of the law did not originally intend the second-hand goods rules to apply to land. However, the option of excluding land from such treatment, which was canvassed in 1999, was not carried through: New Zealand Inland Revenue, *GST: A Review, A Government Discussion Document* (March 1999), Chapter 7.

[C] The Australian GST by Way of Comparison

[1] Non-residential Land

Most supplies of real property, other than residential property, are fully taxed under the Australian GST but some are GST-free (exempt with credit). The original plan was that Australia would fully tax all non-residential land, as is clear in this quote from the original tax reform plans that led to the introduction of GST:

> The construction, sale and leasing of all non-residential land and buildings, whether new or used, will be subject to tax. This treatment will allow virtually all businesses to claim *input tax credits* for the tax payable on such buildings they occupy or own. This will make the purchase or lease of a building effectively 'tax free' for them.[104] (Emphasis in original.)

However, in the law as enacted, some supplies of real property were made GST-free. The list of relevant GST-free supplies currently includes:

- The grant by Government of a freehold or similar interest (essentially ownership) in unimproved land, as well as leases preceding and leading to such grants.[105]
- A supply of land on which a farming business has been carried on for at least 5 years preceding the supply if the purchaser intends to carry on a farming business on the land.[106]
- Supplies equivalent to ownership interests in potential residential land subdivided from a farm.[107]

Most supplies in the second category, and many in the first, would be B2B supplies that would be fully creditable to the purchaser, so that there is no obvious need for GST-free treatment. On the other hand, treating land released by government for residential use as GST-free keeps the underlying land value out of the tax base when the newly developed residences are later sold under the margin scheme. A similar effect arises for the third category, which is clearly a concession to Australia's powerful farming lobby. As well as excluding the underlying value of the land from the tax base, the appreciation resulting from subdividing the land from the farm is also excluded from the tax base. Without this rule, the farmer would either have to supply the land in a fully taxable supply or, more likely, apply the margin scheme and tax only the appreciation on that proportion of the land during the time the farmer had owned the farm.

104. P. Costello, *Treasurer of the Commonwealth of Australia, 'Tax Reform: Not a New Tax, A New Tax System (The Howard Government's Plan for a New Tax System)'*, 97 (August 1998).
105. GST Act 1999 (Aus), ss. 38-445 & 38-450.
106. GST Act 1999 (Aus), s. 38-480.
107. GST Act 1999 (Aus), s. 38-475. Land is *potential residential land* if it is zoned to allow residential use but there is currently no residence on the land. The land from which it is subdivided must be land on which a farming business has been carried on for at least five years. In Canada, such supplies are exempt: see *Excise Tax Act, RSC 1985*, c E-15 (Canada), Schedule V, Part I, s. 9(2).

[2] Exemption for Residential Accommodation

As in New Zealand, Australia exempts supplies of residential accommodation and effectively applies a lower rate to supplies of long-term occupation of commercial accommodation.[108] The key exemption provides that a lease, hire, or licence of *residential premises* is input taxed, but not if the premises are *commercial residential premises* or supplies of accommodation in such premises. Suppliers of long-term *commercial accommodation* can also elect to treat their supplies as input taxed in lieu of applying the lower rate.[109] However, the supplies are input taxed 'only to the extent that the premises are to be used predominantly for *residential accommodation* (regardless of the term of occupation)'.

The boundaries of the exemption thus turn on the definitions of the terms highlighted in italics:

- *Residential premises* means 'land or a building that (a) is occupied as a residence or for residential accommodation; or (b) is intended to be occupied, and is capable of being occupied, as a residence or for residential accommodation; (regardless of the term of the occupation or intended occupation) and includes a floating home'.[110]
- *Commercial residential premises* covers similar ground to the New Zealand concept of a commercial dwelling and includes hotels, motels, inns, hostels, boarding houses, premises used to provide school accommodation, ships mainly hired out in the ordinary course of a business of doing so, ships used to provide entertainment or transport in the ordinary course of a business of doing so, marinas at which one or more of the berths are occupied by ships used as residences, caravan parks, camping grounds, and anything similar.[111]
- *Commercial accommodation* is defined as 'the right to occupy the whole or any part of commercial residential premises' and includes cleaning and maintenance, electricity, gas, air-conditioning or heating, and telephone, television, radio etc., if provided as part of the supply.[112]

The overall effect is that the exemption is less narrowly targeted than the New Zealand exemption. While the New Zealand exemption is targeted only at long-term accommodation, the Australian law also exempts shorter-stay activities such as home-stay, farm-stay, and similar accommodation.[113]

108. GST Act 1999 (Aus), Subdiv 40-B and Div 87.
109. A lease, hire or licence of a marina berth is also input taxed if it is occupied by a ship used for long-term accommodation and the supplier elects to treat the supply as input taxed in lieu of applying the lower rate.
110. GST Act 1999 (Aus), s. 195-1.
111. *Ibid.*
112. GST Act 1999 (Aus), s. 87-15.
113. Commissioner of Taxation (Australia), Goods and Services Tax Ruling GSTR 2000/20 'Goods and Services Tax: commercial residential premises' (21 June 2000), as in force at 12 May 2010.

[3] Exemption for Sales of Residential Property

A sale of real property is input taxed if the property is *residential premises* to be used predominantly for residential accommodation (regardless of the term of occupation).[114] However, it is *not* input taxed if the residential premises are *commercial residential premises* (as defined in the previous section) or *new residential premises*.[115] This approach requires a definition of *new residential premises* and the law provides that premises are new if they:

(a) have not previously been sold as residential premises (other than commercial residential premises) and have not previously been the subject of a long-term lease; or
(b) have been created through substantial renovations of a building; or
(c) have been built, or contain a building that has been built, to replace demolished premises on the same land.[116]

However, residential premises are not new if they have been used to make input taxed supplies of residential accommodation for at least five years since the relevant event that caused them to become new. This is different from the New Zealand approach, which has no notion of 'new' or 'old' dwellings and only exempts the sale of a dwelling if the *supplier* has used it for five years to make exempt supplies of accommodation in the dwelling. The need to determine whether or not a supply of real property is a supply of *new residential premises* adds a level of complexity to the Australian law that is avoided in the New Zealand law.[117]

Other problems with the 'new versus old' approach have also arisen, fuelled by the confused interaction between juridical concepts of real property law and the tax law concepts of residential premises and new residential premises. In a recent case, a property developer developed a combined commercial and residential building (including commercial areas, parking, and residential units) on land owned by a local council. The value added by the developer was not taxed when the developer sold what were clearly new residential units because the complex legal arrangements under which the development took place involved a long-term lease in relation to that part of the development area on which the residential units were located. The Court held that when sold by the developer, the units were not *new residential premises* because they

114. The law treats long-term leases (for a minimum of 50 years) as equivalent to sales.
115. A transitional rule means that new residential premises can be input taxed if they were used for residential accommodation (regardless of the term of occupation) before 2 December 1998 (the date on which the GST law was introduced into Parliament).
116. GST Act 1999 (Aus), s. 40-75(1).
117. Unforeseen interactions with other provisions of the law were used by taxpayers to transform new premises into old. For example, a supply by one member of a GST group to another is treated as if it were not a supply and a supply by the operator of an approved GST joint venture to a participant in the joint venture is not taxed. Within five years of enactment, it became necessary to amend the definition of *new residential* premises ensure that such sales were ignored in deciding whether a subsequent sale was the first supply of new residential premises. GST Act 1999 (Aus), s. 40-75(2A), inserted by *Tax Laws Amendment (2005 Measures No. 2) Act 2005*.

had previously been the subject of a long-term lease, despite the fact that the value of that lease did not include the value of the units.[118] Such a result could easily be avoided if, like the New Zealand law, the Australian law targeted GST at value added to land (including short-term capital gains resulting from development activities) during the course of an economic activity. Instead of focussing on whether the residential units were no longer new because they had 'previously been the subject of a long-term lease', the New Zealand law could have focussed on whether the developer had used the property to make exempt supplies of accommodation in a dwelling for five years. Since it had not, no question of exemption would have arisen.

As noted earlier, Australia uses margin scheme valuation rules for sales of real property, rather than an imputed credit for acquisitions of second-hand goods,[119] but this treatment is optional, applies only to taxable sales of real property, and depends on the agreement of the parties to the transaction. To illustrate the operation of the Australian law on the facts given for Table 8.9, some further assumptions must be made. One question that will arise will be whether TP1 can claim input tax credits for some or all of the improvements supplied to it by builders, on the basis that the improvements relate to the carrying on of TP1's enterprise (the Australian term for taxable activity). If credits are claimed, TP1 will need to work out to what extent they have to be repaid when it on-sells the property in an exempt supply. For the sake of illustration, Table 8.10 presumes that TP1 does claim the credits and then makes a decreasing adjustment to repay 95% of them, on the basis that 5% can be attributed to the making of taxable supplies and the remaining 95% are attributed to the input taxed resale of the property.[120]

In this case, over the five years, the total revenue raised is $ 437,200, less than under both of the New Zealand approaches. It is equal to the tax fraction of the sum of:

- the change in value during the period of ownership by the developer;
- the price of the improvements supplied to the two non-taxable persons (OO2 and RL1); and
- the price of the improvements supplied to TP1, minus the proportion of those improvements that was attributed to taxable supplies made by TP1.

Technically, this is a better result than the New Zealand approach because it clearly excludes the capital appreciation during the time the property was held by TP1, who does not actually add improvements to the property and whose value added is simply a result of capital appreciation. The difference arises because the Australian law exempts all 'old' residential properties, whereas the New Zealand GST does not always do so. However, the postulated situation (in which a residence is used wholly as a place of business without its character being changed) is probably relatively uncommon and the fact that the Australian GST might arrive at a better result in such cases comes at the cost of the complexities already noted in relation to determining whether a supply of real property is or is not *new residential premises*.

118. *Commissioner of Taxation v. Gloxinia Investments (Trustee)* [2010] FCAFC 46 (24 May 2010).
119. GST Act 1999 (Aus), Div 75.
120. This apportionment is required by Div 129.

Table 8.10. Australian Treatment of Land Moving In and Out of the Ring

Supply/Acquisition	*Price*	*Year 1*	*Year 2*	*Year 3*	*Year 4*	*Year 5*
OO1 sells to OO2	550,000					
Builder supplies improvements	77,000	7,000				
OO2 sells to TP1	660,000					
Builder supplies improvements	176,000		16,000			
TP1 claims input tax credit			-16,000			
TP1 sells to RL1 (residential; not new)	880,000					
TP1 makes adjustment for part of previous input credit (estimate)				15,200		
Builder supplies improvements to RL1	165,000			15,000		
RL1 sells to Developer	1,100,000					
Developer sells to new owner-occupiers	5,500,000					400,000
Revenue collected by tax authorities:		7,000	-	30,200	-	400,000

The complexity of the Australian law becomes even more clear when the margin scheme is taken into account. Certainly, the choice to use a margin scheme rather than a second-hand goods credit seems in hindsight to have been a mistake, as was the choice to effectively limit its use to new residential property by denying input tax credits to purchasers of land taxed under the margin scheme. The Division in which the margin scheme is enacted, which originally contained 717 words, has since grown to 4,848 words.[121] This compares with the New Zealand second-hand goods credit which, while it too has grown, still achieves its objectives in only 431 words. Most of the changes to the Australian margin scheme were required in order to respond to what might well have been predicted at the outset: taxpayers entered into a range of schemes to reduce the margin as much as possible. Such schemes involved intentionally making a non-taxable supply of the property before it became new residential premises but after most of the increase in value had occurred (e.g., by making a supply within a GST group or Joint Venture, or making a GST-free supply of a going concern, before selling to consumers). It is not surprising then, that the Australian Treasury released a discussion paper canvassing options for improvement, including the option of changing to the New Zealand model.[122] But as noted, it is not just the margin scheme that adds complexity but also the choice to target the exemption using a distinction between residential property that is and is not 'new'. On balance, the New Zealand approach is to be preferred.

121. See GST Act 1999 (Aus), Div 75 as at 6 January 2000 compared with at 1 July 2010.
122. See Treasury (Australia) *GST Margin Scheme Review – Consultation Paper* (12 May 2009).

[D] Zero Rating of B2B Supplies of Land in New Zealand

Both in New Zealand and in Australia, land transactions have created significant problems with both avoidance and evasion and a significant percentage of the disputes that come before the courts relate to real property transactions.[123] These problems mean that the full taxation model can result in significant losses to GST revenue, losses that are exacerbated by the nature of the property development industry. Developments are carried out by special purpose entities that are wound up after the completion of the development. Inputs are heavily front-loaded: in early stages of development the developers are in a net refund position and it is only towards the end of the development, when sales are completed, that output tax exceeds input tax.

Phoenix schemes, in which the supplier disappears before paying the GST but the customer remains entitled to the input tax credit, caused a significant loss of revenue in New Zealand, a consequence not discussed in *The Modern VAT*.[124] Other schemes were entered into to take advantage of timing mismatches between cash and accruals accounting: taxpayers entered into land transactions with deferred settlement terms, thereby attempting to fund the property development from the taxpayer's purse by generating large input tax credit claims (for purchasers who were accounting on an accruals basis) years in advance of the time when the output tax would be payable (by vendors who were accounting on a cash basis).[125]

As a result, New Zealand recently made sweeping changes to its GST treatment of real property. The initial proposal was to move to a domestic reverse charge for all B2B sales of land.[126] As well as the use of tax-aggressive structures to abuse the input tax credit entitlement, the Government was concerned about the effects of the high value of land, the infrequency with which it is traded, and the cost to suppliers of funding their GST output tax between the time when they are required to account for GST and the time when they are paid by the recipient.[127] Submissions in response to the proposals recommended zero-rating rather than a domestic reverse charge, the former being more consistent with the existing GST, particularly in light of the fact that New Zealand had already moved to zero-rating B2B financial supplies.[128] These recommendations were accepted and the legislation eventually enacted zero-rates all B2B supplies that include a supply of land.[129]

123. For a survey of the more important decisions in New Zealand, see Smith (n. 48 above).
124. Ebrill et al. (n. 19 above).
125. The scheme was eventually defeated in the Courts, but not without significant costs in pursuing litigation to the Supreme Court of New Zealand: *Ch'elle Properties (NZ) Limited v. Commissioner of Inland Revenue* (2004) 21 NZTC 18, 618.
126. *Options for strengthening GST neutrality* (n 80 above); *GST: Accounting for land and other high-value assets* (n 35 above). The proposals also suggested applying a domestic reverse charge to all supplies of going concerns and to transactions with a GST-exclusive value of $ 50 million or more.
127. Payment of the typical 10% deposit on land transactions generally triggers liability for the entire output tax.
128. Inland Revenue (New Zealand), *Changes to the GST Rules*, 23 Tax Information Bulletin 28–45 (2011) which cites ease of compliance as the main reason for preferring zero-rating.
129. All of the provisions noted in the following discussion were incorporated into GST Act 1985 (NZ), with effect from 1 April 2011, by *Taxation (GST and Remedial Matters) Act 2010*. The

A taxable supply of land is zero-rated if:[130]

> the supply wholly or partly consists of land, being a supply—
>
> (i) made by a registered person to another registered person who acquires the goods with the intention of using them for making taxable supplies; and
> (ii) that is not a supply of land intended to be used as a principal place of residence of the recipient of the supply or a person associated with them under section 2A(1)(c);

A new definition provides that 'land':[131]

> (a) includes—
> (i) an estate or interest in land:
> (ii) a right that gives rise to an interest in land:
> (iii) an option to acquire land or an estate or interest in land:
> (iv) a share in the share capital of a flat-owning or office-owning company, as defined in section 121A of the Land Transfer Act 1952:
>
> (b) does not include—
> (i) a mortgage:
> (ii) a lease of a dwelling:
> (iii) an interest in land in circumstances where the supply is made periodically and 25% or less of the total consideration specified in the agreement, in addition to any regular payments, is paid or payable under the agreement in advance of or contemporaneously with the supply being made:

The zero-rating depends not only on the recipient being registered for GST, but also on the use to which it intends to put the property. The law requires the recipient to provide the supplier with a statement regarding the key criteria (registration status, use to make taxable supplies, and non-use as a principal place of residence) and the supplier may rely on the statement.[132] If the recipient is not in fact registered for GST, it will be liable to pay GST on the supply and will not be entitled to an input tax credit, unless it becomes registered for GST and uses the land to make taxable supplies.[133] Where the recipient intends to use the land partly to make taxable supplies and partly to make exempt supplies, the supply will be zero-rated but the recipient will be required to account for output tax to the extent of the exempt use.[134] Where a dwelling to be used as a principal place of residence is included in a larger supply of land, the supplier must

---

original recommendations regarding high-value transactions were dropped but the recommendations regarding supplies of going concerns were effectively incorporated into the changes relating to land by providing that any B2B supply that *includes* a supply of land will be zero-rated. This will cover many supplies of going concerns.

130. GST Act 1985 (NZ), s. 11(1)(mb).
131. GST Act 1985 (NZ), s. 2(1).
132. GST Act 1985 (NZ), 78F.
133. GST Act 1985 (NZ), ss. 5(23), 10(7B), & 20(4B).
134. GST Act 1985 (NZ), s. 20(3J). Confirmation that it is not necessary that the recipient intends to use the land solely to make taxable supplies can be found in: 'Changes to the GST Rules' (n. 128 above), 29.

treat the sale as two separate supplies, zero-rating only that part that is not the dwelling and taxing or exempting the dwelling, as appropriate.[135]

The landscape of the New Zealand GST treatment of immovable property transactions has been radically changed now that these zero-rating rules are in force.

- Most supplies of immovable property between registered persons will be tax free. Because of the broad definition of land, this will include supplies of *profits à prendre* such as mining rights or rights to harvest timber, and equitable interests in land such as easements and restrictions on use.[136]
- Most commercial leases will be taxable supplies.[137]
- A limited number of recipients will reverse charge part of the GST to themselves when they acquire immovable property. This will apply mainly to banks making exempt supplies of financial services and to property that includes both a dwelling and other land, if the recipient intends to use the dwelling to make exempt supplies of accommodation or for personal occupation and the other land to make taxable supplies.
- Where land consists of a dwelling that the recipient or an associate will use as a principal place of residence, the dwelling will be excluded from the zero-rating.
- Timing benefits and detriments will no longer arise and phoenix schemes will be less attractive because the main source of input tax credits (the immovable property itself) will no longer be taxed. Where they do continue, the impact of such schemes on the GST revenue will be diminished.

Immovable property will be taxed when:

(i) sold to an unregistered person;
(ii) sold to a registered person, who will use the property:
    - as a principal place of residence (of the person or the person's associates);
    - solely for private purposes; or
    - solely to make exempt supplies of accommodation in a dwelling.[138]

The effect of these changes is dramatic to say the least. In respect of immovable property transactions, it is effectively equivalent to converting the New Zealand GST into something akin to a retail sales tax.

135. GST Act 1985 (NZ), s.5(15). See also 'Changes to the GST Rules' (n. 128 above), 29.
136. 'Changes to the GST Rules' (n. 128 above), 29.
137. This is the effect of paragraph (b)(iii) of the definition of 'land' cited above.
138. It is hard to conceive of a bank that would make only exempt B2C supplies of financial services, so a supply to a bank will be zero-rated and the bank will reverse charge to impose VAT on itself for an appropriate proportion to reflect the extent the land will be used to make exempt supplies.

§8.06 CONCLUSIONS

Section §8.05[A] set out the following recommendations by the authors of *The Modern VAT*:

(1) Construction services and materials should be fully taxed;
(2) Sales of commercial properties should be fully taxable, effectively raising no revenue;
(3) Sales of new residential properties should be taxed; and
(4) Resales of owner-occupied housing should be exempt, with no credits allowed for improvements purchased by owner-occupiers.[139]

What can we learn from the New Zealand and Australian experience that might cause us to modify these recommendations? From both countries, we can learn that recommendations (2) and (3) can lead to significant problems with avoidance and evasion. While recommendation (2) is an effective mechanism for minimizing cascading, raising no revenue except to the extent that immovable property is an input to exempt supplies (of which both countries have a very limited number), the risks of evasion that come with full taxation might justify the adoption of the new New Zealand approach of zero-rating B2B supplies. From Australia, we can learn that a literal application of recommendation (3) can lead to legal complexity, which itself leads to further risks of avoidance and evasion. From both countries, we can see that recommendations (1) and (4) are achievable, and that resales of leased residences should be included in recommendation (4). We can also see that approaches to determining the extent to which leased housing falls within recommendation (4) can vary, with a narrower approach being taken by New Zealand in order to target the exemption at supplies equivalent to owner-occupation, while a broader approach is taken in Australia in order to limit the number of small taxpayers who will be treated as businesses that are required (or allowed) to engage with the tax system by taxing their supplies of accommodation. The experience of both countries shows that the silence of the recommendations on the treatment of mere investment needs to be addressed, as does the treatment of movements of land into and out of the ring.

In section §8.03, I suggested that a VAT should tax only improvements to land and not the underlying land itself, which is unconsumable. Although neither New Zealand nor Australia appears to have specifically designed their GST treatment of immovable property with the objective of preventing the imposition of GST on the savings/investment element of land, both have partially achieved this effect by excluding or exempting sales of immovable property by mere investors, owner-occupiers, and residential landlords, thereby removing from the tax base the capital appreciation on immovable property during the time it is held by such persons, except to the extent that it results from taxed improvements. Both countries treat the short-term capital appreciation resulting from registration of development plans and

139. Ebrill et al. (n. 19 above), 98–99.

subdivisions of title as part of the tax base, even though this is more appropriately treated as the creation of a new form of unconsumable immovable property, rather than as improvements to the land capable of future consumption. Australia also exempts the capital appreciation on residential property once it is no longer new by treating the supply of non-new residential property as exempt. For simplicity, New Zealand taxes capital appreciation on residential land held by registered persons as part of their taxable activity (rather than as a mere investment independent of the taxable activity), except where the supplier uses the property for exempt leasing for more than five years.

Up to this point, this is not, after all, so distant from the design features of the European VAT. In the words of Advocate General Jacobs:[140]

> Under the Directive the supply and leasing of immovable property are in principle exempt from VAT. Those exemptions reflect the particular difficulties in applying VAT to such goods. Unlike ordinary goods, land is not the result of a production process; moreover, buildings, once constructed, may change hands many times during their life, often without being subject to further economic activity. Under the Directive the charge to VAT is therefore limited in principle to the supply of building land or of new buildings and the land on which they stand. The preparation of land for development entails economic activity enhancing the value of the land; and the supply of a new building marks the end of a production process. Thereafter repeated taxation of immovable property each time it is sold would not be justified. The same applies to the letting of such property, which is normally a comparatively passive activity not entailing significant added value; although an economic activity for the purposes of Article 4 of the Directive, the letting of immovable property is therefore in principle exempt from tax.
>
> However, while generally exempting the leasing or letting of immovable property, Article 13B(b) also provides for exclusion of certain transactions from exemption. The common feature of those transactions is that they entail more active exploitation of the immovable property justifying further taxation in addition to that levied upon its initial sale.

Advocate General Jacobs discussed the relationship between the exemption for leasing and the exception from that exemption for hotel accommodation, which was the subject-matter of the case, and then went on to say, in giving his answers to the questions posed to the Court:

> (7) – Supplies consisting in the alteration or repair of buildings are in any event separately taxable as supplies of services.
>
> (8) – Member States are permitted to grant taxable persons the right to opt to tax the supply or letting of immovable property under Article 13C of the Directive. The option is provided for with commercial property in mind. A vendor or lessor may prefer taxation of the supply or letting of commercial property to a taxable person who uses the property for the purposes of his economic activity and therefore has the right to deduct the tax charged. The vendor or lessor will then himself have the

140. Opinion of Mr Advocate General Jacobs in Case C-346/95, *Elisabeth Blasi v. Finanzamt München* [1998] ECR I-481.

> right to deduct any VAT incurred on the purchase, leasing, alteration or refurbishment of the property. The incurring of irrecoverable VAT by taxable persons in relation to the property is thereby avoided.
>
> (9) – It may be noted however that it was thought necessary to include an express provision in Article 4(2) of the Directive to make it clear that the 'exploitation of tangible ... property for the purpose of obtaining income therefrom on a continuing basis shall also be considered an economic activity' within the meaning of the Directive.

While the underlying logic is not dissimilar, two key features distinguish the EU VAT Directive approach from the approach taken by Australia and New Zealand. The most important difference is the latter countries' full taxation of all non-residential land and leasing, which more fully achieves the objective of ensuring input tax deductibility and preventing over-taxation and cascading. The second major difference is that both Australia and New Zealand prevent the capital appreciation in the hands of excluded persons from re-entering the tax base. Australia does so incompletely because of its use of an optional, constrained margin scheme; New Zealand does so incompletely because its second-hand goods credit, when applied to land, does not include the specific transitional function that is included in the Australian margin scheme. So long as Europe continues with widespread exemption, there may be no need to address the over-taxation that results from a failure to consider the re-entry of taxed land into the production chain, but any move to fully taxing commercial property will require careful consideration of the appropriate rules to deal with land moving back into the sphere of commercial activities.

From the above summary, the following list of more specific recommendations for the treatment of immovable property can be made:

(1) All construction services and materials should be fully taxed.
(2) No revenue should be collected on B2B supplies of non-residential property, other than when it is used to make exempt supplies. To achieve this, either:
    (a) the supplies should be fully taxed; or
    (b) the supplies should be zero-rated, with partially exempt purchasers required to reverse charge VAT.

    The zero-rating option is to be preferred because it gives better protection against evasion. Where the choice for full taxation is made, the law should incorporate design features to minimize the risks of evasion.
(3) B2C supplies of non-residential property should be fully taxed.
(4) B2B and B2C sales of residential property should be taxed but limits should be put on the extent to which tax is applied to capital appreciation that is not attributable to improvements. This can be achieved by:
    (a) only taxing when the property is 'new';

(b) only taxing if the sale is made in the course of the supplier's taxable (non-exempt) activities, with an exception for land used for residential leasing for a specified period;[141] or
(c) any other acceptable method.[142]

(5) B2C supplies of residential accommodation that are equivalent to owner-occupation of housing should be exempt.
(6) C2C supplies (sales and leases) of immovable property should be outside the scope of the tax and therefore effectively exempt, with no credits allowed for improvements.
(7) C2B sales of immovable property should be creditable, except to the extent that the purchaser will use the property to make exempt supplies. (In other words, an imputed 'second-hand goods' credit should be allowed.)
(8) A person should be treated as a 'consumer' for the purposes of the above recommendations if the person is unregistered, holds the property as a mere investment, is a residential landlord, occupies the property as a residence, or otherwise holds the property for private purposes.

141. The shorter the specified period, the more effectively the non-consumable element is excluded from the tax base.
142. An alternative not discussed in this paper, which might be suitable for developing countries, would be to treat all supplies of residential property as exempt, denying credits to the builder or developer who sells the property and requiring it to charge itself tax on the value of its salaries and wages. This could in fact more clearly exclude the pure capital appreciation due to changes in land title. It would also have the added benefit of not requiring refunds to be paid to property developers, a big advantage for an industry that can be notoriously difficult to tax effectively. On the other hand, for those whose perspective is that VAT is in reality a tax on business, the non-taxation of the developer's profit might seem objectionable.

PART V

Exemptions for Insurance and Financial Services

CHAPTER 9

VAT and Financial Services: Competing Perspectives on What Should Be Taxed

Harry Grubert and Richard Krever*

§9.01 INTRODUCTION

The taxation of financial services under a value added tax (VAT) presents both conceptual and practical challenges. This has resulted in a large literature and much controversy. This paper has two features. First, it analyses the application of a VAT to all major types of financial services, including investment services, consumer and business loans, payment services, credit cards and two types of pooling arrangements: gambling and insurance. The ways in which the VAT applies to these transactions frequently will vary depending on the type of service. A second feature of the paper is that it considers the appropriate VAT treatment of the transactions from the perspective of two views of 'consumption', the concept at the heart of the tax base for a VAT and all other consumption taxes. The paper also reviews the practical problems in implementing some of the conclusions, the policies that various governments have adopted and the proposals that have been put forward.

The alternative views share a common starting point – the VAT is a form of consumption tax with the aim of taxing final consumption. They also jointly recognize the practical limitations of a transaction-based consumption tax in contrast with the theoretically equivalent benchmark personal expenditure tax. The benchmark personal expenditure tax, sometimes referred to as a personal cash flow consumption tax, measures consumption in each tax period as total income derived in the period less

* This chapter was originally published in *Tax Law Review* 65 (2012): 199–239. Permission for republication is gratefully acknowledged. Any views expressed in this paper are those of the authors personally and do not reflect the views of the US Treasury Department. The authors are grateful to Alan Viard, who played a critical role in shaping the views of one co-author, and Ben Lockwood, who commented on the conference presentation of an earlier version of this chapter.

amounts spent to derive more income and amounts invested in savings.[1] All income not applied to one of these two purposes is presumed to be used for consumption. In contrast, a transaction-based consumption tax is imposed at the time consumption takes place. In the case of the VAT, the tax is collected from a registered supplier who may not know the purpose to which the supply of goods or services will be put. The structural features of the VAT, and particularly its reliance on registration to allocate the burden of tax to final consumption and to provide relief from tax for other acquisitions, make it difficult to engineer the appropriate outcome in a number of transactions involving financial supplies.

Unfortunately the benchmark personal expenditure tax does not provide firm guidance on the proper treatment of financial services. The conventional discussion of the equivalence of various types of consumption taxes does not consider financial services. In the usual description of the personal expenditure tax, any borrowing is treated as a dis-saving and included in the tax base and interest payments and the repayment of debt are treated as deductible contributions to savings.[2] The interest and principal would go to the saver who provided the funds and can now spend the proceeds on consumption. The basic writings on the expenditure tax, however, do not explicitly address the question of interest deductions where the borrowing involves financial services and embedded in the interest payments is a component to pay for these services.[3] The character of this component thus remains uncertain.

The divergence between the two views of consumption results from different focal points for identifying what constitutes consumption. The traditional expenditure view of consumption starting from the expenditure tax base (consumption is income minus amounts invested in savings) considers consumption solely from the perspective of the person making an expenditure, without regard to the impact of the outgoing on the person receiving funds or other persons. It is a broad view of consumption, catching any application of a person's resources apart from investment or savings. Under the traditional expenditure tax view, if the person making a payment for a supply cannot show that the outgoing was incurred directly in the course of generating income or acquiring an investment, it is assumed the expenditure was for private consumption.[4]

A different view of consumption, enjoying a respected heritage stretching back three and a half centuries to the work of Thomas Hobbes[5] and almost a century and a

1. The most important modern exposition of the expenditure tax is considered to be I. Fisher, *Income in Theory and Income Taxation in Practice*, 5 Econometrica 1 (1937), later refined by N. Kaldor, *An Expenditure Tax* (1955) (Gregg Revivals 1993); and Institute for Fiscal Studies, *The Structure and Reform of Direct Taxation*, 33–39, 150–204 (George Allen & Unwin 1978) available at www.ifs.org.uk/docs/meade.pdf [hereinafter Meade Report].
2. E.g., US Treasury Department, *Blueprints for Basic Tax Reform* (Washington, DC: Department of the Treasury 1977), 124–125; Meade Report (n. 1 above), 178; W.D. Andrews, *A Consumption-Type or Cash Flow Personal Income Tax*, 87 Harv. L. Rev. 1113, 1153–1154 (1974).
3. See Blueprints (n. 2 above), 124–125; Meade Report (n. 1 above), 151.
4. Cf. Blueprints (n. 2 above), 119–120, 135.
5. T. Hobbes, *Leviathan* (1651), 238–239 (R. Tuck ed., Cambridge University Press 1991).

half to John Stuart Mill,[6] and reappearing in much modern consumption tax literature,[7] relies on the conventional economists' utilitarian view based on total consumption in the country. In contemporary terms, this equates to a measurement of national consumption for national accounts purposes. This utilitarian view starts with a potential consumption pie comprising all available goods and services in society and identifies an individual's consumption as uses of real resources from the pool available to all participants in the economy.[8] If the application of personal resources does not remove goods or services from the pool, making them unavailable to others, the outgoing is not viewed as a payment for consumption.[9] The transfer of resources between people does not enter into the calculation of consumption under the social pool view.[10]

Another way of reaching this Hobbesian or social view of consumption is by way of a 'Pareto optimal' analysis. The Pareto optimal perspective seeks to maximize private utility subject to the government budget or resource constraint.[11] The policy is optimal in the sense that it aims to leave individual consumers with the maximum economic resources possible without making the government worse off. As Pareto optimal analysis focuses on the allocation of social resources, the analysis is not concerned with personal utility if maximizing personal utility does not involve an extraction of resources from the social pool (and thus making them unavailable to others or the government). The basic rule is that the expenditure on financial services should not bear tax to the extent the services generate increments in economic capacity so there is no net drain of resources available to society.

The differences between these two views might be seen in the simple case of a gift. In traditional income tax and consumption tax analysis, a cash gift is considered income to the recipient (the person enjoys an increase in economic capacity) and consumption to the donor.[12] In terms of the benchmark personal expenditure tax, the taxpayer has incurred an outgoing that was not applied to savings or investment and is thus treated as consumption. As the economic power transferred by this person could have been used to acquire goods or services in the market, it is assumed the donor must have derived utility equal to the goods or services forgone in favour of the gift.[13] The

6. J. S. Mill, *Principles of Political Economy* (1848), 34–35 (W.J. Ashley ed., Longman's, Green & Co. 1936).
7. See, e.g., C. Fried, *Right and Wrong*, 147 (Harvard University Press 1978); Kaldor (n. 1 above), 53; Andrews (n. 2 above), 1166; B.H. Fried, *Fairness and the Consumption Tax*, 44 Stan. Law Review 961, 962, 1016–1017 (1992).
8. E.g., Kaldor (n. 1 above), 53.
9. *Ibid.*
10. See K.C. Burke & G.P. McCouch, *A Consumption Tax on Gifts and Bequests?*, 17 Va Tax Rev. 658, 664-665 (1998).
11. J.M. Henderson & R.E. Quandt, *Microeconomic Theory: A Mathematical Approach*, 225 (2d ed.) (McGraw-Hill 1971) ('An allocation is Pareto-optimal if production and distribution cannot be reorganized to increase the utility of one or more individuals without decreasing the utility of others.').
12. See J.M. Dodge, *Beyond Estate and Gift Tax Reform: Including Gifts and Bequests in Income*, 91 Harv. L. Rev. 1177, 1199 (1978).
13. This approach was advocated by one of the strongest proponents of an expenditure tax, Kaldor (n. 1 above), 204–205.

social pool or Pareto optimal view, in contrast, would not consider the gift to be consumption by the donor as it does not reduce the consumption opportunities of anyone else.[14] There is no extraction from the consumption pie until the recipient uses the funds to acquire goods or services.

The two views of consumption yield different tax bases and, if one assumes that consumption is an appropriate measure of ability to pay, different measurements of ability to pay. Under the broader personal view, consumption and ability to pay are based on the exercise of command over resources. Under the social pool view, ability to pay is measured in terms of actual use of resources by an individual.

The two views of consumption also yield different perspectives of neutrality. The personal view of consumption seeks to achieve neutrality in terms of an individual's spending by imposing the same tax burden on all applications of income other than investment in savings. Under this view, the taxpayer should bear the same tax whether he uses income to acquire services or goods or gives away the money. The social pool view of consumption, in contrast, is not concerned exclusively with neutrality in terms of an individual deciding how to apply her resources. Rather, it also looks at neutrality in terms of the cost to the government of alternative consumption choices and accepts that the consumption tax can be non-neutral in terms of an individual's consumption choices. In part, the distinction arises because the government, and investors, have discount rates different from consumer borrowers and therefore evaluate cash flows differently. Financial services create a wedge between these discount rates.

The discussion in the following sections illustrates how these alternative perspectives apply to the key types of supplies encompassed within the VAT concept of 'financial supplies', a generic term used to describe a range of supplies including the supply of ownership rights in legal persons and relationships (shares in companies and mutual funds and interests in fixed trusts), the supply of financial pooling services such as insurance, and three types of supplies associated with loans: the supply of credit to borrowers, the supply of financial assets to lenders, and the supply of intermediary services linking borrowers and lenders.[15]

With a limited number of exceptions, countries using a VAT-style consumption tax treat all of these types of financial supplies as 'exempt' supplies, the misnamed description for supplies that attract no explicit tax liability but which nevertheless bear a tax burden as the supplier cannot recover VAT imposed on acquisitions related to the

14. Burke & McCouch (n. 10 above), 664–665; see also J.E. Stiglitz, *Pareto Efficient and Optimal Taxation and the New Welfare Economics*, in *Handbook of Public Economics*, 991, 1035 (vol. 2, A.J. Auerbach & M. Feldstein eds., North Holland 1987) ('Since giving increases the utility of both the giver and receiver it is doubly blessed …').
15. G.S. Cooper & R.J. Vann, *Implementing the Goods and Services Tax*, 21 Sydney Law Review 337, 387–388 (1999). Financial intermediary services are sometimes divided into four classifications: intermediation between suppliers and users of financial capital ('deposit-taking intermediation'); intermediation between persons with different exposures and/or tastes for risk ('risk intermediation'); intermediation between persons with exposure to similar risks ('the insurance function'); and intermediation between buyers and sellers of commodities, currencies and/or debt and equity securities ('brokerage services'). See C. Bakker & P. Chronican, *Financial Services and the GST—A Discussion Paper*, 7–12 (Victoria University Press for the Institute of Policy Studies 1985); T. Edgar, *Exempt Treatment of Financial Intermediation Services Under a Value-Added Tax: An Assessment of Alternatives*, 49 Can. Tax J. 1133, 1137 (2001).

supplies. The unrecognized tax is treated by suppliers as a cost of business and passed on to customers in the form of higher prices. As a consequence, both final consumers and intermediate enterprises along the production and sales chain who acquire exempt supplies are 'input taxed', meaning they bear an embedded tax in every exempt acquisition.

A common view is that the current treatment leads to under-taxation of consumers who face a tax burden equal to the tax on inputs used by the financial service provider, without any further tax amount for the value added by the service provider, and over-taxation of businesses who should be able to recover all tax imposed on inputs under a true consumption tax.[16] The alternative views of consumption noted earlier converge to support a conclusion that no taxation should apply to supplies of investment assets and services ancillary to the acquisition of investments, while they diverge to yield very different conclusions in respect to intermediary services provided to individuals borrowing for personal consumption purposes and some pooling transactions such as gambling or insurance.[17]

§9.02 REVIEW OF THE RECENT CONCEPTUAL LITERATURE

The economic literature on the optimal taxation of financial services under a consumption tax almost exclusively focuses on investment-savings services. The papers reviewed in this section rely on more or less formal mathematical models. In the parts that follow, we show that the basic issues can be illustrated in straightforward arithmetic examples that cover the wide range of financial services. They also illustrate the implications of the different views of a consumption tax.

Harry Grubert and James Mackie start with the individual's intertemporal budget constraint in a two-period model.[18] The individual has an endowment E in labour units that can be consumed now (consumption in period 1 = $C1$) or saved for next period ($C2$). In the no-tax case, $E = C1 + S$. There is a financial cost per dollar of the saving or capital good to acquire it. The saving S therefore buys $S/(1+f)$ of the capital good. The return on the saving asset is r. In the no-tax case, S therefore is able

16. The negative economic consequences of this over-taxation including cascading and vertical integration are reviewed in I. Lejeune, D. Stevens & M. Killer, *The International Direction in the VAT Treatment of Financial Services*, in *Value Added Tax and Direct Taxation*, 673, 678–687 (M. Lang, P. Melz & E. Kristoffersson eds., IBFD 2009).
17. The economic debate surrounding these viewpoints is summarized in D. Monacelli & M. Grazia Pazienza, *VAT Exemption of Financial Services in the EU: An Assessment of the Italian Case*, paper presented at the 63rd Congress of the International Institute of Public Finance, 2007, 1–3, available at www.editorialexpress.com/cgi-bin/conference/download. cgi?db_name=IIPF63 &paper_id=212. Many of the key contributions to the debate are set out in E. McCann & T. Edgar, *VAT Treatment of Interest and Financial Services with Competitive Banking and Insurance Sectors*, 30 Tax Notes Intl. 791, 792–794 (26 May 2003). Edgar concludes it will be difficult to assert with conviction that one or the other should be followed, and he proposes a half-way approach that would retain the current exempt treatment of financial supplies but build into the system provisions that would allow for taxation of some types of supplies based on pricing structures rather than the possible nature of the service to the recipient. Edgar (n. 15 above), 1168–1170.
18. H. Grubert & J. Mackie, *Must Financial Services Be Taxed Under a Consumption Tax?*, 53 Natl. Tax J. 23, 26 (2000) (discussion in the text is drawn from pages 26–28).

to buy $S(1 + r)/(1 + f)$ consumption goods in period two. Substituting for S in the original budget constraint, it becomes, $E = C1 + C2(1 + f)/(1 + r)$. The financial fee adds to the cost of future consumption and offsets some of the gross return. The trade-off between current and future consumption is 1 unit now versus $(1 + r)/(1 + f)$ next period.

With a VAT, if the tax-exclusive rate is t, the budget constraint is $E = C1(1 + t) + S$. If the financial fee is not taxed, a given amount of S will now be able to buy the same amount of the saving good as in the no-tax case, namely $S/(1 + f)$ and the individual's pretax income in the second period will therefore be the same. These proceeds will equal the amount spent on consumption in period 2, $(1 + t)C2$. Therefore S will be able to buy $(1/(1 + t))S(1 + r)/(1 + f) = C2$ units of consumption in period 2. Using this relationship to solve for S as a function of $C2$ and substituting for S in the budget constraint, the budget constraint now becomes $E = (1 + t)C1 + (1 + t)C2(1 + r)/(1 + f)$. But we can divide through by $(1 + t)$ and get $E/(1 + t) = C1 + C2(1 + r)/(1 + f)$. The tax is therefore the equivalent of a lump sum tax and the no-tax trade-off between present and future consumption is preserved.

Grubert and Mackie extended this argument beyond investment services to include consumer loans and insurance.[19] They did not consider, however, the government's budget constraint and implicitly assumed that the government would accept any choice of consumption patterns individuals find optimal even if the financial service costs used resources without any compensating increase in output from society's point of view.

Robin Boadway and Michael Keen criticized Grubert and Mackie for stressing that financial services do not enter directly into the utility function, but their solution is in fact very close to the one proposed by Grubert and Mackie.[20] Their main departure is to note the implicit assumption in Grubert and Mackie that the financial fee f is a linear (proportional) function of the asset acquired. They state that if there is any fixed element, it should be subject to the VAT.[21] That is not surprising. The tax in that case would become the equivalent of a lump sum tax. This non-linearity issue may arise in other contexts like the price of various sizes of machines.

Boadway and Keen did not apply their solution to financial services like consumer loans and insurance. They also did not explicitly consider the government's budget constraint.

Alan Auerbach and Roger Gordon relied on the equivalence between a VAT and a flat wage tax plus a tax on initial capital.[22] They stated that not taxing the fee 'ignores the presence of real inputs used in the production of financial services. If a labor-income tax in fact is equivalent to a VAT, then use of these inputs should not change when one tax is replaced by the other tax.'[23] The same argument can be made,

19. Grubert & Mackie (n. 18 above), 31-36.
20. R. Boadway & M. Keen, *Theoretical Perspectives on the Taxation of Capital Income and Financial Services*, in *Taxation of Financial Intermediation: Theory and Practice for Emerging Economies*, 31, 61-65 (P. Honohan ed., The World Bank 2003).
21. Boadway & Keen (n. 20 above), 62.
22. A.J. Auerbach & R.H. Gordon, *Taxation of Financial Services Under a VAT*, 92 Am. Econ. Rev. 411 (May 2002).
23. Auerbach & Gordon (n. 22 above), 412.

however, for the taxation of inputs used to produce machines. They did not explain why the tax treatment of investment services and machines should be different. In fact, both the worker producing the machine and the one offering the financial service are taxed when they consume.

One difference between Auerbach and Gordon on the one hand, and both Grubert and Mackie and Boadway and Keen on the other, is that Auerbach and Gordon model the financial fee as part of the price of the consumption good, not the cost of the investment.[24] Their argument therefore may fit consumer loan services or transaction services for consumer goods better than investment services. They also assume a given real discount rate without specifying how this relates to real rates of return in society after investment service costs. By contrast, the present chapter suggests that a complete analysis must describe how the government's cost of funds relates to private sector net returns.

In a recent paper, Ben Lockwood presents a general, formal model of investment intermediation by banks.[25] He also adds payment services, but he assumes that they are used only for consumption, not the purchase of investments.[26] He shows that under some circumstances, such as when payment services are a fixed percentage of consumption, there is a basic indeterminacy in determining which taxes are optimal because a tax on payment services is equivalent to an increased tax on consumption.[27] In general, however, Lockwood finds that a zero tax on investment intermediation is optimal.[28]

Lockwood's most general model assumes that payment services provided by banks are a substitute for the consumer's own leisure time,[29] which creates the familiar second-best problem because leisure cannot be taxed. As expected, this leads to a tax on payment services lower than the tax on consumer goods because it induces the individual to enjoy less untaxed leisure, and it is in fact zero in one not unreasonable case.[30]

Lockwood also introduces a model of bank monitoring in which banks can vary the amount of investment services they provide by varying the intensity with which they monitor the operations of their business borrowers.[31] He finds that if a bank has monopoly power in providing monitoring, a Pigouvian tax on intermediation services is optimal.[32] But this Pigouvian tax is really separate from the subject of this paper because the analysis suggests that Lockwood would impose the tax even if the VAT rate is zero.

24. Auerbach & Gordon (n. 22 above), 412–413.
25. Ben Lockwood, *How Should Financial Intermediation Services Be Taxed?*, University of Warwick Economics Department, Research Paper Series No. 948, 2010, available at www2.warwick.ac.uk/fac/soc/economics/research/workingpapers/2010/twerp_948.pdf.
26. Lockwood (n. 25 above), 7.
27. Lockwood (n. 25 above), 23.
28. Lockwood (n. 25 above), 17–22.
29. Lockwood (n. 25 above), 7.
30. Lockwood (n. 25 above), 15–16.
31. Lockwood (n. 25 above), 17–18.
32. Lockwood (n. 25 above), 5.

§9.03 OWNERSHIP ASSETS AND DERIVATIVE INSTRUMENTS

The supply of ownership assets (such as shares, units in fixed trusts, or interests in mutual funds) or derivative instruments (such as options and convertible notes) is commonly characterized as a type of financial supply.[33] Under any legal or economic test, there is no consumption character to the acquisition of investment assets and in theory this type of supply should raise few conceptual issues from a VAT perspective. The only practical question is how the transactions can be made tax-free in the context of the mechanics of an operational VAT. The question of appropriate VAT treatment of services ancillary to the acquisition of assets may involve some borderline characterizations that make articulation of the optimal benchmark more difficult.

[A] VAT and Services Ancillary to the Acquisition of Investments

On their face, ancillary services are simply part of the cost of acquiring an investment or savings, analogous to the stamp duty or the title registration fee incurred on real property purchases in some jurisdictions. As indicated above, that is the conclusion of most of the conceptual literature.[34] A personal perspective analysis would leave these services tax-free as there is no net expenditure by the investor; the use of services to acquire alternative investments is simply a cost related to the substitution of one type of savings with another type. A Pareto analysis approach would support this view, as it is presumed an investor would only incur costs for ancillary services such as brokerage if the average anticipated return from investments was at least equal to the risk-free rate of return available through government debt plus the cost of the ancillary services to access the alternative investments. If this is the case, the most efficient allocation of capital will generate higher returns for the investor and, via eventual taxation of the gains, for the government. In other words, while there is an extraction from the social pool by the investor using investment services, there is a compensating increase in taxable output through the more efficient allocation of the investment capital. Imposing a tax on part of the cost of acquiring the investment would amount to double taxation, reducing the return and distorting investment choices, discouraging the optimal investment, and leaving both the individual and government worse off.

This can be illustrated with a simple example. An individual has 100 units of value that he can save. Assume that the return on government bonds that the individual saver could always buy without having to pay a financial service fee is 10%. An investment intermediary charges 2% of the principal to manage the account. The saver would require a net return of at least 10% so a saver would use the investment manager only if the gross return on the investment is at least 12%. If the fee is not taxed, the saver will make the most efficient decision on whether to save and also in choosing between alternative investments. The government does not lose anything if the saver opts for financial advice and an alternative investment rather

33. E.g., S. Poddar, *VAT on Financial Services – Searching for a Workable Compromise*, in *GST in Retrospect and Prospect*, 179, 193–194 (R. Krever and D. White eds., Thomson Reuters 2007).
34. See text accompanying notes 18–24.

than no advice and the government bond. Even if the gross return is exactly 12%, the saver's consumption in the second period would be 110, the same as if the saver had bought the government bond, and the government's tax revenue from the consumption is the same. Furthermore, the government is also indifferent between the individual saving or not saving because it earns its normal borrowing cost if the individual defers consuming.

The view that services ancillary to the acquisition of savings investments are part of the cost of savings is not universally held, however. As noted in the review above,[35] an alternative view considers the ancillary and indirect cost of acquiring an investment as part of the ultimate consumption from investment returns and not the cost of saving.[36] The different conclusions reflect the different starting points for each approach. The first approach, which would provide similar tax treatment to the person who incurs a brokerage fee to buy a machine and the person who incurs the fee to buy shares in the entity that will buy the machine, seeks to distinguish consumption from savings at the time of investment. The second approach would treat the brokerage fee paid in the course of acquiring shares as part of the consumption if the investor ultimately plans on using the investment returns to buy consumption goods or services, and works back from a model based on tax mix change rather than one that looks directly at what is acquired with the outgoing.

[B] Removing VAT from Investments

The benchmark personal expenditure tax would leave the supply of ownership assets or derivative instruments free of tax. The challenge in the context of a transaction-type tax such as the VAT is how to achieve the benchmark. Removing tax from investments is relatively simple in alternative consumption taxes. The expenditure tax automatically exempts investments from tax by subtracting amounts spent on savings from the tax base. The retail sales tax can avoid tax on savings by suspending the tax on the supply of investment assets and associated services. But the VAT uses a unique process to eliminate tax on supplies that are not acquired for final consumption, initially treating every supply as a supply for final consumption, imposing tax across the board and then rebating the tax back to registered customers who did not acquire the asset in the course of personal consumption. Since registered customers are limited to persons carrying on a business or enterprise, passive investors are normally excluded from the rebate system and have no way of recovering costs incurred directly or indirectly in respect of the acquisition of financial assets.

35. See text accompanying notes 22-24.
36. The alternative view is illustrated in Auerbach & Gordon (n. 22 above), 412-413, who model the service fee as part of the price of the consumption good. The approach appears to find favour with de la Feria and Lockwood. See R. de la Feria & B. Lockwood, *Opting for Opting In? An Evaluation of the European Commission's Proposals for Reforming VAT on Financial Services*, 31 Fiscal Studies 171, 175 (2010). In contrast, Grubert & Mackie (n. 18 above), 25-28, model the fee as part of the cost of the investment asset. The approach taken by Boadway & Keen (n. 20 above), 62, is not dissimilar from that of Grubert and Mackie in this respect. See text accompanying notes 20-23.

The rule that VAT registration is limited to business enterprises arose initially as a consequence of the adoption of the VAT in Europe as a replacement for the business turnover tax then in use.[37] The target group for the replacement tax comprised the active businesses that were already registered for turnover tax purposes. Eligibility for registration and input tax credits or refunds remained limited as courts interpreted the definitions of business and enterprise narrowly.[38] Attempts have been made in some jurisdictions to extend the registration system to particular types of passive investors[39] but for the most part they remain ineligible for direct relief.

Using the ordinary VAT process - imposing tax on all supplies and registering customers entitled to a refund of tax to remove the tax burden on supplies of investment assets - is not a practicable solution. No VAT system could cope with the registration of every individual in the nation who holds investments and the subsequent claims for refunds of tax imposed on the supply of the investments. The logistics of registering this number of people, processing returns, auditing questionable claims and processing refunds would be overwhelming. Relief from consumption taxation could only be provided by eliminating tax on the supply of the asset in the first place. In the VAT, this can be done by treating the supply as a zero-rated supply (no tax is imposed on the supply and the supplier is entitled to full credit for all tax incurred on inputs used to make the supply).

There are two possible impediments to the use of zero-rating as a means of eliminating the tax on investments. It may be feasible to overcome the first, identifying appropriate types of financial assets to be subject to a zero-rating rule (shares, options, interests in investment trusts, and the like), but compiling an exhaustive list could be difficult. Also, care would be needed to ensure that the process does not create avoidance opportunities. An example would be the use of an interposed company to acquire personal consumption assets - creating a company to acquire a summer home or winter ski chalet, for example. If the issuance of shares to the company owner is to be treated as a zero-rated supply, complementary rules would be needed to ensure all benefits provided to shareholders or related persons (such as use of company assets) are taxable supplies.

The second issue, if a mechanism such as zero-rating were adopted to eliminate tax on investments by non-registered people, is how to identify qualifying ancillary

37. See, e.g., R.F.W. van Brederode, *Systems of General Sales Taxation*, 8 (Kluwer Law International 2009); K. James, *Exploring the Origins and Global Rise of VAT*, in *The VAT Reader*, 15, 16 (Tax Analysts 2011); R. Krever, *Designing and Drafting VAT Laws for Africa*, in *VAT in Africa*, 9, 15 (R. Krever ed., Pretoria University Press 2008).
38. An extreme early example was the decision of the Court of Justice of the European Union ('CJEU') in Case C-60/90, *Polysar Investments Netherlands BV v. Inspecteur der Invoerrechten* [1991] ECR I-3111, para. 13, ruling that a holding company was not entitled to input tax credits because it was not carrying on an enterprise. Realizing the damage that would be inflicted if the approach were allowed to stand, the CJEU retreated significantly from the extreme position in subsequent cases. See Case C-142/99, *Floridienne SA & Berginvest SA v. Belgium* [2000] ECR I-9567, para. 17; Case C-16/00, *Cibo Participations SA v. Directeur régional des impôts du Nord-Pas-de-Calais* [2001] ECR I-06663, para. 20; Case C-29/08, *Skatteverket v. AB SKF* [2009] ECR I-10413, para. 41.
39. Australia, for example, expressly included the activity of real property leasing in the definition of an 'enterprise' in addition to the normal business test. A New Tax System (Goods & Services Tax) Act, 1999, s. 9-20(1)(c)(Austl.), available at www.comlaw.gov.au/ Details/c2011c00924.

expenses, particularly where the type of service such as legal, accounting, or investment advice, is a type used for both personal consumption and the acquisition or maintenance of investments or where the service itself may contain a consumption element. Consider, for example, the investor who chooses a broker who charges 20% more than her discount counterpart, provides identical advice to the discount broker, but has a great sense of humour and provides service with such charm and wit that the investor is more than happy to pay for the premium brokerage service. Is the premium fee attributable to personal consumption by the investor over and above the investment advice and brokerage service? Or, is the difference between the two services akin to the difference between a veneer desk and a solid wood desk acquired by two different enterprises with the owner of the second business acknowledging his preference for the more expensive desk because he prefers to work on the aesthetically superior but functionally equivalent equipment?

There may be marginal personal consumption elements in a wide range of business and investment expenses. With few exceptions, however, both the income tax and consumption tax systems adopt a 'business and investment judgment' approach of not seeking to second guess the judgment of the business person or investor.[40] The exceptions are cases where it is assumed most of the expense is for personal consumption, the classic examples being food and entertainment expenditures supposedly connected with business activities. In these cases, particularly where the expense is one such as meals that the person would have incurred even if there were no business activity, tax systems often treat the entire expense or a substantial portion of it as personal consumption.[41] Subject to these exceptions, it is assumed that any personal element in business and investment acquisitions such as that of the investor who opts for the more costly kibitzer broker or the one with the more expensive desk is marginal and can be left out of the income tax or consumption tax without damage to the integrity of the taxes. Quite likely, the untaxed personal element, if any, is offset by higher returns or higher productivity in any case as the investor visits the broker more often and the businessperson spends more hours at the desk.

§9.04 LOANS

Loans enjoy a number of features that distinguish them from other types of financial supplies and supplies more generally and that consequently give rise to unique issues in the world of VATs. A key distinguishing feature is that the movements of loan funds

40. Section 162(a) allows a deduction for all 'ordinary and necessary' expenses paid or incurred in carrying on a trade or business. The Supreme Court has interpreted the ordinary and necessary limitation as '[I]mposing only the minimal requirement that the expense be "appropriate and helpful" for "the development of the [taxpayer's] business." The principal function of the term "ordinary" in § 162(a) is to clarify the distinction, often difficult, between those expenses that are currently deductible and those that are in the nature of capital expenditures, which, if deductible at all, must be amortized over the useful life of the asset'. *Commissioner v. Tellier*, 383 U.S. 687, 689 (1966) (quoting *Welch v. Helvering*, 290 U.S. 111, 113 (1933)).
41. See, e.g., IRC § 274(n) (limiting amount allowable as a deduction for any expense for food or beverages and any activity that is generally considered to constitute entertainment to 50% of the amount of such expense).

do not reflect consumption as is the case with, say, payments to merchants for the acquisition of goods or services. A loan creates an asset or type of savings for the lender and a debt obligation for the borrower but these bookkeeping annotations would not affect tax liability in a consumption tax. Rather, it is the use to which funds are put that should determine tax liability. So long as the lender acquires and retains a savings asset (a right to repayment of principal and payment of interest or discount while the loan is outstanding), the lender has merely augmented savings or altered the form of prior savings. The borrower, on the other hand, has had a 'dis-saving' (repayment of a loan is akin to saving) but should incur no consumption tax if the borrowed funds are used to acquire investments or are applied to business purposes.

The only significant conceptual debate encountered in the analysis of a VAT and intermediary supplies arises with respect to supplies to those who borrow for private consumption purposes. In this case, the two different views of what constitutes consumption yield different outcomes, ironically with the broader, personal expenditure tax view of consumption suggesting these services should not be taxed when provided to unregistered persons using borrowed funds for private consumption and the narrower Hobbesian view suggesting that intermediary services should be taxed in these circumstances. The broad view would treat the cost of financial intermediary services as part of an individual's personal non-taxable cost of shifting the time of consumption while the Pareto optimal view would treat intermediary services as a separate incidence of taxable consumption.

A second unique feature of loan transactions is the fact that those on opposite sides of the transaction often share the same financial services. While there are some direct connections between lenders and borrowers, as is the case, for example, with individuals who acquire debentures directly from corporations, most loans are provided through financial intermediaries, primarily banks, that provide a financial intermediary service of linking lenders and borrowers. The cost of this intermediary service is borne by both the lenders and borrowers and collected implicitly by the intermediary through the interest rate spread between a lower interest rate paid to depositors and higher interest rate charged to borrowers as compared with the rate they would have struck in a direct loan.

And finally, financial arrangements involving loans differ from most other transactions in the extent to which so many of the parties involved are not registered for VAT purposes. All private depositors and private borrowers investing or borrowing outside a business will be unregistered persons.

[A] Loans to Registered and Unregistered Borrowers: The Pure Interest Component

While the appropriate treatment in a VAT of financial intermediation expenses embedded in the cost of borrowing by final consumers is a matter of some debate, there is no dissent from the view that VAT should not be levied on pure interest charges. The case for not taxing interest charges is not entirely intuitive, however. To the lay person, interest paid for the use of money from a bank resembles, on its face, rental charges for the use of any other asset lent to a customer by a provider of rental goods. If consumption paid for by way of lease payments for a rental car is subject to VAT, why shouldn't payments for the 'rental' of money be treated similarly?

The answer is that the consumer using a rental car has tangible consumption while the receipt of loan funds in itself involves no consumption. The money can be used for consumption - the purchase of goods or services - but mere receipt of loan funds does not give rise to consumption. The basis for not taxing pure interest can best be illustrated with an example of a consumer expecting income of $ 110 in the following year and having the choice of borrowing in Year one to consume now or waiting until Year two to consume when the income is available. If the pure interest rate (the government's borrowing rate) is 10% and the consumer can borrow directly from the lender without incurring any expense for the services of a financial intermediary, a loan of $ 100 would be repaid with interest for a total cost of $ 110 the following year. A consumer thus has a choice of borrowing to buy $ 100 of goods and services today using borrowed funds or $ 110 of supplies next year using his own funds.

At first glance, it might be thought that the $ 10 interest payable for use of the borrowed funds looks to be the price the consumer has been willing to pay to shift the time of consumption. In this sense, the interest payment is the cost of choosing when to consume, which looks like a form of consumption akin to consuming goods or services. If, however, the effect of the time value of money is considered, the case for taxing pure interest falls away. If interest were subject to consumption tax at 20%, the consumer who borrows would be charged a 20% consumption tax on the initial $ 100 used to buy goods and services and then a further consumption tax on the $ 10 interest charge the following year when the loan is repaid. The tax paid would be $ 20 in Year one and $ 2 in Year two or $ 22 in total. In contrast, if consumption is deferred until the following year when $ 110 of goods and services are purchased, the consumer will pay $ 22 tax in Year two. It can be seen that the consumer would end up paying $ 22 in either case but most of it is paid a year earlier in the borrowing case. From the government's perspective, much of the tax from the borrower has been collected far earlier than the tax paid by the person who defers consumption. Once the time value of money is considered (the benefit to the government of collecting $ 20 tax a year earlier), it can be seen that the government ends up with more tax from the person who borrowed to accelerate consumption.

It would be impossible to maintain this disequilibrium. Since the government would be in a better position if interest were subject to consumption tax and consumers borrowed to accelerate consumption, there would be an inducement for the government to lower its tax on interest and encourage more accelerated consumption. But this policy would eventually lead to the elimination of the tax on interest.

To understand the process, it is convenient to consider the impact of the government's lowering of the tax in two steps. The first step is the reduction in tax at the initial borrowing level. This change would have no efficiency implications because it is a pure transfer from the government to the consumer. The consumer gains exactly what the government gives up.

The second step is the increased borrowing by the consumer in response to the lower tax. The consumer would not lose from this because it is a voluntary choice in response to the new trade-off between present and future consumption. The government would clearly be better off because of the increased borrowing and the consumer would be no worse off, yielding a net gain in national welfare. The government therefore would continue to lower its tax rate because national welfare would continue to increase until the tax falls to zero. It is only then that no further gains can be obtained. It follows that an initial attempt to impose consumption tax on interest would trigger a process that ultimately would lead to the elimination of the tax.

If interest is not subject to consumption tax, the consumer who borrows to fund accelerated consumption faces a $ 20 tax burden in Year 1 while the one who defers will bear a $ 22 burden in Year 2. In present value terms, the tax liability from accelerated and deferred consumption is the same. Unlike the case where the interest is taxed, if the interest is not taxed the tax system would have no effect on consumption decisions. The government, too, is indifferent between present or future consumption.

The time value of money can also be illustrated with the example of how VAT systems deal with consumer durables. When a consumer buys a durable (an asset with a life extending for several years), the purchase is similar to the acquisition of savings that is gradually drawn upon for consumption over a period of time. The consumption that derives from purchasing a durable is not the acquisition of the asset itself but the use of it over its life. It would be impossible, however, to impose consumption tax as the asset is consumed, even if the value of annual consumption could be accurately measured. The buyers of consumer durables are not registered and it would be very complicated to provide every consumer with a refund of VAT incurred on purchase of durables and periodic collection of tax from them as the assets were used. The solution is to tax the upfront acquisition of the asset, as the initial value of the asset is equal to the present value of periodic consumption over the life of the asset, and the tax levied on that purchase price is the present value of the tax that would have been payable if each period's consumption were measured and taxed separately.[42] This system is also self-correcting for private sales and purchases of used goods. The vendor recoups the value of VAT paid on any unused consumption as the market value of private-use used goods is based on the depreciated after-tax cost of goods, and the purchaser of used goods effectively bears the cost of the tax recouped by the seller.[43]

Thus, once the time value of money is taken into account, it can be seen that the person who shifts consumption forward and consumes less but pays tax on the consumption sooner ultimately enjoys the same economic benefit as the person who consumes more later but must postpone consumption by one year in order to do this. Put another way, in a consumption tax world, a consumer who accelerates consumption or defers consumption will have less to consume after tax than she would in a no-tax world, but the relative value of current to deferred consumption is identical if no tax is levied on the interest paid by the borrower until the lender uses it to consume.[44]

42. Blueprints (n. 2 above), 10.
43. The modern VAT used in jurisdictions such as Australia and Canada extends this treatment to residential premises, subjecting only the first sale of housing to tax. See Austl. GST Act (n. 39 above), s. 40-65, available at www.comlaw.gov.au/Details/c2011c00924; Excise Tax Act, R.S.C., C.E 15 ss. 123(1), 165 (1985) (Can.).
44. Edgar (n. 15 above), 1138-1144.

[B] Charges for Intermediary Services to Consumer Borrowers

The key question with respect to the taxation of financial services is therefore not the treatment of pure interest borne by private borrowers – the price of bringing forward consumption (and a tax liability) – but rather the financial intermediary charges that are bundled into interest.

If it is concluded that VAT should be imposed on intermediary supplies provided to all borrowers, those borrowing to derive more income (borrowing for business purposes) and those borrowing to make investments (borrowing for savings purposes) should be able to recover any VAT imposed, just as they do VAT imposed on other business inputs. The structure of the VAT may raise practical impediments – it may be difficult to identify the value of the intermediary service provided to any particular borrower, needed to supply a tax invoice and determine entitlement to an input tax credit, and in the case of unregistered borrowers using loan funds to make investments, there may be no mechanism to enable the borrower to recover the VAT, but it is likely these technical issues can be solved. The initial question, however, is whether the fees for intermediary services should be subject to a tax on consumption.

Perspectives on the character of financial intermediary services fall into two camps. One view is that all costs incurred to accelerate consumption are elements of an individual borrower's time preference value.[45] Under this view, the price for the intermediary service would be considered an ancillary charge for the provision of credit similar to interest and be excluded from consumption tax in the same way as interest.[46] This approach assumes that the present value of future consumption varies from borrower to borrower (largely dependent on their personal risk profiles, their need to access intermediary services, and the relative cost of arranging the loan given its size) and that any intermediary fees incorporated into the interest charged are simply further costs of bringing forward consumption that should be treated similarly to the pure interest rate.[47] The assumption under this view, thus, is that there is no utility to the borrower from these charges; rather, they are a means to an end, which is acceleration of actual consumption.[48] Whatever components are included in the borrower's cost of shifting consumption, the present value of VAT on accelerated consumption and the larger amount of VAT on deferred consumption will always be equal in economic terms to the borrower.

Under the contrasting social pool view of consumption, the intermediary cost would be dissected from the other costs borne by the borrower to shift the time of consumption and treated as the price of acquiring a separate taxable service.[49] While

45. See, e.g., Grubert & Mackie (n. 18 above), 23–25.
46. Grubert & Mackie (n. 18 above), 23–24.
47. N.-C. Chia & J. Whalley, *The Tax Treatment of Financial Intermediation*, 31 J. Money, Credit & Banking 704, 704–705 (1999).
48. Chia & Whalley (n. 47 above), 705; Grubert & Mackie (n. 18 above), 24. Employing a slightly different mode of analysis, William Jack also concludes that intermediary fees incorporated into interest spreads should not be taxed. W. Jack, *The Treatment of Financial Services Under a Broad-Based Consumption Tax*, 53 Natl. Tax J. 841, 842 (2000).
49. R. Carrol & A.D. Viard, *Value Added Tax: Basic Concepts and Unresolved Issues*, 126 Tax Notes 1117, 1125 (1 March 2010).

the individual might regard the higher interest charge incorporating an intermediary fee as the cost of shifting consumption forward, unlike interest, this fee is used to acquire actual services.[50] If the consumer-borrower were not acquiring these services, the capital and labour used to provide the services would be used to provide taxable goods or services to other persons. In other words, the acquisition uses real resources from the pool of economic resources and thus would amount to consumption under the social pool perspective.[51]

Importantly, the personal view, which treats intermediary charges as part of the cost of shifting the time of consumption (and hence yielding no separate utility to the borrower), does not consider the impact of the transaction from the government's perspective nor the revenue constraints that the government might face if intermediary services are not subject to tax. The present value of accelerated consumption (using borrowed funds) or deferred consumption will be the same for the consumer, which means the value of tax paid on accelerated consumption should equal the tax paid on deferred consumption. A problem arises, however, because the government has a discount rate different from the consumer's, one that does not include the consumer's intermediary costs.

In contrast to payments for pure interest borne by private consumers, which shifts the time of consumption but utilizes no real resources, payments for financial intermediary services are used to acquire real labour and capital inputs. Had the consumer chosen to defer consumption and spend the funds on other services, the alternative acquisitions would be subject to tax. For tax revenues from accelerated or deferred consumption to be equal, therefore, the acquisition of financial intermediary services by the person who accelerates consumption must be taxed in the same manner as the acquisition of non-financial services by the person who defers consumption. Only in this way will the total tax paid by the person who accelerates consumption equal the tax paid by the person who defers consumption and the decision to accelerate or defer consumption have no impact on the government's revenue constraint.

The revenue constraint consideration that arises in the case of the borrower is not mirrored in the case of the depositor or investor. There is a similar use of real resources, but the saver is not acquiring these inputs as an alternative to other forms of consumption. Rather the saver is acquiring the inputs in the course of saving for future consumption. As the anticipated gross return on the investment will be larger than the return anticipated from investments made without reliance on investment services, the government loses no revenue by treating the fees for investment services as part of the

50. Carrol & Viard (n. 49 above).

51. It has been suggested that the portion of the embedded financial services fee that compensates the intermediary for risk of default by the borrower is not payment for any service provided by the intermediary and the portion of the implicit fee representing compensation for risk should not be subject to tax, even if one concludes that the service fee to consumer borrowers should otherwise be subject to VAT. Carrol & Viard (n. 49 above), 1125. This view has not been widely supported, perhaps because the assumption of risk is in fact a central element of financial intermediary services. See A. Schenk, *Taxation of Financial Services Under a Value Added Tax: A Critique of the Treatment Abroad and the Proposals in the United States*, 9 Tax Notes Intl. 823, 831–832 (12 September, 1994).

cost of the investment. In contrast, borrowing for consumption does not yield extra taxable output to make up for the resources used in providing the service.

This can be illustrated with an example that adds a service cost to the pure interest case discussed above.[52] In that case, the pure interest rate (the government's risk-free cost of capital) was 10%. If a 2% service charge was added to the interest charge, the borrower would pay a total of $ 112 in Year 2 rather than $ 100 in Year 1. This individual's personal cost of accelerating consumption would be 12% and in a tax-free world, the choice would be between $ 100 of consumption in Year 1 or $ 112 of consumption in Year 2. With a tax-inclusive tax rate of 20% and no tax on the financial service, the choice would be between $ 80 of consumption in Year 1 or $ 89.60 in Year 2. The trade-off remains the same as in the no-tax case because 89.60/80 = 112/100 = 1.12. On this basis Grubert and Mackie, and by implication Boadway and Keen, concluded that not taxing the service fee is efficient and maintains neutrality between accelerated and deferred consumption.[53] The tax appears to be the equivalent of a lump sum tax because the trade-off between present and future consumption is the same as in the no-tax case.

But introducing the government's budget constraint shows that the Grubert-Mackie/Boadway-Keen conclusion does not apply to consumer loans. The individual's choice between present and future consumption is based on a discount rate that includes a service fee. The government's discount rate does not include the 2% discount fee used in this example as it can borrow directly, without the need for a financial intermediary. Unlike private consumer borrowers, a government does not need to be examined initially and continuously monitored to attract loan funds. Consider what happens if the individual consumes a dollar less in the Year 1 and could therefore consume $ 1.12 more in Year 2. The government therefore would lose $ .10 of revenue in the Year 1 and gain $ .112 more in Year 2. It therefore would be better off because it would get a return of 12% and its normal cost of borrowing is only 10%. The government in this case could start raising the tax on the fee to induce the individual to defer consumption.

Then, as above, it is convenient to divide the effect of the government's raising its tax on the service into two steps. The first step is the effect of imposing the tax on the amount of financial services the consumer-borrower uses before the government starts imposing its tax. That is now a simple transfer of funds from the consumer to the government that leads to no overall welfare loss. The government would be better off exactly by the amount the individual would be worse off. The second step is the effect of the individual deferring consumption because accelerated consumption is now relatively more expensive. The prospective borrower would be no worse off if she chooses to consume less in Year 1 because it is a voluntary response to a new trade-off between present and future consumption. The government, however, would be better off.

The government could continue to raise its tax rate on the financial services until it is equal to the normal rate on other consumption. At that point the tax on

52. See Section §9.04[A].
53. Boadway & Keen (n. 20 above), 61–65; Grubert & Mackie (n. 18 above), 24.

intermediary services from borrowings is exactly equal to the tax it would collect if consumers chose not to borrow and instead consume in Year 2. The government no longer benefits from further deferral of consumption. Any further rise in the tax rate on intermediary services would cause the government to lose more tax revenue on reduced borrowing than it would enjoy on the deferred consumption. The government's loss would be greater than any gain the consumer would obtain by reacting to the higher tax. At the point at which the tax settles, the prospective borrower would face the true social cost of borrowing, including the resources used in providing the service.

The revenue constraint consideration is significant. If resources used to provide financial intermediary services are not taxed and alternative consumption is, the tax treatment will by itself distort consumption decisions, with further distortions caused by the government's need to impose higher taxes on services that are taxed to maintain revenues that would have been realized with lower rates imposed on a broader base. The revenue constraint consideration has altered the views of one of the present authors who has argued there is no personal utility from the use of financial intermediary services by consumer borrowers and has led him to suggest nevertheless that the services should be taxed.[54]

[C] Leases

Another argument used to make the case for taxing borrowers on the cost of intermediation services is based on the comparison of the person who borrows to buy a consumer durable and the person who leases the durable. If lease payments are subject to VAT while explicit financial services are not taxed (or are only input taxed as exempt financial supplies, as at present), there would appear to be inconsistent treatment between the lessee and the person who borrowed to buy the same asset.[55]

The comparison between leases and financial supplies is only directly relevant in respect of one type of lease that contains a notional loan element and, incorporated into that loan, a financial intermediary charge. This is a 'finance loan', based on a sale of an asset with vendor-provided finance. Although the transaction is in substance a conventional amortizing loan (based on blended payments of interest and principal repayment), in form it takes the legal title of a 'lease' and the blended loan payments are labelled 'lease' payments in the contract.

Finance leases take two forms. Some are designed as 'balloon' payment transactions where the 'lease' period is for less than the effective life of the purchased asset and the borrower/lessee makes a balloon payment at the end of the lease equal to the difference between the principal repaid at that point and the market value (if the market value is less than the principal repaid, the lender/lessor refunds the difference). Others are structured as 'effective life leases' with a similar adjustment made at the end of the lease.

54. The Hobbesian (Pareto optimal) analysis of consumer loans here differs from Grubert & Mackie (n. 18 above).
55. J.M. Mintz, *Taxing Financial Activity*, 58 Bull. Intl. Tax. 99, 108 (2004).

In this case in which the lease is the equivalent of a loan, the different perspectives on whether loan services should be taxed apply. Finance leases are to be contrasted with operating leases, which are simple rental services involving no transfer of ownership (and attendant risks) to the lessee and no element of financial supply with an accompanying financial intermediary charge.[56] Operating leases, devoid of loan elements and implicit financial intermediary charges, are fully taxed under the VAT as the entire rental cost borne by the lessee is for consumption of the service provided;[57] there is no explicit financing or purchase of property involved.[58]

Accounting principles look beyond the notional title of the financing arrangements as 'leases' and treat them as blended payment loans for financial accounting purposes.[59] Financial accounting characterization is followed in some jurisdictions for VAT (and income tax) purposes.[60] In these cases the notional 'lease' payments are treated as financial supplies.[61] In most jurisdictions, financial supplies fall into the category of exempt (input taxed) supplies.[62] This means the financial intermediary component of the borrower/lessee's payments is subject to input tax that cannot be recovered by business borrowers, leading to over-taxation of these enterprises.[63] At the same time, depending on the view of consumption one takes, consumer borrowers may be undertaxed for the reasons reviewed earlier.[64]

In other countries, the notional form of the transaction as a 'lease' is respected for VAT purposes, and the so-called 'lease' payments are subject to tax as if they were ordinary operating lease payments.[65] Registered customers may benefit if they acquire an asset by way of a finance lease in a jurisdiction that treats a finance lease as if it were an operating lease. Had the transaction been structured as an explicit loan, it would be an exempt supply and the intermediary financial service of the lender would be subject to input taxation in most jurisdictions.[66] If the loan is characterized as a lease payment, the borrower/ lessee will be subject to VAT on the full lease payment and at the same time will be entitled to offsetting credits for the full amount of the VAT.[67] Treating a finance loan as if it were an operating lease is thus a simple backdoor way for VAT jurisdictions to remove all VAT from the financial service provided to business customers under current rules.[68]

56. M. Fletcher et al., *Leasing in Development: Guidelines for Emerging Economies*, 2–4 (International Finance Corporation 2005) available at rru.worldbank.org/Documents/Toolkits/Leasing/Leasing_in_Development_Full.pdf.
57. See Fletcher et al. (n. 56 above), 44–48.
58. Fletcher et al. (n. 56 above), 2.
59. Fletcher et al. (n. 56 above), 31.
60. L. Burns & R. Krever, *Taxation of Income from Business and Investment*, in *Tax Law Design and Drafting*, 597, 661 (vol. 2, V. Thuronyi ed., International Monetary Fund 1998).
61. Fletcher et al. (n. 56 above), 21.
62. Fletcher et al. (n. 56 above), 48.
63. *Ibid.*
64. See Section §9.04[A].
65. Burns & Krever (n. 60 above), 660.
66. See Fletcher et al. (n. 56 above), 49, tbl.3–4.
67. Burns & Krever (n. 60 above), 660–661.
68. *Ibid.*

If the customer of a finance lease is a final consumer and the jurisdiction treats the finance lease as an operating lease for VAT purposes, the lessee will pay VAT on the full amount of the lease payment, including the notional interest component and the financial intermediary fee component of the notional loan.[69] From the personal expenditure tax point of view, a VAT on the initial price of the asset and no tax on the financial service is equivalent to a VAT on the lease payments as in an operating lease.[70] The reason is that the personal expenditure tax view considers the individual's discount rate to be the appropriate basis for evaluating future payments.[71] From the perspective of a final consumer, treating a finance lease as an operating lease yields the same outcome as treating it as a sale and loan in terms of present values based on the consumer's discount rate. The consumer's discount rate is higher than the government's because it includes the cost of financial intermediation over and above the government borrowing rate. Even though it might appear that the consumer has to pay more tax if the finance lease is treated as an operating lease and a full VAT is paid on the lease payments that include the cost of financial intermediation, this is offset by the fact that the consumer will evaluate the future payments with a higher discount rate.

At this point, the personal expenditure tax and Hobbesian views agree that the full taxation of lease payments is the correct policy. The Hobbesian view takes the government's budget constraint and its borrowing costs into consideration. It therefore regards the characterization of a finance lease as an operating lease for VAT purposes as a move to the appropriate tax treatment of the arrangement. From the government's point of view, the present value of taxes on the lease payments exceeds the upfront tax on the value of the asset because the lease payments reflect the financial intermediation costs in addition to the pure interest component. The Hobbesian view would regard the full taxation of the lease payments as applying to the correct measure of consumption – the government bond rate applied to the principal, the depreciation of the asset, *and* the financial service cost.

Of course, the substantive difference between finance leases and operating leases may be unimportant for the purposes of the analysis of a VAT in contrast to its importance for the analysis of a balance sheet. The main difference between the leases is who bears the price risk for the asset at the end of the lease.[72] In the finance lease, the lessee bears the risk and in the operating lease the lessor bears the risk.[73] The payment under the operating lease will therefore include compensation to the lessor for bearing this risk.[74] The other components of the lease payments, namely the interest, depreciation, and the financial service cost, are the same.[75] If there is no uncertainty

69. See Fletcher et al. (n. 56 above), 49, tbl.3-4; 50, fig.3-6(a).
70. See S. Cnossen, *A VAT Primer for Lawyers, Economists, and Accountants*, 124 Tax Notes 687, 689 (17 August 2009).
71. *Ibid.*
72. Fletcher et al. (n. 56 above), 3, tbl.1-1.
73. *Ibid.*
74. Fletcher et al. (n. 56 above), 2.
75. Fletcher et al. (n. 56 above), 17–18.

over the future value of the asset or the leases extend to the end of its useful life, the substantive difference disappears.[76]

[D] Transaction Services

Banks provide various kinds of transactions services to depositors. Were ownership of a loan asset in the form of a bank account or term deposit, the only benefit derived by a depositor as a consequence of the intermediary charge collected by financial institutions, it would be simple to conclude that the fee is incurred wholly for the acquisition of an investment and therefore should be shielded from VAT.[77] Normally, however, tacked on to a deposit account are a range of services that allow the investor to withdraw some of his or her savings for the purpose of investment elsewhere or consumption. These include access to the account in various locations via ATMs, internet transfer options, direct debit cards, automatic payment systems and cheque facilities.[78]

In some cases, financial institutions impose explicit charges for withdrawals from savings while in others they are collected implicitly as a reduction in the interest rate paid on the deposits.[79] However the fees are charged, the cost of withdrawal services varies with the ease of withdrawal.[80] Accounts paying the highest returns usually have the most restrictions on withdrawals, often accompanied by explicit withdrawal fees, while those paying lower returns provide progressively greater access to withdrawals.[81] The extreme case is the zero interest account that provides unlimited cheque or withdrawal facilities. In this case, viewed in isolation, the depositor appears to derive no benefit from saving apart from safeguarding the deposit. Most likely, however, the depositor using a no-interest chequing account would also hold another higher-interest savings account with fewer or no chequing options. The sacrifice in cash income in the no-interest chequing account is an implicit payment for the transaction services.

There are two views on the character of implicit or explicit charges imposed for withdrawal services. Under one view, the cost of retrieving savings should be coloured

76. Fletcher et al. (n. 56 above), 33, 35.
77. Hoffman, Poddar, and Whalley would tax households on financial services related to both borrowing and deposits, though the rationale for extending the tax to savings by unregistered businesses is not made clear. See L. Arthur Hoffman, S.N. Poddar & J. Whalley, *Taxation of Banking Services under a Consumption Type, Destination Basis VAT*, 40 Natl. Tax J. 547, 552–553 (1987).
78. See, e.g., Deposit Agreement and Disclosures, Bank of America pts. XIX & XXII. https://www3.bankofamerica.com/efulfillmentODAO/new_window_np.cfm?appURL=https://www2.bankofamerica.com/efulfillment/&showdaddoc=91-11-2000ED&daddoc2use=20110805&type=1&view=htm (last visited 16 June 2012) (providing online banking and funds transfer services).
79. Compare Bank of America (n 78 above), pt. VI.F (charging fees for certain withdrawals from savings accounts), with pt. VI.D (fixing interest payment to interest-bearing saving account's daily balance).
80. Bank of America (n. 78 above), pt. VII.H (imposing 1% penalty on early withdrawals from CDs with less than twelve months terms and imposing 3% penalty on early withdrawals from CDs with terms of twelve months or more).
81. *Ibid.*

by the use to which the withdrawn amounts are put. Under this view, the cost of a cheque or ATM withdrawal (or the implicit fee embedded in the lower interest rate on deposits) should be subject to tax if the withdrawn amount is applied to final consumption and exempt from tax if it is reinvested elsewhere or used to cover business or investment expenses.

Under the alternative view, the service of returning part of the investment to the depositor provides no consumption benefit to the investor but rather it is through the application of the returned funds that the investor converts her savings into consumption.

Perhaps one way to resolve this difference is to consider the nature of the withdrawal service. If the service is simply a direct return of investment, and withdrawals through a particular type of account incur a service fee, the fee can be seen as the cost of accessing savings, a service that involves no direct consumption and which therefore should not bear tax. By way of contrast, other withdrawal methods may involve both a withdrawal of funds from savings plus a delivery service. Thus, for example, an ATM fee is primarily a charge for delivery of cash to the depositor's location. Similarly, a charge for the use of a cheque is a charge for the delivery of withdrawn funds to the account of the beneficiary of the cheque. To the extent the charge associated with the withdrawal of savings is a fee for the convenient delivery of an investment return the account holder has received a service distinct from withdrawal.[82] For example, an individual may keep a small balance in a no-interest chequing account in order to make day-to-day consumption purchases. The forgone interest in this case is an implicit charge for withdrawal and delivery services and should be taxed as part of the cost of final consumption. On the other hand, in the case of an interest-bearing asset with no transaction privileges, any charge for final liquidation and withdrawal should be treated like any investment cost.

Importantly, the conceptual question of whether the service of returning funds to the depositor amounts to consumption or is ancillary to a further savings investment is separate from the question as to whether a VAT could accommodate different tax outcomes if it is decided that the character of withdrawal transaction services depends on the use to which withdrawn funds are put. It may be impossible in the context of a VAT regime to provide alternative treatments for withdrawal expenses depending on the use to which the funds are put as the financial institution has no way of knowing how the goods or services bought with a cheque, ATM withdrawal, or online transfer will be used.

[E] Credit Card Services

Credit card issuers offer a variety of services to cardholders and to the merchants that accept the cards as payment. Merchants are provided with payment transaction

82. In contrast to Lockwood, we are here abstracting from the individual's labour-leisure trade-off. See Lockwood (n. 25 above), 3. If the more convenient, more costly transaction mode induces the individual to give up untaxed leisure and work more, second-best considerations would suggest a lower VAT on the service. This is a complication applying to many types of taxes.

services that include the credit card providers' sale-enhancing services (bringing credit card customers to the retailers) and payment systems (enabling the retailers to avoid problems with non-sufficient-funds cheques). Cardholders are provided with implicit loans for the 'no-interest' grace period if the merchant is paid by the credit card company when the transaction is processed and the convenience of a payment system. They may also enjoy ancillary benefits such as loyalty points.

The services provided by credit card issuers to cardholders and to merchants are therefore a combination of transactions, payment services and loans, and to the extent payments are attributable to the latter, they will cover both explicit or implicit interest and financial intermediary fees. The analysis provided earlier of the optimal VAT treatment of each of these types of services therefore should apply to fees and charges associated with the use of credit cards. The problem arises because the different services require disparate tax treatment, and it is difficult to match any of the payments with a particular service or component of a service. The interest charges for loan balances are a combination of pure interest, which should not be taxed, and the bank's service fee, which should be taxed, at least under the Hobbesian view. The merchant's fee payable to the card issuer when the transaction is processed includes payment for the transaction services and the consumer's implicit interest during the grace period. The annual fee is presumably for the privilege of using any of these services and a surcharge payable by the consumer may also be for any of these services.

Disputes have arisen regarding the character for VAT purposes of three types of charges associated with credit card use: annual fees by cardholders, explicit surcharges paid by consumers to merchants when settling an account with a credit card in some jurisdictions, and the charges paid by retailers to credit card providers. Only the last of these is universal, though the first is not uncommon. In a few jurisdictions retailers are allowed to pass the charges they pay to credit card providers on to customers by way of a surcharge.[83] Where this is not allowed,[84] retailers recover the cost of their fees to card issuers by embedding the expense in higher prices for goods or services, a process that leads to customers paying cash subsidizing those paying with credit cards.

The fee paid by the retailer is often treated as the cost of a non-financial taxable service,[85] allowing the merchant to recover the tax as an input tax credit.[86] In contrast, the surcharge sometimes is treated as part of the cost of the underlying goods or services and imbued with the same character as the underlying service or goods. That is, it is assumed the merchant in effect has a dual pricing system, selling the same goods or services at a higher price if the customer wishes to pay by credit card. If the acquisition is entitled to a tax expenditure subsidy and treated as a zero-rated, exempt,

83. This is the case in Australia, for example.
84. See, e.g., Cal. Civ. Code § 1748.1 (West 2009) (prohibiting surcharges for credit card payments); Colo. Rev. Stat. § 5-2-212 (2002) (same).
85. See *Costco Wholesale Canada v. The Queen* [2009] TCC 134, para. 44 (Can.).
86. See *Costco* (n. 85 above).

or concessional rate supply, that treatment applies to both the payment for the goods or services and surcharge for payment by way of credit card.[87]

Viewed from the personal consumption perspective, this policy of attributing the character of the underlying supply to the credit card surcharge is questionable – the customer is clearly willing to pay a premium for the use of a particular payment system over and above the cost of the goods or services supplied. In these circumstances, the customer must perceive a benefit separate from the supply that could have been purchased for a lower cost with cash.

Viewed from a Pareto optimal perspective, the outcomes are problematic, but no more so than any alternatives available. The merchant's fee to the credit card company and the surcharge paid by the retail customer to the retailer when paying by credit card are in part intended to cover the interest and intermediary services portions of the implicit loan for the grace period made to the retail customer. It is, however, impossible to dissect the payment and identify exactly what part of the merchant's fee or the customer's surcharge serves any particular purpose. In these circumstances, the practice of treating merchants' fees to card companies as consideration for taxable supplies and retail customers' surcharges as part of the cost of acquiring underlying goods and services, or alternatively as separate taxable supplies, may yield the only practical outcome. In a sense, the implicit loan is no different than the implicit credit provided by the utility company that bills subscribers in arrears at the end of the billing period or the grace period handed customers by the tradesperson or professional who bills a client rather than demanding cash at the time of the service. For similar practical reasons, no attempt is made to dissect these invoices into fees for services and implicit interest components.

[F] Reforming the VAT on Financial Intermediary Services

There is still no agreement on the appropriate VAT treatment of financial intermediary supplies to consumer borrowers, and the lack of consensus may help explain in part why many commentators have advocated treating consumer loans as exempt supplies, leaving them partially taxed.[88] Concern that input taxation of these supplies creates a bias towards vertical integration and in-house provision of services that could be acquired from possibly more efficient external suppliers of these supplies has led some advocates of the exempt treatment to suggest financial institutions be allowed partial input tax credits, to reduce the tax burden on all or selected outsourced inputs to the supplies,[89] an approach now used in Australia.[90] Clearly a preferable solution would be to tax the value in full if it is concluded the services should be taxed when provided to

87. See, e.g., *In re Waverley Council v. Federal Commissioner of Taxation* (2009) 73 ATR 243, 247–50 (Austl.) (holding that the surcharge imposed on a credit card user was a cost of acquiring the zero-rated service for which the consumer was paying).
88. Edgar (n. 15 above), 1193.
89. Edgar (n. 15 above), 1187.
90. The partial input tax credit for outsourced acquisitions is a feature of the Australian GST system. Austl. GST Act (n. 39 above), Div. 70.

consumer borrowers, with full input tax credits to the service providers, or to remove all tax if it is concluded the services should not be taxed.

While there may be some debate in respect of the appropriate tax treatment of intermediary services to consumer borrowers, there is little debate as to the need to remove the VAT from intermediary supplies to depositors and business borrowers.[91] This outcome follows automatically in the context of an expenditure tax and is relatively easy to achieve in a transaction tax such as a retail sales tax that suspends all tax on business-to-business transactions. There is, however, no simple way to fit loan transactions into the standard VAT system as it is impossible to calculate the value of a supply of intermediary loan financial services on a transaction-by-transaction basis, a cornerstone principle of the VAT where the charge is levied through a margin on interest rates paid and payable.[92]

It is, however, possible to determine the value of the services indirectly at the level of the financial institution providing intermediary services and then collect VAT from the service provider. Four methods of applying VAT in this way have been devised: a 'subtraction' calculation, an 'addition' calculation, a 'cash flow' calculation and a 'reverse-charge' calculation.[93]

The subtraction method is based on the calculation from business accounts of value added as gross revenue less allowable purchases.[94] The addition calculation measures the value of intermediation services using a formula based on taxable income plus wages and salaries.[95] The cash flow method measures the value of intermediation services by tracking the gross cash flows of the financial intermediary – the deposits it receives and repays and the loans it makes and those that are repaid.[96] The reverse-charge method involves a financial intermediary notionally imposing tax on the

91. Edgar (n. 15 above), 1147–1149, 1153.
92. No similar problem arises with financial services for explicit fees but surprisingly only South Africa has included all these services in the ordinary VAT system. See Poddar (n. 33 above), 188.
93. For a description of the first three calculations, see S. Cnossen, *VAT Treatment of Financial Services*, in *International Studies in Taxation: Law and Economics*, 91 (G. Lindencrona, S.-O. Lodin & B. Wiman eds., Kluwer Law International 1999). See also P.-P. Gendron, *VAT Treatment of Financial Services: Assessment and Policy Proposal for Developing Countries*, 62 Bull. Intl Tax. 494, 499–501 (2008) (a review that also includes additional alternatives); A. Kerrigan, *The Elusiveness of Neutrality—Why Is It So Difficult to Apply VAT to Financial Services?*, 21 Intl. VAT Monit. 102, 105–107 (2010) (describing all four methods). For a comprehensive description of cash flow options, see S. Poddar & M. English, *Taxation of Financial Services Under a Value-added Tax: Applying the Cash-flow Approach*, 50 Natl. Tax. J. 89 (1997).
94. The Philippines came very close to adopting a system based on the subtraction method but ultimately retreated from the proposal, in part because of the difficulty in allocating the tax to business customers via tax invoices. See M.M. Guevara, *A Better Alternative Tax for the Financial Sector*, www.iticnet.org/Download.aspx?QSDOCID=115 (last visited 16 June 2012).
95. Israel applies the addition method to tax financial services. See D. Gliksberg, *Israel's Value Added Tax Law*, 3 International VAT Monitor 2 (July 1992).
96. This approach was first proposed in Poddar & English (n. 93 above), 92–97. Ernst & Young prepared a further study on this approach for the Commission of the European Communities in 1994. Ernst & Young, *Treatment of Financial Services Under a VAT: Further Exploration of the Cash-flow Method of Taxation*, in *Value Added Tax: A Study of Methods of Taxing Financial and Insurance Services*, 73–126 (European Commission 1996), available at ec.europa.eu/taxation_customs/resources/documents/taxation/vat/key_documents/reports_published/methods_taxing.pdf.

implicit intermediary service charge it passes on to depositors through lower interest and issuing a tax invoice to itself so it can recover the tax from the intermediary charge it bundles into the interest payable by borrowers.[97]

While there are isolated instances in which some of these alternatives have been seriously contemplated or, more rarely, adopted, none has had widespread acceptance. This is partly a consequence of path determinacy. The first VATs in EU Member States classified financial supplies as exempt supplies only for historical reasons (this was equivalent to the system used in predecessor taxes)[98] and the precedent was followed in the Sixth Directive,[99] the binding European Commission law that subsequently governed the design for all European VATs and established a mould that has been followed since internationally.[100]

Another factor that may explain the continuing preference for exempt treatment of loans in VAT jurisdictions is the difficulty of allocating VAT to individual customers if the tax base is calculated on the basis of total supplies by the intermediary service provider. If the VAT cannot be attributed to each customer in a tax invoice, business borrowers would be unable to claim input tax credits and would bear far more VAT than is the case with the current rule treating the supplies as input taxed supplies. The same would be true of unregistered individual depositors and individuals borrowing for investment purposes, all of whom should be paying less tax than they now do, not more. While proposals have been developed for the allocation of VAT under the cash flow version of a VAT on financial intermediaries[101] and it appears tax invoices for individual borrowers may also be possible under the reverse-charge system,[102] no jurisdiction has been willing to test the theories in practice.

The economic costs of this additional, sometimes cascading, over-taxation may be significant.[103] Businesses that rely on services from a chain of other businesses that employ financial services bear more embedded VAT than businesses in a chain that do not rely on banking services to the same extent, leaving the first type of business less competitive. Also, to reduce the level of non-claimable taxes they must pass on to customers, financial institutions are likely to become more vertically integrated, using their own labour to provide a wide range of services that could be more efficiently provided by external specialist organizations and in the process raising the cost to

97. See H.H. Zee, *A New Approach to Taxing Financial Intermediation Services under a Value-Added Tax*, 58 Natl Tax J. 77, 86–88 (2005) (proposing this system).
98. See van Brederode (n. 37 above), 138–139.
99. Council Directive 77/388, OJ L145/1 of 1977 (EEC) ('the Sixth Directive'), replaced by Council Directive 2006/112, OJ L347/1 of 2006 (EC) ('the EU VAT Directive').
100. V. Sloane, *The Sixth Directive*, Tax J. 9, 9 (June 14, 2008).
101. See Commission of the European Communities, *Proposal for a Council Directive Amending Directive 2006/112/EC on the Common System of Value Added Tax, as Regards the Treatment of Insurance and Financial Services*, COM(2007) 747 final (Nov. 28, 2007) [hereinafter Directive Proposal]; Commission of the European Communities, *Proposal for a Council Regulation Laying Down Implementing Measures for Directive 2006/112/EC on the Common System of Value Added Tax, as Regards the Treatment of Insurance and Financial Services*, COM(2007) 746 final (Nov. 28, 2007) [hereinafter Regulation Proposal].
102. See Zee (n. 97 above), 86–88.
103. Gendron (n. 93 above), 498–499 (discussing the economic problems of the exemption system).

customers of their services.[104] It may also favour foreign suppliers over internal suppliers,[105] who are able to recover all their input taxes,[106] although in practice the supposed advantage should be completely offset by the import VAT collected from the customer.[107]

In the absence of proven examples of new systems that can relieve business borrowers of tax, in the short term alternative solutions that fit directly into the current VAT system appear to be the most logical reform route. Limited attempts have been made to do this in the EU, where individual countries currently have the option to treat some types of financial supplies as taxable supplies,[108] an approach encouraged by the European Banking Federation.[109] More recently, the European Commission has proposed changes to EU law to shift the power to opt for taxation of financial services from EU Member States to financial institutions, subject to common rules to be incorporated in the EU VAT Directive.[110] The practical difficulties with these proposals may not be insurmountable, but they are considerable[111] and experts have suggested that an alternative approach, used by two countries – Singapore and New Zealand – may be preferable,[112] adding technical rationales to the theoretical case that has been made in Europe for a zero-rating system for supplies to business.[113]

---

104. See Gendron (n. 93 above), 498 (discussing the incentive to self-supply).
105. A. Schenk, *Taxation of Financial Services (Including Insurance) under a United States Value Added Tax*, 63 Tax L. Rev. 409, 419 (2010).
106. *Ibid.* This is because they are supplying, from their perspective, exported services, normally qualifying for a zero-rate, thus allowing them to recover all input taxes incurred to make the supply.
107. VAT systems normally collect VAT on imported goods from the importer and on imported services from the receiving customer, at least where the customer makes exempt supplies such as financial supplies. See, e.g., UK HM Revenue & Customs, Notice 702/9, VAT: Imports Customs Procedures with Economic Impact, End Use Relief and Free Zones, at 5 (2005). The rules that collect VAT from customers of imported services are known as 'reverse-charge' rules.
108. These rules are described in S. Nathoeni & T. Braakman, *Option for Taxation of Financial Services – Is It an Option?*, 21 Intl. VAT Monit. 113, 115–117 (2010). See also Cnossen (n. 93 above), 98–99 (examining the option in the context of several EU countries).
109. For a comprehensive review of the issues raised by the option-to-tax approach, see Ernst & Young, *Design and Impact of the 'Option to Tax' System for Application of VAT to Financial Services* (Report prepared for the European Banking Federation) (2009), available at www.ebf-fbe.eu/uploads/documents/publications/Reports/Others/D1925_EBF_-_EY_Final_Report_28_October_2009_TB-NT-2009-01580-01-E.pdf.
110. The EU proposals are the most recent in a debate over the optimal taxation of financial supplies under the European VAT that stretches back over two decades. The key stages are summarized in R. de la Feria, *The EU VAT Treatment of Insurance and Financial Services (Again) Under Review*, 16 EC Tax Rev. 74, 74–89 (2007). For the most recent 'opt in' proposal, see Eur. Comm'n, Directive Proposal (n. 101 above); Eur. Comm'n, Regulation Proposal (n. 101 above).
111. Many of the issues are canvassed in Ernst & Young (n. 109 above).
112. The New Zealand and Singapore regimes are described in L. Burns, *Consumption Taxation of Supplies of Financial Services in the Asia-Pacific Region*, 14 Asia-Pacific Tax Bull. 352, 354–355 (2008).
113. See, e.g., H. Huizinga, *A European VAT on Financial Services*, 17 Econ. Policy 497 (2002); A. Schenk & H.H. Zee, *Treating Financial Services Under a Value Added Tax: Policy Issues and Country Practices*, 22 Tax Notes Intl. 3309 (June 25, 2001), updated as *Financial Services and the Value-Added Tax*, in *Taxing the Financial Sector: Concepts, Issues, and Practices*, 60 (H.H. Zee ed., International Monetary Fund 2004).

These two jurisdictions have retained the exempt supply treatment of financial supplies for non-commercial borrowers but relieve business borrowers from any VAT on their acquisitions of intermediary services by directly or indirectly treating the supplies to VAT-registered borrowers as zero-rated supplies.[114] Whatever system might be adopted for loan intermediary services provided to non-business borrowers, the zero-rated route appears to be the optimal solution in terms of simplicity and effectiveness for removing any consumption taxes from non-personal loans made to registered businesses. It has been suggested that the zero-rating rule is flawed when applied to businesses that in turn make both taxable and exempt supplies (by removing any tax from the exempt supplies),[115] but this observation is probably most useful as a case for reviewing the rationale and design of the exempt supplies that might be made by customers of a financial institution.[116]

Australia recently proposed an alternative approach that would impose VAT on financial institutions based on the value of their intermediary services using an additive calculation while excluding supplies to registered businesses.[117] The proposal achieves the desired neutrality of non-taxation for business customers but increases the tax burden imposed on unregistered investors. Depending on the view one takes of consumer borrowers, it would lead to greater over-taxation or more appropriate full taxation of these users of financial intermediary services compared to the current input taxation system.

§9.05 POOLING SERVICES

Financial intermediaries providing 'pooling' services offer a fundamentally different service from those linking savers and borrowers. In the pooling case, a group of people agree that each member of the group will contribute to a common pool and the proceeds of the pool will be distributed to select members of the pool - the winners with the lucky numbers in collective gambling transactions such as a lottery or the losers suffering catastrophe in the case of insurance. In the case of both types of pooling

114. The background to the New Zealand regime is set out in Policy Advice Division of the Inland Revenue Department, *GST and Financial Services: A Government Discussion Document* (Policy Advice Division of the Inland Revenue Department 2002), available at taxpolicy.ird.govt.nz/sites/default/files/2002-dd-gst-financial-services.pdf. See also A. Maples, *The Zero-Rating of Financial Services and Introduction of a Reverse Charge in New Zealand (At Last!)*, 58 Bull. Intl. Tax. 213, 214–215 (2004); M. Pallot & D. White, *Improvements to the GST Treatment of Financial Services—The Proposed New Zealand Approach*, 13 Intl. VAT Monitor 481, 482–19 (2002); M. Pallot, *GST and Financial Services - Rating Zero-Rating*, in *GST in Retrospect and Prospect* (n. 33 above), 163.
115. See, e.g., Schenk (n. 51 above), 840–841.
116. Apart from designating financial supplies as exempt supplies, most countries use exemptions primarily as a means of subsidizing preferred types of consumption such as food, education, and health services. The use of randomly imposed input taxation as a means of providing concessionally-priced goods or services is difficult to sustain.
117. The proposals grew out of a tax review that explicitly excluded changes to the GST from the terms of reference so the proposal adopted a new term for the VAT applied to financial intermediaries, a 'financial transactions tax'. See Australia's Future Tax System Review Panel, *Australia's Future Tax System: Report to the Treasurer* (December 2009), available at www.taxreview.treasury.gov.au.

(more so for insurance than lottery pooling), there will be some investment of pooled funds by the service provider prior to the payout to enhance the value of the distribution relative to the amount provided initially by way of insurance premiums or lottery ticket cost.

In one case users of the pooling are risk takers and in the other they are risk averse but in both cases a large group of contributors provide the funds that a much smaller subset will use to acquire goods and services. The size of the insurance premium will reflect the actuarially determined likelihood of some of the participants in the pool becoming entitled to compensation for losses. In the case of lotteries, by way of contrast, the price of participation is usually fixed and the number of participants and number of winners will normally determine the value of distribution for each level of winner. The cost of the pooling service for both lotteries and insurance is the difference between the revenue received by the service provider (either from the scheme participants or as investment income) and the amount paid out to the winners or losers, as the case may be.

As is the case with financial intermediary services, real resources are used to provide these pooling services without any compensating increase in taxable consumption somewhere else and the portion of premiums or ticket cost used to pay for the pooling services should be subject to tax. From a Pareto optimal point of view, however, looking at consumption only in terms of the acquisition of resources from the social pool, the bulk of the lottery ticket cost or insurance premium that provided the funds paid to the winners of the lottery or those suffering casualty losses should not be taxed (ie., the premium or cost apart from the slice retained by the lottery intermediary or insurer for the pooling services). The rationale for this conclusion is similar to that applicable to consumer loans, which are analytically similar to insurance and lotteries. Consumer loans shift consumption between periods of time, lotteries shift consumption from one person to another, and insurance shifts consumption between states of the world, that is, from good (no accident) to bad. Neither the pure interest in the loan case nor the insurance premiums or lottery ticket price (net of the cost of the service) in the pooling case gives rise to consumption in the sense of taking real resources out of the economy. Consumption takes place when loan proceeds, insurance proceeds or lottery prizes are spent on goods or services.

A very different result would follow, however, if consumption is viewed from the personal perspective of the insured or lottery ticket buyer. From this perspective, the full premium or full lottery ticket cost may yield utility and consumption benefits equal in value to the alternative consumption that could have been acquired with the payment, even though the contribution to the redistribution pool does not in itself lead to the acquisition of real goods or services withdrawn from the economy.

[A] Lotteries and Gambling

While it is conceivable that an enterprise with a 'system' could acquire lottery tickets as part of a business[118] or apply its capital to gambling activities rather than conventional business pursuits, it can safely be assumed that most gambling lottery tickets are acquired by individuals exercising final consumption choices. The cost of the financial intermediation or pooling service are clearly an incident of personal consumption and should bear VAT. The value of this service is easily measured as the difference between the amount collected from lottery participants and the amount paid out to winners. Imposing tax on this amount has proved a simple way to tax the service.[119] Since all participants are assumed to be final consumers, there is no need to attribute the VAT payable for the purpose of allocating input tax credits.

Limiting VAT to the fee for pooling services provided by a lottery (or other gambling) provider yields an optimal outcome from a Hobbesian or Pareto optimal perspective. This view looks only to the application of lottery winnings to acquire goods or services – that is, to acquire a slice of the economic pie. The supply of funds to the pool and the distribution from the pool to the winner are ignored under this approach. If ten people each bought $ 11 lottery tickets and the lottery organizer distributed $ 100 and retained $ 10 as the fee for pooling services, the only acquisition out of the economic pie is the $ 10 of services; the $ 100 winnings remain to be spent. The outcome also achieves neutrality from the government's perspective. Leaving aside possible social concerns over expenditures on gambling, the government has no interest in encouraging or discouraging gambling if VAT is imposed only on the cost of the pooling service because the tax on the service plus the tax on the spending of the proceeds amount to the same revenue it would have collected if the lottery ticket buyer had chosen to buy 'normal' consumer goods instead of a lottery ticket. Furthermore, taxing only the service preserves the individual's trade-off between consuming the 'normal' consumer goods and enjoying the possibility of consuming in the favourable winning state of nature.

This is not the outcome if the personal perspective of consumption is adopted. The personal perspective seeks to tax (and in the progressive expenditure tax, redistribute) the exercise of economic power through consumption choices, not the use of real resources from the social pool. Under this perspective, there is a case for imposing VAT on the entire amount wagered by a person acquiring a lottery ticket or otherwise gambling rather than limiting the tax base to the fee for the intermediation service. If one starts with the assumption that most ticket buyers (to cite one of the most widespread forms of gambling) realize they are not likely to win, from the perspective of the ticket buyer the purchase of a lottery ticket is an exercise of consumption. That is, most ticket buyers presumably recognize the fact that the odds

118. For a colourful example, see *International Lotto Fund v. Virginia State Lottery Department* 20 F.3d 589, 590 (4th Cir. 1990); A. Wagenbrenner, *Court May Not Stop Withholding on Australian Lottery Winners*, 177 Journal of Accountancy 26 (June 1994).

119. This is the approach used in Australia, which imposes a tax on lottery 'revenues'. See 'GST and Gambling' (Australian Taxation Office), www.ato.gov.au/content/11991.htm.

are against them and are willing to part with the cash in the knowledge that it is likely not to be returned. Since the money could have been spent on other consumption, it can be assumed that the intangible benefits of holding a ticket – the thrill of being in the game, the chance to fantasize how the winnings might be spent, and so forth – were equal in value to the alternative forms of consumption available to the purchaser for the same cost. The fact that the ticket buyer chose to gamble with his money rather than buy certain goods and services supports the conclusion that the intangible gratification of participating in a lottery was equal in value to any alternative form of consumption available to participants. If this is the case, it might be argued that the full cost of a lottery ticket should be subject to tax, not just the portion that represents the cost of financial intermediation. This conclusion is strengthened if economic neutrality is considered, as any alternative applications of the funds apart from the acquisition of investments would be subject to tax, and in a neutral tax world, non-taxation of lottery consumption would amount to a tax expenditure or subsidy for this form of consumption.

The logic behind this approach is identical to the rationale explained earlier for treating gifts as consumption under the expenditure tax – the application of funds for any purpose other than investment or savings is a form of consumption from the perspective of the donor who made a consumption choice to give money away rather than spend it to acquire goods or services. The value of the gift to the donor is, as described earlier, the face value of the funds donated, which is also the value of the goods or services that could have been acquired as an alternative to the gift.

At the end of the day, the appropriate VAT treatment of lottery and gambling expenditures will turn on whether a personal perspective or Hobbes/Pareto use of real resources from the social pool perspective of consumption is preferred. This, in turn, will depend on one's view as to the appropriate base for consumption taxation – extractions from the social pool or the exercise of economic power through the application of income or savings. While the broader view of consumption favoured by expenditure tax advocates cannot be applied to gifts in the VAT world (gift giving does not fall within the limited scope of the VAT applying to commercial activities of registered persons), from a purely technical perspective it would be possible to apply the broader view of consumption to lotteries and gambling. In the VAT world, however, in practice (at least in those countries that impose VAT on lotteries and other gambling) only the value of intermediary pooling services is used as the VAT base, not the gross expenditures on gambling.[120]

[B] Casualty Insurance

Insurance premiums paid to an insurer (the pooling agent) include two components – the portion that will be paid as a benefit to the policy holders who suffer losses and the charge for the pooling services offered by the insurer. The latter should be taxed in a

120. See, e.g., Austl. GST Act (n 39 above), s. 126-10; see generally A. Schenk, *Gambling and Lotteries*, in *VAT in Africa* (n. 37 above), 47.

benchmark VAT (and recovered by business policy holders). The ideal treatment of the former is less clear.

As with other types of financial services, the theoretical issues with insurance only arise in respect of final consumers acquiring the services. VAT imposed on the cost of casualty insurance services provided to business customers should be fully recovered. For historical reasons, the traditional European VAT continues to treat casualty insurance and insurance pooling services as exempt supplies.[121] There is, however, general recognition that history alone explains retention of this rule; the treatment has never been defended on policy grounds.[122] For business customers, this policy distorts business decisions and leads to cascading over-taxation of business inputs.

The appropriate VAT treatment of intermediary pooling charges (the excess of insurance premiums over amounts paid as benefits) is relatively straightforward from both a Pareto perspective and personal perspective. Under both types of analysis the services should be fully subject to tax when acquired by private consumers, and treating these services as exempt supplies, as is done in Europe,[123] amounts to under-taxation of the consumption. To avoid this outcome, the intermediary pooling service of insurers is treated as an ordinary taxable supply in some modern VAT systems, although several different systems are used to calculate the value of this service and impose tax on it.[124]

Less clear is the optimal treatment of the part of the insurance premium that will be passed on to a claimant as an insurance benefit. Claimants are compensated for VAT-inclusive amounts and the premiums from which the insurance benefits are paid therefore must include an amount to cover the VAT value in the benefits. VAT paid by an insurance beneficiary when a replacement asset is acquired is thus funded by all policy holders. Is there any rationale for expecting policy holders to pay VAT on the premiums that already include an amount earmarked to pay the VAT to be paid on a replacement asset?

From a Pareto perspective, no explicit VAT should be imposed on the portion of the premium used to fund benefits when these funds are deposited into the pool. The only extraction from the social pool takes place when the claimant uses insurance proceeds to purchase a replacement vehicle. At that point, the car dealer will remit the appropriate VAT and the cost of that VAT will have been borne implicitly by all those paying premiums.

---

121. EU VAT Directive (n. 99 above); see generally Schenk (n. 105 above).
122. Schenk (n. 105 above), 437.
123. EU VAT Directive (n 99 above), Art. 135(1)(a) (examining insurance, reinsurance transactions and related services).
124. For example, in New Zealand, insurers calculate their output GST liability by deducting the notional amount of GST that would otherwise be applicable to insurance payouts made in the period. Goods and Services Tax Act, 1985, s. 20(3)(d) (N.Z.), available at www.legislation.govt.nz/act/public/1985/0141/71.0/DLM81035.html. Similarly, in Australia, the supply of general insurance is taxable and, while the settlement of a claim does not give rise to a liability on an insured party that is registered, the insurer receives a reduction in its GST liability in respect of settlements paid to insured parties that do not receive an input tax credit for the premium. Austl. GST Act (n. 39 above), ss. 78-5–78-10.

The answer may be different if the personal expenditure perspective is adopted. If the purchase of an insurance policy cannot be regarded as a form of savings by a policy holder, it will be treated as personal consumption under the benchmark expenditure tax. The key question, therefore, is whether insurance is a type of savings. One way of considering the question is to compare the person paying insurance premiums with the person who chooses to self-insure. If the person acquiring insurance pays a $ 10 premium each year plus 17% VAT, the self-insurer could put the same total amount, $ 11.70, in a savings account to be drawn down if the vehicle is stolen. If both the insured person and the self-insured person have their cars stolen after ten years, they end up in the same position - with a new car and no savings remaining, an outcome consistent with the characterization of premiums as a form of savings. On the other hand, if the cars are not stolen, the saver has $ 117 in the bank (plus accrued interest) at the end of ten years and the insured person has nothing to show apart from ten worry-free years, an outcome that challenges the characterization of premiums as akin to savings.

If insurance coverage is not savings, it will be considered consumption from the personal expenditure perspective. Although there may be no extraction from the social pool when the premium is paid, the insured person clearly believes she has acquired a benefit equal in value to the cost of the premium, presumably the comfort of knowing the value of the asset has been protected. From a Pareto perspective there is only one lot of consumption (the actual purchase of a replacement asset) but from the personal perspective there may be two with the insured person initially paying the price of sleeping better knowing a risk has been covered.

Another starting point for analysing insurance premiums might be to compare them with warranty expenses. In addition to the price charged for a profitable sale of goods, a manufacturer may impose an explicit fee for warranty coverage or embed the fee in a higher price charged for the goods. The price of goods purchased with a warranty includes the cost of the goods net of the warranty plus the expected cost of the replacement plus the service charge for administering the warranty program. In most VAT systems, replacements for goods sold under warranty provided for no additional charge are out-of-scope supplies (i.e., they fall outside the definition of taxable supplies).[125] Any tax incurred by the warranty provider for inputs used to honour the warranty will be fully recovered. As a result, the tax levied on the initial sale of an item sold with a warranty will be the only tax borne by the buyer.

The outcome mirrors that of insurance in most jurisdictions where there is also a single liability to VAT, though in the insurance case this is levied when an asset is repaired or replaced rather than when the insurance coverage is provided.[126] VAT rules for warranties are not consistent as some systems lack a mechanism for the guarantor

125. See, e.g., Revenue Legislation Services, Indirect Taxes Division, *VAT Guide* 38 *(Revenue Legislation Services, Indirect Taxes Division 2008), available at revenue.ie/en/tax/vat/leaflets/vatguide_2008.pdf (discussing treatment under Irish law).*

126. E.g., UK HM Revenue & Customs, Notice 701/36 Insurance, para. 5.1 (2011), available at customs.hmrc.gov.uk/channelsPortalWebApp/channelsPortalWebApp.portal?_nfpb=true&_pageLabel=pageVAT_ShowContent&id=HMCE_CL_000129&propertyType=document (noting treatment in the United Kingdom).

to recover the VAT component of a refund where the guarantor is a manufacturer without a direct contractual relationship with the customer.[127] Leaving this anomaly aside, however, the general rule is that where a warranty provider in effect self-insures, VAT is charged only one time in respect of two transactions, the initial payment for coverage and the subsequent provision of warranty goods and services. This outcome is consistent with the Pareto optimal view of consumption as there is only a single allocation of labour and capital resources resulting from the warranty payment. Because there is no tax on the replacement good, the one-time tax on the initial sale is equivalent in the insurance case to a tax on the service cost plus the tax on the consumption from the insurance proceeds.

Another way of regarding the warranty arrangement that would be consistent with the current VAT treatment is to consider the combined initial purchase and warranty as a single contract for service over a period. For example, a customer purchasing an item with a three-year warranty would be treated not as the purchaser of a tangible asset but instead as the buyer of the guaranteed use of the asset for three years with the purchase price being the cost of providing that service. As there are no further charges over the service (warranty) period, VAT is imposed only one time, the outcome consistent with Pareto optimal analysis.

The warranty analogy goes some way to providing an answer to the question of how casualty insurance should be taxed if the starting point is the Pareto optimal analysis. The benchmark treatment remains elusive if the personal perspective is adopted.

§9.06 CONCLUSION

Analyses of generic 'financial supplies' are complicated by the fact that the term is used to describe such a wide variety of supplies ranging from actual intangible investment assets such as bonds or shares, the supply of services to effect the transfer of these assets, ancillary supplies such as the supply of advice, the supply of credit funds, the supply of intermediary services to depositors and borrowers that make these credit funds available, the supply of pooling services for gamblers and insurance policy holders, and the provision of gambling opportunities and insurance coverage.

Different types of financial supplies raise different conceptual issues, which in turn demand disparate policy responses. The issues are further complicated by the fact that there is no universal agreement on the benchmarks by which the taxation of financial supplies should be evaluated. Analysis from a social or Pareto perspective and analysis from a personal or benchmark expenditure tax perspective may yield very different recommendations.

---

127. Refunds and cancelled transactions are normally addressed through 'adjustment events' but the adjustment event formula in some VAT laws will not cover transactions where a consumer purchases from a retailer but receives a rebate or refund from the manufacturer. See, e.g., *Electrical Goods Importer v. Federal Commissioner of Taxation* (2009), 74 ATR 982, 998 (Austl.) (disallowing an adjustment on a cash-back payment made from a manufacturer directly to the customer). The Australian government subsequently modified its legislation to include these payments in the adjustment events formula – see Austl. GST Act (n. 39 above), s. 134-5.

It is clear, however, that under either perspective the current regimes that partially tax supplies of intermediary services overtax business borrowers and lenders and individual depositors while systems that partially tax investment services overtax both business and individual investors. Solutions to these problems vary in terms of complexity. More significant, perhaps, is the fact that a principled response, however, would come at a financial cost, which may make implementation somewhat more problematic from a political perspective.

Chapter 10

Further Thoughts on Reforming the VAT: Treatment of Financial Intermediation Services

Howell H. Zee

§10.01 INTRODUCTION

The literature on the VAT treatment of financial services has witnessed such a rapid growth in the past decade and a half that there are now multiple surveys of this literature - each, not surprisingly, emphasizing different aspects of and providing different perspectives on the subject.[1] The existence of these surveys has largely obviated the need to review the conceptual issues involved as well as describe in broad terms actual country practices observed around the world (implementation details of such practices would, of course, require knowledge at the administrative level). Hence, in this short paper I forgo any attempt at surveying yet again the literature and instead focus directly on making the case for my recent proposal to fully tax financial services

1. To cite but a recent few from both the legal and economics professions: T. Edgar, *The Search for Alternatives to the Exempt Treatment of Financial Services under a Value Added Tax*, in *GST in Retrospect and Prospect*, 123–153 (R. Krever & D. White eds., Thomson Reuters 2007); R. de la Feria, *The EU VAT Treatment of Insurance and Financial Services (Again) under Review*, 2 EC Tax Rev. 74–89 (2007); P. Gendron, *Value-Added Tax Treatment of Financial Services: An Assessment and Policy Proposals for Developing Countries*, International Tax Program, University of Toronto: ITP Paper No. 0701 (2007); A. Schenk & O. Oldman, *Value Added Tax: A Comparative Approach* (Cambridge University Press 2007); and H. Zee, *VAT Treatment of Financial Services: A Primer on Conceptual Issues and Country Practices*, 34 Intertax 458–474 (2006). In addition, there is also a survey prepared by the staff of the Commission of the European Communities: European Commission, *'Background Paper Requested by the Council Presidency; Origin: Commission – DG Taxation and Customs Union; Subject: Financial and Insurance Services'*, TAXUD/2414/08 (Brussels: EC, 2008).

under the VAT – the so-called modified reverse-charging (MRC) approach,[2] especially regarding its practicability and the differences between it and its chief conceptual rival: the cash-flow approach proposed by Poddar and English.[3]

A point that is well understood by most specialists, but is nevertheless worth stressing for the general reader in any discussion of the problem of taxing financial services under the VAT, is that the problem has nothing to do with the nature of the VAT per se and everything to do with the particular transaction-based method – the crediting of input tax against output tax – adopted by most countries to implement the VAT. This method requires the identification of both input and output prices on which to impose the VAT on a transaction-by-transaction basis.[4] Naturally, financial intermediation services (FIS) – an important and significant subset of all financial services that is typically priced on the basis of margin spreads rather than explicit fees – would run into trouble with the credit method, so the standard country practice, including the European Union (EU), is to exempt such services from the VAT. However, other methods – most notably the accounts-based addition or subtraction method – certainly could have been used to implement the VAT and thus tax FIS providers just like other providers of goods and services without encountering the above problem that is unique to the credit method.[5] From this point of view, it is perhaps not too unreasonable to attribute much of the blame for the problem on the EU when it comes to the VAT treatment of financial services: its choice of the credit method in designing a common VAT for the Union, as laid down in its Sixth VAT Directive of 1977, served for better or worse for an extended period of time as the standard VAT model for other countries to follow. Unfortunately, if the results of the recent EU-wide review of its VAT system as regards financial services are any indication, the source of the original problem is unlikely to be the place from which a fully satisfactory solution would emerge.

While acknowledging the distortions that have been created by the VAT exemption of most financial services, and that full taxation of such services is the only way to restore neutrality to the VAT system, the proposed revisions to the EU's VAT in this

2. For details of the MRC approach and worked numerical examples, see H. Zee, *A New Approach to Taxing Financial Intermediation Services under a Value-Added Tax*, 53 Natl. Tax J. 77–92 (2005).
3. S. Poddar & M. English, *Taxation of Financial Services under a Value-Added Tax: Applying the Cash-Flow Approach*, 50 Natl. Tax J. 9–111 (1997). The details of the cash-flow approach, especially regarding its implementation based on a system of tax calculation accounts (TCA), are elaborated in Commission of the European Communities, *The TCA System—A Detailed Description* (EC 2000).
4. It is perhaps worth noting that a VAT invoice system is not a necessary ingredient of the credit method. Japan's VAT (known as the consumption tax), for example, is implemented using the credit method without invoices (although the authorities have recently started to require claims of input tax credits on large transactions above a specified threshold be supported by invoices). The adoption of this invoiceless credit method in Japan has led a number of western VAT observers to erroneously characterize its VAT as being implemented using the accounts-based subtraction method.
5. Of course, these other methods have their own limitations (although unrelated to the taxation of FIS), real or perceived. The addition method, which computes value-added as the sum of wages and profits, renders the VAT too much like an income tax (which it of course is, as explained in n. 16 below) in both appearance and collection. The subtraction method is workable only if the VAT has a single rate.

area by the responsible body are disappointingly limited largely to legal and administrative measures,[6] leaving little doubt that exemption would remain the main approach to how most financial services are to be treated under the VAT. Most significantly, full taxation was ruled out as a policy option from the outset of the review, ostensibly due to a lack of appetite by Member States to revisit that option.[7] It is clear that such a sentiment stemmed largely from the negative experiences concerned parties had had with the field-testing conducted in the late 1990s of the cash-flow approach using the TCA system, which was regarded by most as too complex and administratively costly to justify its adoption.[8]

Since the MRC approach is also a full taxation approach, to render it a viable and attractive policy option one has to make a compelling argument that full taxation is preferable to any of the existing country practices not only on theoretical grounds, but also on grounds of cost-benefit considerations.[9] In other words, one has to establish the case that it is not simply a repackaged version of the cash-flow approach. This is the primary objective of the present paper. The next section takes up the relevant issues. Section §8.03 concludes the paper with some brief remarks.

§10.02 ASPECTS OF REFORMING THE VAT TREATMENT OF FIS

As noted earlier, the objective of both the cash-flow and MRC approaches is to effect full taxation of FIS on a transaction-by-transaction basis.[10] While it could be argued that both approaches are capable of delivering the theoretically correct outcome, this

6. See Commission of the European Communities, *'Proposal for a Council Directive Amending Directive 2006/112/EC on the Common System of Value Added Tax, as Regards the Treatment of Insurance and Financial Services'* COM (2007) 747 final (Brussels: EC, 2007); and Commission of the European Communities, *'Proposal for a Council Regulation Laying Down Implementing Measures for Directive 2006/112/EC on the Common System of Value Added Tax, as Regards the Treatment of Insurance and Financial Services'* COM (2007) 746 final (Brussels: EC, 2007). The proposed revisions fall under three headings: (1) clarification of existing rules; (2) broadening the scope of the existing option to tax; and (3) introduction of a VAT cost-sharing group that would allow supplies provided by the group to its members to be VAT exempt (the focus of this last heading is presumably on certain non-exempt financial services). Among these, perhaps the only substantively significant revision is to extend the option to tax to insurance services. For a description of the (lukewarm) reaction to the proposals, see C. Amand, *VAT on Financial Services: The Unanswered Questions*, 9 ERA Forum 357–376 (2008).
7. See Commission of the European Communities, *'Consultation Paper on Modernising Value Added Tax Obligations for Financial Services and Insurances'* (Brussels: EC, 2006). This consultation paper effectively defined the set of policy options that would later be considered for formulating revision proposals.
8. Of course, revenue concerns could also add to the reluctance of at least some EU Member States in pursuing comprehensive VAT reform in this area. However, as explained below, such concerns, if true, would be fundamentally misguided from a reform perspective.
9. Full taxation in the present context refers to the full integration of financial services consumed by both businesses and households into the VAT net using the credit method, not necessarily taxing such services at a particular (such as the standard) VAT rate.
10. Financial services provided with explicit fees could presumably be taxed, if desired, under the standard credit method (with appropriate modifications if necessary, such as those found in Australia and New Zealand as regards non-life insurance; see Zee (n. 1 above) for an explanation). Hence, such services do not require, in the main, special approaches for their VAT treatment.

equivalence in outcome is true only in a particular sense (further discussed below). Moreover, the methods used by the two approaches to achieve their (common) objective differ not only in administrative terms, but also substantively. The discussions in this section proceed along in three stages: making the case for full taxation, making the case for the MRC approach and considering the benefit and cost of reforming the VAT treatment of FIS.

[A] Case for Full Taxation

It is well known that exempting FIS from the VAT would engender two types of distortions. First, for business users of such services, the credit chain would be broken, and the unrecoverable input VAT would lead to either a bias towards backward vertical integration or forward cascading. Second, for household users, FIS would be under-taxed (relative to the standard VAT rate).[11] Before tackling these distortion issues, however, one issue that should be set aside at the outset is the revenue consequence of moving from exemption to full taxation of FIS. Such a move may or may not entail a revenue loss,[12] and hence could possibly be constrained by budgetary considerations. Whatever the revenue outcome, it is not a relevant issue in the context of discussing the structural aspects of a tax designed specifically to avoid, or at least minimize, tax distortions prior to the consumption stage. For otherwise, what is to prevent the broadening of the scope of exemption to non-financial services or even goods, all in the name of revenue?

If the concern has to do with distortions on the business side alone, neutrality could be easily restored with practically no additional administrative complexity by zero-rating all FIS (not limited to just business-to-business (B2B) transactions of such services, as has been done in New Zealand).[13] Of course, by removing all tax elements from FIS, this zero-rating option could aggravate the under-taxation of household consumption of FIS. Hence, the central challenge in bringing FIS to full taxation lies with the household – not business – side of the problem. Practices of fixed partial input tax recovery, such as those found in Australia and Singapore, are half-way measures

11. With exemption, household consumption of FIS would still contain some tax element. Thus, whether such consumption is considered under-taxed would depend on one's view on the proper rate at which it should be taxed (further discussed below).
12. With full taxation, there is a revenue loss associated with allowing FIS providers to recover their input tax and a revenue gain from taxing the value-added of such providers. The overall outcome is thus entirely an empirical question and likely to vary from country to country.
13. Limiting zero-rating to B2B transactions would be somewhat more costly administratively, as there would then be the need for FIS providers to differentiate their transactions with businesses from those with households to determine the share of recoverable input VAT. New Zealand's implementation of the B2B zero-rating actually entails even more administrative complication than the simple need of differentiating between business and household users of FIS: zero-rating is not allowed even with respect to a business user unless the latter meets a threshold test of making non-exempt supplies.

that do not completely resolve distortions on either side, and thus cannot necessarily be regarded as solutions superior to the zero-rating option.[14]

Discussions in the literature on household consumption of FIS have been confused and confusing. A number of writers have proposed that it should not be taxed – frequently on the basis of a flawed understanding of underlying concepts. Unfortunately, counter-propositions advanced by those holding the opposing view have, more often than not, also been incomplete or at times misleading. While it is not the intention of the present paper to survey all the issues raised in this debate, it would nevertheless be useful to examine the core of the position held by the no-tax camp, which seems to be the belief that the nature of intertemporal intermediation of consumption (as performed by FIS) is fundamentally different from that of temporal intermediation of consumption (as performed by, for example, transportation services). Such a belief would then be manifest in one or in a combination of the following (possibly interrelated) arguments: (1) FIS are not proper objects of taxation because they merely intermediate consumption (across time periods) but are not targets of consumption themselves; (2) taxing FIS, which involves taxing interest, would distort savings; (3) VAT, being a consumption tax, should not include interest in its base (a variation of this argument is that at least a part of interest represents the pure time value of money and not the value of consumption, and should thus not be taxed under a VAT); and (4) taxing interest would violate the VAT's neutrality of taxing consumption over time (this neutrality is sometimes illustrated by using a version of the consumer's budget constraint which shows the intertemporal equivalence between a flat-rate consumption tax and a lump-sum tax on exogenous income, the latter being non-distortive on relative prices).

As it turns out, none of the foregoing arguments stand up well under close scrutiny. The fundamental theory of intertemporal choice indicates that the objects of choice are consumption in different periods and not savings, and the interest rate (or more specifically, the reciprocal of an appropriately stated interest factor) represents nothing more than the relative price between current and future consumption. Stated in this way, current and future consumption should be treated exactly like two different goods or services. Moreover, since real resources are used in the provision of FIS (as evidenced by the fact that they are a component of a country's aggregate value of output), their value-added is ultimately embedded in the value of future consumption in the same way the value of transportation services would be embedded in the value of the transported goods.[15] Of course, taxing interest (or more accurately, putting a tax

14. The EU's rejection of both the zero-rating and fixed partial input tax recovery options in its latest review seems to rest on two concerns: their negative revenue consequences and their non-neutralities. See the background paper issued by the Commission of the European Communities, '*Impact Assessment: Amending Directive 2006/112/EC on the Common System of Value Added Tax, as Regards the Treatment of Insurance and Financial Services*', SEC (2007) 1554 (Brussels: EC, 2008). Just why non-neutralities stemming from exemption are less of a concern than those from zero-rating and fixed partial input tax recovery has not been made clear.
15. Put differently, had there been no FIS, the value of future consumption would have been lower for every unit of current consumption forgone, due to an efficiency loss in transforming savings into investments.

on the relative price of future consumption) would alter the value of the trade-off between current and future consumption, but this is no different from the case when an ordinary good or service is taxed and its associated relative price changed as a result.

The argument that interest should be excluded from the base of a consumption tax fails to appreciate the fact that the terms 'consumption tax' and 'income tax' are simply just labels.[16] Economically, a consumer's income and consumption are fundamentally linked by the existence of budget constraints, both period-by-period and intertemporally. While taxing future consumption would directly raise its relative price, taxing interest would have the same qualitative effect - albeit indirectly - by reducing the available resources for such consumption.[17] Indeed, there is nothing inherently sacred about interest - itself just a relative price variable - that should render it immune to taxation. The more interesting issue is instead at what rate interest should be taxed. Unfortunately, this question cannot be addressed on *a priori* grounds, for the answer ultimately depends, as it usually does with such questions, on own- and cross-price elasticities of demand and supply functions of goods and services both temporally and intertemporally.[18]

What about the argument that taxing interest would break the equivalence between a flat-rate consumption tax and a lump-sum income tax? The validity of this argument hinges on the unsatisfactory assumption of the existence of exogenous income. Once it is recognized that in a general equilibrium framework income is determined endogenously by factor supplies, the aforementioned equivalence would no longer hold, and one is back in the earlier situation in which demand and supply elasticities play a crucial role in determining the optimal tax rates across goods and services on the one hand, and across consumption over time on the other. In such a framework, a flat-rate tax on consumption is generally not optimal. That it is common

16. An obvious case in point is that value-added is nothing but the sum of factor payments (wages to labour and interest and profits to capital). The common tendency to classify the VAT as a consumption rather than an income tax is entirely due to its widely adopted method of collection (i.e., the credit method) rather than any substantive economic rationale. Indeed, it would be difficult to imagine that the VAT would be regarded as a consumption tax if it were collected using the addition method. Of course, the combined base of the corporate income tax (CIT) and personal income tax (PIT) found in most countries tends to be broader than the base of a typical VAT, due to the lack of capital expensing under the CIT and the taxation of capital income under the PIT. Nevertheless, this practical gap in the two tax bases should not obscure the fundamental fact that there is a substantial degree of conceptual overlap between taxing income and taxing consumption. For elaborations of such an overlap, see H. Zee, *Taxing Capital Income in a Globalized World*, 27 Tax Notes Intl. 1185–1211 (2002).
17. This can be seen clearly from examining a simple standard two-period budget constraint of the form: $y = c_1 + c_2 \cdot (1+t)/[1 + r \cdot (1-\tau)]$, where y is given income, r is given interest rate, c_i is consumption in period i, t is the tax rate on c_2, and τ is the tax rate on interest. A straightforward manipulation yields: $(y - c_1)/c_2 = (1+t)/[1 + r \cdot (1-\tau)]$. The left hand side of the equation represents the ratio of savings to future consumption. The consumption tax is seen to increase the ratio on the right hand side by raising its numerator, while the interest tax produces the same qualitative effect on the ratio by reducing its denominator. The exact relationship between t and τ that would render the left hand side unchanged can be derived once the current and future consumption functions are known.
18. On the optimal taxation of savings and consumption, see A. Atkinson & A. Sandmo, *Welfare Implications of the Taxation of Savings*, 90 Econ. J. 528–549 (1980).

to argue for a uniform VAT rate in real-world policy discussions has much more to do with administrative considerations rather than theoretical underpinnings.

Having established the compelling case for the full taxation of FIS - be they consumed by businesses or by households - one is still confronted with the fundamental problem of designing a practicable mechanism for effecting such an outcome. Only two alternatives have so far been advanced in the literature: the cash-flow and MRC approaches. The case for the latter over the former is presented below.

[B] Case for the MRC Approach

Since the bulk of FIS in an economy is provided by the lending and deposit-taking activities of banks, for ease of reference such activities will be used throughout to frame the discussion, although the analysis is conceptually applicable to other FIS that are typically provided on the basis of margin spreads rather than explicit fees.

The central tenet of the cash-flow approach is the recognition that the value-added of any particular intermediation service provided by a bank can be measured by subtracting the total cash outflow from the total cash inflow associated with a given transaction. To subject such a transaction to VAT using the credit method, all a bank has to do would be to collect VAT on the cash inflow (output tax) and claim a credit on VAT paid on the cash outflow (input tax). Assuming an unchanging VAT rate, the VAT on the principal of the transaction (which is included in cash-flow calculations) is self-reversing when the transaction is unwound (e.g., a loan is repaid or a deposit is withdrawn), thus leaving only the VAT on the applicable interest margin. In this way, FIS are effectively taxed on a transaction-by-transaction basis just like other goods and services. Clearly, for this approach to work, each transaction must be tracked over its entire life, not only by the bank, but also by the transaction's counterparty on a cash-flow basis to enable it (a borrower or depositor) to properly pay tax and claim credits if it is a VAT-registered business (no tracking is needed by a non-registered counterparty to the transaction, such as a household, since it cannot claim credits under normal VAT rules anyway).

Assuming both borrower and depositor are registered businesses, it is immediately obvious from the above description that the VAT on the interest margin paid by the bank associated with a loan transaction supported by a deposit transaction would be exactly offset by tax credits claimed by the counterparties to the two transactions in the aggregate, but not separately.[19] To interpret this result as representing the correct

19. Consider a simple example where both the loan and deposit transactions unwind in two periods. Upon unwinding, the VAT on the cash flows associated with the principal in either transaction would wash out, but the borrower would end up in a net VAT credit position (arising from his interest payment) while the depositor would be liable to a positive net VAT payment (arising from his interest receipt). The difference between the tax positions of the borrower and depositor in the second period is nevertheless exactly equal (with a reverse sign) to the tax on the interest margin realized by the bank in the same period. This equality means that the government derives no net revenue in the aggregate from the two transactions, which is as it should be (as the bank's intermediation service in the present context is a business input).

outcome of how the bank's intermediation service is shared between the borrower and depositor individually, one must take into consideration the fact that the tax consequences arising from the principal of each transaction get washed out in nominal terms but not in present-value terms, because the associated cash flows (in opposite directions) occur in different periods. If a common interest rate that lies between the loan and deposit rates is used for the present-value calculations for both the borrower and depositor, then both counterparties to the two transactions would necessarily end up in a tax credit position (in present-value terms) separately without affecting the aggregate credit amount - each credit position representing the tax on the share of intermediation service consumed by the respective counterparty.

While the use of the TCA system as described[20] would indeed substantially reduce the compliance burden of the cash-flow approach,[21] it does not alter the fundamental property of this approach, which is that it would deliver only an arguably correct theoretical outcome in present-value terms. The outcome is merely arguably - not necessarily - correct because questions could be raised about which interest rate should be used in the present-value calculations,[22] and why the same rate should be applicable to all borrowers and depositors alike.[23] These are substantive issues that still seem to await a full investigation. Moreover, an approach whose validity rests on present-value terms is at complete variance with the machinations of a standard credit-method VAT. Hence, its adoption could hardly be considered as capable of providing a seamless integration of VAT treatments of FIS and of other goods and services.

In contrast, the MRC approach has none of the substantive concerns associated with the cash-flow approach. Like the latter, it recognizes that the value-added of a bank's intermediation service is the relevant interest spread between the lending and deposit rates. Unlike the latter, it directly taxes the lending and deposit rates to arrive at, respectively, the bank's output and input taxes (the difference is remitted to the

20. See 'The TCA System—A Detailed Description' (n. 3 above).
21. TCA is basically a bookkeeping system, to be entirely maintained by banks, that allows for the suspension of VAT (with interest) on the principal of lending and deposit transactions, thus avoiding the need to collect and credit tax on cash flows associated with the principal of such transactions. As banks would be responsible for informing their VAT-registered business customers of their tax positions each period, separate tracking by the latter on their transactions with the former would no longer be necessary. The TCA system also allows for adjustments to the basis of any principal if the tax rate were to change before a transaction is unwound.
22. Note that without using the TCA system, the choice of the interest rate would only affect interpretation of the outcome. With the use of the TCA system, actual outcome would be affected by the choice, since suspended VAT on principal amounts is carried in the books with interest applying the chosen rate.
23. The preferred rate of the *'The TCA System—A Detailed Description'* (n. 3 above) for this purpose is the risk-free rate on short-tern government paper that would normally lie between the bank's loan and deposit rates. The justification for this choice is that it represents the pure time value of money. By using such a rate to determine the carrying interest on the principal of loans and deposits in the TCA system, borrowers would effectively be taxed on the interest spread between the loan and risk-free rates, and depositors taxed on the interest spread between the risk-free and deposit rates. However, as argued earlier, the conceptual underpinning of any relationship between the VAT base regarding FIS and the time value of money is suspect.

government as VAT revenue), without regard to the principal of any lending and deposit transaction. By ignoring the principal, the MRC approach completely sidesteps present-value considerations and obviates the need for any party (bank, borrower or depositor) to track cash flows of a transaction over its life. Furthermore, since the input tax on the deposit rate is to be collected by the bank through a reverse-charge mechanism, depositors – many of whom are households – are completely relieved from the burden of collecting tax on their deposits. The output tax collected by the bank from borrowers is creditable as usual by the latter if they are VAT-registered businesses. The machinations of the foregoing system thus result in taxing FIS on a transaction-by-transaction basis in accordance with standard VAT rules. To borrowers and depositors – be they businesses or households – the system's integration with the credit-method VAT is seamless.

There are, however, two substantive problems with adopting the above system without modification. First, since borrowers pay tax on the loan rate, the base used for their tax calculations clearly exceeds that of the bank's interest margin. Second, depositors bear no-tax burden, although they clearly share with borrowers on the consumption of intermediation service provided by the bank. Rectifying the first problem hinges on finding a way to credit the input tax collected from depositors through reverse-charging by the bank against the output tax imposed on borrowers on a transaction-by-transaction basis. A fundamental innovation of the MRC approach is the accomplishment of such an objective through the use of a franking mechanism much like that found in an imputation system to frank dividends under the corporate income tax.[24] The end result is one where the tax burden on borrowers matches exactly the VAT on the bank's interest margin. All other aspects of the system are unaffected.

Addressing the second problem is a relatively easy matter. Suppose the percentage share of the interest margin to be attributed to depositors has been decided. The bank would then reduce its interest payment to each depositor by the tax on this share, accompanied by a VAT invoice that would allow a VAT-registered depositor to claim a credit for this tax. At the same time, the credit against the output tax on each borrower is stepped up by the same percentage amount as the interest payment to the depositor is reduced. In essence, such a procedure can be used to divvy up the interest margin between borrowers and depositors in whatever share that is deemed appropriate. Moreover, as the procedure has no-tax implications for the bank, the MRC approach as proposed in Zee (2005)[25] argues for allowing the bank itself to decide the share of the interest margin that could be attributed to depositors. The bank's decision would only affect how the tax on its FIS is shared between household (as well as unregistered business) borrowers and depositors; it would have no impact on its VAT-registered

24. Under the imputation system, the franking mechanism is used to ensure that dividends eligible for tax credit in the hands of shareholders against their personal income tax have in fact been distributed from profits already taxed under the corporate income tax. In an analogous fashion, under the MRC approach, the franking mechanism is used to ensure that credits granted to borrowers to reduce the VAT on their loan interest have in fact been derived from reverse charges on deposit interest. For details on the operation of the latter franking mechanism, see Zee (n. 2 above).
25. See Zee (n. 2 above).

business customers. It is further argued that competition among banks would produce an outcome that is sustained by market forces rather than tied arbitrarily to a particular risk-free rate.

[C] Benefit and Cost of Reform

While the case for full taxation of household consumption of FIS – and the adoption of the MRC approach as a means to achieve this outcome – is conceptually compelling, there remains the question that must be asked in evaluating the merits of any tax reform, which is whether the benefit to be had from the reform would justify its cost. In the present context, the specific question is whether the removal of the distortions caused by the VAT exemption of FIS is worth the price of subjecting FIS to taxation under a new system. This is fundamentally an empirical question, and its answer would require knowledge of the costs of both the exemption-induced distortions and compliance of the MRC approach. Unfortunately, as rightfully emphasized in the recent survey by Timothy Edgar,[26] little is known about either. Nevertheless, a reasonably strong case could be made for carrying out the reform, even if it is made in a state of relative empirical ignorance.

Broadly speaking, two different contexts can be identified in which economic distortions arise with regard to household consumption of FIS under the exemption approach. The first context relates to the availability of the multitude of different FIS within the financial sector that can be expected to have a high degree of cross-substitutability among them. The current non-uniformity in their VAT treatments (e.g., some taxable and some exempt) is thus likely to have entailed a high efficiency cost. Full taxation of FIS would reduce much of this non-uniformity and result in possibly large efficiency gains. The second context relates to the non-uniformity in VAT treatments of FIS and of other non-financial services. Since the degree of cross-substitutability between them can be expected to be low, little economic harm would be done if the tax burden on FIS is raised under full taxation. Hence, the overall economic benefit that could be reaped from the kind of reform under consideration could well be significant.[27]

26. See Edgar (n. 1 above).
27. It is perhaps useful at this point to clarify an issue raised by Timothy Edgar in his commentary on this paper and by others elsewhere in the literature concerning the issue of the price vs. income elasticity of household consumption of FIS. There is nothing in theory to suggest that the demand for FIS cannot be both price and income elastic. Indeed, as is well known, the total impact of a price change on such demand (as measured by the ordinary price elasticity) combines two separate effects: a substitution effect (as measured by the compensated price elasticity) and an income effect (as measured by the income elasticity). As long as FIS are normal (i.e., their income elasticity is positive, which would be a reasonable assumption), the two effects reinforce each other. Hence, a high (low) ordinary price elasticity would not be inconsistent with a high (low) income elasticity. For policy analyses, the ordinary price elasticity would be relevant for discussing the revenue impact of reform, while the compensated price elasticity would be relevant for discussing the reform's efficiency gains (or distortion abatement). In this paper, the focus is on the latter, so the reference to the cross-substitutability of FIS has to do with the compensated price elasticity of such services.

It is difficult to reliably assess the compliance cost of the MRC approach, since it is as yet untested in the field. However, one could be reasonably confident that its compliance burden is substantially below that of the cash-flow approach – for one simple reason. At the heart of the MRC approach are two elements: reverse-charging and a franking mechanism – both of which are familiar tax concepts as well as tax practices that can be found in a large number of countries. Reverse-charging on deposits can be easily implemented by banks with hardly any additional compliance cost. The franking mechanism is a little more involved, but its operation is straightforward and can easily be computerized – especially in a sector with a relatively high level of IT competency. Additionally, unlike the cash-flow approach, the MRC approach requires no tracking of the principal of every lending and deposit transaction, with or without a TCA system. The likely reason for the complexity encountered in the field-testing the former in the EU is thus absent with the latter.

§10.03 CONCLUDING REMARKS

In a world of globally mobile capital and financial services such as at present, the tax treatment of a country's financial sector has important implications for its ability to attract investments and promote growth. Exempting FIS under the VAT is an antiquated approach that is urgently in need of reform. A country that adheres to this approach risks putting its financial sector in a greatly disadvantageous position vis-à-vis others that have taken steps to redress the inherently distortive nature of exemptions under the VAT's credit method. However, even in these latter countries, the reform measures taken so far have only been partial and have left much to be desired.

Two new proposals have appeared in the literature within the past decade and a half that seem capable of overcoming a fundamental difficulty with taxing FIS on a transaction-by-transaction basis under the VAT implemented using the credit method. One proposal – the cash-flow approach – offers only an arguably, not a necessarily – correct outcome in present-value terms. Its integration with the regular VAT system operating in other sectors of the economy is thus not seamless. Field testing of this approach in the EU suggests that it could be administratively costly to adopt.

The second proposal – the MRC approach – is untested but its design seems to show promise in terms of both its conceptual underpinnings and practical feasibility, especially regarding its ability to offer a seamless integration with the regular VAT treatment of goods and non-financial services. It also seems to deliver an outcome that is less susceptible to conceptual challenge than that of the cash-flow approach. Hence, at a minimum, it deserves a chance for a field test to prove its ware.

Comment: Is the Comprehensive Application of Cash-Flow Taxation Necessary to Integrate Financial Services into an Invoice/Credit VAT?

Timothy Edgar

I INTRODUCTION

The treatment of financial services under an invoice/credit VAT hardly suffers from a lack of attention. Beginning in the late 1980s, there is some early conceptual and technical design work on the subject, the most important of which is probably that of Bakker and Chronican,[1] who thoroughly canvassed a range of alternatives to exemption in a short monograph that was published in the run-up to the adoption of the GST in New Zealand. The development of alternatives to exemption nonetheless appeared to remain in the 'too hard basket' until the publication of an article by Poddar and English[2] in which they build on some earlier work to describe versions of a system of cash-flow taxation as a comprehensive reform alternative to exemption. Their article seemed to spark a lively debate in the literature, with policy implications, over the taxable status of the household consumption of financial services. It also seemed to spark what is now a relatively deep survey literature, whereby the relevant policy issues presented by financial services under an invoice/credit VAT are canvassed and reform alternatives to exemption are examined.

1. C. Bakker & P. Chronican, *Financial Services and GST* (Victoria University Press for the Institute of Policy Studies 1985).
2. S. Poddar & M. English, *Taxation of Financial Services under a Value-Added Tax: Applying the Cash-Flow Approach*, 50 Natl. Tax. J. 89–111 (1997).

Howell Zee's paper[3] avoids the tradition of survey papers and, instead, emphasizes the design features and case for his modified reverse charging ('MRC') system as a workable cash-flow approach intended to realize the full taxation of financial services.[4] This comment goes beyond Zee's narrower focus and highlights a particular competing alternative to cash-flow taxation that is comprehensive in the sense that it addresses the perceived distortions attributable to the exempt treatment of both business and household consumption of financial services. Zee focuses on his MRC system as a first-best approach within the cash-flow family. As an alternative to Poddar and English's truncated tax calculation account ('TCA'), Zee's MRC is most likely an improvement for many of the reasons he emphasizes. However, as outlined recently by Poddar,[5] the reform alternative highlighted here is much more incremental and not quite as conceptually clean as cash-flow taxation. But in addressing the distortions commonly associated with exemption, it may fit well with the current composition of the financial sector while avoiding the same level of compliance and administrative costs of cash-flow taxation as a fundamental reform.

To provide some conceptual context for the comments that follow, I draw on Donald Rumsfeld's famous taxonomy of knowledge:[6]

> As we know, these are known knowns. These are things we know we know. We also know there are known unknowns. That is to say we know there are some things we do not know. But there are also unknown unknowns, the ones we don't know we don't know.

II KNOWN KNOWNS

Under the category of 'known knowns', there are four propositions relevant to the treatment of financial services under a VAT:

(1) the pure time-value return to savings is properly non-taxable under a VAT in order to ensure consistency of treatment of current and deferred consumption;
(2) the principal technical design issue presented by financial services under an invoice/credit VAT is the allocation of implicit or margin-based charges to consumers (both households and businesses);
(3) the household consumption of financial services is consumption, with the debate in the literature centred on its status as taxable; and

3. H. Zee, 'Further Thoughts on Reforming the VAT: Treatment of Financial Intermediation Services', Ch. 10, this volume.
4. See also H. Zee, *VAT Treatment of Financial Services: A Primer on Conceptual Issues and Country Practices*, 34 Intertax 458–474 (2006): and H. Zee, *A New Approach to Taxing Financial Intermediation Services under a Value-Added Tax*, 58 Natl. Tax J. 77–92 (2005).
5. S. Poddar, *VAT on Financial Services – Searching for a Workable Compromise*, in *GST in Retrospect and Prospect*, 179–204 (R. Krever & D. White eds., Thomson, Brookers Ltd. 2007).
6. Donald Rumsfeld, US Secretary of Defence, 12 February 2002, Department of Defence News Briefing.

(4) zero-rating and cash-flow taxation are the two principal alternatives to exemption that are broadly consistent with an invoice/credit VAT in the sense that they explicitly address the need to measure and allocate prices on a transactional basis among consumers of financial services.

To elaborate just a little on these propositions, conventional wisdom holds that financial services are properly taxable under a VAT, while the return to savings should remain non-taxable in order to avoid distorting the choice between present and deferred consumption. The commonly-cited rationale for the application of exempt, rather than taxable, treatment of financial services under a VAT is a perceived inability to identify and measure, on a transactional basis, those intermediation charges that are not explicit but are embedded in financial margins: that is, they take the form of the difference in price (the 'spread') between short and long positions assumed by a financial intermediary with its customers. In the apparent absence of an ability to impute financial margins to consumers of financial services on any means other than a formulaic basis, tax policymakers have tended to exempt a range of financial services from a VAT and deny any credit for offsetting tax on associated inputs consumed by the service provider.

A taxable characterization of the household consumption of financial services appears to be based on the proposition that the provision of such services, like the provision of any other services, uses up real resources and creates value added. Non-taxable characterization is limited to the consumption of financial services by registered businesses, which should be able to expense the associated charges. Difficulties in allocating implicit prices for expensing purposes are seen, however, to preclude this first-best treatment. Grubert and Mackie[7] challenged this conventional wisdom and argued that a non-taxable characterization of the consumption of financial services should extend equally to households and businesses on the basis that such consumption does not enter the consumer utility function. Jack[8] focuses on the efficiency properties associated with the form of the prices charged for the household consumption of financial services to suggest a narrower range of such consumption that should be considered non-taxable. In particular, he articulates three general categories of financial charges and their associated consumption tax treatment, which are said to follow from an efficiency-based analysis. Auerbach and Gordon[9] reject any non-taxable characterization by showing that the application of a VAT to the real resources consumed by the financial sector should not distort prices where the same costs remain and would otherwise be taxed under an equivalent labour-income tax. Rousslang[10] similarly accepts the premise that the real resources used up in the delivery

7. H. Grubert & J. Mackie, *Must Financial Services Be Taxed under a Consumption Tax?*, 53 Natl. Tax J. 23–40 (2000).
8. W. Jack, *The Treatment of Financial Services under a Broad-Based Consumption Tax*, 53 Natl. Tax J. 841–851 (2000).
9. A.J. Auerbach & R.H. Gordon, *Taxation of Financial Services under a VAT*, 92 Am. Eco. Rev. 411–416 (2002): .
10. D.J. Rousslang, *Should Financial Services be Taxed under a Consumption Tax? Probably*, 55 Natl. Tax J. 281–291 (2002).

of financial services should, as an initial proposition, be subject to VAT. In the absence of empirical evidence to show that consumers would increase their borrowing requirements in response to the application of a VAT to financial services, he argues that the better view is that financial services should probably be taxed under a VAT consistent with other sectors.

Zee correctly observes that this confusion in the literature over the taxable status of the household consumption of financial services arises because proponents of the non-taxation of savings complements implicitly are looking for an optimal tax regime, which recognizes the complementary and substitution relationships in setting tax rates. As Rousslang emphasizes, the absence of any empirical evidence that would support the choice of an optimal rate of VAT for financial services probably means that full taxation of such services remains the appropriate default position. This leaves the well-known boundary under a VAT between non-taxable interest charges and charges for taxable financial services. It also means that comprehensive zero-rating is problematic, leaving some form of cash-flow taxation as an alternative to partial reform measures that modify exemption in an attempt to address a perceived distortion of the pattern of consumption of financial services by businesses, as well as a perceived distortion of the pattern of production of financial service providers.

III KNOWN UNKNOWNS

As I have emphasized elsewhere,[11] the overall significance and direction of accepted distortions associated with exemption remain unclear. Yet, the choice of partial reform alternatives to address one or more distortions depends critically on empirical knowledge that we know we do not have. We are left, therefore, to make policy choices in a veil of empirical ignorance operating on intuitions and casual empiricism. We also know, however, that the choice of a comprehensive cash-flow approach entails unknown compliance and administrative costs, as well as revenue effects. This raises the following three questions under the category of 'known unknowns' as critically relevant to the choice of reform of exemption.

(1) Is the business consumption of financial services price elastic or income elastic?
(2) Is the household consumption of financial services price elastic or income elastic?
(3) To what extent is the form of prices for financial services substitutable?

The policy significance of each of these three questions is touched on in Zee's paper. On the assumption that both business and household consumption are price elastic, he proposes his MRC to eliminate VAT on the former and impose it on the latter. His MRC would also address the self-supply bias, which is similarly premised on an empirical

11. T. Edgar, *The Search for Alternatives to Exempt Treatment of Financial Services under a Value Added Tax*, in *GST in Retrospect and Prospect*, 131–161 (R. Krever & D. White eds., Thomson Reuters 2007).

assumption of price elasticity in the consumption of financial services. The fact that the income effect may dominate one or both forms of consumption really does not matter to the choice of cash-flow taxation as an alternative to exemption with targeted relief measures such as an Australian or Singaporean-style reduced input tax credit.

But if, in fact, the household consumption of financial services is income elastic, tax policymakers might be able to realize revenue without any efficiency losses and without incurring the administrative and compliance costs associated with cash-flow taxation, even where those costs might be muted somewhat by Zee's MRC. In exploring this possibility, the substitutability of the form of prices is an important empirical unknown. More particularly, if there are sufficient non-tax constraints on substitutability, we could follow the South African lead and rely on the form of prices to draw the boundary between taxable and exempt status and relieve much of the pressure on definitional issues focused on administrative and cash-management services as well as agency and advisory services.[12] It can also be adopted as a means of offsetting possible revenue loss associated with a move to non-taxation of the business consumption of financial services.[13]

But why stop there? An obvious competing alternative to cash-flow taxation, suggested by Huizinga[14] and Poddar,[15] would combine the zero-rating of the business consumption of financial services with:

- the taxation of explicit fees charged to households; and
- the taxation of financial margins charged to households on an aggregate or pooled basis using a cash-flow base.

Indeed, this particular comprehensive reform is arguably the principal competitor to Zee's MRC version of cash-flow taxation, but with administrative and compliance costs associated with the identification of business and household consumption of financial services rather than the application of a reverse charge mechanism and the tracking of quasi-franking credits as a means to allocate financial margins for input credit purposes. As suggested in the next section, this identification task may not be as difficult as we might think, given the current composition of the financial sector.

12. E. McCann & T. Edgar, *VAT Treatment of Interest and Financial Services with Competitive Banking and Insurance Sectors*, 30 Tax Notes Intl. 791–808 (2003).
13. See, in this respect, H. Huizinga, *A European VAT on Financial Services?*, 35 Econ. Policy 499–526 (2002) (suggesting that looseness in the use of formulas for allocation of input costs by financial service providers means that business consumption is already largely zero-rated in the EU). See also R. de la Feria & B. Lockwood, *Opting for Opting In? An Evaluation of the European Commission's Proposals for Reforming VAT on Financial Services*, 31 Fisc. Stud. 171–202 (2010) (arguing that the European Commission's recently proposed option to tax is functionally equivalent to the zero-rating of the business consumption of financial services where firms cannot coordinate their behaviour, and providing some upper-bound estimates of possible revenue loss).
14. See Huizinga (n. 13 above).
15. See Poddar (n. 5 above).

IV UNKNOWN UNKNOWNS

By definition, there can be nothing to say under the category of 'unknown unknowns'. Perhaps the best that I can do here is to suggest some possible sources. For example, it is certainly the case that we do not know where or when the next innovative idea may come along to provoke a substantial reassessment of conventional thinking in the same way that Poddar and English did with their TCA system.[16] Another source is the structure of the financial sector at any given point in time. That is, structural changes to the financial sector can affect standard policy issues under VAT systems in unanticipated ways. That said, financial intermediation continues to take three broad forms that are treated differently for income tax purposes[17] and might also be treated differently for VAT purposes. In fact, it may be the case that only one of these three forms requires the application of Zee's MRC to tax fully the household consumption of financial services, while eliminating taxation of business consumption of the same services. The following comments are subject, of course, to unanticipated structural changes, including regulatory changes, in the financial sector that can alter the composition of the delivery of financial intermediation in a manner that can make it difficult to segregate household and business consumption, which is critical to the application of the zero-rating of business consumption of financial services in the form of margin-based charges alongside the taxation of explicit fees on an invoice/credit basis and the taxation of margin-based charges on a pooled or aggregate basis for households.

One form of financial intermediation, which can be referred to as 'the insurance function', involves the smoothing of consumption from good to bad states, with intermediaries using the law of large numbers to spread risk. With property and casualty insurance, we know that cash-flow taxation does not require the application of either the truncated TCA or the MRC to ensure taxation of the household consumption of such services while eliminating taxation of business consumption. Under the New Zealand-style approach, insurance premiums are subject to VAT with input credits for business consumers. Output tax is charged on claim payouts. This approach is arguably nothing more than a specific application of Zee's MRC system but without quasi-franking credits to allocate margins, which are considered instead to be borne rateably by all insureds. In fact, this approach is really a reverse charge mechanism without the modifications proposed by Zee. This form of cash-flow taxation of property and casualty insurance on a pooled margin basis can be maintained if household consumption is income elastic and business consumption is price elastic; it provides input credit relief for business consumption presumably on the basis that property and casualty insurance business is exclusively margin-based such that the form of prices cannot be altered to free up input credits. With life insurance, technical design issues

16. See Australia Tax Review Panel, *Australia's Future Tax System: Report to the Treasurer*, 309–311 (Commonwealth of Australia 2009)) (suggesting adoption of an addition-method consumption tax on financial services as a replacement for exemption).
17. E.D. Kleinbard, *Competitive Convergence in the Financial Services Market*, 81 Taxes 225–260 (2003).

focused on the need to separate the insurance from the savings function have been seen to necessitate the application of exemption to both. But this unqualified application of exemption is defensible only where it is applied to the household consumption of financial services generally, including property and casualty insurance. Application of exemption presumably eliminates tax-driven bundling and cross-subsidization, but at the possible cost of some distortion of the pattern of household consumption and savings. It would seem that this possible distortion could be solved by applying the subtraction method on a pooled basis to the household consumption of life insurance while zero-rating business consumption, provided the two can be readily segregated. If so, although the TCA or MRC systems of cash-flow taxation can, in principle, be applied to life insurance, it is not clear that such application is necessary.

Much the same proposition can be posited with market-risk intermediation traditionally performed by broker-dealers. This type of financial intermediation is with the market in the sense that risk associated with changes in the value of assets and liabilities are altered by transacting with counterparties. In performing this function, broker-dealers may act as intermediaries, taking offsetting positions with different counterparties or they may provide liquidity to the market by assuming positions on their own account through their proprietary trading desks. Because much of the former type of risk intermediation occurs with business consumers, it is an obvious candidate for zero-rating of margin-based charges. With proprietary trading, it is not clear that such a function should be taxable unless the provision of liquidity to the market generally can be characterized as taxable, in which case, the end user is indeterminate.

The one type of intermediation in which the application of Zee's MRC might be required to fully tax household consumption while eliminating the taxation of business consumption is the maturity transformation function traditionally associated with retail banking.[18] Because households and businesses can be on either side of this form of intermediation, segregating the two in order to apply taxation on an aggregate basis for households would seem to be problematic. The alternative to application of the MRC approach is to tax explicit charges while zero-rating margin-based charges for businesses and exempting the same charges for households. In this respect, fund management should be included as another form of maturity transformation, but with the notable difference that charges in this case tend to take the form of explicit management fees. Application of cash-flow taxation also appears unnecessary for wholesale banking, not because of the dominance of explicit fees over margin-based charges, but rather because zero-rating of business consumption could be readily applied.

18. Because the MRC ignores capital account cash flows, it would treat the default risk premium embedded in interest cash flows as part of financial margins rather than compensation for expected loan defaults.

EUCOTAX Series on European Taxation

(1) Peter HJ Essers, Guido JME de Bont & Eric CCM Kemmeren (eds), *The Compatibility of Anti-Abuse Provisions in Tax Treaties with EC Law*, 1998 (ISBN 90-411-9678-1).
(2) Gerard TK Meussen (ed.), *The Principle of Equality in European Taxation*, 1999 (ISBN 90-411-9693-5).
(3) Michael Lang (ed.), *Tax Treaty Interpretation*, 2001 (ISBN 90-411-9857-1).
(4) Pasquale Pistone, *The Impact of Community Law on Tax Treaties: Issues and Solutions*, 2002 (ISBN 90-411-9860-1).
(5) René Offermanns, *The Entrepreneurship Concept in a European Comparative Tax Law Perspective*, 2002 (ISBN 90-411-9887-3).
(6) Michael Lang & Mario Züger, *Settlement of Disputes in Tax Treaty Law*, 2002 (ISBN 90-411-9904-7).
(7) Carlo Pinto, *Tax Competition and EU Law*, 2003 (ISBN 90-411-9913-6).
(8) Michael Lang, Hans-Jörgen Aigner, Ulrich Scheuerle & Markus *Stefaner, CFC Legislation, Tax Treaties and EC Law*, 2004 (ISBN 90-411-2284-2).
(9) Mattias Dahlberg, *Direct Taxation in Relation to the Freedom of Establishment and the Free Movement of Capital*, 2005 (ISBN 90-411-2363-6).
(10) Michael Lang, Judith Herdin & Ines Hofbauer, *WTO and Direct Taxation*, 2005 (ISBN 90-411-2371-7).
(11) Dennis Weber, *Tax Avoidance and the EC Tray Freedoms: A Study of the Limitations under European Law for the Prevention of Tax Avoidance*, 2005 (ISBN 90-411-2402-0).
(12) Félix Alberto Vega Borrego, *Limitations on Benefits Clauses on Double Taxation Conventions*, 2005 (ISBN 90-411-2370-9).
(13) Michael Lang, Josef Schuch & Claus Staringer, *ECJ-Recent Developments in Direct Taxation*, 2006 (ISBN 90-411-2509-4).
(14) Reuven S. Avi-Yonah, James R. Hines Jr. & Michael Lang, *Comparative Fiscal Federalism. Comparing the European Court of Justice and the US Supreme Court's Tax Jurisprudence*, 2007 (ISBN 978-90-411-2552-1).
(15) Christiana HJI Panayi, *Double Taxation, Tax Treaties, Treaty-Shopping and the European Community*, 2007 (ISBN 978-90-411-2658-0).
(16) Dennis Weber, *The Influence of European Law on Direct Taxation: Recent and Future Developments*, 2007 (ISBN 978-90-411-2667-2).
(17) Michael Lang & Pasquale Pistone, *The EU and Third Countries: Direct Taxation*, 2007 (ISBN 978-90-411-2665-8).
(18) Oskar Henkow, *Financial Activities in European VAT: A Theoretical and Legal Research of the European VAT System and Preferred Treatment of Financial Activities*, 2007 (ISBN 978-90-411-2703-7).
(19) Michael Lang (ed.), *Tax Compliance Costs for Companies in an Enlarged European Community*, 2008 (ISBN 978-90-411-2666-5).

(20) Michael Lang (ed.), *Source versus Residence. Problems Arising from the Allocation of Taxing Rights in Tax Treaty Law and Possible Alternatives,* 2008 (ISBN 978-90-411-2763-1).
(21) Ioanna Mitroyanni, *Integration Approaches to Group Taxation in the European Internal Market,* 2008 (ISBN 978-90-411-2779-2).
(22) Rolf Eicke, *Tax Planning with Holding Companies. Repatriation of US Profits fromEurope:Concepts, Strategies, Structures,* 2008 (ISBN978-90-411-2794-5).
(23) Peter Essers et al. (ed.), *The Influence of IAS/IFRS on the CCCTB, Tax Accounting, Disclosure and Corporate Law Accounting Concepts: 'A Clash of Cultures',* 2008 (ISBN 978-90-411-2819-5).
(24) Tonny Schenk-Geers, *International Exchange of Information and the Protection of Taxpayers,* 2009 (ISBN 978-90-411-3142-3).
(25) Raymond Adema, *UCITS and Taxation: Towards Harmonization of the Taxation of UCITS,* 2009 (ISBN 978-90-411-2839-3).
(26) Michael Lang, Jianwen Liu & Gongliang Tang (eds), *Europe–China Tax Treaties,* 2010 (ISBN 978-90-411-3216-1).
(27) Michael Lang, Pasquale Pistone, Josef Schuch & Claus Staringer (eds), *Procedural Rules in Tax Law in the Context of European Union and Domestic Law,* 2010 (ISBN 978-90-411-3376-2).
(28) Sjaak J.J.M. Jansen, *Fiscal Sovereignty of the Member States in an Internal Market: Past and Future,* 2011 (ISBN 978-90-411-3403-5).
(29) Dennis Weber & Bruno da Silva, *From Marks & Spencer to X Holding: The Future of Cross-Border Group Taxation,* 2011 (ISBN 978-90-411-3399-1).
(30) Claus Bohn Jespersen, *Intermediation of Insurance and Financial Services in European VAT,* 2011 (ISBN 978-90-411-3732-6).
(31) Sabine Heidenbauer, *Charity Crossing Borders: The Fundamental Freedoms' Influence on Charity and Donor Taxation in Europe,* 2011 (ISBN 978-90-411-3813-2).
(32) Michael Lang, et al., *The Future of Indirect Taxation: Recent Trends in VAT and GST Systems around the World,* 2012 (ISBN 978-90-411-3797-5).
(33) Harm van den Broek, *Cross-Border Mergers within the EU: Proposals to Remove the Remaining Tax Obstacles,* 2012 (ISBN 978-90-411-3824-8).
(34) Michael Lang, et al. (eds), *Tax Treaty Case Law around the Globe – 2011,* 2012 (ISBN 978-90-411-3876-7).
(35) Dennis Weber (ed.), *CCCTB: Selected Issues,* 2012 (ISBN 978-90-411-3872-9).
(36) Daniël Smit, *EU Freedoms, Non-EU Countries and Company Taxation,* 2012 (ISBN 978-90-411-4041-8).
(37) Rita de la Feria, *VAT Exemptions: Consequences and Design Alternatives,* 2013 (ISBN 978-90-411-3276-5).

Lightning Source UK Ltd.
Milton Keynes UK
UKHW021106291019
352474UK00003B/111/P

9 789041 132765